WJ IV Clinical Use and Interpretation

WJ IV Clinical Use and Interpretation

Scientist-Practitioner Perspectives

Edited by

Dawn P. Flanagan
Department of Psychology
St. John's University
New York, NY, USA

Vincent C. Alfonso
School of Education
Gonzaga University
Spokane, WA, USA

ELSEVIER

AMSTERDAM • BOSTON • HEIDELBERG • LONDON
NEW YORK • OXFORD • PARIS • SAN DIEGO
SAN FRANCISCO • SINGAPORE • SYDNEY • TOKYO

Academic Press is an imprint of Elsevier

Academic Press is an imprint of Elsevier
125, London Wall, EC2Y 5AS.
525 B Street, Suite 1800, San Diego, CA 92101-4495, USA
225 Wyman Street, Waltham, MA 02451, USA
The Boulevard, Langford Lane, Kidlington, Oxford OX5 1GB, UK

Notices
Knowledge and best practice in this field are constantly changing. As new
research and experience broaden our understanding, changes in research methods,
professional practices, or medical treatment may become necessary.

Practitioners and researchers must always rely on their own experience and
knowledge in evaluating and using any information, methods, compounds, or
experiments described herein. In using such information or methods they should
be mindful of their own safety and the safety of others, including parties for whom
they have a professional responsibility.

To the fullest extent of the law, neither the Publisher nor the authors, contributors, or
editors, assume any liability for any injury and/or damage to persons or property as a
matter of products liability, negligence or otherwise, or from any use or operation of
any methods, products, instructions, or ideas contained in the material herein.

ISBN: 978-0-12-802076-0

British Library Cataloguing-in-Publication Data
A catalogue record for this book is available from the British Library

Library of Congress Cataloging-in-Publication Data
A catalog record for this book is available from the Library of Congress

Typeset by MPS Limited, Chennai, India
www.adi-mps.com

Contents

3. A Special Validity Study of the Woodcock–Johnson IV: Acting on Evidence for Specific Abilities
Christopher R. Niileksela, Matthew R. Reynolds, Timothy Z. Keith and Kevin S. McGrew

4. Woodcock–Johnson IV Scoring and Reporting Online Program Review
Scott L. Decker, Emma Kate C. Wright and Tayllor E. Vetter

7. Strengths and Weaknesses of the Woodcock–Johnson IV Tests of Cognitive Abilities: Best Practice from a Scientist–Practitioner Perspective

W. Joel Schneider

10. **Use of the Woodcock–Johnson IV Tests of Cognitive Abilities in the Diagnosis of Intellectual Disability**
    Randy G. Floyd, Isaac L. Woods, Leah J. Singh and Haley K. Hawkins

11. **Use of the Woodcock–Johnson IV Tests of Cognitive Abilities and Achievement in the Assessment for Giftedness**
    Steven I. Pfeiffer and Jordy B. Yarnell

List of Contributors

Vincent C. Alfonso School of Education, Gonzaga University, Spokane, WA, USA

Karen E. Apgar Eugene (Oregon) School District 4J, Eugene, OR, USA

Wendi L. Bauman Johnson Department of Psychology and Philosophy, Texas Woman's University, Denton, TX, USA

Scott L. Decker Department of Psychology, University of South Carolina, Columbia, SC, USA

Rosemary I. Devine Department of Psychology, St. John's University, Jamaica, NY, USA

Yi Ding Graduate School of Education, Fordham University, New York, NY, USA

Ron Dumont School of Psychology, Fairleigh Dickinson University, Teaneck, NJ, USA

Dawn P. Flanagan St. John's University, New York, NY, USA

Randy G. Floyd Department of Psychology, The University of Memphis, Memphis, TN, USA

Haley K. Hawkins Department of Psychology, The University of Memphis, Memphis, TN, USA

Timothy Z. Keith Department of Educational Psychology, University of Texas, Austin, TX, USA

Benjamin J. Lovett Department of Psychology, State University of New York at Cortland, Cortland, NY, USA

Denise E. Maricle Department of Psychology and Philosophy, Texas Woman's University, Denton, TX, USA

Nancy Mather Department of Disability and Psychoeducational Studies, University of Arizona, Tucson, AZ, USA

Erin M. McDonough St. John's University, New York, NY, USA

Ryan J. McGill Department of Psychology and Philosophy, Texas Woman's University, Denton, TX, USA

Kevin S. McGrew Institute for Applied Psychometrics, St. Joseph, MN, USA

Daniel C. Miller Department of Psychology and Philosophy, Texas Woman's University, Denton, TX, USA

Christopher R. Niileksela Department of Educational Psychology, Joseph R. Pearson Hall, University of Kansas, Lawrence, KS, USA

Juan A. Ortiz Department of Psychology, St. John's University, Jamaica, NY, USA

Samuel O. Ortiz Department of Psychology, St. John's University, Jamaica, NY, USA

Steven I. Pfeiffer Department of Educational Psychology and Learning Systems, College of Education, Florida State University, Tallahassee, FL, USA

Justin L. Potts Eugene (Oregon) School District 4J, Eugene, OR, USA

Matthew R. Reynolds Department of Educational Psychology, Joseph R. Pearson Hall, University of Kansas, Lawrence, KS, USA

W. Joel Schneider Department of Psychology, Illinois State University, Normal, IL, USA

Leah J. Singh Department of Psychology, The University of Memphis, Memphis, TN, USA

Laura M. Spenceley Department of Counseling and Psychological Services, State University of New York at Oswego, Oswego, NY, USA

Tayllor E. Vetter Department of Psychology, University of South Carolina, Columbia, SC, USA

Robert Walrath Doctoral Program in Counseling and School Psychology, Rivier University, Nashua, NH, USA

Barbara J. Wendling Independent Consultant, Dallas, TX, USA

John O. Willis Department of Education, Rivier University, Nashua, NH, USA

Isaac L. Woods Department of Psychology, The University of Memphis, Memphis, TN, USA

Emma Kate C. Wright Department of Psychology, University of South Carolina, Columbia, SC, USA

Jordy B. Yarnell Department of Educational Psychology and Learning Systems, College of Education, Florida State University, Tallahassee, FL, USA

Preface

The Woodcock-Johnson IV (WJ IV) is an extensive revision of its predecessor, expanded in depth, breadth, cognitive complexity, and online scoring. It is widely used for assessing the cognitive, academic, and oral language abilities of children, adolescents, and adults. The WJ IV includes extensive examiner and technical manuals, but little else has been published to date on this new battery. Therefore, a need exists for documenting its clinical utility, particularly from a scientist-practitioner perspective. To address this need, *WJ IV Clinical Use and Interpretation* presents a wide variety of exemplary clinical applications of the WJ IV from its authors as well as numerous leading experts in assessment-related fields, including learning disabilities, school psychology, and neuropsychology.

The WJ IV is introduced in Part I of this book, with emphasis on how to interpret the range of scores and composites, as well as variation and comparison procedures, that are available. Additionally, Part I addresses the instructional implications of the diverse range of tests comprising the WJ IV. Ding and Alfonso describe the organization, content, and psychometric properties of the WJ IV in Chapter 1 and Dumont, Willis, and Walrath provide comprehensive coverage of how to interpret scores, composites, and intra-individual analysis options for the WJ IV in Chapter 2. Following these chapters, Niileksela, Reynolds, Keith, and McGrew present the results of a special validity study using the standardization data of the WJ IV, demonstrating that broad cognitive abilities referenced by CHC theory are important for explaining broad and narrow aspects of academic achievement. In Chapter 4, Decker, Wright, and Vetter provide detailed instruction on how to use the new WJ IV online scoring. Next, Maricle and Johnson (Chapter 5) and Mather and Wendling (Chapter 6) describe instructional implications from the WJ IV Tests of Cognitive Abilities and Tests of Academic Achievement, respectively. Part I concludes with a thoughtful and jocular summary of the strengths and weaknesses of the WJ IV tests of cognitive abilities (Chapter 7) by Schneider.

The clinical and diagnostic utility of the WJ IV is discussed in Part II of this book. In Chapter 8, McDonough and Flanagan provide a research-based framework for using and interpreting the WJ IV within the context of a referral for suspected learning disability in school-age children, with emphasis on the pattern of strengths and weaknesses (PSW) approach. Diagnosis of learning disabilities in adulthood using the WJ IV is described in detail by Lovett and Spenceley in Chapter 9. While McDonough and Flanagan's approach to learning disability identification is in line with IDEIA and its attendant regulations, Lovett and Spenceley's focus is on use of the DSM-5 criteria for diagnosing learning disorder and understanding disability as reflected in the ADA. The most up-to-date information on diagnosis of Intellectual Disability and assessment of Giftedness using the WJ IV is described by Floyd, Woods, Singh, and Hawkins (Chapter 10) and Pfeifer and Yarnell (Chapter 11), respectively.

Use of the WJ IV in evidence-based assessment approaches is presented in Part III of this book. In Chapter 12, Ortiz, Ortiz, and Devine tackle the complex issues surrounding the use of the WJ IV in the assessment of students from culturally and linguistically diverse backgrounds. Next, Miller, McGill, and Johnson review the application of the WJ IV from a neuropsychological perspective (Chapter 13). Specifically, these authors present a re-classification of the WJ IV tests into a neuropsychological conceptual framework, which allows for additional interpretive options. This section and book concludes with a well thought out and "ready-for-implementation" approach for use of the WJ IV in an RTI service delivery model by Apgar and Potts (Chapter 14).

As editors, we thank all those who contributed to this volume for their expertise, time, and adherence to the scientist-practitioner model. In addition to the chapter authors, we are also grateful to the staff at Academic Press for their expertise, guidance, and pleasant and cooperative working style, most especially Barbara Makinster, Caroline Johnson, and Nikki Levy. These individuals helped to develop what we believe is a volume of the finest quality possible. Finally, we express sincere gratitude to Kristine Lin for her editorial assistance as well as her dedication and commitment to this project.

Dawn P. Flanagan
Vincent C. Alfonso

Chapter 1

Overview of the Woodcock-Johnson IV: Organization, Content, and Psychometric Properties

Yi Ding[1] and Vincent C. Alfonso[2]

[1]*Graduate School of Education, Fordham University, New York, NY, USA* [2]*School of Education, Gonzaga University, Spokane, WA, USA*

The purpose of this chapter is to provide an overview of the organization, content, and psychometric properties of the Woodcock-Johnson IV (WJ IV; Schrank, McGrew, & Mather, 2014a). The WJ IV family of instruments is composed of the WJ IV Tests of Cognitive Abilities (WJ IV COG; Schrank, McGrew, & Mather, 2014b), WJ IV Tests of Achievement (WJ IV ACH; Schrank, Mather, & McGrew, 2014a), and WJ IV Tests of Oral Language (WJ IV OL; Schrank, Mather, & McGrew, 2014b). These revised instruments provide a comprehensive set of norm-referenced and individually administered tests of cognitive, academic achievement, and oral language abilities, respectively.

According to Mather and Wendling (2014b), there are several factors to consider in order to summarize the significant advances in the WJ IV family of instruments. First, the WJ IV assessment system used a theory-based approach to design state-of-the-art instruments. Specifically, the WJ IV allows examiners to explore the strengths and weaknesses of individuals through the measurement of their cognitive, academic, and linguistic abilities via the Cattell–Horn–Carroll (CHC) theory of abilities (Carroll, 1993; Horn & Noll, 1997; Schneider & McGrew, 2012). Second, it complements the response to intervention (RtI) approach, which was not emphasized in the Woodcock-Johnson III (WJ III; Woodcock, McGrew, & Mather, 2001a). Third, the WJ IV enhances the methodology to examine variations and ability/achievement comparisons. Fourth, the WJ IV focuses on the important broad CHC abilities and narrow CHC abilities that are important for academic success, whereas the WJ III focused primarily on the broad CHC abilities. Fifth, the WJ IV family of instruments was designed

WJ IV Clinical Use and Interpretation. DOI: http://dx.doi.org/10.1016/B978-0-12-802076-0.00001-3

with ease of administration and scoring as well as flexibility in mind. Thus, novice examiners can use the tests with confidence, especially those who are familiar with the WJ III. The WJ IV also allows experienced examiners access to a wide range of interpretive options to enhance and individualize their evaluations based on the needs of their examinees (see Dumont, Willis, & Walrath, in this volume, and McDonough & Flanagan in this volume, for more information on interpretive options available on the WJ IV). Examiners can use the cognitive, achievement, and oral language batteries as independent batteries or use them in conjunction with one another.

THEORETICAL UNDERPINNINGS OF THE WJ IV

The WJ IV was designed based on the structure of abilities known as CHC theory. The CHC theory of abilities is based on the integration of two independently derived theories; namely, the Cattell–Horn Gf–Gc theory (Horn & Noll, 1997) and Carroll's three stratum theory (Carroll, 1993). A brief overview of CHC theory is provided next. The interested reader is referred to Alfonso, Flanagan, and Radwan (2005), Flanagan, Ortiz, and Alfonso (2013), McGrew (2005), and Schneider and McGrew (2012) for detailed discussions on the history of CHC theory.

The Gf–Gc theory is a model that has been developed and enhanced by Cattell, Horn, and their research associates over the past 60 years. Cattell's early contribution to Gf–Gc theory concluded that Spearman's g could be best explained by dividing the general g factor into fluid intelligence (Gf) and general crystallized intelligence (Gc) (Cattell, 1941, 1943). The Gf factor has been described as fluid reasoning (Cattell–Horn) or fluid intelligence (Carroll) and is a measure of the abilities to reason, form concepts, and solve problems (using unfamiliar information or novel procedures). Fluid reasoning/intelligence requires basic reasoning processes (deductive and inductive reasoning); manipulation of abstract concepts, rules, and logical relations; demands mental flexibility (shifting mental gears); and requires deliberate and flexible control of attention. It also involves adaptive and new learning capabilities and is related to mental operations and processes. Fluid reasoning/intelligence is more dependent on the physiological structures (e.g., cortical and lower cortical regions) that support intellectual behavior than is crystallized intelligence. Finally, fluid reasoning/intelligence increases until sometime during adolescence and then it slowly declines.

The Gc factor has been described as acculturation knowledge (Cattell–Horn) or crystallized intelligence (Carroll). It is a measure of the breadth and depth of knowledge of culture, understanding of social norms, and the storage and retrieval of previously acquired knowledge. Gc is the ability to communicate one's knowledge, particularly in verbal format, and includes the use of declarative and procedural knowledge. The development of acculturation knowledge or crystallized intelligence involves overlearned and well-established cognitive functions and is related to mental products and achievements. *Gc* is highly influenced by formal and informal educational factors.

From 1965 to the early 1990s, the original *Gf–Gc* model was extended by Horn (1965, 1991) with new factors such as short-term acquisition and retrieval or short-term memory (SAR or *Gsm*), visual perception or processing (*Gv*), auditory processing (*Ga*), tertiary storage and retrieval or long-term storage and retrieval (TSR or *Glr*), and speed of processing (*Gs*) (Alfonso et al., 2005). In addition, Horn described correct decision speed or *Gt*, quantitative ability (*Gq*), and broad reading/writing (*Grw*) as the Cattell–Horn model became an eight-factor model (including *Gf* and *Gc*) (Alfonso et al., 2005; Horn & Blankson, 2005).

Carroll's three stratum theory (1993) was developed based on exploratory factor analyses of more than 400 different datasets that included the important and classic factor-analytic experiments of abilities. In short, Carroll developed a three-tier model of cognitive abilities that are differentiated from general to narrow domains. The broadest level (stratum III) corresponds to a general intelligence or *g*. The broad level (stratum II) includes the following broad abilities: fluid intelligence (*Gf*), crystallized intelligence (*Gc*), general memory and learning (*Gy*), broad visual perception (*Gv*), broad auditory perception (*Gu*), broad retrieval ability (*Gr*), broad cognitive speediness (*Gs*), and decision/reaction time/speed (*Gt*). The narrow level (stratum I) includes a large number of narrow abilities such as inductive reasoning and lexical knowledge. Carroll's work provides a content and hierarchical structure to organize the mass of literature on abilities since Spearman's contribution (McGrew, 2009).

Based on mutual consensus, the integration of the two independently and empirically supported theories was named CHC theory. McGrew (2005) provided historical details of the origin of CHC theory, and the CHC taxonomic umbrella has increasingly obtained public recognition and influence since 1999 (Alfonso et al., 2005; McGrew, 2009). Today, CHC theory encompasses 16 broad abilities and more than 80 narrow abilities (Flanagan, Alfonso, Ortiz, & Dynda, 2013; Flanagan, 2013; Schneider & McGrew, 2012). The WJ IV was developed based on the most recent iteration of CHC theory and moves test development beyond CHC theory as it was conceived in the WJ III. In addition to the emphasis on broad CHC abilities, the WJ IV also addresses the narrow CHC abilities. Some tests are designed to reflect specific cognitive complexity through the influence of two or more narrow abilities, which allows in-depth clinical interpretations and customization of evaluations (see McGrew, LaForte, & Schrank, 2014, for a thorough review of the theoretical underpinnings and cognitive complexity of the WJ IV). Table 1.1 provides broad and narrow CHC ability classifications offered by the test authors and independently by Ortiz, Flanagan, and Alfonso (2015). In general there is a high level of agreement between the broad and narrow CHC classifications offered by the test authors and those by Ortiz et al. (see also Maricle & Johnson, in this volume;

TABLE 1.1 Broad and Narrow CHC Classifications of WJ IV Tests by the Authors and Ortiz et al. (2015)

Battery/Test Name (Number)	WJ IV Authors' Broad and Narrow CHC Ability Classifications	Ortiz et al. (2015) Broad and Narrow CHC Ability Classifications
WJ IV COG		
Oral Vocabulary (1)	*Gc*-VL, LD	*Gc*-VL
Number Series (2)	*Gf*-RQ, I	*Gf*-RQ
Verbal Attention (3)	*Gwm*-WM, AC	*Gsm*-MW
Letter-Pattern Matching (4)	*Gs*-P	*Gs*-P
Phonological Processing (5)	*Ga*-PC, LA; *Glr*-FW	*Ga*-PC; *Glr*-FW
Story Recall (6)	*Glr*-MM; *Gc*-LS	*Glr*-MM
Visualization (7)	*Gv*-Vz	*Gv*-Vz
General Information (8)	*Gc*-K0	*Gc*-K0
Concept Formation (9)	*Gf*-I	*Gf*-I
Numbers Reversed (10)	*Gwm*-WM, AC	*Gsm*-MW
Number-Pattern Matching (11)	*Gs*-P	*Gs*-P
Nonword Repetition (12)	*Ga*-PC, UM; *Gwm*-MS	*Gsm*-MS; *Ga*-UM
Visual-Auditory Learning (13)	*Glr*-MA	*Glr*-MA
Picture Recognition (14)	*Gv*-MV	*Gv*-MV
Analysis-Synthesis (15)	*Gf*-RG	*Gf*-RG
Object-Number Sequencing (16)	*Gwm*-WM	*Gsm*-MW
Pair Cancelation (17)	*Gs*-P; *Gwm*-AC; *Gv*-SS	*Gs*-P
Memory for Words (18)	*Gwm*-MS	*Gsm*-MS
WJ IV ACH		
Letter-Word Identification (1)	*Grw*-RD	*Grw*-RD
Applied Problems (2)	*Gq*-A3; *Gf*-RQ	*Gq*-A3; *Gf*-RQ
Spelling (3)	*Grw*-SG	*Grw*-SG
Passage Comprehension (4)	*Grw*-RC	*Grw*-RC
Calculation (5)	*Gq*-A3	*Gq*-A3
Writing Samples (6)	*Grw*-WA	*Grw*-WA
Word Attack (7)	*Grw*-RD; *Ga*-PC	*Grw*-RD; *Ga*-PC
Oral Reading (8)	*Grw*-RD, V	*Grw*-RD
Sentence Reading Fluency (9)	*Grw*-RC; *Gs*-RS	*Grw*-RS

(Continued)

TABLE 1.1 Broad and Narrow CHC Classifications of WJ IV Tests by the Authors and Ortiz et al. (2015) (Continued)

Battery/Test Name (Number)	WJ IV Authors' Broad and Narrow CHC Ability Classifications	Ortiz et al. (2015) Broad and Narrow CHC Ability Classifications
Math Facts Fluency (10)	Gq-A3; Gs-N	Gs-N
Sentence Writing Fluency (11)	Grw-WA; Gs-WS	Grw-WS
Reading Recall (12)	Grw-RC; Glr-MM	Grw-RC; Glr-MM
Number Matrices (13)	Gf-RQ	Gf-RQ
Editing (14)	Grw-EU	Grw-EU
Word Reading Fluency (15)	Grw-RC; Gs-RS	Grw-RS
Spelling of Sounds (16)	Grw-SG; Ga-PC	Grw-SG
Reading Vocabulary (17)	Grw-RC; Gc-VL	Grw-RC; Gc-VL
Science (18)	Gkn-K0; Gc-K1	Gkn-K1
Social Studies (19)	Gkn-K0; Gc-K2, A5	Gkn-K2, A5
Humanities (20)	Gkn-K0; Gc-K2	Gkn-K2
WJ IV OL		
Picture Vocabulary (1)	Gc-VL, LD	Gc-VL
Oral Comprehension (2)	Gc-LS	Gc-LS
Segmentation (3)	Ga-PC	Ga-PC
Rapid Picture Naming (4)	Glr-NA, LA	Glr-NA
Sentence Repetition (5)	Gwm-MS; Gc-LS	Gsm-MS
Understanding Directions (6)	Gwm-WM; Gc-LS	Gsm-MW
Sound Blending (7)	Ga-PC	Ga-PC
Retrieval Fluency (8)	Glr-FI, LA	Glr-FI
Sound Awareness (9)	Ga-PC	Ga-PC

Notes: Gf = fluid reasoning; Gc = crystallized intelligence; Gkn = domain-specific knowledge; Gv=visual processing; Gwm =short-term working memory; Gsm = short-term memory; Glr = long-term storage and retrieval; Ga = auditory processing; Gs =processing speed; Gq = quantitative knowledge; Grw = reading and writing; RQ = quantitative reasoning; I = induction; RG = general sequential reasoning; VL = lexical knowledge; LD = language development; K0 = general (verbal) knowledge; LS = listening ability; K1 = general science information; K2 = knowledge of culture; A5 = range of geography knowledge; MV = visual memory; Vz = visualization; SS = spatial scanning; MW = working memory; WM = working memory capacity; AC = attentional control; MS = memory span; MA = associative memory; FI = ideational fluency; NA = naming facility; LA = speed of lexical access; FW = word fluency; MM = meaningful memory; PC = phonetic coding; UM = memory for sound patterns; P = perceptual speed; N = number facility; A3 = math achievement; RD = reading decoding; RS = reading speed; SG = spelling ability; RC = reading comprehension; V = verbal (printed) language comprehension; WA = writing ability; WS = writing speed; EU = English usage knowledge. McGrew et al. (2014) replaced Gsm with Gwm because they believe that Gwm is "a broad cognitive ability, consistent with current neuroscience research that posits a dynamic system for both temporary storage and manipulation of information in human cognition", p.4. The interested reader is referred to McGrew et al. for details regarding the decision to replace Gsm with Gwm.

Mather & Wendling, in this volume; Miller, McGill, & Johnson, in this volume; Niileksela, Reynolds, Keith, & McGrew, in this volume; and Schneider, in this volume, for additional discussions regarding the abilities measured by the WJ IV).

ORGANIZATION OF THE WJ IV COG, WJ IV ACH, AND WJ IV OL

WJ IV COG

The WJ IV COG tests are included in two batteries: the Standard Battery (Tests 1–10) and the Extended Battery (Tests 11–18) (Mather & Wendling, 2014b). The WJ IV offers the flexibility for examiners to use the Standard Battery alone or in conjunction with the Extended Battery. Table 1.2 lists the WJ IV COG tests that compose the standard and extended batteries as well as the cognitive composites, CHC factors, and narrow ability and other clinical clusters that can be derived from each battery. The CHC factors, narrow ability clusters, and other clinical clusters provide the primary interpretative information for examiners to

---

TABLE 1.2 WJ IV COG Batteries/Tests, Cognitive Composites, CHC Factors, and Narrow Ability and Other Clinical Clusters

Standard Battery	Extended Battery
Test 1: Oral Vocabulary	Test 11: Number-Pattern Matching
Test 2: Number Series	Test 12: Nonword Repetition
Test 3: Verbal Attention	Test 13: Visual-Auditory Learning
Test 4: Letter-Pattern Matching	Test 14: Picture Recognition
Test 5: Phonological Processing	Test 15: Analysis-Synthesis
Test 6: Story Recall	Test 16: Object-Number
Test 7: Visualization	Sequencing
Test 8: General Information	Test 17: Pair Cancelation
Test 9: Concept Formation	Test 18: Memory for Words
Test 10: Numbers Reversed	**CHC Extended Factors**: Fluid
Cognitive Composites: General Intellectual	Reasoning (*Gf*) and Short-Term
Ability, Brief Intellectual Ability, and *Gf–Gc*	Working Memory (*Gwm*)
CHC Factors: Comprehension-Knowledge (*Gc*),	**Narrow Ability and Other Clinical**
Comprehension-Knowledge Extended (*Gc*-Ext;	**Clusters:** Quantitative Reasoning
includes Test 1: Picture Vocabulary from the WJ	(RQ), Auditory Memory Span
IV OL), Fluid Reasoning (*Gf*), Short-Term Working	(MS; includes Test 2: Sentence
Memory (*Gwm*), Cognitive Processing Speed (*Gs*),	Repetition from the WJ IV OL),
Auditory Processing (*Ga*), Long-Term Retrieval	Number Facility (N), Perceptual
(*Glr*), and Visual Processing (*Gv*)	Speed (P), and Cognitive Efficiency
Narrow Ability Cluster: Vocabulary (VL/LD;	(Standard and Extended)
includes Test 1: Picture Vocabulary from the WJ	
IV OL)	

identify an individual's strengths and weaknesses. Most CHC factors and clinical clusters are composed of two tests. Additional tests are required to create an extended version of some of the CHC factors and one clinical cluster listed in Table 1.2. For example, in order to create an extended *Gf* cluster the examiner must administer Test 15: Analysis-Synthesis. In order to create an extended *Gc* cluster, the examiner must administer Test 1: Picture Vocabulary from the WJ IV OL. Table 1.3 provides brief descriptions of the WJ IV COG tests.

Mather and Wendling (2014b) indicated that the WJ IV COG includes several changes from the Woodcock-Johnson III Tests of Cognitive Abilities (WJ III COG; Woodcock, McGrew, & Mather, 2001b). First, the WJ IV COG includes six new or modified tests measuring information-processing abilities such as Test 1: Oral Vocabulary, Test 3: Verbal Attention, Test 4: Letter-Pattern Matching, Test 5: Phonological Processing, Test 7: Visualization, and Test 12: Nonword Repetition. Second, the WJ IV COG provides narrow ability clusters such as Number Facility and Perceptual Speed. Third, some tests from the WJ III COG have been moved to the WJ IV OL including Rapid Picture Naming and Sound Blending. Fourth, several tests from the WJ III COG are no longer included in the WJ IV such as Visual-Auditory Learning-Delayed, Auditory Attention, and Planning. Fifth, name changes have been applied to some tests to address better the task requirements (e.g., Visual Matching was renamed Number-Pattern Matching and Spatial Relations was renamed Visualization). Sixth, broad and narrow CHC abilities are included to facilitate more in-depth diagnostic evaluation. Seventh, there are three options to measure general intellectual ability. The General Intellectual Ability (GIA) can be derived from a core set of tests (Tests 1–7, see Table 1.2) and provides the foundation for the intra-cognitive variation procedure. The Brief Intellectual Ability (BIA) can be derived from Tests 1–3 (Table 1.2) and the new *Gf–Gc* composite is composed of Tests 1, 2, 8, and 9 (Table 1.2) and allows examiners to recapture the ability-achievement discrepancy model.

WJ IV ACH

The WJ IV ACH is a revised and expanded version of the Woodcock-Johnson III Tests of Achievement (WJ III ACH; Woodcock, McGrew, & Mather, 2001c). According to Mather and Wendling (2014a), there are several features of the WJ IV ACH that were not part of the WJ III ACH. First, the WJ IV ACH has three parallel forms of the Standard Battery to reduce examinees' familiarity and over-practice with specific test items and one form of the Extended Battery, whereas the WJ III ACH only had two parallel forms of the Standard Battery. Second, in comparison to the WJ III ACH, the WJ IV ACH has seven new tests, such as Test 8: Oral Reading, which increases coverage of assessment and provides more options for interpretation. Third, some of the oral language tests that were previously included in the WJ III ACH (i.e., Picture Vocabulary, Oral Comprehension, Understanding Directions, and Sound Awareness) are now

TABLE 1.3 WJ IV COG Test Descriptions

Test Number and Name	Test Description
1: Oral Vocabulary	The examinee provides synonyms and antonyms for words spoken by the examiner.
2: Number Series	The examinee provides the missing number in a series of numbers.
3: Verbal Attention	The examinee listens to an intermingled series of animals and digits from an audio recording and answers questions about the series posed by the examiner.
4: Letter-Pattern Matching	The examinee locates and circles two identical letter patterns in a row of six patterns.
5: Phonological Processing	The examinee provides a word with a specific phonemic element in a specific location, names as many words as possible that begin with a specific sound within 1-min limit, and substitutes part of a word to create a new word.
6: Story Recall	The examinee recalls as many details of increasingly complex stories presented via an audio recording.
7: Visualization	The examinee identifies the two or three parts that form a complete target shape and identifies the two block patterns that match the target pattern.
8: General Information	The examinee answers questions related to general information and knowledge.
9: Concept Formation	The examinee views a complete stimulus set and must derive the rule from each item.
10: Numbers Reversed	The examinee repeats in reverse order numbers spoken by the examiner.
11: Number-Pattern Matching	The examinee locates and circles the two identical numbers in rows of six numbers.
12: Nonword Repetition	The examinee listens to a nonsense word and then repeats the word exactly how it is presented.
13: Visual-Auditory Learning	The examinee learns, stores, and retrieves a series of visual-auditory associations.
14: Picture Recognition	The examinee recognizes a subset of previously presented pictures within a field of distracting pictures.
15: Analysis-Synthesis	The examinee is given instructions by the examiner on how to perform increasingly complex procedures.
16: Object-Number Sequencing	The examinee listens to a series of digits and words presented via an audio recording, reorders the information, and repeats the objects first in order then the digits in order.
17: Pair Cancellation	The examinee locates and marks a repeated pattern as quickly as possible within a 1-min time limit.
18: Memory for Words	The examinee repeats lists of unrelated words in the same sequence as presented by the examiner.

Adapted from Mather and Wendling (2014b).

TABLE 1.4 WJ IV ACH Academic Areas, Batteries/Tests, and Clusters

Academic Area	Standard Battery (Forms A, B, and C)	Extended Battery
Reading	Test 1: Letter-Word Identification Test 4: Passage Comprehension Test 7: Word Attack Test 8: Oral Reading Test 9: Sentence Reading Fluency **Clusters**: Reading, Broad Reading, Basic Reading Skills, Reading Fluency	Test 12: Reading Recall Test 15: Word Reading Fluency Test 17: Reading Vocabulary **Clusters**: Reading Comprehension, Reading Comprehension-Extended, Reading Rate
Mathematics	Test 2: Applied Problems Test 5: Calculation Test 10: Math Facts Fluency **Clusters**: Mathematics, Broad Mathematics, Math Calculation Skills	Test 13: Number Matrices **Cluster**: Math Problem Solving
Writing	Test 3: Spelling Test 6: Writing Samples Test 11: Sentence Writing Fluency **Clusters**: Written Language, Broad Written Language, and Written Expression	Test 14: Editing Test 16: Spelling of Sounds **Cluster**: Basic Writing Skills
Academic Knowledge		Test 18: Science Test 19: Social Studies Test 20: Humanities
Cross-Domain Clusters	Academic Skills Academic Fluency Academic Applications Brief Achievement Broad Achievement	Academic Knowledge Phoneme–Grapheme Knowledge

included in the WJ IV OL. Fourth, the procedures related to ability/achievement comparisons have been simplified and have enhanced flexibility for examiners. Finally, the scholastic/achievement comparison procedure has replaced the achievement/achievement discrepancy procedure. There are six aptitude clusters: two for reading, two for math, and two for writing.

Table 1.4 illustrates the academic areas, batteries/tests, and clusters included in the WJ IV ACH. The Standard Battery is composed of 11 tests (Tests 1–11) and the Extended Battery is composed of 9 tests (Tests 12–20). The Extended Battery can be used in conjunction with any form of the Standard Battery. The Standard Battery provides a set of scores for broad domains, whereas the Extended Battery allows in-depth diagnostic evaluation of an individual's strengths and weaknesses. Table 1.5 provides brief descriptions of the WJ IV ACH tests.

TABLE 1.5 WJ IV ACH Test Descriptions

Test Number and Name	Test Description
1: Letter Number Identification	The examinee identifies letters in print and reads aloud individual words.
2: Applied Problems	The examinee analyzes and solves math problems.
3: Spelling	The examinee draws lines, traces letters, produces upper and lowercase letters, and spells words that are presented orally.
4: Passage Comprehension	The examinee reads a passage and identifies the missing word in text.
5: Calculation	The examinee performs mathematical computations such as addition, subtraction, geometry, and calculus.
6: Writing Samples	The examinee writes sentences that are evaluated for their quality of expression.
7: Word Attack	The examinee produces sounds for single letters and reads aloud nonsense or low-frequency words.
8: Oral Reading	The examinee reads aloud sentences that increase in difficulty.
9: Sentence Reading Fluency	The examinee reads simple sentences quickly and silently and decides whether the statement is true or false.
10: Math Facts Fluency	The examinee solves simple addition, subtraction, and multiplication facts as quickly as possible within a 3-min time limit.
11: Sentence Writing Fluency	The examinee is asked to formulate and write simple sentences quickly using a given stimulus picture and given set of words.
12: Reading Recall	The examinee reads a short story silently and then recalls the details of the story.
13: Number Matrices	The examinee identifies a missing number in a matrix.
14: Editing	The examinee identifies and corrects errors in a written passage.
15: Word Reading Fluency	The examinee is asked to mark the two words that go together in each row within a 3-min time limit.
16: Spelling of Sounds	The examinee spells nonsense words or low-frequency words presented via an audio recording.
17: Reading Vocabulary	The examinee reads words and provides either a synonym or antonym for the word.
18: Science	The examinee answers questions related to anatomy, biology, chemistry, geology, medicine, and physics.
19: Social Studies	The examinee answers questions related to history, economics, geography, government, and psychology.
20: Humanities	The examinee answers questions related to art, music, and literature.

Adapted from Mather and Wendling (2014a).

The WJ IV ACH allows for flexible use of different sets of tests to yield clusters in Reading, Written Language, Mathematics, Academic Skills, Academic Applications, and Brief Achievement, which provide the basis for intra-achievement variation comparisons (Mather & Wendling, 2014a). An examiner does not have to administer all of the tests or complete all of the assessment options for a given examinee. Rather, examiners should be guided by the referral questions, interview data, observations, previous assessment data, and the like to determine what WJ IV tests to administer. Indeed, the WJ IV ACH offers a tool chest whereby examiners can use different combinations of tools to individualize and customize the evaluation based on the needs of the examinee. There are 22 clusters listed in Table 1.4 and they are the primary sources of interpretative information to determine inter- and intra-individual strengths and weaknesses, to assist progress monitoring, and to facilitate appropriate educational placement.

WJ IV OL

The WJ IV OL is a new addition to the WJ family of instruments. However, many of the tests found on the WJ IV OL were included in the WJ III COG or the WJ III ACH. Several characteristics of the WJ IV OL include the following: (i) the WJ IV OL has been co-normed with the WJ IV COG and the WJ IV ACH; (ii) the tests included in the WJ IV OL offer measures of various areas of oral language, such as listening comprehension, oral expression, and auditory memory span; (iii) the WJ IV OL includes English and Spanish tests; (iv) Tests 1–4 of the WJ IV OL provide the basis for the intra-oral language variations procedure; and (v) the WJ IV OL provides an oral language ability/achievement procedure to determine the discrepancy between oral language ability and predicted achievement (Mather & Wendling, 2014c). Table 1.6 lists the tests and clusters included in the WJ IV OL and Table 1.7 provides brief descriptions of the WJ IV OL tests. The WJ IV OL provides three Spanish tests that are parallel to the English versions. The Spanish test format has the same test format as the English test format; however, the test items are different.

CONTENT OF THE WJ IV COG, WJ IV ACH, AND WJ IV OL

Brief Description of Broad and Narrow CHC Abilities and Composition of WJ IV COG Factors and Clusters

The WJ IV COG includes indicators of broad and narrow CHC abilities and other clinical clusters. Although broad abilities are important, narrow abilities and other clinical clusters are emphasized because of their clinical utility, predictive values of academic achievement, and alignment with contemporary advances in neurocognitive studies (McGrew, 2012; McGrew & Wendling, 2010).

Comprehension-Knowledge (*Gc*) includes indicators of the breadth and depth of one's acquired knowledge, verbal communication, and the ability to

TABLE 1.6 WJ IV OL English and Spanish Tests and Clusters

English Tests	Spanish Tests
Test 1: Picture Vocabulary	Test 10: Vocabulario sobre dibujos
Test 2: Oral Comprehension	Test 11: Comprensión oral
Test 3: Segmentation	
Test 4: Rapid Picture Naming	
Test 5: Sentence Repetition	
Test 6: Understanding Directions	Test 12: Comprensión de indicaciones
Test 7: Sound Blending	
Test 8: Retrieval Fluency	
Test 9: Sound Awareness	
WJ IV OL Clusters	**Cross-Battery Clusters**
Oral Language, Broad Oral Language, Oral Expression, Listening Comprehension, Phonetic Coding, Speed of Lexical Access, Lenguaje oral, Amplio lenguaje oral, Comprensión auditiva	Vocabulary, Comprehension-Knowledge-Extended, Auditory Memory Span

apply and reason using previously learned experiences and knowledge (Cattell, 1941, 1943). The *Gc* factor is believed to include declarative and procedural knowledge. Declarative knowledge refers to acquired facts, understanding of rules, concepts, social norms, and relationships and is often presented through the verbal modality (Mather & Wendling, 2014b). Procedural knowledge refers to specific skills such as those used in driving, drawing, and playing musical instruments. The *Gc* factor on the WJ IV COG includes Test 1: Oral Vocabulary and Test 8: General Information which are measures of declarative knowledge (Mather & Wendling, 2014b).

Fluid Reasoning (*Gf*) is the broad ability involved in reasoning, forming concepts, and solving problems using unfamiliar information or in novel situations (Cattell, 1941, 1943). It includes inductive, deductive, and quantitative reasoning and is considered as a mixture of many mental operations, such as identifying relations, forming concepts, and recognizing patterns (Horn, 1991). Fluid Reasoning involves minimal effects of learning and acculturation and often requires deliberate and flexible control of attention and concentration to solve problems. The *Gf* factor on the WJ IV COG includes Test 2: Number Series and Test 9: Concept Formation. When Test 15: Analysis-Synthesis is administered, a Fluid Reasoning-Extended cluster is obtained.

TABLE 1.7 WJ IV OL Test Descriptions

Test Number and Name	Test Description
1: Picture Vocabulary	The examinee identifies pictures of objects.
2: Oral Comprehension	The examinee listens to a short audio-recorded passage and then supplies the missing word using syntactic and semantic cues.
3: Segmentation	The examinee listens to words and identifies the word parts (e.g., compound words, phonemes).
4: Rapid Picture Naming	The examinee names pictures as quickly as possible within a 2-min time limit.
5: Sentence Repetition	The examinee repeats words, phrases, and sentences presented from an audio recording.
6: Understanding Directions	The examinee listens to a sequence of audio-recorded instructions and then points to various objects in a colored picture according to those instructions.
7: Sound Blending	The examinee listens to a series of syllables or phonemes and blends the sounds into a word.
8: Retrieval Fluency	The examinee names as many examples as possible from a given category within a 1-min time limit.
9: Sound Awareness	The examinee deletes word parts and phonemes from words presented orally.
10: Vocabulario sobre dibujos	The examinee identifies pictures of objects in Spanish.
11: Comprensión oral	The examinee listens to a short audio-recorded passage in Spanish and then supplies the missing word using syntactic and semantic cues.
12: Comprensión de indicaciones	The examinee listens to a sequence of audio-recorded instructions in Spanish and then points to various objects in a colored picture according to those instructions.

Adapted from Mather and Wendling (2014c).

Long-Term Retrieval (*Glr*) refers to the ability to store information and fluently retrieve it minutes, hours, days, or even years later (Schneider & McGrew, 2012). The efficiency of Long-Term Retrieval is determined by the amount of information that can be stored and the rate and fluency that one can retrieve and access the information and is the processing mechanism that transfers information from immediate awareness to the stores of declarative and procedural knowledge (Carroll, 1993; Horn, 1965, 1991). The *Glr* factor on the WJ IV COG includes Test 6: Story Recall and Test 13: Visual-Auditory Learning.

Visual Processing (*Gv*) pertains to the ability to perceive, analyze, synthesize, and think with visual patterns and involves the ability to store and recall visual representations via visual imagery and visual memory (Carroll, 1993; Horn, 1965, 1991). This broad ability includes a number of specific, narrow, visual, or spatial abilities, such as the ability to manipulate objects and patterns mentally, visual imagery, and visual memory (Schneider & McGrew, 2012). The *Gv* factor on the WJ IV COG includes Test 7: Visualization and Test 14: Picture Recognition.

Auditory Processing (*Ga*) refers to the ability to encode, synthesize, and discriminate auditory stimuli and to process and discriminate speech sounds (Carroll, 1993; Horn, 1965, 1991). *Ga* tasks often tap phonological awareness, phonological processing, phonological sensitivity, and coding at the phoneme level (Schneider & McGrew, 2012). The *Ga* factor on the WJ IV COG includes Test 5: Phonological Processing and Test 12: Nonword Repetition.

Tasks that require examinees to perform automatic, simple, and repetitive cognitive tasks with sustained attention and concentration are indicators of Cognitive Processing Speed (*Gs*) (Carroll, 1993; Horn, 1991; Horn & Blankson, 2005). Typically, these tasks require rapid processing without much thinking. *Gs* is one aspect of cognitive efficiency. The *Gs* factor on the WJ IV COG includes Test 4: Letter-Pattern Matching and Test 17: Pair Cancellation.

Short-Term Working Memory (*Gwm*) includes indicators of the ability to apprehend and hold information in immediate awareness and then use or manipulate that information to carry out a task within a short period of time (Carroll, 1993; Horn, 1965, 1991). *Gwm* is believed to be very limited and information is typically held for a few seconds before it is forgotten. The *Gwm* factor on the WJ IV COG includes Test 3: Verbal Attention and Test 10: Numbers Reversed. When Test 16: Object-Number Sequencing is administered, a Short-Term Working Memory-Extended cluster is obtained.

The WJ IV COG provides additional narrow CHC ability clusters and other clinical clusters for examiners to provide in-depth information for clinical diagnostic purposes. The WJ IV COG includes five narrow CHC ability clusters and one clinical cluster (i.e., Cognitive Efficiency).

The narrow ability Perceptual Speed (*Gs*:P) is emphasized in the WJ IV COG because of its clinical relevance. Perceptual Speed refers to the ability to work on simple and mechanical clerical tasks that use visual symbols as the stimuli, such as matching numbers and letters (Schneider & McGrew, 2012). It is related to orthographic processing, visual scanning, visual decoding, and encoding. The Perceptual Speed cluster on the WJ IV COG includes Test 4: Letter-Pattern Matching and Test 11: Number-Pattern Matching.

The narrow ability Quantitative Reasoning (*Gf*:RQ) includes indicators of inductive and deductive reasoning skills that involve numbers, mathematical relations, and numerical operations (Carroll, 1993; Cattell, 1941, 1943). The Quantitative Reasoning cluster on the WJ IV COG includes Test 2: Number Series and Test 15: Analysis-Synthesis.

Auditory Memory Span (*Gwm*:MS) is a narrow ability of working memory and refers to the ability to hold auditory information in immediate format (Carroll, 1993; Horn, 1991). Auditory Memory Span tasks often require examinees to hold verbal information in immediate memory and then repeat the information in the sequence presented (McGrew et al., 2014). This cluster on the WJ IV COG includes Test 18: Memory for Words from the WJ IV COG and Test 5: Sentence Repetition from the WJ IV OL.

Number Facility (*Gs*:N) is a narrow ability that involves fluency with numbers, such as number pattern comparison or manipulation of numbers in working memory (Schneider & McGrew, 2012). This cluster on the WJ IV COG includes Test 10: Numbers Reversed and Test 11: Number-Pattern Matching.

Vocabulary (*Gv*:VL) is lexical knowledge or knowledge of the definitions of words and the concepts that underlie them (Carroll, 1993; Cattell, 1941, 1943). There are two tests that measure Vocabulary including Test 1: Oral Vocabulary from the WJ IV COG and Test 1: Picture Vocabulary from the WJ IV OL.

The Cognitive Efficiency cluster on the WJ IV COG involves Cognitive Processing Speed (*Gs*) and Short-Term Working Memory (*Gwm*). The combination of these abilities provides a diagnostic index that assesses one's sustained attention, the ability to hold and manipulate information in conscious awareness to problem solve, and the automaticity to perform tasks rapidly and accurately (Mather & Wendling, 2014b; McGrew et al., 2014). Deficits in the area of cognitive efficiency might result in constrained performance on complex cognitive tasks. The Cognitive Efficiency standard cluster on the WJ IV COG includes Test 4: Letter-Pattern Matching under the *Gs* factor and Test 10: Numbers Reversed under the *Gwm* factor. The administration of Test 3: Verbal Attention (*Gwm*) and Test 11: Number-Pattern Matching (*Gs*) yields a Cognitive Efficiency-Extended cluster.

Brief Description of Additional Broad CHC Abilities and Composition of WJ IV ACH Clusters

The WJ IV ACH includes two broad CHC abilities that are not found or measured on the WJ IV COG; namely, Quantitative Knowledge (*Gq*) and Reading-Writing (*Grw*). Quantitative Knowledge was recognized as a distinct CHC ability after Horn's work (1988, 1989) and refers to the ability to comprehend quantitative concepts and relationships and to manipulate numerical symbols (Carroll, 1993; Cattell, 1943). Tasks addressing *Gq* often tap elements of mathematics (e.g., addition and subtraction) and applications of mathematical thinking (e.g., word problem solving, measurement, and statistics). WJ IV ACH tests that tap *Gq* include Test 2: Applied Problems, Test 5: Calculation, and Test 10: Math Facts Fluency.

Grw was the latest addition to the broad CHC abilities (Carroll & Maxwell, 1979; Woodcock, 1998), although consistent with Cattell's (1943) thinking regarding *Gc*. This ability includes tasks that require examinees to decode words, spell words, read and comprehend text, and write sentences, paragraphs, and stories.

WJ IV ACH tests that tap *Grw* include Test 1: Letter-Word Identification, Test 3: Spelling, Test 4: Passage Comprehension, Test 6: Writing Samples, Test 7: Word Attack, Test 8: Oral Reading, Test 9: Sentence Reading Fluency, Test 11: Sentence Writing Fluency, Test 16: Reading Recall, Test 14: Editing, Test 15: Word Reading Fluency, Test 16: Spelling of Sounds, and Test 17: Reading Vocabulary.

Reading Clusters

The WJ IV ACH includes seven reading clusters, four of which use tests from the Standard Battery and three of which require additional tests from the Extended Battery (Mather & Wendling, 2014a). The Reading cluster provides a measure of reading achievement via an individual's ability to decode words and the ability to comprehend meaning of text while reading. It is composed of Test 1: Letter-Word Identification and Test 4: Passage Comprehension. The Broad Reading cluster yields a measure of overall reading achievement and taps into the areas of reading decoding (Test 1: Letter-Word Identification), reading comprehension (Test 4: Passage Comprehension), and reading speed (Test 9: Sentence Reading Fluency). The Basic Reading Skills cluster includes indicators of sight vocabulary, phonics, and structural analysis skills. This cluster includes Test 1: Letter-Word Identification and Test 7: Word Attack. The Reading Comprehension cluster is a broad measure of reading comprehension and taps reading comprehension, vocabulary, and reasoning and includes Test 4: Passage Comprehension from the Standard Battery and Test 12: Reading Recall from the Extended Battery. Examiners who would like to generate the Reading Comprehension-Extended cluster must also administer Test 17: Reading Vocabulary from the Extended Battery.

The Reading Fluency cluster is a measure of several aspects of reading fluency including prosody, automaticity, and accuracy. It includes Test 8: Oral Reading and Test 9: Sentence Reading Fluency. Finally, the Reading Rate cluster is a measure of automaticity with reading at the word and sentence levels. It includes Test 9: Sentence Reading Fluency from the Standard Battery and Test 15: Word Reading Fluency from the Extended Battery.

Mathematics Clusters

There are four math clusters on the WJ IV ACH. Three clusters are composed of tests from the Standard Battery and one cluster requires a test from the Extended Battery (Mather & Wendling, 2014a). The Mathematics cluster includes tasks that measure problem solving and computational skills. This cluster includes Test 2: Applied Problems and Test 5: Calculation. The Broad Mathematics cluster is a comprehensive measure of math achievement that involves problem solving, number facility, automaticity, and reasoning skills. It includes Test 2: Applied Problems, Test 5: Calculation, and Test 10: Math Facts Fluency. The Math Calculation Skills cluster includes indicators of computational skills and fluency with basic math facts. This cluster includes Test 5: Calculation and Test 10: Math Facts Fluency. The Math Problem Solving cluster yields a measure of mathematical knowledge and reasoning. Tasks on this cluster require examinees to problem solve, analyze, and reason. This cluster includes Test 2: Applied Problems from the Standard Battery and Test 13: Number Matrices from the Extended Battery.

Written Language Clusters

The WJ IV ACH includes four written language clusters. Three of them are composed of tests from the Standard Battery and one of them requires tests from the Standard Battery and the Extended Battery (Mather & Wendling, 2014a). The Written Language cluster, an indicator of written language achievement, requires examinees to spell single words and to write sentences of increasing complexity. This cluster is composed of Test 3: Spelling and Test 6: Writing Samples. The Broad Written Language cluster yields a comprehensive measure of written achievement. The tasks require examinees to spell single words, write fluently, and write with quality of expression. It is composed of Test 3: Spelling, Test 6: Writing Samples, and Test 11: Sentence Writing Fluency. The Basic Writing Skills cluster includes indicators of basic writing skills through isolated format and contextually related format. Tasks on this cluster require examinees to spell single words and to identify and correct errors in spelling, punctuation, and capitalization. This cluster includes Test 3: Spelling from the Standard Battery and Test 14: Editing from the Extended Battery. Finally, the Written Expression cluster requires examinees to produce meaningful written expression and taps fluency of written production. It is composed of Test 6: Writing Samples and Test 11: Sentence Writing Fluency.

Cross-Domain Clusters

The WJ IV ACH provides seven cross-domain clusters. The Brief Achievement and Broad Achievement clusters require administration of tests from the Standard Battery. The other five clusters, including Academic Skills, Academic Fluency, Academic Applications, Academic Knowledge, and Phoneme–Grapheme Knowledge, require combinations of tests from the Standard Battery and Extended Battery. Based on the Academic Skills, Academic Fluency, and Academic Application clusters, examiners can identify significant strengths and weaknesses of examinees across various academic domains. Space limitations preclude a description of the cross-domain clusters; however, the interested reader is referred to Mather and Wendling (2014a) who provide details regarding the purpose, composition, and diagnostic utility of these cross-domain clusters.

Brief Description and Composition of WJ IV OL Clusters

The WJ IV OL includes nine clusters: six from the English tests and three from the Spanish tests (Mather & Wendling, 2014c). The Spanish clusters are designed in parallel format to three of the English clusters to ensure accurate comparison of an examinee's proficiency in English and Spanish. Additional clusters may be obtained by using the combination of tests from the WJ IV OL and the WJ IV COG.

The Oral Language cluster includes indicators of an individual's lexical knowledge, listening ability, and verbal comprehension. It includes Test 1: Picture

Vocabulary and Test 2: Oral Comprehension. The name of the parallel Spanish cluster is Lenguaje oral and includes Test 10: Vocabulario sobre dibujos and Test 11: Comprensión oral. The Broad Oral Language cluster taps an individual's lexical knowledge, listening ability, verbal comprehension, syntactic knowledge, working memory, and auditory memory span. This cluster is composed of Test 1: Picture Vocabulary, Test 2: Oral Comprehension, and Test 6: Understanding Directions. The name of the parallel Spanish cluster is Amplio lenguaje oral and includes Test 10: Vocabulario sobre dibujos, Test 11: Comprensión oral, and Test 12: Comprensión de indicaciones.

The Oral Expression cluster includes indicators of lexical knowledge, language development, and syntactic knowledge. It is composed of Test 1: Picture Vocabulary and Test 5: Sentence Repetition. The Listening Comprehension cluster taps an individual's listening ability and verbal comprehension. This cluster includes Test 2: Oral Comprehension and Test 6: Understanding Directions. Its parallel Spanish cluster is called Comprensión auditiva and includes Test 11: Comprensión oral and Test 12: Comprensión de indicaciones.

The Phonetic Coding cluster includes Test 3: Segmentation and Test 7: Sound Blending and taps an individual's auditory processing abilities, including analysis and synthesis of phonological information. The Speed of Lexical Access cluster was constructed to include indicators of an examinee's efficiency and fluency in retrieving words. It includes tasks that tap lexical knowledge, listening ability, and verbal comprehension skills. It is composed of Test 4: Rapid Picture Naming and Test 8: Retrieval Fluency.

The WJ IV OL includes three additional clusters that require the administration of tests from the WJ IV COG (Mather & Wendling, 2014c). The Vocabulary cluster includes Test 1: Picture Vocabulary from the WJ IV OL and Test 1: Oral Vocabulary from the WJ IV COG and provides information regarding an individual's expressive vocabulary, lexical knowledge, and verbal reasoning. The Comprehension-Knowledge-Extended cluster includes Test 1: Picture Vocabulary from the WJ IV OL and Test 1: Oral Vocabulary and Test 8: General Information from the WJ IV COG. Finally, the Auditory Memory Span cluster includes tasks that require examinees to hold auditory information in immediate awareness and is composed of Test 5: Sentence Repetition from the WJ IV OL and Test 18: Memory for Words from the WJ IV COG.

STANDARDIZATION CHARACTERISTICS AND PSYCHOMETRIC PROPERTIES OF THE WJ IV

The *Standards for Educational and Psychological Testing*[1] (Standards; American Educational Research Association, American Psychological Association, &

---

1. The most recent edition of the *Standards for Educational and Psychological Testing* (American Educational Research Association, American Psychological Association, & National Council on Measurement in Education, 2014) was not available at the time the Woodcock-Johnson IV (Schrank et al., 2014a) was under construction.

National Council on Measurement in Education, 1999) guided the norming and technical analyses for the WJ IV (McGrew et al., 2014). In this section, we provide a brief description of the standardization characteristics and psychometric properties of the WJ IV including reliability, floors and ceilings, and validity evidence. Although the objective of this section of the chapter is largely to apprise readers of what data they will and will not find in the *WJ IV Technical Manual* (McGrew et al., 2014) to support the use of the WJ IV in the assessment of individuals' cognitive, achievement, and oral language abilities, we offer preliminary comments or reviews of these data to initiate conversations about the psychometric rigor of the WJ IV. Several sources were used to assist us in making these preliminary comments or reviews of the psychometric data provided in the technical manual, including Alfonso and Flanagan (2009), Bracken (1987), Emmons and Alfonso (2005), Flanagan and Alfonso (1995), Flanagan, Ortiz, Alfonso, and Mascolo (2006), Hammill, Brown, and Bryant (1992), and Kranzler and Floyd (2013).

Standardization Characteristics

The WJ IV normative data are based on a single sample that was administered the cognitive, achievement, and oral language tests between December 2009 and January 2012. Thus, the normative data are recent and considered meaningful and useful for diagnostic purposes for many years to come. The national standardization sample included 7416 participants, consisting of 664 preschoolers (ages 2–5 years), 3891 K-12 students, 775 adults with college/university-level education, and 2086 adults. With the exception of age 2 years, each 1-year age interval between 3 and 19 years consisted of at least 200 individuals. Between ages 20 and 80+ years the range of participants was 117 (80+ years) to 759 (20–29 years) with an average of 343 participants per 10-year age interval. By most standards, the number of participants per age interval is considered good. Nevertheless, examiners should be aware of the lower number of participants at the lowest and highest age intervals.

The sample represented 100 geographically diverse communities from 46 states and the District of Columbia. A stratified sampling design was used to control for many community and examinee variables including census region, sex, country of birth, race, ethnicity, community type, parent education, type of school, type of college, educational attainment, employment status, and occupational level of adults in the labor force. According to McGrew et al. (2014), the demographic features and community characteristics matched those of the general US population using the 2010 Census projections. Close examination of the data indicated, however, that for several variables the percentage in the US population and percentage in the norm sample differed by more than 5 percentage points (e.g., college and university norming sample, college type; public 2-year and adult norming sample, country of birth 20–29 years).

Because there were sizeable differences between the US population estimates and the norming sample on several standardization sample characteristics, examinee weighting was used. Complete details of the weighting procedures are found in McGrew et al. (2014). There does not seem to be consensus on what constitutes good or sufficient match of demographic variables to census data. In our opinion, the stratified sampling design of the WJ IV is impressive especially given the number of community and examinee variables. Therefore, we believe that the match of the demographic characteristics of the normative samples to the US population is good overall. Nevertheless, examiners may want to review Tables 3.2–3.5 in McGrew et al. to determine for themselves if their examinee's characteristics are adequately represented in the normative sample before weighting procedures were applied as this may assist in qualifying test results of specific examinees.

Reliability[2]

According to McGrew et al. (2014), the goal for WJ IV cluster reliability was set at 0.90 or higher and the goal for WJ IV test reliability was set at 0.80 or higher. Tables 1.8–1.10 provide the median internal consistency reliability coefficients for all clusters of the WJ IV COG, WJ IV ACH, and WJ IV OL together with the corresponding age range. Approximately 91% of the median internal consistency reliability coefficients for the WJ IV clusters are ≥0.90 and thus regarded as good. The remaining 9% are regarded as adequate. A review of WJ IV median internal consistency reliability coefficients for all nonspeeded WJ IV tests indicated that 44% are ≥0.90, 54% are between 0.80 and 0.89, and 2% are ≤0.80. Thus, 98% of the WJ IV nonspeeded tests demonstrate median internal consistency reliability coefficients ≥0.80 meeting the goal set by the authors. We believe that 44% of the coefficients are good, 54% are adequate, and 2% are inadequate.

A different procedure was used to determine the reliability of the WJ IV speeded tests. According to McGrew et al. (2014), a test–retest reliability study was conducted with all WJ IV speeded tests. Participants in three separate age groups (i.e., 7–11 years, 14–17 years, and 26–79 years) were administered the eight speeded tests two times with a 1-day interval in between test administrations which is regarded as good for speeded tests. The numbers of participants in the three groups ranged between 46 and 50 and are rather low for a test–retest reliability study and considerably lower than the number of participants used to determine the internal consistency reliability coefficients for the nonspeeded tests discussed above. In addition, no other details were provided about the test–retest reliability study participants, which makes replication of the study impossible. A review of the 24 test–retest reliability coefficients for all speeded

---

2. In this chapter we discuss briefly internal consistency reliability and test–retest reliability of the WJ IV (Schrank et al., 2014a). McGrew et al. (2014) also discuss alternate-forms equivalence for the WJ IV ACH (Schrank, Mather, et al., 2014a) battery which has three parallel forms.

TABLE 1.8 Median Internal Consistency Reliability Coefficients for the WJ IV COG Clusters with Corresponding Age Range in Years

WJ IV COG Cluster	Median Internal Consistency Reliability Coefficient	Age Range in Years
General Intellectual Ability	0.97	5–80+
Brief Intellectual Ability	0.94	5–80+
Gf–Gc Composite	0.96	5–80+
Comprehension-Knowledge	0.93	4–80+
Comprehension-Knowledge-Extended	0.94	4–80+
Fluid Reasoning	0.94	5–80+
Fluid Reasoning-Extended	0.96	5–80+
Short-Term Working Memory	0.91	3–80+
Short-Term Working Memory-Extended	0.93	5–80+
Cognitive Processing Speed	0.94	4–80+
Auditory Processing	0.92	3–80+
Long-Term Retrieval	0.97	2–80+
Visual Processing	0.86	2–80+
Quantitative Reasoning	0.94	5–80+
Auditory Memory Span	0.90	2–80+
Number Facility	0.90	3–80+
Perceptual Speed	0.93	4–80+
Cognitive Efficiency	0.93	4–80+
Cognitive Efficiency-Extended	0.95	4–80+
Reading Aptitude A	0.89	4–80+
Reading Aptitude B	0.90	3–80+
Math Aptitude A	0.89	5–80+
Math Aptitude B	0.89	5–80+
Writing Aptitude A	0.89	4–80+
Writing Aptitude B	0.90	3–80+

TABLE 1.9 Median Internal Consistency Reliability Coefficients for the WJ IV ACH Clusters with Corresponding Age Range in Years

WJ IV ACH Cluster	Median Internal Consistency Reliability Coefficient	Age Range in Years
Reading	0.95	2–80+
Broad Reading	0.97	5–80+
Basic Reading Skills	0.95	5–80+
Reading Comprehension	0.93	5–80+
Reading Comprehension-Extended	0.96	5–80+
Reading Fluency	0.96	5–80+
Reading Rate	0.96	5–80+
Mathematics	0.96	5–80+
Broad Mathematics	0.97	5–80+
Math Calculation Skills	0.97	5–80+
Math Problem Solving	0.95	5–80+
Written Language	0.94	4–80+
Broad Written Language	0.95	5–80+
Basic Writing Skills	0.95	7–80+
Written Expression	0.92	5–80+
Academic Skills	0.97	5–80+
Academic Applications	0.96	4–80+
Academic Fluency	0.97	5–80+
Academic Knowledge	0.95	2–80+
Phoneme–Grapheme Knowledge	0.94	5–80+
Brief Achievement	0.97	2–80+
Broad Achievement	0.99	5–80+

WJ IV tests across the three age groups indicated that 92% are ≥0.80 and thus regarded as adequate and 8% are <0.80 and regarded as inadequate. There are no other test–retest reliability coefficients reported in McGrew et al. Clearly, additional test–retest reliability studies are needed to determine the stability of

TABLE 1.10 Median Internal Consistency Reliability Coefficients for the WJ IV OL Clusters with Corresponding Age Range in Years

WJ IV OL Cluster	Median Internal Consistency Reliability Coefficient	Age Range in Years
Oral Language	0.90	2–80+
Broad Oral Language	0.92	2–80+
Oral Expression	0.89	2–80+
Listening Comprehension	0.90	2–80+
Phonetic Coding	0.95	3–80+
Speed of Lexical Access	0.89	2–80+
Vocabulary	0.93	4–80+

the WJ IV tests and clusters. These studies should include sufficient numbers of participants, provide details regarding participants' characteristics (e.g., geographic region, sex, social economic status), and demonstrate at least adequate test–retest reliability coefficients (Alfonso & Flanagan, 2009). Interested readers may want to review detailed information regarding reliability of the WJ IV in McGrew et al. (2014, pp. 87–117 and pp. 253–305).

Floors and Ceilings[3]

WJ IV test and cluster floors and ceilings are not discussed by McGrew et al. (2014). However, Floyd, Woods, Singh, and Hawkins (in this volume) discuss the adequacy of the WJ IV COG tests that contribute to the GIA and *Gf–Gc* composites as well as the adequacy of floors of the composites themselves because of their importance in the diagnosis of intellectual disability (ID). If tests and composites do not have adequate floors (i.e., yield normative scores that effectively discriminate among various degrees of functioning at the lower extremes of an ability continuum), overestimates of ability may occur and subsequent services may not be provided for those who need them the most (i.e., low

---

3. Another important test characteristic and one that is related to floors and ceilings is item gradients which refer to the density of items across a test's latent trait scale. We do not discuss the WJ IV's test item gradients because norms tables are not provided; rather, all derived test scores are provided via online scoring without access to test score distributions. The interested reader is referred to Bracken (1987), Flanagan and Alfonso (1995), and Alfonso and Flanagan (2009) for discussions on item gradients and item gradient violations.

functioning individuals). According to Floyd et al., "In sum, although the WJ IV GIA and the *Gf–Gc* Composite can produce sufficiently low norm-referenced scores to identify ID beginning age 5-0 years, some of their constituent tests do not do so until early in the sixth year. As a result, it cannot be recommended that the WJ IV be used to assess for ID in low functioning children younger than age 6-0 years."

It is important that practitioners have information on WJ IV test and composite floors and ceilings in order to make valid diagnostic (e.g., ID and gifted and talented, see Pfeiffer & Yarnell, in this volume) and placement decisions (e.g., special education). Although it is difficult for practitioners to determine floor and ceiling effects on the WJ IV because norms tables are not available for review, the WJ IV publisher or authors are strongly encouraged to provide data on the adequacy of floors and ceilings for all WJ IV tests and composites via an assessment service bulletin or other outlet.

Validity

Schneider (in this volume) called the *WJ IV Technical Manual* by McGrew et al. (2014) "a mammoth slab of awesome and a *tour de force*." We could not agree more. In fact, it is probably the most comprehensive technical manual ever written for a norm-based, individually administered ability battery. As such, reviewing and discussing the validity evidence for this chapter would most likely require a separate book! Therefore, we provide a very broad overview of the validity evidence found in the *WJ IV Technical Manual* as well as some preliminary comments regarding the quality of the evidence (for additional discussions of WJ IV validity evidence, see Floyd et al., in this volume; Maricle & Johnson, in this volume; Niileksela et al., in this volume; Schneider, in this volume). Garnering evidence for the validity of test score interpretation, unlike many other psychometric properties discussed in this chapter, is an ongoing process that is technically never completed; thus, the validity of test score interpretation for the WJ IV will be a topic for practitioners and researchers for years to come (Urbina, 2014).[4]

Given that the WJ IV authors used the 1999 *Standards* (AERA, APA, & NCME) to guide the norming and technical analyses for the WJ IV, our overview and preliminary comments on the quality of the validity evidence are presented according to the strands of validity evidence detailed in the 1999 *Standards* that include (i) test content; (ii) response processes; (iii) internal structure; (iv) relations to other variables; and (v) consequences of testing.

Evidence based on test content. Details regarding WJ IV test design and developmental procedures are explicitly and thoroughly covered in chapter 2 of McGrew et al. (2014). Topics addressed include test specifications update,

---

4. Urbina (2014) provides an excellent treatise on the essentials of validity.

development of new WJ IV tests, augmentation of item pools for existing tests, expert reviews, scale and item pool development, the norming study, item bias analyses, postnorming item revisions, creation of the final test forms, and test accommodation and adaptation design considerations.

The *WJ IV Technical Manual* (McGrew et al., 2014) also provides thorough and clear discussions on the theoretical underpinnings of the WJ IV which is contemporary CHC research and theory. CHC theory is the leading empirically derived theory of ability testing today and has been described earlier in this chapter as well as in many chapters of this volume. The WJ IV is one of several ability tests that operationalizes this theory and probably the only one that comes close to covering the theory in its complete form via its three batteries (see figure 5.1, p. 122, in McGrew et al. for a mapping of the CHC abilities measured by the WJ IV).

In addition to professional judgments regarding the relevance of item content to specific domains, McGrew et al. (2014) used a statistical technique called multidimensional scaling (MDS) to evaluate test content characteristics. The WJ IV may be the only ability battery that has used MDS to map relationships between and among variables and represents an advancement in demonstrating evidence based on test content. Developmental patterns of WJ IV ability clusters are discussed along with several growth curves on pages 136–142 in McGrew et al. According to McGrew et al., these "growth curves illustrate that the unique abilities measured by the WJ IV follow different developmental courses or trajectories over the age span from childhood to geriatric levels" (p. 136).

Evidence based on response processes. Validity evidence based on response processes refers to "the fit between the construct and the detailed nature of performance or response actually engaged in by examinees" (AERA et al., 1999, p. 12). Urbina (2014) stated, "While it is true that with the aid of brain imaging techniques, such as functional magnetic resonance, it is now possible to ascertain what areas of the brain are activated during some mental tasks and thus to directly observe what is happening in the brain, most of the information about response processes that is attainable comes from other sources" (p. 184) such as protocol analysis, data on the timing of item responses, and analysis of the criteria applied by scorers.

Although validity evidence based on response processes is seemingly not addressed directly in McGrew et al. (2014), information regarding descriptions of the ability constructs measured by the WJ IV as well as stimulus response characteristics, task requirements, and inferred cognitive processes is provided in Tables 5.2–5.4 (see pp. 124–129). In addition, McGrew et al. discussed (albeit briefly) test accommodation and adaptation design considerations for individuals with various disabilities, and each WJ IV examiner's manual (Mather & Wendling, 2014a, 2014b, 2014c) provides lists of accommodations and cautions for interpreting test scores when these accommodations are used. Additional information regarding evidence based on response processes via empirical studies and sources recommended by Urbina (2014) is required for the WJ IV and can be provided by the authors of the instrument as well as by independent researchers.

Evidence based on internal structure. According to McGrew et al. (2014), there are two forms of internal structure validity evidence for the WJ IV: patterns of intercorrelations among tests and clusters and exploratory and confirmatory multivariate statistical methods. Appendices E and F of the *WJ IV Technical Manual* (McGrew et al.) provide the intercorrelations among the WJ IV tests and clusters by age, respectively. A perusal of these intercorrelations indicated that the patterns of correlations are consistent with developmental and psychometric theory. WJ IV users are encouraged to review the intercorrelations especially for the age group(s) of examinees they typically assess. A simple rule to keep in mind is that indicators of the same construct (e.g., *Gf* with *Gf*) should be more highly correlated than indicators of different constructs (e.g., *Gf* with *Ga*) (Campbell & Fiske, 1959).

Regarding exploratory and confirmatory factor analyses, McGrew et al. (2014) reported a three-stage structural validity analysis of the WJ IV. The first stage consisted of split-sample random sample generation whereby the six age-differentiated norm groups were randomly split into separate model development and model cross-validation samples of approximately equal size. Stage two involved examination of the model development samples via cluster analysis, exploratory principal components analysis, and multidimensional scaling analysis. Finally, stage three consisted of confirmatory structural model cross-validation whereby model fit evaluation was conducted via multiple goodness of fit indices. As stated earlier, space limitations preclude a detailed review and evaluation of WJ IV validity evidence especially of internal structure. It appears, however, that the WJ IV structure is consistent with the theory-based model upon which it was designed. Additional research must be conducted to determine the extent to which the WJ IV structure represents well the theoretical and research underpinnings of CHC theory and beyond. The interested reader is referred to pages 149–185 of McGrew et al. for a very detailed discussion of the internal structure evidence of the WJ IV.

Evidence based on relations with other variables. Fifteen studies were conducted with the various WJ IV batteries and other measures of cognitive, oral language, and achievement abilities to demonstrate concurrent validity. These studies are described and discussed on pages 185–209 of McGrew et al. (2014). Table 5.23 on page 186 in McGrew et al. presents demographic information for all study participants. The number of participants ranged from a low of 49 to a high of 177. Individuals as young as 3 years of age and as old as 82 years of age participated in the studies. The breadth and depth of these concurrent validity studies are impressive. For example, the test and cluster scores from the WJ IV COG, WJ IV OL, and WJ IV ACH were correlated with six other measures of cognitive abilities, four other measures of oral language, and three other measures of achievement.

In addition to the 15 studies conducted to demonstrate concurrent validity, another nine studies were conducted to demonstrate discriminant validity.

Groups of individuals with various clinical diagnoses, such as those identified as gifted, intellectually disabled, and learning disabled, participated in these studies. Tables 5.39 and 5.40 in McGrew et al. (2014) provide inclusion criteria for each special groups study and demographic characteristics of the group participants, respectively. Summary statistics for each of the nine clinical validity studies are provided on pages 213–216 in McGrew et al. Although these studies provide initial discriminant validity evidence for the WJ IV, more studies are required to demonstrate that the WJ IV tests and clusters can be useful in differential diagnosis of clinical disorders (Floyd et al., in this volume).

Evidence based on consequences of testing. This strand of validity evidence is typically not addressed in technical manuals of ability tests, in part, because it requires many years of test use to determine the consequences of using these instruments via treatment or utility studies. McGrew et al. (2014) did not address validity evidence based on consequences of testing, even though the *Standards* state that scores on tests and decisions made based on them produce the intended consequences (AERA et al., 1999). In reviews of the *Stanford-Binet Intelligence Scales, 5th Edition* (SB5; Roid, 2003) and the *Battelle Developmental Inventory, 2nd Edition* (BDI-II; Newborg, 2005), Alfonso and Flanagan (2009) and Alfonso, Rentz, and Chung (2010) included data on classification analyses with exceptional groups such as individuals with intellectual disability, learning disabilities, autism, and speech and language delays as preliminary evidence of consequential validity. As mentioned above in the evidence of validity based on relations with other variables, McGrew et al. provided a good starting point regarding use of the WJ IV in differential diagnosis of exceptional groups. Nevertheless, this strand of validity evidence requires additional data to support the consequential validity of the WJ IV.

SUMMARY

This chapter included an overview of the organization, content, and psychometric properties of the WJ IV. A brief review of CHC theory and theoretical underpinnings of the WJ IV, description of WJ IV tests, and composition of WJ IV clusters were also presented. Although we included only preliminary comments or reviews for several psychometric properties of the WJ IV, they may form the basis of more comprehensive reviews and evaluations by other researchers and practitioners. All told, we believe that the WJ IV family of instruments is an exceptional contribution to the field of ability assessment. A thorough read of the chapters in this volume will provide users of the WJ IV with a very good understanding of each battery and how to use them individually or in some combination to garner information about their examinees' functioning so that evidence-based interventions can be recommended confidently. We also suggest that users read all materials available on the WJ IV including the technical manual, examiners' manuals, and assessment service bulletins available via the Riverside Publishing Company website to ensure responsible test use and score interpretation.

REFERENCES

Alfonso, V. C., & Flanagan, D. P. (2009). Assessment of preschool children: A framework for evaluating the adequacy of the technical characteristics of norm-referenced instruments. In B. Mowder, F. Rubinson, & A. Yasik (Eds.), *Evidence based practice in infant and early childhood psychology* (pp. 129–166). Hoboken, NJ: John Wiley & Sons.

Alfonso, V. C., Flanagan, D. P., & Radwan, S. (2005). The impact of the Cattell–Horn–Carroll theory on the assessment of cognitive abilities. In D. P. Flanagan & P. L. Harrison (Eds.), *Contemporary intellectual assessment: Theories, tests, and issues* (2nd ed., pp. 185–202). New York, NY: Guilford.

Alfonso, V. C., Rentz, E. A., & Chung, S. (2010). Review of the Battelle Developmental Inventory—Second Edition. *Journal of Early Childhood and Infant Psychology, 6*, 21–40.

American Educational Research Association (AERA), American Psychological Association (APA), & National Council on Measurement in Education (NCME). (1999). *Standards for educational and psychological testing.* Washington, DC: AERA.

American Educational Research Association (AERA), American Psychological Association (APA), & National Council on Measurement in Education (NCME). (2014). *Standards for educational and psychological testing.* Washington, DC: AERA.

Bracken, B. A. (1987). Limitations of preschool scales and standards for minimal levels of technical adequacy. *Journal of Psychoeducational Assessment, 5*, 313–326.

Campbell, D. T., & Fiske, D. W. (1959). Convergent and discriminant validation by the multitrait-multimethod matrix. *Psychological Bulletin, 56*, 81–105.

Carroll, J. B. (1993). *Human cognitive abilities: A survey of factor-analytic studies.* New York, NY: Cambridge University Press.

Carroll, J. B., & Maxwell, S. E. (1979). Individual differences in cognitive abilities. *Annual Review of Psychology, 30*, 603–640.

Cattell, R. B. (1941). Some theoretical issues in adult intelligence testing. *Psychological Bulletin, 38*, 592.

Cattell, R. B. (1943). The measurement of adult intelligence. *Psychological Bulletin, 40*, 153–193.

Dumont, R., Willis, J. O., & Walrath, R. (2016). Clinical interpretation of the Woodcock-Johnson IV Tests of Cognitive Abilities, Academic Achievement, and Oral Language. In D. P. Flanagan, & V. C. Alfonso (Eds.), *WJ IV clinical use and interpretation.* San Diego, CA: Academic Press, in this volume.

Emmons, M. R., & Alfonso, V. (2005). Critical review of the technical characteristics of current preschool screening batteries. *Journal of Psychoeducational Assessment, 23*, 111–127.

Flanagan, D. P., & Alfonso, V. C. (1995). A critical review of the technical characteristics of new and recently revised intelligence tests for preschool children. *Journal of Psychoeducational Assessment, 13*, 66–90.

Flanagan, D. P., Alfonso, V. C., Ortiz, S. O., & Dynda, A. M. (2013). Cognitive assessment: Progress in psychometric theories of the structure of cognitive abilities, cognitive tests, and interpretive approaches to cognitive test performance. In D. Saklofske & V. Schwean (Eds.), *Oxford handbook of psychological assessment of children and adolescents* (pp. 239–285). New York, NY: Oxford University Press.

Flanagan, D. P., Ortiz, S. O., & Alfonso, V. C. (2013). *Essentials of cross-battery assessment* (3rd ed.). Hoboken, NJ: John Wiley & Sons.

Flanagan, D. P., Ortiz, S. O., Alfonso, V. C., & Mascolo, J. T. (2006). *The achievement test desk reference: Comprehensive assessment and learning disabilities* (2nd ed.). Boston, MA: Allyn and Bacon.

Floyd, R. G., Woods, I. L., Singh, L. J., & Hawkins, H. K. (2016). Use of the Woodcock-Johnson IV in the diagnosis of intellectual disability. In D. P. Flanagan, & V. C. Alfonso (Eds.), *WJ IV clinical use and interpretation.* San Diego, CA: Academic Press, in this volume.

Hammill, D. D., Brown, L., & Bryant, B. R. (1992). *A consumer's guide to test in print* (2nd ed.). Austin, TX: PRO-ED.

Horn, J. L. (1965). *Fluid and crystallized intelligence: A factor analytic and developmental study of the structure among primary mental abilities.* Champaign: University of Illinois. Unpublished doctoral dissertation.

Horn, J. L. (1988). Thinking about human abilities. In J. R. Nesselroade & R. B. Cattell (Eds.), *Handbook of multivariate psychology* (2nd ed., pp. 645–865). New York, NY: Academic Press.

Horn, J. L. (1989). Models for intelligence. In R. Linn (Ed.), *Intelligence: Measurement, theory, and public policy* (pp. 29–73). Urbana, IL: University of Illinois Press.

Horn, J. L. (1991). Measurement of intellectual capabilities: A review of theory. In K. S. McGrew, J. K. Werder, & R. W. Woodcock (Eds.), *WJ-R technical manual* (pp. 197–232). Rolling Meadows, IL: Riverside.

Horn, J. L., & Blankson, N. (2005). Foundations for better understanding of cognitive abilities. In D. P. Flanagan & P. L. Harrison (Eds.), *Contemporary intellectual assessment: Theories, tests, and issues* (2nd ed., pp. 41–68). New York, NY: Guilford Press.

Horn, J. L., & Noll, J. (1997). Human cognitive capabilities: Gf-Gc theory. In D. P. Flanagan, J. L. Genshaft, & P. L. Harrison (Eds.), *Contemporary intellectual assessment: Theories, tests, and issues* (pp. 53–91). New York, NY: Guilford Press.

Kranzler, J. H., & Floyd, R. G. (2013). *Assessing intelligence in children and adolescents: A practical guide.* New York, NY: Guilford Press.

Maricle, D., & Johnson, W. L. (2016). Instructional implications from the Woodcock-Johnson IV Tests of Cognitive. In D. P. Flanagan, & V. C. Alfonso (Eds.), *WJ IV clinical use and interpretation.* San Diego, CA: Academic Press, in this volume.

Mather, N., & Wendling, B. J. (2016). Instructional implications from the Woodcock-Johnson IV Tests of Academic Achievement. In D. P. Flanagan, & V. C. Alfonso (Eds.), *WJ IV clinical use and interpretation.* San Diego, CA: Academic Press, in this volume.

Mather, N., & Wendling, B. J. (2014a). *Examiner's manual: Woodcock-Johnson IV Tests of Achievement.* Rolling Meadows, IL: Riverside.

Mather, N., & Wendling, B. J. (2014b). *Examiner's manual: Woodcock-Johnson IV Tests of Cognitive Abilities.* Rolling Meadows, IL: Riverside.

Mather, N., & Wendling, B. J. (2014c). *Examiner's manual: Woodcock-Johnson IV Tests of Oral Language.* Rolling Meadows, IL: Riverside.

McDonough, E., & Flanagan, D. P. (2016). Use of the Woodcock-Johnson IV in the diagnosis of specific learning disabilities in school-age children. In D. P. Flanagan, & V. C. Alfonso (Eds.), *WJ IV clinical use and interpretation.* San Diego, CA: Academic Press, in this volume).

McGrew, K. S. (2005). The Cattell–Horn–Carroll theory of cognitive abilities. In D. P. Flanagan & P. L. Harrison (Eds.), *Contemporary intellectual assessment: Theories, tests, and issues* (2nd ed., pp. 136–181). New York, NY: Guilford Press.

McGrew, K. S. (2009). Editorial: CHC theory and the human cognitive abilities project: Standing on the shoulders of the giants of psychometric intelligence research. *Intelligence, 37,* 1–10.

McGrew, K. S. (2012). *Implications of 20 years of CHC cognitive-achievement research: Back to the future and beyond CHC.* Paper presented at the Richard Woodcock Institute, Tufts University, Medford, MA.

McGrew, K. S., LaForte, E. M., & Schrank, F. A. (2014). *Technical manual: Woodcock-Johnson IV.* Rolling Meadows, IL: Riverside.

McGrew, K. S., & Wendling, B. J. (2010). Cattell–Horn–Carroll cognitive-achievement relations: What we have learned from the past 20 years of research. *Psychology in the Schools*, *47*, 651–675.

Miller, D. C., McGill, R., & Johnson, W. L. (2016). Neurocognitive applications of the Woodcock-Johnson IV. In D. P. Flanagan, & V. C. Alfonso (Eds.), *WJ IV clinical use and interpretation*. San Diego, CA: Academic Press, in this volume.

Newborg, J. (2005). *Battelle Developmental Inventory, 2nd ed.* Itasca, IL: Riverside Publishing.

Niileksela, C., Reynolds, M., Keith, T. Z., & McGrew, K. S. (2016). A special validity study of the WJ IV: Acting on evidence for specific abilities. In D. P. Flanagan, & V. C. Alfonso (Eds.), *WJ IV clinical use and interpretation*. San Diego, CA: Academic Press, in this volume.

Ortiz, S. O., Flanagan, D. P., & Alfonso, V. C. (2015). *Cross-battery Assessment Software System (X-BASS) (Version 1.0) [Computer software]*. Hoboken, NJ: John Wiley & Sons.

Pfeiffer, S., & Yarnell, J. (2016). Use of the Woodcock-Johnson IV Tests of Cognitive Abilities and Achievement in the assessment for giftedness. In D. P. Flanagan, & V. C. Alfonso (Eds.), *WJ IV clinical use and interpretation*. San Diego, CA: Academic Press, in this volume.

Roid, G. H. (2003). *Stanford-Binet Intelligence Scales, 5th ed.* Itasca, IL: Riverside Publishing.

Schneider, J. W. (2016). Strengths and weaknesses of the Woodcock-Johnson IV Tests of Cognitive Abilities: Best practice from a scientist-practitioner perspective. In D. P. Flanagan, & V. C. Alfonso (Eds.), *WJ IV clinical use and interpretation*. San Diego, CA: Academic Press, in this volume.

Schneider, W. J., & McGrew, K. (2012). The Cattell–Horn–Carroll model of intelligence. In D. Flanagan & P. Harrison (Eds.), *Contemporary intellectual assessment: Theories, tests, and issues* (3rd ed., pp. 99–144). New York, NY: Guilford Press.

Schrank, F. A., Mather, N., & McGrew, K. S. (2014a). *Woodcock-Johnson IV Tests of Achievement*. Rolling Meadows, IL: Riverside.

Schrank, F. A., Mather, N., & McGrew, K. S. (2014b). *Woodcock-Johnson IV Tests of Oral Language*. Rolling Meadows, IL: Riverside.

Schrank, F. A., McGrew, K. S., & Mather, N. (2014a). *Woodcock-Johnson IV*. Rolling Meadows, IL: Riverside.

Schrank, F. A., McGrew, K. S., & Mather, N. (2014b). *Woodcock-Johnson IV Tests of Cognitive Abilities*. Rolling Meadows, IL: Riverside.

Urbina, S. (2014). *Essentials of psychological testing* (2nd ed.). Hoboken, NJ: John Wiley & Sons.

Woodcock, R. W. (1998). Extending Gf–Gc theory into practice. In J. J. McArdle & R. W. Woodcock (Eds.), *Human cognitive abilities in theory and practice* (pp. 137–156). Mahwah, NJ: Lawrence Erlbaum.

Woodcock, R. W., McGrew, K. S., & Mather, N. (2001a). *Woodcock-Johnson III*. Rolling Meadow, IL: Riverside.

Woodcock, R. W., McGrew, K. S., & Mather, N. (2001b). *Woodcock-Johnson III Tests of Cognitive Abilities*. Rolling Meadows, IL: Riverside.

Woodcock, R. W., McGrew, K. S., & Mather, N. (2001c). *Woodcock-Johnson III Tests of Achievement*. Rolling Meadows, IL: Riverside.

Chapter 2

Clinical Interpretation of the Woodcock–Johnson IV Tests of Cognitive Abilities, Academic Achievement, and Oral Language

Ron Dumont[1], John O. Willis[2] and Robert Walrath[3]

[1]School of Psychology, Fairleigh Dickinson University, Teaneck, NJ, USA [2]Department of Education, Rivier University, Nashua, NH, USA [3]Doctoral Program in Counseling and School Psychology, Rivier University, Nashua, NH, USA

Despite the easily recognizable continuity from the *Woodcock–Johnson Psychoeducational Battery* (Woodcock & Johnson, 1989) to the *Woodcock–Johnson IV* (WJ IV; Schrank, McGrew, & Mather, 2014c), with important traces from the *Woodcock Reading Mastery Tests* (Woodcock, 1973) and the *Goldman–Fristoe Woodcock Auditory Skills Test Battery* (Goldman, Fristoe, & Woodcock, 1974), the WJ IV offers new tests, new composites, a new organizational structure, many new interpretive options, and scoring conducted exclusively "in the cloud," as well as the expected fine tuning of the various tests and items. Some of the updates and outright changes necessitate alterations in our approach to clinical interpretation of the *WJ IV*, which we attempt to outline in this brief chapter.

TESTS OF COGNITIVE ABILITIES, ACHIEVEMENT, AND ORAL LANGUAGE

The *Woodcock–Johnson IV* est omnis divisa est in partes tres (Caesar, 2008): *Woodcock–Johnson IV Tests of Cognitive Abilities* (WJ IV COG; Schrank, McGrew, & Mather, 2014d; 10 Standard Battery and 8 Extended Battery tests), *Woodcock–Johnson IV Tests of Achievement* (WJ IV ACH; Schrank, Mather, & McGrew, 2014a; 11 Standard Battery and 9 Extended Battery tests), and

WJ IV Clinical Use and Interpretation. DOI: http://dx.doi.org/10.1016/B978-0-12-802076-0.00002-5

Woodcock–Johnson IV Tests of Oral Language (WJ IV OL; Schrank, Mather, & McGrew, 2014b; 9 English and 3 Spanish tests). Two of the Cognitive tests (Oral Vocabulary and Memory for Words) can be added to two of the Oral Language tests (Picture Vocabulary and Sentence Repetition) to form Vocabulary and Auditory Memory Span composites to be reported with either the Tests of Cognitive Abilities or the Tests of Oral Language. Table 2.1 shows the configuration of the three WJ batteries.

The two composites with tests from two WJ IV batteries illustrate an essential point: best practice in clinical interpretation of the WJ IV often first requires judicious use of tests from all three batteries, even if your primary interest in an evaluation may be limited to cognitive abilities only, academic achievement, or oral language. Tests from each battery provide essential information in the other domains and should be used, as necessary, to provide that information. For example, if the practitioner is especially interested in a complete understanding of an examinee's verbal abilities, he/she may want to include not only the Comprehension-Knowledge (*Gc*) tests from the WJ IV COG (Oral Vocabulary and General Information) and the Picture Vocabulary and Sentence Repetition from the WJ IV OL, but also Memory for Words from the WJ IV COG; Oral Comprehension and Understanding Directions from the WJ IV OL, and the reading, writing, Science, Social Studies, and Humanities tests from the WJ IV ACH. We consider it penny wise and pound foolish to have and use only one or two of the three WJ IV batteries. Although there are several pairs of cognitive ability and achievement measures that have been administered to samples of examinees to facilitate comparison of ability and achievement, the WJ IV (and its predecessors) is the only instrument that measures cognitive, achievement, and oral language abilities with three interconnected batteries all normed on a single, very large sample of examinees and provides not only intra-ability comparisons within the three batteries, but also five types of ability/achievement comparisons.

Further, there are many useful comparisons of tests that are alike and different. Mather and Jaffe (2015) discuss many such useful comparisons. For just one example, the examiner can contrast Reading Vocabulary and Passage Comprehension from the WJ IV ACH with, respectively, Oral Vocabulary from the WJ IV COG and Oral Comprehension from the WJ IV OL. The pairs of tests are almost identical in format (the vocabulary tests even more so than on the *Woodcock–Johnson III Normative Update* (WJ III; Woodcock, Schrank, McGrew, & Mather, 2005)), except for the difference between oral or oral-and-print presentation for the oral tests and presentation in print alone for the reading tests. Rather than a broad comparison between oral language and reading or between cognitive ability and reading, the examiner can focus on almost identical comprehension tasks that differ only in who does the reading. Further, each task in each pair was normed on the same large sample of examinees. If the examiner is going to use the WJ IV at all, it would be negligent to pass up the unique insights available from judicious use of "selective testing" from the three batteries.

TABLE 2.1 WJ IV Tests of Cognitive, Achievement, and Oral Language Abilities by Tests, Global Measures, and Clusters

WJ IV Tests of Cognitive Abilities

Tests	Global Measure	Cluster/Test		
Oral Vocabulary	**GEN INTELLECTUAL ABIL**	**COMP-KNOWLEDGE (Gc)**	**AUDITORY PROCESS (Ga)**	**QUANTITATIVE REASONING**
Number Series	Oral Vocabulary	Oral Vocabulary	Phonological Processing	Number Series
Verbal Attention	Number Series	General Information	Nonword Repetition	Analysis–Synthesis
Letter-Pattern Matching	Verbal Attention	**FLUID REASONING (Gf)—(3)**	**L-TERM RETRIEVAL (Glr)**	**NUMBER FACILITY**
Phonological Processing	Letter-Pattern Matching	Number Series	Story Recall	Numbers Reversed
Story Recall	Phonological Processing	Concept Formation	Visual-Auditory Learning	Number-Pattern Matching
Visualization	Story Recall	Analysis–Synthesis (3)		
General Information	Visualization		**VISUAL PROCESSING (Gv)**	**PERCEPTUAL SPEED**
Concept Formation	General Information	**S-TERM WORK MEM (Gwm)—(3)**	Visualization	Letter-Pattern Matching
Numbers Reversed	Concept Formation	Verbal Attention	Picture Recognition	Number-Pattern Matching
Number-Pattern Matching[a]	**Gf-Gc COMPOSITE**	Numbers Reversed		
Nonword Repetition	Oral Vocabulary	Object-Number Sequencing (3)		
Visual-Auditory Learning	Number Series			
	General Information			

(Continued)

TABLE 2.1 WJ IV Tests of Cognitive, Achievement, and Oral Language Abilities by Tests, Global Measures, and Clusters (Continued)

WJ IV Tests of Cognitive Abilities

Tests	Global Measure	Cluster/Test	
		COG PROCESS SPEED (Gs)	**COG EFFICIENCY—(Ext)**
Picture Recognition	Concept Formation		Verbal Attention
Analysis–Synthesis		Letter-Pattern Matching	Letter-Pattern Matching
Object-Number Sequencing			Numbers Reversed
Pair Cancellation		Pair Cancellation	Number-Pattern Matching (EXT)
Memory for Words[a]			

WJ IV Tests of Achievement

Tests	Global Measure	Cluster/Test		
		READING	**MATHEMATICS**	**ACADEMIC SKILLS**
Letter-Word Identification	**BRIEF ACHIEVEMENT**	Letter-Word Identification	Applied Problems	Letter-Word Identification
Applied Problems	Letter-Word Identification	Passage Comprehension	Calculation	Spelling
Spelling	Applied Problems			Calculation
Passage Comprehension	Spelling	**BROAD READING**	**BROAD MATHEMATICS**	
Calculation	**BROAD ACHIEVEMENT**	Letter-Word Identification	Applied Problems	**ACADEMIC FLUENCY**
Writing Samples				

Word Attack	Letter-Word Identification	Passage Comprehension	Calculation	Sentence Reading Fluency
Oral Reading	Applied Problems	Sentence Reading Fluency	Math Facts Fluency	Math Facts Fluency
Sentence Reading Fluency	Spelling	**BASIC READING SKILLS**	**MATH CALCULATION SKILLS**	Sentence Writing Fluency
Math Facts Fluency	Passage Comprehension	Letter-Word Identification	Calculation	**ACADEMIC APPLICATIONS**
Sentence Writing Fluency	Calculation	Word Attack	Math Facts Fluency	Applied Problems
Reading Recall	Writing Samples			Passage Comprehension
Number Matrices	Sentence Reading Fluency	**READING COMPREHENSION**	**MATH PROBLEM SOLVING**	Writing Samples
Editing	Math Facts Fluency	Passage Comprehension	Applied Problems	
Word Reading Fluency	Sentence Writing Fluency	Reading Recall	Number Matrices	**ACADEMIC KNOWLEDGE**
Spelling of Sounds		**READING COMP (Ext)**	**WRITTEN LANGUAGE**	Science
Reading Vocabulary		Passage Comprehension	Spelling	Social Studies
Science		Reading Recall	Writing Samples	Humanities
Social Studies		Reading Vocabulary		**PHONEME–GRAPHEME KNOW**
Humanities				

(Continued)

TABLE 2.1 WJ IV Tests of Cognitive, Achievement, and Oral Language Abilities by Tests, Global Measures, and Clusters (Continued)

WJ IV Tests of Achievement

Tests	Global Measure	Cluster/Test	
		READING FLUENCY	
		Oral Reading	
		Sentence Reading Fluency	
		READING RATE	
		Sentence Reading Fluency	
		Word Reading Fluency	
		BROAD WRITTEN LANGUAGE	Word Attack
		Spelling	Spelling of Sounds
		Writing Samples	
		Sentence Writing Fluency	
		BASIC WRITING SKILLS	
		Spelling	
		Editing	
		WRITTEN EXPRESSION	
		Writing Samples	
		Sentence Writing Fluency	

WJ IV Tests of Oral Language

Tests	Cluster/Test
Picture Vocabulary	**ORAL LANGUAGE**
Oral Comprehension	Picture Vocabulary
Segmentation	Oral Comprehension
Rapid Picture Naming	
Sentence Repetition	**BROAD ORAL LANGUAGE**
Understanding Directions	Picture Vocabulary
Sound Blending	Oral Comprehension
Retrieval Fluency	Understanding Directions
Sound Awareness	
	ORAL EXPRESSION
	Picture Vocabulary
	Sentence Repetition
	LISTENING COMP
	Oral Comprehension
	Understanding Directions
	PHONETIC CODING
	Segmentation
	Sound Blending
	SPEED of LEXICAL ACCESS
	Rapid Picture Naming
	Retrieval Fluency
	VOCABULARY
	Picture Vocabulary
	Oral Vocabulary[b]
	AUDITORY MEMORY SPAN
	Sentence Repetition
	Memory for Words[b]

Notes: Most Gf–Gc clusters are formed by combining one test from tests 1 through 7 with one test from 8 through 14. For example, Gc is the combination of tests 1 and 8. The exception to these pairing is the Cognitive Processing Speed (Gs) composite that is made by combining tests 4 and 17.
[a]Number-Pattern Matching and Memory for Words do not contribute to any of the Core Gf–Gc clusters.
[b]Oral Vocabulary and Memory for Words are tests from the WJ IV Tests of Cognitive Abilities.

EVALUATING WITH A PURPOSE

Far too often, and not necessarily in line with best practice, we use the same instrument or even the same subset of subtests, tests, or composites for every evaluation. The evaluation should be uniquely designed for the situation: the characteristics of the examinee, the examinee's circumstances, and the referral questions. For example, if the only referral question were to rule out intellectual disability, the 18 WJ IV COG tests or even the 7 tests needed for the General Intellectual Ability (GIA) may be overkill. The four *Gf–Gc* Composite tests or three Brief Intellectual Ability (BIA) tests should suffice (if no disabilities or disadvantages rendered any of the tests inappropriate for the individual).

Referral Questions

We believe that examiners should actively solicit and quote referral questions from parents, teachers, specialists, and the examinee and then copy and paste those questions into the Conclusions section of their report and attempt to answer each one (even, if necessary, with "I don't know"). It is helpful to be aware of referral "concerns," but the evaluation should be guided by actual questions that are potentially answerable. The examiner may develop additional follow-up questions that should be answered.

Referral questions can guide the selection of evaluation instruments and procedures. If, for example, the referral question asks why the student has difficulty writing four-page essays, then brief writing tests (such as Spelling, Spelling of Sounds, Writing Samples, Sentence Writing Fluency, and Editing) can identify or rule out weaknesses in basic writing skills as likely causes of the problem. However, if basic writing skills are intact, the examiner would need to explore further with formal or informal samples of longer writing productions. On the other hand, if reading, writing, and listening are all proved to be intact and there are no referral questions in those areas, there would be little need to administer the usual battery of auditory processing tests (Phonological Processing, Nonword Repetition, Sound Blending, Sound Awareness, Word Attack, and Spelling of Sounds).

Specific Purposes

The referral may include specific requests, such as a *Diagnostic and Statistical Manual*, Fifth Edition (DSM-5; American Psychiatric Association, 2013) diagnosis, determination of legal competence, an Individuals with Disabilities Education Act (IDEA) disability identification, a recommendation for an educational or therapeutic placement, or prescription for a specific remedial reading program. The intended outcomes can then help drive the choice of evaluation instruments and procedures. With 50 tests, the WJ IV can provide much or all of the requisite testing data for such purposes, but the examiner must first determine what kinds of information are necessary for the purpose before selecting the appropriate tests.

History

The history sections of many evaluation reports seem to be careful, accurately typed, but mindless exercises in summarizing data without considering the implications of those data. The referral questions and intended outcomes need to be considered in the context of the examinee's personal, familial, social, emotional, medical, educational, and vocational history. We often see for example, lists of tests previously taken by the examinee without any discussion of the results (and, therefore, without later comparisons with current results).

Choice of Instruments and Procedures

When we have thoughtfully considered referral questions, requested outcomes, and the examinee's history, we should be able to select appropriate WJ IV and other instruments and specific tests to answer the questions and provide the requested information without introducing construct-irrelevant variance (Flanagan, Ortiz, & Alfonso, 2013, pp. 18–20; Messick, 1989, 1995) for the examinee. For example, if the examinee has a history of poor visual acuity and visual tracking, the Letter-Pattern Matching and Pair Cancellation tests might be excellent measures of the functional severity of the visual problems, but they would be terrible means of measuring g for that individual. For that individual, the BIA or Gf–Gc Composite would be a better measure of g than would be the GIA, which includes Letter-Pattern Matching. If we find ourselves administering the same procedures over and over again, we are probably not assessing very thoughtfully or usefully.

LEVELS OF INTERPRETATION

The WJ IV offers several types of scores and several levels of interpretation. When examiners use the online scoring to calculate results, they are offered a multitude of reporting options for those results. Figure 2.1 shows the options available: 11 different types of numerical scores (Percentile Ranks [PRs, with and without confidence bands], Age Equivalents [AE, with and without confidence bands], Grade Equivalents [GE, with and without confidence bands], Relative Proficiency Indexes [RPI], Standard Scores [SS, with and without confidence bands], Normal Curve Equivalents [NCE], Stanines, Standard T-Scores, z-scores, W Scores, and W difference scores) and three types of descriptive results (Cognitive Academic Language Proficiency [CALP], Proficiency, Developmental Zones).

Although it is not listed in the "Score Selection Template," the online score report does provide an option to print out raw scores—the actual scores the

> *Score Selection Template Name* * *(50 character max)*
>
> ☐ Percentile Rank w/ Band   ☐ Proficiency
> ☐ Percentile Rank   ☐ NCE
> ☐ CALP   ☐ Stanine Score
> ☐ Age Equivalent (AE)   ☐ T Score
> ☐ Grade Equivalent (GE)   ☐ z-score
> ☐ Relative Proficiency Index ☐ W Score
>   (RPI)   ☐ Developmental Zones
> ☐ Standard Score w/ Band   ☐ W Difference
> ☐ Standard Score   ☐ Age Equivalent Band

FIGURE 2.1   WJ IV score selection template.

TABLE OF SCORES
Woodcock-Johnson IV Tests of Cognitive Abilities (Norms based on age 9-8)

CLUSTER/Tests	W	AE	GE	RPI	SS	PR	z	T	Stanine	NCE
GEN INTELLECTUAL ABIL	481	7-8	2.2	63/90	77	7	-1.50	35	2	18
Oral Vocabulary	473	6-6	1.1	39/90	70	2	-2.02	30	1	7
Number Series	482	8-8	3.2	74/90	92	30	-0.52	45	4	39
Verbal Attention	484	8-0	2.6	73/90	89	24	-0.72	43	4	35
Letter-Pattern Matching	485	8-1	2.7	54/90	88	22	-0.77	42	3	34
Phonological Processing	481	6-8	1.3	57/90	76	6	-1.57	34	2	17
Story Recall	480	6-7	1.1	67/90	78	7	-1.46	35	2	19
Visualization	489	8-2	2.7	82/90	92	30	-0.53	45	4	39
COMPOSITE	476	7-3	1.9	52/90	77	6	-1.52	35	2	18
Oral Vocabulary	473	6-6	1.1	39/90	70	2	-2.02	30	1	7
Number Series	482	8-8	3.2	74/90	92	30	-0.52	45	4	39
General Information	464	5-1	<K.0	20/90	67	1	-2.18	28	1	4
Concept Formation	486	7-11	2.5	73/90	90	25	-0.67	43	4	36
COMP-KNOWLEDGE (Gc)	468	5-11	K.5	29/90	65	1	-2.34	27	1	1

FIGURE 2.2   WJ IV printout of Ellie's scores selected by the examiner.

program uses to calculate all results—but only by choosing Examinee Data Record, under "Report Type." The typical score report used by examiners does not allow for the reporting of the raw scores. Examiners must not blindly accept that the printout results are accurate. Human error when entering the raw data will result in inaccuracies. Without the raw scores on the printout, there is no easy way to check that the raw scores entered match the record form. We must always compare the record form to the actual data-input page of the online program.

Figure 2.2 shows results, based upon age-based norms, for the assessment of pseudonymous Ellie. The examiner has chosen to report nine different types of numerical scores. Some (e.g., SS and PR) may be easily recognizable while others (e.g., W, RPI, NCE) are less common. Each type of score is a way to represent Ellie's performance on the WJ IV tests. Understanding each will allow the examiner to make an informed choice of what to, or not to, report and interpret.

Along with the options for reporting different types of scores, the scoring program also provides the examiner information regarding two types of *difference score* information: *variations* and *comparisons*. While *variation* scores describe a person's results in terms of a pattern of strengths and weaknesses, *comparison* scores examine whether the examinee's performance is outside the range of predicted scores. Table 2.2 shows the WJ IV variation procedures.

TABLE 2.2 Variation Procedures Available by Composites

| Composite | Variation | | | |
| | Intra- | | | Academic |
	Cognitive	Achievement	Oral Language	Skills/Fluency/Applications
COMP-KNOWLEDGE (*Gc*)	√			
COMP-KNOWLEDGE (Ext)	√			
FLUID REASONING (*Gf*)	√			
FLUID REASONING (Ext)	√			
S-TERM WORK MEM (*Gwm*)	√			
S-TERM WORK MEM (Ext)	√			
COG PROCESS SPEED (*Gs*)	√			√
AUDITORY PROCESS (*Ga*)	√		√	
L-TERM RETRIEVAL (*Glr*)	√			
VISUAL PROCESSING (*Gv*)	√			
QUANTITATIVE REASONING	√			
AUDITORY MEMORY SPAN	√			
PERCEPTUAL SPEED	√			√

(Continued)

TABLE 2.2 Variation Procedures Available by Composites (Continued)

	Variation			
	Intra-			Academic
Composite	Cognitive	Achievement	Oral Language	Skills/Fluency/Applications
VOCABULARY	√			
ORAL LANGUAGE	√			
PHONETIC CODING	√			
SPEED of LEXICAL ACCESS	√			
BASIC READING SKILLS	√	√		
READING COMPREHENSION	√	√		
READING COMP (Ext)	√	√		
READING FLUENCY	√	√		
READING RATE	√	√		√
MATH CALCULATION SKILLS	√	√		
MATH PROBLEM SOLVING	√	√		
BASIC WRITING SKILLS	√	√		
WRITTEN EXPRESSION	√	√		
ACADEMIC SKILLS	√			√
ACADEMIC FLUENCY	√			√
ACADEMIC APPLICATIONS	√			√
ORAL EXPRESSION	√		√	
LISTENING COMP	√		√	
PHONETIC CODING	√		√	
SPEED of LEXICAL ACCESS	√		√	
VOCABULARY	√		√	

The examiner must exercise judgment and self-restraint in selecting those options that are best suited to answer the referral questions, respond to the referral requests, and make sense to the various readers of the report. Different purposes require different scores. A dozen pages of myriad scores and analyses are overwhelming to most readers. Some examiners have fallen into the pernicious habit of simply adding a page or two of text to the computer printout from the WJ III or other instruments, a habit that should not be perpetuated with the WJ IV. For the use of future evaluators, we may want to append the WJ IV printout to our report, but, if we report scores at all, we need to select the most useful and appropriate ones and insert them in the report.

Age-Based Norms versus Grade-Based Norms

As far as we know, the WJ IV and its predecessors are unique in providing cognitive ability and achievement (and now oral language) scores based on norms for the examinee's age and based on norms for the examinee's current grade placement. This valuable feature requires the examiner to choose thoughtfully the most appropriate norms for each evaluation and, in text and in all tables of scores, to remind the reader which norms are being used. Each can be valuable, but may also lead to confusion. Take for example Ellie, who is 9 years, 8 months old, but in the second grade because she began school later than usual (entering first grade when she was 7) and then was retained in the first grade. She began the second grade 2 years older than most of her classmates. Figure 2.3 shows Ellie's GIA score based on her chronological age (9-8) and her grade (2-7). Her age-based GIA is 77 (PR=7, Low) and her grade-based GIA is 94 (PR=34, Average). The examiner will probably need to report both scores. The age-based (GIA 77) is comparable to the Full Scale IQ or other total score from most tests of cognitive ability and must be taken into consideration. However, if the examiner or the evaluation team intends to compare Ellie's academic achievement to her intellectual ability with grade-based achievement scores, then the grade-based ability score (GIA 94) must be used.

TABLE OF SCORES
Woodcock-Johnson IV Tests of Cognitive Abilities (Norms based on grade 2.7)

CLUSTER/Tests	AE	GE	RPI	SS (95% Band)	SS	PR
GEN INTELLECTUAL ABIL	7-8	2.2	85/90	94 (88-100)	94	34

TABLE OF SCORES
Woodcock-Johnson IV Tests of Cognitive Abilities (Norms based on age 9-8)

CLUSTER/Tests	AE	GE	RPI	SS (95% Band)	SS	PR
GEN INTELLECTUAL ABIL	7-8	2.2	63/90	77 (70-84)	77	7

FIGURE 2.3   Ellie's WJ IV GIA scores in AE, GE, RPI, SS with 95% confidence bands, and PRs by norms for her age and by norms for her current grade placement.

We must never use one set of norms for cognitive abilities and a different set of norms for achievement. That would be like saying that Ellie (who is of normal size for her age) was of average height for her age but much too heavy for her grade. Grade-based achievement scores can be compared only to grade-based cognitive ability scores. Often, we need to report scores by both sets of norms. It is not reasonable to expect a third grader of any age to perform fifth-grade math. However, it is also not reasonable to retain a child in a grade a couple of times because of reading problems and then blithely report that the child's reading scores are in the average range for her grade.

Raw Scores

Raw scores (the points earned on the items attempted and passed plus the point values of non-administered items below the basal or the points earned on the items within a specified block of items on tests such as Story Recall, Reading Recall, or Writing Samples) have very limited utility. They are only ordinal measurements (7 is greater than 6 and less than 8). They are not equal units (items vary in difficulty) and cannot be manipulated arithmetically. They are sometimes used to indicate progress over time for very low-scoring examinees or to assert at least minimal progress when SS remain stagnant or fall, but *W* scores (Woodcock, 1978; Woodcock & Dahl, 1971) are much better.

Raw scores should almost never be included in reports. They confuse and mislead readers, who insist on attempting to assign nonexistent meanings to the Raw Scores. What does a Raw Score of 42 mean? Was it 42 correct out of 42 items or 42 out of 967 items? Was the Raw Score of 42/48 for this third grader obtained on a block of test items designed for third graders or on a test designed for grades K through 12?

As noted earlier, raw scores are entered into the WJ IV online scoring program, but unless the examiner chooses the Examinee Data Record, under Report Type, the score report does not show those scores. Several WJ IV tests (e.g., Oral Vocabulary) have separate sections, each of which requires the examiner to calculate raw scores for each individual part. Do not make the mistake of believing that a raw score of 12 on the first section, and a raw score of 20 on the second section mean that the child performed better on the second section.

W Scores and *W* Diff

W scores are the underlying metric of the WJ IV. The *W*-scale is an equal-interval scale on which a given interval represents the same difference (e.g., amount of growth) in the specific trait measured, regardless of where that interval is along the scale or what is being measured. The *W*-scale for each test is centered on a value of 500, which has been set to approximate the average performance at age 10 years, 0 months. For each age and grade group in the WJ IV norming sample, the median *W* ability value was identified. This median *W* score corresponds to the difficulty level at which 50% of the group responded correctly and 50% responded incorrectly. That median value, the reference W, is the score against which the performance of a person within that age or grade group is compared. The difference between a person's obtained W score and his or her peer group's reference W is called the W difference (W diff). The W difference is the value from which SS, PR, and RPI are derived.

Raw scores are converted first to W scores and then transformed into SS. Figure 2.2 shows that Ellie's GAI SS was 77. Note that Ellie's W score for the GIA is 481. Table C-1 in the WJ IV *Technical Manual* (McGrew, LaForte, & Schrank, 2014, p. 279) shows that for 9-year-olds (Ellie's reference group), the reference W score is 495. Ellie's W diff score is -14 (W score—W reference score). Since the *SD* in W units for GIA at age 9 is 9.23, Ellie's z-score is -1.52 ($z = W$ difference/SD). To generate a SS with a mean (M) of 100 and an SD of 15, one multiplies Ellie's z-score (-1.52) by the standard deviation of the SS (in this case WJ IV SS have standard deviations of 15), and then subtract the obtained number from the mean of the test which is 100. When this is done, the result is 77.25 which converts to a rounded SS of 77. Luckily, all this is done by the online scoring software algorithms!

Age- and Grade-Equivalent Scores

AE and GE scores are very popular and very misleading scores. An examinee could make errors on very easy items because of carelessness or specific weaknesses and pass very difficult items, resulting in a GE score well above the level of the early errors and far below the student's general functioning level (Willis, 1977). It is profoundly misleading to report that a student who passed most eighth grade items was working at a fourth-grade level.

Wechsler (1949, pp. 2–3) carefully explained the reasons for not using mental ages (MA) on the *Wechsler Intelligence Scale for Children* (WISC), but later yielded and provided them (Wechsler, 1951). There are many problems with GE and AE (or "MA") scores. AEs and GEs are not equal units (e.g., one year's growth at age 6 or grade 1 vs. one year's growth at age 16 or grade 11). They cannot be added, subtracted, multiplied, or divided, so one cannot validly calculate a mean. GEs assume steady progress throughout a given grade in school. On many instruments, AEs and GEs are interpolated and extrapolated. The single-month organization of the WJ IV norms tables, however, may eliminate this issue (McGrew et al., 2014, p. 82). At the extremes, AEs and GEs are silly ("You're awfully tall for a 27-year-old"). High-school level GEs for basic skills have limited or no other meaning. The same AEs or GEs on different tests often do not reflect the same levels of ability, a potential problem when comparing WJ IV scores to scores on other tests. Even if an AE of 10:0 accurately reflects the typical performance of a child on her 10th birthday, it would not mean that a 6-year-old, a 10-year-old, and a 14-year-old all achieving that AE would function similarly. AEs and GEs tend to magnify small differences. For example, the estimated GEs for Passage Comprehension on Form A of the WJ IV ACH for raw scores of 40–43 (4 items) progress from GE 8.6 to 12.6 (4 grades from the end of middle school to the end of high school). AEs and GEs encourage comparisons with inappropriate groups.

Many authorities (International Reading Association, 1982; Reynolds, 1981; Smith, n.d.) have recommended avoiding GE and AE or MA scores. Mather and Wendling (2014a, p. 79) explain why GE on the WJ IV are more useful and trustworthy than those on other tests. Despite their clear explanation, and because of the frequent misinterpretation of these scores, we recommend avoiding AE and GE.

Relative Proficiency Index

The RPI is based on the W difference score. The W score (Woodcock, 1978; Woodcock & Dahl, 1971) allows item difficulty and person ability to be measured on the same scale. The W difference score allows computation of the examinee's probable degree of success on tasks at age or grade level, or the examinee's RPI. Jaffe (2009) provides a very clear explanation of RPIs on the WJ III. The RPI provides very different information than the SS and PR because the RPIs also take into account how widely spread or tightly clumped a particular ability is in the population. For example, in Figure 2.2, we see that Ellie's scores are almost identical for Verbal Attention (SS 89, PR 24) and Letter-Pattern Matching (SS 88, PR 22). However, Ellie's RPI is 73/90 for Verbal Attention but only 54/90 for Letter-Pattern Matching. Even though her scores were about equidistant from the mean for her age and at about the same rank order among her peers, her accuracy in Verbal Attention was 73% at a difficulty level at which the average child her age was 90% accurate, but her speed and accuracy on Letter-Pattern Matching were only 54% compared to 90% for the average child of her age.

If we report RPIs, we need to explain them to the reader. For example, "RPI scores show the proficiency (speed, accuracy, reading comprehension, or whatever is being measured) that Ellie would demonstrate at a level of difficulty where other children the same age [or 'in the same grade'] would demonstrate 90% proficiency. For example an RPI of 75/90 would mean that on tasks at which other students of the same age [or 'grade'] would be 90% proficient, Ellie would probably be only 75% proficient." It is always essential to remind readers, in text and tables, whether scores are reported based on the examinee's age, the examinee's grade, or both.

Standard Scores

The WJ IV (like its predecessors) uses SS with a mean of 100 and standard deviation of 15 for all tests and composites. This decision simplifies interpretation of evaluation results. If we report SS, we need to explain them to the reader.

For instance, "SS range from about 0 to about 200. The middle 50% of SS falls between 90 and 110, a reasonable definition of the average range of scores."

Confidence Bands

Inevitably, there are many sources of measurement error built into tests. If a person took the same test over and over an infinite number of times without tiring and without benefiting from the practice, the person would not obtain the same score. Instead, there could be a wide range of scores. The extent to which a test would produce similar scores if the test were taken repeatedly is known as *reliability*. Every test and every composite on the WJ IV has its own measured reliability. The more reliable a test, the smaller the range of scores is. Based upon the actual reliability of a test or composite, the obtained scores should be surrounded by the *standard error of measurement* (SE_m). Whatever the resulting range of scores is, the examiner can assume that the "true score" would, with a certain level of confidence (e.g., $95\% = 1.96\ SE_m$), fall within that range. The score that a person earns on any actual administration of the WJ IV is called the *obtained score*, and should not be confused with the *True score* of that student.

It is very important to remember how limited the meaning of true score really is. The entire test may be invalid for its purpose, or it may be invalid for any particular person. A child with a profound, bilateral hearing loss would have a true score on the WJ IV GIA, but it would not be a "true" measure of the child's intelligence. A child with a vision and memory problem may obtain a true score for attempting to choose the answer on the multiple-choice Visualization test of the WJ IV, but it would not be a "true" measure of the person's intelligence. The only sense in which a true score" is "true" is that it gives the average (Mman) of all the scores a particular person may receive—even on a test that does not truly assess the child's ability.

From this discussion, there are three especially important points. First, obtained scores are only approximations; one can never know the true score. Second, the true score is not true ability in the capacity being studied, merely the statistical abstraction of the person's most likely score on a test that may or may not be a valid measure of the capacity. Third, the SE_m measures only the statistical error of the test under good testing conditions. Error introduced by noise, interruptions, fire drills, evacuations, fatigue, hunger, anxiety, and examiner blunders would be *in addition to* the known SE_m.

When an examiner recognizes that the obtained scores of the WJ IV are just that—obtained—and correctly decides to report scores as a range of scores (confidence bands), the WJ IV online scoring allows the choice of 68%, 90%, or 95% confidence. As seen in Figure 2.4, Ellie's obtained GIA was 77, but with 95% confidence the examiner could say that Ellie's intellectual ability falls between 70 and 84. This acknowledges that there is no way to know Ellie's "true score" (the toils of Sisyphus would pale by comparison to the infinite retestings).

TABLE OF SCORES
Woodcock-Johnson IV Tests of Cognitive Abilities (Norms based on age 9-8)

CLUSTER/Tests	AE	EASY	to DIFF	SS (95% Band)	PR (95% Band)
GEN INTELLECTUAL ABIL	7-8	6-9	8-10	77 (70-84)	7 (2-15)
Oral Vocabulary	6-6	5-8	7-5	70 (58-81)	2 (<1-10)
Number Series	8-8	7-11	9-7	92 (83-102)	30 (12-55)
Verbal Attention	8-0	7-0	9-6	89 (77-101)	24 (7-53)
Letter-Pattern Matching	8-1	7-6	8-10	88 (74-102)	22 (4-56)
Phonological Processing	6-8	5-11	8-0	76 (66-87)	6 (1-20)
Story Recall	6-7	5-4	8-7	78 (67-89)	7 (1-24)
Visualization	8-2	6-5	11-2	92 (81-103)	30 (11-57)
COMPOSITE	7-3	6-6	8-4	77 (71-83)	6 (3-13)

FIGURE 2.4   Ellie's WJ IV GIA composite and tests with 95% confidence bands.

Examiners need to decide the point at which the search for certainty makes the confidence band so wide that it is meaningless; for instance, "We are 99.9999% certain that this score is included in a band around the True score that is 175 points wide, ranging from profound intellectual disability to extreme giftedness." If an examiner chooses the 68% confidence, there is a 32% chance that the score being described fell outside the range and we do not know in which direction it missed. It is a little disturbing to contemplate meeting one's *Maker* and having to confess to diagnostic errors in 32% of one's evaluations. That is a very high stakes game of *Battleship*.

If we report confidence bands (which we should, at least in the appended table of test scores), we need to explain them to the reader. For example, "Even on the very best tests, scores can never be perfectly reliable. Lucky and unlucky guesses, momentary lapses of concentration, narrowly beating or missing time limits, and other factors cause some variability in scores, just by pure chance. The 95% confidence band shows how much scores are likely to vary 95% of the time just by pure chance."

Percentile Ranks

PRs are not equal units, so they cannot be added, subtracted, multiplied or divided. They tell the percentage of same-age or same-grade (to the month on the WJ IV) persons in the norming sample who scored the same as or lower than the examinee. Unlike most instruments, which just assign PR to SS by normal curve statistics (e.g., an SS of 77 is always PR 6), the WJ IV used a special procedure (McGrew et al., 2014, p. 83) so that an SS of 77 may be associated with a PR slightly higher or lower than 6. Note that in Figure 2.2 the GIA and the *Gf–Gc* Composite have the same SS of 77, but different PRs: GIA is 7, but the *Gf–Gc* Composite is 6.

Look at the *z*-score associated with each of the scores of 77. For the GIA the *z*-score is −1.50, while for the *Gf–Gc* Composite the associated *z*-score is

−1.52. A *z*-score of −1.50 converts to a PR of 6.68 (rounded to 7) while a *z*-score of −1.52 is associated with a PR of 6.43 (rounded to 6). The PRs and SSs are transformed from the actual underlying "real-world skew of score distribution."

If we report PRs, we need to explain them to the reader. For instance, "PRs tell the percentage of children of the same age [or 'in the same grade'] whose scores were the same as José's or lower. For example, a PR of 7 would mean that José scored as high as or higher than 7 percent of students her age [or 'in her grade'] and lower than the other 83 percent."

Examiners should not ever use the % sign in an abbreviation for PR (e.g., % or %ile)! This error encourages the already-too-likely confusion of PR with "percent correct." We have seen this confusion occur many times in evaluation team meetings. A PR of 68 is a pretty strong score in the highest one-third of all scores. However, 68% correct on a well-designed and fair classroom test would be fairly dismal. If you cannot spell out percentile rank, use some other abbreviation, such as "PR."

Normal Curve Equivalents

NCEs were developed to solve the problem of PRs being unequal units. The unequal units for PRs are a problem because they prevent examiners from doing any arithmetic, such as finding an average score, with PRs. Unequal units (like the proverbial apples and oranges) cannot be added or subtracted, much less multiplied or divided.

NCEs, like PRs, range from 1 to 99 with 50 in the middle. However, they are equal-unit SSs (with an $X=50$ and an $SD=21.06$). NCEs can be added and subtracted, and some theorists allow them to be multiplied and divided, so they are popular for comparing pre-test and post-test scores and are required by some government agencies for measuring progress.

Pre- and post-test comparisons are risky business under the best of circumstances. Such comparisons can safely be done only with genuinely equivalent forms of the same edition of the same test (except under Item Response Theory, in which nonequivalent forms can be equated if the same item difficulty scale is used for both).

Furthermore, merely holding the same relative position (the same score) in the norming sample looks like no gain, but actually represents improvement for a student who has been falling behind and does demonstrate a higher absolute level of achievement. For example, a student with an NCE of 33 by Fall Norms on a reading test in September may again score a 33 by Spring Norms when a genuinely equivalent form of the test is given the following spring. At first glance, it may appear that no gain in reading skill occurred. However, this is not the case. The child had to develop greater reading skill to maintain the same position in the group of students who were, as a whole, making reading skill gains during the year. The student did not catch up with any other students, but did make progress, just as the marathon runner who is in 57th place in a pack of

60 runners at the one-mile mark and remains in 57th place at the 26-mile mark did some serious running for the intervening 25 miles, despite not passing any other runners and probably being much farther behind the leaders by the end of the race.

Stanines

Stanines (short for "standard nines," but pronounced with a long a) are a nine-point, mostly equal-unit scoring system. Stanines divide the scores into nine units. The units are centered around the mean of the distribution of the scores of the norming sample. For Stanines, the $X=5$, and the SD is 1.96, so Stanines 3 and 7 are 1 SD from the mean.

Stanines offer several advantages over other scoring systems. They are easy to explain and understand (a virtue for student evaluation conferences in which a lot of information needs to be explained in very little time). Stanines have essentially equal units for arithmetic purposes. Further, they are so broad that they may effectively convey the reality that test scores are imprecise and should thus be interpreted cautiously. Having 99 PRs or 120 SSa seems to give an impression of more precision than tests really can offer.

The disadvantage of Stanines arises from that same broadness. Errors frequently occur at the margins so that minor differences can be overemphasized. For instance, as seen in Ellie's report (Figure 2.2), her SS of 88 for Letter-Pattern Matching is in Stanine 3, Below Average, while the 92 for Number Series is in Stanine 4, Average. The use of Stanines gives a false impression that the SSs of 88 and 92 (or even 89) are far apart (Stanines 3 and 4, respectively) when they are really practically identical. This weakness also applies, of course, to classification labels.

z-Scores

A z-score (also known as a z-value, standard score, and normal score) is used to describe a particular score in terms of where it fits into an overall group of scores. In other words, a z-score is an ordinary score transformed so that it better describes the location of that score in a distribution. A z-score has an $X=0$ and an $SD=1$. Although z-scores are the basis for all SS, they by themselves are seldom used on psychological and educational tests.

Standard T-Scores

Standard T-scores, like many normalized scores, are used to tell individuals how far their score is from the mean. Standard T-scores have an $X=50$ and an $SD=10$. Therefore, if a student's raw score were converted to a standard T-score and his/her standard T-score was 60, it would in turn mean that his/her score was 10 points above the mean. One advantage of using a standard T-score rather than a z-score is that standard T-scores are relatively easy to explain to parents when reporting the student's assessment scores. On the WJ IV, examiners can obtain the standard T-scores for each test and cluster by choosing it as an option in the scoring template.

Conditional Probability or the Whole Does Not Equal the Sum of Its Parts

Examiners are often surprised and confused when they discover that some of the composite scores they obtain on the WJ IV (and other tests) seem intuitively to be out of the ordinary, given the scores that are combined to create the composites. For example, Figure 2.5 shows Ellie's Auditory Processing (Ga) composite score. She obtained an SS of 67 (PR=1), based upon her performance on two tests (Phonological Processing, SS=76, PR=6 and Nonword Repetition, SS= 71, PR=2). How can we explain that the composite score is lower than either of the two scores that make it up?

This phenomenon has been present for years and occurs on all tests of cognitive abilities, although it is more obvious on tests such as the Woodcock–Johnson where all tests and composites scores use a common metric ($X=100$, $SD=15$). On most tests (not just the WJ IV), composite scores are calculated using sophisticated statistical procedures, not simply the averaging of the "parts." For the WJ IV, a thorough explanation of those procedures is provided in Chapter 3 (pp. 59–86) of the *Technical Manual* (McGrew et al., 2014).

The Auditory Processing composite SS is not the average of its parts (Phonological Processing and Nonword Repetition). The lower Auditory Processing composite SS is explained in part by "conditional probability," or a description of the chance that a certain phenomenon (a set of low scores occurring together) will occur. Using Ellie's SSs as the example, first ask what are the chances that any child would have an SS of 76 on Phonological Processing? In other words, what percent of the population would we expect to have obtained that same score as Ellie? The PR tells us that the score occurs in about 6% of the population.

TABLE OF SCORES
Woodcock-Johnson IV Tests of Cognitive Abilities (Norms based on age 9-8)

CLUSTER/Tests	AE	GE	RPI	SS (95% Band)	SS	PR
AUDITORY PROCESS (Ga)	5-11	K.5	41/90	67 (59-75)	67	1
Phonological Processing	6-8	1.3	57/90	76 (66-87)	76	6
Nonword Repetition	4-10	<K.0	26/90	71 (62-79)	71	2

FIGURE 2.5   Ellie's WJ IV Auditory Processing (Ga) composite and tests with 95% confidence bands.

Second, what are the chances that any child would have a SS of 71 on the Nonword Repetition? Again, the PR tells us that this occurs in about 3% of the population. Now, the final question is, what are the chances that a child would have low scores on each of the two tests of the Auditory Processing composite at the same time? In this case, the probability of this specific result occurring in the population is only about 1%.

In order to explain this issue better to anyone not especially attuned to, or interested in the statistical reasons for the results, a decathlon analogy might be useful:

> *It is unusual to be able to sprint or run hurdles very fast. It is unusual to be able to jump very high or very long. It is unusual to be able to fling heavy objects long distances. It is unusual to be able to pole vault great heights. It is unusual to be able to run 1.5 km in just over 4 min. It is VERY unusual to be able to do all 10 of those things well. Ten moderately high scores on the decathlon events make a VERY high total score. It is the combination that makes it unusual.*

When interpreting performance on a test composite (or a decathlon event), it is always useful to understand that having one very high (or low) score is itself unusual, but having several high (or low) scores at the same time is even more unusual. The total score must reflect the usualness, or in these cases, the unusualness of the total performance.

CATEGORICAL DESCRIPTORS

SS Descriptors

The WJ IV uses the following labels to describe SSs within specific ranges:

> *Very Low (60 and below), Low (70–79), Low Average (80–89), Average (90–110), High Average (111–120), Superior (121–130), and Very Superior (131 and above). Qualitative descriptors are only suggestions and are not empirically based. The labels used by the WJ IV may not be the same as used on other tests (e.g., Wechsler Scales).*

Note that there currently is no way to obtain the SS category descriptors from the online scoring program. Other choices (e.g., RPI levels, CALP descriptions) are readily available from the score template choices (Figure 2.1).

Cognitive Academic Language Proficiency

Cognitive Academic Language Proficiency (CALP), as opposed to Basic Interpersonal Communication Skills (BICS) (Cummins, 2003), is an important issue in assessment of individuals for whom English is not their first language and for persons with communication disorders and delays. The WJ IV offers CALP levels (ranging from 1 [Extremely Limited] to 6 [Very Advanced]) as a scoring option for tests involving oral and written language. An "Instructional Implication" for proficiency at grade or age level (Nearly Impossible to Extremely Easy) is provided for each CALP level. Obviously, we should select CALP descriptors and report and explain them when we assess persons whose first language is not Standard English. However, CALP descriptions can also be very helpful when we assess individuals with oral language disorders and intellectual disabilities. Figure 2.6 shows a portion of Ellie's CALP scores and interpretation levels.

Proficiency Level

Proficiency level categories are used to describe the RPI scores, not the SSs. Those descriptors, with their corresponding RPIs are Very Advanced (100), Advanced (98–99), Average to advanced (96–98), Average (82–95), Limited to Average (67–81), Limited (24–66), Very Limited (3–23), and Extremely Limited (0–2).

Developmental Levels

The Developmental Zones suggest the level at which tasks will be easy for a person and the level at which tasks will be difficult, and may be used to describe a person's present level of functioning. As with Proficiency level descriptors described above, the Developmental Zones refer to the RPI scores, not the SSs. The Developmental Zone descriptors, with their corresponding RPIs are Very Advanced (100), Advanced (98–99), Age-appropriate to Advanced (96–98), Age-appropriate (82–95), Mildly Delayed to Age-appropriate (67–81), Mildly Delayed (24–66), Moderately Delayed (3–23), and Severely Delayed (0–2). Figure 2.7 shows a portion of Ellie's score report with both Proficiency and Developmental Zones reported.

Cognitive-Academic Language Proficiency (CALP) Scores and Interpretation

CLUSTER	W	WDiff	RPI	CALP	Interpretation
COMP-KNOWLEDGE (Gc)	468	-28	29/90	3	Limited
COMP-KNOWLEDGE (Ext)	465	-32	22/90	2	Very Limited
ORAL LANGUAGE	464	-33	20/90	2	Very Limited
BROAD ORAL LANGUAGE	469	-29	28/90	3	Limited

FIGURE 2.6   Ellie's WJ IV CALP scores and interpretation.

TABLE OF SCORES
Woodcock-Johnson IV Tests of Cognitive Abilities (Norms based on age 9-8)

CLUSTER/Tests	SS	PR	Proficiency	DZ
GEN INTELLECTUAL ABIL	77	7	Limited	Mildly Delayed
Oral Vocabulary	70	2	Limited	Mildly Delayed
Number Series	92	30	Limited to Average	Mildly Delayed to Age-Appropriate
Verbal Attention	89	24	Limited to Average	Mildly Delayed to Age-Appropriate

FIGURE 2.7   Sample of Ellie's Proficiency and Developmental Zone (DZ).

GROUPS OF TESTS

The WJ IV is explicitly designed to, among other purposes, assess a broad array of Cattell–Horn–Carroll (CHC) broad and narrow abilities (McGrew et al., 2014; see also Flanagan et al., 2013). Many of the test groupings are CHC broad or narrow abilities.

General Intellectual Ability

The GIA SS is derived from the WJ IV COG tests 1–7 (Oral Vocabulary, Number Series, Verbal Attention, Letter-Pattern Matching, Phonological Processing, Story Recall, and Visualization). It is the first unrotated principal component and accounts for the most overall variance in performance on the tests and is considered the best overall predictor of school achievement or other outcome related to cognitive ability (Mather & Wendling, 2014b; Schrank et al., 2014d). Unlike most intelligence tests, the GIA includes a measure of *Ga* and gives similar (but differentiated) weightings to *Gf*, *Gc*, *Gv*, *Gwm*, *Glr*, and *Gs*, an important consideration when comparing scores on different instruments. Psychometric *g* may be ubiquitous in intelligence tests (Schneider & McGrew, 2012), but it is not measured the same way on different tests (Flanagan et al., 2013).

Brief Intellectual Ability

The BIA SS is derived from equal weighting of the first three tests from the WJ IV COG (Oral Vocabulary, Number Series, and Verbal Attention) and is considered most suitable for screening or brief evaluation uses. Two of the tests require focused attention, which may make the BIA a poor measure of *g* for an examinee with attention problems.

Gf–Gc Composite

The *Gf–Gc* Composite is derived from four tests of the WJ IV COG (Oral Vocabulary, Number Series, General Information, and Concept Formation) and is designed to provide an estimation of cognitive ability based on the two highest *g* loaded factors (Schrank et al., 2014d). It can be used in ability-achievement discrepancy analysis, as part of the procedures to identify gifted and intellectually disabled populations, and in identifying overall intellectual potential. As the name indicates, this composite includes only *Gf* and *Gc* abilities, which warrants consideration as a measure of *g* for examinees with auditory, attention, visualization, or memory deficits, such as students with specific learning disabilities.

Note that the WJ IV *Technical Manual* does not provide information to aid the evaluator in deciding when or how to use the *Gf–Gc* Composite in place of the GIA. What constitutes a significant difference between the GIA and the *Gf–Gc* Composite: 5, 10, or 15 points? Must the scores from the four individual tests of the *Gf–Gc* Composite be relatively close to each other (however close that should be) and at the same time relatively discrepant from the tests that make up the GIA?

Comprehension Knowledge (*Gc*)

The standard *Gc* cluster includes two tests from the WJ IV COG (Oral Vocabulary and General Information). An extended cluster is available by adding the Picture Vocabulary test from the WJ IV OL. This cluster represents a person's acquired knowledge and the ability to communicate and reason using this knowledge. *Gc* obviously carries a considerable cultural loading and significant linguistic demand (Flanagan et al., 2013, pp. 287–350) and must be used cautiously for anyone for whom English is not the first language, who has had limited exposure to US culture, or who has a communication disorder. *Gc* provides valuable information about such individuals, but may not be assessing *g* very accurately. Low scores on *Gc* would suggest the need for further assessment with the WJ IV OL.

Fluid Reasoning (*Gf*)

The standard *Gf* cluster includes two tests from the WJ IV COG (Number Series and Concept Formation). An extended cluster is available by adding the Analysis–Synthesis test from the same battery. This cluster provides an indication of a person's ability to reason, conceptualize, and problem-solve using novel information and procedures (Schrank et al., 2014d). Many researchers (Flanagan et al., 2013; Schneider & McGrew, 2012) consider *Gf* to be almost identical to *g*. Examiners need, however, to examine the apparent sources of errors on Number Series and Concept Formation to be certain that low scores are primarily attributable to weak intellectual ability rather than other factors, such as numerical facility or oral language.

Short-Term Working Memory (*Gwm*)

The standard *Gwm* (previously labeled *Gsm*) cluster includes two tests from the WJ IV COG (Verbal Attention and Numbers Reversed). An extended cluster is available by adding the Object-Number Sequencing test from the same battery. This cluster is an indication of cognitive efficiency and the ability to hold and manipulate information while maintaining attentional control (Schrank et al., 2014d). *Gwm* is an essential ability for most fluid reasoning tasks and many academic skills and should be assessed and interpreted in most evaluations.

Auditory Memory Span (*Gwm*-MS)

The *Gwm*-MS cluster comprises the Memory for Words test of the WJ IV COG and the Sentence Repetition test of the WJ IV OL. It measures the ability to hold auditory information in immediate, short-term memory. It is sensitive to the impact of language and requires the same interpretive considerations as *Gc*, especially if *Gwm*-MS is significantly weaker than *Gsm*.

Cognitive Processing Speed (*Gs*)

The *Gs* cluster is derived from two tests from the WJ IV COG (Letter-Pattern Matching and Pair Cancellation). Another indicator of cognitive efficiency, this cluster indicates the ability to perform simple and complex cognitive tasks quickly and efficiently. Judicious interpretation of this cluster helps illuminate the causes of poor academic fluency, such as slow cognitive processing speed or incompletely mastered academic achievement skills, which would require different interventions.

Perceptual Speed (*Gs*-P)

The *Gs*-P cluster also includes Letter-Pattern Matching, but pairs it with Number-Pattern Matching to assess clerical speed in comparing symbols, an important aspect of orthographic processing, which should be considered whenever difficulties are found in reading, writing, or math, especially in fluency in those skills.

Auditory Processing (*Ga*)

The *Ga* cluster is derived from two tests from the WJ IV COG (Phonological Processing and Nonword Repetition) and indicates the ability to discriminate, as well as the ability to encode and synthesize auditory stimuli (Schrank et al., 2014d). Assessment of *Ga* abilities is essential to a comprehensive evaluation of reading and writing achievement (Farrall, 2012).

Long-Term Retrieval (*Glr*)

The *Glr* cluster includes two tests from the WJ IV COG (Story Recall and Visual-Auditory Learning). Unlike the WJ III, these two tests no longer allow for a "delayed" recall trial. This cluster indicates the ability to store and later efficiently retrieve information that has passed through working memory (*Gsm*). Efficient retrieval of information from memory is an essential skill for reading, writing, and math. Slow retrieval can interact with a short memory span (*Gwm*) and slow cognitive processing speed (*Gs*) to cause dysfluent academic skills and to undermine academic applications (Wolf et al., 2002).

Visual Processing (*Gv*)

The *Gv* cluster is derived from two tests from the WJ IV COG (Visualization and Picture Recognition) and represents the ability to perceive, process, and manipulate visual patterns. There is limited research (Flanagan et al., 2013; Schneider & McGrew, 2012) to suggest that Gv plays much of a role in academic achievement, but clinical experience suggests that severe deficits in Gv can impair academic functioning in most areas (e.g., mental visualization as a component of reading comprehension). Low scores on Gv may suggest further assessment of basic visual perceptual and visual-motor abilities.

Number Facility

The Gs-N cluster contributes to the understanding of a narrow ability of fluency with numbers. It includes the Numbers Reversed and Number-Pattern Matching tests from the WJ IV COG.

Cognitive Efficiency

The standard Cognitive Efficiency cluster includes two tests from the WJ IV COG (Letter-Pattern Matching and Numbers Reversed). An extended cluster is available by adding Verbal Attention and Number-Pattern Matching from the same battery. This cluster samples Gs and Gsm cognitive processes and represents the individual's ability to hold and manipulate information, control attention, and perform tasks quickly and accurately (Schrank et al., 2014d). This cluster holds specific importance in the diagnosis and/or understanding of attentional problems, specific learning disabilities, or neurological impairments.

Oral Language Clusters

Oral language is fundamental to school achievement. A comprehensive assessment of achievement is seldom complete without tests from the WJ IV OL, which includes nine oral language clusters using tests from the standard and extended batteries. Six are based on the English language tests and three from the Spanish tests. **The Oral Language** cluster includes the Picture Vocabulary and Oral Comprehension tests to measure lexical knowledge, listening, and verbal comprehension abilities. The Spanish equivalent of this cluster is **Lenguaje oral.** To add working and auditory memory span abilities, the **Broad Oral Language** cluster combines the two Oral Language tests with the Understanding Directions test. The Spanish equivalent is **Amplio lenguaje oral**. Clinical experience suggests that Understanding Directions is especially sensitive to difficulties with listening attention. The **Oral Expression** cluster includes Picture Vocabulary and Sentence Repetition tests to illuminate lexical and syntactical knowledge and language development. The **Listening Comprehension** cluster includes the Oral Comprehension and Understanding Directions tests to measure listening ability and verbal comprehension. The Spanish equivalent is **Comprensión auditiva**. The **Phonetic Coding** cluster includes the Segmentation and Sound Blending tests to measure phonological awareness and auditory processing. Finally, the **Speed of Lexical Access** cluster combines the Rapid Picture Naming and Retrieval Fluency tests to measure retrieval efficiency together with long-term storage.

Reading Clusters

The WJ IV ACH includes seven reading clusters using tests from the standard and extended batteries. The **Reading** Cluster includes the Letter-Word Identification and Passage Comprehension tests to assess reading achievement in decoding and text comprehension. **Broad Reading** adds the silent Sentence Reading Fluency test to the **Reading** cluster to include reading speed. **Basic Reading Skills** includes the Letter-Word Identification and Word Attack tests to measure sight vocabulary, phonics, and structural analysis (Schrank et al., 2014d). **Reading Comprehension** includes Passage Comprehension and Reading Recall (from the Extended Battery) to assess comprehension, reasoning, and long-term retrieval. Adding the Reading Recall test from the Extended Battery yields the **Reading Comprehension-Extended** cluster to measure comprehension, vocabulary and reasoning. The **Reading Fluency** cluster includes the Oral Reading and Sentence Reading Fluency tests to assess cognitive processing speed and reading fluency and accuracy.

Finally, the **Reading Rate** cluster utilizes the Sentence Reading Fluency and Word Reading Fluency (from the Extended Battery) tests to measure fluency at the word and sentence levels. Each of these tests measures an important reading skill, so evaluators will often need to use all of the tests for a comprehensive reading assessment. In addition, it is often valuable to compare Reading Vocabulary (ACH) with Oral Vocabulary (COG) and Passage Comprehension (ACH) with Oral Comprehension (OL). The formats of the tests in each pair are almost identical with the only difference being in who does the reading. A thorough assessment of phonics skills might include comparisons among Spelling, Spelling of Sounds, Letter-Word Identification, and Word Attack to help differentiate between phonics skills and memorized words. Mather and Jaffe (2015) offer further information on such comparisons.

Math Clusters

The WJ IV ACH includes four math clusters using tests from the standard and extended batteries. **Mathematics** includes the Applied Problems and Calculation tests to measure math problem solving related to computations and problem solving. **Broad Mathematics** adds the Math Facts Fluency test to include automaticity of math facts. Comparison of accuracy with automaticity is often helpful. The **Math Calculation Skills** cluster utilizes Calculation and Math Facts Fluency tests to assess computation and automaticity with basic math facts. Finally, the **Math Problem Solving** cluster includes Applied Problems and Number Matrices from the Extended Battery to measure math problem solving, analysis, and reasoning. The Number Facility cluster can add useful information.

Written Language Clusters

The WJ IV ACH includes four Written Language clusters using tests from the standard and extended batteries. The **Written Language** cluster includes the Spelling and Writing Samples tests to measure single-word spelling and expressive writing. **Broad Written Language** adds the Sentence Writing Fluency test to include fluency of production. The **Basic Writing Skills** cluster includes the Spelling test and Editing from the Extended Battery to measure writing skills that include identifying errors in spelling, punctuation, grammar, and word usage analysis (Schrank et al., 2014d). Finally, the **Written Expression** cluster combines the Writing Samples and Sentence Writing Fluency tests to assess meaningful writing and cognitive processing speed as it related to writing fluency. The Written Language tests provide a thorough analysis of basic writing skills. To assess extended written production, the examiner must solicit classroom writing samples (with clear provenance regarding number of drafts, sources of assistance, etc.) or administer a longer writing test or information writing sample.

Cross-Domain Clusters

The WJ IV ACH includes seven cross-domain clusters using tests from the standard and extended batteries. **Brief Achievement** and **Broad Achievement** clusters measure the examinee's performance in reading, writing, and math at a screening and more comprehensive level. The **Academic Skills** cluster provides an overall score of basic achievement using the Letter-Word Identification, Spelling, and Calculations tests. The **Academic Fluency** cluster utilizes Sentence Reading Fluency, Math Facts Fluency, and Sentence Writing Fluency tests to create an overall measure of academic fluency. The **Academic Applications** cluster includes the Applied Problems, Passage Comprehension, and Writing Samples tests, which provide opportunities to apply academic skills to problem solving. Some examinees demonstrate differences among Academic Skills, Fluency, and Applications rather than differences among overall Reading, Writing, and Mathematics achievement. These three clusters are sometimes the key to understanding a student's academic difficulties. The **Academic Knowledge** cluster uses Science, Social Studies, and Humanities from the Extended Battery to give a broad sample of a person's knowledge in these three content areas. This information should be compared to findings from the OL battery and from the *Gc* cluster in the COG battery. Finally, the **Phoneme–Grapheme Knowledge** cluster includes Word Attack and Spelling of Sounds from the Extended Battery to evaluate sound and common orthographic patterns in decoding and encoding tasks.

Scholastic Aptitude Clusters

For examiners who wish to compare achievement to cognitive ability, there are three choices. The worst is a direct comparison of scores on intelligence and achievement tests, which makes the false assumption that the expected achievement should be the same as the tested cognitive ability. A better means is comparison of achievement scores with achievement predicted by regression from a cognitive ability score (or, even better, based on actual data from examinees who took both tests) (McLeod, 1968, 1974). As far as we know, the Woodcock–Johnson continues to be the only individually administered instrument that predicts achievement from specific scholastic aptitudes rather than a total score on an intelligence test. This process has been considerably refined in the WJ IV so that each of six reading, four mathematics, and four writing clusters is predicted by a combination of four COG tests that are highly correlated with the achievement area and supported by research, but do not share similar content. For example, Reading, Broad Reading, Reading Comprehension, Reading Fluency, and Reading Rate are compared to a predictor consisting of Oral Vocabulary, Phonological Processing, Concept Formation, and Number-Pattern Matching. Note that Letter-Pattern Matching is excluded because of similar content. The aptitude cluster for Basic Reading Skills, however, includes Oral Vocabulary, Phonological Processing, and Number-Pattern Matching, but Verbal Attention is used rather than Concept Formation. If an examiner wishes (or is required) to compare ability and achievement, these Scholastic Aptitude/Achievement Comparisons offer a refined way to do so.

EXAMPLES OF TEST SELECTION FOR SPECIFIC ISSUES

The 50 WJ IV tests permit examiners to tailor the assessment process for each individual with special attention to suspected or known disabilities. Two examples follow.

Autism Spectrum Disorders

The breadth, depth, and flexibility of the WJ IV offer an array of options for the evaluation of Autism Spectrum Disorders (ASD). McGrew et al. (2014) provide limited information regarding the performance of children with ASD on the WJ IV. However, there are a number of options from the available tests, using a cross-battery assessment approach (Flanagan et al., 2013), to investigate known patterns of strengths and weaknesses within this population

Children with ASD often demonstrate an uneven cognitive profile and splinter skills that increase the difficulty of accurate assessment (Fleury et al., 2014). There is support for patterns of weaknesses in auditory or linguistic processing (Cashin & Barker, 2009) and strengths in visual types of information processing. Oral Vocabulary and Nonword Repetition (WJ IV COG), for example, may shed light on auditory/language processing difficulties, while Visualization and Picture Recognition (WJ IV COG) would be expected to reveal strengths.

Difficulties in executive functioning (McCloskey, Perkins, & Van Divner, 2009) may be assessed using Concept Formation, Verbal Attention, and Pair

Cancellation (WJ IV COG). Weak central coherence in ASD suggests a focus on detailed rather than global processing (Fleury et al., 2014), which may be seen in weak performance on Concept Formation and Analysis–Synthesis (WJ IV COG). In academic achievement, this may be seen with higher scores on Letter-Word Identification and Word Attack compared to Passage Comprehension (WJ IV ACH). Writing Samples (WJ IV ACH) would also be expected to be relatively weak.

As children with ASD often exhibit strengths in rote learning and memory and weak working memory (Riccio, Sullivan, & Cohen, 2010), Story Recall, Memory for Words, Numbers Reversed, Visual-Auditory Learning, and Object-Number Sequences (WJ IV COG) may also be useful to tease out particular strengths and weaknesses in this area.

Attention–Deficit/Hyperactivity Disorder

Similarly, the flexibility of the WJ IV can contribute to a more focused assessment of difficulties with Attention–Deficit/Hyperactivity Disorder (ADHD), with several tests across batteries that measure CHC broad and narrow band abilities (short-term working memory [*Gwm*], working memory capacity [WM], attentional control [AC] and Memory Span [MS]) across visual and auditory modalities. This is a significant strength compared to the WJ III, which had limited sampling of these abilities (Strickland & Watkins, 2015).

On the WJ IV COG, auditory or verbal measures of working memory and attention include Verbal Attention, Object-Number Sequencing, and Memory for Words; and on the WJ IV OL, Sentence Repetition. Visual measures of working memory include Pair Cancellation on the WJ IV COG and Understanding Directions on the WJ IV OL. Verbal Attention, Numbers Reversed, and Object-Number Sequencing combine to create an extended interpretative cluster for Short-Term Working Memory (*Gwm*), while Memory for Words and Sentence Repetition combine to make an interpretive cluster for Auditory Working Memory (WM). Memory for Words (WJ IV COG) and Sentence Repetition (WJ IV OL) combine across batteries to create the narrow band interpretive cluster for Memory Span (MS).

Most important in consideration of ADHD is the construct of "Attentional Control" or AC (McGrew et al., 2014) that is a refinement of Carroll's (1993) "ability to attend" and defines a more cohesive construct of attention as it related to cognition and academic achievement. Verbal Attention, Numbers Reversed, and Pair Cancellation, all tests from the WJ IV COG, combine to create the AC interpretative cluster.

CONCLUSION

The WJ IV COG, ACH, and OL batteries offer powerful interpretive and diagnostic capabilities, especially when selected tests and clusters from all three batteries are used in a thoughtfully planned assessment based on referral questions, the examinee's history, and the purpose of the assessment. The various clusters, the several types of score and levels of interpretation, and the *variation* and *comparison* scores can and should be used judiciously for different purposes; examiners need to understand all of the options and should not fall into the habit of using only one set of clusters, one type of score, one level of interpretation, or one type of difference score as each is best suited to specific purposes. In many instances, examiners would do best to select two or three types of scores or more than one level of interpretation to provide a complete picture of the examinee's functioning and answer the referral questions.

However, it is also important not to overwhelm the reader with a report full of mysterious information that may be irrelevant to the purpose of the evaluation. For most purposes, raw scores, z-scores, W scores, and AE and GE are just clutter in a report. CALP scores, for example, may be essential for one evaluation and irrelevant for another. In some cases, though, it may be essential, for example, to provide PRs and RPIs or to report scores by age norms and grade norms.

REFERENCES

American Psychiatric Association. (2013). *Diagnostic and statistical manual of mental disorders* (5th ed.). Arlington, VA: Author.

Caesar, G. I. (2008). *C. Iuli Cæsaris commentariorum do bello Gallico.* Retrieved from <http://thelatinlibrary.com/caesar/gall1.shtml>.

Carroll, J. (1993). *Human cognitive abilities: A survey of factor-analytic studies.* New York, NY: Cambridge University Press.

Cashin, A., & Barker, P. (2009). The triad of impairment in autism revisited. *Journal of Child and Adolescent Psychiatric Nursing*, *22*(4), 189–193. http://dx.doi.org/10.1111/j.1744-6171.2009.00198.x.

Cummins, J. (2003). BICS and CALP: Origins and rationale for the distinction. In C. B. Paulston & G. R. Tucker (Eds.), *Sociolinguistics: The essential readings* (pp. 322–328). London: Blackwell.

Farrall, M. L. (2012). *Reading assessment: Linking language, literacy, and cognition.* Hoboken, NJ: Wiley.

Flanagan, D. P., Ortiz, S. O., & Alfonso, V. (2013). *Essentials of cross-battery assessment* (3rd ed.). Hoboken, NJ: Wiley.

Fleury, V. P., Hedges, S., Hume, K., Browder, D. M., Thompson, J. L., Fallin, K., et al. (2014). Addressing the academic needs of adolescents with Autism Spectrum Disorder in secondary education. *Remedial and Special Education*, *35*(2), 68–79. http://dx.doi.org/10.1177/0741932513518823.

Goldman, R., Fristoe, M., & Woodcock, R. W. (1974). *The Goldman–Fristoe–Woodcock auditory skills test battery.* Circle Pines, MN: American Guidance Service.

International Reading Association (1982). Misuse of grade equivalents: Resolution passed by the Delegates Assembly of the International Reading Association, April 1981. *Reading Teacher*, January, p. 464. Retrieved from <http://www.myschoolpsychology.com/wp-content/uploads/2015/04/IRA-on-grade-equivalents-1981.pdf>.

Jaffe, L. E. (2009). *Development, interpretation, and application of the W score and the relative proficiency index (Woodcock–Johnson III Assessment Service Bulletin No. 11)*. Rolling Meadows, IL: Riverside Publishing. Retrieved from <http://www.riverpub.com/products/wjIIIComplete/pdf/WJ3_ASB_11.pdf>.

Mather, N., & Jaffe, L. (2015). *Woodcock–Johnson IV: Recommendations, reports, and strategies*. Hoboken, NJ: Wiley.

Mather, N., & Wendling, B. J. (2014a). *Examiner's manual: Woodcock–Johnson IV tests of achievement*. Rolling Meadows, IL: Riverside.

Mather, N., & Wendling, B. J. (2014b). *Examiner's manual: Woodcock–Johnson IV tests of cognitive abilities*. Rolling Meadows, IL: Riverside.

McCloskey, G., Perkins, L., & Van Divner, B. (2009). *Assessment and intervention for executive function difficulties*. New York, NY: Routledge.

McGrew, K. S., LaForte, E. M., & Schrank, F. A. (2014). *Technical manual: Woodcock–Johnson IV*. Rolling Meadows, IL: Riverside.

McLeod, J. (1968). Reading expectancy from disabled readers. *Journal of Learning Disabilities*, *1*, 97–105.

McLeod, J. (1974). Educational underachievement: Toward a defensible psychometric definition. *Journal of Learning Disabilities*, *12*(5), 322–330.

Messick, S. (1989). Validity. In R. L. Linn (Ed.), *Educational measurement* (3rd ed., pp. 13–103). New York, NY: Macmillan.

Messick, S. (1995). Validity of psychological assessment: Validation of inferences from persons' responses and performances as scientific inquiry into score meaning. *American Psychologist*, *50*(9), 741–749.

Reynolds, C. R. (1981). The fallacy of "two years below grade level for age" as a diagnostic criterion for reading disorders. *Journal of School Psychology*, *19*(4), 350–359.

Riccio, C., Sullivan, J., & Cohen, M. (2010). *Neuropsychological assessment and intervention for childhood and adolescent disorders*. Hoboken, NJ: Wiley.

Schneider, J., & McGrew, K. S. (2012). The Cattell–Horn–Carroll model of intelligence. In D. P. Flanagan & P. L. Harrison (Eds.), *Contemporary intellectual assessment: Theories, tests and issues* (3rd ed., pp. 99–144). New York, NY: Guilford Press.

Schrank, F. A., Mather, N., & McGrew, K. S. (2014a). *Woodcock–Johnson IV tests of achievement*. Rolling Meadows, IL: Riverside.

Schrank, F. A., Mather, N., & McGrew, K. S. (2014b). *Woodcock–Johnson IV tests of oral language*. Rolling Meadows, IL: Riverside.

Schrank, F. A., McGrew, K. S., & Mather, N. (2014c). *Woodcock–Johnson IV*. Rolling Meadows, IL: Riverside.

Schrank, F. A., McGrew, K. S., & Mather, N. (2014d). *Woodcock–Johnson IV tests of cognitive abilities*. Rolling Meadows, IL: Riverside.

Smith, M. (n.d.). *The Hippocratic Oath and grade equivalents* (MetaMetrics Position Paper 1330L). Retrieved from MetaMetrics website: <http://cdn.lexile.com/m/uploads/positionpapers/TheHippOathandGrdEquiv.pdf>.

Strickland, T., & Watkins, M. W. (2015). Structure of the Woodcock–Johnson III cognitive tests in a referral sample of elementary school students. *Psychological Assessment* Advance online publication: http://dx.doi.org/10.1037/pas0000052.

Wechsler, D. (1949). *Wechsler Intelligence Scale for Children (WISC)*. New York, NY: The Psychological Corporation.

Wechsler, D. (1951). Equivalent test and mental ages for the WISC. *Journal of Consulting Psychology, 15*(5), 381–384.

Willis, J.O. (1977). Overall Achievement Test—Cumulative Evaluation Reflecting Educational Ability Level (OAT-CEREAL). *NH Personnel and Guidance Journal*, 6, 1, 9. Retrieved from <http://www.myschoolpsychology.com/testing-information/misuse-of-grade-equivalents/>.

Wolf, M., O'Rourke, A. G., Gidney, C., Lovett, M., Cirino, P., & Morris, R. (2002). The second deficit: An investigation of the independence of phonological and naming-speed deficits in developmental dyslexia. *Reading and Writing, 15*(1–2), 43–72. http://dx.doi.org/10.102 3/A:1013816320290.

Woodcock, R. W. (1973). *Woodcock reading mastery tests*. Circle Pines, MN: American Guidance Service.

Woodcock, R. W. (1978). *Development and standardization of the Woodcock–Johnson psycho-educational battery*. Rolling Meadows, IL: Riverside.

Woodcock, R. W., & Dahl, M. N. (1971). *A common scale for the measurement of person ability and test item difficulty*. Circle Pines, MN: American Guidance Service. (AGS Paper No. 10.)

Woodcock, R. W., & Johnson, M. B. (1989). *Woodcock–Johnson psycho-educational battery— Revised*. Allen, TX: DLM Teaching Resources.

Woodcock, R. W., McGrew, K. S., Schrank, F. A., & Mather, N. (2005). *Woodcock–Johnson III normative update*. Rolling Meadows, IL: Riverside Publishing.

Chapter 3

A Special Validity Study of the Woodcock–Johnson IV: Acting on Evidence for Specific Abilities

Christopher R. Niileksela[1], Matthew R. Reynolds[1], Timothy Z. Keith[2] and Kevin S. McGrew[3]

[1]*Department of Educational Psychology, Joseph R. Pearson Hall, University of Kansas, Lawrence, KS, USA* [2]*Department of Educational Psychology, University of Texas, Austin, TX, USA* [3]*Institute for Applied Psychometrics, St. Joseph, MN, USA*

Validity of test score interpretation is an essential component of educational and psychological test development. The modern conceptualization of validity goes far beyond the popular notion of whether a test "measures what it purports to measure" (Kelley, 1927, p. 14). Validity is not a single number or set of numbers, but includes a range of interrelated components, including the reality of constructs measured by tests and whether those constructs are causally related to individual differences in test scores (Borsboom, Mellenbergh, & Heerden, 2004), how test scores are related to other constructs (Campbell & Fiske, 1959), how well test scores predict future outcomes, the generalizability of test scores across populations, and the consequences of how test scores are interpreted (Messick, 1995). Valid test score interpretation ultimately falls on the shoulders of the test users, and test users must rely on validity evidence to guide test score interpretation. The purpose of this study is to contribute to the validity evidence of the Woodcock–Johnson IV (WJ IV; Schrank, McGrew, & Mather, 2014c) by examining the relations between latent cognitive abilities and achievement skills measured by the WJ IV.

VALIDITY EVIDENCE WITH THE WJ IV

The WJ IV is an individually administered assessment system of co-normed tests that includes three test batteries designed to measure psychometric intelligence (WJ IV Tests of Cognitive Abilities [WJ IV COG]; Schrank, McGrew, & Mather, 2014d), oral language (WJ IV Tests of Oral Language [WJ IV OL]; Schrank, Mather, & McGrew, 2014b), and academic achievement (WJ IV Tests

WJ IV Clinical Use and Interpretation. DOI: http://dx.doi.org/10.1016/B978-0-12-802076-0.00003-7
65

of Academic Achievement [WJ IV ACH]; Schrank, Mather, & McGrew, 2014a). See Chapter 1 for a description of the tests and psychometric properties of the WJ IV.

The WJ IV *Technical Manual* (McGrew, LaForte, & Schrank, 2014) provides extensive validity evidence based on the *Standards for Educational and Psychological Testing* (American Educational Research Association [AERA], American Psychological Association [APA], National Council on Measurement in Education [NCME], 1999). Validity evidence is presented for test content and response processes (e.g., expert review and multidimensional scaling [MDS]), developmental evidence (e.g., cross-sectional growth curves), the internal structure of the scores (e.g., cluster analysis, MDS, exploratory and confirmatory factor analyses using calibration and validation samples), the relations of test scores with other variables (e.g., correlations with other major cognitive, academic, and oral language tests), and test criterion (e.g., test score differences across disability groups). Additionally, the developers included procedures to evaluate bias and fairness in testing (e.g., differential item functioning and diversity expert review).

The WJ IV is based on the Cattell–Horn–Carroll (CHC) theory of human cognitive abilities, a taxonomy of cognitive abilities that has been strongly supported in research (Reynolds, Keith, Flanagan, & Alfonso, 2013; Schneider & McGrew, 2012). CHC theory had an important influence on the Woodcock–Johnson—Third Edition (WJ III; Woodcock, McGrew, & Mather, 2001) and was an important guiding theoretical structure for the WJ IV. In addition to CHC theory, recent developments in psychological and neuropsychological research were also used during the revision of the WJ IV COG to expand on the constructs measured by the tests. For example, Short-Term Memory (*Gsm*) is now called Short-Term Working Memory (*Gwm*) to emphasize the substantial influence of working memory on learning (Geary, 2011), and this change is reflected in the use of more complex Working Memory tasks for the *Gwm* cluster (McGrew et al., 2014, pp. 4–5). The tests that comprise the Auditory Processing (*Ga*) cluster on the WJ IV COG are completely new and were specifically developed to emphasize complex phonological processing, which is strongly related to reading development (Melby-Lervåg, Lyster, & Hulme, 2012). Several other tests were added or changed to increase the *cognitive complexity*, or information processing demands of tests (i.e., increasing the cognitive load or attentional control required for a test, Marshalek, Lohman, & Snow, 1983) to increase the ecological validity of the tests.

VALIDITY AND COGNITIVE-ACHIEVEMENT RELATIONS

CHC theory has had a significant influence on the development and revision of almost all major cognitive and academic test batteries over the past 25 years (Keith & Reynolds, 2010). Similarly, research focused on understanding how the CHC cognitive ability constructs influence academic achievement outcomes (henceforth, cognitive-achievement relations) has increased during that time (McGrew & Wendling, 2010). The assumption is that cognitive abilities are an important component of academic skill development. It is well known that general intelligence, or psychometric g, has an important influence on all types of psychological and educational variables, including general academic achievement (Jensen, 1998; Kaufman, Reynolds, Liu, Kaufman, & McGrew, 2012). Nonetheless, research has also supported the notion that specific cognitive abilities fully mediate the influence of g on academic skills, and they even influence academic skills beyond g (Elliott, Hale, Fiorello, Dorvil, & Moldovan, 2010; Floyd, Keith, Taub, & McGrew, 2007; Hajovsky et al., 2014; McGrew, Flanagan, Keith, & Vanderwood, 1997; though see Glutting, Watkins, Konold, & McDermott, 2006; Parkin & Beaujean, 2012). Cognitive-achievement relations research provides an empirical basis for determining relevant strengths and weaknesses that promote or inhibit learning for an individual (McGrew et al., 1997). This research has subsequently influenced recent models of specific learning disability (SLD) identification. Methods commonly referred to as *patterns of strengths and weaknesses* (PSW, e.g., Flanagan, Alfonso, & Mascolo, 2011; see Chapters 9 and 10) have focused the use of assessment data to build an understanding of cognitive and academic strengths and weaknesses.

Previous cognitive-achievement relations research has primarily used structural equation modeling (SEM) to estimate multiple structural relations among latent cognitive and academic variables, and much of this research used the Woodcock–Johnson—Revised (WJ R, Woodcock & Johnson, 1989; see Flanagan, 2000; Keith, 1999; McGrew et al., 1997; Vanderwood, McGrew, Flanagan, & Keith, 2002) and WJ III (Benson, 2008; Floyd et al., 2007; Taub, Floyd, Keith, & McGrew, 2008). Other major test batteries have been used (Elliott et al., 2010; Hajovsky et al., 2014; Parkin & Beaujean, 2012), but no studies have used the WJ IV. The release of the WJ IV provides an opportunity to investigate cognitive-achievement relations with a new, nationally representative sample, using new measures and constructs that have been developed or revised for the WJ IV. Cognitive-achievement relations on the WJ IV can be compared to previous research with the WJ R and WJ III to determine whether these relations are specific to certain tests or are related to the constructs measured by the tests.

PREVIOUS RESEARCH ON COGNITIVE-ACHIEVEMENT RELATIONS

The consistency of cognitive-achievement relations across different studies has been summarized comprehensively by Flanagan, Ortiz, and Alfonso (2013) and by McGrew and Wendling (2010). We will briefly summarize previous cognitive-achievement relations research, focusing primarily on studies that used the WJ R and WJ III.

Comprehension-Knowledge (*Gc*) and *Gwm*[1] have shown important influences on reading in previous research (Evans, Floyd, McGrew, & Leforgee, 2001; Floyd et al., 2007; Floyd, Meisinger, Gregg, & Keith, 2012). Processing Speed (*Gs*) and Long-Term Retrieval (*Glr*) have also been shown to have important influences on reading, primarily during early reading development (Evans et al., 2001; Floyd et al., 2007, 2012). *Ga* has also been related to reading, especially the narrow *Ga* ability Phonetic Coding (e.g., Flanagan, 2000; Keith, 1999; McGrew et al., 1997; Vanderwood et al., 2002). Phonetic Coding influenced reading on the WJ III (Evans et al., 2001), but broad *Ga* was only influential on reading for older adults (Floyd et al., 2007, 2012). This difference is likely due to the broader representation of narrow CHC abilities on the WJ III *Ga* cluster (i.e., Phonetic Coding and Resistance to Auditory Stimulus Distortion) as opposed to the WJ R *Ga* cluster (i.e., two Phonetic Coding tasks).

Fluid Reasoning (*Gf*), *Gc*, and *Gs* have been shown to influence math achievement in latent (Taub et al., 2008) and observed variable models (Floyd, Evans, & McGrew 2003; McGrew & Hessler, 1995). Floyd et al. (2003) also found that *Gwm* had a moderate influence on math, whereas *Glr* and *Ga* had small influences on math for younger children. For writing achievement, McGrew and Knopik (1993) found that *Gc*, *Gs*, and *Ga* had the most consistent influences on writing achievement, and *Gf* was related to writing at younger ages (i.e., 5–12 years). Floyd, McGrew, and Evans (2008) found similar results with the WJ III, where *Gc*, *Gs*, and *Gwm* had the most consistent influences on writing, but they also found small influences from *Glr*, broad *Ga*, and Phonetic Coding on writing. In contrast to McGrew and Knopik (1993), Floyd et al. (2008) found that *Gf* had a moderate influence on writing, but only in later adolescence.

Considering the patterns of cognitive-achievement relations across studies, it is apparent that some cognitive abilities have influences across multiple academic skills, whereas other cognitive abilities have influences on specific academic skills. These have been referred to as *domain-general* and *domain-specific* abilities, respectively (McGrew, 2012). In cognitive-achievement relations research using the WJ, examples of domain general abilities are *Gc*, *Gs*, and *Gwm* because they influence multiple academic skills (i.e., reading, writing, and math). Examples of domain specific abilities would be *Gf*, which has specific influences on math (and maybe writing), and *Ga*, which has specific influences on reading and writing. *Glr* also appears to be a domain general ability, but primarily at early ages. This suggests that age also moderates the magnitude of cognitive-achievement relations (McGrew & Wendling, 2010). For example, the influence of *Gc* on basic reading skills tends to increase with age, whereas the influences *Gs* and *Ga* (especially Phonetic Coding) tend to decrease with age (Evans et al., 2001). *Gs* and *Ga* are especially influential in the development

---

1. Although previous studies with the WJ R and WJ III referred to Short-Term Memory as *Gsm*, for consistency we will use *Gwm* when referring to either *Gsm* on the WJ R and WJ III or *Gwm* on the WJ IV.

of basic reading skills because young readers tend to decode words by identifying letter sounds in each word, whereas older readers are able to immediately recognize whole words (i.e., orthographic mapping, Ehri, 2014), making *Ga* and *Gs* less influential on reading skills.

CURRENT STUDY

The purpose of this study was to investigate cognitive-achievement relations on the WJ IV across the lifespan. This study was designed to answer the following questions: (i) What cognitive-achievement relations are present on the WJ IV? and (ii) Are the cognitive-achievement relations from the WJ IV consistent with previous research? Based on the results, recommendations for assessment and interpretation will be made.

METHOD

Participants and Instrument

Data from all individuals ages 6 years and older from the WJ IV norming sample were used for this study ($N = 6612$). This was a stratified random sample that was representative of the United States population according to the 2010 US Census. The sample was divided into separate age groups consistent with the validity studies in the WJ IV *Technical Manual* (McGrew et al., 2014): ages 6–8 years ($n = 954$), ages 9–13 years ($n = 1573$), ages 14–19 years ($n = 1685$), ages 20–39 years ($n = 1251$), and ages 40–90 years ($n = 1149$). The norming sample for the WJ IV used a planned missing data design, where all participants completed a subset of the tests in the battery, and data for missing tests were imputed (McGrew et al., 2014, pp. 67–71). The complete imputed dataset of standard scores from WJ IV COG, WJ IV OL, WJ IV ACH, and the research tests not included in these batteries was used in this study.

Analysis Plan

Cognitive abilities. SEM was used for all analyses. A higher-order latent variable model of cognitive abilities based on CHC theory and consistent with the WJ IV was developed (McGrew et al., 2014). The model included general intelligence (*g*) as a second-order factor, seven broad abilities (*Gc*, *Gf*, *Gwm*, *Glr*, *Gs*, *Ga*, Visual Processing [*Gv*]), and one narrow ability (Speed of Lexical Access [LA]) as first-order factors. The broad abilities that were included have been well-established in cross-battery factor analytic research using the WJ III (Phelps, McGrew, Knopik, & Ford, 2005; Reynolds et al., 2013) and in the WJ IV validity studies (McGrew et al., 2014). LA was included as a new ability proposed by the WJ IV authors for inclusion in the CHC taxonomy based on evidence from the construct and concurrent validity studies for the WJ IV. LA appeared to measure a unique ability not included in CHC cognitive-achievement research and not measured in other major intelligence and language batteries (McGrew et al., 2014). These cognitive factors were the explanatory variables in our SEM models that included cognitive and achievement variables.

Academic skills. Seven narrow academic factors were examined in this study: Basic Reading Skills, Reading Comprehension, Reading Rate, Basic Writing Skills, Written Expression, Math Calculation Skills, and Math Applications.[2] Narrow academic skills were evaluated because they are more consistent with the skill areas identified in definition of SLD in the Individuals with Disabilities Education Improvement Act (IDEIA, 2004). These academic skills were used as outcome variables in our SEM models that included cognitive and achievement variables.

Factorial invariance. Invariance tests were used to determine if the factor loadings for the cognitive and academic constructs measured by the WJ IV were proportionally equal across age groups (i.e., factorial invariance; Meredith, 1993). Corresponding factor loadings (first- and second-order) were constrained to be equal across age groups. If invariance of first- and second-order factor loadings was tenable, structural relations (i.e., cognitive-achievement relations) were compared across age groups.

Cognitive-achievement relations. Cognitive-achievement relations were analyzed for the reading, math, and writing factors. Cognitive variables were modeled as explanatory variables, and the academic factors were modeled as outcome variables. For reading, the three narrow reading factors (i.e., Basic Reading Skills, Reading Rate, and Reading Comprehension) were included in one model, for writing the two narrow writing factors (i.e., Basic Writing Skills, Written Expression) were included in one model, and for math the two narrow math factors (i.e., Math Calculation Skills, Math Applications) were included in one model. For each academic area, the analysis used the following sequence:

1. **Direct effects of g on academic skills.** Direct paths were included from g to each narrow academic skill factor. Previous research used similar analyses to compare whether using g as a single predictor of academic skills is sufficient for predicting performance on an academic task, rather than including direct paths from other broad and narrow cognitive abilities (cf. Glutting et al., 2006; Vanderwood et al., 2002). The comparison of this model with subsequent models tests whether g is the only important cognitive ability for explaining academic skills (Glutting et al., 2006; Parkin & Beaujean, 2012).
2. **Direct effects of broad CHC abilities on academic skills.** Direct paths were included from the broad CHC abilities to academic skills. The broad

---

2. The name *Math Applications* is intended to highlight the application of math calculation and knowledge to solving problems, a narrower skill than Quantitative Knowledge (*Gq*) or Mathematical Achievement (A3, see Schneider & McGrew, 2012). We wanted the name of this factor to describe math problem solving accurately, therefore, we decided to use the term *Math Applications.*

CHC abilities that had statistically significant influences on academic skills were identified using backward elimination (Floyd et al., 2007; Taub et al., 2008). First, direct paths were included from all of the broad CHC abilities to each academic skill. Paths with negative relations to the academic skills were eliminated one by one. After all of the negative paths were removed, paths that were not statistically significant ($p > .05$) were removed, starting with the smallest path coefficient. Once all broad CHC ability cognitive-achievement relations were statistically significant, paths that had theoretical reasons to be retested (e.g., they were identified in previous research) or those suggested by modification indexes (MI > 10, $p < .001$) were added into the model to determine if they had been inadvertently removed. Finally, a direct path from g to the academic skills was added to determine if a direct effect from g should also be included in this model.

3. **Direct effects of broad CHC abilities on specific academic tests**. The WJ IV *Technical Manual* suggested that several academic tests loaded directly on broad CHC cognitive abilities (McGrew et al., 2014). Direct paths from broad CHC abilities to individual academic tests were included in the models to determine if these specific effects were statistically significant after accounting for the direct effects of broad CHC abilities on the narrow academic factors (e.g., Is the direct path from Gs to Word Reading Fluency statistically significant after accounting for the direct path of Gs on the Reading Rate factor?).

4. **Age invariance of cognitive-achievement relations**. Last, we tested whether developmental trends in the magnitude of cognitive-achievement relations were present in the WJ IV tests by constraining all corresponding cognitive-achievement relations in the models to be equal across age groups. A statistically significant degradation in model fit suggested that the strength of cognitive-achievement relations were different across the lifespan.

Model Evaluation

Models were estimated using maximum likelihood estimation (MLE). Standalone model fit was evaluated using χ^2, Comparative Fit Index (CFI), Tucker–Lewis Index (TLI), Root Mean Square Error of Approximation (RMSEA), and Standardized Root Mean Square Residual (SRMR). The Akaike Information Index (AIC), Bayesian Information Index (BIC), and sample size-adjusted Bayesian Information Index (aBIC) were used for comparing nonnested models. Change in χ^2 ($\Delta \chi^2$) was used as the primary determination of a statistically significant change in model fit when comparing nested models. The ΔCFI was used to compare models for factorial invariance because the $\Delta \chi^2$ is highly sensitive to small changes in model fit with large sample sizes. A criterion of .01 for the ΔCFI was used, where a decrease in CFI greater than .01 suggests that invariance is not tenable (Chen, 2007; Cheung & Rensvold, 2002).

In confirmatory factor analyses (CFA) in the WJ IV *Technical Manual* (McGrew et al., 2014, pp. 167–170), model fit indexes were worse than suggested by conventional rules of thumb when using MLE (Schermelleh-Engel, Moosbrugger, & Müller, 2003). The authors suggested poorer fit may have been due to the large number of variables, significant complexity in the model, and the presence of multicollinearity among variables (McGrew et al., 2014, footnote on p. 222). Additionally, this poor fit may have been the result of using an imputed dataset. Previous research with the WJ III showed substantial differences in model fit in studies using the covariance matrices compared to those that used the original dataset with missing values (cf. Floyd et al., 2007; Keith, Reynolds, Patel, & Ridley, 2008; Taub et al., 2008). The WJ IV *Technical Manual* also reported fit indexes for the models using the *scale-free least squares* (SFLS) estimator (Blunch, 2008), which had better fit than MLE. All models were re-estimated using SFLS. SFLS estimation does not provide fit indexes for the CFI or TLI. Consistent with the WJ IV *Technical Manual*, we report the Adjusted Goodness of Fit Index (AGFI) and the Parsimony-Adjusted Normed Fit Index (PNFI) for MLE and SFLS.

RESULTS

Cognitive Abilities Model

Two cross loadings were included *a priori* in the cognitive abilities model: Nonword Repetition loaded on *Ga* and *Gwm*, and Phonological Processing loaded on *Ga* and LA. Nonword Repetition is a measure of memory for sound patterns (McGrew et al., 2014), thus loaded on both *Ga* and *Gwm*. Phonological Processing includes three subtests, one of which is Word Fluency. Word Fluency requires the examinee to think of as many words as possible that start with a specific letter sound in 1 minute. This subtest also measures Speed of Lexical Access and is similar in task requirements to Retrieval Fluency, thus Phonological Processing loaded on both *Ga* and LA.[3] Several test and factor residual covariances consistent with those in the WJ IV *Technical Manual* were included to account for similar test content or response processes.[4] The cognitive abilities model is presented in Figure 3.1.

Academic Skills

The seven narrow academic skills examined in this study were included in a measurement model. Five narrow academic factors (Reading Comprehension,

---

3. Retrieval Fluency is an ideational fluency task that requires individuals to retrieve words from different categories. The Word Fluency subtest of Phonological Processing requires individuals to retrieve words based on initial sounds; thus, words are retrieved based on phonological codes rather than ideational categories.
4. A full description of residual covariances in the model is available from the first author.

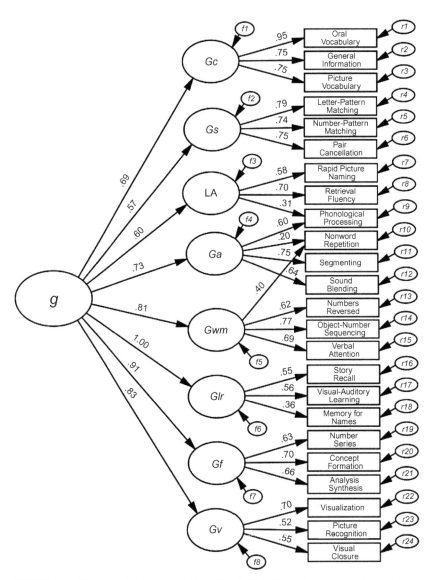

FIGURE 3.1 Cognitive abilities model. *Note*: Standardized factor loadings are shown for ages 9–13 years. Residual covariances are not shown for clarity.

Reading Rate, Math Calculation Skills, Basic Writing Skills, and Written Expression) were similar to clusters available on the WJ IV (Figure 3.2, see also Chapter 1). Two narrow academic factors (Basic Reading Skills and Math Applications) were slightly different than the clusters available on the WJ IV. These changes were made after the initial measurement model of academic

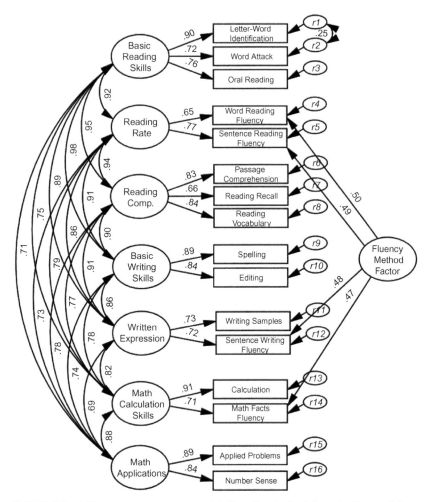

FIGURE 3.2 Achievement measurement model. *Note*: Standardized factor loadings and factor correlations are shown for ages 9–13 years.

skills was developed. Changes centered on two tests: Oral Reading and Number Matrices. On the WJ IV, Oral Reading (a measure of reading accuracy) is combined with Sentence Reading Fluency (a measure of reading rate) to create a Reading Fluency composite. This pairing of rate and accuracy is consistent with fluency composites on other standardized reading fluency tests (e.g., Gray Oral Reading Tests—Fifth Edition; Wiederhold & Bryant, 2012). Oral Reading was initially included with the Reading Rate tests (i.e., Sentence Reading Fluency and Word Reading Fluency) to be more consistent with the WJ IV scoring. Oral Reading is scored on reading accuracy rather than reading rate, suggesting that it is a measure of decoding. Indeed, when Oral Reading cross-loaded on the

Reading Rate and Basic Reading Skills factors, the cross-loading showed that Oral Reading was better modeled as a test on the Basic Reading Skills factor (loadings between .69 and .78) over the Reading Rate factor (loadings between .10 and .11); therefore, Oral Reading was included on the Basic Reading Skills factor.

Applied Problems and Number Matrices comprise a Math Problem Solving cluster on the WJ IV ACH. We also included the Number Sense test on this factor. Number Sense is a research test that is included on the WJ IV Early Cognitive and Academic Development Battery[5] (WJ IV ECAD; Schrank, McGrew, & Mather, 2015). Further analysis suggested that Number Matrices was better modeled with Number Series (a *Gf* test) as a Quantitative Reasoning (RQ) factor in the cognitive model.[6] After this change, Applied Problems and Number Sense were included on the Math Applications achievement factor. This full achievement measurement model is presented in Figure 3.2.

Factorial Invariance

The model of cognitive abilities was fit to all age groups in a multigroup model. Model fit indexes using MLE were generally below conventional rules for adequate fit (Table 3.1, Model 1). Fit indexes using SFLS were adequate (Table 3.2, Model 1).[7] The second-order factor loading for *Glr* on *g* was slightly greater than one for most groups. This factor loading was constrained to one by setting the residual variance for *Glr* to zero for all groups, which did not result in a statistically significant degradation in model fit (Table 3.1, Model 2). When equality constraints were added to the first-order factor loadings there was a statistically significant degradation in model fit according to the $\Delta\chi^2$, but the ΔCFI was <.01 (Table 3.1, Model 3). There was not a statistically significant degradation in model fit when equality constraints were added to the second-order factor loadings (Table 3.1, Model 4). Invariance was tenable for first- and second-order factor loadings in the cognitive abilities model (Keith, 2015, chap. 19).

Next, all of the achievement factors were included in a multigroup measurement model to test the invariance of first-order factor loadings. A method factor was included in this model to account for the covariance between the academic fluency tests. This method factor included loadings on all four fluency tests that were set to be equal to each other, and the method factor was uncorrelated with the other factors. This model had adequate fit for MLE and SFLS (Tables 3.1 and 3.2, Model 5). When equality constraints were added to the first-order factor

---

5. Normative data were available for Number Sense across the lifespan, even though this test is only available on the WJ IV EACD.

6. RQ in this study was similar to the *Gf*-RQ (fluid intelligence—quantitative reasoning) factor included in the WJ IV *Technical Manual* (p. 165).

7. Table 3.1 includes all fit indexes for MLE. Table 3.2 includes corresponding fit indexes for SFLS and MLE. Although Table 3.1 is referenced throughout, the fit indexes for SFLS on corresponding models from Table 3.1 are in Table 3.2.

TABLE 3.1 Model Tests for Cognitive-Achievement Relations

	χ^2 (df)	$\Delta\chi^2$ (Δdf)	p	CFI	TLI	RMSEA	SRMR	AIC	BIC	aBIC
Factorial Invariance: Cognitive Model										
1) Configural model	13,539.37 (1150)			.848	.818	.090	.049	1254388	1257583	1256089
2) Set $g{\rightarrow}Glr$ to zero	13,548.42 (1155)	9.05 (5)	.107	.848	.819	.090	.049	1254387	1257548	1256070
3) First-order loadings equal	13,714.60 (1227)	166.18 (72)	.000	.847	.828	.088	.056	1254409	1257081	1255832
4) Second-order loadings equal	13,747.51 (1255)	32.91 (28)	.239	.847	.832	.087	.059	1254386	1256867	1255707
Factorial Invariance: Achievement Model										
5) Configural Model	5636.71 (405)			.944	.917	.099	.042	795022	797425	796307
6) First-order loadings equal	5764.23 (441)	124.52 (36)	.000	.943	.923	.096	.055	795075	797243	796229
Cognitive-Achievement Relations for Reading Factors										
7) g effects only	40,357.99 (2280)			.747	.725	.112	.078	1652459	1655993	1654341
8) Broad CHC effects only[a]	35,460.13 (2250)			.780	.757	.106	.069	1647621	1651359	1649611
9) Broad+specific effects	33,545.73 (2230)	1914.40 (20)	.000	.792	.769	.103	.066	1645746	1649621	1647809
10) Add $Gf{\rightarrow}RdgCmp$	33,322.43 (2225)	223.31 (5)	.000	.794	.770	.103	.065	1645533	1649441	1647614
11) Age invariance	33,444.47 (2281)	122.04 (56)	.000	.793	.775	.102	.067	1645543	1649071	1647421

Cognitive-Achievement Relations for Writing Factors

	χ²(df)	Δχ²(Δdf)	p	CFI	TLI	RMSEA	SRMR	AIC	BIC	aBIC
12) g effects only	27,162.18 (1738)			.772	.752	.105	.071	1458191	1461127	1459754
13) Broad CHC effects only[a]	24,649.52 (1721)			.795	.774	.100	.066	1455712	1458764	1457337
14) Add Gs→SntWrtFl	24,577.27 (1716)	72.25 (5)	.000	.795	.774	.100	.066	1455650	1458736	1457293
15) Add g→WrtSmp	24,211.17 (1711)	366.10 (5)	.000	.798	.777	.100	.064	1455294	1458414	1456955
16) Age invariance	24,264.12 (1740)	52.96 (29)	.004	.798	.781	.099	.065	1455289	1458211	1456845

Cognitive-Achievement Relations for Math Factors

	χ²(df)	Δχ²(Δdf)	p	CFI	TLI	RMSEA	SRMR	AIC	BIC	aBIC
17) g effects only	25,230.21 (1857)			.809	.791	.098	.067	1500868	1504015	1502543
18) Broad CHC effects only[a]	22,374.85 (1831)			.832	.814	.092	.062	1498065	1501388	1499834
19) Broad+specific effects	21,528.84 (1821)	846.01 (10)	.000	.839	.821	.090	.060	1497238	1500630	1499044
20) Free all broad effects	21,506.98 (1817)	21.86 (4)	.000	.839	.820	.091	.061	1497225	1500643	1499045
21) Age invariance	21,586.38 (1857)	79.40 (40)	.000	.839	.824	.090	.062	1497224	1500371	1498900

Notes: All fit statistics in this table are estimated using MLE. Compare all models to previous model unless otherwise noted. χ² (df) = Chi-Square; Δχ² (Δdf) = Change in Chi-Square; CFI = Comparative Fit Index; TLI = Tucker–Lewis Index; RMSEA = Root Mean Square Error of Approximation; SRMR = Standardized Root Mean Square Residual; AIC = Akaike Information Index; BIC = Bayesian Information Index; aBIC = Adjusted Bayesian Information Index; RdgCmp = Reading Comprehension; SntWrtFl = Sentence Writing Fluency; WrtSmp = Writing Samples; Age Invariance = Invariance of cognitive-achievement relations across all age groups.
[a]Δχ² cannot be used because these models are not nested.

TABLE 3.2 Model Tests for Cognitive-Achievement Relations: MLE and SFLS Results

	MLE		SFLS	
	AGFI	**PNFI**	**AGFI**	**PNFI**
Factorial Invariance: Cognitive Model				
1) Configural model	.821	.698	.981	.817
2) Set $g{\to}Glr$ to zero	.822	.701	.981	.821
3) First-order loadings equal	.830	.743	.980	.870
4) Second-order loadings equal	.834	.759	.979	.888
Factorial Invariance: Achievement Model				
5) Configural model	.840	.635	.995	.673
6) First-order loadings equal	.850	.690	.994	.732
Reading				
7) g effects only	.719	.679	.965	.886
8) Broad CHC effects only	.737	.699	.974	.883
9) Broad+specific effects	.746	.704	.976	.877
10) Add $Gf{\to}$RdgCmp	.745	.703	.977	.876
11) Age invariance	.750	.720	.977	.897
Writing				
12) g effects only	.755	.701	.968	.888
13) Broad CHC effects only	.770	.714	.973	.885
14) Add $Gs{\to}$SntWrtFl	.770	.712	.974	.882
15) Add $g{\to}$WrtSmp	.770	.713	.974	.880
16) Age invariance	.773	.725	.974	.895
Math				
17) g effects only	.772	.730	.975	.891
18) Broad CHC effects only	.794	.740	.980	.883
19) Broad+specific effects	.798	.742	.980	.879
20) Free all broad effects	.798	.741	.981	.877
21) Age invariance	.801	.756	.980	.896

Notes: MLE = Maximum Likelihood Estimation; SFLS = Scale-free Least Squares; AGFI = Adjusted Goodness of Fit Index; PNFI = Parsimony-Adjusted Normed Fit Index; RdgCmp = Reading Comprehension; SntWrtFl = Sentence Writing Fluency; WrtSmp = Writing Samples; Age Invariance = Invariance of cognitive-achievement relations across all age groups.

loadings, there was a statistically significant degradation in model fit for the $\Delta\chi^2$, but the ΔCFI was <.01 (Table 3.1, Model 6). Invariance was tenable. These results suggest that the factor loadings in the WJ IV cognitive and achievement models were proportionally equal across the lifespan. These equality constraints on factor loadings were included on all subsequent models.

Reading

Cognitive-achievement models were estimated with Basic Reading Skills, Reading Rate, and Reading Comprehension factors as outcome variables.[8]

Direct effects of *g* on reading factors. The direct effects of *g* on Basic Reading Skills (.74–.80), Reading Rate (.61–.68), and Reading Comprehension (.84–.91) were strong for all age groups. Model fit indexes were poor using MLE, but acceptable for SFLS (Tables 3.1 and 3.2, Model 7).

Direct effects of broad CHC abilities on reading factors. After the backward elimination procedure, paths from *Gc*, *Ga*, and *Gs* to Basic Reading Skills and to Reading Comprehension were statistically significant for all groups, and paths from *Gc*, *Gs*, and LA to Reading Rate were statistically significant for all groups. This model fit substantially better than the model that included only the direct effect of *g* on the reading factors (Table 3.1, Model 8). A path from *g* to each of the reading factors was added to the model, but this path was not statistically significant. The effects of *g* on the reading factors were completely mediated by the broad CHC abilities, suggesting that broad CHC abilities have important influences on reading achievement.

Direct effects of broad CHC abilities on specific reading tests. Several direct effects from broad CHC abilities to specific reading tests were suggested in the WJ IV *Technical Manual*, suggesting direct effects of broad CHC abilities on individual tests beyond the effects of broad CHC abilities on the academic factors.[9] These direct effects included paths from *Gc* to Passage Comprehension and Reading Vocabulary, *Ga* to Word Attack, and *Gs* to Word Reading Fluency.[10] Adding direct paths from cognitive abilities to these four reading tests resulted

---

8. It is important to note that reading skills (e.g., decoding, fluency, comprehension) are not separate abilities that are independently developed; rather, they are likely linked together causally (Floyd et al., 2007; Hajovsky et al., 2014). We examined narrow reading factors that were simply correlated without specifying structural relations among the reading constructs, which was beyond the purpose of this study.

9. Paths from *Glr* to academic skills were not included in any models because the second-order factor loading for *Glr* on *g* was 1.0; *Glr* had no unique variance that could be differentiated from *g*.

10. The higher order model in the WJ IV *Technical Manual* (pp. 164–165) included paths from *Gs* to both Word Reading Fluency and Sentence Reading Fluency. A path from *Gs* to both Reading Rate tests and the Reading Rate factor would result in an underidentified model. The effect from *Gs* to Word Reading Fluency was larger in the *Technical Manual*, which is why it was initially chosen to load on *Gs*. As a follow-up, a path from *Gs* to Sentence Reading Fluency instead of Word Reading Fluency was included, but this path was negative. *Gs* appears to influence Word Reading Fluency beyond its effect on Reading Rate, but not Sentence Reading Fluency.

in a statistically significant improvement in model fit (Table 3.1, Model 9). All of these paths were statistically significant across all groups.

Including direct effects to individual tests altered some of the findings with the broad CHC abilities. The influence of *Gc* on the Reading Comprehension factor decreased substantially, and was statistically significant for only two groups (ages 9–13 years and 40–90 years). Additionally, there was a significant improvement in model fit when a path from *Gf* to Reading Comprehension, as suggested by the MIs, was included (Table 3.1, Model 10).

Age invariance of cognitive-achievement relations for reading. There was a statistically significant degradation in model fit when all paths from broad CHC abilities to the reading factors were constrained to be equal across age groups (Table 3.1, Model 11), supporting the presence of developmental differences in the strength of cognitive-achievement relations. Thus, the effects of the broad abilities on achievement factors change with age, consistent with previous research and developmental patterns in learning development.

Final model for reading. The final model for reading included direct paths from *Gc*, *Gs*, and *Ga* on Basic Reading Skills, with a direct path from *Ga* to Word Attack. Direct paths were included from *Gc*, *Gs*, and LA to Reading Rate, with a direct path from *Gs* to Word Reading Fluency. Finally, paths from *Gf*, *Gc*, *Gs*, and *Ga* to Reading Comprehension were included, with direct paths from *Gc* to Passage Comprehension and Reading Vocabulary. Standardized coefficients for the cognitive-reading relations are in Table 3.3. An example of cognitive-achievement relations for Basic Reading Skills only is presented in Figure 3.3.

TABLE 3.3 Standardized Coefficients for Cognitive-Achievement Relations for Reading Factors

	Ages 6–8 Years	Ages 9–13 Years	Ages 14–19 Years	Ages 20–39 Years	Ages 40–90 Years
Basic Reading Skills					
Total Indirect Effect of g on Basic Reading Skills Factor					
g→Basic Reading Skills	.69	.65	.70	.71	.73
Direct Effects on Basic Reading Skills Factor					
Gc→Basic Reading Skills	.39	.52	.53	.44	.57
Gs→Basic Reading Skills	.23	.20	.09	.18	.13
Ga→Basic Reading Skills	.32	.25	.33	.32	.24

(Continued)

TABLE 3.3 Standardized Coefficients for Cognitive-Achievement Relations for Reading Factors (Continued)

	Ages 6–8 Years	Ages 9–13 Years	Ages 14–19 Years	Ages 20–39 Years	Ages 40–90 Years
Total, Direct, and Indirect Effects on Basic Reading Skills Tests					
Ga→Word Attack[a]	.52 (.35/.16)	.42 (.30/.13)	.46 (.30/.16)	.45 (.29/.16)	.41 (.28/.13)
Reading Rate					
Total Indirect Effect of g on Reading Rate Factor					
g→Reading Rate	.59	.57	.60	.58	.63
Direct Effects on Reading Rate Factor					
Gc→Reading Rate	.22	.23	.25	.16	.24
Gs→Reading Rate	.58	.60	.55	.60	.54
LA→Reading Rate	.12	.14	.12	.14	.14
Total, Direct, and Indirect Effects on Reading Rate Tests					
Gs→Word Reading Fluency[a]	.67 (.30/.37)	.66 (.31/.35)	.60 (.28/.32)	.67 (.32/.35)	.65 (.33/.33)
Reading Comprehension					
Total Indirect Effect of g on Reading Comprehension Factor					
g→Reading Comprehension	.68	.62	.64	.66	.71
Direct Effects on Reading Comprehension Factor					
Gf→Reading Comprehension	.25	.34	.46	.49	.35
Gc→Reading Comprehension	*.04*	.08	*−.04*	*−.07*	.11
Gs→Reading Comprehension	.17	.15	*.04*	.13	.08
Ga→Reading Comprehension	.37	.24	.28	.21	.30
Total, Direct, and Indirect Effects on Reading Comprehension Tests					
Gc→Passage Comprehension[a]	.41 (.39/.02)	.46 (.41/.05)	.46 (.48/−.02)	.46 (.49/−.03)	.51 (.45/.06)
Gc→Reading Vocabulary[a]	.60 (.58/.02)	.63 (.60/.03)	.64 (.65/−.02)	.61 (.63/−.02)	.67 (.63/.04)

[a]*Values outside the parentheses are total effects from broad CHC abilities to specific subtests, and values inside the parentheses are direct and indirect effects, respectively. Values that are underlined and italicized are not statistically significant at the p < .05 level.*

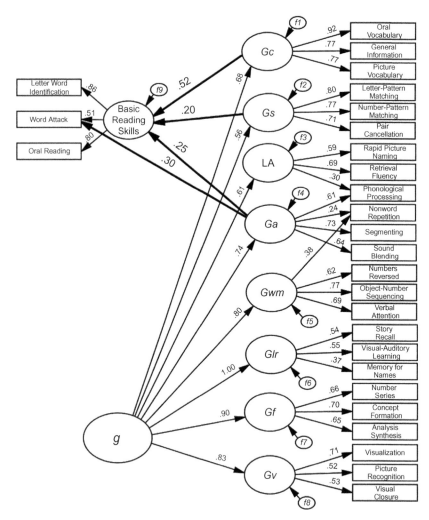

FIGURE 3.3 Example of cognitive-achievement relations for Basic Reading Skills. *Note*: Standardized factor loadings are shown for ages 9–13 years. Residual variances and covariances are not shown for clarity. Cognitive-achievement relations for Reading Rate and Reading Comprehension were also estimated in this model, but are not shown for clarity.

Writing

Cognitive-achievement models were estimated with Basic Writing Skills and Written Expression factors as outcome variables.

Direct effects of *g* on writing factors. The direct effect of *g* was large for Basic Writing Skills (.77–.82) and Written Expression (.78–.84) (Table 3.1, Model 12).

Direct effects of broad CHC abilities on writing factors. After the backward elimination procedure, paths from *Gc*, *Gs*, and *Gwm* to Basic Writing Skills were statistically significant. The broad CHC abilities related to Written Expression differed slightly across the age range. Paths from *Gv* and *Gs* to Written Expression were statistically significant across all age groups, and the path from LA to Written Expression was statistically significant for ages 6–8 years and ages 9–14 years only. This model fit much better than the model that only included direct effects of *g* on the writing factors (Table 3.1, Model 13). A path from *g* to both writing factors was added to the model, but this path was negative or not statistically significant. The influence of *g* on the writing factors was completely mediated by the broad CHC abilities. For writing, as well as reading, the broad CHC abilities appear to have important influences on writing achievement.

Direct effects of broad CHC abilities on specific writing tests. A direct path from *Gs* to the Sentence Writing Fluency test was suggested in the WJ IV *Technical Manual*. Adding this path resulted in a statistically significant improvement in model fit, and this path was statistically significant across all age groups (Table 3.1, Model 14). MIs suggested a direct influence of *g* on the Writing Samples test across all age groups. When this path was added, there was a statistically significant improvement in model fit (Table 3.1, Model 15).

Age invariance of cognitive-achievement relations for writing. Setting the paths from corresponding broad CHC abilities to the writing factors to be equal across age groups resulted in a statistically significant degradation in model fit (Table 3.1, Model 16), suggesting developmental differences in cognitive-achievement relations for writing.

Final model for writing. The final model for writing included *Gc*, *Gs*, and *Gwm* effects on Basic Writing Skills, and *Gs*, *Gv*, and LA effects on Written Expression, with direct effects of *g* on Writing Samples and *Gs* on Sentence Writing Fluency. Standardized coefficients for cognitive-writing relations are in Table 3.4.

Math

Cognitive-achievement models were estimated with Math Calculation Skills and Math Applications factors as outcome variables.

Direct effects of *g* on math factors. The direct effects of *g* were very large on Math Calculation (.75–.83) and on Math Applications (.87–.90) (Table 3.1, Model 17).

Direct effects of broad CHC abilities on math factors. After the backward elimination procedure, paths from *Gc*, *Gs*, and RQ to Math Calculation Skills were statistically significant across all age groups. For Math Applications, the pattern of cognitive-achievement relations differed slightly across the age range. *Gc* and RQ were related to Math Applications across all age groups.

TABLE 3.4 Standardized Coefficients for Cognitive-Achievement Relations for Writing Factors

	Ages 6–8 Years	Ages 9–13 Years	Ages 14–19 Years	Ages 20–39 Years	Ages 40–90 Years
Basic Writing Skills					
Total Indirect Effect of g on Basic Writing Skills Factor					
g→Basic Writing Skills	.70	.68	.72	.74	.77
Direct Effects on Basic Writing Factor					
Gc→Basic Writing	.46	.48	.53	.52	.52
Gs→Basic Writing	.24	.22	.15	.22	.18
Gwm→Basic Writing	.27	.29	.29	.25	.29
Written Expression					
Total Indirect Effect of g on Written Expression Factor					
g→Written Expression	.57	.60	.61	.50	.64
Direct Effects on Written Expression Factor					
Gs→Written Expression	.32	.39	.32	.27	.40
LA→Written Expression	.13	.11	*.00*	*.00*	*.00*
Gv→Written Expression	.32	.38	.47	.39	.41
Total, Direct, and Indirect Effects on Written Expression Tests					
g→Writing Samples[a]	.64 (.35/.29)	.51 (.23/.29)	.61 (.38/.23)	.56 (.35/.21)	.65 (.36/.29)
Gs→Sentence Writing Fluency[a]	.50 (.27/.23)	.48 (.20/.27)	.49 (.30/.19)	.54 (.38/.16)	.60 (.22/.28)

[a]*Values outside the parentheses are total effects from broad CHC abilities to specific subtests, and values inside the parentheses are direct and indirect effects, respectively. Values that are underlined and italicized are not statistically significant at the $p < .05$ level.*

Gf was related to Math Applications in all age groups except ages 6–8 years, *Gs* was related to Math Applications in all age groups except ages 20–39 years, and *Gv* was related to Math Applications in all age groups except ages 20–39 years and ages 40–90 years. This model fit much better than the model that only included *g* as a predictor of the math factors (Table 3.1, Model 18). A path from *g* to each of the math factors was added to the model to determine if *g* had a direct effect on the math factors, but was not statistically significant; the effect of *g* on the math factors was completely mediated by the broad cognitive abilities. Consistent with reading and writing achievement, broad CHC abilities had important influences on math achievement.

Direct effects of broad CHC abilities on specific math tests. Direct paths from RQ to the Applied Problems test and from *Gs* to the Math Facts Fluency test were suggested in the WJ IV *Technical Manual*. Adding these paths resulted in a statistically significant improvement in model fit (Table 3.1, Model 19), and these paths were statistically significant across all groups. Adding these paths changed the magnitude of the effects from broad CHC abilities to the Math Applications factor. The paths from the broad CHC abilities on the Math Applications factor (i.e., *Gc*, *Gs*, *Gf*, RQ, and *Gv*) were freed for all groups to reevaluate the effects (Table 3.1, Model 20). The results indicated that *Gc*, *Gs*, RQ, and *Gv* were related to Math Applications across all ages, and *Gf* was related to Math Applications for all groups except ages 6–8 years and ages 20–39 years (Table 3.1, Model 21). There were no changes in cognitive-achievement relations for the Math Calculation factor.

Age invariance of cognitive-achievement relations for math. Setting the cognitive-achievement relations to be equal across age groups resulted in a statistically significant degradation in model fit (Table 3.1, Model 22), suggesting developmental differences in cognitive-achievement relations across the lifespan. As expected, the magnitude of the effects of the broad abilities on broad and specific math achievements change depending on age.

Final model for math. The final model for Math included paths from *Gc*, *Gs*, and RQ to Math Calculation, with a direct path from *Gs* to Math Facts Fluency. For Math Applications, there were paths from *Gc*, *Gf*, *Gs*, RQ, and *Gv*, and a direct path from RQ to the Applied Problems test. The path from *Gf* to Math Applications was not statistically significant for ages 6–8 years or ages 20–39 years. Standardized coefficients for cognitive-math relations are in Table 3.5. An example of the model of cognitive-achievement relations for Math Applications is in Figure 3.4.

INTERPRETING COGNITIVE-ACHIEVEMENT RELATIONS WITH THE WJ IV

We used SEM to investigate cognitive-achievement relations on the WJ IV. We set out to answer two questions: (i) What cognitive-achievement relations are

TABLE 3.5 Standardized Coefficients for Cognitive-Achievement Relations for Math Factors

	Ages 6–8 Years	Ages 9–13 Years	Ages 14–19 Years	Ages 20–39 Years	Ages 40–90 Years
Math Calculation Skills					
Total Indirect Effect of g on Math Calculation Skills Factor					
g→Math Calculation Skills	.73	.70	.74	.74	.76
Direct Effects on Math Calculation Skills Factor					
Gc→Math Calculation Skills	.07	.08	.11	.08	.11
Gs→Math Calculation Skills	.40	.35	.32	.25	.23
RQ→Math Calculation Skills	.57	.63	.61	.68	.67
Total, Direct, and Indirect Effects on Math Calculation Skills Tests					
Gs→Math Facts Fluency[a]	.58 (.37/.21)	.53 (.36/.17)	.48 (.32/.17)	.47 (.34/.13)	.45 (.33/.12)
Math Applications					
Total Indirect Effect of g on Math Applications Factor					
g→Math Applications	.80	.77	.80	.80	.83
Direct Effects on Math Applications Factor					
Gc→Math Applications	.27	.32	.33	.34	.35
Gs→Math Applications	.19	.19	.19	.10	.10
Gf→Math Applications	*.12*	.17	.11	*.11*	.22
RQ→Math Applications	.28	.17	.23	.35	.24
Gv→Math Applications	.18	.20	.19	.12	.11
Total, Direct, and Indirect Effects on Math Applications Tests					
RQ→Applied Problems[a]	.49 (.31/.18)	.45 (.34/.11)	.48 (.33/.15)	.55 (.32/.23)	.47 (.31/.16)

[a]Values outside the parentheses are total effects from broad CHC abilities to specific subtests, and values inside the parentheses are direct and indirect effects, respectively. Values that are underlined and italicized are not statistically significant at the p < .05 level.

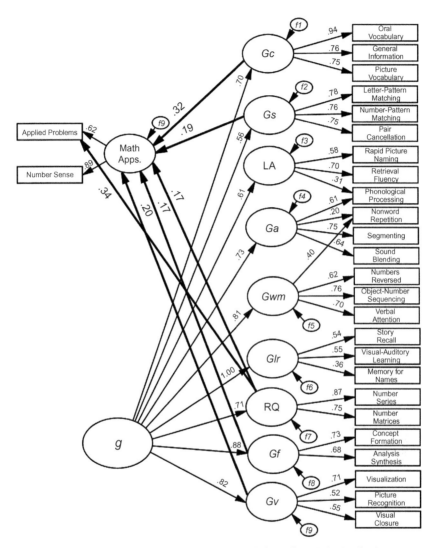

FIGURE 3.4 Example of cognitive-achievement relations for Math Applications. *Note*: Standardized factor loadings are shown for ages 9–13 years. Residual variances and covariances are not shown for clarity. Cognitive-achievement relations for Math Calculation Skills were also estimated in this model, but are not shown for clarity.

present on the WJ IV? and (ii) Are cognitive-achievement relations from the WJ IV consistent with previous research? We will answer these questions as they relate to each of the narrow academic skills examined in this study and provide recommendations for interpretation of the WJ IV based on the results.

Basic Reading Skills

What cognitive-achievement relations were found for Basic Reading Skills?
There were strong influences of *Gc* (standardized path coefficients ranged from
.39 to .57),[11] moderate to strong influences from *Ga* (.24–.33), and weak to
moderate influences of *Gs* (.09–.23) on Basic Reading Skills. There was also a
strong direct influence from *Ga* on the Word Attack test (.28–.35). Finally, the
indirect effect of *g* (i.e., the effect of *g* that was mediated by broad CHC abilities) was strong (.65–.73).

    Were results for Basic Reading Skills consistent with previous research?
Consistent with WJ III research (Evans et al., 2001; Floyd et al., 2012), the
influence of *Gc* on Basic Reading Skills was strong and appeared to increase
with age, where the smallest influence was for ages 6–8 years (.39) and the
largest was for ages 40–90 years (.57). The increasing influence of *Gc* on Basic
Reading Skills may be related to the development of orthographic mapping of
words (Ehri, 2014), where words and their meanings are automatically recognized and do not need to be decoded. In other words, *Gc* may have a greater
influence on Basic Reading Skills as reading develops because identifying
single words becomes declarative knowledge (i.e., immediate recognition of
words) rather than procedural knowledge (i.e., active decoding of words).

    There was a moderate to strong influence from *Ga* on Basic Reading Skills
across all age groups. This finding is consistent with WJ R research (Flanagan,
2000; McGrew et al., 1997; Keith, 1999; Vanderwood et al., 2002), but inconsistent with WJ III research (Evans et al., 2001; Floyd et al., 2007). The *Ga*
tasks on the WJ IV are new and very different than those on the WJ R or the WJ
III. The WJ IV *Ga* tests are more cognitively complex (McGrew et al., 2014)
and they measure access to an individual's lexicon via phonological codes
(i.e., Phonological Processing) and memory for sound patterns (i.e., Nonword
Repetition). The *Ga* factor in this study included two additional Phonetic Coding
tests from the WJ IV OL, Sound Blending and Segmentation, weighting this factor heavily toward phonological skills. The greater focus on complex phonological processing on the WJ IV is likely the reason for the strong influence of *Ga* on
Basic Reading Skills across the lifespan. There was also a strong influence from
Ga on the Word Attack test across all groups, consistent with previous research
using the WJ R (Flanagan, 2000; Keith, 1999; McGrew et al., 1997; Vanderwood
et al., 2002). The total effect of *Ga* on Word Attack was strong (.41–.52), with
strong direct effects (.28–.53) and moderate indirect effects (.13–.16). Overall,
Ga has a strong influence on nonsense word decoding, which requires the active
decoding of words using phonetic coding skills.

---

11. Standardized path coefficients above .05 were considered weak, those that were approximately
    .15 were considered moderate, and those greater than .25 were considered strong. These inter-
    pretations have been used in previous research on cognitive-achievement relations (Floyd et al.,
    2012; Taub et al., 2008; cf. Keith, 2015, chap. 4).

The influence of *Gs* on Basic Reading Skills was weak to moderate, a finding consistent with WJ III research (Evans et al., 2001; Floyd et al., 2007). This influence tended to be largest for younger ages, consistent with hypotheses that *Gs* is especially important when basic academic skills are developing (Floyd et al., 2007; McGrew & Wendling, 2010).

Finally, the indirect effect of *g* on Basic Reading Skills was strong, consistent with previous research (Floyd et al., 2007). Although *g* was a strong predictor of Basic Reading Skills in the *g* only model, model fit was substantially better when direct effects from broad CHC abilities were included in the model. This suggests that broad CHC abilities have important direct influences on academic skills, whereas the influence of *g* is indirect and mediated by the broad CHC abilities. This finding was consistent across reading, writing, and math models. The influence of *g* should not be understated; it is clearly a strong predictor of all academic skills. Identifying the broad CHC abilities that mediate the effects of *g* and also uniquely influence academic skills may provide a better understanding for why individuals have difficulties in specific academic domains that are not explained by global difficulties in cognitive functioning.

Recommendations for Basic Reading Skills. The assessment of *Gc*, *Ga*, and *Gs*, as operationally defined by the WJ IV, is important to consider when a student has difficulties with Basic Reading Skills. These three abilities had important influences on Basic Reading Skills across the lifespan, and it is possible that difficulties in one or more of these areas may partially explain concurrent difficulties in Basic Reading Skills. The current results suggest that the influence of *Ga* on Basic Reading Skills for the WJ IV is stronger than previous versions of the WJ, potentially making this a very useful cluster for understanding difficulties in Basic Reading Skills. Additionally, the assessment of *Ga* may be especially important when there are suspected difficulties with phonics skills, difficulties that may be evidenced by low scores on Word Attack.

Reading Rate

What cognitive-achievement relations were found for Reading Rate? *Gs* (.54–.60) had strong influences, *Gc* (.16–.25) had moderate to strong influences, and LA (.12–.14) had weak influences Reading Rate. There was a strong (.28–.33) direct influence from *Gs* on the Word Reading Fluency test. Finally, the indirect effect of *g* on Reading Rate was strong across all age groups (.57–.63).

Were results for Reading Rate consistent with previous research? Reading Rate is a new cluster on the WJ IV that has not been examined in previous WJ research. The Reading Rate factor represents shared variance between tests that require the rapid recognition of words and their meanings (Word Reading Fluency) and the rapid determination of the accuracy of short sentences (Sentence Reading Fluency). These are measures of silent reading fluency, a skill that differs from other reading fluency tests that typically measure oral reading.

The influence of *Gs* on Reading Rate was strong across all age groups, indicating that the ability to quickly and efficiently perform simple cognitive tasks generalizes to speeded reading tasks. Additionally, there was a strong direct effect from *Gs* on Word Reading Fluency. The total effect of *Gs* on Word Reading Fluency was very large (.60–.67), and the direct and indirect effects of *Gs* on Word Reading Fluency were similar in magnitude (.28–.33, .32–.37, respectively). The strong influence of *Gs* on Reading Rate and Word Reading Fluency is consistent with research showing that processing speed is one of the many important cognitive abilities related to reading fluency (Hudson, Pullen, Lane, & Torgerson, 2009).

The influence of *Gc* on Reading Rate may be explained by the pervasive influence of *Gc* on language-related tasks, but may be partially explained by the nature of the tests on this factor. Word Reading Fluency requires vocabulary knowledge to determine which two words are conceptually similar, and Sentence Reading Fluency requires a person to have general knowledge about the world to answer simple *Yes* and *No* questions. Individuals who lack a depth of vocabulary knowledge may have more difficulty on these tasks, especially on Word Reading Fluency.

The influence of LA on Reading Rate is consistent with previous research that has found an influence of rapid automatized naming (RAN) on reading (Lervåg & Hulme, 2009; Wolf & Bowers, 1999). This relation is also consistent with research and theory suggesting that the quality of lexical representation and the efficiency with which lexical information is accessed strongly influences reading (LaBerge & Samuels, 1974; Perfetti, 1985, 2007). The ability to access lexical information efficiently and accurately from memory would likely help readers quickly recognize words and their meaning, increasing the rate of performance on these types of tasks. Reading Rate was not only influenced by general processing speed (i.e., *Gs*), but also by the speed at which individuals are able to access their lexicon (i.e., LA). Finally, the indirect effect of *g* on Reading Rate was strong, similar to Basic Reading Skills. This suggests that the influence of *g* is still important (although indirect), even for academic fluency tasks.

Recommendations for Reading Rate. Overall, Reading Rate on the WJ IV appears to be strongly influenced by *Gs*, but also has influences from *Gc* and LA. It is also possible that difficulties with Reading Rate may also be due to difficulties with Basic Reading Skills (e.g., slow or inaccurate decoding), which may not present as difficulties in *Gs*, *Gc*, or LA. Therefore, it is necessary to consider the developmental progression of reading and how basic reading skills (e.g., decoding) can influence other reading skills (e.g., reading comprehension, see Floyd et al., 2012; Hajovsky et al., 2014). When there are difficulties in Reading Rate, it is be important to be aware of potential difficulties in *Gs*, *Gc*, and LA, as well as other reading skills. More research on the Reading Rate factor is warranted to better understand what it measures.

Reading Comprehension

What cognitive-achievement relations were found for Reading Comprehension? *Gf* (.25–.49) had strong, *Ga* (.21–.37) had moderate to strong, and *Gc* (−.07–.11) and *Gs* (.04–.17) had weak to moderate influences on Reading Comprehension. Additionally, *Gc* had strong direct influences on the Passage Comprehension (.39–.49) and Reading Vocabulary (.58–.63) tests. Finally, the indirect effect of *g* on Reading Comprehension was strong for all groups (.62–.71).

Were results for Reading Comprehension consistent with previous research? The strong influence of *Gf* on Reading Comprehension is inconsistent with previous WJ research (Evans et al., 2001; Floyd et al., 2012). The influence of *Gf* on Reading Comprehension was considered tentative in McGrew and Wendling's (2010) synthesis of cognitive-achievement relations research, although other research supports the importance of inference skills for reading comprehension (Cain & Oakhill, 1999; Cain, Oakhill, & Bryant, 2004; Fuchs et al., 2012). It is important to note that the influence of *Gf* was not statistically significant until *Gc* was directly associated with Passage Comprehension and Reading Vocabulary. Once the *Gc* influences were controlled for on those two tests, *Gf* strongly influenced the Reading Comprehension factor. Adding these direct effects to specific tests may account for the inconsistent findings across WJ studies.

Changes in the *Gf* factor on the WJ IV, specifically the inclusion of Number Series as a *Gf* test, may also explain its strong influence on Reading Comprehension. We re-estimated the final reading model without Number Series on the *Gf* factor, and the effect of *Gf* on Reading Comprehension was much smaller (.06–.28) and only statistically significant in three of the five age groups. Two hypotheses may explain this change in effect size when Number Series is included as an indicator of *Gf*. First, the WJ R and WJ III *Gf* factor tests in prior cognitive-achievement research were Concept Formation and Analysis-Synthesis, both of which are controlled learning tasks that include examiner feedback (i.e., external scaffolding was provided to the examinee). Number Series is not a controlled learning task (i.e., no external scaffolding), making it a fundamentally different type of task. Second, when analyzed from information and cognitive processing perspectives, number series tasks can exert significant cognitive load on working memory and require complex relational integration (Bertling, 2012), which may partially explain the influence of *Gf* on Reading Comprehension. Number Series is included as the primary test of *Gf* on the WJ IV, and the relation between *Gf* and Reading Comprehension should be interpreted using Number Series as part of the *Gf* factor.

Gs and *Ga* also influenced Reading Comprehension. These two influences were present in previous research with the WJ III (Evans et al., 2001; Floyd et al., 2007, 2012), although the influences of *Ga* on Reading Comprehension were stronger and more consistent across the lifespan in the current study than previous research with the WJ. This stronger influence may be due to the new *Ga* tests on the WJ IV, which are more cognitively complex measures of auditory processing that those measures used in the prior WJ R and WJ III research studies.

Similar to previous research, *Gc* had a strong influence on Reading Comprehension (Evans et al., 2001; Floyd et al., 2012; Quinn, Wagner, Petscher, & Lopez, 2014; Reynolds & Turek, 2012), although this influence disappeared when *Gc* directly influenced two of the three tests that were associated with the Reading Comprehension factor (i.e., Passage Comprehension and Reading Vocabulary). This was not surprising given that these two tests were directly associated with *Gc* in previous research with the WJ R (Vanderwood et al., 2002) and both of these tests require access to acquired background knowledge. Reading Recall does not require the individual to access acquired background knowledge, but simply retell what he/she read (i.e., Meaningful Memory recall). Other research suggests that different reading comprehension tests do not necessarily measure the same skills (Cutting & Scarborough, 2006; Eason, Goldberg, Young, Geist, & Cutting, 2012; Keenan, Betjemann, & Olson, 2008). For example, Eason et al. (2012) found that higher level cognitive skills (i.e., inferential language and executive functioning) were more strongly related to reading comprehension questions that required inference, but not to reading comprehension questions that only required recall of facts.

Finally, the indirect influence of *g* on Reading Comprehension was strong across groups, consistent with previous research (Floyd et al., 2012). Again, there is no doubt that *g* is a strong predictor of Reading Comprehension. By modeling direct effects of broad CHC abilities on the Reading Comprehension factor and specific Reading Comprehension tests, we were able to obtain a more nuanced understanding of how both *g* and broad CHC abilities influence Reading Comprehension on the WJ IV.

Recommendations for Reading Comprehension. *Gc, Gf, Ga,* and *Gs* were especially influential on Reading Comprehension. This analysis suggests that *Gf, Ga,* and *Gs* have important influences on reading comprehension *in general*, whereas *Gc* has important influences on *specific* aspects of reading comprehension that required the examinee to access acquired background knowledge (i.e., Passage Comprehension and Reading Vocabulary). These results highlight the importance of understanding what specific tests measure and how different cognitive abilities may influence performance on those tests. Based on these results, it is possible that someone with low scores on *Gc* may perform poorly on Passage Comprehension and Reading Vocabulary, but may have less difficulty with Reading Recall. Although the current study provides some understanding of the differences in cognitive-achievement relations using reading comprehension tests from the WJ IV, more research is needed to understand better what is measured by different reading comprehension tests.

Basic Writing Skills

What cognitive-achievement relations were found for Basic Writing Skills? *Gc* (.46–.53) and *Gwm* (.25–.29) had strong influences on Basic Writing Skills, and *Gs* (.15–.24) had moderate influences on Basic Writing Skills. The indirect effect of *g* on Basic Writing Skills was strong (.68–.77) for all groups.

Were results for Basic Writing Skills consistent with previous research? The influences of *Gc* and *Gs* on Basic Writing Skills were consistent with previous research using the WJ R and WJ III (Floyd et al., 2008; McGrew & Knopik, 1993). *Gc* had a large effect on Basic Writing Skills, which is likely due to the pervasive influence *Gc* has across language tasks. The influence of *Gs* on Basic Writing Skills likely represents the importance of fast and efficient processing that influences performance across all academic skills, including basic and higher level writing skills (Floyd et al., 2008; McGrew & Knopik, 1993).

The influence of *Gwm* on Basic Writing Skills was moderate to strong across age groups, consistent with WJ III research (Floyd et al., 2008), though not with WJ R research (McGrew & Knopik, 1993). *Gwm* on the WJ IV is more cognitively complex than previous versions of the WJ, and it focuses primarily on tests of Working Memory, rather than tests of Working Memory and Memory Span. Previous researchers identified Working Memory as having an important influence on writing (Berninger, 1999; Swanson & Berninger, 1996), possibly due to the monitoring and coordination of multiple skills (e.g., retrieval of words and spellings from long-term memory, transcription of the words from memory to paper) required for writing (Berninger, 1999). Finally, the indirect influence of *g* on Basic Writing Skills was strong across the lifespan, again supporting the important influence of *g* and broad CHC abilities.

Recommendations for Basic Writing Skills. *Gc*, *Gwm*, and *Gs* have important influences on Basic Writing Skills on the WJ IV, and should be considered as potential cognitive difficulties that explain deficits in the basic mechanics of writing. Writing is a complex skill that requires the coordination of several cognitive and motor processes, resulting in multiple potential areas that could cause writing difficulties for an individual. Although the current results suggest that there are some cognitive abilities that can potentially explain some of these difficulties, other research on cognitive-achievement relations with writing is lacking. We hope that these results assist in identifying some of the potential areas of difficulty that are related to Basic Writing Skills that will be helpful for practitioners and guide future research.

Written Expression

What cognitive-achievement relations were found for Written Expression? There were strong influences from *Gv* (.32–.47) and *Gs* (.27–.40) on Written

Expression across all groups, and there was a weak influence from LA (.11–.12) on Written Expression for ages 6–8 years and ages 9–13 years. There was also a moderate to strong influence from *Gs* on the Sentence Writing Fluency test (.20–.38) and a moderate to strong influence from *g* (.23–.38) on the Writing Samples test. Finally, there was a strong indirect effect of *g* on Written Expression (.50–.64).

Were results for Written Expression consistent with previous research? Neither McGrew and Knopik (1993) nor Floyd et al. (2008) found *Gv* to influence Written Expression on previous versions of the WJ. Writing clearly involves the integration of visual-motor and orthographic processing skills (Jones & Christensen, 1999) and visual processing has been identified as a possible cognitive ability deficit related to writing disabilities (Niileksela & Reynolds, 2014; Sandler et al., 1992), although little research has been completed in this area (Flanagan et al., 2013). It is unknown why there was such a strong influence of *Gv* on Written Expression in the current study, especially since *Gv* has not influenced Written Expression in previous research with the WJ. Although the modification of Visualization on the WJ IV (i.e., 2-D Spatial Relations subset plus 3-D Block Rotation subtest) from the single 2-D Spatial Relations test in the WJ R and WJ III may account for this new finding, more research on the influence of *Gv* and writing is needed to fully understand this relation.

Gs had a strong influence on Written Expression across the lifespan, consistent with previous research with the WJ R (McGrew & Knopik, 1993) and the WJ III (Floyd et al., 2008). Similar to Basic Writing Skills, the influence of *Gs* on Written Expression may be related to the development of automaticity in academic skills, which may help free attentional resources and improve monitoring for what is being written (Floyd et al., 2008). This is consistent with research showing that automaticity in letter writing is a strong predictor of written expression (Jones & Christensen, 1999). There was a moderate to strong direct effect from *Gs* (.20–.38) to the Sentence Writing Fluency test. The indirect effect of *Gs* on Sentence Writing Fluency was moderate to strong (.16–.28), and the total effect of *Gs* on Sentence Writing Fluency was strong (.48–.60). Sentence Writing Fluency requires the rapid production of sentences, and similar to other academic fluency tests it is not surprising that *Gs* would influence performance on these tasks.

There was also a weak, but statistically significant relation between LA and Written Expression, but only for ages 6–8 years and ages 9–13 years. RAN has been related to written expression in elementary school (Kim, Al Otaiba, Wanzek, & Gatlin, 2015), and efficient access to lexical information would likely help individuals write more effectively if they are able to retrieve words and ideas easily from memory (Perfetti, 2007).

There was a moderate to strong direct effect from *g* to Writing Samples (.20–.38). The total effect from *g* on Writing Samples was large (.48–.60) and the indirect effect from *g* was moderate to large (.16–.28). Writing is arguably the most complex of all academic skills (Mather, Wending, & Roberts, 2009), requiring the integration of a number of cognitive abilities (Jones & Christensen, 1999). Although it makes theoretical sense that Writing Samples may be directly related to *g* given the complexity of writing in general, it is difficult to know what exactly this relation means given that *g* is a highly abstract construct that is difficult to define by specific test characteristics (Jensen, 1998). The WJ IV *Technical Manual* suggested an influence from *Glr* to Writing Samples, but *Glr* was perfectly correlated with *g* in this analysis, making it impossible to differentiate the influence of *Glr* from *g*. It is possible that this lack of differentiation between *g* and *Glr* in the current study explains this difference.

The indirect effect of *g* on Written Expression was strong across all groups (.50–.64). Interestingly, this effect was not as strong as the indirect effect of *g* on Basic Writing Skills (.68–.77). A strong influence of *g*, whether direct or indirect, would certainly be expected given the complexity of writing, but this may not be as strong as some would expect.

Recommendations for Written Expression. Overall, *Gv* and *Gs* appear to be important cognitive abilities to consider when there are concerns about Written Expression with the WJ IV. These results also suggest that *g* has a direct influence on Writing Samples and *Gs* has a direct influence on Sentence Writing Fluency. Similar to the results from Basic Writing Skills, these analyses represent some of the first cognitive-writing relations research using latent variables and CHC theory. Although the results are interesting and consistent with some previous research, these results should be interpreted cautiously. More research is necessary to better understand cognitive-achievement relations with writing.

Math Calculation Skills

What cognitive-achievement relations were found for Math Calculation Skills? There were strong influences from RQ (.57–.68), moderate to strong influences from *Gs* (.23–.40), and a weak influence from *Gc* (.07–.11) on Math Calculation Skills. There was a strong direct influence from *Gs* on the Math Facts Fluency test (.32–.37). Finally, there was a strong indirect effect from *g* on Math Calculation Skills for all groups (.70–.76).

Were results for Math Calculation Skills consistent with previous research? The current results were consistent with the syntheses of research by Flanagan et al. (2013) and McGrew and Wendling (2010), both of whom identified *Gs*, *Gc*, and *Gf* as commonly found influences on math achievement. We found the influence of RQ (a narrow ability under *Gf*) on Math Calculation Skills to be strong in the current study. It is not surprising that RQ was related to Math Calculation Skills given that RQ represents "The ability to reason, either with induction or deduction, with numbers, mathematical relations, and operators" (Schneider & McGrew, 2012, p. 112). Although performance on RQ does not necessarily require knowledge of advanced mathematical operations, it appears that those who are able to reason well with numbers also have strong calculation skills.

The strong influence of *Gs* on Math Calculation Skills is consistent with previous research using the WJ III (Floyd et al., 2003; Taub et al., 2008) and the WJ R (McGrew & Hessler, 1995). Fast and efficient processing of information may be especially important for math calculation because those who can solve simple operations quickly may be able to free cognitive resources for solving more complex parts of a problem (Fuchs et al., 2006; McGrew & Hessler, 1995). There was also a direct effect from *Gs* to the Math Facts Fluency test, consistent with the influence of *Gs* on the academic fluency tests for reading and writing in the current study. The total and direct effects of *Gs* on Math Facts Fluency were strong (.45–.53, .32–.37, respectively), whereas the indirect effect of *Gs* on Math Facts Fluency was weak to moderate (.12–.21).

The influence of *Gc* on Math Calculation Skills was generally weak. Floyd et al. (2003) found a weak to moderate influence of *Gc* on Math Calculation Skills with the WJ III, although the strength of this influence increased with age. McGrew and Hessler (1995) reported that *Gc* had the strongest influence of all the broad CHC abilities on Math Calculation Skills for the WJ R. The use of RQ in the cognitive abilities model in the current study may partially explain this inconsistency. RQ was not included in previous WJ research, and it is possible that RQ is explaining variance in Math Calculation Skills that was previously explained by *Gc*. In fact, when the final math model was re-estimated without RQ (i.e., RQ was removed from the model, and a path from *Gf* to Math Calculation Skills was added), the influence of *Gc* on Math Calculation Skills increased substantially (from .07–.11 to .23–.31). Again, this suggests that the addition of an RQ test (i.e., Number Series) as a primary indicator of *Gf* may have an important impact on the measurement of *Gf* and how well it predicts academic skills on the WJ IV. Finally, the indirect effect of *g* on Math Calculation Skills was strong across all groups, consistent with previous research that indicates a strong relationship between *g* and mathematics achievement (Glutting et al., 2006; Keith, 1999; Taub et al., 2008).

Recommendations for Math Calculation Skills. Overall, these results suggest that RQ, *Gs*, and *Gc* have important influences on Math Calculation Skills, and these are especially important to examine if there are concerns about Math Calculation Skills on the WJ IV. The inclusion of RQ in the model suggests that this narrow ability under *Gf* has an especially strong influence on Math Calculation Skills and would be very important to consider in an evaluation. More research on how narrow *Gf* abilities (i.e., RQ, Induction, General Sequential Reasoning; Schneider & McGrew, 2012) influence Math Calculation Skills is warranted to better understand how these abilities influence the development of math calculation skills.

Math Applications

What cognitive-achievement relations were found for Math Applications?
Gc (.27–.35) had strong influences, RQ (.17–.35) had moderate to strong

influences, and Gs (.10–.19), Gf (.11–.22), and Gv (.11–.20) had weak to moderate influences on Math Applications. There was also a large direct influence from RQ on the Applied Problems test (.31–.34). The indirect effect of g on Math Applications was very strong across all groups (.77–.83).

Were results for Math Applications consistent with previous research?
Gc has been identified as an important influence of Math Applications in previous research with the WJ (Floyd et al., 2003; Keith, 1999; Taub et al., 2008). Gc may influence Math Applications because verbal mediation is often necessary to solve word problems (Koedinger & Nathan, 2004), and Math Applications is considered to be a specific area of acquired knowledge under Gc (i.e., Mathematics Achievement; Schneider & McGrew, 2012). The strong relation between RQ and Math Applications was also not surprising given the nature of RQ discussed previously. Other research has identified the importance of reasoning skills on math achievement (Fuchs et al., 2006). Similar to Math Calculation Skills, future research should more closely examine the relationships between Math Applications, RQ, and other narrow Gf abilities.

There were moderate relations from Gf, Gv, and Gs on Math Applications. The influences of Gf and Gs are consistent with previous research with the WJ R (Keith, 1999) and WJ III (Floyd et al., 2003; Taub et al., 2008). Similar to other academic areas, perhaps Gs is related to Math Applications because fast and efficient processing likely frees up cognitive resources for more complex thinking. The influence of Gf on Math Applications is consistent with previous research that has found that verbal and nonverbal reasoning tests have unique influences on arithmetic word problems (Fuchs et al., 2006). It is important to note that RQ and Gf had unique influences on Math Applications in the current study, suggesting that both verbal and numerical reasoning Gf tasks had unique influences Math Applications on the WJ IV.

The influence from Gv to Math Applications in the current study is inconsistent with previous WJ research (Keith, 1999; McGrew & Hessler, 1995; Taub et al., 2008). Flanagan et al. (2013) suggest that the lack of an influence from Gv on math achievement in previous cognitive-achievement relations research may be due to the skills that are measured on math achievement tests and Gv tests. It is possible that the changes in Gv to the WJ IV discussed previously may explain our findings. Other research suggests Gv is important for math skills. For instance, visual–spatial skills have been shown to be predictive of math skills in elementary school (Assel, Landry, Swank, Smith, & Steelman, 2003; Hegarty & Kozhevnikov, 1999), strong visual–spatial skills are related to subsequent careers in science, technology, engineering, and math (STEM) domains (Wai, Lubinski, & Benbow, 2009), and visual–spatial skills have been identified as deficits in students with SLD in math (Pieters, Desoete, Roeyers, Vanderswalmen, & Van Waelvelde, 2012). Finally, the indirect effect of g on Math Applications was very strong across groups, consistent with previous research indicating a strong relation between math achievement and g mentioned previously. The indirect effect of g for Math Applications is especially interesting given these results, which suggests that g influences Math Applications through a variety of broad CHC abilities.

Recommendations for Math Applications. These results suggest that a variety of cognitive abilities influence Math Applications, including RQ, *Gf*, *Gs*, *Gc*, and *Gv*. These abilities should be considered when there are concerns about performance in Math Applications when using the WJ IV. In addition to these cognitive abilities, it would also be important to consider whether there are difficulties with Math Calculation Skills, which may in turn influence performance on Math Applications. Similar to the progression of reading skill development, basic math skills (e.g., arithmetic) likely influence performance on more complex math skills (e.g., word problems; Fuchs et al., 2006).

Overall Summary of Cognitive-Achievement Relations with the WJ IV

Table 3.6 summarizes all cognitive-achievement relations from the current study. Narrow academic skills and specific tests that were influenced by cognitive abilities are in rows and broad and narrow CHC cognitive abilities are in columns. Cognitive-achievement relations were specified as *Strong*, *Moderate*, or *Weak* depending on the most consistent findings across the lifespan. When considering the effects across all analyses, it is clear that *Gc* and *Gs* had a pervasive influence across almost all academic skills on the WJ IV. This is consistent with previous research indicating that *Gc* and *Gs* are domain general abilities that influence multiple academic skills (McGrew, 2012; McGrew & Wendling, 2010). Also consistent with previous research, there was evidence for domain-specific influences on academic skills. *Ga* was specifically related to reading skills, *Gf* was specifically related to Reading Comprehension and Math Applications (more complex academic skills), and RQ was specifically related to math achievement. There were several novel findings in this study that suggest possible domain specific influences, including the influence of *Gv* on Written Expression and Math Applications, and the influence of LA on Reading Rate and Written Expression. One unique contribution of this study compared to research with the WJ III was the inclusion of direct effects of broad CHC abilities on specific tests, suggesting that specific cognitive abilities have influences on specific academic tests. *Ga* had a direct influence on Word Attack, RQ had a direct influence on Applied Problems, *g* had a direct influence on Writing Samples, *Gc* had direct influences on Passage Comprehension and Reading Vocabulary, and *Gs* had a direct influence on most of the academic fluency tests. Hopefully, this table provides a useful overview of the complete results of this study.

One of the most significant inconsistencies with previous research was the lack of a relation from *Gwm* to the reading or math factors. In previous research, *Gwm* has been identified as a domain general ability that has important influences across all academic skills (McGrew, 2012), including reading (Cain et al., 2004; Evans et al., 2001; Floyd et al., 2007, 2012), math

TABLE 3.6 Summary of Cognitive-Achievement Relations Across Academic Skills

	g	Gc	Gwm	Gs	Gf	RQ	Gv	Ga	LA
Direct Effects of Broad CHC Abilities on Narrow Achievement Factors									
Basic Reading Skills		Strong		Moderate				Strong	
Reading Rate		Moderate		Strong					Weak
Reading Comprehension		Weak		Weak	Strong			Strong	
Basic Writing Skills		Strong	Strong	Moderate					
Written Expression		Strong		Strong			Strong		Weak
Math Calculation Skills		Weak		Strong		Strong			
Math Applications		Strong		Moderate	Weak	Moderate	Moderate		
Direct Effects of Broad CHC Abilities on Specific Achievement Tests									
Word Attack				Strong				Strong	
Word Reading Fluency				Strong					
Passage Comprehension		Strong							
Reading Vocabulary		Strong							
Sentence Writing Fluency				Strong					
Writing Samples	Strong								
Math Facts Fluency				Strong					
Applied Problems						Strong			

Note: Only achievement tests with direct influences from broad CHC abilities are included in the table. It is important to note that the indirect influence from g was strong across all achievement factors.

(Floyd et al., 2003, Geary, 2011), and writing (Swanson & Berninger, 1996). *Gwm* was only related to Basic Writing Skills in the current study. It is not known at this time why *Gwm* was not related to math or reading in this study, although this difference may be due to the increase in cognitive complexity for other tests on the WJ IV. In other words, by deliberately increasing the cognitive load and complexity of processing required on tests not on the *Gwm* factor (e.g., increasing the working memory, attentional control, and executive function demands on tests; Lohman & Lakin, 2011), this may be contributing to working memory variance via other tests (e.g., Phonological Processing; Nonword Repetition; Visualization; Number Series).

Validity and Cognitive-Achievement Relations with the WJ IV

There are two ways in which the results of these analyses contribute to the validity of the WJ IV. First, many of the findings were consistent with previous research, especially research with the WJ R and WJ III. This consistency across different versions of the WJ tests provides some evidence that the cognitive abilities and academic skills measured by the WJ batteries have been relatively consistent across time. Additionally, many of the results from this study are consistent with cognitive-achievement relations research using other batteries (Elliott et al., 2010; Hajovsky et al., 2014), suggesting that the CHC factors from the WJ IV may generalize to other test batteries (Reynolds et al., 2013). Despite some significant changes to the WJ IV, these results suggest that the measurement of CHC constructs on the WJ IV is not a radical departure from previous versions.

Second, even though this study had many consistencies with previous research, there were also several novel findings that support the validity of the changes made to the WJ IV. The increase in cognitive complexity and a greater focus on cognitive abilities important for learning appear to have influenced the magnitude of some cognitive-achievement relations. One of the most significant changes on the WJ IV was to the *Ga* factor. *Ga* on the WJ IV focuses on complex phonological processing, skills that are important for reading. The influence of *Ga* on Basic Reading Skills and Reading Comprehension was strong across all age groups. This influence was not present in previous research with the WJ III (Floyd et al., 2007) and this increase in the magnitude of *Ga* on reading supports the validity of the changes to *Ga*. Other results also support changes and additions to the WJ IV. For instance, the new ability LA had unique influences on Reading Rate and Written Expression, the inclusion of Number Series on *Gf* appears to have influenced the measurement of *Gf*, which in turn influenced how well it predicts some academic skills (e.g., Reading Comprehension), and *Gv* had influences on Math Applications and Written Expression, a novel finding not identified in previous research with the WJ. Although some of these results are novel and more research is necessary, this study helps provide some evidence that the changes made to the WJ IV have resulted in potentially useful improvements to the constructs measured by the WJ IV. We hope these results help others better understand the WJ IV and its utility for assessing cognitive and academic skills.

Limitations and Future Directions

There are several important limitations in the current study. First, we tested cognitive-achievement relations with one type of model, the higher-order model. Some have argued that cognitive-achievement relations results differ when using a higher order model or a bifactor (nested factor) model (Beaujean, Parkin, & Parker, 2014). Space does not permit a detailed discussion regarding this issue, but higher order models tend to model g as a source trait. This is how we generally conceptualize g and we consider the higher order model to be consistent with one of the guiding pillars of CHC theory, three-stratum theory (Carroll, 1993, pp. 625–626). Second, model fit using MLE was generally lower than acceptable standards. Although we discussed some reasons why this may have occurred (e.g., imputed data set, complex models), a better understanding of why model fit for the WJ IV was not consistent with previous versions of the WJ and other test batteries is needed. Finally, most of our results help understand cognitive-achievement relations for WJ IV ACH clusters available on the scoring program. Two of our achievement factors were slightly different than those available on the WJ IV scoring program (i.e., Basic Reading Skills, Math Applications), which may limit the generalization of some results into practice. Although these factors are not available as clusters on the scoring program for the WJ IV, we believe that this study helps provide a stronger understanding of what the tests measure and how cognitive abilities influence those tests.

The current results provide some preliminary evidence for cognitive-achievement relations with the WJ IV, but much work still needs to be done. One of the most important goals of future research should be to examine how narrow achievement skills within specific academic areas (e.g., reading) influence each other. For example, research has shown that basic reading skills has a direct influence on reading comprehension, and some of the cognitive abilities that influence reading comprehension are indirect through basic reading skills (Floyd et al., 2012; Hajovsky et al., 2014). Considering the developmental sequence of academic skills, understanding how cognitive-achievement relations change when models include structural relations among basic academic skills and higher level academic skills will help researchers and practitioners better understand academic skill development. Second, cognitive-achievement relations using cross-battery methods (Flanagan et al., 2013) is greatly needed. Research has shown that the tests from several major cognitive test batteries measure the same broad CHC abilities (Reynolds et al., 2013), but cognitive-achievement relations research has typically been limited to a single test battery (Beaujean et al., 2014; Elliott et al., 2010; Floyd et al., 2007; Hajovsky et al., 2014). Using a cross-battery approach will help clarify inconsistent findings across previous cognitive-achievement relations studies, and will provide a better understanding of how cognitive abilities influence academic skills without the confound of using a single test battery.

CONCLUSIONS

As discussed in the introduction, the validity of test score interpretation is multifaceted and ongoing. This study extended the validity evidence of the WJ IV by examining cognitive-achievement relations on the new version of the test, comparing it to previous cognitive-achievement relations research, and providing some preliminary interpretive recommendations that may help researchers and practitioners better understand the WJ IV. Among the most important findings of this study is that the broad cognitive abilities referenced by CHC theory are important for explaining broad and narrow aspects of academic achievement. The abilities that are important are understandable from CHC theory and generally consistent with previous research. There were also developmental changes in cognitive-achievement relations, and these differences are generally consistent with theory and previous research. Although further research will be necessary, we believe this study provides a preliminary understanding of cognitive-achievement relations with the WJ IV.

CONFLICT OF INTEREST DISCLOSURE

Kevin S. McGrew has a financial (royalty) interest in the WJ IV Battery as a WJ IV coauthor.

ACKNOWLEDGMENT

We would like to thank Riverside Publishing for access to the WJ IV data to conduct this study.

REFERENCES

American Educational Research Association, American Psychological Association, & National Council on Measurement in Education, (1999). *Standards for educational and psychological testing.* Washington, DC: American Educational Research Association.

Assel, M. A., Landry, S. H., Swank, P., Smith, K. E., & Steelman, L. M. (2003). Precursors to mathematical skills: Examining the roles of visual-spatial skills, executive processes, and parenting factors. *Applied Developmental Science, 7,* 27–38.

Beaujean, A. A., Parkin, J., & Parker, S. (2014). Comparing Cattell–Horn–Carroll factor models: Differences between bifactor and higher order factor models in predicting language achievement. *Psychological Assessment, 26*(3), 789–805.

Benson, N. (2008). Cattell–Horn–Carroll cognitive abilities and reading achievement. *Journal of Psychoeducational Assessment, 26*(1), 27–41.

Berninger, V. W. (1999). Coordinating transcription and text generation in working memory during composing: Automatic and constructive processes. *Learning Disability Quarterly, 22*(2), 99–112.

Bertling, J. P. (2012). Measuring reasoning ability: Applications of rule-based item generation (Unpublished doctoral dissertation). Westfälische Wilhelms-Universität Münster: Münster, Germany.

Blunch, N. (2008). *Introduction to structural equation modeling using SPSS and AMOS*. Thousand Oaks, CA: Sage.

Borsboom, D., Mellenbergh, G. J., & van Heerden, J. (2004). The concept of validity. *Psychological Review*, *111*(4), 1061–1071.

Cain, K., Oakhill, J., & Bryant, P. (2004). Children's reading comprehension ability: Concurrent prediction by working memory, verbal ability, and component skills. *Journal of Educational Psychology*, *96*, 31–42.

Cain, K., & Oakhill, J. V. (1999). Inference making ability and its relation to comprehension failure in young children. *Reading and Writing*, *11*(1), 489–503.

Campbell, D. T., & Fiske, D. W. (1959). Convergent and discriminant validation by the multitrait-multimethod matrix. *Psychological Bulletin*, *56*(2), 81–105.

Carroll, J. B. (1993). *Human cognitive abilities: A survey of factor analytic studies*. New York, NY: Cambridge University Press.

Chen, F. F. (2007). Sensitivity of goodness of fit indexes to lack of measurement invariance. *Structural Equation Modeling: A Multidisciplinary Journal*, *14*(3), 464–504.

Cheung, G. W., & Rensvold, R. B. (2002). Evaluating goodness-of-fit indexes for testing measurement invariance. *Structural Equation Modeling*, *9*(2), 233–255.

Cutting, L. E., & Scarborough, H. S. (2006). Prediction of reading comprehension: Relative contributions of word recognition, language proficiency, and other cognitive skills can depend on how comprehension is measured. *Scientific Studies of Reading*, *10*(3), 277–299.

Eason, S. H., Goldberg, L. F., Young, K. M., Geist, M. C., & Cutting, L. E. (2012). Reader–text interactions: How differential text and question types influence cognitive skills needed for reading comprehension. *Journal of Educational Psychology*, *104*, 515–528.

Ehri, L. C. (2014). Orthographic mapping in the acquisition of sight word reading, spelling memory, and vocabulary learning. *Scientific Studies of Reading*, *18*(1), 5–21.

Elliott, C. D., Hale, J. B., Fiorello, C. A., Dorvil, C., & Moldovan, J. (2010). Differential Ability Scales-II prediction of reading performance: Global scores are not enough. *Psychology in the Schools*, *47*(7), 698–720. http://dx.doi.org/10.1002/pits.20499.

Evans, J. J., Floyd, R. G., McGrew, K. S., & Leforgee, M. H. (2001). The relations between measures of Cattell–Horn–Carroll (CHC) cognitive abilities and reading achievement during childhood and adolescence. *School Psychology Review*, *31*(2), 246–262.

Flanagan, D. P. (2000). Wechsler-based CHC cross-battery assessment and reading achievement: Strengthening the validity of interpretations drawn from Wechsler test scores. *School Psychology Quarterly*, *15*(3), 295–329.

Flanagan, D. P., Alfonso, V. C., & Mascolo, J. T. (2011). A CHC-based operational definition of SLD: Integrating multiple data sources and multiple data-gathering methods. In D. P. Flanagan & V. C. Alfonso (Eds.), *Essentials of specific learning disability identification* (pp. 233–298). Hoboken, NJ: Wiley.

Flanagan, D. P., Ortiz, S. O., & Alfonso, V. C. (2013). *Essentials of cross-battery assessment*. Hoboken, NJ: Wiley.

Floyd, R. G., Evans, J. J., & McGrew, K. S. (2003). Relations between measures of Cattell–Horn–Carroll (CHC) cognitive abilities and mathematics achievement across the school-age years. *Psychology in the Schools*, *40*(2), 155–171.

Floyd, R. G., Keith, T. Z., Taub, G. E., & McGrew, K. S. (2007). Cattell–Horn–Carroll cognitive abilities and their effects on reading decoding skills: g has indirect effects, more specific abilities have direct effects. *School Psychology Quarterly*, *22*(2), 200–233. http://dx.doi.org/10.1037/1045-3830.22.2.200.

Floyd, R. G., McGrew, K. S., & Evans, J. J. (2008). The relative contributions of the Cattell–Horn–Carroll cognitive abilities in explaining writing achievement during childhood and adolescence. *Psychology in the Schools*, *45*(2), 132–144. http://dx.doi.org/10.1002/pits.20284.

Floyd, R., Meisinger, E., Gregg, N., & Keith, T. (2012). An explanation of reading comprehension across development using models from Cattell–Horn–Carroll theory: Support for integrative models of reading. *Psychology in the Schools*, *49*(8), 725–743.

Fuchs, D., Compton, D. L., Fuchs, L. S., Bryant, V. J., Hamlett, C. L., & Lambert, W. (2012). First-grade cognitive abilities as long-term predictors of reading comprehension and disability status. *Journal of Learning Disabilities*, *45*(3), 217–231.

Fuchs, L. S., Fuchs, D., Compton, D. L., Powell, S. R., Seethaler, P. M., Capizzi, A. M., et al. (2006). The cognitive correlates of third-grade skill in arithmetic, algorithmic computation, and arithmetic word problems. *Journal of Educational Psychology*, *98*, 29–43.

Geary, D. C. (2011). Cognitive predictors of achievement growth in mathematics: A 5-year longitudinal study. *Developmental Psychology*, *47*(6), 1539–1552.

Glutting, J. J., Watkins, M. W., Konold, T. R., & McDermott, P. A. (2006). Distinctions without a difference: The utility of observed versus latent factors from the WISC-IV in estimating reading and math achievement on the WIAT-II. *The Journal of Special Education*, *40*(2), 103–114.

Hajovsky, D., Reynolds, M. R., Floyd, R. G., Turek, J. J., Keith, T. Z., & Hitchcock, J. (2014). A multigroup investigation of latent cognitive abilities and reading achievement relations. *School Psychology Review*, *43*, 385–406.

Hegarty, M., & Kozhevnikov, M. (1999). Types of visual–spatial representations and mathematical problem solving. *Journal of Educational Psychology*, *91*, 684–689.

Hudson, R. F., Pullen, P. C., Lane, H. B., & Torgesen, J. K. (2009). The complex nature of reading fluency: A multidimensional view. *Reading & Writing Quarterly*, *25*, 4–32.

Individuals with Disabilities Education Improvement Act (IDEIA) of 2004, PL 108–446.

Jensen, A. R. (1998). *The g factor: The science of mental ability.* Westport, CT: Praeger.

Jones, D., & Christensen, C. A. (1999). Relationship between automaticity in handwriting and students' ability to generate written text. *Journal of Educational Psychology*, *91*(1), 44–49.

Kaufman, S. B., Reynolds, M. R., Liu, X., Kaufman, A. S., & McGrew, K. S. (2012). Are cognitive *g* and academic achievement *g* one and the same *g*? An exploration on the Woodcock–Johnson and Kaufman tests. *Intelligence*, *40*, 123–138.

Keenan, J. M., Betjemann, R. S., & Olson, R. K. (2008). Reading comprehension tests vary in the skills they assess: Differential dependence on decoding and oral comprehension. *Scientific Studies of Reading*, *12*, 281–300.

Keith, T. Z. (1999). Effects of general and specific abilities on student achievement: Similarities and differences across ethnic groups. *School Psychology Quarterly*, *14*(3), 239–262.

Keith, T. Z. (2015). *Multiple regression and beyond: An introduction to multiple regression and structural equation modeling* (2nd ed.). New York, NY: Routledge.

Keith, T. Z., & Reynolds, M. R. (2010). Cattell–Horn–Carroll abilities and cognitive tests: What we've learned from 20 years of research. *Psychology in the Schools*, *47*(7), 635–650. http://dx.doi.org/10.1002/pits. 20496.

Keith, T. Z., Reynolds, M. R., Patel, P. G., & Ridley, K. P. (2008). Sex differences in latent cognitive abilities ages 6 to 59: Evidence from the Woodcock–Johnson III Tests of Cognitive Abilities. *Intelligence*, *36*, 502–525. http://dx.doi.org/10.1016/j.intell.2007.11.001.

Kelley, T. L. (1927). *Interpretation of educational measurements.* New York, NY: World Book Company.

Kim, Y. -S., Al Otaiba, S., Wanzek, J., & Gatlin, B. (2015). Toward and understanding of dimensions, predictors, and the gender gap in written expression. *Journal of Educational Psychology*, *107*(1), 79–95. http://dx.doi.org/10.1037/a0037210.

Koedinger, K. R., & Nathan, M. J. (2004). The real story behind story problems: Effects of representations on quantitative reasoning. *The Journal of the Learning Sciences, 13*(2), 129–164.

LaBerge, D., & Samuels, S. J. (1974). Toward a theory of automatic information processing in reading. *Cognitive Psychology, 6*, 293–323.

Lervåg, A., & Hulme, C. (2009). Rapid automatized naming (RAN) taps a mechanism that places constraints on the development of early reading fluency. *Psychological Science, 20*(8), 1040–1048.

Lohman, D. F., & Lakin, J. M. (2011). Intelligence and reasoning. In R. J. Sternberg & S. B. Kaufman (Eds.), *The Cambridge handbook of intelligence* (pp. 419–441). New York: Cambridge University Press.

Marshalek, B., Lohman, D. F., & Snow, R. E. (1983). The complexity continuum in the radex and hierarchical models of intelligence. *Intelligence, 7*, 107–127.

Mather, N., Wendling, B., & Roberts, R. (2009). *Writing assessment and instruction for students with learning disabilities* (2nd ed.). Hoboken, NJ: Wiley.

McGrew, K. S. (2012, September). *Implications of 20 years of CHC cognitive-achievement research: Back-to-the- future and beyond CHC*. Paper presented at the Richard Woodcock Institute, Tufts University, Medford, MA.

McGrew, K. S., Flanagan, D. P., Keith, T. Z., & Vanderwood, M. (1997). Beyond *g*: The impact of *Gf–Gc* specific cognitive abilities research on the future use and interpretation of intelligence tests in the schools. *School Psychology Review, 26*, 189–210.

McGrew, K. S., & Hessler, G. L. (1995). The relationship between the WJ-R *Gf–Gc* cognitive clusters and mathematics achievement across the life-span. *Journal of Psychoeducational Assessment, 13*(1), 21–38.

McGrew, K. S., & Knopik, S. N. (1993). The relationship between the WJ-R *Gf–Gc* cognitive clusters and writing achievement across the life-span. *School Psychology Review, 22*, 687–695.

McGrew, K. S., & Wendling, B. J. (2010). Cattell–Horn–Carroll cognitive-achievement relations: What we have learned from the past 20 years of research. *Psychology in the Schools, 47*, 651–675. http://dx.doi.org/10.1002/pits.20497.

McGrew, K. S., LaForte, E. M., & Schrank, F. A. (2014). Technical Manual: *Woodcock–Johnson IV*. Rolling Meadows, IL: Riverside.

Melby-Lervåg, M., Lyster, S. A. H., & Hulme, C. (2012). Phonological skills and their role in learning to read: A meta-analytic review. *Psychological Bulletin, 138*(2), 322–352.

Meredith, W. (1993). Measurement invariance, factor analysis, and factorial invariance. *Psychometrika, 58*(4), 525–543.

Messick, S. (1995). Validity of psychological assessment: Validation of inferences from persons' responses and performances as scientific inquiry into score meaning. *American Psychologist, 50*(9), 741–749. http://dx.doi.org/10.1037/0003-066X.50.9.741.

Niileksela, C. R., & Reynolds, M. R. (2014). Global, broad, or specific cognitive differences? Using a MIMIC model to examine differences in CHC abilities in children with learning disabilities. *Journal of Learning Disabilities, 47*(3), 224–236.

Parkin, J. R., & Beaujean, A. A. (2012). The effects of Wechsler Intelligence Scale for Children—Fourth Edition cognitive abilities on math achievement. *Journal of School Psychology, 50*(1), 113–128.

Perfetti, C. (2007). Reading ability: Lexical quality to comprehension. *Scientific Studies of Reading, 11*(4), 357–383.

Perfetti, C. A. (1985). *Reading ability*. London: Oxford University Press.

Phelps, L., McGrew, K. S., Knopik, S. N., & Ford, L. (2005). The general (*g*), broad, and narrow CHC stratum characteristics of the WJ III and WISC-III tests: A confirmatory cross-battery investigation. *School Psychology Quarterly, 20*(1), 66–88.

Pieters, S., Desoete, A., Roeyers, H., Vanderswalmen, R., & Van Waelvelde, H. (2012). Behind mathematical learning disabilities: What about visual perception and motor skills? *Learning and Individual Differences, 22*, 498–504.

Quinn, J. M., Wagner, R. K., Petscher, Y., & Lopez, D. (2014). Developmental relations between vocabulary knowledge and reading comprehension: A latent change score modeling study. *Child Development, 86*(1), 159–175.

Reynolds, M. R., Keith, T. Z., Flanagan, D. P., & Alfonso, V. C. (2013). A cross-battery, reference variable, confirmatory factor analytic investigation of the CHC taxonomy. *Journal of School Psychology, 51*(4), 535–555.

Reynolds, M. R., & Turek, J. J. (2012). A dynamic developmental link between verbal comprehension-knowledge (*Gc*) and reading comprehension: Verbal comprehension-knowledge drives positive change in reading comprehension. *Journal of School Psychology, 50*(6), 841–863.

Sandler, A. D., Watson, T. E., Footo, M., Levine, M. D., Coleman, W. L., & Hooper, S. R. (1992). Neurodevelopmental study of writing disorders in middle childhood. *Journal of Developmental & Behavioral Pediatrics, 13*(1), 17–23.

Schermelleh-Engel, K., Moosbrugger, H., & Müller, H. (2003). Evaluating the fit of structural equation models: Tests of significance and descriptive goodness-of-fit measures. *Methods of Psychological Research Online, 8*(2), 23–74.

Schneider, W. J., & McGrew, K. S. (2012). The Cattell–Horn–Carroll model of intelligence. In D. P. Flanagan & P. L. Harrison (Eds.), *Contemporary intellectual assessment: Theories, tests, and issues* (3rd ed., pp. 99–144). New York, NY: Guilford Press.

Schrank, F. A., Mather, N., & McGrew, K. S. (2014a). *Woodcock–Johnson IV tests of achievement.* Rolling Meadows, IL: Riverside.

Schrank, F. A., Mather, N., & McGrew, K. S. (2014b). *Woodcock–Johnson IV tests of oral language.* Rolling Meadows, IL: Riverside.

Schrank, F. A., McGrew, K. S., & Mather, N. (2014c). *Woodcock–Johnson IV.* Rolling Meadows, IL: Riverside.

Schrank, F. A., McGrew, K. S., & Mather, N. (2014d). *Woodcock–Johnson IV tests of cognitive abilities.* Rolling Meadows, IL: Riverside.

Schrank, F. A., McGrew, K. S., & Mather, N. (2015). *Woodcock–Johnson IV tests of early cognitive and academic development.* Rolling Meadows, IL: Riverside.

Swanson, L., & Berninger, V. (1996). Individual differences in children's working memory and writing skills. *Journal of Experimental Child Psychology, 63*, 358–385.

Taub, G. E., Floyd, R. G., Keith, T. Z., & McGrew, K. S. (2008). Effects of general and broad cognitive abilities on mathematics achievement. *School Psychology Quarterly, 23*(2), 187–198. http://dx.doi.org/10.1037/1045-3830.23.2.187.

Vanderwood, M. L., McGrew, K. S., Flanagan, D. P., & Keith, T. Z. (2002). The contribution of general and specific cognitive abilities to reading achievement. *Learning and Individual Differences, 13*(2), 159–188.

Wai, J., Lubinski, D., & Benbow, C. P. (2009). Spatial ability for STEM domains: Aligning over fifty years of cumulative psychological knowledge solidifies its importance. *Journal of Educational Psychology, 101*(4), 817–835.

Wiederhold, J. L., & Bryant, B. R. (2012). *Gray oral reading test—fifth edition.* Austin, TX: Pro-Ed.

Wolf, M., & Bowers, P. G. (1999). The double-deficit hypothesis for the developmental dyslexias. *Journal of Educational Psychology, 91*(1), 415–438.

Woodcock, R. W., & Johnson, M. B. (1989). *Woodcock–Johnson psycho-educational battery—revised.* Chicago: Riverside.

Woodcock, R. W., McGrew, K. S., & Mather, N. (2001). *Woodcock–Johnson III.* Rolling Meadows, IL: Riverside Publishing.

Chapter 4

Woodcock–Johnson IV Scoring and Reporting Online Program Review

Scott L. Decker, Emma Kate C. Wright and Tayllor E. Vetter
Department of Psychology, University of South Carolina, Columbia, SC, USA

INTRODUCTION

The Woodcock–Johnson (WJ) series of batteries is known for innovative advancements in testing technology. The online scoring feature of the WJ IV (Schrank, McGrew, & Mather, 2014a) may prove to be yet another major advancement in the use of test technology. Traditionally, test score technology was based on printed tables and required users to find information manually within these tables. The WJ III (Woodcock, McGrew, & Mather, 2001) was one of the first commercially available measures to use computer software for scoring. Although the use of computer software to score tests is commonplace today, it was not without controversy. Indeed, any change in technology often requires some period of time for accommodation. Similarly, the use of online web-based scoring requires some accommodation, which is beneficial, as well as challenging.

The goal of this chapter is to provide a practical overview of the online scoring software (Schrank & Dailey, 2014) used with the WJ IV. The first part provides an overview of basic functions that are most frequently used. The second part covers some more advanced features of the online scoring software. The chapter concludes with a brief discussion of clinical and ethical implications that arise in the use of online scoring systems.

MINIMAL SYSTEMS REQUIREMENTS

Although online scoring systems provide benefits over standalone software options, there are still some technological barriers. The WJ IV online scoring and reporting platform has the following minimum system requirements:

WJ IV Clinical Use and Interpretation. DOI: http://dx.doi.org/10.1016/B978-0-12-802076-0.00004-9
107

Operating System	Web Browser	Other Required Software	Additional Requirements
Windows® 8	• Internet Explore® 10 or higher • Firefox® 21 or higher • Google Chrome™ 27 or higher	Adobe® Reader 10 or higher	• Processor: 1 GHz Pentium dual core or higher • Memory: 1 GB RAM or higher • 1024 × 768 screen resolution
Windows 7	• Internet Explore® 9 or higher • Firefox® 21 or higher • Google Chrome™ 27 or higher		For Optimal Performance: • Processor: 2 GHz Pentium dual core or higher • Memory: 2 GB RAM or higher • 1366 × 768 screen resolution
Apple™ OS X 10.7	• Safari™ 5.0 or higher • Firefox® 21 or higher		
Apple™ OS X 10.8	• Safari™ 6.0 or higher • Firefox® 21 or higher		

Basic Functionality

The WJ IV scoring program (version 1.2) allows online scoring and reporting in an easy-to-use format that can be found at www.wjscore.com. It's anticipated that most users will exclusively use the WJ IV scoring program to generate standard scores from score reports. Therefore, we have provided a step-by-step guide outlining this process. Additionally, to better navigate the WJ IV's online program, a brief description of the program's layout and functions are discussed based on the four main tabs presented on the website, which are *Dashboard, Reports, Administration*, and *Resources*. Finally, information regarding help with the online scoring program is briefly described.

Step-by-Step Guidelines for Obtaining Standard Scores

1. Add Examinee:

   a. Under the *Dashboard* tab, click Add Examinee in the My Recent Examinees box.

   b. Add the information as prompted, such as demographics and general examinee information. Press Save at the bottom of the page.

   c. These actions automatically redirect the user to the *Administration* tab where examinee information is displayed and test records can be added.

At the bottom of page, select Add Test Record and select the appropriate WJ IV test before entering scores.

d. *Note*: Once routed to the *Administration* tab, examiners have the option to revise the previously entered information using the Edit Examinee option. Additionally, users are able to move the examinee to a different case folder or a shared folder by using the Move Examinee and/or Share Examinee options.

2. **Enter Data**:
   a. Enter test administration information and insert the raw data into the appropriate subtest box for each measure.

3. **Save or Commit Test Record**:
   a. Choose to Save or Commit Test Record (see Implications for Practice section of this chapter for more information on committing a test record).
   b. Note: examiners must commit test records before creating a report and before the software program will generate standard scores.
   c. A test record may be edited up to 90 days after committing it before it becomes permanent.
   d. If the user wants to add another test record, manually return to the *Dashboard* to select the previously created examinee within the Recent Examinees box, and add the new test record.

4. **Create Report**:
   a. After committing a test record, select the *Reports* Tab, to view the Create Reports option.
   b. Select the Report Type that fits the needs of the examiner (e.g., Score Report), and select the appropriate examinee within the Examinee Selection box.
   c. Customize the report by selecting the appropriate features that fit the needs of the current evaluation (see *Report Customization* section under *Advanced* functionality for more information on specific customizable features).
   d. Choose to Run Report or Save to My Reports.
   e. Note: Saved reports are only available for a total of 14 days within the WJ IV scoring system. Make sure to save a copy of the report to your computer.
   f. Saved reports can be found on the *Dashboard* tab within the My Saved Reports box.

Basic Layout and Functions

In order to understand the different functions permitted on the WJ IV scoring and reporting program, it is important to comprehend what permissions are allowed for the three types of users, which are account holder, administrator, and examiner. The account holder is the key communication coordinator for Houghton Mifflin Harcourt-Riverside (HMH-Riverside) and a given organization. This individual is able to use and manage all functions of the online program. An administrator can add examiners, review caseload folders, and perform the same functions of an examiner on the program. Compared to account holders and administrators, examiners have limited capabilities, which only include recording test results and generating reports, as well as adding caseload folders, examinees, and test records. An examiner is only able to access records or caseload folders that the examiner self-created, while an account holder or administrator can access all content created by the account holder's organization. This difference in permission between users also means that examiners are able to share examinee cases with other examiners, but not administrators or the account holder, as these users already can see every case associated with an organization. With this understanding of the permissions associated with different users within an organization, detail on functions of the four main tabs is presented.

The *Dashboard* is the first tab and is displayed after the user signs into the program and presents previously entered information (i.e., caseload folders, recent examinees, saved reports, etc.), as well as the option to add new content. The key areas on the Dashboard, which appear in designated boxes, include Caseload Folders, My Recent Examinees, Shared Caseload Folders, Messages from Riverside, Messages from the Account Holder, and My Saved Reports (see Figure 4.1 for a screenshot showing each of these areas). The Caseload Folders box on the Dashboard tab allows a quick view of folders that users create to organize their cases. When a user selects a case folder, the individual cases are then displayed below in the My Recent Examines box of the Dashboard. This box shows the first and last name of the individual case, as well as several icons. The icons listed under the examinee column of this box allow a user to edit an examinee's information, move the examinee to an alternate case folder, or share an examinee with another examiner or administrator. The icons under the Test Record column of the box allow the user to add a new test record or delete a previously entered record. Additionally, it is important to note that when selecting the option to share an examinee, the individual initiating the share is allowed to select permissions that let the other individual view the examinee, edit the examine, view the test records, or edit the test records. Once the examinee has been shared with another examiner, the examinee's case can be viewed under the shared examiner's My Shared Folder box on the Dashboard tab. Another key feature on the Dashboard tab includes the Messages from Riverside box, which provides a platform for the HMH-Riverside to communicate critical information regarding the online scoring and reporting program. For example, HMH-Riverside may indicate that a new version of the online program has gone live and list new features of the most recent version. Additionally, the Dashboard tab has a Messages from the Account Holder box. This box facilitates communication from the account holder of an organization to any administrator or examiner associated with that organization. Finally, the last box of the Dashboard tab is the My Saved Reports box.

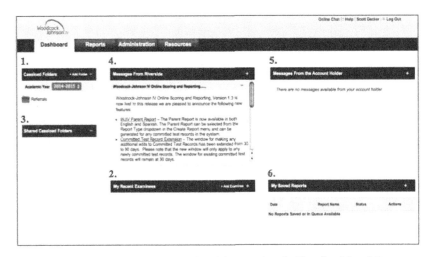

FIGURE 4.1   Layout of the *Dashboard* Tab. Brief summaries of utility of each box follow:
1. *Caseload Folders* box: where users can have a quick view of the folders that they create to organize cases.
2. *My Recent Examinees* box: where individual cases are located, and where users can add examinees, edit examinee information, move examinees to other case folders, or share examinees with other users.
3. *My Shared Folder* box: where shared examinees are located.
4. *Messages from Riverside* box: platform for HMH-Riverside to communicate information about the scoring program.
5. *Messages from the Account Holder* box: where messages from the account holder of an organization to other administrators or examiners within that organization appear.
6. *My Saved Reports* box: where users' saved reports are located.

The second main tab, *Reports*, has three options: Create Report, Data Export, and Report Options (see Figure 4.2 for a screenshot showing each of these areas). The first option under Reports, Create Report, is self-explanatory. Users are allowed to select from a menu of report types (profile report, roster report, score report, etc.) and options to create custom reports. The Data Export option allows users to generate a file that can be used to create a .txt file of data from reports to the user's computer. The last option under Reports, Report Options, allows the user to customize discrepancy cut-offs and the confidence bands for reports (see Figure 4.3 for a screenshot of this area). Further, it allows the user to include either the individual's last name in a report or use the individual's ID number instead. (For additional information regarding specifics within each of the three options, please refer to the Advanced Functionality section of this chapter and view the Report Customization subsection.)

The third tab, *Administration*, provides a platform for the key communication coordinator for HMH-Riverside to use and manage all functions of the online program through five main options: Account Holder Messages, Manage

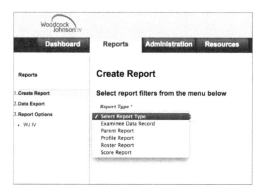

FIGURE 4.2 The *Reports* Tab. A brief description of each option under *Reports* follows:
1. *Create Report* option: where users can select desired report type.
2. *Data Export* option: where users can generate files that can be used to create .txt files of the data.
3. *Report Options* option: where users can customize discrepancy cut-offs and confidence bands for reports.

Test Records, Manage Examinees, Manage Caseload Folders, and Manage Examines (see Figure 4.4 for a screenshot showing each of these areas). The Account Holder Messages section allows the administrator to create or edit/delete messages that display on the Dashboard of the website and facilitate communication with associated examiners or users of the account holder (i.e., administrator). Due to a maximum limit of 10 messages from an administrator, the option to set a date and time for the message to appear and disappear on an associated user's Dashboard is provided, as well as the option to edit and delete a currently displayed message. The second option under the *Administration* tab is Manage Test Records, which shows the account holder/administrator the number of available, saved, and committed test records. Also, the option to order additional test records falls in this section of the website. A contact phone number and a link to find a local sales representative is found at the top of the page that displays the number of available, saved, and committed test records. When ordering additional records, if the company a user works for has more than one account with HMH-Riverside it is important to specify the specific account and the Account Holder to avoid electronic test records from being placed within another account. Once an order has been placed, electronic test records will show up within the associated software account, and hard-copy protocols will be mailed. The Manage Examinees option allows all user types to add, search and edit, or search for deleted test records. The fourth option, Manage Caseload Folders, allows all user types to add new caseload folders or to search/edit current caseload folders. Again, permissions granted to examiners will only allow these users to search through his or her examinees or caseload folders, unlike the account holder or administrator who can search through all

1. Select the *Reports* tab at the top of the window, and then click on the **Report Options** within the *Reports* tab.

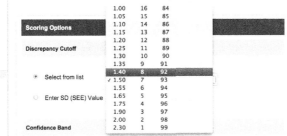

2. On the **Report Options** page, the scoring and other available report options are listed. Users can select the desired discrepancy cutoff from the list option.

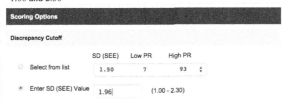

3. Users also have the option to enter manually a standard deviation value between 1.00 and 2.30

FIGURE 4.3   Report Options Visual Guide

1. Select the *Reports* tab at the top of the window, and then click on the **Report Options** within the *Reports* tab.
2. On the **Report Options** page, the scoring and other available report options are listed. Users can select the desired discrepancy cut-off from the list option.
3. Users also have the option to enter manually a standard deviation value between 1.00 and 2.30.

examinees and caseload folders for the entire organization. Finally, the Manage Examiners option allows the administrator to add a new examiner by entering in the examiner's first and last name, email, status, role, username, and data export permissions for the new examiner. Note that the status option indicates that the examiner is actively using the WJ IV, the role option allows the account holder to grant administrative access to the new examiner, and the data export permission can be edited to allow the examiner permission to download WJ IV data.

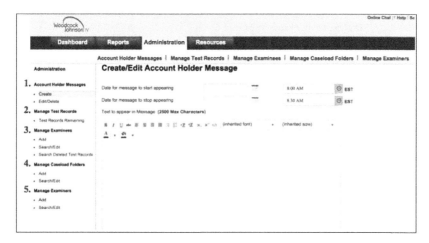

FIGURE 4.4 The *Administration* Tab. A description of each of the options under this tab follows.

1. *Account Holder Messages* option: where the administrator can edit/delete messages that appear under the *Dashboard* tab.
2. *Manage Test Records* option: where the account holder/administrator can view the amount of available, saved, and committed test records.
3. *Manage Examinees* option: where all user types can add, search, and edit test records, as well as search for deleted test records.
4. *Manage Caseload Folders* option: where all user types can add new caseload folders or search/edit current caseload folders.
5. *Manage Examiners* option: where the administrator can add a new examiner and edit access information for new examiners.

The fourth and final main tab of the WJ IV online program is the *Resources* tab (see Figure 4.5 for a screenshot of this tab). This tab provides several download-able PDF documents to provide assistance in the usage of the WJ IV program. The provided PDFs include report and score interpretation guides for the WJ IV Tests of Achievement (WJ IV ACH; Schrank, Mather, & McGrew, 2014a), WJ IV Tests of Oral Language (Schrank, Mather, & McGrew, 2014b), and WJ IV Tests of Cognitive Abilities (Schrank, McGrew, & Mather, 2014b), the WJ IV *Technical Manual* (McGrew, LaForte, & Schrank, 2014), a User's Guide for online scoring and reporting, and HMH-Riverside Policy documents like the WJ IV Terms of Use, WJ IV Business Associate Agreement, and WJ IV Privacy Policy.

Help Options

In addition to the *Resources* tab, the WJ IV online program offers other resources for assistance, just in case users experience difficulty in navigating the site. First, users can receive assistance by clicking the *Help* option in the Banner in the upper right-hand corner of the window. Within the *Help* tab, users can search a specific topic or browse through the *Help* contents and select the resources that address

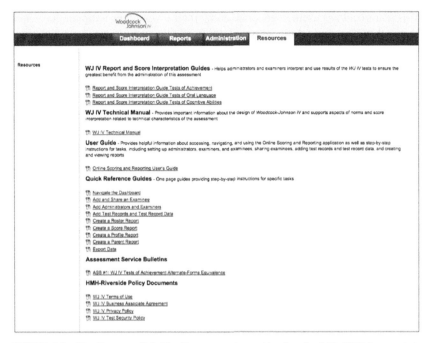

FIGURE 4.5   The *Resources* Tab. The *Resources* tab provides downloadable PDF documents to assist users with the navigation and use of the WJ IV online scoring program.

needed information. The *Help* option also provides detailed "Quick Guides" to address frequently asked questions with step-by-step visual guides. The online program also offers assistance through the *Online Chat* option in which users can connect with HMH Customer Service representatives for questions and technical support. Furthermore, if no representatives are available, users have the option of sending an email query to the customer service representatives.

Advanced Functionality

The WJ IV online scoring and reporting program has developed options for the user to tailor how data can be used by creating options to customize report generation and export data.

Report Customizations

Under the *Report* tab, the first of the three main functions is the Create Report option. This option includes several different features that can be customized by the user when generating reports. This option includes the following features: Score Selection Template, Options, Variations, Comparisons, Grouping Option, and Output Format. The first feature is the Score Selection Template.

This feature allows users to generate either their own unique template for which scores they want to include within a report, or they can use the default settings which includes age equivalent (AE), relative proficiency index (RPI), Standard Score with Band, and W scores. When creating a unique template, users are able to name the template so that in the future they can select their customized template from a drop-down list when using this function.

The next customizable feature on the *Report* tab is the Options feature. When generating a report using the new software, the default of this feature includes GIA scores, Comprehension-Knowledge-Extended, Fluid Reasoning-Extended, Short-Term Working Memory-Extended, Cognitive Efficiency-Extended, Reading Comprehension-Extended, and Broad Achievement. The only selection that is not included within the default settings of this feature is the inclusion of BIA scores, which can be selected to include either the BIA only if GIA is not also included, or include the BIA even if GIA is also included. This feature was previously called "Select Optional Scores" on the WJ III scoring software and included the GIA/BIA scores as the default selection, with the option to include BCA-Low Verbal Cluster, Total Achievement Cluster, and Pre-Academic Extended Cluster.

Another customizable feature on the *Report* tab is the Variations feature. The default selections for this feature include: Intra-Cognitive Variations, Intra-Oral Language Variations, Intra-Achievement Variations, and Academic Skills/Fluency/Applications Variations. This was previously called "Select Variations" on the WJ III scoring software and included the Intra-COG and/or Intra-Ach as the default selection, with the option to select Intra-Individual (COG & ACH) or None for no variations.

The next customizable feature is the Comparisons feature. The default selections for this feature include: *Gf–Gc* Composite/Other Ability Comparisons, GIA/Achievement Discrepancy Procedure, Oral Language/Achievement Comparisons (Either or both language(s) when available), Academic Knowledge/Achievement Comparisons, and Scholastic Aptitude/Achievement Comparisons. The only option not listed under the default settings pertains to the Oral Language/Achievement Comparisons, where it is possible to select to have an English Oral Language (OL) cluster only, a Spanish OL cluster only, or to use the default selection, which is either or both language(s) when available. This was previously called "Select Discrepancies" on the WJ III scoring software, and it was included in the Predicted Achievement/Achievement comparison as its default setting with the Oral Language/Achievement, Intellectual Ability/Achievement, and GIA (Std)/Cognitive Clusters discrepancy options.

Finally, the last two customizable features on the *Reports* tab are the Grouping Option and the Output Format features. These are new features that were not included within the WJ III scoring software. The Grouping Option allows users to select how the subtests are presented on the generated report. The selections include listing test in numerical order separately from clusters, listing test under clusters (where singleton test appear separately), and listing test under clusters and also in numerical order. The Output Format allows users to make the generated report a PDF, webpage, or word document.

Data Export

Another interesting feature of the WJ IV online program is the "Data Export" option. This option is located under the *Reports* tab, and it is actually not discussed within the WJ IV User's Guide for Online Scoring and Reporting. Information on utilizing this feature can be found in a PDF document under "Quick Guides" when selecting the "Help" option in the top right corner of the website. This feature was created to help users easily export WJ IV data into a third party program like Microsoft Excel, SPSS, etc., which would be convenient for researchers or for examiners with large quantities of data. However, when exploring and attempting to use the Data Export option, several concerns surfaced.

First, when creating an export and downloading the data file, the content shows up under the My Saved Reports box of the *Dashboard* tab, and it is not easily exported into other programs. The downloadable file can be opened as a .txt file or a webpage, but the content does not transpose appropriately into a third party program. Again, when searching for additional information on how to use this feature, the website did not adequately indicate how to take the data from its downloadable form and import it into another program. Also, when entering in a name or title for the Data Export, a previously used name is not permitted, which is likely included as a safeguard against writing over an earlier data export. However, the option to delete a previous export name is not intuitive. Users cannot simply use the delete icon next to a report within the My Saved Reports box of the Dashboard. To delete a previously used report name permanently from the online system, users must go to the *Reports* tab, and then select "Data Export," then use the drop-down menu to select a previously entered export name. Once the previous export name has been highlighted, "Edit Data Export" appears in blue text above the drop-down menu. If the users click on "Edit Data Export," they are then given the option to delete the export. Due to the limited amount of information on this feature, and its currently non-user-friendly state, it is recommended that HMH-Riverside provide additional direction on usage and update the feature in the next version of the WJ IV's online program.

Implications for Practice

In order to increase user understanding and awareness, implications for clinical practice are examined by exploring critical strengths and weaknesses of the new WJ IV scoring and reporting program.

Test Security

Test security has always been an important issue to practitioners. However, test security has been traditionally relegated to securing physical materials. With the advent of online test scoring, security issues will likely be a primary consideration for many practitioners. The general data security features for the WJ IV can be found online at: http://www.riversidepublishing.com/products /wj-iv/pdf/WJIV_Technical_Overview_7_1_14.pdf.

As a brief summary, HMH-Riverside and their vendors take a variety of precautions to protect the users' data physically and online by using the latest measures to defend their servers. HMH-Riverside's partnered vendor meets the highest security standards in the industry for data integrity and related processes by strictly monitoring physical access to the data center, requiring authentication to access all information, proactively attending to system vulnerabilities, and ensuring that infrastructure changes are accurate and logged. Additionally, HMH-Riverside implements premium protective software against viruses, as well as advanced firewall technology to provide protection against potential intruders. The company also ensures efficient recovery processes for client data by backing up all servers and databases regularly. Overall, HMH-Riverside employs extensive actions in order to guarantee the security of its users' data, and are constantly monitoring this process in order to keep the data protected at all times.

Confidentiality

With technology moving into the digital era, the push for services to be wide-spread through online programs and applications raises several critical concerns regarding confidentiality and security of test information. First, when providing a platform for practitioners to score and report testing online, it becomes convenient to complete work anywhere that has Internet access. Best practice would be to complete scoring and reporting at a job site, but the convenience of accessing scoring programs from any computer that has internet capabilities may lead practitioners to work in less secure environments. Additionally, the online nature of scoring and reporting programs such as the new WJ IV poses concerns with confidentiality.

If practitioners drift from best practice and use the WJ IV program outside of a secure environment, it is possible for an unauthorized individual to view data. The software does appear to log a user out automatically after approximately 20 min of nonuse, which was likely created to safeguard information and to combat issues with confidentiality. However, 20 min of nonuse is ample time for an unauthorized individual to view content on the computer if a practitioner steps away. Further, in the digital age there is the additional threat of data being breached, even if this event is unlikely to occur. However, as previously discussed, HMH-Riverside has taken steps to safeguard security of data within the online scoring program.

Another concern with confidentiality regarding the WJ IV scoring and reporting program involves the account holder and administrator's level of access to examinee information and records. The account holder and administrator(s) are able to view all examinee information. These individuals are not obtrusively viewing content on the *Dashboard* tab unless they intentionally click through different shared folders or search for examinees under the *Administration* tab. However, the level of access that an account holder or administrator has to an individual's personal information raises a critical concern regarding whether the WJ IV is adhering to the protection of personal information based on the Health Insurance Portability and Accountability Act (HIPPA). This is especially salient when considering that an administrator or account holder may simply be a technology assistant within a school district or another individual who is less familiar with privacy laws like HIPPA and the Federal Educational Rights and Privacy Act (FERPA). Individuals with this level of access should receive HIPPA training in order to avoid potential issues with confidentiality of information, and organizations should use caution in determining who has access as an administrator or account holder.

An additional concern regarding confidentiality pertains to the Shared Caseload feature of the WJ IV scoring and reporting program. The WJ IV team has sought to limit issues with confidentiality within this feature through the use of permission options. First, examiners are only able to view cases from an organization that were created by the examiner. Second, if cases are to be shared in the organization, HMH-Riverside recommends that the original examiner only allow the shared examiner viewing permissions when using the Shared Casefolder option. This permissions option prevents the shared examiner from making changes to the examinee's data, which facilitates communication between examiners. This may also prevent errors when practitioners write-up scores for an official evaluation report, where perhaps the original examiner reported scores that may have been changed by the shared examiner without the original examiner's knowledge.

Online Nature

There are several critical strengths and weaknesses that the WJ IV scoring and reporting program highlights when considering the online nature of the program. One key strength of the new WJ IV scoring program is that the Shared Caseload Folders feature and Messages Boards facilitate easy communication between the publisher and an organization, as well as within an organization. This is especially true when considering the Shared Caseload Folders feature, where practitioners can jointly complete an evaluation or view previous records through sharing an examinee and/or an examinee's test record with another examiner. An example of how this could be appropriately utilized might be when one examiner completes the cognitive component of the WJ IV, while another administers the achievement and/or the oral language test. However, despite this strength in the online nature of the WJ IV scoring program, there are serious concerns related to the online nature of the program when considering connectivity.

Specifically, if users are not connected to the Internet then there is no way to score and report findings from testing. This could be problematic for schools located in rural or poor communities that may have limited resources that could prevent access to high speed Internet. While most public schools report having internet access, only 80% of these schools report being satisfied with their internet services, primarily due to the slow speed of their internet services. Furthermore, rural schools reported dissatisfaction with internet speed more than other schools (Federal Communications Commission, 2010). Most school psychologists are located at more than one school, with a survey study reporting that approximately 25% of school psychologists have a psychologist to student ratio of 1:1500 (Bramlett, Murphy, Johnson, Wallingsford, & Hall, 2002). With so many students to survey, internet connectivity issues or wireless fidelity (Wi-Fi) issues may be especially problematic for school psychologists working from laptops, and this would only add to work-related stress. This potential issue would unnecessarily add time to the evaluation process, which is already challenged by deadlines. HMH-Riverside has indicated that a mobile application will be developed that does not require the Internet. However, this currently unreleased application would likely require cellular data, which would cause similar issues if problems with connectivity are present.

Mobile Application (App)

The WJ IV mobile app is a unique addition to the WJ IV scoring program. Users can download the application to their mobile devices, such as a phone or tablet, in order to input or collect data without an internet connection. However, internet access is still needed if the examiner desires to commit data, generate reports, and have access to any normative data. Additionally, HMH-Riverside ensures that the same data protection used for the WJ IV scoring program will be applied to the mobile app security. The WJ IV mobile app was made available to download in the Spring of 2015.

"Committing" a Test Record

One critical concern regarding clinical practice that may arise with the new WJ IV scoring and reporting software is the "commitment" of a test record (i.e., finalizing the test record). When creating a new test record, an examiner can enter and save scores to be updated or changed at a later time. There does not appear to be a time limit regarding how long a test record can be saved. However, once a test record has been "committed" the administration date cannot be changed, but scores and other information can be edited up to 90 days before the test record is locked and permanent. Originally, the software only permitted editing for 30 days, so the 90-day window is an improvement. Despite this change, one potential concern regarding the finalization of the test administration upon "committing" the record is that the normative range could potentially change based on the examinee's date of birth. A likely explanation for why the WJ IV provides this window for change is that users are unable to view standard scores until the test record is committed. Without this window for change, it would be difficult for examiners to determine whether or not an examinee would need additional supplemental subtests (e.g., a cross-battery assessment, spoiled subtest).

Research and Data Usage

As a related concern to committing a test record, normative databases for psychological tests should be verified for accuracy by researchers. Traditionally, printed tables provided easy access to investigating normative patterns in measures. Researchers, as well as clinicians, could get a feel for how the mean score changes across age. Additionally, the degree of differences in raw score points could be analyzed to determine whether a few raw scores influence the standard scores. Although the use of computerized scoring software made it more difficult to investigate changes across ages, raw scores could be entered into the software program to map out changes in standard scores across development.

With the advent of online scoring software that requires "committing" a test record, the empirical investigation of normative values becomes more difficult. Scores cannot be independently evaluated without paying a test record fee for each scoring. At best, scores could be evaluated for a single age by uncommitting a test record within the 90-day period. While this setup likely provides a profitable business model, it creates additional impediments to the open evaluation of normative databases.

As a final issue, there is uncertainty in how the data collected for scoring purposes is to be used. Archived data presents a tremendous wealth of information that can be used by researchers. "Big data" movements have arrived for numerous other disciplines in which inert data are mined to produce useful information. Because the use of an online scoring system requires the transfer and storage of data to remote servers, this inevitably raises issues on the appropriate use and access of data by third parties. How de-identified data can be used is unclear, but this will likely be an issue of interest for many clinicians. Whether or not archived data collected during online scoring procedures can be used for research purposes or to monitor testing practices in different states or school districts may also be an issue in need of clarification.

Appropriate use of archived data is not a unique to the practice of psychological testing. However, what is unique is that psychological testing is now entering an era of networked systems in which the transfer of information is a standard component of practice. Such capabilities provide a host of benefits, but are not risk free. Clinicians are advised to be aware and mindful, not only of the tremendous benefits emerging in the technological advancements of psychological testing, but also of the risk inherent in the use of these new technologies.

REFERENCES

Bramlett, R. K., Murphy, J. J., Johnson, J., Wallingsford, L., & Hall, J. D. (2002). Contemporary practices in school psychology: A national survey of roles and referral problems. *Psychology in The Schools*, *39*(3), 327–335.

Federal Communications Commission. (2010). E-rate program and broadband usage survey. Retrieved from <http://transition.fcc.gov/010511_Eratereport.pdf>.

McGrew, K. S., LaForte, E. M., & Schrank, F. A. (2014). *Technical manual: Woodcock Johnson IV*. Rolling Meadows, IL: Riverside.

Schrank, F. A., & Dailey, D. (2014). *Woodcock–Johnson online scoring and reporting [Online format]*. Rolling Meadows, IL: Riverside.

Schrank, F. A., Mather, N., & McGrew, K. S. (2014a). *Woodcock–Johnson IV Tests of Achievement*. Rolling Meadows, IL: Riverside.

Schrank, F. A., Mather, N., & McGrew, K. S. (2014b). *Woodcock–Johnson IV Tests of Oral Language*. Rolling Meadows, IL: Riverside.

Schrank, F. A., McGrew, K. S., & Mather, N. (2014a). *Woodcock–Johnson IV*. Rolling Meadows, IL: Riverside.

Schrank, F. A., McGrew, K. S., & Mather, N. (2014b). *Woodcock–Johnson IV Tests of Cognitive Abilities*. Rolling Meadows, IL: Riverside.

Woodrock, R. W., McGrew, K. S., & Mather, N. (2001). *Woodcock–Johnson III*. Itasca, IL: Riverside.

Chapter 5

Instructional Implications from the Woodcock–Johnson IV Tests of Cognitive Abilities

Denise E. Maricle and Wendi L. Bauman Johnson
Department of Psychology and Philosophy, Texas Woman's University, Denton, TX, USA

The purpose of this chapter is to explore instructional implications from the Woodcock–Johnson IV Tests of Cognitive Abilities (WJ IV COG; Schrank, McGrew, & Mather, 2014a). Enhancing cognitive or intellectual abilities in children has been a topic of great interest in education and rehabilitation. Children's cognitive impairments affect their ability to achieve developmental milestones not previously attained, impact school achievement, and restrict their ability to participate in age appropriate social activities. Thus, questions such as the following arise:

> *"What are the instructional implications of knowing a child's strengths and weaknesses within his/her cognitive ability profile?"*
> *"What does the WJ IV COG tell us about how to instruct a child with a particular cognitive deficit or combination of cognitive deficits?"*
> *"What intervention(s), accommodations, compensation, or remediation would be most effective for an individual child with a specific pattern of strengths, weaknesses, or deficits?"*

This chapter reviews the literature and research applicable to the WJ IV COG's relationship to academic achievement and instructional implications that may then be derived.

WJ IV

The WJ IV (Schrank, McGrew, & Mather, 2014b) is described elsewhere in this text (see Ding & Alfonso, this volume). Briefly, for the purposes of this chapter, the WJ IV consists of three separate instruments measuring cognitive, language, and achievement abilities. Although there are three distinct instruments, one of

WJ IV Clinical Use and Interpretation. DOI: http://dx.doi.org/10.1016/B978-0-12-802076-0.00005-0

which is devoted primarily to the measurement of cognitive abilities, all three instruments were designed to work in concert to assess cognitive, language, and achievement constructs. The WJ IV authors indicate that the design blueprint for the WJ IV differed significantly from the previous version (Schrank et al., 2014b). For example, the Woodcock–Johnson III (Woodcock, McGrew, & Mather, 2001) emphasized constructing relatively pure broad CHC (Cattell–Horn–Carroll) factors, whereas the WJ IV introduces the idea of cognitive complexity and narrow abilities as more predictive of CHC factors and academic performance. Issues with regard to the WJ IV's standardization, psychometric characteristics, and factor structure have yet to be identified and researched by independent examiners. Currently, professionals must rely on what is provided in the *WJ IV Technical Manual* (McGrew, LaForte, & Schrank, 2014).

A specific concern for the authors of this chapter is the factor analytic methodology used to establish the structure of the WJ IV. From the information included in the technical manual it would appear that depending on the methodology applied different factor structures were elicited, including exploratory methods that resulted in a 3-factor model (auditory–linguistic dimension, figural–visual dimension, quantitative–numeric dimension) and a 5-factor model (Gc, Gs, Grw, $Gq + Gf$, Gwm); and confirmatory methods that resulted in three models showing equal fit acceptability (Model 1 = g; Model 2 = 9 broad factors; Model 3 = 4 narrow abilities, 8 broad factors, and g). Thus, from the information available in the manual, it is unclear exactly what the factor structure of the WJ IV is and thus, what aspects of the CHC theoretical model should be applied interpretively. This appears to be compounded by the lack of clarity surrounding the "evolution" of CHC theory.

THE EVOLUTION OF CHC THEORY AND ITS RELATIONSHIP TO THE WJ IV

The CHC theory of cognitive abilities has evolved over the past 20 years, serves as the theoretical foundation for cognitive assessment, and has been applied to the majority of published cognitive measures. A significant amount of research has been conducted on the relationship of cognitive abilities with instruction and academic achievement. McGrew and Wendling (2010) provide a thorough summary of the past 20 years of research on CHC and achievement.

The WJ IV reflects changes to CHC theory postulated most recently in work by Schneider and McGrew (2012, 2013) and apparently operationalized in the WJ IV. The WJ IV authors note that "this revision represents a significant advance in the measurement of cognitive, linguistic, and achievement abilities" (Mather & Wendling, 2014, p. 1). The primary changes to the CHC constructs applied to the WJ IV appear to be in the conceptualization of the narrow abilities that comprise the broad factors as measured by various WJ IV subtests, a reconceptualization of Auditory Processing (Ga), and the refinement of ideas around short-term or working memory (Gwm). Additionally, the WJ IV introduces or returns to the idea of cognitive complexity. Cognitive complexity is not a novel concept and has its roots in personal construct psychology as proposed by James Bieri in 1955. Cognitive complexity is related to the problem of task impurity, which has been a topic in cognitive and neuropsychological assessment for many years. There really is no such thing as a pure measure of a specific cognitive skill, often several skills are needed to complete successfully a complex cognitive task. The WJ IV authors appear to circumvent the task impurity topic by deciding that some of its tasks are "intended" to be cognitively complex. Thus, the first seven subtests of the WJ IV COG are considered to be "the most" cognitively complex, the best measures of "*g*," and the most predictive of their respective CHC factors (McGrew et al., 2014, p. 8–9). The authors of the WJ IV are clear about the fact that all the CHC factor clusters and composite clusters are different, in varying degrees, to how they were in the WJ III, and that the two versions are not comparable.

These changes to CHC theory and the WJ IV are recent, and therefore, very little independent research or research by anyone other than the authors is available regarding these new suppositions. Additionally, recent research on CHC theory posits other conceptualizations of CHC constructs. For example, Schneider and McGrew in their 2012 review of the literature articulated a 16-factor model containing over 80 narrow abilities, which Schneider and McGrew grouped into six major categories (i.e., reasoning, acquired knowledge, memory and efficiency, sensory, motor, and speed and efficiency). Flanagan, Ortiz, and Alfonso (2013) have within their cross-battery approach classified all the subtests of the major achievement, cognitive, and neuropsychological batteries according to the specific CHC broad ability being measured, using the CHC taxonomy of 13 broad factors and a multitude of narrow abilities. Additionally, Flanagan and Alfonso (2011) and Flanagan, Alfonso, and Dixon (2014) have even expanded ideas within the cross-battery approach to address the integration of CHC theory with neuropsychological perspectives. The cross-battery classification system is based on using empirically strong or moderate measures of CHC abilities with limited factorial complexity or impurity (Flanagan et al., 2013). It is unclear as to how the WJ IV ideas about cognitive complexity might be integrated into this popular taxonomy and classification system. Miller (2013) has merged CHC constructs into his theory of neuropsychological assessment in an effort to understand better cognitive processing strengths and weaknesses in children and adolescents from a neuropsychological perspective. Although it is possible to view these approaches as distinct, they seem to be far from mutually exclusive, and could also be viewed as complementary.

It is important to note that no one "owns" CHC theory. Therefore, its interpretation, evolution, and applicability to various cognitive measures is open to interpretation. What is important to know, however, is that the ideas to date regarding the evolution of CHC and the structure of the CHC factors postulated by researchers such as McGrew, Mather, Schneider, Flanagan, Miller, or Woodcock are disparate and lacking in supportive research. Therefore, suppositions about the new relationships among CHC factors or about CHC factors as measured by the WJ IV need to be based on what is known about the old relationships from the last 20 years of research.

WJ IV COG

The WJ IV COG consists of 18 tests divided into two batteries (Standard and Extended). The first seven tests comprise the General Intellectual Ability index (GIA) which is the primary measure of "g", although the WJ IV introduces a $Gf–Gc$ Composite (comprised of two Gf subtests and two Gc subtests), which the authors note is considered a better measure of "g" and the best estimate of intellectual ability, as well as a better predictor of academic achievement. They indicate that if a discrepancy method is used for SLD identification, the $Gf–Gc$ Composite is the best measure to utilize for the "ability" score. The prevailing CHC factor structure of Gc, Gf, Gwm, Gs, Ga, Glr, and Gv persists and to obtain factor composites, the examiner continues to need to give one test from the standard battery and one test from the extended battery. However, the WJ IV authors indicate that the tests for each factor in the standard battery are the best predictors of their respective CHC factor; therefore, it would not necessarily be essential to obtain a factor composite to interpret a specific cognitive construct.

The WJ IV also provides new narrow ability clusters (Quantitative Reasoning, Auditory Working Memory Span, Number Facility, Perceptual Speed, and Vocabulary) and a clinical cluster (Cognitive Efficiency, which is comprised of $Gs + Gwm$), but gives no real guidance as to how to apply them. An interesting addition is the reintroduction of Scholastic Aptitude Clusters (SAC), which the WJ IV indicates can be used to predict performance in specific academic areas and may be utilized as a foundation for a Pattern of Strengths and Weaknesses (PSW) approach to the identification of learning disabilities. The SACs were designed to "predict academic performance and for time-efficient, referral-focused or domain-specific assessment" (Schrank et al., 2014a, p. 20). For each curricular area, there are four test scores from the WJ IV COG that in combination produce the best prediction of a particular achievement area. For example, for predicting overall reading achievement, the four WJ IV COG tests include Oral Vocabulary, Phonological Processing, Concept Formation, and Number Pattern Matching. How the examinee performs on these four tests should predict how he/she will perform on reading measures. Predictions were determined via multiple regression and the extant literature and research (McGrew & Wendling, 2010). The predictions were made only with the WJ IV COG and Woodcock–Johnson IV Tests of Achievement (Schrank et al., 2014a), but it could be assumed that it would hold true in a cross-battery approach as well, although there is no supporting research at this time.

RELATIONSHIP OF COGNITION AND ACHIEVEMENT

Historically, general intelligence has been regarded as the best predictor of achievement across all academic domains (Deary, Strand, Smith, & Fernandes, 2007). According to Mather and Wendling (2015), the WJ IV COG measures the most important cognitive abilities for learning. The WJ IV COG facilitates documenting a child's relative strengths and weaknesses to assist in the determination of a disability or to decide appropriate instructional approaches or interventions. The *WJ IV Interpretation and Instructional Interventions Program* (WIIIP™; Schrank & Wendling, 2015) provides suggestions to remediate limited academic proficiency by directly linking assessment data to evidence-based instruction. The WJ IV publisher touts this program as containing over 500 research-based interventions. Linking assessment to instruction or intervention can assist Individualized Education Program teams in making informed and effective decisions about the education program of a specific student. Mascolo, Alfonso, and Flanagan (2014) thoroughly discuss planning, selecting, and tailoring interventions to individual children. Mascolo et al. indicate that planning and selecting interventions is the process of identifying evidence-based interventions. However, tailoring interventions requires the examiner to understand the individual's pattern of cognitive and academic strengths and weakness as well as how this pattern interacts with classroom environment, instructional factors and materials, and individual variables, all of which can facilitate or inhibit learning.

However, a definitional problem exists within the intervention literature surrounding the terminology used to refer to remediation, compensation, modification and accommodation, and intervention; although these terms have been defined comprehensively by Mascolo et al. (2014). Nevertheless, some educational professionals tend to use these terms interchangeably, and fail to differentiate between them. Further confusion is added with loosely defined terms such as strategies and instructional practices, and how these are applied to an individual child. Instructional practices are typically defined as prescribed instructional procedures that are systematically implemented, whereas, strategies are instructional practices that are not prescribed nor systematically implemented, but may be applied for an individual child. For example, Direct Instruction (Englemann & Carnine, 1982) would be considered an instructional practice as it usually includes specific curricular materials that contain explicit, systematic step-by-step instructions for teaching. In contrast, strategies are instructional techniques that are applied to an individual child such as cooperative learning or mediated scaffolding (Shapiro, 2011).

An accommodation is an alteration in the way a task is presented, but it does not alter the task or the expectations of the task. Accommodations are designed to provide equity, not advantage. Accommodations are adaptations, usually physical or environmental, so that the child can be successful in the regular education classroom. Examples of accommodations include extended time, frequent breaks, preferential seating, reduction of environmental distraction (e.g., a cubicle or carrel), use of varied teaching approaches or instructional practices (peer tutoring), highlighting material, or breaking down complex projects into smaller more manageable steps. Thus, changes in instructional practices may fit under the concept of accommodation. In comparison, a modification alters the instruction, content, expectations for success, or assessment practices for the individual. It frequently fundamentally alters or lowers the standards or expectations and/or changes the task. For example, modifications might include modified curriculum, adapted materials, differential grading, or changes in location, assignments (reducing the amount of work completed in an assignment or not requiring homework), scheduling (attending part-time), or level of instruction (e.g., attending a lower reading group). In contrast, an intervention is a specific skill-building strategy that is implemented and monitored to improve, develop, or remediate a target skill (academic or behavioral) and frequently involves changing instructional environments.

So, how are these different? Accommodations level the playing field, modifications change the playing field, and interventions remediate or teach a skill. Accommodations and modifications are compensatory, whereas intervention is remedial. Compensation includes procedures, techniques, and strategies intended to minimize or bypass the impact of the individual's cognitive or academic deficit. Remediation is the attempt to ameliorate the cognitive or academic deficit (Mascolo et al., 2014).

During the past decade, there has been substantial movement toward the use of evidence-based interventions in schools. The foundation behind evidence-based practice is that practitioners utilize only those practices and interventions that have been proven through data-based research to be effective in improving outcomes for individuals when implemented with fidelity. But what exactly constitutes evidence-based? Implementing interventions that are supported by research can be challenging for many reasons including the fact that research findings do not always generalize to every problem or setting. What is found to be effective in a laboratory or controlled setting may not be as effective in a more natural setting, and frequently interventions are not rigorously studied (Gettinger & Doescher Hurd, 2011).

Regardless, a skilled clinician can often discern a number of instructional implications or needed accommodations/modifications by evaluating the individual's performance on measures of cognition and achievement. Deriving instructional implications or needed accommodations requires interpreting obtained scores from cognitive and academic measures within the context of information gathered through record review, interview, and observation. Error analysis and careful observation of the individual's test taking process can provide valuable information about their cognitive reasoning and problem-solving skills. There is a plethora of literature available regarding academic-based accommodations, modifications, instructional approaches, and interventions (Fletcher, Lyon, Fuchs, & Barnes, 2007; Mascolo et al., 2014; Shapiro, 2011; Shinn & Walker, 2010; Swanson, Harris, & Graham, 2013; Wendling & Mather, 2008).

Cognitive rehabilitation is common with children who have sustained a neurological insult and has a long standing history as an effective intervention practice in pediatric neuropsychology (Cicerone et al., 2005; Laatsch et al., 2007). However, the use of rehabilitation techniques for the development or remediation of foundational cognitive skills in the general population of school children is still in its infancy (Limond & Leeke, 2005), despite the increase in research in cognitive neuroscience and clinical rehabilitation (Ponsford, 2004). Cognitive rehabilitation focuses on the re-attainment of mental abilities following neurological insult. Limond and Leeke (2005) suggest that clinically cognitive rehabilitation "denotes a systematic intervention designed to compensate for, or ameliorate, the impact of cognitive and/or behavioral difficulties following acquired brain injury" (p. 339). The foundational premise is that cognition is a neurophysiologically based function that is modifiable through therapeutic rehabilitation. The goals of cognitive rehabilitation are to enhance the individual's cognitive functioning and improve the person's ability to function in all aspects of daily life. Intervention usually takes the form of restoration/remediation, which focuses on restoring or improving the specific cognitive function by eliminating or reducing the underlying cognitive impairment, or compensation where the focus is on adapting to the presence of the cognitive deficit and acquiring compensatory skills or using assistive devices to accommodate for the deficit (Eslinger & Oliveri, 2002). Treatment may be process specific, focused on improving a particular cognitive domain such as memory, language, attention, or executive functions (EFs), or skill-based and aimed at improving performance of a specific activity, such as word retrieval.

Neuropsychological assessment is the foundation for treatment planning (Bergquist & Malec, 2002). Practitioners in the field are able to provide information as to the nature of the individual child's cognitive strengths and weaknesses through neuropsychological assessment. Information about the individual's neurocognitive abilities, academic skills, and psychosocial functioning forms the basis for designing interventions. There is a linkage between assessment and intervention, where competent evaluation leads to effective intervention. Typically the use of strengths is recommended to compensate for deficits and often direct retraining of certain deficits is recommended (Semrud-Clikeman, 2001).

NEUROCOGNITIVE AND CHC CONSTRUCTS RELEVANT TO ACADEMIC ACHIEVEMENT

In the past decade, research on the relationship between cognitive abilities, neuropsychological constructs, and specific academic skills has converged with research on cognitive-academic relationships within the context of CHC theory and using CHC specific instruments. Additionally, the more recent integration of CHC theory with neuropsychological theory and research in the emerging field of school neuropsychology has contributed to the understanding of how CHC constructs and neuropsychological constructs relate to each other, providing the astute clinician with greater options for interpretation as well as a broader base of research to inform their practice (Flanagan & Alfonso, 2011; Flanagan et al., 2013; Flanagan, Ortiz, Alfonso, & Mascolo, 2006; Fletcher et al., 2007;

Mascolo et al., 2014; McGrew & Wendling, 2010; Miller, 2013). A significant amount of literature and research has established that cognitive processes are relevant to learning and academic success. This connection between cognition and achievement is well documented; therefore only a brief overview is provided here.

Comprehension-Knowledge (*Gc*). Comprehension-Knowledge (*Gc*) represents acquired knowledge, which is one's cumulative knowledge of facts and associations. Comprehension-Knowledge is significantly associated with language development and comprehension as well as cultural and environmental exposure. Comprehension-Knowledge is believed to increase with age and throughout adulthood regardless of formal education. Evidence suggests that increasing knowledge can positively influence cognitive and academic performance, and that increasing *Gc* is one of the easiest constructs with which to intervene. Building vocabulary and background knowledge (general information and factual information) can be explicitly taught through techniques such as word instruction, monitored practice, word development and analysis strategies, or semantic mapping.

Fluid Reasoning (*Gf*). Fluid reasoning is the ability to solve unfamiliar problems using logical reasoning (Schneider & McGrew, 2012). It involves the ability to reason, form concepts and solve problems using novel information or unfamiliar procedures. Inductive and deductive reasoning are the hallmarks of *Gf*. Fluid reasoning has a strong relationship to working memory, as working memory is responsible for solving fluid reasoning problems. Working memory allows the individual to engage in multistep problem-solving, to control the focus of attention, and to adapt, change or modify as needed. Being able to hold more information in a state of activation improves the ability to complete complex tasks such as reading comprehension or applied math reasoning. Although fluid reasoning is considered by many to be mostly an innate capacity, individuals can be taught strategies for reasoning and problem-solving. For instance, instruction in philosophy and logical thinking or reasoning was frequently part of the educational curriculum until the mid-twentieth century. Current instructional strategies, such as teaching categorization, connecting concepts to prior knowledge, guided practice, and story mapping, have been shown to improve fluid reasoning skills (Flanagan, Alfonso, & Mascolo, 2011; Mather & Jaffe, 2015). Cooperative teaching approaches, reciprocal teaching methodologies, and metacognitive strategy instruction have all proven useful at improving *Gf* skills.

Visual–Spatial Processing (*Gv*). Visual–spatial processing (*Gv*) pertains to the complex processing of visual information, such as perceiving complex visual patterns, visualizing objects from different orientations, being able to assemble or deconstruct objects from their respective parts to form multidimensional shapes or objects, or using the mind's eye to visualize objects in space (Schneider & McGrew, 2012). Visualization, which is the ability to perceive complex patterns and mentally simulate transformations of visual–spatial material, is the core component of *Gv*. Tasks of *Gv* frequently use simultaneous processing skills as these skills allow the individual to recognize patterns, integrate information, and see the whole or the big picture (the gestalt).

Although *Gv* does not show a strong relationship with the other cognitive factors or to academic functions, it is a necessary ability for abstract mathematical functions, such as geometry, and the orthographic aspects of written language. There is research to suggest that *Gv* is a necessary precursor to higher order processes required in the fields of science, technology, and engineering (Lubinski, 2010; Wai, Lubinski, & Benbow, 2009). Instructional supports for *Gv* deficits often take the form of modifications such as relying on auditory cueing to supplement visual information, or providing visual supports, such as graphic organizers or graph paper.

Auditory Processing (*Ga*). Auditory processing allows us to distinguish between sounds and to hear differences in sounds or speech. While it is a precursor to language comprehension, it is not the same thing as language comprehension (Schneider & McGrew, 2012). *Ga* is related to reading, particularly the ability to use phonics to sound out words. Skilled readers do not sound out familiar words; they retrieve the word sounds from memory, whereas with poor readers the process of mapping sounds to letters is effortful and prone to error. Schneider and McGrew posit that *Ga* should be given greater credence or importance within CHC theory and that *Ga* is a critical latent cognitive factor relevant to "*g*" and to academic success. The WJ IV also provides more emphasis on *Ga* in the WJ IV COG and in the Woodcock–Johnson IV Tests of Oral Language (WJ IV OL; Schrank, Mather, & McGrew, 2014b).

Short-Term Working Memory (*Gwm*). The research is clear that short-term memory capacity and working memory skills are critical to academic success (Alloway, 2009; Dehn, 2008; Swanson, Zheng, & Jerman, 2009) and the ability to complete successfully complex cognitive tasks. Short-term memory capacity or immediate memory capacity is the amount of information that can be retained at one time. Working memory span or capacity involves the maintenance of information in mind while deploying attentional resources to manipulate the information. Strategies that teach how to focus attention can lessen the demand on working memory capacity. For example, shortened instructions or directions, using lists of steps or written directions, and breaking multistep problems into manageable components can be effective accommodations.

Long-Term Storage and Retrieval (*Glr*). Long-term storage and retrieval (*Glr*) can be defined as the ability to acquire, store, consolidate, and retrieve information over time. Associative memory, meaningful memory, and retrieval are the core characteristics of *Glr*. An individual learns to associate new information with previously acquired information or knowledge, and then efficiently retrieves the learned information from memory. *Glr* is distinguished from *Gc* in that it reflects the process of memory (e.g., learning efficiency), rather than the breadth of stored knowledge, which is characteristic of *Gc*. For example, retrieval is from the knowledge stores of *Gc*, but the ease of the retrieval of information is independent of measures of *Gc* (McGrew & Wendling, 2010).

Associative memory is an important ability for early reading as it is needed for development of the alphabetic principle and phonemic awareness (McGrew & Wendling, 2010). Naming fluency, or word retrieval fluency is a key predictor of early reading achievement and has been associated with reading comprehension problems. More is known about rapid automatized naming (RAN) than any of the other associative memory skills. Reading involves the ability to retrieve from memory the meaning of words and then construct meaning from the entire set of words. Slow retrieval fluency impairs fluid reading, making it more effortful. Poor retrieval fluency disrupts attentional resources and negatively impacts reasoning and problem solving. Instructional strategies to aid in *Glr* deficits look similar to those applied for short-term or working memory deficits. For example, using repeated practice and review, teaching memory strategies, or providing flow charts and study guides (Mascolo et al., 2014).

Cognitive Processing Speed (*Gs*). Cognitive processing speed consists of separate specific skills. Perceptual speed is the speed at which visual stimuli can be compared or matched, and is a core element of *Gs*. Other cognitive processing speed narrow abilities include rate of test taking, number facility, reading speed, and writing speed (Schneider & McGrew, 2012). Overall, cognitive processing speed is the speed, automaticity, and fluency with which a person can perform an attention demanding task. Cognitive processing speed allows one to perform a task without using attentional resources, thus, providing more cognitive resources for higher order thinking tasks.

Cognitive processing speed is very sensitive to aging, neurological injury, and fluctuations in alertness. It is also heavily influenced by individual strengths and weaknesses in attention, and a number of other variables can factor into *Gs* deficits as well (such as fatigue, or response style). Interventions for *Gs* tend to focus on compensating for deficits, such as providing extended time for work completion, reducing the quantity of work required, or teaching planning and time management strategies.

READING, MATHEMATICS, AND WRITTEN LANGUAGE

It is beyond the scope of this chapter to discuss all the relevant information regarding reading, mathematics, and written language. Practitioners and educators should be cognizant of the development of academic skills in each curricular area, developmental trajectories involved in learning such skills, assessment of academic achievement, the neurobiology behind learning and the development of academic skills, as well as the intervention approaches deemed effective for various academic skill deficits. Numerous relevant texts are available to discuss these areas in greater detail. A more thorough review of the implications for low achievement and applicability of specific interventions can be found in Mascolo et al. (2014), Mather and Wendling (2015), Salvia, Ysseldyke, and Bolt (2012), Shapiro (2011), Shaywitz and Shaywitz (2011), Shinn and Walker

(2010), and Swanson et al. (2013). For the purposes of this chapter only a brief review is provided.

Reading

Emergent literacy was a termed coined by Marie Clay in 1966 to refer to the process of becoming literate. Children develop the precursors for literacy such as oral language, vocabulary, and concepts about print, before they even walk into a classroom. Language development is one of the critical components to developing literacy. Exposure to language development opportunities not only builds vocabulary and sentence formulation skills, but also fosters analytical reasoning skills and problem solving.

McGrew and Wendling (2010) report that *Gc*, *Ga*, *Gs*, and *Gwm* have a consistent and significant relationship with reading achievement. *Gc* is strongly related to basic reading skills and reading comprehension, and its contribution increases with age. The contribution of *Ga* to reading success is primarily through the narrow ability of phonemic awareness and phonetic coding, which is critical to basic reading skills. Phonetic coding (*Ga*) and *Gc* are strongly related to reading, even after the weighty effect of "*g*" is accounted for (Feifer, 2011a; Flanagan et al., 2006; McGrew & Wendling, 2010). Memory skills, such as *Gwm* and *Glr*, are also important for the development of reading skills. For example, working memory has been shown to correlate at all ages and short-term immediate memory has been related to reading comprehension at the secondary level and the prediction of reading achievement (Feifer, 2011a). Associative memory and retrieval fluency have been able to predict reading failure. Associative memory and naming facility are critical during the early years, whereas meaningful memory is associated more with reading comprehension in the middle years (Feifer, 2011a).

Research indicates that the correlation of *Gwm* with reading increases with age where as *Glr* and *Gs* decrease with age. *Gs* is related to reading fluency or reading rate, which has been found to be important to reading comprehension. Children with deficits in reading fluency often have difficulties with reading comprehension that are directly related to their inability to decode words quickly and accurately (Shapiro, 2011). However, the question as to whether a subgroup of reading disability can be identified specifically by deficits in reading fluency alone has not been researched adequately. *Gf* has been linked to reading comprehension but not decoding, which makes sense if reading comprehension is defined as the ability to extract meaning from text. Although it is common to observe the presence of difficulties with copying or matching visual designs in children with disabilities, *Gv* or visual–spatial processing appears to make no significant contribution to reading, other than in orthographic coding (Fletcher et al., 2007; McGrew & Wendling, 2010). Although not a specific CHC factor, attention appears to play a critical role in phonological processing such that it may be necessary to consider the role of attentional mechanisms in the reading process (Shaywitz & Shaywitz, 2011).

The WJ IV COG includes an SAC that is designed to predict performance in Reading, Broad Reading, Reading Comprehension, Reading Fluency, and Reading Rate. This SAC consists of Test 1: Oral Vocabulary, Test 5: Phonological Processing, Test 9: Concept Formation, and Test 11: Number Pattern Matching. A second SAC is designed to predict Basic Reading Skills and consists of Test 1: Oral Vocabulary, Test 3: Verbal Attention, Test 5: Phonological Processing, and Test 11: Number Pattern Matching.

Reading is a complex activity involving several component skills. The acquisition of phonological awareness skills is one of the most important because it is a critical skill involved in successful reading and spelling performance. Phonemic awareness is a specific skill comprised of subskills such as alliteration (initial sounds), blending, segmenting, deleting, substituting, and manipulating sounds. Phonemic awareness is the ability to hear, identify, and manipulate individual sounds within spoken words. Poor readers often evidence deficits in phonemic awareness and rapid naming (retrieval fluency); however, it is phonological memory that distinguishes good readers from poor readers (Muter & Snowling, 1998; Swanson, 1992; Velluntino et al., 1996). Word reading encompasses the concepts of word recognition (sight words) and word identification skills used to access strategies to aid in reading a word. The goal of word reading is automaticity, wherein words are recognized effortlessly. In reading disabilities, deficits in word recognition are often a core characteristic which in turn involves deficits in phonological awareness and the metacognitive understanding that words heard and read have internal structures based on sound (Shapiro, 2011). This awareness of the phonological structure of language forms the basis for accurate recognition of known words needed for basic reading, reading comprehension, spelling, and written expression. Children who develop automaticity expend less cognitive effort trying to figure out the printed material. The skill of reading fluency is critical to increasing the rate at which text is translated into spoken language. Reading fluency is the bridge between word decoding and reading comprehension.

Delayed readers pass through the acquisition stages of reading, but do so at a slower rate. Children with reading disabilities display deficits in areas such as phonemic awareness orthographic processing, working memory (particularly phonological memory) and retrieval fluency. Furthermore, significant research on the neuropsychological correlates of reading is now available (Shaywitz & Shaywitz, 2011) and current evidence suggests genetic transmission, although no specific genetic marker has yet been discovered. Neuroimaging studies suggest that reading disabilities are related to the failure of left hemisphere posterior brain systems to function properly. Additionally, functional MRI (fMRI) studies have demonstrated the importance of memory systems in individuals with reading disabilities (Shaywitz et al., 2007) and evidence is beginning to emerge that many of these individuals compensate for poor reading by memorizing words.

There are many resources available regarding effective reading instruction (Joseph, 2006; Mascolo et al., 2014; Shapiro, 2011), accommodations, interventions, and remediation. The National Reading Panel (National Reading Panel, 2000) found that explicit daily phonemic awareness instruction was effective in promoting the acquisition of decoding skills and supported the transfer of skills to spelling words. Reading rate and fluency is often the target of reading interventions, despite limited research as to its efficacy. Two approaches are often used, repeated guided oral reading, and independent silent reading. The NRP (2000) failed to find conclusive evidence that increased independent reading improves fluency. However, the NRP found that repeated guided reading had a positive impact on word recognition, reading rate, and reading comprehension, the latter of which is the most important component of reading (Gettinger & Doescher Hurd, 2011). The NRP also found that explicit instruction in vocabulary was associated with better reading comprehension; however, word knowledge alone is not sufficient for comprehension. Reasoning and problem-solving are also necessary for students to construct meaning from the written text. The NRP found that self-monitoring strategies, cooperative learning strategies, the use of graphic or semantic organizers, story mapping, and teaching strategies that incorporated Socratic questioning and summarization skills were helpful in facilitating effective reading comprehension skills.

Mathematics

Disorders in mathematics have not received the same attention and emphasis in the literature and research as reading disorders, although a significant amount of research is now available on the neuropsychological bases of math disabilities (Geary, Hoard, & Bailey, 2011; Maricle, Psimas-Fraser, Muenke, & Miller, 2010). A report by the National Mathematics Advisory Panel (2008) indicated that understanding mathematical concepts, operations, and relationships; having the ability to carry out the sequential steps to solve math computation and word story problems; and the automatic recall of math facts and information is necessary to achieve proficiency in mathematics.

Achievement in mathematics is strongly related to acquired knowledge of mathematics (e.g., *Gq* and *Gc*). Mathematics appears to be especially vulnerable to learning difficulties as it is presented and learned in a cumulative scaffolded manner. Since mathematics instruction is cumulative, failing to understand the foundational concepts will result in difficulties mastering more complex concepts that build upon that foundation (Butterworth, 2008). Additionally, students who initially show early high achievement in math may not continue to be successful, due to the developmental trajectories of neuropsychological constructs needed at more advanced levels. Within the special education and learning disabilities literature, a child may be determined to have a disability in either math calculation or math problem solving, or both (Flanagan, & Alfonso, 2011; Fletcher et al., 2007).

Within the research on CHC and specific cognitive domains that influence the ability to perform mathematically, the research suggests that different cognitive factors are at play at different developmental periods. McGrew and Wendling (2010) reported that *Gf*, *Gc*, and *Gs* correlated consistently with math skills and math reasoning. Geary et al. (2011) also reported that *Gf*, *Gc*, and *Gs* correlate highly with basic math skills and math problem-solving. They noted developmental differences in the contributions of these cognitive factors, with *Gc* increasing with age, *Gs* being strongest only in the elementary years, and *Gf* being consistently important across all ages. Another study found that *Gs* is the best predictor of arithmetic competence at age 7 years and that *Gf* is an important correlate of math reasoning (Geary, Hoard, Byrd-Green, Nugent, & Numtee, 2007). A study conducted by Floyd, Evans, and McGrew (2003) found that *Gc*, *Gf*, *Gs*, and *Glr* were most associated with performance on math tasks and often deficient in children with math disabilities. Moreover, *Gq* (quantitative knowledge) along with *Gc* (comprehension-knowledge) plays a role in the ability to perform calculations at all ages, but is particularly important at early ages.

The WJ IV COG provides an SAC (Mather & Wendling, 2014) that encompasses the academic clusters of Mathematics, Broad Mathematics, and Math Calculation Skills. This SAC consists of Test 1: Oral Vocabulary, Test 2: Number Series, Test 7: Visualization, and Test 17: Pair Cancellation. The WJ IV COG provides a second SAC for Math Problem Solving. This SAC consists of Test 1: Oral Vocabulary, Test 7: Visualization, Test 10: Numbers Reversed, and Test 15: Analysis-Synthesis.

Mathematical performance can also be affected by a variety of neuropsychological factors (such as memory or processing speed) and affective factors (such as anxiety). fMRI studies have implicated four primary brain regions in mathematical thinking and processing. The inferior frontal gyrus has been implicated in the breaking down of larger quantities into smaller quantities; the angular gyrus appears to be the seat of symbolic representation and responsible for the visual–spatial recognition of numbers and digits; the occipital–temporal regions of the left hemisphere appear to be involved in the automaticity of number recognition; and the left inferior parietal region posterior to the angular gyrus appears to be responsible for analyzing magnitude and performing calculations (Maricle, Johnson, & Avirett, 2010).

Memory, and in particular working memory, is important in math performance (Fletcher et al., 2007; Swanson et al., 2009). All math tasks from the simplest calculations to the more complex problem-solving or quantitative reasoning tasks require memory skills such as immediate memory span, working memory, and long-term retrieval (Dehn, 2008). Children with math disorders tend to be able to store and retrieve information similarly to typically developing children; however, they have difficulty holding the information in mind while manipulating it, which is the hallmark of working memory (Swanson & Beebe-Frankenberger, 2004). In addition, EFs that involve strategy knowledge, concept formation, and inferential thinking contribute to successful math problem-solving skills. Processing speed (*Gs*) appears related to automaticity and *Glr* appears to be related to the fluid retrieval of math knowledge, such as memorized math facts (Flanagan et al., 2013). *Gs* and more specifically perceptual speed (*Gs*-P) contributes to math functioning across all ages. Visual processing or *Gv* appears related to math tasks that require higher level skills, such as geometry, but does not appear to be related to the performance of basic math skills (McGrew & Wendling, 2010).

The literature and research supporting neuropsychologically based interventions for mathematics are limited (Maricle et al., 2010). Collectively, the research supports the effectiveness of systematic and explicit methods of math instruction (Gersten, Chard, & Jayanthi, 2009). For children and adolescents with deficits in basic math skills, explicit instruction, demonstration, and guided practice, as well as strategies involving self-regulation and mnemonic devices, have been found useful. For example, constant time delay (CDT; Wolery, Anthony, Caldwell, Synder, & Morgante, 2002) is an instructional procedure designed to enable students to succeed through systematic, predictable, near-errorless instruction. Research also supports the use of problem-solving interventions and working memory interventions to address the underlying EFs involved in mathematics. Visual representation techniques such as Concrete-Representation-Abstract (CRA; Hudson & Miller, 2006) have been useful in developing conceptual and symbolic knowledge in mathematics. Finally, class-wide practices such as peer tutoring, peer assisted learning, and reciprocal peer tutoring have been found to be effective (Mascolo et al., 2014).

Writing

Written language is a highly sophisticated ability that requires the integration of a multitude of cognitive capacities (Feifer, 2011b). Writing proficiency is critical to long-term academic success. Writing involves planning, drafting, editing, and revising, and good writers employ many strategies to generate written text. The cognitive constructs of executive functioning are activated in writing; specifically working memory, attentional control, inhibition, decision-making, and self-monitoring. The capacity to sustain attention to a written language task allows the individual to retain and hold his/her thoughts long enough to transcribe them (Amtmann, Abbot, & Berninger, 2008). Working memory is also critical to language success in that the ability to recall spelling rules, remember grammatical procedures, maintain sentence structure and punctuate correctly, as well as retain thoughts and ideas in mind in order to arrange words syntactically and semantically are critical to effective writing. Written expression, more than any other academic skill places great demand on EFs (Feifer). Teaching an array of strategies aimed at increasing executive functioning coupled with strategies to assist the person to organize thoughts and ideas can improve academic performance in written language (Feifer & DeFina, 2002).

Writing is multidimensional, language-based, and developmental. Written language skills are the last to develop after language comprehension, speech, and reading. Although the neurological research on written language is limited, the anterior supermarginal gyrus at the intersection of the temporal-parietal lobes and the angular gyrus which is found near the posterior parietal-occipital interface have been implicated in different types of writing deficits (Feifer, 2011b). Similarly, there is limited research on the relationship of CHC abilities and written language skills. Berninger (2011), Flanagan et al. (2013), and Floyd, McGrew, and Evans (2008) report that written language requires the cognitive skills of *Gc*, *Gs*, *Gwm*, *Gf*, *Glr*, and *Ga*. Specifically, Berninger implicates *Gs* in the automaticity of written language production; *Ga* in the phonetic coding ability needed for spelling of sounds; and *Gwm* for the memory span required to hold information in mind while engaged in the writing process.

The WJ IV COG provides an SAC (Mather & Wendling, 2014) that encompasses the academic clusters of Written Language, Broad Written Language, and Written Expression. This SAC consists of Test 1: Oral Vocabulary, Test 5: Phonological Processing, Test 6: Story Recall, and Test 11: Number Pattern Matching. The WJ IV COG provides a second SAC for Basic Writing Skills. This SAC consists of Test 1: Oral Vocabulary, Test 3: Verbal Attention, Test 5: Phonological Processing, and Test 11: Number Pattern Matching.

Writing instruction that is explicit and teaches strategies that individuals can apply to self-regulate their writing have proven efficacious (Berninger, 2008; Graham & Perin, 2007; Hooper, Knuth, Yerby, Anderson, & Moore, 2009; Troia, 2009). Graham and Perin (2007) performed a meta-analysis of studies involving research on explicit instruction, instructional supports, and specific modes of instruction. The results of Graham and Perin's meta-analysis elucidated three conclusions. First, specific strategy instruction appears to be the most effective type of intervention. Simply teaching distinct or isolated skills will not be effective; rather, teaching the student how to implement a set of skills within the context of writing is needed. For example, teaching a COP strategy that involves first reviewing writing for capitalization errors (C), then reviewing for organizational deficits (O), and finally reviewing for punctuation (P). Self-Regulated Strategy Development (SRSD; Harris & Graham, 1999) is another example of an approach used to teach students to plan, draft, and revise text. It involves explicit strategy instruction and has been shown to have a moderate effect on the improvement of students' writing quality. Graham and Perin also advocate for early writing instruction, particularly the development of vocabulary, as well as the use of context and meaningfulness in writing.

NEUROCOGNITIVE CONSTRUCTS: EFS AND WORKING MEMORY

Three neurocognitive constructs or abilities are consistently implicated in overall academic achievement, and specifically in reading, writing, and mathematics. EFs, working memory, and attention are all reported to play a critical role in other cognitive abilities as well as in academic success. Miller (2013) labels these three constructs as cognitive facilitators/inhibitors, and posits that they play a role in the effective deployment of other cognitive skills and academic abilities. The reader is referred to recent literature for excellent summaries of the research regarding EFs and working memory, including Anderson, Jacobs, and Anderson (2008), Davis (2013), Dehn (2008), Goldstein, Naglieri, Princiotto, and Otero (2014), Hunter and Sparrow (2012), Mascolo et al. (2014), McCloskey and Perkins (2013), and Miller (2013). A brief review of the relationship of EF and working memory to cognitive assessment and the derivation of interventions to address deficits are provided here. However, due to the enormous amount of literature and research available regarding attention, and the lack of space within this chapter to distill such information into a more manageable form, the relationship of attention with academic skills is not addressed.

Executive Functions

Although the term EF has been in use for the past several decades, there is no universally accepted definition, or list of cognitive factors that comprise EFs. In addition, competing models or theories of executive functioning abound (Jurado & Roselli, 2007). EFs are a conglomeration of a wide range of cognitive skills and abilities including planning, working memory, attention, inhibition, self-monitoring, self-regulation, and initiation. This multidimensional and complex reciprocal nature of EF makes developing a mutually acceptable and cohesive definition challenging (Goldstein et al., 2014; Hughes, 2011; Hunter & Sparrow, 2012; Maricle et al., 2010). While there is general consensus in the research literature that EF consists of separate, but related cognitive processes, there is no consensus as to what comprises the components of EF. Despite the difficulties with definition, many school-based psychoeducational or neuropsychological evaluations now attempt to address some aspect of EF (Hunter & Sparrow, 2012), often treating EF as a singular cognitive capacity. Rather, EF is better viewed on a spectrum or as a continuum, and while a single skill area in EF may not show a deficit, the cumulative effect of multiple EF deficits can result in significant impairment. Like EF, executive dysfunction is not unitary.

Neuropsychological research has given us a greater understanding of the neural substrates and integrated circuitry involved in executive functioning. The processes of EF are associated with the anterior regions of the frontal lobe or prefrontal cortex (PFC); however, how exactly the frontal lobes support executive functioning remains controversial (Hughes & Graham, 2008; Jacobs, Harvey, & Anderson, 2011; Raposo, Mendes, & Marques, 2012; Tamnes et al., 2010). The PFC attends, integrates, formulates, executes, monitors, modifies, and judges. The two hallmark functions of the PFC and EF are cognitive flexibility and inhibition. The dorsolateral PFC (dPFC) primarily regulates the cognitive aspects of EFs involved in metacognition such as problem-solving, planning, and memory (Zilmer, Spiers, & Culbertson, 2008). Damage to the dPFC tends to result in deficits in attentional control, regulation, and integration. The orbitofrontal PFC and anterior cingulate circuit (ACC) have been implicated in the emotional–motivational aspects of executive functioning. The proximity and interconnectivity between the dorsolateral and orbitofrontal PFC and the ACC suggests that they interact to support EFs.

EFs are developmental, and there is an interaction between cortical development and the manifestation of EFs (Hunter, Edidin, & Hinkle, 2012; Maricle et al., 2010). Different aspects of EF appear to emerge at different stages of development, display different developmental trajectories, increase in sophistication over time, and reach maturation at different chronological ages. Given the lack of definitional congruence and the complexity of EFs, developmentally appropriate assessment becomes challenging. The integrative nature of frontal lobe functioning makes it difficult to parse out the specific cognitive functions being used in each task. Nearly all cognitive tasks require some type of EF skill, and it is difficult to isolate a single EF skill as these tasks are particularly vulnerable to task impurity. Additionally, environmental factors can influence EF performance, such as the structure of the testing situation, or fatigue. Finally, what constitutes a deficit in EF relative to typically developing peers, overall intellectual functioning, or neurocognitive modality, is unclear.

CHC theory does not view EFs as a cognitive construct or domain, rather it is viewed through the lens of cognitive processes such as *Gf* and *Gs*. The WJ IV COG does not directly assess EF, rather concerns about EF functioning need to be derived from the individual's performance on tasks of *Gf*, *Gwm*, and *Gs*.

The development and use of skills needed for reading, writing, and mathematics is heavily dependent upon the effective deployment of EFs (Jacobson & Mahone, 2011; McCloskey & Perkins, 2013), but the traditional definitions of academic achievement have not included a direct reference to EF (Salvia et al., 2012). Children and adolescents with EF deficits may present with academic, social, or behavioral difficulties such as the inability to maintain attention, control impulses, maintain effort, engage in mental planning and problem-solving, manage time, organize and execute tasks, or self-monitor. Recent research on the relationship of EF to reading (Gathercole, Alloway, Willis, & Adams, 2006; Menghini, Finzi, & Benassi, 2010; Velluntino, Fletcher, Snowling, & Scanlon, 2004) suggests EF accounts for additional variance in reading performance even when phonological correlates are accounted for, so that EF appears to exert a moderating effect on performance. Although EF correlates with math achievement, very little research is actually available. A few longitudinal studies have shown that EF performance is predictive of later math achievement (Bull, Espy, & Weibe, 2008; Clark, Pritchard, & Woodward, 2010; Johnson, Humphrey, Mellard, Woods, & Swanson, 2010). Only a few studies (Altemeier, Abbott, & Berninger, 2008; Altemeier, Jones, & Berninger, 2006) have addressed the relationship of EF with written language. These studies suggest that successful writing and the skills needed to produce a cohesive narrative require the higher order skills that comprise EF.

The majority of research on EF intervention is with adults, involves single case design, and focuses on recovery from neurological insult. Little research is available to support effective interventions for EF in children, although several recent publications purport to offer academic interventions for EF (Dawson & Guare, 2004, 2014; Slomine, Locascio, & Kramer, 2012). Slomine et al. provide a comprehensive review of the intervention research related to EF. Environmentally focused interventions where adults modify the environment to provide support, control, and reinforcement have the most support within the intervention literature. Environmental adjustments might include increasing the structure and routine of the classroom, providing clear classroom expectations, rules, and consequences, structuring tasks into manageable increments, providing explicit instruction, and teaching strategies for planning and problem-solving. Environmental management essentially replaces the role of the frontal lobes through external structure. Many school-wide programs teach cognitive awareness, metacognitive strategies, and EF strategies using direct instruction and apply techniques such as of cooperative learning and peer tutoring (Dawson & Guare, 2014; Goldstein et al., 2014; Metzler, 2014; Slomine et al., 2012).

Cognitive rehabilitation often takes the form of direct retraining of cognitive abilities where tasks are designed to provide practice in underlying cognitive abilities, such as attention or inhibition. Mahone and Slomine (2007) discuss teaching skills that are coached, rehearsed and practiced within the environment in which they are to be performed. A promising approach is self-instructional training where children are taught self-talk and self-regulation. A specific strategy with some evidence for effectiveness is a program by Graham and Harris (2003) called SRSD (Feeney & Ylvisaker, 2008). Other programs with some research basis include Sohlberg and Mateer's (1987) Attention Process Training (APT), Butter and Copeland's (2002) Cognitive Remediation Program, COGMED, Captain's Log, and Destination Reading and Math (Rabiner, Murray, Skinner, & Mahone, 2010).

Working Memory

Working Memory has been one of the most studied cognitive constructs. Historically, working memory has been conceptualized as an active memory system that is responsible for the temporary maintenance and processing of information (Dehn, 2008). Working memory is the ability to hold information in mind and manipulate it for brief periods of time during complex cognitive tasks. Theoretical models of working memory proliferate and differ in their views of the nature, structure, and function of working memory (Maricle, Miller, & Mortimer, 2011). It is difficult to define working memory and disentangle it from related cognitive processes such as attention, processing speed or reasoning. Working memory is often subsumed under the umbrella of EFs. Regardless of how it is classified, working memory is a major cognitive process underlying thinking and learning. A significant amount of research on the neurobiology of working memory is available. Neuroimaging research has found common and unique brain regions responsible for working memory performance. For the most part, the brain areas implicated in memory are widespread and dependent on the type of memory being assessed. Memory appears to be a parallel distributed process with separate systems for verbal and visual modalities (Semrud-Clikeman & Teeter-Ellison, 2009). Working memory has been linked to the dPFC and ventrolateral PFC, which appear to be responsible for the monitoring and maintenance of information. Most imaging research suggests that increased activation in the PFC is associated with increasing working memory demand (Fassbender et al., 2011; Marvel & Desmond, 2010). Additionally, the hippocampus has been implicated in memory storage and the retrieval of information from the memory systems.

The WJ IV COG directly measures short-term working memory (*Gwm*) and long-term storage and retrieval (*Glr*). On the WJ IV COG short-term working memory (*Gwm*) was reconceptualized from its previous incarnation as *Gsm* on the WJ III, and subtests were modified and changed to reflect this refined conceptualization. The authors note that *Gwm* is an aspect of cognitive efficiency and that it reflects the capacity to maintain information and to manipulate information, as well as the efficiency of attentional control during the process (Mather & Wendling, 2014). The *Gwm* cluster consists of Test 3: Verbal Attention and Test 10: Numbers Reversed. Verbal Attention is a new subtest that requires the examinee to listen to an intermingled series of animals and digits, and then answer a specific question regarding the sequence. It is purported to be a measure of controlled EF or attentional control. Numbers Reversed is a classic working memory task and was retained from the previous version. The Auditory Working Memory test from the WJ III was renamed Object Number Sequencing and placed in the extended battery as an additional test measuring short-term auditory working memory. Object Number Sequencing is classified as a measure of working memory capacity within the *Gwm* CHC factor. The WJ IV COG long-term storage and retrieval factor (*Glr*) was also reconfigured. The Story Recall test was transferred to the WJ IV COG from the WJ III ACH and Visual–Auditory Learning was relegated to the extended battery. Finally, the WJ IV COG offers two clinical clusters or narrow ability clusters that could be related to *Gwm*, Auditory Memory Span and Cognitive Efficiency. Auditory Memory Span encompasses Memory for Words from the WJ IV COG and Sentence Repetition for the WJ IV OL. Cognitive Efficiency combines *Gwm* and *Gs* using the Verbal Attention, Letter-Pattern Matching, Numbers Reversed and Number Pattern Matching subtests. Research regarding these reconceptualized and reconfigured WJ IV factors is now needed.

A half century of psychological and educational research has provided solid evidence for the relationship between memory skills, such as short-term or immediate memory capacity, working memory, long-term storage and retrieval, and learning (Dehn, 2008; Entwhistle & Shinaver, 2014; Gathercole, Lamont, & Alloway, 2006; Miller & Blasik, 2010). Working memory is the gate-keeper of learning; everything that is learned and remembered must pass through working memory. Therefore, it stands to reason that working memory capacity and efficiency determines the extent and rate of learning. Relationships between working memory and specific areas of academic achievement are well established (Alloway, 2009; Carretti, Borella, Cornoldi, & De Beni, 2009; Swanson & Beebe-Frankenberger, 2004; Swanson, Jerman, & Zheng, 2008; Swanson et al., 2009), but the effectiveness of working memory interventions at improving academic achievement has not been widely researched.

Glisky and Glisky (2002) summarize evidence-based memory interventions currently being used in practice. Interventions are organized into four groups: practice and rehearsal, mnemonic strategies, environmental supports or external aids, and domain specific for learning. Practice and rehearsal interventions are exemplified by the idea of spiral curriculum wherein ideas are revisited repeatedly. Glisky and Glisky note that practice, review, and specific instruction in memory strategies such as mnemonics can drastically improve performance. Dehn (2014), DeJong (2010), and Elliot, Gathercole, Alloway, Holmes, and Kirkwood (2010) all recommend reducing cognitive load (amount of time and effort required to process information) as an effective way to support working memory in the classroom. Methods for reducing cognitive load included manipulating how information or materials are presented and taught, adapting the time needed for task completion (e.g., self-pacing), changing the extent or amount of external structure, using effective teaching strategies such as rehearsal, review, chunking, and mnemonics, and/or providing systematic structured teaching such as with direct instruction.

Several research studies have examined the effects of working memory training on cognition, but only a few have examined the transfer of such training to academic performance. Morrison and Chein (2011) suggest that working memory training can improve working memory capacity and shows promise for transfer to other tasks beyond what was manipulated in their particular study. Several studies (Diamond & Lee, 2011; Holmes, Gathercole, & Dunning, 2009; Klingberg, Forssberg, & Westerberg, 2002; Thorell et al., 2009) have utilized computerized adaptive working memory tasks (COGMED) to demonstrate that cognitive training can be used to improve working memory and reasoning. Entwhistle and Shinaver (2014) provide a good review of the COGMED research. Additionally, two studies reported working memory training having a positive effect on reading comprehension (Dahlin, 2010) and mathematics (Holmes et al., 2009).

SUMMARY AND CONCLUSIONS

The WJ IV provides the professional with the means to identify cognitive strengths and weaknesses, to ascertain academic skills and deficits, and to link cognitive performance with academic performance. Furthermore, the WJ IV has attempted to link cognitive and academic performance to instruction with the new *WJ IV Interpretation and Instructional Interventions Program* (WIIIP™; Schrank & Wendling, 2015). According to its authors, the WIIIP™ has been designed to link assessment data with evidence-based instruction and contains over 500 research-based interventions.

In reality, although the data supporting the link between cognitive performance and academic difficulties are strong, the data supporting interventions used to remediate cognitive skills and the corresponding improvement of academic achievement is still very limited. Still, research examining the relationships between cognitive intervention or remediation and academic outcomes is beginning to emerge. For instance, promising research by Shaywitz (2003) demonstrated that neuroimaging could be used to document neurological changes in the brain of a child with a reading disability subsequent to interventions in reading. However, considerably more research is needed. Even with evidence supporting the connection between the assessment process and interventions, the selection of a particular intervention or teaching strategy should not be based on the assessment data alone (Shapiro, 2011). Best practice would encourage using multiple sources of data to select and tailor instructional practices and interventions for each individual child.

REFERENCES

Alloway, T. (2009). Working memory but not IQ predicts subsequent learning in children with learning difficulties. *European Journal of Psychological Assessment, 25*(2), 92–98.

Altemeier, L. E., Abbott, R. D., & Berninger, V. W. (2008). Executive functions for reading and writing in typical literacy development and dyslexia. *Journal of Clinical Experimental Neuropsychology, 30*, 588–606.

Altemeier, L. E., Jones, J., Abbott, R. D., & Berninger, V. W. (2006). Executive functions in becoming writing readers and reading writers: Note taking and report writing in third and fifth grades. *Developmental Neuropsychology, 29*(1), 161–173.

Amtmann, D., Abbott, R., & Beringer, V. (2008). Identifying and predicting classes of response to explicit, phonological spelling instruction during independent composing. *Journal of Learning Disabilities, 41*(3), 218–234.

Anderson, V., Jacobs, R., & Anderson, P. J. (2008). *Executive functions and the frontal lobes: A lifespan perspective*. NY: Taylor & Francis.

Bergquist, T. E., & Malec, J. F. (2002). Neuropsychological assessment for treatment planning and research. In P. J. Eslinger (Ed.), *Neuropsychological interventions: Clinical research and practice* (pp. 38–58). NY: Guilford Press.

Berninger, V. (2008). Evidenced based written language instruction during early and middle childhood. In R. Morris & N. Mather (Eds.), *Evidenced based interventions for students with learning and behavioral challenges* (pp. 215–235). NY: Lawrence Erlbaum Associates.

Berninger, V. (2011). Evidenced-based differential diagnosis and treatment of reading disability with and without comorbidities in oral language, writing, and math. In D. P. Flanagan & V. C. Alfonso (Eds.), *Essentials of specific learning disability identification* (pp. 203–232). Hoboken, NY: John Wiley & Sons.

Bull, R., Espy, K. A., & Weibe, S. A. (2008). Short-term memory, working memory, and executive functioning in preschoolers: Longitudinal predictors of mathematical achievement at age 7 years. *Developmental Neuropsychology, 33*(3), 205–208.

Butter, R. W., & Copeland, D. R. (2002). Attentional processes and their remediation in children treated for cancer: A literature review and the development of a therapeutic approach. *Journal of the International Neuropsychological Society, 8*(1), 115–124.

Butterworth, B. (2008). Developmental dyscalculia. In J. Reed & J. Warner-Rogers (Eds.), *Child neuropsychology: Concepts, theory and practice* (pp. 357–374). Malden, MA: Wiley- Blackwell.

Carretti, B., Borella, E., Cornoldi, C., & De Beni, R. (2009). Role of working memory in explaining the performance of individuals with specific reading comprehension difficulties: A meta-analysis. *Learning and Individual Differences, 19*(2), 245–251.

Cicerone, K. D., Dahlberg, C., Malec, J. F., Langenbahn, D. M., Felicetti, T., Kniepp, S., et al. (2005). Evidenced based cognitive rehabilitation: Updated review of the literature from 1998–2002. *Archives of Physical Medicine and Rehabilitation, 86*(8), 1681–1691.

Clark, C. A. C., Pritchard, V. E., & Woodward, L. J. (2010). Preschool executive functioning abilities predict early mathematics achievement. *Developmental Psychology, 46*(5), 1176–1191.

Dahlin, K. (2010). Effects of working memory training on reading in children with special needs. *Reading and Writing, 24*(4), 479–491.

Davis, A. (2013). *Handbook of pediatric neuropsychology.* NY: Springer.

Dawson, P., & Guare, R. (2004). *Executive skills in children and adolescents: A practical guide to assessment and intervention.* NY: Guilford.

Dawson, P., & Guare, R. (2014). Interventions to promote executive development in children and adolescents. In S. Goldstein & J. A. Naglieri (Eds.), *Handbook of executive functioning* (pp. 427–443). NY: Springer.

Deary, I. J., Strand, S., Smith, P., & Fernandes, C. (2007). Intelligence and educational achievement. *Intelligence, 35*(1), 13–21.

Dehn, M. J. (2008). *Working memory and academic learning: Assessment and intervention.* NY: John Wiley & Sons.

Dehn, M. J. (2014). Supporting and strengthening working memory in the classroom to enhance executive functioning. In S. Goldstein & J. A. Naglieri (Eds.), *The handbook of executive functioning* (pp. 495–507). NY: Springer.

DeJong, T. (2010). Cognitive load theory, educational research, and instructional design: Some food for thought. *Instructional Science, 38*(2), 105–134.

Diamond, A., & Lee, K. (2011). Intervention shown to aid executive function development in children 4–12 years old. *Science, 333*(6045), 959–964.

Elliot, J. G., Gathercole, S. E., Alloway, T. P., Holmes, J., & Kirkwood, H. (2010). An evaluation of a classroom-based intervention to help overcome working memory difficulties and improve long-term academic achievement. *Journal of Comparative Education and Psychology, 9*(3), 237–250.

Englemann, S., & Carninc, D. (1982). *Theory of instruction.* NY: Irvington.

Entwhistle, P. C., & Shinaver, C. (2014). Working memory training and COGMED. In S. Goldstein & J. A. Naglieri (Eds.), *The handbook of executive functioning.* NY: Springer.

Eslinger, P. J., & Oliveri, M. V. (2002). Approaching interventions clinically and scientifically. In P. J. Eslinger (Ed.), *Neuropsychological interventions: Clinical research and practice* (pp. 3–15). NY: Guilford Press.

Fassbender, C., Schweiter, J. B., Cortes, C. R., Tagaments, M. A., Windsor, T. A., Reeves, G. M., et al. (2011). Working memory in ADHD is characterized by a lack of specialization of brain function. *PLoS One, 6*(11), 1–11.

Feeney, T., & Ylvisaker, M. (2008). Context-sensitive cognitive-behavioral supports for young children with TBI: A second replication study. *Journal of Positive Behavior Interventions, 10*(2), 115–128.

Feifer, S. G. (2011a). How specific learning disabilities manifest in reading. In D. P. Flanagan & V. C. Alfonso (Eds.), *Essentials of specific learning disability identification.* Hoboken, NY: John Wiley & Sons.

Feifer, S. G. (2011b). The neuropsychology of written language disorders. In A. S. Davis (Ed.), *Handbook of pediatric neuropsychology*. NY: Springer.

Feifer, S. G., & DeFina, P. D. (2002). *The neuropsychology of written language disorders: Diagnosis and intervention*. Middletown, MD: School Neuropsych Press.

Flanagan, D. P., & Alfonso, V. C. (2011). *Essentials of specific learning disability identification*. Hoboken, NJ: John Wiley & Sons.

Flanagan, D. P., Alfonso, V. C., & Dixon, S. G. (2014). Cross battery approach to the assessment of executive functions. In S. Goldstein & J. A. Naglieri (Eds.), *Handbook of executive functioning* (pp. 379–409). NY: Springer.

Flanagan, D. P., Alfonso, V. C., & Mascolo, J. T. (2011). A CHC-based operational definition of SLD: Integrating multiple data sources and multiple data-gathering methods. In D. P. Flanagan & V. C. Alfonso (Eds.), *Essentials of specific learning disability identification* (pp. 233–298). Hoboken, NJ: John Wiley & Sons.

Flanagan, D. P., Ortiz, S. O., & Alfonso, V. C. (2013). *Essentials of cross battery assessment* (3rd ed.). Hoboken, NJ: John Wiley & Sons.

Flanagan, D. P., Ortiz, S. O., Alfonso, V. C., & Mascolo, J. T. (2006). *Achievement test desk reference: A guide to learning disability identification* (2nd ed.). Hoboken, NJ: Wiley.

Fletcher, J. M., Lyon, G., Fuchs, L. S., & Barnes, M. A. (2007). *Learning disabilities: From identification to intervention*. NY: Guilford.

Floyd, R. G., Evans, J. J., & McGrew, K. S. (2003). Relations between measures of Cattell–Horn–Carroll (CHC) cognitive abilities and mathematics achievement across the school age years. *Psychology in the Schools*, *40*(2), 155–177.

Floyd, R. G., McGrew, K. S., & Evans, J. J. (2008). The relative contributions of the CHC cognitive abilities in explaining writing achievement during childhood and adolescence. *Psychology in the Schools*, *45*(2), 132–144.

Gathercole, S. E., Alloway, T. P., Willis, C., & Adams, N. M. (2006). Working memory in children with reading disabilities. *Journal of Experimental Child Psychology*, *93*(3), 265–281.

Gathercole, S. E., Lamont, E., & Alloway, T. P. (2006). Working memory in the classroom. In S. Pickering (Ed.), *Working memory and education*. Elsevier Press.

Geary, D. C., Hoard, M. K., & Bailey, D. H. (2011). How SLD manifests in mathematics. In D. P. Flanagan & V. C. Alfonso (Eds.), *Essentials of specific learning disability identification* (pp. 43–64). Hoboken, NJ: John Wiley & Sons.

Geary, D. C., Hoard, M. K., Byrd-Green, J., Nugent, L., & Numtee, C. (2007). Cognitive mechanisms underlying achievement deficits in children with mathematical learning disabilities. *Child Development*, *78*, 1343–1459.

Gersten, R., Chard, D., & Jayanthi, M. (2009). Mathematics instruction for students with learning disabilities: A meta-analysis of instructional components. *Review of Educational Research*, *79*(3), 1202–1242.

Gettinger, M., & Doescher Hurd, H. (2011). Developing and implementing evidenced-based academic interventions. In A. S. Davis (Ed.), *Handbook of pediatric neuropsychology*. NY: Springer.

Glisky, E. L., & Glisky, M. L. (2002). Learning and memory impairments. In P. J. Eslinger (Ed.), *Neuropsychological interventions: Clinical research and practice*. NY: Guilford.

Goldstein, S. J., Naglieri, J. A., Princiotto, D., & Otero, T. M. (2014). Introduction: A history of executive functioning as a theoretical and clinical construct. In S. Goldstein & J. A. Naglieri (Eds.), *The handbook of executive functioning* (pp. 3–12). NY: Springer.

Graham, S., & Harris, K. R. (2003). Students with learning disabilities and the process of writing: A meta-analysis of SRSD studies. In H. L. Swanson, K. R. Harris, & S. Graham (Eds.), *Handbook of learning disabilities* (pp. 323–344). NY: Guilford.

Graham, S., & Perin, D. (2007). A meta-analysis of writing instruction for adolescent students. *Journal of Educational Psychology*, *99*(3), 445–476.

Harris, K. R., & Graham, S. (1999). Programmatic intervention research: Illustrations from the evolution of self-regulated strategy development. *Learning Disability Quarterly*, *22*(4), 251–262.

Holmes, J., Gathercole, S. E., & Dunning, D. L. (2009). Adaptive training leads to sustained enhancement of poor working memory in children. *Developmental Science*, *12*(4), 9–15.

Hooper, S., Knuth, S., Yerby, D., Anderson, K., & Moore, C. (2009). A review of science supported writing instruction with implementation in mind. In S. Rosenfield & V. Berninger (Eds.), *Implementing evidenced-based interventions in school settings* (pp. 49–83). NY: Oxford University Press.

Hudson, P., & Miller, S. P. (2006). *Designing and implementing mathematics instruction for students with diverse learning needs*. Boston, MA: Allyn & Bacon.

Hughes, C. (2011). Changes and challenges in 20 years of research into the development of executive functions. *Infant Child Development*, *20*(3), 251–271.

Hughes, C., & Graham, A. (2008). Executive functions and development. In J. Reed & J. Warner-Rogers (Eds.), *Child neuropsychology: Concepts, theory and practice*. NY: Wiley-Blackwell.

Hunter, S. J., Edidin, J. P., & Hinkle, C. D. (2012). The developmental neurobiology of executive functions. In S. J. Hunter & E. P. Sparrow (Eds.), *Executive function and dysfunction: Identification, assessment and treatment* (pp. 17–36). Cambridge, UK: Cambridge University Press.

Hunter, S. J., & Sparrow, E. P. (2012). *Executive function and dysfunction: Identification, assessment and treatment*. Cambridge, UK: Cambridge University Press.

Jacobs, R., Harvey, A. S., & Anderson, V. (2011). Are executive skills primarily mediated by the prefrontal cortex in childhood? Examination of focal brain lesions in childhood. *Cortex*, *47*(7), 808–824.

Jacobson, L. A., & Mahone, E. M. (2011). Educational implications of executive dysfunction. In S. J. Hunter & E. P. Sparrow (Eds.), *Executive function and dysfunction: Identification, a assessment and treatment*. Cambridge, UK: Cambridge University Press.

Johnson, E. S., Humphrey, M., Mellard, D. F., Woods, K., & Swanson, H. (2010). Cognitive processing deficits and students with specific learning disabilities: A selective meta-analysis of the literature. *Learning Disability Quarterly*, *33*(1), 3–18.

Joseph, L. M. (2006). *Understanding, assessing, and intervening on reading problems: A guide for school psychologists and other educational consultants*. Bethesda, MD: NASP.

Jurado, M. B., & Roselli, M. (2007). The elusive nature of executive functions: A review of our current understanding. *Neuropsychology Review*, *17*(3), 213–233.

Klingberg, T., Forssberg, H., & Westerberg, H. (2002). Increased brain activity in frontal and parietal cortex underlies the development of visual–spatial working memory capacity in childhood. *Journal of Cognitive Neuroscience*, *14*(1), 1–10.

Laatsch, L., Harrington, D., Hotz, G., Marcantuono, J., Mozzoni, M. P., Walsh, V., et al. (2007). An evidenced based review of cognitive and behavioral rehabilitation treatment studies in children with acquired brain injury. *Journal of Head Trauma Rehabilitation*, *22*(4), 248–256.

Limond, J., & Leeke, R. (2005). Practitioner review: Cognitive rehabilitation for children with acquired brain injury. *Journal of Child Psychology and Psychiatry*, *46*(4), 339–352. http://dx.doi.org/10.1111/j.1469-7610.2004.00397.

Lubinski, D. (2010). Spatial ability and STEM: A sleeping giant for talent identification and development. *Personality and Individual Differences*, *49*(4), 344–351.

Mahone, E. M., & Slomine, B. S. (2007). Managing dysexecutive disorders. In S. J. Hunter & J. Donders (Eds.), *Pediatric neuropsychological interventions: A critical review of science & practice*. London: Cambridge University Press.

Maricle, D. E., Johnson, W., & Avirett, W. (2010). Assessing and intervening in children with executive function disorders. In D. C. Miller (Ed.), *Best practices in school neuropsychology: Guidelines for effective practice, assessment, and evidenced-based intervention* (pp. 521–549). Hoboken, NJ: Wiley & Sons, Inc.

Maricle, D. E., Miller, D. C., & Mortimer, J. (2011). Memory tests in pediatric neuropsychology. In A. S. Davis (Ed.), *Handbook of pediatric neuropsychology* (pp. 275–292). NY: Springer.

Maricle, D. E., Psimas-Fraser, L., Muenke, R. C., & Miller, D. C. (2010). Assessing and intervening with children with math disorders. In D. C. Miller (Ed.), *Best practices in school neuropsychology: Guidelines for effective practice, assessment, and evidenced- based intervention* (pp. 521–549). Hoboken, NJ: Wiley & Sons.

Marvel, C. L., & Desmond, J. E. (2010). Functional topography of the cerebellum in verbal working memory. *Neuropsychology Review, 20*(3), 271–279.

Mascolo, J., Flanagan, D. P., & Alfonso, V. C. (2014). A systematic method of analyzing assessment results for tailoring interventions (SMAAARTI). In J. T. Mascolo, V. C. Alfonso, & D. P. Flanagan (Eds.), *Essentials of planning, selecting, and tailoring interventions for unique learners*. Hoboken, NJ: John Wiley & Sons.

Mather, N., & Jaffe, L. E. (2015). *Woodcock–Johnson IV: Reports, recommendations, and strategies*. Hoboken, NJ: John Wiley & Sons.

Mather, N., & Wendling, B. J. (2014). *Examiner's manual. Woodcock–Johnson IV Tests of Achievement*. Rolling Meadows, IL: Riverside.

Mather, N., & Wendling, B. J. (2015). *Essentials of WJ IV tests of achievement*. Hoboken, NJ: John Wiley & Sons.

McCloskey, G., & Perkins, L. A. (2013). *Essentials of executive functions assessment*. Hoboken, NJ: John Wiley & Sons.

McGrew, K. S., LaForte, E. M., & Schrank, F. A. (2014). *WJ IV technical manual*. Rolling Meadows, IL: Riverside.

McGrew, K. S., & Wendling, B. J. (2010). Cattell–Horn Carroll cognitive-achievement relations: What we have learned from the past 20 years of research. *Psychology in the Schools, 47*(7), 651–675.

Menghini, D., Finzi, A., Benassi, R., et al. (2010). Different underlying neurocognitive deficits in developmental dyslexia: A comparative study. *Neuropsychologia, 48*(4), 863–872.

Metzler, L. (2014). Teaching executive functioning processes: Promoting metacognition, strategy use, and effort. In S. Goldstein & J. A. Naglieri (Eds.), *The handbook of executive functioning* (pp. 445–473). NY: Springer.

Miller, D. C. (2013). *Essentials of school neuropsychological assessment* (2nd ed.). Hoboken, NJ: John Wiley & Sons.

Miller, J. A., & Blasik, J. L. (2010). Assessing and intervening with children with memory and learning disorders. In D. C. Miller (Ed.), *Best practices in school neuropsychology: Guidelines for effective practice, assessment, and evidence-based intervention*. NJ: John Wiley & Sons.

Morrison, A. B., & Chein, J. M. (2011). Does working memory training work? The promise and challenges of enhancing cognition training of working memory. *Psychonomic Bulletin and Review, 18*(1), 46–60.

Muter, V., & Snowling, M. (1998). Concurrent and longitudinal predictors of reading: The role of metalinguistic and short-term memory skills. *Reading Research Quarterly, 33*(4), 320–337.

National Mathematics Advisory Panel, (2008). *Report of task group on instructional practices*. Washington, DC: US Department of Education.

National Reading Panel, (2000). *Teaching children to read*. Washington, DC: National Institute of Child Health and Development.

Ponsford, J. (2004). *Cognitive and behavioral rehabilitation: From neurobiology to clinical practice*. New York, NY: Guilford Press.

Rabiner, D. L., Murray, D. W., Skinner, A. T., & Mahone, P. S. (2010). A randomized trial of two promising computer-based interventions for students with attention difficulties. *Journal of Abnormal Child Psychology, 38*(1), 131–142.

Raposo, A., Mendes, M., & Marques, J. F. (2012). The hierarchical organization of semantic memory: Executive function in the processing of superordinate concepts. *NeuroImage, 59*, 1870–1878.

Salvia, J., Ysseldyke, J., & Bolt, S. (2012). *Assessment in special education*. NY: Wadsworth.

Schneider, W. J., & McGrew, K. S. (2012). The Cattell–Horn–Carroll model of intelligence. In D. Flanagan & P. Harrison (Eds.), *Contemporary intellectual assessment: Theories, tests and issues* (pp. 99–144) (3rd ed.). NY: Guilford.

Schneider, W. J., & McGrew, K. S. (2013). Individual differences in the ability to process information. In B. J. Irby, G. Brown, R. Lara-Alecio, & S. Jackson (Eds.), *The handbook of educational theories* (pp. 767–782). Charlotte, NC: Information Age Publishing, Inc.

Schrank, F. A., McGrew, K. S., & Mather, N. (2014a). *Woodcock–Johnson IV*. Rolling Meadows, IL: Riverside.

Schrank, F. A., Mather, N., & McGrew, K. S. (2014b). *Woodcock–Johnson IV tests of oral language*. Rolling Meadows, IL: Riverside.

Schrank, F. A., & Wendling, B. J. (2015). *WJ IV interpretation and instructional interventions program (WIIIP)*. Rolling Meadows, IL: Riverside.

Semrud-Clikeman, M. (2001). *Traumatic brain injury in children and adolescents: Assessment and intervention*. London, UK: The Guilford Press.

Semrud-Clikeman, M., & Teeter-Ellison, P. A. (2009). *Child neuropsychology: Assessment and interventions for neurodevelopmental disorders* (2nd ed.). NY: Springer.

Shapiro, E. S. (2011). *Academic skills problems* (4th ed.). NY: Guilford.

Shaywitz, B., Skudlarski, P., Holahan, J., Marchione, K., Constable, R., Fulbright, R., et al. (2007). Age-related changes in reading systems of dyslexic children. *Annals of Neurology, 61*, 363–370.

Shaywitz, S. E. (2003). *Overcoming dyslexia: New and complete science-based program for r = reading problems at any level*. NY: Vintage Books.

Shaywitz, S. E., & Shaywitz, B. A. (2011). Dyslexia. In A. S. Davis (Ed.), *Handbook of pediatric neuropsychology*. NY: Springer.

Shinn, M. R., & Walker, H. M. (2010). *Interventions for academic and behavior problems in a three-tier model including RTI*. Bethesda, MD: NASP.

Slomine, B., Locascio, G., & Kramer, M. (2012). Empirical status regarding the remediation of executive skills. In S. J. Hunter & E. P. Sparrow (Eds.), *Executive function and dysfunction: Identification, assessment and treatment*. Cambridge, UK: Cambridge University Press.

Sohlberg, M. M., & Mateer, C. A. (1987). Effectiveness of an attention training program. *Journal of Clinical and Experimental Neuropsychology, 9*(2), 117–130.

Swanson, H. L. (1992). Generality and modifiability of working memory skilled and less skilled readers. *Journal of Educational Psychology, 84*(4), 473–488.

Swanson, H. L., & Beebe-Frankenberger, M. (2004). The relationship between working memory and mathematical problem solving in children at risk and not at risk for serious math difficulties. *Journal of Educational Psychology, 96*(3), 471–491.

Swanson, H. L., Harris, K. R., & Graham, S. (2013). *Handbook of learning disabilities* (2nd ed.). NY: Guilford.

Swanson, H. L., Jerman, O., & Zheng, X. (2008). Growth in working memory and mathematical problem-solving in children at risk and not at risk for math disabilities. *Journal of Educational Psychology, 100*(2), 343–379.

Swanson, H. L., Zheng, X., & Jerman, O. (2009). Working memory, short-term memory, and reading disabilities: A selective meta-analysis of the literature. *Journal of Learning Disabilities, 42*(3), 260–287.

Tamnes, C. K., Ostby, Y., Walhovd, K. B., Westlye, L. T., Due-Tonnessen, P., & Fjell, A. M. (2010). Neuroanatomical correlates of executive functions in children and adolescents: A magnetic resonance imaging (MRI) study of cortical thickness. *Neuropsychologia, 48*(9), 2496–2508.

Thorell, L. B., Lindquist, S., Bergman, S., Nutley, S., Bohlin, G., & Klingberg, T. (2009). Training and transfer effects of executive functions in preschool children. *Developmental Science, 12*(1), 106–113.

Troia, G. (2009). *Writing instruction and assessment for struggling writers: From theory to evidenced-based practices.* NY: Guilford.

Velluntino, F. R., Fletcher, J. M., Snowling, M. J., & Scanlon, D. M. (2004). Specific reading disability: What we have learned in the past four decades. *Journal of Child Psychology and Psychiatry, 45*(1), 2–40.

Velluntino, F. R., Scanlon, D. M., Sipay, E. R., Small, S. G., Pratt, A., & Chen, R. (1996). Cognitive profiles of difficult to remediate and readily remediated poor readers: Early intervention as a vehicle for distinguishing between cognitive and experiential deficits as basic causes of specific reading disability. *Journal of Educational Psychology, 88*(4), 601–638.

Wai, J., Lubinski, D., & Benbow, C. P. (2009). Spatial ability for STEM domains: Aligning over fifty years of cumulative psychological knowledge solidifies its importance. *Journal of Educational Psychology, 101*, 817–835.

Wendling, B., & Mather, N. (2008). *Essentials of evidenced-based academic interventions.* NY: Wiley.

Wolery, M., Anthony, L., Caldwell, N. K., Snyder, E. D., & Morgante, J. D. (2002). Embedding and distributing constant time delay in circle time and transitions. *Topics in Early Childhood Special Education, 22*(1), 14–25.

Woodcock, R. W., McGrew, K. S., & Mather, N. (2001). *Woodcock–Johnson IIII.* Rolling Meadows, IL: Riverside.

Zilmer, E. A., Spiers, M. V., & Culbertson, W. C. (2008). *Principles of neuropsychology* (2nd ed.). Belmont, CA: Thomson.

Chapter 6

Instructional Implications from the Woodcock–Johnson IV Tests of Achievement

Nancy Mather[1] and Barbara J. Wendling[2]

[1]*Department of Disability and Psychoeducational Studies, University of Arizona, Tucson, AZ, USA*
[2]*Independent Consultant, Dallas, TX, USA*

Evaluation should go hand-in-hand with instruction.

(Kirk, Kleibhan, & Lerner, 1978, p. 155)

The central purposes of an educational evaluation are to address and answer the referral question or questions in order to create positive changes in a student's school and home environment. Unfortunately, the emphasis on scores and eligibility criteria has led some practitioners away from using tests as tools for instructional planning or even taking the time to conduct a careful analysis of patterns and errors. Some seem to have forgotten that the central purpose for diagnosing learning difficulties is for treatment, not for classification (Kirk, 1975). It is well known that the earlier struggling students are identified, the better; the longer timely interventions are delayed, the greater the impact on the individual (Snowling & Hulme, 2011).

Standardized tests, such as the Woodcock–Johnson IV (WJ IV; Schrank, McGrew, & Mather, 2014a), are often the beginning of the diagnostic process. Once areas of instructional need have been clearly identified, a more in-depth assessment is often performed, including criterion-referenced testing, curriculum-based measurements, and informal analyses of work samples. Even though standardized test results may need to be supplemented, considerable information can be derived from these tests. Thus, the central purpose of this chapter is to explore instructional implications that can be derived from WJ IV Tests of Achievement (WJ IV ACH; Schrank, Mather, & McGrew, 2014a) results. Although the focus of this chapter is on the interpretive features of the WJ IV ACH, some information is incorporated from the WJ IV Tests of Cognitive

WJ IV Clinical Use and Interpretation. DOI: http://dx.doi.org/10.1016/B978-0-12-802076-0.00006-2
151

Abilities (WJ IV COG; Schrank, McGrew, & Mather, 2014b) and the WJ IV Tests of Oral Language (WJ IV OL; Schrank, Mather, & McGrew, 2014b) that can assist with the formulation of diagnostic hypotheses.

This chapter begins with a discussion of the importance of qualitative observations and quantitative information, as well as consideration of a student's present instructional levels. Next, an explanation is presented illustrating how patterns of cluster and test scores and a comparison of oral language abilities and/or academic knowledge to various areas of achievement can help inform instruction. Then, the relationship between various cognitive factors and academic performance is discussed. Finally, performance and instructional implications are addressed within three broad areas: academic skills, academic fluency, and academic applications. A case study is presented to illustrate how these three clusters can help identify a student's instructional needs.

GENERAL CONSIDERATIONS

A skilled clinician can obtain a variety of instructional implications by evaluating an individual's performance on the WJ IV. Understanding the instructional implications from this battery of tests requires interpreting the obtained scores within the context of information gathered through a review of records, interviews, and observations. Essentially, all the gathered information is then woven into a tapestry that integrates linguistic and cultural factors, educational history and opportunities, genetic factors and family support, prior interventions, social economic status, and emotional and affective factors.

Qualitative Observations and Quantitative Information

Clinical evaluations involve information obtained from interviews and direct observations as well as test scores. Often, the manner in which an individual attempts a task is as important as the resultant score. Two individuals can obtain identical scores but one's performance is indicative of a problem, whereas the other's performance is not. Each test in the WJ IV ACH Standard Battery (Tests 1–11) includes a qualitative observation checklist to help document how the examinee performed on the task. Further, each test record has a Test Session Observations Checklist to gather additional qualitative information about the examinee. In addition, a careful analysis of responses to items often leads to insights regarding intervention. For example, Jessica, a 9-year-old girl, made errors on the Calculation and Math Facts Fluency tests on most of the problems involving a zero (0), such as $3-0=0$. Clearly, Jessica needs to review the concept of zero. Kevin, an eighth-grade student, missed many items involving medial vowel sounds on Word Attack and Spelling of Sounds. One possible educational recommendation is to reteach Kevin these sound-symbol correspondences and then provide practice in reading and spelling.

Although test scores are an aid to interpretation, they cannot replace clinical judgment or the inferences obtained through error analysis and careful observation. Normative scores, such as standard scores (SSs) and percentile ranks, provide peer comparison information (i.e., group standing, rank order) which is only part of the performance picture. Two other types of scores on the WJ IV have particular relevance to instruction: the Relative Proficiency Index (RPI) and the Instructional Zone.

Relative Proficiency Index. Unlike peer comparison scores, the RPI does not indicate where a person stands within a norm group. It provides a statement about the individual's functionality, or quality of performance, on a task. The RPI ranges from 0/90 to 100/90 and compares the individual's performance to average age- or grade-mates who demonstrate 90% proficiency on the task. For individuals with below average proficiency on a task, the RPI describes the degree of impairment. For example, if a student has an RPI of 45/90 on the Spelling test, it would indicate that the student is about half as proficient on this task as average age- or grade-mates. In addition to describing the individual's performance on the task, the RPI predicts how the individual will perform on similar tasks. Sheila, a third-grade student, obtained an RPI of 75/90 on the WJ IV ACH Spelling test. This score means that when average age- or grade-mates experience 90% success on spelling tasks, Sheila is likely to have only 75% success.

The RPI can document a performance deficit that may not be apparent in standard scores and percentile ranks. At times it appears that a contradiction exists between the SS and the RPI. For example, a student may obtain an SS of 92 (average) on the Reading Recall test, but an RPI of 39/90 (limited). These scores provide different information and are not interchangeable. The SS reflects an individual's relative standing within a distribution of age- or grade mates. The RPI is based on the number of W points the person's score falls above or below the median W score (REF W) for his or her age or grade. This means that the RPI is influenced by the characteristics of the underlying ability or trait being measured. When the ability is in a period of rapid growth or development, the RPI may appear deficient even when the SS is average. Periods of rapid growth cover a wide range of W scores, so distance from the median W for an age or grade can be dramatic. When the ability is in a period of slow growth, the SS may appear below average but the RPI is average because the range of the W scores is limited.

The RPI is similar to the familiar Snellen Index used to describe the quality of an individual's visual acuity (Woodcock, 1999). An individual with 20/20 vision is predicted to see an object at a distance of 20 feet as well as a person with normal vision. However, if the person's vision is 20/80, that person needs to be within 20 feet of an object to see it as well as a person with normal vision sees the object from 80 feet. The quality of the individual's visual acuity is described with a criterion-referenced statement. Often the determination of the type of support and services needed is based upon this criterion-referenced

TABLE 6.1 RPI Performance Implications

RPI Range	Skill with Age or Grade Level Tasks	Age/Grade Level Tasks Will Be
100/90	Very Advanced	Extremely Easy
98/90 to 100/90	Advanced	Very Easy
95/90 to 98/90	Average to Advanced	Easy
82/90 to 95/90	Average	Manageable
67/90 to 82/90	Limited to Average	Difficult
24/90 to 67/90	Limited	Very Difficult
3/90 to 24/90	Very Limited	Extremely Difficult
0/90 to 3/90	Extremely Limited	Nearly Impossible

statement. In determining the need for corrective lenses, consideration of the individual's quality of vision is more important than his or her relative standing compared to age- or grade-mates. If a person's vision is impaired, the individual will benefit from corrective lenses regardless of relative standing with peers. Like the Snellen Index, the RPI provides a criterion-referenced statement of an individual's performance. An RPI of 75/90 or lower suggests the individual will find the task to be difficult, whereas an RPI of 96/90 or greater suggests the individual will find the task to be easy. Table 6.1 provides information about the performance implications of the RPI.

Instructional Zone. The WJ IV ACH Instructional Zone (called the Developmental Zone on the WJ IV COG and WJ IV OL) is designed to estimate the instructional level ranging from an easy to difficult level. The RPI is used to establish this zone. An RPI of 96/90 represents the Easy, or independent, level and an RPI of 75/90 represents the Difficult, or frustration, level. The interpretation of this zone is similar to the criteria used in informal reading inventories. Betts (1946) described three levels of reading performance: independent, instructional, and frustration. Thus, a critical factor for effective instruction is to ensure that students have the appropriate level of instructional materials. For example, when a student is asked to read a book without assistance, the assigned book should be at the independent level (99% accuracy). When support is being provided by a teacher or parent, the book should be at the instructional level (95% accuracy).

When an individual's Instructional Zone is far below that of his or her classmates, adaptations and accommodations need to be made. Examples of program modifications include altering the difficulty level of the material, reducing the amount of material to be covered, or increasing the amount and intensity of assistance. Analysis and understanding of a person's present performance levels lead to the selection of appropriate instructional materials and goals. Vygotsky (1978) originally discussed the concept of the "zone of proximal development." This zone refers to an area of learning that is slightly above the person's present performance level: instruction in the zone occurs when a student is helped by a teacher or peer with higher knowledge of the subject. The WJ IV ACH Instructional Zone provides an estimate of where instruction should begin.

Patterns of Cluster and Test Scores

The WJ IV contains several procedures for examining the variability among a person's abilities. Oftentimes, the patterns obtained on the cluster and test scores can help reveal a person's unique strengths and weaknesses. One useful method in the WJ IV ACH is the variation procedure among the three cross-domain clusters. Each cross-domain cluster (Academic Skills, Academic Fluency, and Academic Applications) includes three tests—one from each of the three main academic domains: reading, written language, and mathematics. In addition, three additional clusters that are all timed can be added in: WJ IV ACH Reading Rate, and the WJ IV COG Cognitive Processing Speed and Perceptual Speed clusters. When these clusters are compared, a variety of patterns can exist. Examples include: (a) low basic skills with adequate performance on fluency and application tests; (b) low performance on fluency with adequate performance on skills and application tests; (c) low performance on application tests with adequate performance on skills and fluency tests; (d) variability among areas of performance (e.g., math performance lower than reading); and (e) generalized low or high performance in all three domains.

The results of a student's performance on the cross-domain clusters can have implications for either an Individualized Education Program (IEP) or a 504 accommodation plan. Some students perform poorly on application tasks because of limited knowledge, poor reasoning, low language, or limited exposure to cultural or educational experiences, but have average performance on measures of basic skills and fluency. These students tend to have higher scores on lower order basic skills tests, and lower scores on higher order tests involving language and reasoning. For these students, intervention is directed to building background knowledge, increasing use of strategies, and developing language and problem-solving abilities. These students will tend to require adjustments in the curricular demands (e.g., modifying the difficulty level of the materials). Other students have higher scores on tests involving language and reasoning, but lower performance on measures of basic skills and fluency. These students will tend to require accommodations in the curricular demands (e.g., extended time on exams). Table 6.2 indicates possible program accommodations and instructional implications for individuals who have weaknesses in skills, fluency, and/or applications.

TABLE 6.2 Possible Accommodations and Instructional Implications Based on Cross-Domain Cluster Results

Cross-Domain Cluster Results	Accommodations	Instructional Implications
Skills lower than Fluency and Applications	No penalty for poor skills (e.g., poor spelling)	Provide direct instruction in deficient skills
Fluency lower than Skills and Applications	Extend time or shorten assignments	Provide activities to promote automaticity (e.g., speed drills)
Applications lower than Skills and Fluency	Modify the instructional level	Provide instruction to build acquired knowledge; teach use of strategies

Clearly, all students with academic disabilities will not exhibit these exact profiles. As a general observation, students with "specific" learning disabilities tend to perform lower on measures of basic skills and fluency, and higher on measures of application and oral language. Students with language impairments tend to perform lower on measures of application and oral language, and higher on measures of basic skills and fluency. Three patterns of specific learning disabilities are discussed below: reading, written language, and mathematics. These patterns reflect the general findings in the research literature and are not based on specific findings with the WJ IV.

Reading disability. Because the most common referral for educational testing is difficulty learning to read, a major focus of this chapter is on reading disabilities. Analysis of test scores can help the evaluator determine whether an individual has dyslexia (an impairment in phoneme/grapheme knowledge, rapid word recognition, and spelling) or if the reading difficulties are best explained by other factors (e.g., limited instruction or low oral language abilities). A common profile for students with dyslexia shows higher performance on reading tasks that involve more context (e.g., Passage Comprehension and Reading Recall) than on tasks relying on the application of phoneme–grapheme correspondences (e.g., Word Attack and Spelling of Sounds). Clark and Uhry (1995) indicated that older students with reading disabilities who have had remediation often exhibit the following pattern of scores: listening comprehension > reading comprehension > decoding words in text > decoding words in isolation > spelling/reading nonwords. Using WJ IV ACH and WJ IV OL tests, this pattern would translate as: Oral Comprehension > Passage Comprehension > Oral Reading > Letter–Word Identification > Spelling of Sounds, and Word Attack. Similarly, Goldsmith-Phillips (1994) explains that individuals with phonological dyslexia "...will have the greatest difficulty with reading nonwords and the most success with passage comprehension, which is a more cognitively loaded task. The task of word identification will be at an intermediate level because the words may have been learned by Gestalt" (p. 97).

Writing disability. For students with specific writing disabilities, a similar pattern is often apparent. They obtain their highest score on Writing Samples, which requires expression of ideas, lower scores on Sentence Writing Fluency and Editing, and their lowest scores on the Spelling test (real words) and the Spelling of Sounds test (nonwords). Some individuals with writing disabilities have coexisting reading difficulties, whereas others do not.

Math disability. In math performance, individuals are likely to have higher scores on the Applied Problems and Number Matrices tests, measures of mathematical reasoning, and lower scores on measures of fluency and basic skills such as the Calculation and Math Facts Fluency tests. Individuals with math disabilities often understand concepts, but have trouble memorizing facts and the various steps involved in algorithms.

Comparison of Oral Language and Academic Knowledge to Academic Performance

Insights can be gained about instructional needs by examining the relationships between oral language and achievement. When using only the WJ IV ACH, the orally administered Academic Knowledge cluster (Science, Social Studies, and Humanities) can be used to predict academic performance. When using the WJ IV OL and the WJ IV ACH together, the Broad Oral Language cluster can be used to predict academic performance. These ability-achievement discrepancy procedures are described in more detail in the manuals (Mather & Wendling, 2014a, 2014b, 2014c), as well as in *Essentials of WJ IV Tests of Achievement* (Mather & Wendling, 2015). These types of comparisons are particularly relevant for deciding if the instructional focus needs to be directed to general oral language proficiency or specific academic skills (reading, writing, or mathematics). Comparing listening comprehension measures to reading and writing performance can help determine the source of the weakness (Johnson, 1998) and the need for specific skill instruction.

This type of comparison can also provide evidence for establishing a reading disability; as in these cases, oral comprehension is significantly higher than reading performance (Clark & Uhry, 1995; Goldsmith-Phillips, 1994). Essentially, what distinguishes individuals with a reading disability from other poor readers is that their listening comprehension ability is higher than their ability to decode words (Rack, Snowling, & Olson, 1992). Although some students have adequate decoding and poor reading comprehension, students with poor comprehension but adequate word recognition have comprehension problems that are general to language comprehension rather than specific to reading (Spencer, Quinn, & Wagner, 2014). These students would be more accurately classified as having a language impairment, rather than a specific reading disability.

For students with a specific reading disability or dyslexia, intervention is directed toward improving basic reading and writing skills rather than overall language development. If all language skills are low, the intervention is directed toward improving all aspects of language development. Many examples of recommendations and possible interventions are available in: *Essentials of Evidence-Based Academic Interventions* (Wendling & Mather, 2009), *Essentials of Dyslexia: Assessment and Intervention* (Mather & Wendling, 2012), and *Woodcock–Johnson IV: Reports, Recommendations, and Strategies* (Mather & Jaffe, 2016). In addition, the *Woodcock Interpretation and Instructional Interventions Program* (WIIIP; Schrank & Wendling, 2015) uses WJ IV test results to identify recommended interventions and accommodations.

Performance Implications of the Cattell–Horn–Carroll (CHC) Cognitive Factors

The results of an individual's performance on the seven WJ IV COG CHC abilities can help explain why the student is struggling in certain aspects of school. For example, low Comprehension-Knowledge (*Gc*) influences reading comprehension (Floyd, Meisinger, Gregg, & Keith, 2012), whereas low Auditory Processing (*Ga*) may influence the development of decoding (word reading) and encoding (spelling) abilities. Table 6.3 presents the seven CHC abilities measured in the WJ IV COG, gives descriptors of those abilities, lists the achievement areas that are most significantly related to these abilities (Evans, Floyd, McGrew, & Leforgee, 2001; Flanagan, Ortiz, & Alfonso, 2013; McGrew & Wendling, 2010), and provides example instructional recommendations. One caution to keep in mind is that the relationship of cognitive factors to academic performance changes with age and stage of development. For example, McGrew and Wendling (2010) found that fluid reasoning (*Gf*), acquired knowledge (*Gc*), and processing speed (*Gs*) abilities were significantly related to math achievement, but the *Gc* relationship increased with age, whereas the *Gs* relationship decreased with age. *Gf* was related consistently and significantly across all ages.

Another note of caution is applicable to the conflicting results reported in studies that explore the significance of the relationship between specific cognitive abilities and academic performance. One reason for contradictions may be due to specification error or the inclusion of a limited number of important variables. For example, phonemic awareness and rapid automatized naming (RAN) tasks have been described as the "double-deficit hypothesis" or two important correlates of reading failure (Wolf & Bowers, 1999). Conceivably, the importance of these abilities may diminish when other possible correlates (e.g., working memory, processing speed) are included in the design. Although considerable progress has been made in our understanding of how cognitive abilities relate to academic performance, continued research is needed to document and further clarify the relationships among a broad range of cognitive abilities and achievement.

TABLE 6.3 Possible Performance Implications of the Seven CHC Cognitive Factors

CHC Cognitive Factor	Descriptors	Achievement Area	Sample Recommendations
Comprehension-Knowledge (Gc)	Acquired knowledge Vocabulary Information	Reading Comprehension Written Expression Math Problem Solving	Specific instruction in vocabulary Relate new learning to prior knowledge
Fluid Reasoning (Gf)	Inductive and deductive reasoning Problem-solving	Math Problem Solving Reading Comprehension Written Language	Teach problem-solving techniques and strategies Use concrete to abstract sequence of instruction
Long-Term Retrieval (Glr)	Memorization Fluency of retrieval Association and retrieval	Basic Reading Skills Basic Writing Skills Math Calculation Skills	Provide overlearning, review, and repetition Teach memory strategies
Auditory Processing (Ga)	Phonological awareness Blending and segmentation	Basic Reading Skills Basic Writing Skills	Provide specific training in rhyming, sound blending, and segmentation
Visual Processing (Gv)	Spatial relations Visual imagery Visual memory	Mathematics Reading Comprehension	Verbally describe graphics Use manipulatives Teach to visualize what is being read to enhance comprehension
Cognitive Processing Speed (Gs)	Automaticity Visual scanning Perceptual speed	Basic Reading Skills Math Calculation Skills Basic Writing Skills	Limit the amount of work Provide rate-building activities
Short-Term Working Memory (Gwm)	Sequential memory Immediate awareness Limited capacity	Basic Reading Skills Math Calculation Skills Basic Writing Skills	Keep directions short Provide compensatory aids Teach memory strategies

ACADEMIC SKILLS

Academic basic skills are lower order tasks that become automatic with repeated practice, such as knowing the multiplication facts or spelling words with ease. These abilities involve perceptual and motoric processes that are critical for school success. When these low-level processes become routine and automatic, they require minimal attentional resources (Schneider & Shiffrin, 1977). In analyzing a student's performance on basic skills, the evaluator should consider what strategies the student employs and how quickly the student responds. In addition, the evaluator should attempt to discern if patterns exist among the incorrect responses. Table 6.4 identifies the cognitive, oral language, and achievement clusters that may provide relevant information when interpreting performance on the basic skills clusters.

TABLE 6.4 Clusters to Consider When Interpreting Performance in Academic Skills

Academic Skills Cluster/Tests	Relevant Achievement Clusters	Relevant Cognitive Clusters
Academic Skills Letter–Word Identification Calculation Spelling	Academic Fluency Academic Applications Basic Reading Skills Math Calculation Skills Basic Writing Skills	Comprehension-Knowledge Long-Term Retrieval Cognitive Processing Speed Short-Term Working Memory
Basic Reading Skills Letter–Word Identification Word Attack	Phoneme/Grapheme Knowledge Reading Comprehension	Auditory Processing Comprehension-Knowledge Long-Term Retrieval Cognitive Processing Speed Short-Term Working Memory
Math Calculation Skills Calculation Math Facts Fluency	Math Reasoning	Comprehension-Knowledge Fluid Reasoning Long-Term Retrieval Cognitive Processing Speed Short-Term Working Memory Visual Processing
Basic Writing Skills Spelling Editing	Phoneme/Grapheme Knowledge Written Expression	Auditory Processing Comprehension-Knowledge Long-Term Retrieval Cognitive Processing Speed Short-Term Working Memory

Phonological Awareness

Although phonological awareness is an aspect of oral language, it may be placed under the category of basic skills because a substantial body of research supports the link between phonological processing abilities and the subsequent development of reading and spelling skills (Lyon, 1995; Perfetti, 1992; Torgesen, 1992, 1993; Wagner & Torgesen, 1987). Deficits in phonological skills have been identified as the major cause of severe reading problems (Ehri, 1998; Morris et al., 1998; Wagner, Torgesen, Laughon, Simmons, & Rashotte, 1993). Results from longitudinal studies suggest that 75% of the children who struggle with reading in third grade, particularly with the development of phonological awareness, will still be poor readers by the end of high school (Francis, Shaywitz, Stuebing, Shaywitz, & Fletcher, 1996; Lyon, 1998). Another longitudinal study of nearly 4000 students found that children who are not proficient readers by third grade are four times more likely to leave school without a diploma than proficient readers (Hernandez, 2012). Thus, early interventions that promote the development of phonological awareness and basic reading skills are critical.

The WJ IV COG includes two measures of phonological abilities: Phonological Processing and Nonword Repetition. The Phonological Processing test consists of three subtests: Word Access, Word Fluency, and Substitution. In Word Access, the examinee is required to provide a real word that includes a specified phoneme in a stated location (i.e., beginning, middle, or end of the word); in Word Fluency the examinee is required to name as many words as possible in 1 minute that begin with a specific phoneme; and in Substitution the examinee is required to substitute a word part or phoneme to create a new word. The Nonword Repetition test requires the examinee to listen to and then repeat nonwords that increase in length and difficulty. Performance on this type of task is closely associated with language development (Nation & Hulme, 2011). If a more in-depth analysis of phonological awareness abilities is needed, two tests from the WJ IV OL, Segmentation and Sound Blending, can be administered to obtain the Phonetic Coding cluster. In addition, the Sound Awareness test on the WJ IV OL, a screening test designed primarily for younger students, may also be administered to assess the abilities to rhyme words and delete phonemes.

Phonological awareness is an important underlying linguistic ability for reading and spelling unfamiliar words. Phonetic coding, an aspect of auditory processing (*Ga*), is especially important in kindergarten through third grade (McGrew & Wendling, 2010). Reading unfamiliar words requires blending skill and is required to arrive at a unified pronunciation of the parts; spelling unfamiliar words requires segmentation skill; one must pull apart the phonemes so that the graphemes can be selected (Ehri, 2000). The ability to blend individual sounds into spoken words and segment spoken words into their individual sounds are two central phonological awareness abilities that lead to fluent word recognition and enable comprehension (Allor & Chard, 2011).

Nonword Reading and Spelling

Considerable research has confirmed that poor readers have more difficulty reading and spelling nonwords (also called nonsense words or pseudowords) than do normally developing readers (Rack et al. 1992; Siegel & Ryan, 1988). The WJ IV ACH has two tests that measure the ability to read and spell nonwords—Word Attack and Spelling of Sounds. These two tests are particularly helpful for determining a student's knowledge of phoneme–grapheme correspondences (knowledge of spoken and written symbols). When combined, the tests form the "Phoneme–Grapheme Knowledge" cluster, which is particularly relevant to the documentation of a reading disability.

Phonological dyslexia is often described as an impairment in nonword reading (Coltheart, 1996). Although the reading of nonwords is sometimes described as a phonological coding test, both phonology and orthography are required (Johnson, 1998). The ability to pronounce and spell nonwords requires knowledge of phonology (the sound system) and orthography (the spelling system). Orthographic coding, the ability to recall letters and letter strings, is important to reading and spelling success (Berninger, 1996). The English language is described as a "deep orthography" because of the inconsistencies and complexities of the match between the phonemes (speech sounds) and the graphemes (letters or letter groups that represent the phonemes).

Several abilities are required to pronounce a nonword that has regular phoneme–grapheme correspondence and corresponds to English spelling rules, including phonological, orthographical, and morphological knowledge. Phonological awareness helps readers associate the phonemes with the graphemes; orthographic awareness of the graphemes within words helps readers apply this knowledge to decoding unfamiliar written words; and morphological awareness helps readers recognize common patterns, such as prefixes and suffixes (Berninger & Wolf, 2009).

Consider the skills that are needed to pronounce the nonword "tramble," similar to a multisyllabic nonword on the WJ IV Word Attack test. Nonword reading involves the following three stages: (a) grapheme parsing, which requires converting a letter or letter group into a grapheme string; (b) phoneme assignment, which requires determining what phoneme corresponds to each of the graphemes; and (c) phoneme blending, which requires converting the phonemes into a single, unified form (Coltheart, 1996). The first two stages involve orthography and morphology, whereas the third stage involves phoneme manipulation. Therefore, a difficulty in nonword reading can result from weaknesses in orthographic and morphological awareness, rather than poor phonological awareness.

By administering the WJ IV COG Phonological Processing and Nonword Repetition tests and the WJ IV OL Segmentation, Sound Blending, and Sound Awareness tests, the evaluator can determine if the individual has difficulties on a variety of phonological tasks. The evaluator can also determine if nonword reading is lower than word reading by comparing results on the Word Attack test to the results on the Letter–Word Identification test. If the individual's score is significantly higher on Letter–Word Identification than on Word Attack, this would suggest that the individual recognizes some real words because of prior experience and print exposure, but has not yet fully mastered phoneme/grapheme relationships. In analyzing spellings on the Spelling of Sounds test, the evaluator should note whether the writer records a plausible grapheme for each phoneme in the word. For example, an individual who writes "fich" for the nonword "fitch" demonstrates good sound knowledge (phonology), but more limited knowledge of English spelling patterns (orthography), as the /ch/ sound in a one-syllable word with a short vowel is spelled "-tch." If the individual does not have difficulty with tasks involving phonemic blending and segmentation, low performance on Word Attack and Spelling of Sounds is likely more indicative of limited exposure to printed material or a weakness in orthography and morphology.

Some students can obtain scores that fall within the average range on non-word reading tests, but their performance is still compromised by their speed of word recognition. Younger students who are slow to develop decoding skills may eventually read nonwords accurately, but they will still read slowly (Holopainen, Ahonen, & Lyytinen, 2001). Older students who have had intensive reading intervention are likely to obtain average nonword reading scores, but their speed of word perception is compromised. In describing the reading performance of college students with dyslexia, Bruck (1998) reported that for college students with dyslexia, the average latency to pronounce a nonword was 2019 milliseconds, whereas the average latency for age-matched controls and reading-matched controls was 882 and 839, respectively.

Similarly, Wilson and Lesaux (2001) found that although college students with dyslexia had age-appropriate performance on standardized measures of reading and spelling, their performance was still compromised on phonological processing measures and measures involving speed. For example, a student may obtain an average SS on the Letter–Word Identification test because this score is based on number of words read correctly and does not take into account the manner in which the reader approached the task. The student may eventually pronounce the word correctly after several attempts and repeated self-corrections. In considering an older student with a history of reading difficulties and reading interventions, average reading test scores do not rule out the need for services, including appropriate accommodations, nor should services be denied on the basis of a lack of ability-achievement discrepancy (Wilson & Lesaux, 2001). With older readers, college students, and adults, the speed of decoding is often more impaired than accuracy. In a study investigating 200 Dutch college students with ($N = 100$) and without dyslexia ($N = 100$), Callens, Tops, and Brysbaert (2012) found that with the exception of spelling, the reading and writing deficits of the students with dyslexia were larger for speed related measures than for accuracy related measures. Thus, an evaluator should consider the person's performance on the WJ IV ACH Reading Rate cluster, as well as any significant difference in scores between the Basic Reading Skills and Reading Rate clusters.

Basic Writing Skills

Handwriting, spelling, and knowledge of the rules of written language underlie performance in basic writing skills. Writing speed (automaticity of handwriting) has been found to be a good predictor of performance on more complex written language tasks (Berninger, 1996). Automatic letter formation permits the writer to focus on the ideas and organization needed in the writing process.

Spelling difficulties appear to result from weaknesses in phonology, orthography, and morphology. Individuals with spelling difficulties often have difficulty analyzing and memorizing the sounds, syllables, and meaningful parts of words. In addition, poor spellers may also experience difficulty learning math facts and math operation signs, further reflecting difficulty learning and memorizing symbolic codes (Moats, 1995).

Basic Math Skills

As with reading, mathematics involves basic skills, fluency, and problem solving. Some students have difficulty primarily with computational skills, such as adding, subtracting, and multiplying. One common characteristic for individuals with limited basic math skills is difficulty memorizing and recalling math facts. Many individuals with learning disabilities have persistent difficulty memorizing basic number facts in all four operations despite great effort and adequate understanding (Fleischner, Garnett, & Shepherd, 1982). Some individuals demonstrate deficits in fundamental arithmetic operations, even though they evidenced adequate reasoning, language, and visual processing skills (Novick & Arnold, 1988). This difficulty with the acquisition of basic math skills is referred to as dyscalculia. One of the most consistent behavioral characteristics of this learning disorder is the individual's difficulty learning and retrieving math facts from memory (Price & Ansari, 2013). Thus, for a student struggling with basic math skills, an evaluator would want to review his or her performance on the WJ IV ACH Calculation and Math Facts Fluency tests.

Instructional Implications for Academic Skills

Students with weaknesses in basic skills often need specific accommodations in the classroom. Some students will require shortened assignments, whereas some will require extended time. Others will need to use technology to help reduce the impact of deficiencies in basic skills. The type and availability of instructional supports for students with disabilities also vary from school district to district (Decker, 2012).

Phonological awareness. Students with low performance on measures of phonological awareness should engage in a variety of tasks that will increase skill acquisition. Tasks should be ordered by the difficulty level: rhyme, alliteration, blending, segmentation, and manipulation (Ball, 1993; Chafouleas, Lewandowski, Smith, & Blachman, 1997). Table 6.5 provides definitions and examples of these five types of phonological awareness tasks. Chafouleas et al. found that 90% of children are able to perform most of these tasks by the age of 7 years. The most important abilities for reading and spelling performance, however, are the abilities to blend and segment sounds.

Phoneme/grapheme knowledge. Students with weaknesses in phoneme–grapheme knowledge will require specific instruction in the alphabetic system. For students with weaknesses in phonology, explicit instruction in phonemic awareness should be coupled with instruction in letter–sound relationships (Calfee, 1998). By the end of kindergarten, children should be able to blend and segment sounds and use sounds to spell simple words (Chard & Dickson, 1999).

TABLE 6.5 Definitions and Examples of Five Types of Phonological Awareness Tasks

Task	Definition	WJ IV Test	Example
Rhyming			
Identification	Identifies words that end alike, or rhyme	Sound Awareness	Which two words end alike or rhyme? (Rat, horse, cat)
Production	Produces word that rhymes with a target word	Sound Awareness	Tell me a word that rhymes with "big"
Alliteration	Identifies words that have the same sound (beginning, middle, or ending sounds)		Which two words begin with the same sound? (boy, baby, car)
Blending	Combines individual syllables or sounds into a whole word Pushes sounds together	Sound Blending	Tell me the word I'm trying to say: (/t/../a/../b/../l/)
Segmentation	identifies the two words in compound words, syllables in a word, or phonemes in a word Pulls sounds apart	Segmentation	How many syllables are in "carpenter"? How many sounds do you hear in the word "dog"?
Manipulation	Deletes the sounds in a word	Sound Awareness	Say "hat" without the /h/

As a first step for increasing phoneme–grapheme knowledge, students must grasp the alphabetic principle, which is the understanding that the letters of the alphabet represent the discrete sounds of speech (Liberman, Shankweiler, & Liberman, 1989). The beginning reader must discover that words have an internal phonemic structure that is represented by letters (graphemes). They then must be able to apply this knowledge. Students with word recognition and spelling problems require explicit instruction and practice in reading and spelling single words (Berninger et al., 2000; Berninger & Wolf, 2009) which can often be accomplished by using a synthetic phonics approach.

With synthetic phonics instruction, the student is explicitly taught the relationship between letters and sounds. After sounds are taught in isolation, the student is then taught how to blend the letter sounds together to pronounce words. Once the student can blend single phonemes, additional graphemes are introduced and emphasis is placed on learning to chunk or break words into their basic parts. The goal of this instruction is to help children understand, as much as possible, why English words are pronounced and spelled the way that they are. Because learning to read and learning to spell are closely related and rely on the same knowledge sources, instruction should be designed so that "their acquisition is mutually facilitative and reciprocal" (Ehri, 2000, p. 34). In addition, individuals with reading difficulties need extensive practice applying their knowledge of letter–sound relationships to the task of spelling (Grossen, 1997).

Initial reading instruction is supported with the use of decodable text that consists primarily of words with regular sound-symbol relationships and a few sight words that are taught systematically. This type of text allows beginning readers to integrate their knowledge within the context of connected reading and to practice and apply their developing knowledge of letter–sound correspondences to text. As phoneme–grapheme knowledge increases, attention is directed to recognizing common English spelling patterns, and building reading speed. Even with adequate instruction, older students with a history of reading and spelling difficulties will often require the accommodation of extended time on tasks that require lengthy reading or writing.

Basic math skills. For instruction in basic math skills, the evaluator should first determine the reasons for poor performance. Is low performance a result of not knowing the meaning of the signs, not following the steps in the algorithm, or something as basic as a lack of knowledge of one-to-one correspondence or counting skills? Success in math, more than any other academic area, is predicated on acquiring the prerequisite skills and knowledge. Prerequisites include concepts such as shape and form, size and length, one-to-one correspondence, and counting. If students do not understand early mathematical concepts, they will have difficulty acquiring concepts that are taught later in the developmental sequence. For example, an understanding of one-to-one correspondence is necessary for meaningful counting. Any gaps in the student's mastery of the developmental sequence of mathematical concepts or skills must be addressed. In general, remediation should include concrete materials that can be manipulated, structured presentations using small steps, and specific verbalization of instructions followed by conversion into mathematical symbols. In addition, a variety of aids have proven useful in remediation, including number lines and Cuisenaire Rods (Harrison & Harrison, 1986; Herbert, 1985; Suydam, 1984).

The language of mathematics is a critical element affecting performance. Students should not be expected to use symbols until they understand their meaning. The signs in mathematics indicate the relationship between the numbers and how they should be manipulated. If the student does not pay attention to or understand the meaning of the sign, he or she will be unsuccessful in solving the problem. For some students, color coding math signs can draw attention to the operation.

The visual–spatial aspects of an arithmetic problem can also impact performance. To solve math problems, the student must understand that the numbers go left to right, top to bottom, and that solutions often go right to left. Careful explanation must be given each time a new process is introduced. No assumptions can be made about what the student does and does not know. Memory span and working memory can also interfere with calculation if the student has difficulty memorizing math facts and retaining the sequence of steps necessary for solving the problem. Provision of a cue card with each step can be helpful, as can using visual cues to indicate the starting point and direction in which to work the problem. The WJ IV COG Short-term Working Memory (*Gwm*), Long-Term Retrieval (*Glr*), and Auditory Memory Span clusters may provide valuable information for determining any aspects of memory that are impacting an individual's performance in basic math skills.

ACADEMIC FLUENCY

The WJ IV ACH fluency measures are all timed tests that relate to automaticity and speed of processing. In interpreting performance on the fluency tests, the evaluator should first determine if scores are low in all academic domains or only in one or two academic domains. The student's performance on the WJ IV COG Cognitive Processing Speed cluster or the Perceptual Speed cluster can be compared to the Academic Fluency cluster to determine if the lack of automaticity generalizes to most types of speeded tasks, or applies only to tasks involving a specific type of academic content. In addition, the Academic Fluency cluster can be compared to the WJ IV OL Speed of Lexical Access cluster, to determine if the rate of word retrieval is affecting performance on timed measures as well. If a student has a low score on one or more measures of fluency, the problem could be related to low performance in basic skills, delayed automaticity, slow word retrieval, or a generalized slow response style that is pervasive across all timed tasks.

One caution is in order for interpreting performance on the Academic Fluency tests. The content of the WJ IV ACH reading, math, and writing fluency tests is controlled for difficulty level so that the tests measure automaticity in performance. As the difficulty level of materials increases, a student who was fluent on easy materials may become dysfluent when the vocabulary and conceptual demands increase. In other words, a student may perform automatically on simple tasks, such as solving single-digit addition and subtraction problems on the Math Facts Fluency test, but not have automaticity on tasks of greater complexity, such as solving a problem involving long division on the Applied Problems test. Automaticity occurs when a known procedure is practiced enough times that it is completed with little cognitive effort. Thus, in considering fluency, the difficulty level of the material for the student is a factor. A college student with a reading disability may appear quite fluent on text at the third-grade instructional level, but very dysfluent when reading college-level textbooks. Table 6.6 lists additional clusters to consider when interpreting performance on academic fluency tasks.

Reading Fluency

Reading fluency encompasses accuracy, the speed or rate of reading, and the ability to read materials with expression and comprehension. Some definitions of reading fluency focus more on decoding and speed, whereas others emphasize

TABLE 6.6 Clusters to Consider When Interpreting Performance in Academic Fluency

Academic Fluency Cluster/Tests	Relevant Achievement or Oral Language Clusters	Relevant Cognitive Clusters
Academic Fluency Sentence Reading Fluency Math Facts Fluency Sentence Writing Fluency	Basic Skills (Reading, Mathematics, Written Language) Speed of Lexical Access	Comprehension-Knowledge Cognitive Processing Speed Perceptual Speed Short-Term Working Memory
Reading Fluency Oral Reading Sentence Reading Fluency	Basic Reading Skills Reading Comprehension Speed of Lexical Access	Auditory Processing Comprehension-Knowledge Cognitive Processing Speed Short-Term Working Memory
Math Facts Fluency	Math Calculation Skills Speed of Lexical Access	Comprehension-Knowledge Cognitive Processing Speed Perceptual Speed Short-Term Working Memory
Sentence Writing Fluency	Basic Writing Skills Written Expression Speed of Lexical Access	Auditory Processing Comprehension-Knowledge Cognitive Processing Speed

the role of comprehension. Meyer and Felton (1999) defined fluency as "...the ability to read connected text rapidly, smoothly, effortlessly, and automatically with little conscious attention to the mechanics of reading, such as decoding" (p. 284). Pikulski and Chard (2005) provided a broader definition; they note that efficient, effective word recognition skills permit a reader to construct the meaning of text, read with expression, and comprehend text while reading silently. Thus, how fluently one reads is a strong predictor of comprehension (Chard, Vaughn, & Tyler, 2002).

Children are successful with decoding when the process used to identify words is fast and nearly effortless or automatic. As noted, the concept of automaticity refers to a student's ability to recognize words rapidly with little attention required to the word's appearance. Lack of automaticity causes the attentional system to be overloaded and places heavy demands on memory and adversely affects comprehension. The key to skilled reading, therefore, is the ability to read words automatically by sight (Ehri, 1998).

Some individuals may have developed accurate word pronunciation and spelling skills, as measured on the Letter–Word Identification, Word Attack, Spelling, and Spelling of Sounds tests, but still read or write slowly. For slow readers, their limited fluency can affect performance in the following ways: (a) they read less text than peers and have less time to remember, review, or comprehend the text; (b) they expend more cognitive energy than peers trying to identify individual words; and (c) they may be less able to retain text in memory and less likely to integrate those segments with other parts of the text (Mastropieri, Leinart, & Scruggs, 1999).

A major problem for poor readers is the rapid identification of individual words (Torgesen, Rashotte, & Alexander, 2001). Individuals with dyslexia often display a disruption in word reading automaticity (Olson, 2011) and obtain low scores on measures of reading rate and fluency as well as processing speed, particularly the WJ IV COG Perceptual Speed cluster. This cluster is composed of two tests: Letter-Pattern Matching and Number-Pattern Matching which require the rapid marking of matching letter and number patterns. In addition to perceptual speed measures, a variety of factors can affect reading fluency and rate. Torgesen et al. (2001) explained that the following components can underlie individual differences in the accuracy and rate of oral reading: (a) the number of words recognized by sight; (b) the speed with which sight words are processed; (c) the speed of processes used to pronounce unfamiliar words; (d) the use of context to facilitate speed of word identification; and (e) the rate that word meanings can be accessed.

One additional factor to keep in mind is that the two reading rate tests, Sentence Reading Fluency and Word Reading Fluency, measure silent reading, not oral reading. Although the majority of school research has focused on oral reading, "oral reading should not be allowed to subsume its silent counterpart" (Price, Meisinger, Louwerse, & D'Mello, 2015). Ultimately, as students move through the grades the focus shifts to silent reading. The Oral Reading test is designed to let evaluators assess if the individual can read orally with ease and expression. The silent reading rate tests involve comprehension of simple sentences, as well as the understanding of simple to more complex vocabulary.

Simple measures of oral reading fluency (ORF) do not diagnose the reasons for the difficulty. Allor and Chard (2011) provided the following analogy: "It is critically important to view ORF (whether it is the DIBELS measure or another similar measure) as an indicator of a problem and not a diagnosis. It is comparable to a doctor taking a child's temperature; a fever indicates there is a problem, but it does not inform the doctor as to the best method of treating the problem" (p. 8).

Writing Fluency

As with reading, fluent and automatic basic skills are fundamental to the expression of more complex meaningful writing (Berninger & Wolf, 2009; Graham, Berninger, Abbott, Abbott, & Whitaker, 1997). A number of factors, in addition to automaticity with basic skills, can influence writing fluency: visual-motor abilities, handwriting speed, facility with syntax, and reading ability. Berninger and Richards (2002) described the complexity of writing as "an immense juggling act." In some instances, handwriting speed is the reason for a low score on the Sentence Writing Fluency test.

As with reading and spelling, handwriting proficiency is also developmental. Levine (1987) described several stages of handwriting proficiency: (a) imitation, where young children pretend to write by copying others; (b) graphic presentation, during first and second grade where children learn how to form letters and to write on a line with proper spacing and fine-motor skills become better developed; (c) progressive incorporation, from late second to fourth grade, where letters are produced with less effort; and (d) automatization, in fourth through seventh grade, where children write rapidly and efficiently. In the final stages, children develop personalized styles and increase writing proficiency. If a student has a low score on the Sentence Writing Fluency test, examine the individual's handwriting. An evaluator may compare the quality of handwriting on the Writing Samples test (untimed) to Sentence Writing Fluency test (timed). An evaluator may also consider the individual's performance on the WJ IV COG Perceptual Speed (*Gs*) cluster, and the WJ IV OL Oral Language cluster. Difficulties may be caused by poor motor control or slow handwriting speed, generalized slow processing speed, or difficulty formulating sentences quickly. If oral language abilities are low, then the low Sentence Writing Fluency score may be due to difficulties manipulating syntax resulting in slow sentence formulation.

Math Fluency

As with reading and writing performance, fluency with basic skills is fundamental to success with more complex math (Cawley, 1985; Hasselbring,

Goin, & Bransford, 1987; Kirby & Becker, 1988). A lack of automaticity with basic math facts interferes with performance on higher level skills and is an important predictor of math performance (Meltzer, 1994). Acquisition of basic math skills may be affected by problems similar to those that affect decoding and encoding. A student who has difficulty memorizing basic math facts and developing numerical facility often has difficulty solving mathematical problems. More advanced levels of mathematics require rapid and accurate handling of numerical quantities (Carroll, 1993). Carroll defines numerical facility and explains the importance of this ability to mathematical thinking:

> "…the degree to which the individual has developed skills in dealing with numbers, from the most elementary skills of counting objects and recognizing written numbers and their order, to the more advanced skills of correctly adding, subtracting, multiplying, and dividing numbers with an increasing number of digits, or with fractions and decimals. These are skills that are learned through experiences in the home, school, or even in the workplace. In the early years, skills deal with simple numbers and operations, and the important object is to be able to deal with number problems correctly, at whatever speed. In later years, practice is aimed at handling computations with greater speed as well as accuracy. More complex problems can be dealt with effectively and efficiently only if skills with simple problems are increasingly automatized." (p. 469)

Just as with reading and writing fluency, the lower level skills involved in rapid calculation must become increasingly automatized so that full attention can be devoted to mathematical problem solving.

Instructional Implications for Academic Fluency

The main accommodation typically needed for students with delayed automaticity is extended time. These students are not able to complete work at the rate of many of their classmates. On some occasions, assignments can be shortened or targeted for a certain amount of time, rather than a certain number of pages. For example, the teacher may ask students to read for 20 minutes, regardless of the number of pages that are completed in that time period. Students with low fluency can often benefit from technology, such as listening to recorded books to complete reading assignments.

For intervention when fluency is low, the goal is to establish automaticity; that is, rapid and easy recognition of words, rapid and easy production of letter forms, and rapid recall of math facts. In general, limited fluency and rate in reading, writing, and/or math are addressed through various rate-building and timed activities. A variety of speed drills can be used in which the student is asked to read, or write, or calculate math facts as rapidly as possible over a 1-minute period. For reading lists of words as a 1-minute speed drill, Fischer (1999) suggested using the following general guidelines: 30 correct wpm for first- and second-grade children; 40 correct wpm for third-grade children; 60 correct wpm for mid-third-grade; and 80 wpm for students in fourth grade and above.

Reading fluency. Another well-known procedure for students who read slowly despite adequate word recognition is the repeated reading technique with immediate corrective feedback from a skilled reader (Therrien & Kubina, 2006). For this procedure, the individual reads the same passage aloud three to four times. The time and number of errors are recorded until a predetermined goal is reached or the student is able to read the passage fluently with few mistakes. The provision of immediate corrective feedback increases the effectiveness of repeated readings (Begeny, Daly, & Vallely, 2006).

Research on repeated readings suggests that fluency can be improved as long as students are provided with specific instructions and procedures are used to monitor their progress (Mastropieri et al., 1999; Meyer & Felton, 1999). Repeated readings have also been used as a component of class-wide peer tutoring (Mathes & Fuchs, 1993). In one study of this intervention, pairs of students in one group read continuously over a 10-minute period, while pairs of students in another group read a passage together three times before going on to the next passage. Although both experimental conditions produced higher results than the typical reading instruction, no difference existed between the procedures, suggesting that the main benefit of the intervention is the student reading involvement and the increased time spent in reading (Mastropieri et al., 1999).

Research findings related to effective instruction for reading fluency identify explicit modeling of fluent reading and repeated reading with immediate corrective feedback as highly effective methods (Chard et al., 2002). Additional procedures that can be used to increase rate include rapid word recognition charts (Carreker, 2009), tape-assisted/CD reading, and the *Great Leaps Reading* program (Campbell, 2005).

Writing Fluency. As with reading speed, one goal for writing instruction is to establish automaticity or rapid and easy production of letter forms. Practice contributes to automaticity as the motor patterns needed for legible writing become more firmly established. One technique that may be used to improve writing rate and fluency and to encourage reluctant writers to increase their productivity is daily timed writings (Alvarez, 1983; Douglass, 1984: Houten, Morrison, Jarvis, & MacDonald, 1974). For this procedure, students write about a topic for 5–10 minutes, trying to write more words than they did on the previous day. At the end of the time period, students count the number of words, and record the number of words on the top of the paper. Individual reinforcements can be provided contingent upon performance such as points for an assigned number of letters, words, or sentences.

Math fluency. For automaticity with math facts, daily speed drills may increase the speed and accuracy of recall. One way to help students become more automatic with math facts is to practice with flashcards. First, the teacher would identify the facts that the student does not know. Then the student would practice three unknown facts at a time. The teacher would present the card and ask the student to respond. If the response was longer than 2 seconds, the teacher would tell the student the answer and move on to the next card. Once the student has mastered these three facts, he or she would place them in a pile for review the next day.

Use of a pocket-size facts chart is another helpful technique. Once the student demonstrates speed and accuracy with a fact, it can be removed or blocked out from his or her personal chart. This approach motivates the student to learn another fact and discourages overreliance on the chart. In addition to providing support and instruction, this type of approach builds in a self-monitoring feature.

Another method for increasing speed with math facts is using verbal reasoning strategies to make the task more meaningful. For example, a teacher might demonstrate the strategy of verbalizing the relationship between a known fact and a new fact. "Since $5 + 5$ is $10, 5 + 6$ is 11." Helping the student see relationships between facts or building knowledge of fact "families" reduces the burden on memory.

When working with students with slow rates and limited automaticity with reading, writing, or math facts, more repetition and practice are required for mastery and timed activities that require rapid responses seem most effective. Fluency-building activities should use content in which the student has demonstrated accuracy and makes few errors. As noted by Hasbrouck and Glaser (2011): "Accuracy is first, foremost, and forever the foundation of fluency." In addition, short, frequent periods of practice are better than one long session. Finally, concrete measures of progress, such as charts and graphs, are effective for displaying gains.

ORAL LANGUAGE, KNOWLEDGE, AND ACADEMIC APPLICATIONS

Oral language abilities, acquired knowledge, and reasoning abilities provide the foundation for success in tasks involving comprehension, problem solving, and self-monitoring. Oral language is positively related to success in reading, math, and written language (Gregg, 2001; McGrew & Wendling, 2010; Stanovich, 1986; Wiig & Semel, 1984). The WJ IV OL measures an individual's receptive and expressive oral language abilities, and the WJ IV ACH measures the individual's knowledge of curricular areas. Receptive oral language refers to the ability to understand what is being said or listen with understanding. Expressive oral language refers to the ability to express thoughts and ideas in an appropriate manner through speaking. Low expressive language in preschool children is a strong predictor of subsequent academic difficulties (Bishop & Adams, 1990; Tallal, Curtiss, & Kaplan 1989).

Some students have adequate receptive language, but poor expressive language; they understand what is said to them but have difficulty responding orally. These students tend to have higher scores on measures that involve pointing (such as the WJ IV OL Understanding Directions test) and lower scores on measures involving speaking (such as the WJ IV COG Story Recall test). Other students have poor receptive and expressive language and have difficulties with many linguistic tasks. Language difficulties can affect performance in many domains.

One critical factor that influences oral expression, reading comprehension, written expression, and math problem solving is background knowledge. The attainment of knowledge is an important aim of education and may be the most important predictor of school success (Rolfhus & Ackerman, 1999). The Comprehension-Knowledge (*Gc*) cluster is obtained by combining the WJ IV COG Oral Vocabulary and General Information tests. Picture Vocabulary from the WJ IV OL can be added in to create the Comprehension-Knowledge-Extended cluster. In addition, the Academic Knowledge cluster from the WJ IV ACH provides another measure of background knowledge. These clusters represent estimates of lexical knowledge as well as the knowledge obtained from educational and general life experiences. If a student obtains low scores on measures of oral language and knowledge, the evaluator should consider if the difficulties are related to: (a) poor word retrieval; (b) limited lexical knowledge; (c) lack of exposure and experience; (d) poor memory; (e) limited English proficiency; or (f) a specific language impairment. Several tests from the WJ IV OL can also help an evaluator determine the nature and extent of the linguistic difficulties. For example, performance on the Retrieval Fluency and Rapid Picture Naming tests can be used to measure word retrieval abilities and speed of lexical access.

The WJ IV ACH cluster of Academic Applications includes tests that involve conceptual processes that require the use of procedural knowledge and strategies. These types of tasks are higher order in that they involve linguistic and reasoning abilities that are required for defining words, writing an idea, or solving a verbal math problem. If a student has low performance on application tasks, the first step is to determine which of the following factors are most related to the poor performance: (a) low performance in basic skills; (b) limited oral language proficiency; (c) limited background or procedural knowledge; (d) ineffective or limited instruction; or (e) limited knowledge of or failure to apply strategies. Some individuals with learning disabilities appear to be inflexible and inefficient in applying problem-solving strategies that are required for tasks such as math problem solving. Successful completion of application tasks requires integration of language, procedural (how to) and declarative (factual) knowledge, reasoning abilities, self-monitoring, and self-evaluation. Weaknesses in metacognition, or the ability to think about one's own thinking, also appear to adversely affect the development and use of strategies and impede progress in academic tasks (Kaufman, 2010; Montague, 1997).

Several of the WJ IV COG factors appear related to the ability to perform academic applications (McGrew & Wendling, 2010). Acquired knowledge (*Gc*) and short-term working memory (*Gwm*) have a consistent, significant relationship with reading achievement. The significance of comprehension-knowledge (*Gc*) to reading and writing achievement increases with age. In addition, memory span (the ability to attend to and immediately recall temporally ordered items) appears to influence comprehension. Naming facility, an aspect of long-term retrieval (*Glr*), appears to be related to word-retrieval abilities. Fluid reasoning (*Gf*) is also important to reading comprehension but not to decoding. In contrast, visual processing abilities (*Gv*) have little significance in explaining or predicting reading achievement.

Visual processing abilities *(Gv)* appear, however, to be related to math tasks that require higher level skills and thinking but not to basic math skills (McGrew & Wendling, 2010). Some students have difficulty with the conceptual component of math, such as the abilities involved in learning mathematical concepts and solving story problems. For students with weaknesses in math problem solving, it is important to determine whether language or reading problems are contributing to a mathematics problem, or if the difficulty stems from weaknesses in quantitative knowledge and reasoning. Table 6.7 indicates achievement, oral language, and cognitive clusters to consider when interpreting performance in academic applications.

TABLE 6.7 Clusters to Consider When Interpreting Performance in Academic Applications

Academic Application Cluster/Test	Relevant Achievement or Oral Language Clusters	Relevant Cognitive Clusters
Academic Applications Applied Problems Passage Comprehension Writing Samples	Broad Oral Language Academic Knowledge Academic Skills Academic Fluency	Comprehension-Knowledge Fluid Reasoning Cognitive Processing Speed Short-term Working Memory Auditory Processing Long-term Retrieval
Math Problem Solving Applied Problems Number Matrices	Math Calculation Skills Broad Oral Language	Comprehension-Knowledge Fluid Reasoning Cognitive Processing Speed Short-term Working Memory Visual Processing
Reading Comprehension Passage Comprehension Reading Recall	Basic Reading Skills Academic Knowledge Broad Oral Language Listening Comprehension Oral Expression	Comprehension-Knowledge Short-term Working Memory Auditory Processing
Written Expression Writing Samples Sentence Writing Fluency	Basic Writing Skills Reading Comprehension Academic Knowledge Broad Oral Language Oral Expression	Comprehension-Knowledge Cognitive Processing Speed Short-term Working Memory Auditory Processing

Instructional Implications for Academic Applications

Students with weaknesses in language, knowledge, and/or application tasks often require an adjustment in the difficulty level of the instructional materials to be successful. Rather than providing more time to complete assignments, the content of the assignments needs to be matched to the student's level of linguistic and academic competence. Most students can be successful in school if they learn how to be organized, reflective, and strategic. Regardless of whether a strategy is designed primarily to enhance oral language, knowledge, reading comprehension, written expression, or math problem solving, the following general principles apply (Meltzer, Roditi, & Stein, 1998): (a) teach strategies in the context of the curriculum; (b) teach different strategies so students can choose among strategies; (c) provide a balance between instruction in strategies and skills; (d) encourage students to understand their own learning styles; and (e) show students how to adapt strategies as needed. Effective strategy instruction requires clear descriptions of the strategy; teacher modeling followed by student verbal rehearsal, practice, and extensive feedback; gradual transfer of strategy control to students; and the use of instructional level texts (Jitendra & Gajria, 2011).

Oral language, reading comprehension, written expression. One goal of instruction for students with weaknesses in language and academic applications is to increase background knowledge. A simple strategy for helping students increase their knowledge is called the K–W–L strategy (Ogle, 1986). Three columns are written across the top of a paper: What I Know, What I Want to Learn, and What I Learned. The K–W–L procedure provides an opportunity for the student to organize what is known, to record new information, and then review and rehearse what has been learned.

Another goal for instruction is to help students increase their knowledge of word meanings by bringing vocabulary to life (Beck, McKeown, & Kucan, 2013). As students progress through school, the vocabulary used in their classes becomes increasingly more specialized. Many students benefit from direct instruction in morphology, the meaning units of language, as well as instruction in Latin and Greek roots; this type of instruction can deepen students' understanding of language structure (Henry, 2010). Students can study word origins as well as the various derivations of words to increase their understanding of how common morphemes, such as prefixes and suffixes, alter word meaning. Explicit instruction in a single cognitive strategy (e.g., finding the main idea, questioning) as well as integrated strategies (e.g., collaborative strategic reading) can also help struggling students acquire reading processes that have proven to be effective across content areas (Jitendra & Gajria, 2011). As a cautionary note, if oral language abilities are the primary area of concern, a more comprehensive evaluation by a speech and language therapist is often needed to pinpoint the exact linguistic difficulties and plan a systematic intervention program.

In order to identify effective instructional practices for teaching writing to elementary grade students, Graham, McKeown, Kiuhara, and Harris (2012) conducted a meta-analysis of the writing intervention literature. Examples of effective writing instruction included: strategy instruction, adding self-regulation to strategy instruction, text structure instruction, teaching transcription skills, pre-writing activities, word processing, and comprehensive writing programs. Several other activities also resulted in a statistically significant improvement in the quality of students' writing.

Math reasoning. Students who have difficulty with math problem solving require instruction that focuses on meaning and establishing prerequisite skills and concepts. In a meta-analysis of mathematical intervention research, Gersten et al. (2008) reported that the following approaches were effective for students with learning disabilities: (a) explicit instruction in a strategy with practice and corrective feedback; (b) student verbalization of the solution to the problem; (c) visual representations of the math problems, such as graphs and diagrams; (d) inclusion of carefully selected examples; (e) instruction and practice applying multiple strategies; (f) provision of performance data and recommendations for instruction to teachers; (g) provision of feedback to students on their performance, and (h) cross-age peer tutoring.

Because students progress through different stages of learning at different rates, the teacher needs to identify the stage of learning the student has reached and adjust intervention accordingly. Smith and Rivera (1998) identify the following stages: In the first stage, the student is *acquiring the skill* or learning how to perform the skill, practicing the skill, and becoming increasingly accurate in using the skill. During the second stage, the student becomes *proficient with the skill*—he or she develops the ability to respond more easily while maintaining accuracy. In the third stage, maintenance, the student extends his or her ability to continue to *maintain or use the skill* once mastery is achieved. Some students find this particularly difficult without on-going practice and review. For these students, it is necessary to provide periodic assessment to ensure that the skill is still maintained. *Generalization*, the fourth stage, is the ability to use the skill in different situations. Generalization should occur throughout all stages of learning mathematics and the teacher should create opportunities for students to apply strategies in new situations and model for students the times, places, and situations that the skill can be used. In the final stage, students learn *adaptation* or ways to extend their knowledge and skills through problem solving.

General interventions that assist in teaching mathematics include modeling (particularly useful during the first two stages of instruction), shaping (using reinforcement as the student works toward successive approximations of the skill), drills, rewards for accuracy, and feedback and strategy instruction. Guided practice as students engage in problem solving can be critical. In addition, teachers should teach content thoroughly and not move on with instruction until mastery has been achieved. Unfortunately, many teachers move on to new math material even though students are answering only about 60% of the problems correctly (Jones, Wilson, & Bhojwani, 1997).

Verbal explanations and discussions can also facilitate learning quantitative concepts. As with strategies for reading and writing, students need opportunities to discuss, clarify, and state what is being learned to help increase understanding. In addition, teachers should provide explicit instruction in the language of mathematics including signs, symbols, and terms as well as the vocabulary used to express mathematical ideas. Students who have difficulty using language need to talk through possible answers to word problems so that they can identify and resolve incorrect assumptions (Tobias, 1993).

Students with weaknesses in language, knowledge, and/or reasoning abilities need to have teachers who will establish appropriate expectations, set clear educational goals, and adjust explanations and assignments to the level of the student's understanding. This does not mean setting lowered expectations, but rather realistic expectations: the teacher designs instruction that is challenging yet possible for the student to learn and succeed. As illustrated by Vygotsky's concept of the zone of proximal development, good instruction is one step above a student's present performance level (Vygotsky, 1978).

SAMPLE CASE

Consideration of an individual's cognitive and linguistic strengths and weaknesses in the context of academic performance can provide a meaningful framework for determining instructional implications. The following example illustrates some of the comparisons that can be made within the WJ IV. The three WJ IV ACH cross-domain clusters—Academic Skills, Academic Fluency, and Academic Applications—are used as the focal points for understanding academic performance.

Noel: Age 9-6, Grade 4.6

Noel was referred for an evaluation by her parents who expressed concerns about their daughter's reading and spelling abilities. In addition, the parents were concerned that Noel was spending an inordinate amount of time trying to complete her homework assignments each night. Noel's teacher, Ms. Stein, reported that Noel rarely finished assignments within the time allowed in class which has increased the amount of her nightly homework. Classroom observations in Noel's social studies class also supported that Noel was slow to complete lengthy reading assignments. For this assessment, the evaluator selected the WJ IV because it provides opportunities to analyze patterns of performance between and among cognitive, linguistic, and academic abilities. This process can help the evaluator document specific academic difficulties as well as the underlying cognitive or linguistic abilities that may be impacting performance.

A review of Noel's performance on the three cross-academic clusters indicated significant variations between her Academic Skills, Academic Fluency,

TABLE 6.8 Noel's Cross-Domain Cluster Variations

Variations	Standard Scores			Discrepancy		Interpretation at ± 1.50 SD (SEE)
	Actual	Predicted	Difference	PR	SD	
Academic Skills/Academic Fluency/Academic Applications Variations						
Academic Skills	83	95	−12	4	−1.72	Weakness
Academic Fluency	83	96	−13	6	−1.51	Weakness
Academic Applications	107	85	22	99	+2.47	Strength

and Academic Application clusters. Academic Skills and Academic Fluency were significant weaknesses for Noel while Academic Applications was a significant strength (Table 6.8). This variation procedure compares each cluster to the average of the other two clusters to determine if any significant differences exist. When analyzing Noel's performance, only 4% of her age mates with the same predicted score would have scored as low or lower on Academic Skills. On Academic Fluency, only 6% of her age mates with the same predicted score would have scored as low or lower. On the other hand, only 1% of age mates with the same predicted score would have scored as high or higher on Academic Applications. These strengths and weaknesses are relative to Noel's performance as all of the SSs were in the low average to average range.

An analysis of these findings suggests that Noel's higher level reading, writing, and math skills (e.g., comprehension, expression, and reasoning) are intact and that she may benefit from accommodations such as extended time or shorter assignments on tasks involving basic skills or rapid performance. In contrast, if no penalty exists for basic skills and sufficient time is allotted on tasks, Noel should not need adjustments on tasks involving reasoning and problem solving. To further substantiate these conclusions, it is necessary to examine the tests within each cluster to determine whether the problems are generalized or domain-specific.

Within the Academic Skills cluster (Table 6.9), Calculation with an SS of 114 and an RPI of 98/90 is not an area of concern. In contrast, Noel is demonstrating considerable difficulty with Letter–Word Identification and Spelling. These tests have SSs in the low range (SS = 74) and RPIs of 5/90 and 12/90, respectively, indicating that Noel has very limited proficiency on word reading and spelling.

TABLE 6.9 Noel's Academic Skills Cluster and Test Results

Cluster/Tests	W	AE	RPI	SS (68% Band)
Academic Skills	469	7-11	42/90	83 (81–86)
Letter–Word Identification	446	7-0	5/90	74 (71–76)
Spelling	454	7-0	12/90	74 (70–78)
Calculation	506	11-2	98/90	114 (109–118)

TABLE 6.10 Noel's Academic Fluency Cluster and Test Results

Cluster/Tests	W	AE	RPI	SS (68% Band)
Academic Fluency	463	6-11	28/90	83 (80–86)
Sentence Reading Fluency	420	6-11	1/90	74 (70–79)
Math Facts Fluency	500	10-1	95/90	104 (100–109)
Sentence Writing Fluency	470	7-0	37/90	74 (67–81)

TABLE 6.11 Noel's Academic Application Cluster and Test Results

Cluster/Tests	W	AE	RPI	SS (68% Band)
Academic Applications	500	10-5	94/90	107 (104–111)
Applied Problems	511	12-6	99/90	117 (112–122)
Passage Comprehension	484	8-3	75/90	92 (88–96)
Writing Samples	503	11-8	96/90	109 (105–114)

Similarly, within the Academic Fluency cluster (Table 6.10), Sentence Reading Fluency and Sentence Writing Fluency are problematic, whereas Math Facts Fluency is not. For Academic Skills and Academic Fluency, the criterion-referenced scores (RPIs) indicate that compared to average age mates, Noel is functionally limited in her performance involving basic reading and writing skills especially under timed conditions. The results of an informal reading inventory also supported the conclusion that Noel has limited automaticity with word identification which affects her reading rate.

The tests within the Academic Applications cluster (Table 6.11) indicated performance in the average to high average range on Applied Problems, in the

TABLE 6.12 Noel's Intra-Cognitive Variations

Variations	Standard Scores			Discrepancy		Interpretation at ± 1.50 SD (SEE)
	Actual	Predicted	Difference	PR	SD	
Intra-Cognitive (Extended) Variations						
Comprehension Knowledge (Gc)	132	97	35	99.8	+2.88	Strength
Fluid Reasoning (Gf)	108	101	7	74	+0.64	–
S–T Work Mem (Gwm)	126	100	26	99	+2.24	Strength
Auditory Process (Ga)	71	106	−35	0.1	−3.00	Weakness
L-Term Retrieval (Glr)	78	104	−26	2	−2.16	Weakness
Perceptual Speed	83	104	−21	5	−1.69	Weakness

low average to average range on Passage Comprehension, and in the average range for Writing Samples. This example also illustrates the importance of considering the RPI in addition to the SS. On Passage Comprehension, the SS of 92 is within the average range. However, the RPI of 75/90 indicates "limited" proficiency or mastery of this type of task compared to average age mates. Grade level reading comprehension tasks would be difficult for Noel.

Next, Noel's cognitive and linguistic abilities were examined to determine if any factors can help explain her academic strengths and weaknesses and would assist in determining accommodations and planning an appropriate instructional program. On the intra-cognitive variation procedure (Table 6.12), Noel demonstrated significant strengths in Comprehension-Knowledge (Gc) and Fluid Reasoning (Gf) and significant weaknesses in Auditory Processing (Ga), Cognitive Processing Speed (Gs), and Long-term Retrieval (Glr). Noel's cognitive strengths help explain her strengths in Academic Applications. Her strong knowledge base and reasoning skills facilitate her ability to comprehend, organize her thoughts for writing, and solve math problems.

In contrast, Noel's cognitive weaknesses help explain her difficulties in the reading and writing areas within Academic Skills and Academic Fluency. All three cognitive abilities—auditory processing, cognitive processing speed, and long-term retrieval—have documented relationships to reading and writing, especially in the area of basic skills (McGrew & Wendling, 2010). Further, her

TABLE 6.13 Noel's Intra-Oral Language Variations

Variations	Standard Scores			Discrepancy		Interpretation at ± 1.50 SD (SEE)
	Actual	Predicted	Difference	PR	SD	
Intra-Oral Language (Extended) Variations						
Oral Expression	113	89	24	98	+2.06	Strength
Listening Comp	94	93	1	57	+0.17	–
Phonetic Coding	75	101	−26	3	−1.85	Weakness
Speed of Lexical Access	70	102	−32	1	−2.46	Weakness
Vocabulary	131	89	42	>99.9	+3.75	Strength

significant weakness on the Perceptual Speed cluster provides a possible reason for her lack of fluency.

A review of the WJ IV OL intra-oral language variation procedure indicates that Noel's oral expression and vocabulary scores are in the high average to superior range, respectively, and are significant strengths for her. In addition, Noel's strong vocabulary performance provides supporting evidence for her strength in Comprehension-Knowledge and indicates that her reading and spelling difficulties are not due to limits in acquired knowledge. In contrast, significant weaknesses included the Phonetic Coding cluster, an aspect of phonological awareness, and the Speed of Lexical Access cluster, or ability to retrieve words quickly. These linguistic weaknesses are similar to the cognitive weaknesses identified in Auditory Processing and Cognitive Processing Speed (Table 6.13).

When her Broad Oral Language cluster (SS=106) is used as a predictor in the ability/achievement discrepancy procedure, Noel demonstrated significant discrepancies in Reading, Broad Reading, Basic Reading Skills, Reading Fluency, Academic Skills, and Academic Fluency (Table 6.14). This information provides additional support for documenting her domain-specific weaknesses in reading and writing. In addition, Noel's performance on two oral language clusters, Phonetic Coding and Speed of Lexical Access, was significantly lower than expected based on her Broad Oral Language cluster score. These linguistic abilities are foundational for decoding, encoding, and rapid word recognition which further explains Noel's difficulties in word reading and spelling.

Based on the results of this evaluation as well as qualitative information from parents, teachers, and classroom observations, Noel was determined to be eligible for specific learning disabilities services. An IEP was completed

TABLE 6.14 Noel's Broad Oral Language/Achievement Comparisons

Comparisons	Standard Scores			Discrepancy		Interpretation at ± 1.50 SD (SEE)
	Actual	Predicted	Difference	PR	SD	
Oral Language/Achievement Comparisons						
Reading	80	104	−24	2	−2.01	Yes (−)
Broad Reading	78	104	−26	2	−2.07	Yes (−)
Basic Reading Skills	75	104	−29	1	−2.36	Yes (−)
Reading Fluency	71	104	−33	1	−2.45	Yes (−)
Mathematics	117	103	14	86	+1.06	No
Broad Mathematics	112	104	8	74	+0.63	No
Math Calculation Skills	109	104	5	65	+0.38	No
Written Language	89	103	−14	14	−1.08	No
Broad Written Lang	85	103	−18	9	−1.35	No
Written Expression	93	102	−9	25	−0.66	No
Academic Skills	83	103	−20	6	−1.58	Yes (−)
Academic Fluency	83	103	−20	7	−1.51	Yes (−)
Academic Applications	107	104	3	61	+0.29	No
Phonetic Coding	75	103	−28	2	−1.98	Yes (−)
Speed of Lexical Access	70	103	−33	0.4	−2.65	Yes (−)

for her that addressed her weaknesses in the areas of decoding, encoding, and fluency. The IEP also included several accommodations to support Noel while she received systematic reading and writing instruction. The primary accommodations were: a time limit on homework assignments, no penalty for spelling errors, extended time on tests as needed, and shortened assignments. With the exception of extended time as needed, accommodations were not necessary for higher level tasks involving reasoning and problem solving. The following instructional recommendations were provided.

Reading

1. Use an explicit, synthetic phonics program to improve Noel's phonemic awareness and phonic skills. One example would be the Wilson Reading System®, provided by a teacher with training in this methodology. Provide Noel with 1-hour tutorials at least three times a week. As an alternative, instruction could be delivered using an online reading intervention, such as the Virtual Reading Coach (www.mindplay.com). Noel should spend 30 minutes 5 days a week on this intervention and continue to use the program throughout the summer.
2. Provide additional fluency practice using text that Noel can read with 95% accuracy. Methods include repeated reading with immediate error correction, rapid word recognition charts, timed readings, and modeling fluent reading.
3. Provide Noel with recorded books so that she can access grade level content.

Spelling

1. Use phoneme–grapheme mapping materials to strengthen Noel's understanding of sounds and symbols.
2. Provide a customized or shortened list of words for Noel to study for the weekly spelling test.
3. Use a multisensory approach (seeing, saying, and tracing) to teach Noel how to spell high frequency and irregular words that she misspells in her writing assignments.
4. Teach Noel common spelling rules, the six syllable types, and how to spell common word parts, such as prefixes and suffixes.

CONCLUSION

"The single most important factor in planning for a child with a learning disability is an intensive diagnostic study. Without a comprehensive evaluation of his deficits and assets, the educational program may be too general, or even inappropriate" (Johnson & Myklebust, 1967, p. 50).

The WJ IV is a sophisticated diagnostic instrument that serves as a valuable tool when in the hands of a skilled clinician. By analyzing the results of the WJ IV ACH, an evaluator can determine if the problem is related to generalized low performance, performance on certain types of tasks across the academic domains (skills, fluency, and/or applications), or the difficulties are circumscribed to one area of functioning. Once the cognitive and linguistic factors that both facilitate and inhibit academic performance have been identified, a specific instructional plan can be developed that is designed to address the referral concerns and promote more successful outcomes for the individual.

REFERENCES

Allor, J. H., & Chard, D. J. (2011). A comprehensive approach to improving reading fluency for students with disabilities. *Focus on Exceptional Children, 43*(5), 1–12.

Alvarez, M. C. (1983). Sustained timed writing as an aid to fluency and creativity. *Teaching Exceptional Children, 15,* 160–162.

Ball, E. W. (1993). Assessing phoneme awareness. *Language, Speech, and Hearing Services in Schools, 24,* 130–139.

Beck, I. L., McKeown, M. G., & Kucan, L. (2013). *Bringing words to life: Robust vocabulary instruction* (2nd ed.). New York, NY: Guilford Press.

Begeny, J. C., Daly, E. J., & Vallely, R. J. (2006). Improving oral reading fluency through response opportunities: A comparison of phrase drill error correction and repeated reading. *Journal of Behavioral Education, 15*(4), 229–235.

Berninger, V. W. (1996). *Reading and writing acquisition: A developmental neuropsychological perspective.* Oxford, UK: Westview Press.

Berninger, V. W., & Richards, T. (2002). *Brain literacy for educators and psychologists.* San Diego, CA: Academic Press.

Berninger, V. W., Vaughan, K., Abbott, R. D., Brooks, A., Begay, K., Curtin, G., et al. (2000). Language-based spelling instruction: Teaching children to make multiple connections between spoken and written words. *Learning Disability Quarterly, 23,* 117–135.

Berninger, V. W., & Wolf, B. J. (2009). *Teaching students with dyslexia and dysgraphia: Lessons from teaching and science.* Baltimore, MD: Paul H. Brookes.

Betts, E. A. (1946). *Foundations of reading instruction.* New York, NY: American Book.

Bishop, D. V. M., & Adams, C. (1990). A prospective study of the relationship between specific language impairment, phonological disorders and reading retardation. *Journal of Child Psychology and Psychiatry, 31*(7), 1027–1050.

Bruck, M. (1998). Outcomes of adults with childhood histories of dyslexia. In C. Hulme & R. M. Joshi (Eds.), *Reading and spelling development and disorders* (pp. 179–200). Mahwah, NJ: Lawrence Erlbaum.

Calfee, R. (1998). Phonics and phonemes: Learning to decode and spell in a literature-based program. In J. L. Metsala & L. C. Ehri (Eds.), *Word recognition in beginning literacy* (pp. 315–340). Mahwah, NJ: Lawrence Erlbaum.

Callens, M., Tops, W., & Brysbaert, M. (2012). Cognitive profile of students who enter higher education with an indication of dyslexia. *PLOS ONE, 7*(6), e38081.http://dx.doi.org/10.1371/journal.pone.0038081.

Campbell, K. U. (2005). *Great leaps reading program.* Micanopy, FL: Diarmuid.

Carreker, S. (2009). Teaching reading: Accurate decoding and fluency. In J. R. Birsh (Ed.), *Multisensory teaching of basic language skills* (pp. 141–182) (3rd ed.). Baltimore, MD: Paul H. Brookes.

Carroll, J. B. (1993). *Human cognitive abilities: A survey of factor-analytic studies.* New York, NY: Cambridge University Press.

Cawley, J. F. (1985). Arithmetical word problems and the learning disabled. Paper presented at the Association for Children with Learning Disabilities, International Conference, San Francisco.

Chafouleas, S. M., Lewandowski, L. J., Smith, C. R., & Blachman, B. A. (1997). Phonological awareness skills in children: Examining performance across tasks and ages. *Journal of Psychoeducational Assessment, 15,* 331–347.

Chard, D. J., & Dickson, S. V. (1999). Phonological awareness: Instructional and assessment guidelines. *Intervention in School and Clinic, 34*(5), 261–270.

Chard, D. J., Vaughn, S., & Tyler, B. J. (2002). A synthesis of research on effective interventions for building reading fluency with elementary students with learning disabilities. *Journal of Learning Disabilities, 35*(5), 386–406.

Clark, D. B., & Uhry, J. K. (1995). *Dyslexia: Theory and practice of remedial instruction* (2nd ed.). Baltimore, MD: York Press.

Coltheart, M. (1996). Phonological dyslexia: Past and future. *Cognitive Neuropsychology, 13*(6), 749–762.

Decker, S. (2012). Dimensional integration of assessment outcomes with intervention services for children with specific learning disabilities. *Journal of Applied School Psychology, 28*(2), 175–199.

Douglass, B. (1984). Variation on a theme: Writing with the LD adolescent. *Academic Therapy, 19*(3), 361–363.

Ehri, L. C. (1998). Grapheme–phoneme knowledge is essential for learning to read words in English. In J. L. Metsala & L. C. Ehri (Eds.), *Word recognition in beginning literacy* (pp. 3–40). Mahwah, NJ: Lawrence Erlbaum.

Ehri, L. C. (2000). Learning to read and learning to spell: Two sides of a coin. *Topics in Language Disorders, 20*(3), 19–36.

Evans, J. J., Floyd, R. G., McGrew, K. S., & Leforgee, M. H. (2001). The relations between measures of Cattell–Horn–Carroll (CHC) cognitive abilities and reading achievement during childhood and adolescence. *School Psychology Review, 31*, 246–262.

Fischer, P. (1999). Getting up to speed. *Perspectives, The International Dyslexia Association, 25*(2), 12–13.

Flanagan, D. P., Ortiz, S. O., & Alfonso, V. (2013). *Essentials of cross-battery assessment* (3rd ed.). Hoboken, NJ: Wiley.

Fleischner, J. E., Garnett, K., & Shepherd, M. J. (1982). Proficiency in arithmetic basic fact computation of learning disabled and nondisabled children. *Focus on Learning Problems in Mathematics, 4*, 47–55.

Floyd, R., Meisinger, E., Gregg, N., & Keith, T. (2012). An explanation of reading comprehension across development using models from Cattell–Horn–Carroll theory: Support for integrative models of reading. *Psychology in the Schools, 49*(8), 723–743.

Francis, D. J., Shaywitz, S. E., Stuebing, K. K., Shaywitz, B. A., & Fletcher, J. M. (1996). Developmental lag versus deficit models of reading disability: A longitudinal, individual growth curves study. *Journal of Educational Psychology, 88*(1), 3–17.

Gersten, R., Chard, D. J., Jayanthi, M., Baker, S. K., Morphy, P., & Flojo, J. (2008). *Teaching mathematics to students with learning disabilities: A meta-analysis of the intervention research.* Portsmouth, NH: RMC Research Corporation, Centeron Instruction.

Goldsmith-Phillips, J. (1994). Toward a research-based dyslexia assessment: Case study of a young adult. In N. C. Jordan & J. Goldsmith-Phillips (Eds.), *Learning disabilities: New directions for assessment and intervention* (pp. 85–100). Boston, MA: Allyn and Bacon.

Graham, S., Berninger, V., Abbott, R. D., Abbott, S. P., & Whitaker, D. (1997). Role of mechanics in composing of elementary school students: A new methodological approach. *Journal of Educational Psychology, 89*, 170–182.

Graham, S., McKeown, D., Kiuhara, S., & Harris, K. R. (2012). A meta-analysis of writing instruction for students in the elementary grades. *Journal of Educational Psychology, 104*, 879–896.

Gregg, N. (2001). Written expression disorders. In L. Bailet, A. Bain, & L. Moats (Eds.), *Written language disorders* (2nd ed., pp. 65–98). Austin, TX: Pro-Ed.

Grossen, B. (1997). *30 Years of research: What we now know about how children learn to read.* Santa Cruz, CA: The Center for the Future of Teaching & Learning.

Harrison, M., & Harrison, B. (1986). Developing numeration concepts and skills. *Arithmetic Teacher, 33,* 18–21.

Hasbrouck, J., & Glaser, D. (2011). *Fluency: Understanding and teaching this complex skill: Training manual.* Wellesley Hills, MA: Gibson Hasbrouck & Associates.

Hasselbring, T. S., Goin, L. I., & Bransford, J. D. (1987). Developing automaticity. *Teaching Exceptional Children, 19*(3), 30–33.

Henry, M. K. (2010). *Unlocking literacy: Effective decoding and spelling instruction* (2nd ed.). Baltimore, MD: Paul H. Brookes.

Herbert, E. (1985). One point of view: Manipulatives are good mathematics. *Arithmetic Teacher, 38*(2), 22–23.

Hernandez, D. J. (2012). *Double jeopardy: How third-grade reading skills and poverty influence high school graduation.* Baltimore, MD: Annie E. Casey Foundation.

Holopainen, L., Ahonen, T., & Lyytinen, H. (2001). Predicting delay in reading achievement in a highly transparent language. *Journal of Learning Disabilities, 34*(5), 401–413.

Houten, R. V., Morrison, E., Jarvis, R., & MacDonald, M. (1974). The effects of explicit timing and feedback on compositional response rate in elementary school children. *Journal of Applied Behavior Analysis, 7*(4), 547–555.

Jitendra, A. K., & Gajria, M. (2011). Reading comprehension instruction for students with learning disabilities. *Focus on Exceptional Children, 43*(8), 1–16.

Johnson, D. (1998). Dyslexia: The identification process. In B. K. Shapiro, P. J. Accardo, & A. J. Capute (Eds.), *Specific reading disability: A view of the spectrum* (pp. 137–154). Timonium, MD: York Press.

Johnson, D. J., & Myklebust, H. R. (1967). *Learning disabilities: Educational principles and practices.* New York, NY: Grune & Stratton.

Jones, E. D., Wilson, R., & Bhojwani, S. (1997). Mathematics instruction for secondary students with learning disabilities. *Journal of Learning Disabilities, 30*(2), 151–163.

Kaufman, C. (2010). *Executive function in the classroom.* Baltimore, MD: Paul H. Brookes.

Kirby, J. R., & Becker, L. D. (1988). Cognitive components of learning problems in arithmetic. *Remedial and Special Education, 9*(5), 7–16.

Kirk, S. A. (1975). From labels to action. In S. A. Kirk & M. M. McCarthy (Eds.), *Learning disabilities: Selected ACLD papers* (pp. 39–45). Boston, MA: Houghton Mifflin.

Kirk, S. A., Kleibhan, J. M., & Lerner, J. W. (1978). *Teaching reading to slow and disabled learners.* Boston, MA: Houghton Mifflin.

Levine, M. (1987). *Developmental variations and learning disorders.* Cambridge, MA: Educators Publishing Service.

Liberman, I. Y., Shankweiler, D., & Liberman, A. M. (1989). The alphabetic principle and learning to read. In D. Shankweiler & I. Y. Liberman (Eds.), *Phonology and reading disability: Solving the reading puzzle* (pp. 1–33). Ann Arbor, MI: University of Michigan Press.

Lyon, G. R. (1995). Toward a definition of dyslexia. *Annals of Dyslexia, 45,* 3–27.

Lyon, G. R. (1998). Why reading is not natural. *Educational Leadership, 55*(6), 14–18.

Mastropieri, M. A., Leinart, A., & Scruggs, T. E. (1999). Strategies to increase reading fluency. *Intervention in School and Clinic, 34*(5), 278–283.

Mather, N., & Jaffe, L. E. (2016). *Woodcock–Johnson IV: Reports, recommendations, and strategies.* Hoboken, NJ: Wiley.

Mather, N., & Wendling, B. J. (2012). *Essentials of dyslexia: Assessment and intervention.* Hoboken, NJ: Wiley.

Mather, N., & Wendling, B. J. (2014a). *Examiner's manual. Woodcock–Johnson IV Tests of Cognitive Abilities.* Rolling Meadows, IL: Riverside.

Mather, N., & Wendling, B. J. (2014b). *Examiner's manual. Woodcock–Johnson IV Tests of Oral Language*. Rolling Meadows, IL: Riverside.

Mather, N., & Wendling, B. J. (2014c). *Examiner's manual. Woodcock–Johnson IV Tests of Achievement*. Rolling Meadows, IL: Riverside.

Mather, N., & Wendling, B. J. (2015). *Essentials of WJ IV Tests of Achievement*. Hoboken, NJ: Wiley.

Mathes, P. G., & Fuchs, L. S. (1993). Peer-mediated reading instruction in special education resource rooms. *Learning Disabilities Research & Practice*, *8*, 233–243.

McGrew, K. S., & Wendling, B. J. (2010). CHC cognitive-achievement relations: What we have learned from the past 20 years of research. *Psychology in the Schools*, *47*(7), 651–675.

Meltzer, L. J. (1994). Assessment of learning disabilities: The challenge of evaluating cognitive strategies and processes underlying learning. In G. R. Lyon (Ed.), *Frames of reference for the assessment of learning disabilities: New views on measurement issues* (pp. 571–606). Baltimore, MD: Paul H. Brookes.

Meltzer, L., Roditi, B., & Stein, J. (1998). Strategy instruction: The heartbeat of successful inclusion. *Perspectives (The International Dyslexia Foundation)*, *24*(3), 10–13.

Meyer, M. S., & Felton, R. H. (1999). Repeated reading to enhance fluency: Old approaches and new directions. *Annals of Dyslexia*, *49*(1), 283–306.

Moats, L. C. (1995). *Spelling: Development disability and instruction*. Baltimore, MD: York Press.

Montague, M. (1997). Cognitive strategy instruction in mathematics for students with learning disabilities. *Journal of Learning Disabilities*, *30*(2), 164–177.

Morris, R. D., Stuebing, K. K., Fletcher, J. M., Shaywitz, S. E., Lyon, G. R., Shankweiler, D. P., ... Shaywitz, B. A., (1998). Subtypes of reading disability: Variability around a phonological core. *Journal of Educational Psychology*, *90*, 347–373.

Nation, K., & Hulme, C. (2011). Learning to read changes children's phonological skills: Evidence from a latent variable longitudinal study of reading and nonword repetition. *Developmental Science*, *14*(4), 649–659.

Novick, B. Z., & Arnold, M. M. (1988). *Fundamentals of clinical child neuropsychology*. Philadelphia, PA: Grune & Stratton.

Ogle, D. M. (1986). K–W–L: A teaching model that develops active reading of expository text. *Reading Teacher*, *39*(6), 564–570.

Olson, R. K. (2011). Evaluation of Fast ForWord language effects on language and reading. *Perspectives on Language and Literacy*, *37*(1), 11–15.

Perfetti, C. A. (1992). The representation problem in reading acquisition. In P. B. Gough, L. C. Ehri, & R. Treiman (Eds.), *Reading acquisition* (pp. 145–174). Hillsdale, NJ: Lawrence Erlbaum Associates.

Pikulski, J. J., & Chard, D. J. (2005). Fluency: Bridge between decoding and reading comprehension. *Reading Teacher*, *58*, 510–519.

Price, G. R., & Ansari, D. (2013). Dyscalculia: Characteristics, causes and treatments. *Numeracy*, *6*(1) Article 2. Available at: http://scholarcommons.usf.edu/numeracy/vol6/iss1/art2.

Price, K. W., Meisinger, E. B., Louwerse, M. M., & D'Mello, S. (2015). The contributions of oral and silent reading fluency to reading comprehension. *Reading Psychology*.

Rack, J. P., Snowling, M., & Olson, R. (1992). The nonword reading deficit in developmental dyslexia: A review. *Reading Research Quarterly*, *27*(1), 28–53.

Rolfhus, E. L., & Ackerman, P. L. (1999). Assessing individual differences in knowledge: Knowledge, intelligence, and related traits. *Journal of Educational Psychology*, *91*(3), 511–526.

Schneider, W., & Shiffrin, R. M. (1977). Controlled and automatic human information processing: Detection, search, and attention. *Psychological Review*, *84*(1), 1–66.

Schrank, F. A., Mather, N., & McGrew, K. S. (2014a). *Woodcock–Johnson IV Tests of Achievement*. Rolling Meadows, IL: Riverside.

Schrank, F. A., Mather, N., & McGrew, K. S. (2014b). *Woodcock–Johnson IV Tests of Oral Language*. Rolling Meadows, IL: Riverside.

Schrank, F. A., McGrew, K. S., & Mather, N. (2014a). *Woodcock–Johnson IV*. Rolling Meadows, IL: Riverside.

Schrank, F. A., McGrew, K. S., & Mather, N. (2014b). *Woodcock–Johnson IV Tests of Cognitive Abilities*. Rolling Meadows, IL: Riverside.

Schrank, F. A., & Wendling, B. J. (2015). *Woodcock Interpretive and Instructional Interventions Program (WIIIP)*. Rolling Meadows, IL: Riverside.

Siegel, L. S., & Ryan, E. B. (1988). Development of grammatical sensitivity, phonological, and short-term memory in normally achieving and learning disabled children. *Developmental Psychology*, *24*(1), 28–37.

Smith, D. D., & Rivera, D. P. (1998). Mathematics. In B. Wong (Ed.), *Learning about learning disabilities* (2nd ed., pp. 346–374). San Diego, CA: Academic Press.

Snowling, M. J., & Hulme, C. (2011). Evidence-based interventions for reading and language difficulties: Creating a virtuous circle. *British Journal of Educational Psychology*, *81*(1), 1–23.

Spencer, M., Quinn, J. M., & Wagner, R. K. (2014). Specific reading comprehension disability: Major problem, myth, or misnomer? *Learning Disabilities Research & Practice*, *29*(1), 3–9.

Stanovich, K. E. (1986). Matthew effects in reading: Some consequences of individual differences in the acquisition of literacy. *Reading Research Quarterly*, *21*(4), 360–406.

Suydam, M. N. (1984). Research report: Manipulative materials. *Arithmetic Teacher*, *31*(5), 27.

Tallal, P., Curtiss, S., & Kaplan, R. (1989). The San Diego longitudinal study: Evaluating the outcomes of preschool impairment in language development (Final Report, NINCDS). Washington, DC.

Therrien, W. J., & Kubina, R. M. (2006). Developing reading fluency with repeated reading. *Intervention in School and Clinic*, *41*(3), 156–160.

Tobias, S. (1993). *Overcoming math anxiety*. New York, NY: W.W. Norton & Co.

Torgesen, J. K. (1992). Learning disabilities: Historical and conceptual issues. In B. Y. L. Wong (Ed.), *Learning about learning disabilities* (pp. 3–38). San Diego, CA: Academic Press.

Torgesen, J. K. (1993). Variations on theory in learning disabilities. In G. R. Lyon, D. B. Gray, J. F. Kavanagh, & N. A. Krasnegor (Eds.), *Better understanding learning disabilities: New views from research and their implications for education and public policies* (pp. 153–170). Baltimore, MD: Paul H. Brookes.

Torgesen, J. K., Rashotte, C. A., & Alexander, A. W. (2001). Principles of fluency instruction in reading: Relationships with established empirical outcomes. In M. Wolf (Ed.), *Dyslexia, fluency, and the brain* (pp. 333–355). Timonium, MD: York Press.

Vygotsky, L. S. (1978). *Mind in society*. Cambridge, MA: Harvard University Press.

Wagner, R. K., & Torgesen, J. K. (1987). The nature of phonological processing and its causal role in the acquisition of reading skills. *Psychological Bulletin*, *101*(2), 192–212.

Wagner, R. K., Torgesen, J. K., Laughon, P., Simmons, K., & Rashotte, C. A. (1993). The development of young readers' phonological processing abilities. *Journal of Educational Psychology*, *85*(1), 1–20.

Wendling, B. J., & Mather, N. (2009). *Essentials of evidence-based academic interventions*. Hoboken, NJ: Wiley.

Wiig, E., & Semel, E. (1984). *Language assessment and intervention for the learning disabled*. Columbus, OH: Charles E. Merrill.

Wilson, A. M., & Lesaux, N. K. (2001). Persistence of phonological processing deficits in college students with dyslexia who have age-appropriate reading skills. *Journal of Learning Disabilities, 34*(5), 394–400.

Wolf, M., & Bowers, P. G. (1999). The double-deficit hypothesis for the developmental dyslexias. *Journal of Educational Psychology, 91*(3), 415–438.

Woodcock, R. W. (1999). What can Rasch-based scores convey about a person's test performance?. In S. E. Embretson & S. L. Hershberger (Eds.), *The new rules of measurement: What every psychologist and educator should know* (pp. 106–109). Mahwah, NJ: Lawrence Erlbaum Associates.

Chapter 7

Strengths and Weaknesses of the Woodcock–Johnson IV Tests of Cognitive Abilities: Best Practice from a Scientist–Practitioner Perspective

W. Joel Schneider

Department of Psychology, Illinois State University, Normal, IL, USA

In the competitive marketplace, the major cognitive batteries are pitted against each other. Once they enter our possession, however, they are on the same side, a team of former rivals, united in purpose. There is a sense in which each could do the job of the other reasonably well. Used together, however, their complementary strengths and compensating virtues offer safeguards against the weaknesses and vulnerabilities that each of them would have if used alone. Well-trained and thoughtful professionals may have their favorites, but depending on the needs of the moment, they often have good reasons to select an alternate battery. Even when they start with their preferred tool, they encounter questions that are best answered with follow-up testing from another battery.

There is no final sense in which the Woodcock–Johnson IV Tests of Cognitive Abilities (WJ IV COG; Schrank, McGrew, & Mather, 2014b) is "The Best Cognitive Battery." No test merits such a title. As seen below, however, the WJ IV COG is clearly the best (if not only) choice for particular applications. In some applications, it is merely a good option among many other solid alternatives. As with all other batteries, there are certain assessment questions the WJ IV COG does not answer very well and others it does not answer at all.

What follows is an idiosyncratic review of the strengths and weaknesses of the WJ IV COG's individual tests and of the battery as a whole. Throughout the review, it is assumed that the reader is already familiar with the Cattell–Horn–Carroll (CHC) theory of cognitive abilities (McGrew, 2009; Schneider & McGrew, 2012), the primary theoretical foundation of the WJ IV COG.

WJ IV Clinical Use and Interpretation. DOI: http://dx.doi.org/10.1016/B978-0-12-802076-0.00007-4
191

Water that has been boiled is generally safe to drink, but has an unpleasant taste. Compared to the goal of preventing waterborne disease, improving the taste is a minor concern. Sometimes test developers have to make hard choices, allowing for minor flaws so as to avoid major ones. Critics like me often make much of minor problems in the final product, blissfully unaware of the toil and trouble it took to prevent disaster.

In times of scarcity, we human beings are grateful for whatever we can get. It is in times of plenty that we find plenty to complain about. When indulged, coddled, and pampered, our most bitter resentment is aroused by objects that fall just short of perfection. And even when an item is truly flawless, our most enduring reaction to it is to want more of it than is available. Thus, in cataloging the various strengths and weaknesses of the WJ IV COG, it was important for me to keep a sense of proper perspective. The handwork of mortals cannot be perfect in every dimension simultaneously. With each additional test and each additional feature, the WJ IV COG offers critics like me another nit to pick and many a hair to split. It is like a sumptuous banquet at which the appetizers inspire a sense of mystery and delight, each round of entrees thins the veil between us and the divine, the desserts offer temporary transport to cosmic fulfillment, and at its conclusion we observe that the postprandial coffee is weak and that the decor is plain. It is to this level of shameless greed and ingratitude that I aspire. In this light, when my complaints seem trivial, petty, and vulgar, consider it high praise indeed.

STRENGTHS AND WEAKNESSES: INDIVIDUAL TESTS

Tests of Comprehension/Knowledge (*Gc*)

Oral Vocabulary

In this test, examinees give synonyms and antonyms to words of varying degrees of difficulty. This test is a welcome return to the Oral Vocabulary test from the WJ R Tests of Cognitive Ability (WJ R COG; Woodcock & Johnson, 1989). The WJ R also had a Verbal Analogies test. In the Woodcock–Johnson III Tests of Cognitive Abilities (WJ III COG; Woodcock, McGrew, & Mather, 2001a), Oral Vocabulary and Verbal Analogies were fused together into the Verbal Comprehension test. This fusion was like a composite score from which it was not possible to parse the individual scores. Thankfully, we have a more pure measure of oral vocabulary once again.

This test is quick and easy to administer with straightforward scoring rules. The words are well chosen, with no obvious missteps. Sometimes vocabulary tests contain difficult words from specialist fields, which, to my mind, undermines the utility of the test. In the Oral Vocabulary test, even the most difficult items consist of words with general applicability and usefulness. Most of the words have an abstract quality, having to do with basic dimensions (e.g., size, quantity, proportion, position, and time) and human relations (e.g., roles, emotions, personality, intentions, and evaluations).

A nice feature of this test is that because it requires single-word answers (although there are often many correct single-word answers), it can alert clinicians to possible problems of dysnomia (memory retrieval deficits manifest in word-finding problems). When people appear to know what many of the words mean, but cannot think of single-word responses, follow-up assessment with specialized tests seems warranted.

One of the great features of the WJ IV COG is that related tests are often arranged in a thoughtful hierarchy from measures of simple to complex cognitive functions. From a task analysis perspective, this test is on the simple end of the verbal ability continuum. It is a straightforward measure of vocabulary in which one must identify near synonyms and antonyms for different words. What this test gains in clarity, however, it loses in subtlety. There are few words in English that are truly interchangeable. Students who consult the thesaurus to make their writing sound fancy often embarrass themselves. For example, looking up *many* in a thesaurus we can find words as diverse as *bountiful, crowded, umpteen, varied, loads, frequent, innumerable, bags of*, and *lousy with*. I believe that vocabulary tests are important in the measurement of intelligence not so much to see if a person knows what words mean in general but to see if a person can use words to make important distinctions. Well-designed cloze items and analogies can assess a person's understanding of how related words are used differently (Gellert & Elbro, 2013). Contrasting a person's performance on relatively simple measures of verbal understanding like Oral Vocabulary with more complex measures like Oral Comprehension, Understanding Directions, and tests outside the WJ IV COG can offer helpful insights into a person's difficulties. Note that I am not saying that there is a particular meaning that is evident when Oral Vocabulary is higher than Oral Comprehension or vice versa. There are probably thousands of possible explanations. This is one of the reasons that we still need thoughtful human beings observing evaluees as they approach tasks in diverse ways, according to their unique profile of strengths and weaknesses.

General Information

The *jingle fallacy* is the false idea that things with the same name necessarily refer to the same thing (Aikins, 1902, p. 194; Thorndike, 1904, p. 14). Although the names are quite similar, this test is not at all like the Information subtest of the Wechsler series of intelligence tests. The Wechsler Information subtest covers the same material as the WJ IV COG Humanities, Social Sciences, and Science tests. In contrast, the General Information test measures knowledge about physical objects by asking where would one find them (Where would you find a *rafter*?) and for what they would be used (What is a *bridle* used for?). Note that this test can be seen as a specialized kind of vocabulary test. I may know very well what a bridle does, but I may not know its name. If the *Gc* test correlations from the *Technical Manual* (McGrew, LaForte, & Schrank, 2014) are examined closely, the hypothesis that General Information is more

	General Information	Oral Vocabulary	Picture Vocabulary	Reading Vocabulary	Oral Comprehension	Humanities	Social Studies	Science
General Information		0.71	0.68	0.59	0.53	0.6	0.58	0.4
Oral Vocabulary	0.71		0.7	0.7	0.62	0.6	0.7	0.54
Picture Vocabulary	0.68	0.7		0.61	0.64	0.64	0.68	0.63
Reading Vocabulary	0.59	0.7	0.61		0.65	0.6	0.6	0.58
Oral Comprehension	0.53	0.62	0.64	0.65		0.55	0.58	0.57
Humanities	0.6	0.6	0.64	0.6	0.55		0.64	0.61
Social Studies	0.58	0.7	0.68	0.6	0.58	0.64		0.69
Science	0.4	0.54	0.63	0.58	0.57	0.61	0.69	

FIGURE 7.1 Correlations among the WJ IV COG *Gc* tests in the 9- to 13-year age group.

of a vocabulary test than a general knowledge test is supported. For example, the correlations for ages 9–13 years are above. It is easy to see that General Information, Oral Vocabulary, and Picture Vocabulary form a tight cluster of scores, a finding largely confirmed when I factor-analyzed the correlation matrices from different age groups (Figure 7.1).

Picture Vocabulary

Like General Information, this test measures knowledge about the names of physical objects. It is a good follow-up test if there are questions about a person's performance on General Information.

Oral Comprehension

The test uses the cloze paradigm to measure oral language comprehension. Specifically, it measures the ability to make predictive inferences. For some theorists, making predictive inferences is one of the brain's primary functions (Hawkins & Blakeslee, 2004; Schacter, Addis, & Buckner, 2007). A predictive inference is when a person anticipates what a speaker (or author) is about to say. For example, "My opponent and I disagree about many things, but we both want what is_____ for our country." Our ability to fill in such gaps before a speaker finishes a sentence can be exploited to humorous effect (Groucho Marx was the master of this style of humor: "Before I speak, I have something important to say"). Indeed, much of the pleasure of reading well-written text comes from having our expectations skillfully manipulated so that we feel surprised, shocked, or disappointed when things go unexpectedly wrong and relieved and delighted when they turn out all right after all. Irony and satire are lost on those who cannot make predictive inferences.

Oral Comprehension has a special relationship with Passage Comprehension. Because they have the same format, but are in different modes (oral vs. written), discrepant scores are likely to be meaningful. Again, it is unlikely that discrepant scores signal a single, specific problem. Rather, such discrepancies often function as nonspecific warnings that something warrants our close attention.

Academic Knowledge: Humanities, Social Studies, and Science

These are tests of general knowledge likely to be encountered in formal education. The items are well chosen and can be interpreted in a straightforward manner. It should be noted that performance on these kinds of tests has less to do with mere exposure to the material than it does to having engaged deeply with the material. Except for people whose education was truly deficient, by the end of high school, most people have been exposed repeatedly to almost all of the knowledge tested on such measures. People who have internalized the basic principles and major themes of culture, art, history, and science tend to remember the details. Or rather, the details are remembered because they have been abstracted in memory to represent the basic principles and major themes of these disciplines.

Tests of Fluid Reasoning

Concept Formation

At the core of intelligence is fluid reasoning, and at the core of fluid reasoning is *induction*, the ability to use limited information to discover logical patterns and rule-based behavior. Concept Formation is conceptually well formed. Evaluees try to discover what rule determines which shapes are inside a box and which are outside. The idea behind the test is so simple and elegant that it still amazes me that we had to wait until 1977 before anyone thought of it (Woodcock & Johnson, 1977).

Analysis–Synthesis

This test measures the ability to work with a set of logical rules to deduce new knowledge (what Spearman (1923) called the *eduction of correlates*). This kind of reasoning is at the core of philosophical inquiry, scientific hypothesis testing, mathematical imagination, and the kinds of thought experiments without which democracies fail.

To a degree that is perhaps imprudent of me to admit, Analysis–Synthesis moves me as a work of art. On the surface it is just a simple puzzle. Deeper in, there are mathematical universes awaiting discovery. Not long ago I asked Dick Woodcock if he could think of any way he could have improved upon the various tests he had invented, but for the sake of continuity had been kept the same. He gave thoughtful answers about hard choices that had to be made here and there, but when we came to Analysis–Synthesis, he relaxed and with more than a little pride said, "No, that one I think I got right." I heartily agree.

Number Series+Number Matrices=A Love Story That Doesn't Add Up

Number Series and Number Matrices have a great deal in common—they were practically made for each other. On the WJ III COG, they lived together in a quiet neighborhood called the Diagnostic Supplement to the Woodcock–Johnson III Tests of Cognitive Abilities (WJ III COG DS; Woodcock, McGrew, Mather, & Schrank, 2003). Number Series, though, was living a double life. It had something going on with an Achievement test called Quantitative Knowledge, giving away half its items. This was especially disappointing because on the WJ R ACH, Quantitative Knowledge had been a model of psychometric purity. On the WJ III ACH, it was homewrecker and a sloppy mess.

In the wreckage of this sordid affair, Quantitative Knowledge left town, and Number Series and Number Matrices have called it quits. They moved to separate batteries and are now seeing other tests. Number Series makes up half of the Fluid Reasoning composite in the cognitive battery and Number Matrices makes up half of the Math Problem Solving composite in the achievement battery.

It did not have to be this way. Although I have criticized the WJ III COG and WJ IV COG for creating "Frankentests" that combine qualitatively different item types into a single measure, these tests are of one flesh. For this reason, let them leave their official composites and cleave to each other; so then they are no more twain, but one test. What therefore theory hath joined together, let not practice put asunder. Number Series and Number Matrices should never be interpreted as measuring different abilities. One should not predict or "explain" the other as part of an aptitude cluster. They are neither purely academic nor purely "cognitive," but occupy a weirdish wild space in between.

Tests of Auditory Processing

The WJ batteries have had auditory processing tests since the original 1977 battery. In the transition to the fourth edition, the auditory processing tests have undergone major changes. Incomplete Words is gone. Auditory Attention is no more. I will miss the quirky sounds from the two Sound Patterns tests. Sound Blending and Sound Awareness are the only survivors. The newcomers are a fascinating bunch, mostly measuring aspects of phonological processing, which is known to predict word decoding ability.

Nonword Repetition

For this test, evaluees must repeat back nonsense words of increasing length. The early words are short and sound like words with Old English/Germanic roots (e.g., *protch*). Later words are long, polysyllabic, and sound like Latinate terms with familiar prefixes and suffixes (e.g., *delitrification*). Given that most long words in English are Latinate terms, this seems like a good choice. If long Germanic-sounding words were used (e.g., *watungnuberchteintgesetz*), the test might be a good predictor of learning to speak a Germanic language—but of little else.

There is no need to think of this test as either an auditory processing test or as a memory span test. It is both. The sounds must be correctly perceived, held in memory, and reproduced in speech. If any one of these processes is disrupted, the item is failed. Factor analyses suggest that for most people the difficulty of this task is in holding the information in memory (i.e., it loads primarily on the Memory Span factor). Nevertheless, for people with impaired phonological processing, this task is likely to be more difficult than a simple span test consisting of familiar words and numbers.

Phonological Processing

This test of auditory processing has three distinct item formats:

1. Saying any word that has particular phonemes in specific positions (e.g., "Say a word that ends with the /ts/ sound").
2. In 1 min, saying as many words as possible that begin with a particular sound (e.g., words that begin with the /r/ sound).
3. Substitute phonemes to change one word into another (e.g., "Change /g/ in *fig* to /t/").

Formats 1 and 2 are similar in that one may say any word that comes to mind, and thus are measures of *divergent* production (Guilford, 1967). Specifically, they are measures of lexical access via phonological cues. However, one is a power test and the other is a speed test. Format 3 seems to measure something more akin to what is measured by Sound Awareness, Segmentation, and Sound Blending (i.e., pulling apart and putting together phonemes). In fact, this format was used in one part of the Woodcock–Johnson III Tests of Achievement (WJ III ACH; Woodcock, McGrew, & Mather, 2001b) Sound Awareness test. Theoretically, it seems that it should have stayed there.

Given these differences, it is not clear whether the "cognitive complexity" (McGrew et al., 2014, p. 6) of this subtest comes from the mixed format or from the especially complex cognition needed to complete these tasks. Given that the item formats do not appear to require more complex cognition than that required by very similar tests from other batteries, I suspect that the mixed format is responsible for the multiple cross-loadings in factor analyses and the central position in multidimensional scaling analyses presented in the *Technical Manual*. It would be possible to test this hypothesis if the correlations of the separate components of Phonological Processing were available. Until then, it is hard to know what Phonological Processing scores mean.

Sound Blending and Segmentation

On Sound Blending, evaluees hear words with their syllables and phonemes pulled apart and must guess what the complete word is. In Segmentation, the opposite process occurs: A complete word is given and evaluees must split them by syllables and later by phonemes. Together, these tests make up the Phonetic Coding cluster.

Sound Blending and Incomplete Words was modeled on tests from the *Iowa Test of Psycholinguistic Abilities* (Kirk, McCarthy, & Kirk, 1968). They were thought of as tests of *auditory closure* (Thurstone, 1950), analogous to *visual closure* (e.g., WJ III COG Visual Closure, a test moved to the WJ IV Early Cognitive and Academic Development battery [WJ IV ECAD; Schrank, McGrew, & Mather, 2015]).

Tests of Visual–Spatial Processing

In the transition from the WJ III COG to the WJ IV COG, in a flurry of house-cleaning, underperforming *Ga* tests were removed and potentially useful ones were brought in. Although progress has been made, this kind of restructuring has not occurred to the same degree with *Gv* tests. Although it is clear from many studies that visual–spatial processing predicts important outcomes (Wai, Lubinski, & Benbow, 2009), the utility of the *Gv* tests on the WJ COG batteries specifically has not, to my knowledge, been documented. In particular, there is little evidence that the WJ COG *Gv* tests have an important role in explaining academic achievement (as measured by the WJ batteries). This is not to say that there is anything wrong with the tests, but that there is more work to do. After documenting what the tests measure, the next step is to document what they are measured for. That is, what do the tests tell us about inherently meaningful outcomes? It is possible that the WJ IV COG *Gv* tests are just as they should be, but that the scope of academic achievement measures on the WJ IV ACH needs to be widened such that the influence of *Gv* on achievement can be seen.

Visualization

The WJ III COG Spatial Relations test and the Block Rotation test from the WJ III DS formed the Visualization cluster on the WJ III DS. These tests measure the ability to solve spatial problems in the mind's eye. On the WJ IV COG, these tests are present, but no longer yield separate scores. What was once the Visualization cluster is now the Visualization test. It seems proper to regard this score as a cluster score and thus the usual prohibitions against interpreting subtest scores should not apply.

Picture Recognition

Picture Recognition measures a kind of visual memory in which evaluees are shown line drawings of physical objects and then after a brief exposure, must find them again among distractors. On the WJ III COG, this test was something of a problem because it barely correlated with anything, not even other Gv tests. For example, on the WJ III COG, Picture Recognition and Spatial Relations had a correlation of only 0.19 in the 9- to 13-year age group. Its correlations with other Gv tests were even lower than that!

On the WJ IV COG, there is no longer partial credit on Picture Recognition. On each item, the response is scored as correct or incorrect. The item changes on the WJ IV COG appear to have strengthened its correlations with Visualization (e.g., $r=0.43$ in the 9- to 13-year age group). As was the case in the WJ III COG, Picture Recognition is not just a Gv test, but is a memory test. In various analyses presented in the *Technical Manual*, Picture Recognition has relations with Gv, Glr-Learning Efficiency, Glr-Retrieval Fluency, and even Gwm.

From an information processing perspective, it is easy to imagine why Picture Recognition has relations with various CHC factors. Visual stimuli must be perceived and stored in memory in the learning phase of each item, and then retrieved from memory at the recognition phase. People with good Glr-Learning Efficiency (and Gwm) have an advantage in that they can store more information. However, people with good Gv will be able to store complex visual information as simple gestalts, greatly reducing memory load. I hypothesize that Glr-Retrieval Fluency comes into play on the more difficult items when multiple stimuli must be recognized. If recognition occurs quickly and effortlessly, there is less interference for information being maintained in working memory. Although the test stimuli and the distractor stimuli generally belong to the same category (e.g., cars), with a sufficiently detailed label (e.g., "sedan with the windows down"), some of the visual memory can be converted into verbal memory, hence the greater than anticipated relationship this test has with Visual-Auditory Learning.

Tests of Working Memory Capacity

Working Memory Capacity is the ability to hold raw information in immediate awareness so that that it can be manipulated and transformed into a more useful form (Schneider & McGrew, 2012). Individual differences in working memory capacity appear to arise from two components: the ability to maintain information in primary memory and the ability manipulate the focus of attention to search for information in stored in long-term memory (Unsworth & Engle, 2007).

Verbal Attention

This is a cleverly designed test of working memory capacity. The evaluee hears a series of numbers and animals and then is directed to repeat back a specific number or animal (e.g., "5…turtle…9…6 Tell me the number after turtle."). Because the information is held in memory without having to transform it, this is intended as a *Memory Span* test. In the classic memory span paradigm, evaluees repeat back the entire sequence. Unfortunately, this means that the act of producing the first few items in the sequence can interfere with the memory for the latter items. In Verbal Attention there is only one thing to recall for each item. Thus, there is little self-interference when one answers. However, because the examiner asks a questions, there is likely still some interference. There is evidence that even in classic simple span measures (e.g., Memory for Words) that attentional control mechanisms are required in more difficult items to search for information in long-term memory (Unsworth & Engle, 2007). In an informal confirmatory factor analysis I ran on the correlation matrix for 9–13 years and again for 14- to 19-year olds, Verbal Attention had a strong loading on the Memory Span factor and a substantial secondary loading on the Attentional Control factor.

Memory for Words

In this test evaluees hear a list of unrelated words and repeat them back in the same order. This is a classic memory span test and aside from gaining a few moderately difficult new items, it is largely unchanged from the WJ III COG (McGrew et al., 2014, p. 43).

Sentence Repetition

Sentence Repetition is a simple task in which evaluees repeat back full sentences of increasing length. Aside from a few new difficult items, it is little changed from its predecessor, the WJ III DS Memory for Sentences. Because the test requires no manipulation of information, it is considered a test of memory span. However, it is not a psychometrically pure test. Sentence span tests regularly have substantial loadings on *Gc*. What it lacks in psychometric purity, it gains in face validity. The ability to repeat back what one has just heard is an obviously important ability in a wide variety of circumstances.

Understanding Directions

On this task, evaluees follow increasingly complex verbal instructions related to a picture (e.g., "Point to the window on the left side of the house, but only if there are at least two blue cars on the street. Otherwise point to the girl riding her bicycle."). Because this task requires the coordination and integration of many cognitive operations, this test not only has a primary loading on memory span but also on attentional control and *Gc*.

Numbers Reversed

On this test, evaluees hear a list of single digits and must repeat them back in reverse order. It is a classic test in the classic format. When a Wechsler test is used as the primary battery, Numbers Reversed is a good option to use as a follow-up test when a person performs unexpectedly poorly on Digits Backward. Numbers Reversed is more reliable than Digits Backward because it has more items at each span length.

Object-Number Sequencing

On the Object-Number Sequencing test, evaluees hear an intermixed list of objects and numbers. They repeat the numbers first, in order and then the objects, in order. Because this sorting requires simultaneous storage and processing of information, this test is a strong measure of the attentional control aspects of working memory.

Object-Number Sequencing is the WJ III COG Auditory Working Memory test reborn with a more descriptive name and a better set of scoring rules. In its previous incarnation, there was a way in which partial credit could be awarded. This awarding of partial credit was well intentioned, but occasionally an evaluee used a strategy such that he/she always earned the partial credit score without using much in the way of working memory, thus earning anomalously high scores. This loophole has been closed on the WJ IV COG.

Tests of Learning Efficiency

In CHC Theory (Schneider & McGrew, 2012), there are two intermediate factors of long-term memory ability (*Glr*), learning efficiency (*Gl*) and retrieval fluency (*Gr*), each of which has many specific abilities. On the WJ IV COG, *Gl* is measured with a test of associative memory and a test of meaningful memory. There are no longer any delayed memory tests on the WJ IV COG. Aside from professionals who used the WJ III COG to screen for dementia (if there were any), the delayed memory tests will find few who mourn their passing. The hassle involved in administering them was not worth the meager incremental information they provided.

Visual-Auditory Learning

There are subtests that are perky and pleasant upon first acquaintance, but then reveal surprising depth after extended interaction. Whereas Memory for Faces (now on the WJ IV ECAD) is cute, Visual-Auditory Learning is just adorable. How could anyone not find those rebuses charming? In just a few minutes it is possible to witness how evaluees learn to read! What could be more directly relevant to treatment planning? It might escape notice at first, but there is an underlying logic baked into the code such that it has a helpful set of redundancies that facilitate learning. When I see children smile at certain points in the test, I know that they see what I see. This nuance is what gives the test a sense of lift-off. Furthermore, because the correct answers come in complete sentences, Visual-Auditory Learning is not a test of learning "one damn thing after another." It is a test of intelligence.

Although Visual-Auditory Learning has long been labeled a measure of *associative memory* (Flanagan, Ortiz, & Alfonso, 2013), I am unaware of evidence that specifically links it with the kinds of tests that defined that factor in Carroll's (1993) theory. Those tests generally required learning many paired associates presented all at once and tested all at once. Visual-Auditory Learning uses a structured learning task in which new information is taught and tested incrementally, without ever exceeding a person's working memory capacity. In addition, there are often meaningful associations between the symbols and words in the context of meaningfully coherent sentences. Carroll (1993, pp. 273–274) noted that there is little evidence that associative memory makes much of an independent contribution to the prediction of school learning performance. In contrast, Visual-Auditory Learning has long been one of the better predictors of reading performance. Thus, Visual-Auditory Learning may be a more a test of Carroll's *meaningful memory* factor than has been previously appreciated. Time will tell if this speculation has merit (…that and a few well-designed studies).

Story Recall

On the WJ IV COG, there are tests of memory for symbols, pictures, faces, numbers, sounds, words, sentences, and, at the highest unit of complexity, stories. The Story Recall test is now nicely paired with Reading Recall on the WJ IV ACH so that one can investigate hypotheses about higher level reading comprehension problems in more detail than was previously possible with the WJ III ACH.

Some story memory tests in other ability test batteries have just one or two long stories, which can occasionally result in extremely low scores in inattentive examinees who miss early details and then fail to follow the rest of the story. In contrast, the WJ IV COG Story Recall test is a series of very short stories of increasing complexity. The upside of this format is that it probably results in more accurate scores for those who have minor lapses of attention. The downside is that the stories are so short that they no longer resemble the kinds of situations that such tests are often used to predict performance in (e.g., classroom lectures). Of course, this issue is a matter of mere face validity, which often does not track with predictive validity. I am unaware of the predictive validity of tests like Story Recall in predicting long-term retention of lecture material. I suspect that in such a study the WJ IV COG Story Recall test would fare better than many of its competitors. In many story memory tests, there is not much story and a whole lot of inconsequential detail, which means that the test is essentially a list-learning test. On the WJ IV COG Story Recall test, the number of inconsequential details does rise a bit in the last few stories but most of a person's total score comes from recalling the gist of the story. In a well-taught course, gist learning is far more important than list learning.

Tests of Long-Term Memory Retrieval Fluency

On the WJ IV COG, these tests are measures of what is termed *Lexical Access* in the *WJ IV Technical Manual*. Lexical Access is a specific component of what Cattell (1987) called *Retrieval Capacity* and Carroll (1993) called *Broad Retrieval Ability (Gr)*. In CHC theory, retrieval fluency tests are thought of as aspects of long-term memory. This conceptual linkage is not without empirical support. However, these tests are more highly correlated with *Gs* tests than they are with learning efficiency tests. Failing to appreciate this fact can result in unparsimonious interpretations in which a person is described as having two deficits instead of just one that is manifest in *Gs* tests and *Gr* tests.

Retrieval Fluency

On the test of Retrieval Fluency, evaluees quickly name exemplars of a broad category (e.g., "Name as many plants as you can in 1 min. Go."). This test made up half of the WJ III COG *Glr* cluster. Thankfully, this arrangement is no longer the case. Because of the unusual way in which WJ cluster scores are created, a test with a larger W-score standard deviation contributes more variance to the cluster. In the WJ III COG, the standard deviation of the Visual-Auditory Learning test was two to three times larger than that of Retrieval Fluency. Thus, the *Glr* cluster score was dominated to an unusual degree by Visual-Auditory Learning and the influence of Retrieval Fluency was very small.

Although the item content has not changed, the W-score standard deviation has increased dramatically on the WJ IV COG. Previously its average standard deviation across age groups was 4.42, and now it is 9.34, which is more in line with the standard deviations of other tests. The reason for this welcome change is that the speeded tests on the WJ IV COG use a different method of converting raw scores to W-scores (McGrew et al., 2014, pp. 51–52). The new method eliminates the need for giving bonus points to people who finish early. The implications of the new scoring method are not fully explored, but it appears to improve the psychometric properties of the speeded tests significantly (Kevin McGrew, personal communication, April 27, 2015).

Rapid Picture Naming

On this test, evaluees name an array of line drawings of common objects as quickly as they can. The items are very easy to identify and thus this test measures speed of naming rather than vocabulary. I like the WJ version of this test better than similar measures on other batteries because each object is unique rather than having just a few objects repeated (e.g., the Comprehensive Test of Phonological Processing—Second Edition [Wagner, Torgesen, Rashotte, & Pearson, 2013] Rapid Object Naming subtest). This characteristic makes it a true memory retrieval speed test rather than just a processing speed test.

Tests of Processing Speed

The *processing* in tests of processing speed (*Gs*) probably has more to do with the executive control of attention (Mirsky, Anthony, Duncan, Ahearn, & Kellam, 1991) than with automatic perceptual processing, though both kinds of processing influence test performance. Automatic perceptual processing is more a function of Decision Time (*Gt*) in CHC Theory (Schneider & McGrew, 2012) and is not measured directly in the WJ IV. The Decision Speed test was dropped from the WJ IV COG. I liked the test and am sad to see it go.

Number-Pattern Matching and Letter-Pattern Matching

There are tests that are perfectly serviceable alternatives to other tests intended to measure a particular construct. Number-Pattern Matching (née Visual Matching) is a fine measure of Processing Speed. Because it is so simple, the meaning of a person's score is fairly clear. However, it does not offer the subtle pleasures of a Processing Speed measure like Coding from the Wechsler tests. When I observe someone performing poorly on that test, I obtain a much clearer view of what is going wrong under the hood (or at least I am deluded in thinking I do).

Letter-Pattern Matching is exactly the same as Number-Pattern Matching except that it uses letters instead of numbers. For this reason, I believe that the composite formed from the two tests should not be called *Perceptual Speed*. Instead, they should be thought of variants of the same test. If a narrow ability called *Perceptual Speed* exists, and if there is utility in distinguishing it from *Gs*, then two measures using different methods are needed to measure it with confidence.

Pair Cancellation

On this test, examinees scan an array of simple line drawings for a particular pair of objects in the correct sequence. This test has a small cross-loading on *Gv* for most age groups. This test has displaced Decision Speed to make up the *Gs* cluster.

This test is the same as it was on the WJ III COG and yet it correlates much more highly with *Gs* tests now than it did before. For example, in the 9- to 13-year age group, Pair Cancellation had a 0.23 correlation with Visual Matching. In the same age group on the WJ IV COG, its correlation with Number-Pattern Matching (i.e., Visual Matching) is now 0.57. It appears that the new scoring method for speeded measures has strengthened the validity of Pair Cancellation considerably.

STRENGTHS AND WEAKNESSES: WHOLE BATTERY

The Woodcock–Johnson IV (WJ IV; Schrank, McGrew, & Mather, 2014a) offers major advantages to those who use it as a primary battery. As a secondary battery, it offers a plentiful and diverse range of unique tools for follow-up testing.

The *Technical Manual*

Before July 4, 2001, no one in the sport known as *competitive eating* had ever been able to ingest more than 25 hot dogs in 12 min. On that day, however,

Takeru Kobayashi, a rookie competitor weighing 128 lbs, not only broke that record, he doubled it. Yes, he ate 50 hot dogs and 50 hot dog buns in just 12 min. The crowd was gobsmacked by this display of preternatural talent…

…It was sort of like that for me when I first opened the *WJ IV Technical Manual* (McGrew et al., 2014). I was expecting a great deal—the *WJ III Technical Manual* (McGrew & Woodcock, 2001) had already set the bar for what a technical manual should look like. This one blows that one away. Like other manuals, it has detailed descriptions of the norming process, reliability statistics, and validity studies. This manual, however, has an amazing number of beautiful figures in color. Most importantly, the findings are not merely presented, they are thoughtfully articulated and interpreted. Like the sport of competitive eating, reading technical manuals is not for everyone. This one, though, is a mammoth slab of awesome and a *tour de force*.

The WJ IV's Greatest Weakness

Received wisdom has it that when interviewers ask job candidates "What is your greatest weakness?" the proper response is to give some sort of variant of "Aw shucks! I suppose that when it comes to my greatest strength, I'm a little too awesome for my own good." In the case of the WJ IV, this answer might actually be the truth. Many of its strengths are so strong that even veteran users can feel overwhelmed by the complexity. Although I believe that the scoring output could be streamlined intelligently, I far prefer too much complexity to too little nuance.

The WJ IV leads us to make many distinctions within and between cognitive and academic abilities, but it is not clear that all of these distinctions are consequential. One example among many: On what basis should I distinguish between *Gs* and Perceptual Speed?

The Postprandial Coffee Is Weak…

That is, the online scoring software (Schrank & Dailey, 2014) is not amazing. Like CompuScore before it, it is old fashioned and a little clunky. It is possible to make software smooth, interactive, and lively. At present, it is a slightly awkward online form that spits back static pages. That said, it gets the job done. The advantage of online scoring is that the experience can be improved continuously and new features can be added over time.

…and the Decor Is Plain

I wish that the easel design had been either a little less retro or a whole lot more. I do like the sturdy travel case in which it comes, though.

A Little Co-Norming Goes a Long Way

What is right about the WJ IV has been right right from the beginning in 1977. It is a comprehensive cognitive ability test that is co-normed with a comprehensive academic achievement test. Other test batteries link to achievement batteries with relatively small samples. These smallish linking samples can give us an idea as to how large the intercorrelations between batteries are, but the standard error around those correlations is generally too large to perform structural equation modeling that yields trustworthy results about the complex relations among cognitive and academic abilities. At first this may not seem like much of loss. However, each time it happens it is a missed opportunity for taking academic achievement assessment to the next level of sophistication. For certain kinds of interpretive methods, the WJ IV is the only game in town. However, for this game, not all the features work right out of the box.

The WJ IV COG Comprehension-Knowledge cluster summarizes two tests. The Comprehension-Knowledge Extended cluster summarizes three tests. Depending on how you count, the WJ IV has at least seven tests of Comprehension-Knowledge. There is no cluster score that summarizes them all. As it stands, we are left to aggregate stray scores in our heads. Unfortunately, we humans are famously bad at mental math involving probability (Kahneman, 2011). This problem is not specific to the *Gc* tests, it is a problem with all of the tests. It is a common problem in other batteries, too.

I think that it is time to rethink our approach to cluster/composite scores. Instead of thinking about composite scores as fixed combinations of particular test scores, we should think of them as *updatable* estimates of latent abilities. Estimates should make use of and properly weight all available information. If we have only two tests, we estimate the underlying ability with a fair amount of uncertainty. If we have three tests, the confidence interval around our estimate narrows. With each additional test score, our confidence in our estimate increases. Because the WJ IV is scored entirely online, it would not be difficult to give, in addition to the existing cluster scores, model-based estimates of latent abilities thought to underlie the WJ IV scores (Schneider, 2013). This approach would allow for complex tests with multiple loadings to contribute to multiple scores with realistic weights. This kind of flexibility is easily possible for the WJ IV and could be yet another feature that sets it apart from other batteries.

I wrote supplemental software for the Woodcock–Johnson III (Woodcock, McGrew, & Mather, 2001c) that was whimsically called *The Compositator* (Schneider, 2010). As the six or seven people who ever used it already know, it was a sort of demonstration project of what I thought the next wave of test interpretation tools should look like. I wrote a detailed technical manual hoping that test developers would borrow and extend my ideas. Not only does the software allow clinicians to combine test scores in any way they see fit, they can see the degree to which the tests that make up the score measure a common factor. Thus, their intuitions about what is plausible are informed by psychometric constraints.

With most test batteries, a general ability score is used to predict academic achievement scores. With the WJ IV a variety of prediction methods can be employed to compare various scores (e.g., intra-cognitive, intra-oral, intra-achievement, cross-domain, oral/achievement, scholastic aptitude/achievement, general ability/achievement, and *Gf–Gc*/Other ability). However, the clinician is not allowed to "order off the menu." If your seven *Gc* tests give a different estimate of *Gc* than the single *Gc* test in the Scholastic Aptitude clusters, there is no recourse available to you. I know, I know, the WJ IV offers so many more options for score comparison than any other test, it is embarrassing to ask for even more. Nevertheless, I want more, and I have good reason to want more.

Not only do I want to explain a person's Passage Comprehension score with any combination of cognitive scores that I believe are relevant, I want to combine this information with the person's performance on tests of lower-level academic skills. Consider the model in Figure 7.2. For the sake of illustration, it is simple but it is based on correlations from the 9- to 13-year age group. Two cognitive abilities, Lexical Knowledge and Phonetic Processing, predict three sequentially linked reading abilities. Using this model, we can estimate how far under expectations an individual's reading skills. In Figure 7.2, we can see that given the observed scores, we estimate that the latent Phonetic Processing speed score is 78 with 95% margin of error of 17 and that the latent Lexical Knowledge is 108 with a 95% margin of error of 9. With a low Phonetic Processing score, one might think that the Word Attack score of 75 would be expected. In fact, if the estimated latent scores are accurate, the Word Attack score of 75 is 21 points below expectations, which occurs in less than 4% of the population. That

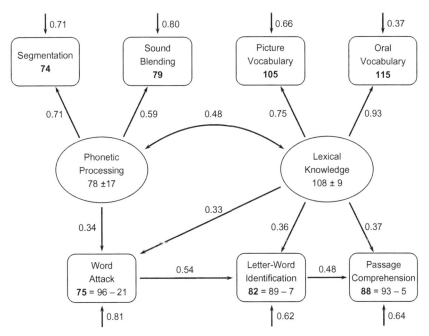

FIGURE 7.2   A simple model of reading ability applied to an individual.

is, even with the poor Phonetic Processing scores, the person's Word Attack skills are unusually low. This means that although poor Phonetic Processing is a partial cause of low Word Attack performance, I need to keep looking for additional causes. After accounting for the unusually low Word Attack score, the other reading scores are not far from expectations.

From this analysis, we can also estimate the expected benefit that would come from remediating the person's Word Attack skills (i.e., for every standard deviation improvement, we can expect more than half a standard deviation gain in Letter–Word Identification and about a quarter of a standard deviation increase in Passage Comprehension). Of course, these are only back-of-the-envelope calculations but they anchor our intuitions in helpful ways.

Of course, this illustration is a very simple model. A more complex model might look like Figure 7.3. Fortunately, with proper software, all the complexity

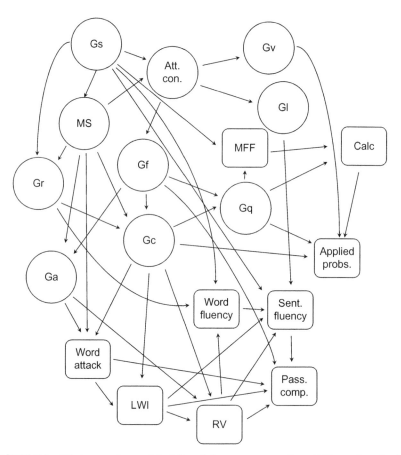

FIGURE 7.3 What a complex model of the relations among cognitive abilities and academic achievement might look like on the WJ IV.

is handled automatically and thus it is not as overwhelming as it might seem at first. Although the WJ IV scoring software, great as it is, does not perform analyses like these, it is fairly easy for a competent programmer to implement them. I understand that few people have the training to interpret these kinds of models. However, I believe that this is the direction in which the field should go, and only co-normed batteries like the WJ IV can take us there.

OVERALL EVALUATION

The original WJ was a true original. In the WJ R, the *R* stood for *Revolutionary*. The WJ III required three batteries to contain all its innovations. The WJ IV now has four. There is nothing else like it in terms of breadth, depth, size, and scope. It has minor flaws here and there, but they are very minor indeed. It is an excellent choice to use as a primary battery or as a secondary battery for cross-battery assessment (Flanagan et al., 2013).

These are exciting times for those of us who love the art and science of cognitive assessment. We have never had so many excellent tests from which to choose. It is clear that test developers are inspired by each other's innovations. Given the history of continuous innovation and frequent updates on the WJ family of tests, it is likely that the WJ IV will improve continuously for the rest of its life cycle.

REFERENCES

Aikins, H. A. (1902). *The principles of logic*. New York, NY: Holt.

Carroll, J. B. (1993). *Human cognitive abilities: A survey of factor-analytic studies*. New York, NY: Cambridge University Press.

Cattell, R. B. (1987). *Intelligence: Its structure, growth and action: Its structure, growth and action*. New York, NY: Elsevier.

Flanagan, D. P., Ortiz, S. O., & Alfonso, V. C. (2013). *Essentials of cross-battery assessment* (Vol. 84). Hoboken, NJ: John Wiley & Sons.

Gellert, A. S., & Elbro, C. (2013). Cloze tests may be quick, but are they dirty? Development and preliminary validation of a cloze test of reading comprehension. *Journal of Psychoeducational Assessment, 31*(1), 16–28.

Guilford, J. P. (1967). *The nature of human intelligence*. New York, NY: McGraw-Hill.

Hawkins, J., & Blakeslee, S. (2004). *On intelligence*. New York, NY: Times Books.

Kahneman, D. (2011). *Thinking, fast and slow*. New York, NY: Macmillan.

Kirk, S. A., McCarthy, J. J., & Kirk, W. D. (1968). *Illinois test of psycholinguistic abilities*. Urbana, IL: University of Illinois Press.

McGrew, K. S. (2009). CHC theory and the human cognitive abilities project: Standing on the shoulders of the giants of psychometric intelligence research. *Intelligence, 37*(1), 1–10.

McGrew, K. S., LaForte, E. M., & Schrank, F. A. (2014). *Woodcock–Johnson IV technical manual*. Rolling Meadows, IL: Riverside.

McGrew, K. S., & Woodcock, J. R. (2001). *Woodcock–Johnson III technical manual*. Rolling Meadows, IL: Riverside.

Mirsky, A. F., Anthony, B. J., Duncan, C. C., Ahearn, M. B., & Kellam, S. G. (1991). Analysis of the elements of attention: A neuropsychological approach. *Neuropsychology Review*, 2(2), 109–145.

Schacter, D. L., Addis, D. R., & Buckner, R. L. (2007). Remembering the past to imagine the future: The prospective brain. *Nature Reviews Neuroscience*, 8(9), 657–661.

Schneider, W. J. (2010). *The Compositator 1.0*. Olympia, WA: WMF Press.

Schneider, W. J. (2013). What if we took our models seriously? Estimating latent scores in individuals. *Journal of Psychoeducational Assessment*, 31(2), 186–201.

Schneider, W. J., & McGrew, K. S. (2012). The Cattell–Horn–Carroll model of intelligence: *Contemporary intellectual assessment: Theories, tests, and issues* (3rd ed.). New York: Guilford Press. (pp. 99–144).

Schrank, F. A., & Dailey, D. (2014). *Woodcock–Johnson online scoring and reporting [Online format]*. Rolling Meadows, IL: Riverside.

Schrank, F. A., McGrew, K. S., & Mather, N. (2014a). *Woodcock–Johnson IV*. Rolling Meadows, IL: Riverside.

Schrank, F. A., McGrew, K. S., & Mather, N. (2014b). *Woodcock–Johnson IV tests of cognitive abilities*. Rolling Meadows, IL: Riverside.

Schrank, F. A., McGrew, K. S., & Mather, N. (2015). *Woodcock–Johnson IV tests of early cognitive and academic development*. Rolling Meadows, IL: Riverside.

Spearman, C. (1923). *The nature of "intelligence" and the principles of cognition*. London: Macmillan.

Thorndike, E. L. (1904). *Theory of mental and social measurements*. New York, NY: The Science Press.

Thurstone, L. (1950). Some primary abilities in visual thinking. *Proceedings of the American Philosophical Society*, 94(6), 517–521.

Unsworth, N., & Engle, R. W. (2007). The nature of individual differences in working memory capacity: Active maintenance in primary memory and controlled search from secondary memory. *Psychological Review*, 114(1), 104–132.

Wagner, R. K., Torgesen, J. K., Rashotte, C. A., & Pearson, N. A. (2013). *Comprehensive test of phonological processing* (2nd ed.). San Antonio, TX: Pearson.

Wai, J., Lubinski, D., & Benbow, C. P. (2009). Spatial ability for STEM domains: Aligning over 50 years of cumulative psychological knowledge solidifies its importance. *Journal of Educational Psychology*, 101(4), 817–835.

Woodcock, R. W., & Johnson, M. (1977). *Woodcock–Johnson psychoeducational battery*. Allen, TX: DLM.

Woodcock, R. W., & Johnson, M. (1989). *Woodcock–Johnson-Revised tests of cognitive abilities*. Chicago, IL: Riverside.

Woodcock, R. W., McGrew, K. S., & Mather, N. (2001a). *Woodcock–Johnson III tests of cognitive abilities*. Itasca, IL: Riverside.

Woodcock, R. W., McGrew, K. S., & Mather, N. (2001b). *Woodcock–Johnson III tests of achievement*. Itasca, IL: Riverside.

Woodcock, R. W., McGrew, K. S., & Mather, N. (2001c). *Woodcock–Johnson III*. Itasca, IL: Riverside.

Woodcock, R. W., McGrew, K. S., Mather, N., & Schrank, F. A. (2003). *Woodcock–Johnson III tests of cognitive abilities diagnostic supplement*. Rolling Meadows, IL: Riverside.

Chapter 8

Use of the Woodcock–Johnson IV in the Identification of Specific Learning Disabilities in School-age Children[*]

Erin M. McDonough and Dawn P. Flanagan
St. John's University, New York, NY, USA

The WJ IV measures a wide range of theory-based abilities and processes and includes numerous variation and comparison procedures, making it a useful set of batteries for the evaluation of children suspected of having a specific learning disability (SLD). According to the WJ IV authors, the *variation* procedures (e.g., intracognitive) describe the child's pattern of strengths and weaknesses (PSW) and the *comparison* procedures (e.g., ability-achievement) are used to determine if the child's performance is outside the range of predicted scores (McGrew, LaForte, & Schrank, 2014). Furthermore, an analysis of the relationships and interactions among the WJ IV ability and skill tests and composites is considered necessary to understand the child's PSW, presumably for the purpose of differentially diagnosing SLD from other disorders (McGrew et al., 2014). While it is certainly true that the WJ IV's variation and comparison procedures will provide valuable information about a child's cognitive, oral language, and achievement abilities from both person-relative and population-relative perspectives, there is little in the way of guidance on how these procedures may be used and interpreted within the context of an independent evaluation of suspected SLD.

The purpose of this chapter is to provide guidance on the use of the WJ IV in the identification of SLD, with a focus on interpretation of the myriad variation and comparison analyses that may be conducted with WJ IV tests and composites. We will offer our guidelines within the context of a research-based

---

[*] Sections of this chapter were adapted from *Essentials of Cross-Battery Assessment*, 3e with permission from Wiley. Copyright 2013, all rights reserved.

WJ IV Clinical Use and Interpretation. DOI: http://dx.doi.org/10.1016/B978-0-12-802076-0.00009-8
211

operational definition of SLD that is consistent with both the federal definition of SLD (34 CFR Part 300.8[c]10) and the third option specified in the procedures for identifying SLD (34 CFR Part 300.309) included in the 2006 regulations that accompany IDEA. This third option involves the evaluation of a PSW that is consistent with the SLD construct, via a combination of tests of cognitive and academic abilities and neuropsychological processes (see Fiorello, Flanagan, & Hale, 2014). Specifically, Flanagan and colleagues' operational definition of SLD will be used as the basic conceptual structure for the independent evaluation of SLD (i.e., Flanagan, Ortiz, & Alfonso, 2013; Flanagan, Ortiz, Alfonso, & Mascolo, 2002). The utility of the WJ IV variation and comparison procedures will be demonstrated within this structure and specific interpretive guidelines will be provided relevant to the identification of SLD. Emphasis will be placed on the sufficiency of a WJ IV evaluation for SLD identification as well as use of the WJ IV variation and comparison procedures to evaluate normative versus deficit functioning, domain-specific weaknesses, average (or better) overall cognitive ability, below average aptitude-achievement consistency, and unexpected underachievement. The information presented in this chapter can serve as a research-based model for completing SLD referrals using the WJ IV.

THE DUAL DISCREPANCY/CONSISTENCY OPERATIONAL DEFINITION OF SLD

The federal definition of SLD does not reflect the best thinking about the SLD construct because it has not changed in over 30 years (Kavale, Spaulding, & Beam, 2009). This fact is surprising, as several decades of investigation into the nature of SLD resulted in numerous proposals over the years to modify the definition (see Kavale et al., for a discussion). As such, Kavale and Forness (2000) asserted that if the field of SLD is to recapture its status as a reliable entity in special education and psychology, then more attention must be paid to the federal definition. Accordingly, Kavale and colleagues proposed a "richer" description of SLD that articulated the boundaries of the term and the class of things to which it belongs. In addition, their definition delineated what SLD is and what it is not. Although not a radical departure from the federal definition, their definition by comparison provides a more comprehensive description of the nature of SLD. Kavale and colleagues' definition is as follows:

> *"Specific learning disability refers to heterogeneous clusters of disorders that significantly impede the normal progress of academic achievement…The lack of progress is exhibited in school performance that remains below expectation for chronological and mental ages, even when provided with high-quality instruction. The primary manifestation of the failure to progress is significant underachievement in a basic skill area (i.e., reading, math, writing) that is not associated with insufficient educational, cultural/familial, and/or sociolinguistic experiences.*

The primary severe ability-achievement discrepancy is coincident with deficits in linguistic competence (receptive and/or expressive), cognitive functioning (e.g., problem solving, thinking abilities, maturation), neuropsychological processes (e.g., perception, attention, memory), or any combination of such contributing deficits that are presumed to originate from central nervous system dysfunction. The specific learning disability is a discrete condition differentiated from generalized learning failure by average or above (>90) cognitive ability and a learning skill profile exhibiting significant scatter indicating areas of strength and weakness. The major specific learning disability may be accompanied by secondary learning difficulties that also may be considered when planning the more intensive, individualized special education instruction directed at the primary problem." (p. 46)

Kavale and colleagues stated that their richer description of SLD "can be readily translated into an operational definition providing more confidence in the validity of a diagnosis of SLD" (p. 46). Following the advice of Kavale and colleagues, Flanagan and colleagues developed the Dual-Discrepancy/Consistency (or DD/C) operational definition of SLD, which captures the nature of SLD as reflected in the federal definition and includes concepts from a variety of other researchers (e.g., Berninger, 2011; Feifer & DeFina, 2005; Fletcher-Janzen & Reynolds, 2008; Geary, Hoard, & Bailey, 2011; Hale & Fiorello, 2004; Hale et al., 2010; Harrison & Holmes, 2012; McCloskey, Whitaker, Murphy, & Rogers, 2012; Naglieri, 2011; Reynolds & Shaywitz, 2009; Siegel, 1999; Stanovich, 1999; Vellutino, Scanlon, & Lyon, 2000).

Because operational definitions represent only temporary assumptions about a concept, they are subject to change (Kavale et al., 2009). Flanagan and colleagues have modified and refined their operational definition periodically over the last decade to ensure that it reflects the most current theory, research, and thinking with regard to (i) the nature of SLD; (ii) the methods of evaluating various elements and concepts inherent in SLD definitions (viz., alternative research-based methods); and (iii) criteria for establishing SLD as a discrete condition separate from undifferentiated low achievement and overall below average ability to think and reason, particularly for the purpose of acquiring, developing, and applying academic skills. The most recent iteration of Flanagan and colleagues' operational definition of SLD (i.e., the DD/C definition) is presented in Table 8.1. This definition encourages a continuum of data gathering methods, beginning with Curriculum Based Measures (CBM) and progress monitoring and culminating in norm-referenced tests of cognitive and academic abilities and neuropsychological processes for students who demonstrate an inadequate response to high-quality instruction and intervention. This type of systematic approach to understanding learning difficulties can emanate from any well-researched theory (see Hale, Wycoff, & Fiorello, 2011; McCloskey et al., 2012).

TABLE 8.1 The Dual Discrepancy/Consistency (DD/C) Operational Definition of SLD

Level	Nature of SLD[a]	Focus of Evaluation	Examples of Evaluation Methods and Data Sources	Criteria for SLD	SLD Classification and Eligibility
					Necessary ⟶
I	Difficulties in one or more areas of academic achievement, including (but not limited to)[b] Basic Reading Skill, Reading Comprehension, Reading Fluency, Oral Expression, Listening Comprehension, Written Expression, Math Calculation, Math Problem Solving.	*Academic Achievement:* Performance in specific academic skills (e.g., *Grw-R* (reading decoding, reading fluency, reading comprehension); *Grw-W* (spelling, written expression); *Gq* (math calculation, math problem solving); *Gc* (communication ability, listening ability).	Response to quality instruction and intervention via progress monitoring, performance on norm-referenced, standardized achievement tests, evaluation of work samples, observations of academic performance, teacher/parent/student interview, history of academic performance, data from other members of Multidisciplinary Team (MDT) (e.g., speech-language pathologist, interventionist, reading specialist).	Performance in one or more academic areas is *weak or deficient*[c] (despite attempts at delivering quality instruction) as evidenced by converging data sources. Results from the WJ IV *intra-achievement variation* procedure may be used as one data source, especially when academic area(s) identified as a weakness has an associated standard score that is weak or deficient.	
II	SLD does not include a learning problem that is the result of visual, hearing, or motor disabilities; of intellectual disability; of social or emotional disturbance; or of environmental, cultural, or economic disadvantage.	*Exclusionary Factors:* Identification of potential primary causes of academic skill weaknesses or deficits, including intellectual disability, cultural or linguistic difference, sensory impairment, insufficient instruction or opportunity to learn, organic or physical health factors, social/emotional or psychological disturbance.	Data from the methods and sources listed at Levels I and III. Behavior Rating Scales; medical records; prior evaluations; interviews with current or past counselors, psychiatrists, etc.	Performance is not *primarily* attributed to these exclusionary factors, although one or more of them may contribute to learning difficulties. (Consider using the *Exclusionary Factors Form*, which may be downloaded from www.crossbattery.com under "resources.")	

III	A disorder in one or more of the basic psychological/neuropsychological processes involved in understanding or in using language, spoken or written; such disorders are presumed to originate from central nervous system dysfunction.	*Cognitive Abilities & Processes:* Performance in cognitive abilities and processes (e.g., Gv, Ga, Glr, Gsm, Gs), specific neuropsychological processes (e.g., attention, executive functioning, orthographic processing; RAN; RAS) and learning efficiency (e.g., associative memory; free recall memory, meaningful memory).	Performance on norm-referenced tests, evaluation of work samples, observations of cognitive performance, task analysis, testing limits, teacher/parent/student interview, history of academic performance, records review.	Performance in one or more cognitive abilities and/or neuropsychological processes (related to academic skill deficiency) is *weak or deficient*[c] as evidenced by converging data sources. Results from the WJ IV *intracognitive variation* and *intra-oral language variation* procedures may be use, especially when cognitive area(s) identified as a weakness has an associated standard score that is weak or deficient.

(Continued)

TABLE 8.1 The Dual Discrepancy/Consistency (DD/C) Operational Definition of SLD (Continued)

Level	Nature of SLD[a]	Focus of Evaluation	Examples of Evaluation Methods and Data Sources	Criteria for SLD	SLD Classification and Eligibility
IV	The specific learning disability is a discrete condition differentiated from generalized learning failure by generally average or better ability to think and reason and a learning skill profile exhibiting significant variability, indicating processing areas of strength and weakness.	*Pattern of Strengths and Weaknesses Marked by a Dual-Discrepancy/ Consistency (DD/C)* Determination of whether academic skill weaknesses or deficits are related to specific cognitive area(s) of weakness or deficit; pattern of data reflects a below average aptitude-achievement *consistency* with otherwise average or better ability to think and reason.	Data gathered at all previous levels as well as any additional data following a review of initial evaluation results (e.g., data gathered for the purpose of hypothesis testing; data gathered via demand analysis and limits testing).	Circumscribed below average aptitude-achievement *consistency* (i.e., related cognitive processes and academic skills are generally about 1 SD below the mean or lower); circumscribed ability-achievement and ability-cognitive aptitude *discrepancies*, with cognitive areas of strength represented by standard scores that are generally ≥90; clinical judgment supports the impression that the student's overall ability to think and reason will enable him or her to benefit from tailored or specialized instruction/intervention, compensatory strategies, and accommodations, such that his or her performance rate and level will likely approximate more typically achieving, nondisabled peers.	*Sufficient for SLD Identification*

						Necessary for Special Education Eligibility
V	Specific learning disability has an adverse impact on educational performance.	Special Education Eligibility[d] Determination of Least Restrictive Environment (LRE) for delivery of instruction and educational resources.	Data from all previous levels and MDT meeting, including parents.	When using the WJ IV comparison and variation procedures the following procedures may be used to support a DD/C pattern: GIA/achievement, Gf-Gc/achievement, or SAPT/achievement discrepancy and Gf-Gc/Other (COG) Ability discrepancy (when ability is at least average and specific academic and cognitive areas of presumed weakness are below average or lower).	Student demonstrates significant difficulties in daily academic activities that cannot be remediated, accommodated, or otherwise compensated for without the assistance of individualized special education services.	

[a]This column includes concepts inherent in the federal definition (IDEA, 2004), Kavale et al.'s (2009) definition, Harrison and Holmes' (2012) consensus definition, and other prominent definitions of SLD (see Sotelo-Dynega, Flanagan, & Alfonso, 2011, for a summary). Thus, all prominent SLD markers are included in this column.

[b]Poor spelling with adequate ability to express ideas in writing is often typical of dyslexia and/or disgraphia. Even though IDEA (2004) includes only the broad category of written expression, poor spelling, and handwriting are often symptomatic of a specific writing disability and should not be ignored (Wendling & Mather, 2009).

[c]Weak performance is typically associated with standard scores in the 85–89 range, whereas deficient performance is often associated with standard scores that are around 1SD below the mean or lower. Interpretations of weak or deficient performance based on standard scores that fall in these ranges are bolstered when they have ecological validity (e.g., when there is evidence that the abilities or processes identified as weak or deficient manifest in everyday classroom activities that require these abilities and processes).

[c]The major specific learning disability may be accompanied by secondary learning difficulties that also may be considered when planning the more intensive, individualized special education instruction directed at the primary problem. For information on linking assessment data to intervention, see Mascolo et al. (2014).

As described in the prior edition of this book, the DD/C definition provides a viable, and arguably necessary, framework for applying the WJ IV variation and comparison procedures in an attempt to understand whether a child's PSW is consistent with the SLD construct. The essential elements in evaluation of SLD in the DD/C operational definition, as illustrated in Table 8.1, include: (i) academic ability analysis, (ii) evaluation of mitigating and exclusionary factors, (iii) cognitive ability and processing analysis, (iv) PSW analysis, and (v) evaluation of interference with learning for purposes of special education eligibility. These elements are depicted as distinct levels in Figure 8.1 and together form the DD/C operational definition of SLD. The WJ IV can be used effectively to gather information and test hypotheses at each level of this operational definition.

It is assumed that the levels of evaluation depicted in Table 8.1 are undertaken after prereferral assessment activities have been conducted and when a focused evaluation of specific abilities and processes through standardized testing is deemed necessary. Evaluation of the presence of a learning disability is based on the assumption that an individual has been referred for testing specifically because of observed learning difficulties. However, prior to formal testing, it is expected that remediation of academic skill weaknesses via a response-to-intervention (RTI) service delivery model was attempted with little success. Moreover, prior to beginning SLD assessment with the WJ IV, other significant data sources should have already been gathered and considered within the context of the intervention activities. These data may include results from informal testing, direct observation of behaviors, work samples, reports from people familiar with the child's difficulties (e.g., teachers, parents), and information provided by the child him- or herself.

Before beginning Level I assessment with the WJ IV, practitioners should decide what type of analyses will be conducted at Levels III and IV. For example, depending on school-district and state department regulations, practitioners may engage in ability/achievement discrepancy analysis, PSW analysis, RTI, or some combination thereof, in the process of SLD determination. Numerous procedures for discrepancy analysis (e.g., General Ability Index [GAI]/achievement comparison) and PSW analysis (e.g., intracognitive variation) are offered by the WJ IV, only some of which may be relevant within the context of individual district and state criteria. Table 8.2 provides a brief description of and purpose for each WJ IV variation and comparison procedure. A review of Table 8.2 shows that only some of the WJ IV variation and comparison procedures are relevant to the DD/C operational definition of SLD. Therefore, if the WJ IV is used within the context of this definition, practitioners should first review Table 8.2 and select a priori the types of variation and comparison procedures that are most appropriate for their purposes. Selecting variation and comparison procedures a priori guards against the scientifically unsupported practice of running multiple analyses in an attempt to find a significant discrepancy, for example, to meet existing criteria.

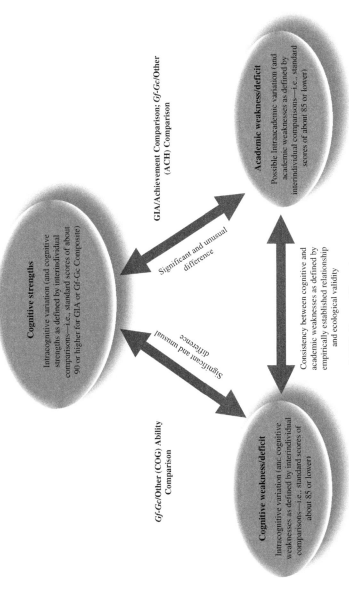

FIGURE 8.1 Selected WJ IV variation and comparison procedures for PSW analysis.

TABLE 8.2 Variation and Comparison Procedures of the WJ IV and Their Relevance to the DD/C Operational Definition of SLD Criteria

Type of WJ IV Analysis Procedure	Description	DD/C Operational Definition of SLD Criteria	Relevance of WJ IV Analysis Procedures to DD/C Criteria
Variation Options			
Intra-Achievement	This procedure uses WJ IV ACH Tests 1 through 6 to calculate intra-achievement variations. For example, the average of five of these tests is used to predict performance on the sixth. The difference between actual and predicted performance on the sixth test is compared to difference score norms to determine if the difference is unusual in the general population. Unusual negative differences are labeled as relative weaknesses and unusual positive differences are labeled as relative strengths. Table 1-6 in the WJ IV Technical Manual (McGrew et al., 2014) provides additional (optional) tests and clusters that may be included in the intra-achievement variation procedure.	Level I Performance in one or more academic areas is *below average or lower* (despite quality attempts at delivering quality instruction) as evidenced by converging data sources.	A relative weakness that is also a *normative* weakness may meet the criterion of "unexpected underachievement" for the child, especially when s/he was expected to perform significantly better in that academic area as predicted by an overall cognitive ability estimate or an oral language estimate in the case of reading achievement. This procedure should be used in conjunction with the GIA/ACH, Gf-Gc/ACH, or OL/ACH comparison procedure. Selection of the comparison procedure(s) to be used with the intra-achievement variation procedure should be done a priori.
Intracognitive	This procedure uses WJ IV COG Tests 1 through 7 to calculate intracognitive variations. For example, the average of six of these tests is used to predict performance on the seventh. The difference between actual and predicted performance on the seventh test is compared to difference score norms to determine if the difference is unusual in the general population. Unusual negative differences are labeled as relative weaknesses and unusual positive differences are labeled as relative strengths. Table 1-4 in the WJ IV Technical Manual (McGrew et al., 2014) provides additional (optional) tests and clusters that may be included in the intracognitive variation procedure.	Level III Performance in one or more cognitive abilities and/or neuropsychological processes (related to academic skill weakness) is *below average or lower* as evidenced by converging data sources.	A relative weakness that is also a *normative* weakness may meet the criterion of a "domain-specific weakness" for the child, especially when other important abilities for learning and academic success are about average or higher. This procedure may be used in conjunction with the Gf-Gc/Other Ability Comparison procedure to support a domain-specific weakness. The finding of a domain-specific weakness that is related to one or more academic weaknesses supports the (Level IV) criterion of "below average cognitive-achievement consistency."

| Intra-Oral Language | This procedure uses WJ IV OL Tests 1 through 4 to calculate intra-oral language variations. For example, the average of three of these tests is used to predict performance on the fourth. Each of the four tests represents a different aspect of oral language, namely expressive vocabulary, listening comprehension, phonological sensitivity, and naming automaticity. Relative strengths and weaknesses are determined in the same manner as in the intra-achievement and intracognitive variation procedures. Table 1-5 in the WJ IV Technical Manual (McGrew et al., 2014) provides additional (optional) tests and clusters that may be included in the intra-oral language variation procedure. | **Level III** Performance in one or more oral language areas is *below average or lower* (despite attempts at delivering quality instruction) as evidenced by converging data sources. | This variation procedure may be selected in addition to the intra-achievement variation procedure, especially when areas of oral expression and listening comprehension are the focus of the referral. Alternatively, an intracognitive analysis that includes oral language may be selected in lieu of this variation procedure. A relative oral language weakness in oral expression or listening comprehension that is also a *normative* weakness may meet the criterion of "unexpected underachievement." A relative weakness in phonological sensitivity or naming automaticity that is also a normative weakness may meet the criterion of domain-specific cognitive weakness. (Note that all OL tests may be included in the intracognitive variation procedure.) The absence of unusual variation coupled with one or more below average or lower scores may suggest the need for a comprehensive speech-language evaluation. |
| Academic Skills/Academic Fluency/Academic Applications | This procedure uses WJ IV ACH tests 1 through 6 and 9 through 11 to compare three academic clusters—skills, fluency, and applications. The average of two academic clusters is used to predict performance on the third. Speed and fluency clusters are included in this analysis automatically when the appropriate tests from the WJ IV COG (i.e., those that make up Gs and P) and WJ IV ACH (i.e., those that make up Reading Rate) are administered. Table 1-7 in the WJ IV Technical Manual (McGrew et al., 2014) provides additional (optional) tests and clusters that may be included in the intracognitive variation procedure. | **Level I** Performance in one or more academic areas is *below average or lower* (despite attempts at delivering quality instruction) as evidenced by converging data sources. | A relative weakness in one of these domains may provide useful information for intervention planning. A relative weakness that is also a *normative* weakness may meet the criterion of "unexpected underachievement" for the child, especially when s/he was expected to perform significantly better in that academic area, as determined via the GIA/achievement or Gf-Gc/ achievement comparisons. |

(Continued)

TABLE 8.2 Variation and Comparison Procedures of the WJ IV and Their Relevance to the DD/C Operational Definition of SLD Criteria (Continued)

Type of WJ IV Analysis Procedure	Description	DD/C Operational Definition of SLD Criteria	Relevance of WJ IV Analysis Procedures to DD/C Criteria
Comparison Procedures			
Academic Knowledge/ Achievement[a]	This procedure uses WJ IV ACH tests 18 through 20, which form the Academic Knowledge cluster—a measure of Gc, or more specifically Gkn. In this procedure, the Academic Knowledge cluster is used as an ability measure to determine if any achievement clusters differ significantly from it. According to the WJ IV authors, no significant difference between academic knowledge and areas of achievement suggests a consistency, whereas a statistically significant difference between academic knowledge and one or more achievement areas suggests the need for a comprehensive evaluation that includes cognitive and language abilities (McGrew et al., 2014).	Not applicable	It is presumed that knowledge of science, social studies, and humanities is gained through both life experiences and formal schooling. Moreover, in school, much of this domain-specific knowledge is acquired mainly through reading after about the 3rd grade. As such, one might expect to find consistency between Academic Knowledge and reading achievement, for example. If Academic Knowledge is either significantly higher or lower than achievement, hypotheses should be generated regarding the specific reasons for those discrepancies and tested systematically. Only the results of such hypothesis testing would be relevant with regard to the DD/C operational definition of SLD criteria.

| Oral Language/ Achievement[a] | The procedure uses the WJ IV Broad Oral Language cluster, which includes expressive and receptive language tests as well as a test of verbal working memory. This procedure allows the Broad Oral Language cluster to be used as the ability measure to determine if any WJ IV ACH reading, math, or written language clusters differ significantly from it. Standard scores from achievement clusters are compared to predicted scores (generated from the Broad Oral Language cluster). A significant difference between predicted and actual performance (where achievement is lower than what was predicted) suggests that the child is not performing academically at a level that would be expected given his/her oral language ability. This procedure may also be considered to be a Gc/ Achievement comparison. Because Gc likely explains the most variance in academic outcome as compared to each of the other major cognitive abilities, a Gc/achievement comparison may be particularly informative if the difference is statistically significant. | Level IV Below Average ability/ achievement consistency | According to the WJ IV authors, this comparison can have "rich interpretive value," primarily because teachers often expect children to perform academically at a level that is commensurate with their oral language ability (McGrew et al., 2014, p. 19). As such, an oral language/achievement consistency would not be considered unexpected from a teacher's perspective; however, an oral language > achievement discrepancy would be considered unexpected (especially in reading). The latter finding would suggest the need to explore other possible explanations for poor academic performance. The intracognitive variation procedure may be helpful in this regard. |

(Continued)

TABLE 8.2 Variation and Comparison Procedures of the WJ IV and Their Relevance to the DD/C Operational Definition of SLD Criteria (Continued)

Type of WJ IV Analysis Procedure	Description	DD/C Operational Definition of SLD Criteria	Relevance of WJ IV Analysis Procedures to DD/C Criteria
Scholastic Aptitude/ Achievement	This procedure is designed to determine whether a small subset of cognitive abilities (i.e., a four-test scholastic aptitude) that is most related to a given academic area (e.g., reading, math, written language) is consistent with or discrepant from that academic area. A consistent relationship between actual and predicted academic performance (based on the scholastic aptitude) indicates that the child is performing at an expected level academically. A discrepant relationship between actual and predicted academic performance indicates that the child is performing at an unexpected level academically (when actual performance is lower than predicted performance). In the latter situation, there may be factors other than cognitive weakness(es) to explain the child's unexpected academic performance. Although we agree with the WJ IV authors' caution that the scholastic aptitude/achievement comparison yields information that is descriptive rather than causal or diagnostic, converging data sources may certainly support a more causal or diagnostic conclusion.	Level IV Below Average Cognitive aptitude/achievement consistency	This comparison procedure may provide information to support the below average cognitive aptitude achievement consistency component of the DD/C model, particularly when the difference is not statistically significant and both the scholastic aptitude and the academic area are below average.

GIA/ Achievement	In this comparison the GIA, which is based on the first principle component (*g*) of the seven tests that comprise it, is used as the predictor and the severity of a discrepancy between any area of achievement or oral language and a predicted score for that area is determined. This comparison procedure is consistent with a traditional ability-achievement discrepancy analysis.	Level IV Cognitive Strength/ Academic Weakness Comparison	In the DD/C model, the PSW pattern includes a statistically significant and unusual difference between predicted and actual performance in the area identified as an academic weakness (where an estimate of *g* is used as the predictor).
Gf-Gc Composite/ Other Ability		Level IV Cognitive Strength/ Academic Weakness Comparison and Cognitive Strength/ Cognitive Weakness Comparison	In the DD/C model, the PSW pattern includes statistically significant and unusual differences between predicted and actual performances in the areas identified as cognitive and academic weaknesses (where an estimate of *g* is used as the predictor).

[a]In the Academic Knowledge/Achievement and Oral Language/Achievement comparison procedures, the predictor is essentially an estimate of the broad Gc ability. Comparing results of these analyses may assist in understanding which aspects of Gc has the most influence on academic performance (i.e., stores of acquired knowledge, as estimated by Academic Knowledge or language development, as estimated by Oral Language).

LEVEL I: ACADEMIC ABILITY ANALYSIS WITH THE WJ IV

Level I focuses on the basic concept of SLD: that underlying processing and/ or memory deficits adversely effected skill development which led to underachievement. In other words, intrinsic cognitive deficits often manifest in observable phenomena, particularly academic achievement. Thus, the first component of the DD/C operational definition of SLD involves documenting that some type of *learning* dysfunction exists. In the DD/C definition, the presence of a *normative deficit* established through standardized testing, and supported through other means such as clinical observations of academic performance, work samples, and parent and teacher reports is a necessary but insufficient condition for SLD determination. Level I includes the first criterion that is considered necessary for determining the presence of SLD. When criteria are met at Levels I through IV, practitioners can be reasonably confident that a diagnosis or classification of SLD is appropriate.

Level I involves comprehensive measurement of the major areas of academic achievement (e.g., reading, writing, and math abilities) or any subset of these areas that is the focus and purpose of the evaluation. The academic abilities depicted at this level are organized according to the eight areas of achievement specified in IDEA (2004). These eight areas are math calculation, math problem solving, basic reading skills, reading fluency, reading comprehension, written expression, listening comprehension, and oral expression. Typically, the eight areas of academic achievement are measured using standardized, norm-referenced tests. A combination of tests from the WJ IV ACH and OL batteries provides for measurement of all eight areas. Nevertheless, it is important to realize that data on academic performance should come from multiple sources (see Table 8.1, Level I, column 4). Following the collection of data on academic performance, it is necessary to determine whether the student has a weakness or deficit in one or more specific academic skills.

A *weakness* is typically defined as performance on standardized, norm-referenced tests that falls *below average* (where average is defined as standard scores between 90 and 110 [inclusive], based on a scale having a mean of 100 and standard deviation of 15). A weakness is associated with standard scores of 85–89 (inclusive). Interpreting scores in this very narrow range usually requires clinical judgment, as abilities associated with these scores may or may not pose significant problems for the individual. A *deficit* is often defined as performance on norm-referenced tests that falls greater than one standard deviation below the mean (i.e., standard scores <85). See Table 5-3 in the WJ IV *Examiner's Manual* (Mather & Wendling, 2014, p. 83) for the classification system recommended for use with the WJ IV and Table 8.3 for one that is recommended for use in evaluations that comprise more than one norm-referenced battery. Because all tests use different classification language, use of one classification system eliminates confusion when reporting results.

Determining whether a student has a weakness or deficit usually involves making normative-based comparisons of the student's performance against a

TABLE 8.3 Standard Scores, Percentile Ranks, and Corresponding Performance Classifications

Result		Classification of Performance	
Standard Score Range	Percentile Rank Range	Descriptive	Normative
≥131	98–99+	Very superior	
121–130	92–97	Superior	Normative strength 16% of population (>+1 standard deviation)
116–120	86–91	Above average	
111–115	76–85	High average	
90–110	25–75	Average	Normal limits 68% of population (≤±1 standard deviation)
85–89	16–24	Low average	
80–84	9–15	Below average	
70–79	3–8	Deficient	Normative weakness 16% of Population (>−1 standard deviation)
≤69	≤2	Very deficient	

Note: The classifications in this table are recommended when describing and reporting scores that were derived from more than one battery.

representative sample of same-age or grade peers from the general population. If weaknesses or deficits in the student's academic performance are not found, then the issue of SLD may be moot because such weaknesses are a necessary component for classification/diagnosis.

Nevertheless, some students who struggle academically may not demonstrate academic weaknesses or deficits on standardized, norm-referenced tests of achievement, particularly very bright students, for a variety of reasons. For example, some students may have figured out how to compensate for their processing deficit(s). Therefore, it is important not to assume that a student with a standard score in the 85–90 range, for example, on a "broad reading" composite is "ok," particularly when a parent, teacher, or the student him- or herself expresses concern. Under these circumstances, a more focused assessment of the CHC abilities and neuropsychological processes related to reading should be conducted.

As Table 8.1 demonstrates, the presence of an academic weakness or deficit established through standardized testing, for example, and corroborated by other data sources, such as CBM, clinical observations of academic performance, and work samples, is a necessary (but insufficient) condition for SLD determination. As such, the first criterion in the DD/C definition (Level I in Table 8.1) is a normative weakness or deficit in academic achievement. At this initial level then, a student's academic performance is compared to that of other individuals included in the WJ IV standardization sample (see Table 8.4). While statistically significant person-relative (or intraindividual) variations may also provide useful information, results of these analyses should not be interpreted as indicators of dysfunction unless one or more of the student's scores falls at the lower end of the normal range of functioning or lower (i.e., standard score around 85 or lower).

The *intra-ability* analyses of the WJ IV (e.g., intra-achievement, intracognitive) reflect statistical rarity in score differences as compared to the general population (based on actual discrepancy norms). However, it is important to remember that statistical rarity (which, unfortunately, is often associated with the term *abnormal*) is not synonymous with abnormality, impairment, or deficiency. Indeed, some deviations from normal or average are *valuable* deviations, and not all rarities are abnormal in the negative sense. Differences between test scores may be statistically significant and even rare, but not necessarily clinically meaningful. Practitioners should always seek to establish meaningful clinical significance as well as statistical significance. "The major weakness of the statistical rarity approach is that it has no values; it lacks any system for differentiating between desirable and undesirable behaviors. Of course, most users of the statistical rarity approach acknowledge that not all rarities should be identified as abnormal" (Alloy, Acocella, & Bootzin, 1996, p. 6).

Furthermore, it is also possible for nonsignificant statistical findings to be clinically meaningful. For example, when conducting variation procedures with the WJ IV, a user might find that a score of 76 on one subtest is not classified as a weakness according to the statistical analyses embedded in the scoring software, while another score of 77 on a subtest is classified as a weakness. According to the classification system described in Table 8.4, both scores are reflective of normative weaknesses or deficits that may very well impede academic performance and/or knowledge acquisition. Therefore, it is important that the user understand how interpretations of scores as strengths and weaknesses are derived by the scoring program so that potentially clinically significant findings are not overlooked (see Dumont and colleagues, this volume).

The WJ IV's intra-achievement variation procedure can be used most effectively to identify a student's *relative* strengths and weaknesses. The information generated from this type of person-relative analysis can be used to develop remedial strategies, educational plans, and specific academic interventions based on the data gathered at Level I. In addition to the intra-academic variation procedure, the WJ IV offers criterion-referenced scores (i.e., Instructional Range, Developmental Level Band, and Relative Proficiency Index) that also may be used to guide the development of educational plans

TABLE 8.4 A Summary of Empirically Supported Relationships Between CHC Abilities and Academic Achievement

	Reading Achievement	Math Achievement	Writing Achievement
Gf	Inductive (I) and general sequential reasoning (RG) abilities play a moderate role in *reading comprehension*.	*Inductive (I) general sequential (RG) and quantitative (RQ) reasoning abilities are consistently very important for math problem solving at all ages.*	Inductive (I) and general sequential reasoning abilities (RG) are consistently related to *written expression* at all ages.
Gc	*Language development (LD), lexical knowledge (VL), and listening ability (LS) are important at all ages for reading acquisition and development. These abilities become increasingly important with age.*	*Language development (LD), lexical knowledge (VL), and listening abilities (LS) are important at all ages. These abilities become increasingly important with age.*	*Language development (LD), lexical knowledge (VL), and general information (K0) are important primarily after about the 2nd grade. These abilities become increasingly important with age.*
Gwm	Memory span (MS) and *working memory capacity (WM)* or attentional control. *Gwm important for overall reading success.*	Memory span (MS) and *working memory capacity (WM)* or attentional control. *Gwm important for overall math success (e.g., math problem solving).*	Memory span (MS) is important to writing, especially *spelling* skills whereas working memory has shown relations with advanced writing skills (e.g., *written expression*). Gwm is important for overall writing success.
Gv	Orthographic Processing (often measured by tests of perceptual speed and speed of lexical access)—*reading fluency.*	Visualization (VZ) is important primarily for higher level or *advanced mathematics* (e.g., geometry, calculus).	Orthographic Processing (often measured by tests of perceptual speed and speed of lexical access)—*spelling.*
Ga	*Phonetic coding (PC) or "phonological awareness/processing" is very important during the elementary school years for the development of basic reading skills.*		*Phonetic coding (PC) or "phonological awareness/processing" is very important during the elementary school years for both basic writing skills and written expression (primarily before about grade 5).*

(Continued)

TABLE 8.4 A Summary of Empirically Supported Relationships Between CHC Abilities and Academic Achievement (Continued)

	Reading Achievement	Math Achievement	Writing Achievement
Glr	*Naming facility (NA) or "rapid automatic naming" (also called speed of lexical access) is very important during the elementary school years.* Associative memory (MA) is also important.	Naming Facility (NA; or speed of lexical access); Associative Memory (MA)—*rapid retrieval of basic math facts (necessary for higher level math problem solving).*	Naming facility (NA) or "rapid automatic naming" *(also called speed of lexical access)* has demonstrated relations with written expression, primarily *writing fluency.*
Gs	*Perceptual speed (P) abilities are important during all school years, particularly the elementary school years.*	*Perceptual speed (P) abilities are important during all school years, particularly the elementary school years.*	*Perceptual speed (P) abilities are important during all school years for basic writing and related to all ages for written expression.*

and interventions. However, population-relative (or interindividual) data are necessary to evaluate a student's performance in the domains assessed at Level I relative to a representative sample of same-age peers from the general population. Information from these scores provides the necessary data to determine whether performance is within or outside of normal limits (i.e., ±1SD from the normative mean) or any other range of ability (e.g., average, high average). Overall, results from both intra- and interindividual ability analyses are important. However, interindividual comparisons are most useful for diagnostic purposes and intraindividual comparisons are most useful for instructional purposes (see Chapter 6).

When weaknesses or deficits in academic performance are found (irrespective of the particular methods by which they are identified), the process advances to Level II.

LEVEL II: EXCLUSIONARY FACTORS—EVALUATION OF POTENTIAL PRIMARY AND CONTRIBUTORY CAUSES OF ACADEMIC SKILL WEAKNESSES OR DEFICITS

Level II involves evaluating whether any documented weaknesses or deficits found through Level I evaluation are or are not primarily the result of factors that may be, for example, largely external to the individual, noncognitive in nature, or the result of a condition other than SLD. Because there can be many reasons for weak or deficient academic performance, causal links to SLD should not be ascribed prematurely. Instead, reasonable hypotheses related to other potential causes should be developed. For example, cultural and linguistic differences are two common factors that can affect both test performance and academic skill acquisition adversely and result in achievement data that appear to suggest SLD (see Ortiz, 2011). In addition, lack of motivation, social/emotional disturbance, performance anxiety, psychiatric disorders, sensory impairments, intellectual disability, and medical conditions (e.g., hearing or vision problems) also need to be ruled out as potential explanatory correlates to any weaknesses or deficits identified at Level I.

Note that because the process of SLD determination does not necessarily occur in a strict linear fashion, evaluations at Levels I and II often take place concurrently, as data from Level II is often necessary to understand performance at Level I. The circular arrows between Levels I and II in Table 8.1 are meant to illustrate the fact that interpretations and decisions that are based on data gathered at Level I may need to be informed by data gathered at Level II. Ultimately, at Level II, the practitioner must judge the extent to which any factors other than cognitive impairment can be considered the *primary* reason for academic performance difficulties. If performance cannot be attributed primarily to other factors, then the second criterion necessary for establishing SLD according to the operational definition is met and assessment may continue to the next level.

It is important to recognize that, although factors such as having English as a second language, may be present and may affect performance adversely, SLD can also be present. Certainly, students who have vision problems, chronic illnesses, limited English proficiency, and so forth, may also have SLD. Therefore, when these or other factors at Level II are present or when they are determined to be *contributing* to poor performance, SLD should not be ruled out. Rather, only when such factors are determined to be *primarily* responsible for weaknesses in learning and academic performance, not merely contributing to them, should SLD, as an explanation for dysfunction in academic performance, be discounted. Examination of exclusionary factors is necessary to ensure fair and equitable interpretation of the data collected for SLD determination and as such, is not intended to *rule in* SLD. Rather, careful examination of exclusionary factors is intended to rule out other possible explanations for deficient academic performance.

One of the major reasons for placing evaluation of exclusionary factors at this (early) point in the SLD assessment process is to provide a mechanism that is efficient in both time and effort and that may prevent the unnecessary administration of additional tests. However, it may not be possible to completely and convincingly rule out all of the numerous potential exclusionary factors at this stage in the assessment process. For example, the data gathered at Levels I and II may be insufficient to draw conclusions about such conditions as intellectual disability, which often requires more thorough and direct assessment (e.g., administration of an intelligence test and adaptive behavior scale).

When gathering data at Level II, the "Test Session Observations Checklist" found on the WJ IV Test Record may be useful. This checklist is a brief behavior rating scale that can be used to document pertinent examiner observations following testing. Examinees are rated on the following seven categories: (i) conversational proficiency, (ii) cooperation, (iii) activity, (iv) attention and concentration, (v) self-confidence, (vi) care in responding, and (vii) response to difficult tasks. Information from this checklist can help describe observed behaviors that may have facilitated or inhibited an examinee's performance. When exclusionary factors have been evaluated carefully and eliminated as possible *primary* explanations for poor academic performance—at least those that can be evaluated at this level—the process may advance to the next level.

LEVEL III: COGNITIVE ABILITY ANALYSIS WITH THE WJ IV

The criterion at this level is similar to the one specified in Level I except that it is evaluated with data from an assessment of cognitive abilities and neuropsychological processes. Analysis of data generated from the administration of standardized tests represents the most common method available by which cognitive and neuropsychological functions in children are evaluated. However, other types of information and data are relevant to cognitive performance (see Table 8.1, Level III, column 4). Practitioners should actively seek out and gather data from other sources as a means of providing corroborating evidence for standardized test findings. For example, when test findings are found to be consistent with the student's performance in the classroom, a greater degree of confidence may be placed on test performance because interpretations of cognitive deficiency have ecological validity—an important condition for any diagnostic process (Flanagan, Alfonso, & Ortiz, 2012; Hale & Fiorello, 2004).

Because new data are gathered at Level III, it is possible to evaluate the exclusionary factors that could not be evaluated earlier (e.g., Intellectual Disability). The circular arrows between Levels II and III in Table 8.1 are meant to illustrate the fact that interpretations and decisions that are based on data gathered at Level III may need to be informed by data gathered at Level II. Likewise, data gathered at Level III is often necessary to rule out (or in) one or more exclusionary factors listed at Level II in Table 8.1. Reliable and valid identification of SLD depends in part on being able to understand academic performance (Level I), cognitive performance (Level III), and the many factors that may facilitate or inhibit such performances (Level II).

The WJ IV's intracognitive variation procedure can be used most effectively to identify a student's *relative* strengths and weaknesses. The information generated from this type of person-relative analysis can be used to inform educational strategies and interventions (see Mascolo, Alfonso, & Flanagan, 2014). However, population-relative (or interindividual) data are necessary to evaluate a student's performance in the cognitive domains assessed at Level III relative to a representative sample of same-age peers from the general population.

Information from these scores provides the necessary data to determine whether performance is within or outside of normal limits (i.e., ±1SD from the normative mean). As with Level I analysis, results from both intra- and interindividual ability analyses are important. However, interindividual comparisons are most useful for identifying cognitive weaknesses or deficits relative to most people. When normative weaknesses or deficits in cognitive performance are found, the process advances to Level IV.

LEVEL IV: THE DUAL DISCREPANCY/CONSISTENCY PSW

This level of evaluation revolves around a theory- and research-guided examination of performance across academic skills, cognitive abilities, and neuropsychological processes to determine whether the student's PSW is consistent with the SLD construct. When the process of SLD identification has reached this level, three necessary criteria for SLD identification have already been met: (i) one or more weaknesses or deficits in academic performance; (ii) one or more weaknesses or deficits in cognitive performance; and (iii) exclusionary factors determined not to be the primary causes of the academic and cognitive weaknesses or deficits. What has yet to be determined is whether the pattern of results is marked by an empirical or ecologically valid relationship between the identified cognitive and academic weaknesses, whether the individual displays generally average ability to think and reason, whether the individual's learning difficulty is domain-specific, and whether the individual's underachievement is unexpected. These four additional SLD markers are described below.

Relationship between Cognitive and Academic Weaknesses

A student with an SLD possesses specific cognitive and academic weaknesses or deficits. When these weaknesses are related empirically or when there is an ecologically valid relationship between them, the relationship is referred to as a *below average cognitive aptitude-achievement consistency* in the DD/C definition. This consistency is a necessary marker for SLD because SLD is caused by cognitive processing weaknesses or deficits (e.g., Hale et al., 2010). Thus, there is a need to understand and identify the underlying cognitive ability or processing problems that contribute significantly to the student's academic difficulties.

The term *cognitive aptitude* within the context of the DD/C definition represents the specific cognitive ability or neuropsychological processing weaknesses or deficits that are empirically related to the academic skill weaknesses or deficits. For example, if a student's basic reading skill deficit is related to cognitive deficits in phonological processing (a narrow *Ga* ability) and rapid automatic naming (a narrow *Glr* ability), then the combination of below average narrow *Ga* and *Glr* performances represents his or her *below average cognitive aptitude for basic reading*. Moreover, the finding of below average performance on measures of phonological processing, rapid automatic naming, and basic reading skill represents a *below average cognitive aptitude-achievement consistency*.

The concept of below average cognitive aptitude-achievement consistency reflects the notion that there are documented relationships between specific cognitive abilities and processes and specific academic skills. Empirically supported cognitive-achievement relationships are summarized in Table 8.4. The finding of below average performance in related cognitive and academic areas is an important marker for SLD in the DD/C definition and in other alternative research-based approaches (e.g., Hale et al., 2011; McCloskey et al., 2012).

In the DD/C definition, the criteria for establishing a below average cognitive aptitude-achievement *consistency* are as follows:

1. "Below average" performance (i.e., less than 90, and more typically at least a standard deviation or more below the mean) in the specific cognitive *and* academic areas that are considered weaknesses or deficits and
2. Either evidence of an empirical relationship between the specific cognitive and academic areas or an ecologically valid relationship between these areas. To validate the relation between the cognitive and academic areas of weakness, practitioners can document the manner in which the cognitive weakness or deficit manifests in academic difficulties in the classroom, for example (see Mascolo et al., 2014, for a comprehensive discussion of general and specific manifestations of cognitive deficits).

When the criteria for a below average cognitive aptitude-achievement consistency are met, there may or may not be a nonsignificant difference between the scores that represent the cognitive and academic areas of weakness. That is, in the DD/C definition, "consistency" refers to the fact that an empirical or ecologically valid relationship exists between the areas of identified cognitive and academic weakness, but not necessarily a nonsignificant difference between these areas. While a nonsignificant difference between the areas of cognitive and academic weakness would be expected, it need not be an inclusionary criterion for SLD. Because many factors facilitate and inhibit performance, a student may perform better or worse academically than his or her cognitive weaknesses may suggest (see Flanagan et al., 2013, for a discussion).

It is important to understand that discovery of consistencies among cognitive abilities and processes and academic skills in the below average (or lower) range could result from intellectual disability or generally below average cognitive ability, which would negate two important markers of SLD—that cognitive weaknesses are domain-specific and that underachievement is unexpected. Therefore, identification of SLD should not rest on below average cognitive aptitude-achievement consistency alone. A student with SLD typically has many cognitive capabilities. Therefore, in the DD/C model, the student must demonstrate a pattern of strengths or overall cognitive ability that is at least average.

Generally Average Ability to Think and Reason (*g*)

A specific learning disability is just that—*specific*. It is not general. As such, the below average cognitive aptitude-achievement consistency ought to be circumscribed and represent a significantly different level of functioning as compared to the student's cognitive capabilities or strengths in other areas. Indeed, the notion that students with SLD are of generally average or better overall cognitive ability is well known and has been written about for decades (e.g., Hinshelwood, 1917; Orton, 1937). In fact, the earliest recorded definitions of learning disability were developed by clinicians based on their observations of individuals who experienced considerable difficulties with the acquisition of basic academic skills, despite their average or above average general intelligence. According to Monroe (1932), "The children of superior mental capacity who fail to learn to read are, of course, spectacular examples of specific reading difficulty since they have such obvious abilities in other fields" (p. 23; cf Mather, 2011). Indeed, "all historical approaches to SLD *emphasize the spared or intact abilities* that stand in stark contrast to the deficient abilities" (Kaufman, 2008, pp. 7–8, emphasis added).

Current definitions of SLD also recognize the importance of generally average or better overall ability as a characteristic of individual's with SLD. For example, the official definition of learning disability of the Learning Disabilities Association of Canada (LDAC) states, in part, "Learning Disabilities refer to a number of disorders which may affect the acquisition, organization, retention, understanding or use of verbal or nonverbal information. These disorders affect learning in individuals who otherwise demonstrate at least average abilities essential for thinking and/or reasoning" (http://www.ldac-acta.ca/en/learnmore/ld-defined.html; see also Harrison & Holmes, 2012).

Unlike some definitions of SLD, such as Canada's (Harrison & Holmes, 2012), the 2006 federal regulations do not explicitly state that student's with SLD have average or better overall ability, although it is implied by the following phrasing: "…(ii) The child exhibits a pattern of strengths and weaknesses in performance, achievement, or both, relative to age, State-approved grade-level standards, or intellectual development, that is determined by the group to be relevant to the identification of a specific learning disability…" Given the vagueness of the wording in the federal regulations, one could certainly infer that this phrase means that the cognitive and academic areas of concern are significantly lower than what is expected relative to same-age peers or relative to otherwise average intellectual development. Indeed, there continues to be considerable agreement that a student who meets criteria for SLD has *some* cognitive capabilities that are at least average relative to most people (e.g., Berninger, 2011; Feifer, 2012; Geary et al., 2011; Hale & Fiorello, 2004; Hale et al., 2011; Harrison & Holmes, 2012; Kaufman, 2008; Kavale & Forness, 2000; Kavale & Flanagan, 2007; Kavale et al., 2009; Mather & Wendling, 2011; McCloskey et al., 2012; Naglieri, 2011). Moreover, the criterion of overall average or better ability in cognitive domains is necessary for differential diagnosis.

By failing to differentially diagnose SLD from other conditions that impede learning, such as intellectual disability, pervasive developmental disorders, and overall below average ability to learn and achieve (e.g., slow learner), the SLD construct loses its meaning and there is a tendency (albeit well intentioned) to accept anyone under the SLD rubric who has learning difficulties for reasons other than specific cognitive dysfunction (e.g., Kavale & Flanagan, 2007; Kavale, Kauffman, Bachmeier, & LeFever 2008; Mather & Kaufman, 2006; Reynolds & Shaywitz, 2009). While the underlying causes of the learning difficulties of all students who struggle academically *should be investigated and addressed*, an accurate SLD diagnosis is necessary because it informs instruction (e.g., Hale et al., 2010). When practitioners adhere closely to the DD/C definition, SLD can be differentiated from other disorders that also manifest as academic difficulty (e.g., Berninger, 2011; Della Toffalo, 2010; Flanagan et al., 2013).

While it may be some time before consensus is reached on what constitutes "average or better ability" for the purpose of SLD identification, a student with SLD, *generally speaking*, ought to be able to perform academically at a level that approximates that of his or her more typically achieving peers when provided with individualized instruction as well as appropriate accommodations, curricular modifications, and the like. In addition, in order for a student with SLD to reach performances (in terms of both rate of learning and level of achievement) that approximate his or her nondisabled peers, he or she must possess the ability to learn compensatory strategies and apply them independently, which often requires higher level thinking and reasoning, including intact executive processes (e.g., Maricle & Avirett, 2012; McCloskey, Perkins, & Van Divner, 2009).

Determining otherwise average or better ability to think and reason (or average or better g) for a student who has a below average cognitive aptitude-achievement consistency is not a straightforward task, however, and there is no agreed upon method for doing so. The main difficulty in determining whether or not an individual with *specific* cognitive weaknesses has otherwise average overall ability or g, is that either the selected cognitive ability battery provides only one total test score or a school district's guidelines limits discrepancy analysis to only one specific score, such as a full scale IQ. On most batteries, the total test score is an aggregate of *all* (or nearly all) abilities and processes measured by the instrument. As such, in many instances, the student's specific cognitive weaknesses or deficits attenuate the total test score on these instruments, which often masks overall cognitive ability or capacity. This problem with ability tests was noted as far back as the 1920s when Orton stated, "it seems probably that psychometric tests as ordinarily employed give an entirely erroneous and unfair estimate of the intellectual capacity of these [learning disabled] children" (1925, p. 582; cf Mather, 2011). Although intelligence and cognitive ability batteries have become more differentiated, offering a variety of specific cognitive ability composites, the manner in which they summarize overall intellectual or cognitive ability remains largely the same as that of their predecessors.

The WJ IV offers more options for estimating overall cognitive ability than some other batteries. It allows for the calculation of a General Intellectual Ability (GIA) score based on seven tests, one from each of the following CHC domains: *Gf, Gc, Glr, Gsm, Gv, Ga,* and *Gs.* However, because students with SLD may have deficits in one or more processing areas (e.g., *Glr, Gsm, Gs*), the GIA may be attenuated and underestimate the student's intellectual capacity. In recognition of this problem, the WJ IV authors included a new ability estimated called the *Gf-Gc* composite. This composite is comprised of two tests of *Gf* and two tests of *Gc.* The *Gf-Gc* composite was offered as an alternative to the GIA when processing deficits attenuate the GIA. However, processing deficits may also attenuate the *Gf-Gc* composite. For example, a student with weaknesses in *Gs* and *Gsm* may have difficulty performing the *Gf* tasks without the assistance of compensatory strategies, thus attenuating the *Gf-Gc* composite. In such a situation, the best estimate of overall ability is likely the aggregate of *Gc, Glr, Gv,* and *Ga,* although calculation of a composite that includes the tests of only these abilities is not an option on the WJ IV. Finally, because of the manner in which the SAPT composites were constructed (e.g., includes tests from four CHC domains, eliminates tests with content similar to criterion measure, includes a cognitively complex test), they provide reasonably proxies of *g.* But again, the SAPT composites may also be attenuated by processing deficits. Careful consideration of the composition of the WJ IV's overall ability composites is necessary for proper interpretation and to render a judgment with regard to the students overall level of cognitive ability.

Even when it is determined that a student has overall average ability to think and reason along with a below average cognitive aptitude-achievement consistency, these findings alone do not satisfy the criteria for a PSW consistent with the SLD construct in the DD/C model. This is because it is not yet clear whether the differences between the score representing overall ability and those representing specific cognitive and academic weaknesses or deficits are statistically significant, meaning that such differences are reliable differences (i.e., not due to chance). Moreover, it is not yet clear whether the cognitive area of weakness is domain-specific and whether the academic area of weakness (or underachievement) is unexpected.

Domain-Specific Cognitive Deficits

SLD has been described as a condition that is domain-specific. In other words, areas of cognitive weakness or deficit are circumscribed, meaning that while they interfere with learning and achievement, they are not pervasive and do not affect all or nearly all areas of cognition. According to Stanovich (1993a,b), "The key deficit must be a vertical faculty rather than a horizontal faculty—a domain-specific process rather than a process that operates across a variety of domains" (p. 279). It is rare to find an operational definition that specifies a criterion for determining that the condition is "domain-specific." Some suggest that this condition is supported by a statistically significant difference between an student's overall (average or better) cognitive ability and a score representing the individual's cognitive area of weakness (e.g., Naglieri, 2011). However, a statistically significant difference between two scores means only that the difference is not due to chance; it does not provide information about the *rarity* or infrequency of the difference in the general population. Some statistically significant differences are common in the general population; others are not. Therefore, to determine if the cognitive area that was identified as a weakness by the evaluator is domain-specific, the difference between the individual's actual and expected performance in this area should be uncommon in the general population.

Unexpected Underachievement

The traditional ability-achievement discrepancy analysis was used to determine if an individual's underachievement (e.g., reading difficulty) was unexpected (i.e., the individual's achievement was not at a level that was commensurate with his or her overall cognitive ability). A particularly salient problem with the ability-achievement discrepancy approach was that a total test score from an intelligence test (e.g., GIA, FSIQ) was used as the estimate of overall ability. However, for individuals with SLD, the total test score was often attenuated by one or more specific cognitive weaknesses or deficits and therefore may have provided an unfair or biased estimate of the individual's actual overall intellectual capacity. Furthermore, when the total test score was attenuated by specific cognitive weaknesses or deficits, the ability-achievement discrepancy was often not statistically significant, which often resulted in denying the student much needed academic interventions and special education services (e.g., Aaron, 1995; Hale et al., 2011). For this reason, as stated earlier, the authors of the WJ IV included the *Gf-Gc* composite as an alternative to the GIA for use in comparison (discrepancy) procedures—an alternative that Flanagan and her colleagues have advocated for many years (e.g., see Appendix H in Flanagan, McGrew, & Ortiz, 2000 and Appendix H in Flanagan et al., 2013; see also the Pattern of Strengths and Weaknesses component of the *Cross-Battery Assessment Software System* [X-BASS], Ortiz, Flanagan, & Alfonso, 2015).

In sum, an individual's scores from a comprehensive evaluation are evaluated at this level of the DD/C definition (Level IV) to determine if they represent a PSW that is consistent with SLD. The pattern that suggests SLD is characterized by *two discrepancies*—one that defines SLD as a domain-specific condition and one that further defines SLD as unexpected underachievement—that is concomitant with a below average cognitive aptitude-achievement *consistency*. Thus, a DD/C PSW is the overarching diagnostic marker of SLD.

LEVEL V: EVALUATION OF INTERFERENCE WITH LEARNING

When the SLD determination process reaches this point, presumably the criteria at each of the previous levels were met. In addition to the PSW requirement for

SLD identification, a basic eligibility requirement contained in both the legal and clinical prescriptions for diagnosing SLD refers to whether the suspected learning problem(s) actually results in significant or substantial academic failure or other restrictions or limitations in daily life functioning.

The legal and diagnostic specifications of SLD necessitate that practitioners review the whole of the collected data and make a professional judgment about the extent of the adverse impact that any measured deficit has on an individual's performance in one or more areas of learning or academic achievement. Essentially, Level V analysis serves as a kind of quality control test designed to prevent the application of an SLD diagnosis in cases in which "real-world" functioning is not in fact impaired or substantially limited as compared to same-age peers in the general population, regardless of the patterns seen in the data.

This final criterion requires practitioners to take a very broad survey not only of the entire array of data collected during the course of the assessment but also of the real-world manifestations and practical implications of any presumed disability. In general, if the criteria at Levels I through IV were met, it is likely that in the vast majority of cases, Level V analysis serves only to support conclusions that have already been drawn. However, in cases in which data may be equivocal or when procedures or criteria other than those specified in the DD/C definition have been utilized, Level V analysis becomes an important safety valve, ensuring that any representations of SLD suggested by the data are indeed manifest in observable impairments in one or more areas of functioning in real-life settings.

Space limitations preclude the inclusion of lengthy case illustrations of how the WJ IV may be used within the context of the DD/C operational definition of SLD. Therefore, the next section will provide only excerpts from a case to illustrate the decision-making process across the five Levels of the DD/C definition when the WJ IV is used. The WJ IV was administered to Andrew, a fifth-grade student who was referred for suspected learning disability in the area of mathematics. Figure 8.1 provides an example of the variation and comparison procedures followed in the SLD identification process.

Summary of a WJ IV Case Report

Level I

According to the DD/C operational definition of SLD, the first necessary criterion to be established is weak or deficient performance in one or more academic areas. Table 8.5 includes Andrew's WJ IV Score Report and shows that his performance in the area of mathematics ranged from weak to deficient. For example, his performance on Calculation was weak (SS = 85) and his performance on Applied Problems was deficient (i.e., SS = 73). It is noteworthy that an intra-achievement analysis is not necessary to identify academic weaknesses. Only a comparison of an individual's obtained standard scores to same-age or grade peers is necessary to establish an academic weakness (when corroborating data

TABLE 8.5 WJ IV Score Report for Andrew

Score Report

Name A N D R E W
Date of Birth: 10/01/2004
Age: 10-0 (COG)
  10-1 (ACH)
Sex: Male
Date of Testing: 10/06/2014 (COG)
  10/25/2014 (ACH)

School:
Teacher:
Grade: 5.2

ID:
Examiners:

TESTS ADMINISTERED
Woodcock-Johnson IV Tests of Cognitive Abilities (Norms based on age 10-0)
Woodcock-Johnson IV Tests of Achievement Form A and Extended (Norms based on age 10-1)

TABLE OF SCORES
Woodcock-Johnson IV Tests of Cognitive Abilities (Norms based on age 10-0)

CLUSTER/Tests	W	AE	RPI	SS (68% Band)
GEN INTELLECTUAL ABIL	492	9-0	83/90	91 (87-95)
Oral Vocabulary	499	10-1	90/90	100 (94-107)
Number Series	466	7-7	28/90	78 (73-84)
Verbal Attention	480	7-7	58/90	83 (77-89)
Letter-Pattern Matching	517	11-2	96/90	107 (97-117)
Phonological Processing	501	10-7	92/90	103 (97-108)
Story Recall	496	10-8	91/90	103 (99-107)
Visualization	498	10-6	91/90	102 (97-108)
Gf-Gc COMPOSITE	493	9-3	85/90	95 (91-98)
Oral Vocabulary	499	10-1	90/90	100 (94-107)
Number Series	466	7-7	28/90	78 (73-84)
General Information	507	12-2	96/90	109 (104-114)
Concept Formation	500	10-4	92/90	102 (98-106)
COMP-KNOWLEDGE (Gc)	503	11-0	94/90	105 (101-110)
Oral Vocabulary	499	10-1	90/90	100 (94-107)
General Information	507	12-2	96/90	109 (104-114)
FLUID REASONING (Gf)	483	8-4	67/90	87 (83-91)
Number Series	466	7-7	28/90	78 (73-84)
Concept Formation	500	10-4	92/90	102 (98-106)
FLUID REASONING 3	489	8-10	79/90	92 (88-95)
Number Series	466	7-7	28/90	78 (73-84)
Concept Formation	500	10-4	92/90	102 (98-106)
Analysis-Synthesis	500	10-8	93/90	103 (98-108)
S-TERM WORK MEM (Gwm)	481	7-7	59/90	82 (76-87)
Verbal Attention	480	7-7	58/90	83 (77-89)
Numbers Reversed	481	7-7	61/90	86 (79-92)
S-TERM WORK MEM 3	478	7-6	58/90	81 (77-85)
Verbal Attention	480	7-7	58/90	83 (77-89)
Numbers Reversed	481	7-7	61/90	86 (79-92)
Object-Number Sequencing	474	7-3	55/90	84 (78-89)

1 of 6

(Continued)

TABLE 8.5 WJ IV Score Report for Andrew (Continued)

ANDREW
October 25, 2014

Score Report

CLUSTER/Tests	W	AE	RPI	SS (68% Band)
COG PROCESS SPEED (Gs)	515	11-4	97/90	108 (102-115)
Letter-Pattern Matching	517	11-2	96/90	107 (97-117)
Pair Cancellation	513	11-7	98/90	108 (102-114)
AUDITORY PROCESS (Ga)	503	11-3	93/90	105 (101-109)
Phonological Processing	501	10-7	92/90	103 (97-108)
Nonword Repetition	504	11-11	94/90	105 (101-110)
L-TERM RETRIEVAL (Glr)	495	9-6	89/90	98 (95-101)
Story Recall	496	10-8	91/90	103 (99-107)
Visual-Auditory Learning	494	8-3	85/90	95 (90-99)
VISUAL PROCESSING (Gv)	500	11-2	92/90	104 (99-110)
Visualization	498	10-6	91/90	102 (97-108)
Picture Recognition	503	12-8	93/90	105 (98-113)
QUANTITATIVE REASONING	483	8-5	69/90	88 (84-92)
Number Series	466	7-7	28/90	78 (73-84)
Analysis-Synthesis	500	10-8	93/90	103 (98-108)
NUMBER FACILITY	495	10-0	90/90	100 (94-105)
Numbers Reversed	481	7-7	61/90	86 (79-92)
Number-Pattern Matching	508	11-4	98/90	111 (102-119)
PERCEPTUAL SPEED	513	11-3	97/90	110 (102-117)
Letter-Pattern Matching	517	11-2	96/90	107 (97-117)
Number-Pattern Matching	508	11-4	98/90	111 (102-119)
COGNITIVE EFFICIENCY	499	9-7	87/90	97 (90-104)
Letter-Pattern Matching	517	11-2	96/90	107 (97-117)
Numbers Reversed	481	7-7	61/90	86 (79-92)
COG EFFICIENCY (Ext)	497	9-9	88/90	98 (93-103)
Verbal Attention	480	7-7	58/90	83 (77-89)
Letter-Pattern Matching	517	11-2	96/90	107 (97-117)
Numbers Reversed	481	7-7	61/90	86 (79-92)
Number-Pattern Matching	508	11-4	98/90	111 (102-119)
Oral Vocabulary	499	10-1	90/90	100 (94-107)
Number Series	466	7-7	28/90	78 (73-84)
Verbal Attention	480	7-7	58/90	83 (77-89)
Letter-Pattern Matching	517	11-2	96/90	107 (97-117)
Phonological Processing	501	10-7	92/90	103 (97-108)
Story Recall	496	10-8	91/90	103 (99-107)
Visualization	498	10-6	91/90	102 (97-108)
General Information	507	12-2	96/90	109 (104-114)
Concept Formation	500	10-4	92/90	102 (98-106)
Numbers Reversed	481	7-7	61/90	86 (79-92)
Number-Pattern Matching	508	11-4	98/90	111 (102-119)
Nonword Repetition	504	11-11	94/90	105 (101-110)
Visual-Auditory Learning	494	8-3	85/90	95 (90-99)
Picture Recognition	503	12-8	93/90	105 (98-113)

2 of 6

(Continued)

TABLE 8.5 WJ IV Score Report for Andrew (Continued)

ANDREW
October 25, 2014

Score Report

CLUSTER/Tests	W	AE	RPI	SS (68% Band)
Analysis-Synthesis	500	10-8	93/90	103 (98-108)
Object-Number Sequencing	474	7-3	55/90	84 (78-89)
Pair Cancellation	513	11-7	98/90	108 (102-114)
Memory for Words	467	6-7	49/90	83 (77-89)

Woodcock-Johnson IV Tests of Achievement Form A and Extended (Norms based on age 10-1)

CLUSTER/Tests	W	AE	RPI	SS (68% Band)
READING	505	11-2	95/90	108 (104-111)
Letter-Word Identification	509	11-5	97/90	108 (104-112)
Passage Comprehension	502	10-11	94/90	104 (99-110)
MATHEMATICS	471	8-1	34/90	79 (76-82)
Applied Problems	466	7-6	21/90	73 (68-79)
Calculation	476	8-7	50/90	85 (81-89)
BROAD MATHEMATICS	472	8-1	34/90	80 (76-83)
Applied Problems	466	7-6	21/90	73 (68-79)
Calculation	476	8-7	50/90	85 (81-89)
Math Facts Fluency	474	8-3	33/90	84 (78-90)
MATH CALCULATION SKILLS	475	8-5	41/90	84 (80-88)
Calculation	476	8-7	50/90	85 (81-89)
Math Facts Fluency	474	8-3	33/90	84 (78-90)
MATH PROBLEM SOLVING	472	7-8	37/90	78 (74-82)
Applied Problems	466	7-6	21/90	73 (68-79)
Number Matrices	478	7-11	57/90	85 (81-90)
WRITTEN LANGUAGE	502	10-8	94/90	105 (101-108)
Spelling	506	10-10	95/90	105 (102-109)
Writing Samples	498	10-5	92/90	102 (97-106)
ACADEMIC SKILLS	497	10-0	89/90	99 (97-102)
Letter-Word Identification	509	11-5	97/90	108 (104-112)
Spelling	506	10-10	95/90	105 (102-109)
Calculation	476	8-7	50/90	85 (81-89)
ACADEMIC APPLICATIONS	489	8-11	78/90	91 (88-95)
Applied Problems	466	7-6	21/90	73 (68-79)
Passage Comprehension	502	10-11	94/90	104 (99-110)
Writing Samples	498	10-5	92/90	102 (97-106)
BRIEF ACHIEVEMENT	493	9-7	84/90	96 (94-99)
Letter-Word Identification	509	11-5	97/90	108 (104-112)
Applied Problems	466	7-6	21/90	73 (68-79)
Spelling	506	10-10	95/90	105 (102-109)
Letter-Word Identification	509	11-5	97/90	108 (104-112)
Applied Problems	466	7-6	21/90	73 (68-79)
Spelling	506	10-10	95/90	105 (102-109)
Passage Comprehension	502	10-11	94/90	104 (99-110)
Calculation	476	8-7	50/90	85 (81-89)

3 of 6

(Continued)

TABLE 8.5 WJ IV Score Report for Andrew (Continued)

ANDREW
October 25, 2014

Score Report

CLUSTER/Tests	W	AE	RPI	SS (68% Band)
Writing Samples	498	10-5	92/90	102 (97-106)
Math Facts Fluency	474	8-3	33/90	84 (78-90)
Number Matrices	478	7-11	57/90	85 (81-90)

	STANDARD SCORES			DISCREPANCY		Interpretation at
VARIATIONS	Actual	Predicted	Difference	PR	SD	+ or -1.50 SD (SEE)
Intra-Cognitive [Extended] Variations						
COMP-KNOWLEDGE (*Gc*)	105	96	9	77	+0.74	--
FLUID REASONING (*Gf*)	87	100	-13	12	-1.17	--
FLUID REASONING 3	92	100	-8	22	-0.78	--
S-TERM WORK MEM (*Gwm*)	82	99	-17	7	-1.48	--
S-TERM WORK MEM 3	81	99	-18	5	-1.62	Weakness
COG PROCESS SPEED (*Gs*)	108	97	11	81	+0.89	--
AUDITORY PROCESS (*Ga*)	105	96	9	79	+0.79	--
L-TERM RETRIEVAL (*Glr*)	98	96	2	55	+0.12	--
VISUAL PROCESSING (*Gv*)	104	97	7	71	+0.55	--
QUANTITATIVE REASONING	88	100	-12	13	-1.12	--
PERCEPTUAL SPEED	110	96	14	85	+1.03	--
Oral Vocabulary	100	96	4	65	+0.37	--
Number Series	78	100	-22	3	-1.82	Weakness
Verbal Attention	83	99	-16	11	-1.25	--
Letter-Pattern Matching	107	97	10	77	+0.75	--
Phonological Processing	103	96	7	72	+0.58	--
Story Recall	103	97	6	67	+0.44	--
Visualization	102	97	5	66	+0.42	--
General Information	109	97	12	81	+0.87	--
Concept Formation	102	100	2	56	+0.16	--
Numbers Reversed	86	99	-13	15	-1.05	--
Number-Pattern Matching	111	97	14	85	+1.03	--
Nonword Repetition	105	97	8	74	+0.65	--
Visual-Auditory Learning	95	97	-2	43	-0.18	--
Picture Recognition	105	98	7	70	+0.52	--
Analysis-Synthesis	103	100	3	60	+0.25	--
Object-Number Sequencing	84	99	-15	10	-1.26	--
Pair Cancellation	108	97	11	79	+0.80	--
Memory for Words	83	99	-16	10	-1.27	--
Number Matrices	85	100	-15	13	-1.14	--

	STANDARD SCORES			DISCREPANCY		Interpretation at
VARIATIONS	Actual	Predicted	Difference	PR	SD	+ or -1.50 SD (SEE)
Intra-Achievement [Extended] Variations						
MATH CALCULATION SKILLS	84	99	-15	7	-1.49	--
MATH PROBLEM SOLVING	78	101	-23	2	-2.11	Weakness

4 of 6

(Continued)

TABLE 8.5 WJ IV Score Report for Andrew (Continued)

ANDREW
October 25, 2014

Score Report

VARIATIONS	Actual	STANDARD SCORES Predicted	Difference	DISCREPANCY PR	SD	Interpretation at + or -1.50 SD (SEE)
Intra-Achievement [Extended] Variations						
Letter-Word Identification	108	94	14	95	+1.65	Strength
Applied Problems	73	101	-28	0.5	-2.55	Weakness
Spelling	105	95	10	86	+1.09	--
Passage Comprehension	104	95	9	84	+0.98	--
Calculation	85	99	-14	9	-1.32	--
Writing Samples	102	96	6	67	+0.45	--
Math Facts Fluency	84	99	-15	10	-1.28	--
Number Matrices	85	101	-16	12	-1.15	--

COMPARISONS	Actual	STANDARD SCORES Predicted	Difference	DISCREPANCY PR	SD	Interpretation at + or -1.50 SD (SEE)
Gf-Gc Composite/Other Ability Comparisons						
S-TERM WORK MEM (Gwm)	82	97	-15	11	-1.25	--
S-TERM WORK MEM 3	81	96	-15	10	-1.30	--
COG PROCESS SPEED (Gs)	108	97	11	80	+0.84	--
PERCEPTUAL SPEED	110	98	12	81	+0.87	--
AUDITORY PROCESS (Ga)	105	97	8	75	+0.69	--
L-TERM RETRIEVAL (Glr)	98	97	1	54	+0.09	--
VISUAL PROCESSING (Gv)	104	97	7	70	+0.52	--
NUMBER FACILITY	100	97	3	58	+0.19	--
COGNITIVE EFFICIENCY	97	97	0	51	+0.02	--
COG EFFICIENCY (Ext)	98	97	1	54	+0.09	--
BRIEF ACHIEVEMENT	96	96	0	52	+0.05	--
READING	108	96	12	86	+1.08	--
MATHEMATICS	79	96	-17	5	-1.67	Weakness
BROAD MATHEMATICS	80	96	-16	5	-1.61	Weakness
MATH CALCULATION SKILLS	84	97	-13	13	-1.12	--
MATH PROBLEM SOLVING	78	96	-18	3	-1.91	Weakness
WRITTEN LANGUAGE	105	97	8	75	+0.68	--
ACADEMIC SKILLS	99	96	3	62	+0.31	--
ACADEMIC APPLICATIONS	91	96	-5	33	-0.44	--

COMPARISONS	Actual	STANDARD SCORES Predicted	Difference	DISCREPANCY PR	SD	Significant at + or -1.50 SD (SEE)
GIA/Achievement Discrepancy Procedure						
BRIEF ACHIEVEMENT	96	92	4	67	+0.45	No
READING	108	93	15	92	+1.40	No
MATHEMATICS	79	92	-13	8	-1.40	No
BROAD MATHEMATICS	80	93	-13	8	-1.43	No

5 of 6

(Continued)

TABLE 8.5 WJ IV Score Report for Andrew   (Continued)

ANDREW
October 25, 2014   **Score Report**

		STANDARD SCORES		DISCREPANCY		Significant at
COMPARISONS	Actual	Predicted	Difference	PR	SD	+ or -1.50 SD (SEE)
GIA/Achievement Discrepancy Procedure						
MATH CALCULATION SKILLS	84	93	-9	17	-0.95	No
MATH PROBLEM SOLVING	78	93	-15	6	-1.53	Yes (-)
WRITTEN LANGUAGE	105	93	12	86	+1.10	No
ACADEMIC SKILLS	99	93	6	76	+0.70	No
ACADEMIC APPLICATIONS	91	92	-1	48	-0.06	No

			STANDARD SCORES		DISCREPANCY		Significant at
COMPARISONS	Actual	SAPT	Predicted	Difference	PR	SD	+ or -1.50 SD (SEE)
Scholastic Aptitude/Achievement Comparisons							
READING	108	107	105	3	59	+0.24	No
MATHEMATICS	79	96	97	-18	3	-1.90	Yes (-)
BROAD MATHEMATICS	80	96	97	-17	3	-1.87	Yes (-)
MATH CALCULATION SKILLS	84	96	97	-13	10	-1.31	No
MATH PROBLEM SOLVING	78	96	97	-19	4	-1.77	Yes (-)
WRITTEN LANGUAGE	105	108	106	-1	46	-0.09	No

Woodcock-Johnson IV Tests of Achievement Form A and Extended Qualitative Observations

Letter-Word Identification: Identified words rapidly and accurately with little effort (automatic word identification skills)

Applied Problems: Appeared to have limited understanding of grade- or age-appropriate math application tasks

Spelling: Spelled words easily and accurately

Passage Comprehension: Appeared to read initial passages easily but appeared to struggle as the reading increased in difficulty (typical)

Calculation: Solved problems slowly and demonstrated less automaticity with the latter items

Writing Samples: Sentences were simple but adequate (typical)

6 of 6

Houghton Mifflin Harcourt.

sources are present). Although not a necessary criterion in the DD/C definition, to evaluate whether Andrew's performance on Applied Problems is unusual, the results of the WJ IV intra-achievement variation may be examined. The intra-achievement analysis in Table 8.5 shows that only 5 out of 1000 age mates, with the same predicted score as Andrew, scored as low as or lower than he scored on Applied Problems. Note that although only Applied Problems emerged as a weakness in the intra-achievement (Extended) Variation analysis in Table 8.5, the standard scores obtained by Andrew on other individual achievement tests (i.e., Calculation, Math Fluency Facts, and Number Matrices) are all at least 1SD below the normative mean, suggesting that they represent normative weaknesses and are areas of concern. As such, the Level I criterion of weak or deficient performance in one or more academic areas is met.

Level II

In the case of Andrew, exclusionary factors were evaluated at Level II via the collection of collateral information. The observed math skill deficits are not attributable to intellectual disability, as evidenced by the GIA and *Gf-Gc* composites of 91 and 95, respectively (see Table 8.5). Andrew's skill deficits in mathematics are also not attributable to cultural or linguistic differences, sensory impairments, insufficient instruction or opportunity to learn, organic or physical health factors, or social/emotional or psychological disturbance. Therefore, the criterion at Level II was met.

Level III

Level III requires evidence of weak or deficient performance in one or more basic psychological/neuropsychological or cognitive processes presumed to originate from central nervous system dysfunction. Therefore, the focus of this level of analysis is on performance on cognitive and neuropsychological measures. Andrew demonstrated deficient performance relative to same age peers in the areas of Short-Term Working Memory (Extended) (SS = 81) and quantitative reasoning (e.g., Number Series SS = 78). Although not a necessary criterion in the DD/C definition, to evaluate whether these score performances are unusual for Andrew, the results of the WJ IV intracognitive variation may be examined. The intracognitive analysis in Table 8.5 shows that only 3% of Andrew's peer group, with the same predicted score as Andrew, scored as low as or lower than he scored on Number Series. Note that although only the Number Series test emerged as a weakness, several other individual cognitive test performances are considered weak or deficient from a normative perspective, namely Verbal Attention (SS = 83), Numbers Reversed (SS = 86), Object-Number Sequencing (SS = 84), Memory for Words (SS = 83), and Number Matrices (SS = 85). Also, note that the Short-Term Working Memory composite of 82 did not emerge as a weakness, but the Short-Term Working Memory (Extended) composite of 81 did emerge as a weakness. This finding demonstrates that when practitioners rely only on the information included in the last column in Table 8.5 (i.e., the column that lists strengths and weaknesses), they will miss important information about how an individual functions relative to same age or grade peers—information that is necessary when determining disability. The standard scores obtained by Andrew on tests of *Gf*-Quantitative Reasoning (i.e., Number Series) and Gwm-Working Memory Capacity (e.g., Verbal Attention, Object-Number Sequencing) are greater than 1SD below the normative mean, suggesting that they represent normative weaknesses and are areas of concern. As such, the Level III criterion of weak or deficient performance in one or more cognitive areas is met.

Level IV

This level of analysis requires (i) determination of whether the observed cognitive weaknesses are domain-specific, meaning that they are discrepant from observed areas of cognitive strength (as represented by a global estimate of *g*); (ii) determination of whether the observed academic weaknesses are unexpected, meaning that they are discrepant from areas of cognitive strength (as represented by a global estimate of *g*); and (iii) the observed cognitive and academic weaknesses are related empirically and that relationship is ecologically valid. In order to meet the discrepancy criterion in conditions i and ii, the difference between actual cognitive and academic performance (in the identified areas of concern) and performance predicted by an estimate of overall ability must be rare (i.e., occurring in less than about 10% of the population).

In the DD/C operational definition of SLD, the estimate of overall ability must be a standard score of 85 or higher. The rationale for a cut score of 85 for the overall ability (*g*) estimate is that for scores less than 85 the upper end of the confidence band (based on one standard error of measurement) is unlikely to extend into the average range of ability. Since average overall ability is a criterion in the DD/C model, individuals with overall ability estimates of less than 85 are not considered to have *specific* learning disabilities under most circumstances (see Flanagan et al., 2013, for a discussion). Because individuals with SLDs often have deficits in cognitive processes that attenuate estimates of overall ability on cognitive batteries, the authors of the DD/C model developed a program that provides an estimate of overall ability, when appropriate, that is not influenced by cognitive areas of weakness (see Flanagan et al., 2013; Ortiz et al., 2015). For example, Andrew has specific cognitive deficits in Gwm and *Gf* that attenuated his WJ IV GAI (SS = 91). Some of the attenuating influences of his cognitive weaknesses on overall ability were eliminated in the calculation of the WJ IV *Gf-Gc* composite (SS = 95), which is why this composite is higher than the GAI. Flanagan and colleagues' program calculates an estimate of overall ability based only on cognitive areas that are not weak or deficient and that estimate is only calculated when the breadth of abilities that can potentially be included is sufficient to render a psychometrically defensible estimate of general ability (Flanagan et al., 2013; Ortiz et al., 2015). Their estimate of general ability is referred to as the Facilitating Cognitive Composite or FCC because it is comprised of only those cognitive performances that are likely to facilitate learning and academic performance. When using Flanagan and colleagues' program for determining SLD following the DD/C model, Andrew's FFC is 105. This standard score represents his overall ability without the attenuating influences of quantitative reasoning and working memory deficits. Because the WJ IV does not have a similar composite, the best estimate of Andrew's overall ability is the *Gf-Gc* composite of 95. In essence, the 95 represents the top oval in Figure 8.1 and is the value that is used as the predictor when determining whether the difference between actual and predicted performance is unusual.

When using the WJ IV to determine whether the observed cognitive weaknesses are discrepant from observed areas of cognitive strength (as represented by the *Gf-Gc* Composite), results from the *Gf-Gc*/Other Ability Comparison should be considered. Table 8.5 shows that none of the cognitive areas were reported as weaknesses, despite the fact that Gwm, for example, is a normative weakness for Andrew relative to same age peers. When weaknesses are not reported in the far right column in Table 8.5, then it is especially important to examine the discrepancy percentile ranks, as these values reflect "base rates" in the population. Andrew's discrepancy percentile rank of 10 on Short-Term Working Memory (Extended) indicates that only 10% of his peer group had the same or larger negative difference score on this composite. This finding meets the criterion of a domain-specific cognitive weakness for Andrew. That is, the difference between Andrew's actual Gwm score of 81 and his predicted score of 96 (a −15 point difference) is unusual in the population (when unusual is defined as occurring in ≤10% of the population).

When using the WJ IV to determine whether the observed academic weaknesses are discrepant from observed areas of cognitive strength (as represented by the *Gf-Gc* Composite), results from the *Gf-Gc*/Other Ability Comparison should be considered. Table 8.5 shows that the Mathematics, Broad Mathematics, and Math Problem Solving composites all emerged as weaknesses. Each of these composites had discrepancy percentile rank values that were less than 10, meaning that the differences between Andrew's performances in these areas and his expected performances (as predicted by his *Gf-Gc* composite) are unusual in the population. Note that the Math Calculation Skills composite of 84 did not emerge as a weakness. However, the tests that make up this composite include skills that are very difficult for Andrew. For example, his Math Facts Fluency Relative Proficiency Index is 33/90, meaning that on similar tasks in which the average fifth-grade student would demonstrate 90% proficiency, Andrew would demonstrate only 33% proficiency. Andrew's facility with basic math facts is very limited. Therefore, even though the Math Calculation Skills Composite did not emerge as a weakness on the WJ IV Score Report in the *Gf-Gc* Composite/Other Ability Comparison (Table 8.5), it is clear that these skills should be targeted for remediation and intervention. Overall, the results of the

Gf-Gc Composite/Other Ability Comparison demonstrate that Andrew's weaknesses in mathematics are unexpected.

To determine whether the observed cognitive and academic weaknesses are related empirically, a consideration of the relations among abilities, processes, and specific academic skills should be considered (see Flanagan et al., 2013; McGrew & Wendling, 2010; for summaries of this research). Table 8.4 shows that working memory capacity and quantitative reasoning correlate highly with math problem solving, for example. Therefore, there is empirical evidence to support a below average cognitive aptitude-achievement consistency in Andrew's pattern of score performances. Moreover, a review of work samples and an interview with Andrew's teacher demonstrated that Andrew's cognitive weaknesses manifest in predictable and expected ways in the classroom (e.g., Andrew cannot solve multi-step math word problems that are presented orally in class).

Overall, the WJ IV Score Report provided information necessary to evaluate whether Andrew's pattern of cognitive and academic strengths and weaknesses is marked by a dual discrepancy and a consistency in a manner suggestive of SLD. A combination of inter- and intraindividual comparisons was considered along with base rate data (in the form of discrepancy percentile values). This information was interpreted within the context of research on the relations among cognitive abilities, processes, and specific academic skills.

CONCLUSIONS

When the criteria at each level of the DD/C operational definition are met, it may be concluded that the WJ IV (and all other) data gathered are sufficient to support a diagnosis of SLD. The operational definition presented in this chapter provides a guide to the process of using and interpreting the WJ IV effectively within the context of SLD referrals. Because the specifications and procedures implied by this definition are grounded in the same theory and research that guided the development of the WJ IV, this instrument is particularly well suited for use in SLD evaluations that subscribe to the DD/C model.

REFERENCES

Aaron, P. G. (1995). Differential diagnosis of reading disabilities. *School Psychology Review*, *24*, 345–360.

Alloy, L. B., Acocella, J., & Bootzin, R. R. (1996). Abnormal psychology: Current. In *Perspectives* (7th ed.). New York: McGraw-Hill.

Berninger, V. W. (2011). Evidence-based differential diagnosis and treatment of reading disabilities with and without comorbidities in oral language, writing, and math: Prevention, problem-solving consultation, and specialized instruction. In D. P. Flanagan & V. C. Alfonso (Eds.), *Essentials of specific learning disability identification* (pp. 203–232). Hoboken, NJ: Wiley.

Della Toffalo, D. A. (2010). Linking school neuropsychology with response-to-intervention models. In *Best practices in school neuropsychology: Guidelines for effective practice, assessment, and evidence-based intervention* (pp. 159–183). Hoboken, NJ: John Wiley & Sons Inc.

Feifer, S. G. (2012). *Integrating RTI with cognitive neuropsychology: A scientific approach to reading*. Presentation given at the Fordham University 4th Annual Assessment Conference, May 11. New York, NY.

Feifer, S. G., & DeFina, P. D. (2005). *The neuropsychology of mathematics: Diagnosis and intervention*. Middletown, MD: School Neuropsych Press.

Fiorello, C. A., Flanagan, D. P., & Hale, J. B. (2014). Response to the special issue: The utility of the pattern of strengths and weaknesses approach. *Learning Disabilities: A Multidisciplinary Journal, 20*(1), 55–59.

Flanagan, D. P., Alfonso, V. C., & Ortiz, S. O. (2012). The cross-battery assessment approach: An overview, historical perspective, and current directions. In D. P. Flanagan & P. L. Harrison (Eds.), *Contemporary intellectual assessment: theories, tests, and issues* (3rd ed.) (pp. 459–483). New York, NY: Guildford Press.

Flanagan, D. P., McGrew, K. S., & Ortiz, S. O. (2000). *The Wechsler intelligence scales and Gf-Gc theory: A contemporary approach to interpretation*. Boston: Allyn and Bacon.

Flanagan, D. P., Ortiz, S. O., & Alfonso, V. C. (2013). *Essentials of cross-battery assessment* (3rd ed.). Hoboken, NJ: Wiley.

Flanagan, D. P., Ortiz, S. O., Alfonso, V. C., & Mascolo, J. (2002). *The Achievement Test Desk Reference (ATDR): Comprehensive assessment and learning disabilities*. Boston: Allyn & Bacon.

Fletcher-Janzen, E., & Reynolds, C. R. (2008). *Neuropsychological perspectives on learning disabilities in the era of RTI: Recommendations for diagnosis and intervention*. Hoboken, NJ: John Wiley & Sons Inc.

Geary, D. C., Hoard, M. K., & Bailey, D. H. (2011). Fact retrieval deficits in low achieving children and children with mathematical learning disability. *Journal of Learning Disabilities, 45*(4), 291–307. http://dx.doi.org/10.1177/0022219410392046.

Hale, J., Alfonso, V., Berninger, V., Bracken, B., Christo, C., Clark, E., et al. (2010). Critical issues in response-to-intervention, comprehensive evaluation, and specific learning disabilities identification and intervention: An expert white paper consensus. *Learning Disabilities Quarterly, 33*(3), 223–236.

Hale, J. B., & Fiorello, C. A. (2004). *School neuropsychology: A practitioner's handbook*. New York, NY: Guilford Press.

Hale, J. B., Wycoff, K. L., & Fiorello, C. A. (2011). RTI and cognitive hypothesis testing for identification and intervention of specific learning disabilities: The best of both worlds: *Essentials of specific learning disability identification* (pp. 173–201). Hoboken, NJ: John Wiley & Sons Inc.

Harrison, A. G., & Holmes, A. (2012). Easier said than done: Operationalizing the diagnosis of learning disability for use at the postsecondary level in Canada. *Canadian Journal of School Psychology, 27*, 12–34.

Hinshelwood, J. (1917). *Congenital word-blindness*. London: H.K. Lewis.

Individuals with Disabilities Education Act (IDEA, 2004). 20 U.S.C § 1400.

Kaufman, A. S. (2008). Neuropsychology and specific learning disabilities: Lessons from the past as a guide to present controversies and future clinical practice. In E. Fletcher-Janzen & C. Reynolds (Eds.), *Neuropsychological perspectives on learning disabilities in an era of RTI: Recommendations for diagnosis and intervention* (pp. 1–13). Hoboken, NJ: Wiley.

Kavale, K. A., & Flanagan, D. P. (2007). Ability-achievement discrepancy, response to intervention, and assessment of cognitive abilities/processes in specific learning disability identification: Toward a contemporary operational definition. In *Handbook of response to intervention: The science and practice of assessment and intervention* (pp. 130–147). New York: NY: Springer Science+ Business Media. http://dx.doi.org/10.1007/978-0-387-49053-3_10.

Kavale, K. A., & Forness, S. R. (2000). What definitions of learning disability say and don't say: a critical analysis. *Journal of Learning Disabilities, 33*, 239–256.

Kavale, K. A., Kauffman, J. M., Bachmeier, R. J., & LeFever, G. B. (2008). Response-to-intervention: Separating the rhetoric of self-congratulation from the reality of specific learning disability identification. *Learning Disability Quarterly, 31*, 135–150.

Kavale, K. A., Spaulding, L. S., & Beam, A. P. (2009). A time to define: Making the specific learning disability definition prescribe specific learning disability. *Learning Disability Quarterly, 32*(1), 39–48.

Maricle, D. E., & Avirett, E. (2012). The role of cognitive and intelligence tests in the assessment of executive functions. In *Contemporary intellectual assessment: Theories, tests, and issues* (3rd ed.) (pp. 820–828). New York: NY: Guilford Press.

Mascolo, J. T., Alfonso, V. C., & Flanagan, D. P. (2014). *Essentials of planning, selecting, and tailoring interventions for unique learners*. Hoboken, NJ: John Wiley & Sons Inc.

Mather, N. (2011). *Let's stop monkeying around: What we know about reading disabilities*. Verona, NY: New York Association of School Psychologists.

Mather, N., & Kaufman, N. (2006). Introduction to the Special Issue, Part Two: It's about the what, the how well, and the why. *Psychology in The Schools, 43*(8), 829–834. http://dx.doi.org/10.1002/pits.20199.

Mather, N., & Wendling, B. J. (2011). How SLD manifests in writing. In *Essentials of specific learning disability identification* (pp. 65–88). Hoboken, NJ: John Wiley & Sons Inc.

Mather, N., & Wendling, B. J. (2014). Examiner's manual: *Woodcock-Johnson IV Tests of Cognitive Abilities*. Rolling Meadows, IL: Riverside.

McCloskey, G., Perkins, L. A., & Van Divner, B. (2009). *Assessment and intervention for executive function difficulties*. New York, NY: Routledge.

McCloskey, G., Whitaker, J., Murphy, R., & Rogers, J. (2012). Intellectual, cognitive, and neuro-psychological assessment in three-tier service delivery systems in schools. In D. P. Flanagan & P. L. Harrison (Eds.), *Contemporary intellectual assessment: Theories, tests and issues* (pp. 852–881) (3rd ed.). New York, NY: Guilford Press.

McGrew, K. S., LaForte, E. M., & Schrank, F. A. (2014). Technical manual: *Woodcock-Johnson IV*. Rolling Meadows, IL: Riverside.

McGrew, K. S., & Wendling, B. J. (2010). Cattell–Horn–Carroll cognitive–achievement relations: What we have learned from the past 20 years of research. *Psychology in the Schools, 47*(7), 651–675.

Monroe, M. (1932). *Children who cannot read: The analysis of reading disabilities and the use of diagnostic tests in the instruction of retarded readers*. Oxford, England: University of Chicago Press.

Naglieri, J. A. (2011). The discrepancy/consistency approach to SLD identification using the PASS theory. In D. P. Flanagan & V. C. Alfonso (Eds.), *Essentials of specific learning disability identification* (pp. 145–172). Hoboken, NJ: Wiley.

Ortiz, S. O. (2011). Separating cultural and linguistic differences (CLD) from specific learning disability (SLD) in the evaluation of diverse students: Difference or disorder? *Essentials of specific learning disability identification* (pp. 299–325). Hoboken, NJ: John Wiley & Sons Inc.

Ortiz, S. O., Flanagan, D. P., & Alfonso, V. C. (2015). *Cross-Battery Assessment Software System (X-BASS) [Computer Software] In development*. New Jersey: John Wiley & Sons, Inc. ISBN: 978-1-119-05639-3.

Orton, S. T. (1937). *Reading, writing and speech problems in children*. New York, NY: WW Norton & Co.

Reynolds, C. R., & Shaywitz, S. A. (2009). Response to intervention: Prevention and remediation, perhaps. Diagnosis, no. *Child Development Perspectives, 3*, 44–47.

Siegel, L. S. (1999). Issues in the definition and diagnosis of learning disabilities: A perspective on Guckenberger v. Boston University. *Journal of Learning Disabilities, 32,* 304–319.

Sotelo-Dynega, M., Flanagan, D. P., & Alfonso, V. C. (2011). Specific learning disabilities: An overview of definitions, classification systems, and methods of identification. In D. P. Flanagan & V. C. Alfonso (Eds.), *Essentials of specific learning disability identification.* Hoboken, NJ: Wiley.

Stanovich, K. (1993a). Discrepancy definitions of reading disability: has intelligence led us astray? *Reading Research Quarterly, 26,* 7–29.

Stanovich, K. E. (1993b). Romance and reality. *Reading Teacher, 47*(4), 280.

Stanovich, K. E. (1999). Educational research at a choice point. *Issues in Education, 5*(2), 267.

Vellutino, F. R., Scanlon, D. M., & Lyon, G. R. (2000). Differentiating between difficult-to-remediate and readily remediated poor readers. *Journal of Learning Disabilities, 33*(3), 223–238.

Chapter 9

Use of the Woodcock–Johnson IV in the Diagnosis of Specific Learning Disabilities in Adulthood

Benjamin J. Lovett[1] and Laura M. Spenceley[2]

[1]Department of Psychology, State University of New York at Cortland, Cortland, NY, USA
[2]Department of Counseling and Psychological Services, State University of New York at Oswego, Oswego, NY, USA

Although learning disabilities (LDs) are neurodevelopmental disorders that first manifest in childhood (Lewandowski & Lovett, 2014a), adults are frequently evaluated for possible LD (Mapou, 2008). A common scenario occurs when someone who was first diagnosed in childhood needs updated documentation of LD, when applying for educational accommodations in college or testing accommodations on a professional licensure exam. In addition, some people begin to have academic difficulty in college or graduate/professional school and seek an LD evaluation for the first time. Finally, LDs may be diagnosed as part of a comprehensive psychological or neuropsychological evaluation when the initial referral concerns go beyond academic problems.

The Woodcock–Johnson IV (WJ IV; Schrank, McGrew, & Mather, 2014b), comprising assessments of cognitive abilities, academic achievement, and oral language skills, is ideal for assessing LDs. Moreover, since the battery is normed on individuals from 2 to 90+ years, it can be used for young adults as well as older individuals (unlike many other batteries), and it can serve to assess children and adolescents as well. In this chapter, we focus on the application of the WJ IV to adults being evaluated for suspected LDs. We begin by discussing more generally how to apply formal criteria for diagnosis of LD in adults, before turning to different models of LD diagnosis and considering how to use the WJ IV with each model.

WJ IV Clinical Use and Interpretation. DOI: http://dx.doi.org/10.1016/B978-0-12-802076-0.00010-4

FORMAL CRITERIA FOR LD IN ADULTHOOD

The most important set of formal criteria for diagnosing LD in adults comes from the *Diagnostic and Statistical Manual of Mental Disorders*, now in its fifth edition (the DSM-5; American Psychiatric Association, 2013). The diagnostic criteria changed a great deal from the previous edition (the DSM-IV-Text Revision; American Psychiatric Association, 2000), and so even experienced clinicians will need to become familiar with the new guidelines. The DSM-5 reorganized virtually all disorders, and their new name for LD (Specific Learning Disorder) is grouped among the "Neurodevelopmental Disorders."

In order to be diagnosed as LD under DSM-5, an individual first must exhibit "difficulties learning and using academic skills, as indicated by" at least one of the following symptoms: "inaccurate or slow and effortful word reading," "difficulty understanding the meaning of what is read," "difficulties with spelling," "difficulties with written expression," "difficulties mastering number sense, number facts, or calculation," and "difficulties with mathematical reasoning" (Criterion A; American Psychiatric Association, 2013, p. 66). This is a fairly lenient criterion, in that even a single deficit (e.g., slow reading or difficulty spelling), without any other deficits, is sufficient. However, no *cognitive* deficits are mentioned as areas of LD, and so if an individual demonstrates deficits in cognitive skills but no deficits in academic skills, he/she would not meet DSM-5 criteria for LD. Therefore, so-called LDs in the areas of processing speed or working memory are not considered LDs under the DSM-5, unless they lead to impaired academic skills in one of the areas above.

The second criterion is rather strict, requiring that at least one of those areas of academic skills be "substantially and quantifiably below those expected for the individual's chronological age, and cause significant interference with academic or occupational performance, or with activities of daily living, as confirmed by individually administered standardized achievement measures and comprehensive clinical assessment" (Criterion B; American Psychiatric Association, 2013, p. 67). Thus, DSM-5 requires *age-based comparisons* rather than comparisons to an individual's education level or IQ. Thus, the person being evaluated must have normative (and not merely relative) deficits in academic skills. The DSM-5 text actually goes further, recommending that "for the greatest diagnostic certainty," clinicians should use a cutoff of "1.5 standard deviations…below the population mean for age, which translates to a standard score of 78 or less, which is below the 7th percentile" (p. 69). In addition, there must be evidence of impairment in real-world settings. In adults, the DSM permits the real-world impairment to be shown through "self-report or report by others."

Third, DSM-5 requires that the "learning difficulties begin during school-age years" (Criterion C; American Psychiatric Association, 2013, p. 67). The text explains further that "the learning difficulties are readily apparent in the early school years in most individuals," but allows that, at times, "the learning difficulties may not manifest fully until later school years" (p. 69). We interpret this to mean that, sometime within the K-12 school years, there should be evidence of impairment, and we should typically see evidence during the elementary school years.

Finally, DSM-5 includes an exclusionary criterion; an individual's learning difficulties should not be "better accounted for by intellectual disabilities, uncorrected visual or auditory acuity, other mental or neurological disorders, psychosocial adversity, lack of proficiency in the language of academic instruction, or inadequate educational instruction" (Criterion D; American Psychiatric Association, 2013, p. 67). This criterion suggests that, in adults, there must at least be informal screening of other disorders that could explain the individual's learning difficulties, as well as a careful history that would exclude social and environmental disadvantage as causes.

Although the DSM-5 is the most prominent source of clinical criteria for diagnosing LD, we should also mention relevant legal criteria. Indeed, the DSM-5 makes clear that meeting clinical criteria for one of its disorders "does not imply that someone with such a condition meets…a specific legal standard (e.g., for competence, criminal responsibility, or disability)" (p. 25). In children, special education laws govern the definition of disabilities, but adults are covered by the Americans with Disabilities Act (ADA). ADA defines a disability as follows: "a physical or mental impairment that substantially limits one or more of the major life activities of such individual" (P.L. 101-336, 1990). Here an "impairment" does not mean *functional* impairment, but instead a condition, such as LD. Thus, an individual would need to have LD *and* the LD would need to limit substantially a major life activity (such as reading). The "substantially limits" requirement has generally been interpreted to mean that an individual's abilities are below those of the average person in the general population (Lovett, Gordon, & Lewandowski, in press).

If the DSM-5 criteria for LD are rigorously applied, and a client meets those criteria, the client should also meet the ADA standard. Given that the DSM-5's Criterion B requires that academic skills be below the average range for someone's age, *and* that those below-average skills cause impairment in real-world settings, this is virtually identical to the ADA's requirement that the individual be substantially limited in a major life activity. Unfortunately, the DSM-5's criteria contain phrasing that could permit clinicians to interpret them in a very lenient manner (Lewandowski & Lovett, 2014b). Therefore, just because an adult presents evidence that a clinician rendered a DSM-5 diagnosis of specific learning disorder, this does not mean that the ADA standard has been met. In sum, clinical (DSM-5) and legal (ADA) criteria must both be considered when determining whether an adult has adequately documented LD.

DIAGNOSTIC MODELS OF LD

There are several prominent, competing models for diagnosing LD (Sotelo-Dynega, Flanagan, & Alfonso, 2011; Taylor, 2014). The different models tend to identify rather different groups of individuals, especially in adults (Proctor & Prevatt, 2003;

Sparks & Lovett, 2009). We discuss three diagnostic models: the low achievement model, the ability–achievement discrepancy model, and the pattern of strengths and weaknesses model. (We do not cover the response-to-intervention model since it has not been used with adults.) We describe each model, as well as how to use the WJ IV to diagnose LD under that model, before considering each model's advantages and limitations.

Low Achievement (Simple Impairment) Model

The simplest LD diagnostic model, at least psychometrically speaking, is the low achievement model. This model makes low academic skills the essence of LD; to have LD, it is necessary to have low academic skills in at least one area, and that alone is almost sufficient to make a diagnosis. The low skills must always be demonstrated on standardized, norm-referenced achievement tests. Some versions of the low achievement model also require additional evidence from educational settings (e.g., low grades, below-average scores on educational accountability tests), early onset, and exclusion of other causes of low academic skills.

Siegel (1999) and Stanovich (1999) each put forth versions of the low achievement model in the context of reading disabilities; each suggested that a below-average score on a measure of either word reading or phonological processing should be the operational definition of a reading disability. A more sophisticated version of the model was developed by Dombrowski, Kamphaus, and Reynolds (2004), who proposed requiring a standard score below 85 on a norm-referenced achievement test as well as "evidence of educational impairment (based on classroom grades, [curriculum-based assessment measures], and teacher reports or ratings)" (p. 367). (These scholars would also require that certain exclusionary criteria be met.) This approach was further discussed by Brueggemann, Kamphaus, and Dombrowski (2008). Finally, the DSM-5 criteria constitute another low achievement model of LD.

Using the WJ IV with low achievement models. The low achievement model says nothing about cognitive skills, except perhaps that intellectual disability should be ruled out if it is suspected. Thus, academic skills are usually the only traits needing formal testing; other assessment tools include a careful history and review of educational records. The WJ IV Tests of Achievement (WJ IV ACH; Schrank, Mather, & McGrew, 2014a) provide well for the formal testing of those academic skills. In the adult normative sample, the cluster scores have reliability coefficients above 0.90 and often above 0.95, and even most of the individual tests have reliability coefficients above 0.90 in that sample (McGrew, LaForte, & Schrank, 2014). In addition, a variety of types of evidence support the validity of inferences from WJ IV ACH scores. Below we discuss exactly how the WJ IV ACH should be used to diagnose LD under the low achievement model.

1. Standard scores ($M = 100$, $SD = 15$) and percentile scores are most useful for diagnostic purposes. Consistent with the DSM-5 definition of LD, age-based WJ IV ACH scores should be used for diagnostic purposes. However, grade-based scores can still be clinically useful. For instance, consider a 21-year-old college senior who is evaluated for possible LD; her age-based WJ IV ACH scores are mostly in the average range with a few scores above the average range, but some of her grade-based scores are below the average range. In that case, a diagnosis of LD would be inappropriate, but the below-average grade-based scores could be useful in giving feedback about why certain college courses are challenging; the grade-based scores could also open the door to a discussion about which courses or careers match the student's pattern of skills.

2. Most of the tests on the WJ IV ACH relate to the DSM-5 areas of LD. Thus, a below-average score on one of the *clusters* would be suggestive of LD. The cluster scores also have higher reliability coefficients, supporting diagnostic use. For instance, an adult whose reading fluency cluster score is sufficiently low may qualify for an LD diagnosis. Although some individual tests map directly on to DSM-5 areas of LD (e.g., Test 2, Applied Problems, maps directly on to the "difficulties with mathematical reasoning" described in DSM-5), evaluators should be cautious in diagnosing LD on the basis of a low score on a single test. In particular, a test's reliability coefficients should be inspected. For instance, the Sentence Reading Fluency test has reliability coefficients that are on the low side for high-stakes individual decision making, and even though the DSM-5 mentions reading fluency as an area of LD, a low Sentence Reading Fluency score would not be as useful diagnostically as a low Reading Fluency Cluster score. When other, corroborating evidence is present (e.g., impairment in real world settings), and a particular subtest yields a sufficiently reliable score, a single low test score may be sufficient.

3. There are several tests on the WJ IV ACH that are not measures of core academic skills, even if they are statistically and conceptually related to academic skills. The final three tests on the extended battery (Science, Social Studies, and Humanities) are among these tests. It may be clinically useful to administer these tests, but low scores should not be taken to be diagnostic of a LD. In addition, there are two tests (Word Attack and Spelling of Sounds) that measure phonological processing; although students with reading disabilities often show deficits in phonological processing, low scores on these tests alone would not be sufficient evidence of LD. If a person is able to read actual words well (as shown by scores on other reading tests), deficits in the ability to read and spell pseudo-words are not evidence of LD under DSM-5.

4. The DSM-5 suggests that an academic skill deficit be quite severe—at least 1.5 standard deviations below the mean—when LD is diagnosed, to ensure high confidence in the diagnosis. However, the DSM-5 also mentions a role for clinical judgment, permitting a "more lenient threshold," as lenient as

1 standard deviation below the mean (a standard score of 85, at the 16th percentile). This more lenient threshold is indeed reasonable "when learning difficulties are supported by converging evidence" (American Psychiatric Association, 2013, p. 69), as they always should be anyway. Standard scores between 85 and 90 present a problem, in that they are below the average range, in the "low average" range, but they do not meet the DSM-5 cutoff. At times, evaluators will even claim that scores between 90 and 95 are "on the low side of average" or something similar. We encourage evaluators to require a score of 85 or below (see Taylor, 2014, p. 129 as well).

Evaluation of low achievement models. Low achievement models have experienced (and weathered) a variety of criticisms. One line of criticism has noted that measuring skills at a single point in time is not sufficiently reliable (Francis et al., 2005). Certainly, it is possible that students who obtain a score below a cutoff one day would receive a score above the cutoff on a different day, or vice versa. However, errors like these are less likely when test scores are combined with other data, especially data of real-world impairment. Moreover, in adults it is not usually feasible to have repeated testing within a brief time interval. Indeed, this criticism would rule out any diagnoses based on a single evaluation, leaving only the RTI approach, which has not been sufficiently developed for use with adults.

Another line of criticism has been that some individuals with LD will not evidence normative deficits in achievement. Mather and Gregg (2006) expressed particular concern about intellectually gifted individuals with LD, who may show average achievement in some areas, but above-average cognitive abilities and achievement in other areas. Such patterns of performance certainly exist, but the question is whether such patterns are consistent with the meaning of "disability." The DSM-5 makes clear that low achievement is a requirement for LD diagnosis, and the ADA definition of disability similarly makes clear that the individual must be "substantially limited." This emphasis on functional impairment is central to the definition of any disability (Lovett et al., in press) and has clear applicability to the LD construct (Lovett, 2011, 2013; Lovett & Lewandowski, 2006). Thus, even if low achievement is not sufficient for LD, it should be required as one component of the diagnosis.

Yet another line of criticism has concerned the arbitrariness of the cutoff for "low" achievement (Stuebing, Fletcher, Branum-Martin, & Francis, 2012). Admittedly, although there is some empirical support for a cutoff at about the 15th percentile (Taylor, 2014), the primary reasons for choosing a particular cutoff are practical ones (Stanovich, 1999). However, we do not view this as inherently problematic. Many medical problems, including most mental disorders, exist on a continuum rather than in a rigid categorical fashion (Haslam, Holland, & Kuppens, 2012). Hypertension is an obvious example of such a diagnosis; the cutoff is set in a semi-arbitrary manner, since it is not as though a systolic blood pressure of 140 mm Hg is mortally dangerous whereas 139 mm Hg is just fine.

LDs are very much the same way, and so while we should seek a uniform cutoff, it is simply not possible to find the one "true" cutoff.

Ability–Achievement Discrepancy Model

The ability–achievement discrepancy model of LD emerged in the federal description of LD as a disorder in a basic psychological process marked by a "severe discrepancy between achievement and intellectual ability" (United States Office of Education, 1977, p. G1082). Unfortunately, the federal description failed to include specific procedures for calculating a discrepancy, and more fundamentally, it did not identify the amount of discrepancy required to evidence LD (Meyer, 2000). Therefore, individual states developed their own methods of calculating an ability–achievement discrepancy, which included standard score differences, regression formulas, and expectancy formulas (Reschly & Hosp, 2004). Maki, Floyd, and Roberson (2015) found that 34 (67%) of states continue to permit the use of a discrepancy model in the diagnosis of LD, even as 10 (20%) states explicitly prohibit this practice. Moreover, in an adult population, this model appears to be commonly utilized (Sparks & Lovett, 2013).

Using the WJ IV with ability–achievement discrepancy models. The various WJ IV batteries are well-suited for use within the context of a discrepancy model of LD identification in an adult population. In the WJ IV, "comparisons" calculate the discrepancy between two standard scores based on a correction for regression toward the mean. The fact that the different parts of the WJ IV are co-normed aids this process. There are two comparisons that use the Woodcock–Johnson IV Tests of Cognitive Abilities (WJ IV COG; Schrank, McGrew, & Mather, 2014c) and WJ IV ACH batteries: General Intellectual Ability/Achievement comparisons, and *Gf–Gc* Composite/Other Ability comparisons (Mather & Wendling, 2014). While the procedures vary slightly for each of these comparisons, the core assumption is that a broad estimate of cognitive ability (either GIA or *Gf–Gc*) can be used to predict achievement. Below we discuss how the WJ IV ACH and WJ IV COG should be used within the discrepancy model.

1. At minimum, the standard batteries for the WJ IV ACH and WJ IV COG should be administered. This will allow for the calculation of cluster scores across both batteries. As previously mentioned, cluster scores provide a more reliable method of assessing skills, and consequently, they support more valid diagnostic decisions. It is also recommended that age-based norms be used as the basis for diagnostic decisions, although grade-based norms may provide additional information for intervention and counseling purposes, as we noted above.

2. An intellectual ability composite must then be chosen for the comparison procedure. The WJ IV COG GIA cluster score is the best index of psychometric *g*, and is derived from seven core tests, whereas the WJ IV

COG *Gf–Gc* composite is derived from four core tests. The WJ IV COG Examiner's Manual suggests that for some individuals with LD, the *Gf–Gc* composite may provide a more accurate measure of broad cognitive ability as it removes the influence of cognitive processing skills that tend to relate to academic deficits, such as processing speed (Mather & Wendling, 2014). We recommend that the GIA be used within an ability–achievement discrepancy model of LD diagnosis. Removing the cognitive processing deficits that may underlie achievement deficits artificially increases the likelihood that a significant discrepancy between ability and achievement will be identified. Moreover, in an adult population, the GIA has been found to be a stronger predictor of WJ IV ACH cluster scores across reading and writing clusters, and all but two mathematics clusters (Schrank, McGrew, & Mather, 2015).

3. While adhering to the discrepancy model, the examiner should compare the GIA score to WJ IV ACH cluster scores using the comparisons procedure. When a significant discrepancy between cognitive ability and an achievement cluster is identified, it becomes useful to consider the level of the area of weakness to ensure DSM-5 criteria are met. While there is flexibility to include clinical judgment, we recommend the academic cluster standard score fall at or below 85 to demonstrate the normative deficits required by the DSM-5.

Evaluation of the Ability–Achievement Discrepancy Model

The psychometric limitations of the ability–achievement discrepancy model are well-documented and include the influence of regression to the mean and the unreliability of difference scores (Sternberg & Grigorenko, 2002; Van den Broeck, 2002). Regression to the mean is an expected artifact of the process of a discrepancy comparison, given measurement error and the imperfect correlation between ability and achievement measures. Thus, if a student obtains a high-average GIA score and a low-average achievement cluster score, repeat testing may find both scores to be in the average range. Perhaps more importantly, the effect produces predictable false positive errors for individuals with IQ scores above 100, as it is likely that achievement scores will more closely approximate the mean, while the opposite effect will occur with individuals with IQ scores less than 100, meaning it is less likely a significant discrepancy between IQ and achievement will be identified (Francis et al., 2005). Without consideration of this phenomenon, the use of a discrepancy model will underidentify LD for individuals with lower global IQ scores, and overidentify LD for individuals with higher global IQ scores (Harrison & Holmes, 2012; see Fletcher, Lyon, Fuchs, & Barnes, 2007 for a comprehensive discussion).

To circumvent these effects, others have proposed a regression-based discrepancy method, which corrects for the correlation between IQ and achievement measures by predicting academic achievement on the basis of ability while accounting for the correlation between the measures and standard deviation of each measure. Unfortunately, regression-based discrepancy scores have also been criticized for failing to differentiate between low achievement and learning disabilities (Dombrowski et al., 2004), and unreliable diagnosis on the basis of the ability score that is selected (Cahan, Fono, & Nirel, 2012).

Low reliability is the second psychometric limitation of difference scores. These scores are influenced not only by the reliability of each of the two measures used to calculate the score, but also the correlation between the two measures being compared (Caruso, 2004). Consequently, difference scores tend to be less reliable than the scores from which they were calculated, especially when the correlation between the measures increases (Sternberg & Grigorenko, 2002). With the moderate to high correlation often found among achievement and intelligence measures (indeed, the WJ IV COG GIA and reading cluster scores correlations range between 0.62 and 0.80 in adults aged 20–39; Schrank et al., 2015), difference scores can be assumed to be unreliable over time and result in poor diagnostic decision making.

Finally, the discrepancy model continues to be implemented with inconsistency, given disagreement over the method of calculation and needed degree of discrepancy. Maki et al. (2015) found that although two-thirds of states continue to support the use of the discrepancy model, 35% of these states do not specify how to determine the discrepancy. While Maki and colleagues' study focused on special education criteria, rather than DSM-5 or ADA requirements, it may help to elucidate the findings at the college level, which suggest inconsistent application of the discrepancy model. Our experience suggests that while the discrepancy model is relatively frequent as part of an evaluation for the presence of LD in an adult population, it is not consistently applied. In addition, Sparks and Lovett (2009) found that in a group of college students previously diagnosed with LD, the rate of classification changed markedly when the discrepancy criterion was modified from liberal (1 *SD* between ability and achievement; 42% identified as LD) to conservative (2 *SD* between ability and achievement; 10% identified as LD).

Pattern of Strengths and Weaknesses Models

Recent focus has shifted away from the simple ability–achievement model in favor of those models that identify LD through *patterns* of cognitive processing strengths and weaknesses (PSW). At the foundation of each PSW approach is the recognition that academic skills and cognitive processes are related (theoretically and statistically), although each PSW approach includes a distinct theoretical framework. Three prominent PSW approaches are briefly discussed below along with a more general discussion of the methods by which the WJ IV can be used with PSW approaches.

Concordance/Discordance Model. Hale and Fiorello (2004) developed the concordance/discordance model (C/DM), which specifies three criteria for identifying LD. First, there must be an identified area of weak academic achievement that is concordant with a weakness in a related neuropsychological process. Second, there must be discordance between the achievement deficits and unrelated neuropsychological processes. Third, discordance must be demonstrated when comparing processing strengths and weaknesses.

The C/DM model does not require a normative area of academic weakness, only a relative weakness, based upon discordance from a cognitive process score. In addition, Hale and Fiorello (2004) cautioned that comparisons can be made on composite scores only if the composite is considered to reflect accurately the broad ability being evaluated. Therefore, when significant variability in performance across subtests within the same cluster exists, subtest comparisons can be appropriate if (i) the reliability estimate for the subtest is high, and (ii) the 99% confidence level is utilized for setting confidence intervals. Hale, Wycoff, and Fiorello (2010) recommended examining empirical support for the relationship between cognitive processes and academic skills, to avoid the practice of arbitrarily selecting the highest cognitive score, lowest cognitive score, and lowest achievement score for contrasts.

Naglieri's Discrepancy/Consistency Model. Naglieri's (1999) Discrepancy/ Consistency Model (D/CM) emerged after the publication of the Cognitive Assessment System (CAS; Naglieri & Das, 1997) and the PASS (Planning, Attention, Simultaneous, and Successive) theory of cognitive processing (Das, Naglieri, & Kirby, 1994). The PASS theory stipulates that four basic psychological processes serve as the foundation for all human cognitive functioning and allow individuals to function in their environment: Planning, Attention, Simultaneous Processing, and Successive Processing (Das et al., 1994). Naglieri (1999) defines *planning* as the ability to determine, select, apply, and evaluate solutions to problems; *attention* is the ability to focus on specific stimuli while also inhibiting responses to other stimuli; *simultaneous* processing requires the individual to integrate separate stimuli into a conceptual group; and *successive* processing occurs when multiple stimuli must be processed in a specific order.

The D/CM method of classifying LD includes three main tenets (Naglieri, 1999, 2010). First, an individual must evidence a substantially below-average processing deficit in one or more of the basic psychological processes, with a *discrepancy* between the area of weakness and other psychological processes. Further, the individual must demonstrate a significant *discrepancy* between the adequate processing scores and lower academic skills in some area. Finally, there should be *consistency* between the area of weakness in cognitive processing and the manifested academic skill deficits. Naglieri (2010) specifies an ipsative and normative comparative framework for identifying deficits in processing. When using the CAS, he notes that, to be termed an area of weakness, one or more of the PASS process scale scores must be (i) significantly weaker than the individual's mean PASS scale score, and (ii) significantly below average (<90 standard score), relative to national norms.

Although the D/CM was developed in conjunction with the CAS (Naglieri & Das, 1997), it can be adapted for use with other cognitive and achievement measures (Naglieri, 2010). Naglieri (2010) stressed the importance of selecting measures that allow for scale-level, rather than subtest-level, comparisons between cognitive processing scores and academic achievement scores. When using a measure other than the CAS, evidence for an LD would be demonstrated through a normatively weak cognitive processing cluster score, which is significantly lower than other cognitive cluster scores. This area of cognitive weakness would significantly under-predict performance in unrelated areas of academic achievement, but would accurately predict performance on a theoretically related area of academic achievement.

Cross-Battery Assessment. The cross-battery assessment (XBA) approach to the conceptualization and diagnosis of LDs arose from the Cattell–Horn–Carroll (CHC) theory of intelligence and the practical need to sample fully the domains of intellectual functioning identified by CHC theory. Largely based on the work of Flanagan et al. (Flanagan & McGrew, 1997; Flanagan, Ortiz, & Alfonso, 2013), the XBA approach allows the evaluator to measure a wide range of cognitive abilities through the use of subtests from different batteries that together sample these abilities more comprehensively than would be permitted through use of a single, fixed cognitive measure (Flanagan et al., 2013).

Within the XBA model, an LD is demonstrated through several criteria (Flanagan, Alfonso, & Mascolo, 2010). First, a normative weakness in one or more areas of academic achievement (such as Basic Reading, Reading Comprehension, Math Calculation) must be demonstrated in the absence of intellectual disability, environmental, economic, and/or educational disadvantage, and motor, visual, or hearing disabilities. Furthermore, the individual must have a normative weakness in one or more basic psychological or neuropsychological processes, despite an otherwise typical cognitive profile. Additionally, there must be a theoretically supported relationship between the deficits in cognitive process and achievement. Finally, these demonstrated cognitive processing and academic deficits have an adverse impact on educational performance.

Using the WJ IV in PSW Models. The WJ IV offers a viable option for use within each of the three PSW models, although doing so requires minor modifications to procedure within the context of each model.

To obtain data sufficient to use the PSW models discussed, we recommend that the WJ IV COG extended (Tests 1–18) battery be administered. This will allow for the calculation of a general intelligence estimate, as well as cognitive cluster scores aligned with the CHC model of intelligence. Similarly, we recommend that for an adult population, WJ IV ACH standard (Tests 1–11) or extended battery (Tests 1–20) be administered to collect achievement data that correspond to the DSM-5 diagnostic criteria for LD. All three PSW models endorse the interpretation of cluster scores, although the XBA and C/DM models allow for more flexibility in creating clusters that represent the seven broad areas of cognitive functioning posited by CHC theory (Flanagan, Alfonso, & Ortiz, 2012; Hale et al., 2010). Further, Flanagan et al. (2012) encouraged the use of co-normed measures of academic achievement and cognitive ability to sample a broad set of skills. Once the relevant measures have been administered, the evaluator must determine the presence of significant discrepancies within and between areas of cognitive and academic functioning. Again, we recommend the use of age-based standard scores to do this.

As indicated above, the method of identifying a significant LD profile varies by the particular PSW model. We believe that this is best illustrated through a hypothetical case study. Consider the example of Tim, a 19-year-old college freshman. His pattern of performance revealed consistently average scores across composites of the WJ IV COG (Tests 1–18) and WJ IV ACH (Tests 1–17), with a few notable exceptions. On the WJ IV COG, Tim obtained average range standard scores on the following clusters: GIA ($SS = 98$), Comprehension-Knowledge ($SS = 102$), Short-Term Working Memory ($SS = 109$), Cognitive Processing Speed ($SS = 104$), Auditory Processing ($SS = 107$), Long-Term Retrieval ($SS = 101$), and Visual Processing ($SS = 104$). In contrast, he obtained a below-average score on the Fluid Reasoning cluster ($SS = 76$). On the Number Series ($SS = 77$) and Concept Formation ($SS = 81$) tests, Tim obtained weaker-than-expected low to low-average range scores. The intra-cognitive variations confirm that Tim's performance across the Fluid Reasoning cluster and component tests was significantly weaker than expected, given his average GIA score.

On the WJ IV ACH, Tim's performance indicated age-appropriate skills across a variety of clusters. He obtained the following average range scores: Reading ($SS = 92$), Broad Reading ($SS = 91$), Basic Reading Skills ($SS = 92$), Reading Comprehension ($SS = 92$), Reading Rate ($SS = 97$), Math Calculation Skills ($SS = 90$), Written Language ($SS = 95$), Broad Written Language ($SS = 94$), Basic Writing Skills ($SS = 92$), and Written Expression ($SS = 97$). In contrast, Tim obtained low and low-average range scores on the Mathematics ($SS = 76$), Broad Mathematics ($SS = 84$), and Math Problem Solving ($SS = 74$) clusters. On the tests that contribute to these clusters, Tim demonstrated relatively stable and below-average performance with few exceptions: Applied Problems ($SS = 76$), Calculation ($SS = 79$), Math Facts Fluency ($SS = 101$), and Number Matrices ($SS = 77$). The intra-achievement variations procedures confirm that Tim's Math Problem Solving cluster and Applied Problems performance was significantly weaker than expected, given his performance across the other academic clusters.

The results of the evaluation indicate that although Tim evidences a wide range of age-appropriate cognitive and academic skills, he also demonstrates notable areas of cognitive and academic weakness. Comparisons between his GIA and achievement clusters confirm his performance on the Mathematics, Broad Mathematics, and Math Problem Solving clusters was significantly weaker than expected, given his global intellectual ability. Moreover, the *Gf* cluster score is lower than expected, using the intra-cognitive variations procedure.

Within the C/DM model (Hale & Fiorello, 2004), Tim's performance is consistent with LD. First, he displays areas of processing strength and weakness. His below-average range Fluid Reasoning cluster score is discordant from his otherwise age-appropriate cognitive processing scores. Tim demonstrated limited variation in his performance across each of the tests within this cluster, meaning the cluster score accurately reflects narrow and broad ability deficits. Furthermore, he displayed a significant academic weakness across several mathematics clusters (Basic Mathematics, Math Problem Solving, and Mathematics) with consistent, weaker-than-expected scores on each of the tests within each cluster. Finally, Tim's deficits in math occur in the context of otherwise typical academic skills. Crucially, the demonstrated academic deficits in math and math problem solving have been shown to be related to deficits in fluid reasoning skills (see McGrew & Wendling, 2010, and Proctor, 2012 for empirical reviews of the relationship between fluid reasoning and math problem solving). In sum, Tim's academic and cognitive weaknesses are theoretically related, and are significantly weaker than expected given his otherwise typical academic skills and cognitive processes, suggesting that he would meet criteria for LD within the C/DM model.

Within Naglieri's (1999) D/CM model, we must first determine whether basic psychological processes are represented by the WJ IV COG composite scores, given that Tim was not administered a measure that directly relates to the PASS theory of cognitive processing (Das et al., 1994). Naglieri (2010) asserts that a cognitive process is "a foundational, neuropsychologically identified ability that provides the means by which an individual functions in this world" (p. 147). Flanagan et al. (2010) indicated that the seven broad cognitive abilities (i.e., *Gf, Gc, Gv, Ga, Glr, Gsm,* and *Gs*) within the CHC theory represent these fundamental processes. Given the strong adherence of the WJ IV COG to CHC theory (McGrew et al., 2014), we proceed to interpret Tim's data within the D/CM model with the assumption that the broad cognitive cluster scores adequately represent distinct cognitive processes. Tim's below-average score on the Fluid Reasoning cluster is normatively weaker than expected for his age and intra-cognitive variations procedures confirm that Tim's fluid reasoning skills are significantly weaker than expected given his otherwise average range cognitive skills. Tim also displayed a significant normative and ipsative deficit in mathematics and math problem solving on the WJ IV ACH. As previously indicated, the relationship between mathematics performance and fluid reasoning has been theoretically supported. Given the discrepancies within Tim's cognitive processing and achievement scores and the consistency between his academic and cognitive deficits, each of which is ipsatively and normatively weaker than expected, Tim appears to meet criteria for LD within the D/CM model.

Finally, if we consider Tim's performance in the context of the XBA approach, it is consistent with LD. Tim's scores on the WJ IV COG suggest that although his global intellectual functioning is age-appropriate, his Fluid Reasoning cluster score indicates significantly weaker reasoning, concept formation, and problem solving skills for his age and other cognitive skills. Tim's low to low-average range performance on the Mathematics, Broad Mathematics, and Math Problem Solving clusters of the WJ IV ACH cannot be considered secondary to an intellectual disability, given his age-appropriate global cognitive ability. As discussed, the theoretical relationship between fluid reasoning and mathematics achievement has been supported in the literature (McGrew & Wendling, 2010; Proctor, 2012). Although our example does not explicitly document several important considerations, such as an adverse impact to educational performance or the absence of the environmental, economic, and/ or educational disadvantage, so long as these criteria were met, Tim appears likely to meet criteria for LD within the XBA framework.

Evaluation of the PSW models. Each of the PSW models described above is designed to identify the specific cognitive processes that underlie academic deficits, to improve the sensitivity and sensitivity of diagnosis, and to inform interventions to target weaknesses in cognitive processes and academic skills (Flanagan et al., 2010; Hale & Fiorello, 2004; Naglieri, 2010). Recent literature supports the claim that specific cognitive functions correlate meaningfully with specific academic skills across the lifespan, and more specifically, in adults with LDs (Floyd, Meisinger, Gregg, & Keith, 2012; McGrew & Wendling, 2010; Proctor, 2012).

Despite the recent attention in the literature to the promise of PSW models, two recent studies have highlighted some potential limitations of these models. Miciak, Fletcher, Stuebing, Vaughn, and Tolar (2014) found that the XBA and C/DM models identified less than 50% of elementary-age students who displayed persistent reading deficits despite the provision of increasingly intensive reading interventions through Tier 2 within an RTI framework. Furthermore, these authors found surprisingly little overlap in the students identified across the two PSW methods. Similarly, using simulated data, Stuebing et al. (2012) found that PSW methods possessed strong specificity (majority of estimates >0.85) and negative predictive values (all estimates >0.90) but demonstrated significantly weaker and more variable sensitivity and positive predictive values. The practical implications from these findings reveal these methods are better suited for ruling out LD, but are much less accurate at identifying individuals with LD. Each group of investigators (Miciak et al., 2014; Stuebing et al., 2012) encouraged caution in adopting PSW models.

In addition, although PSW models of evaluation provide a substantial amount of assessment data, some have questioned whether the data collected can meaningfully inform intervention (Consortium for Evidence-Based Early Intervention Practices, 2010). In a review of extant literature, Kearns and Fuchs (2013) found limited support for cognitively focused interventions, and they noted significant methodological limitations across many of the studies reviewed. Admittedly, some critics of PSW models appear to identify the models with earlier ability–achievement discrepancy approaches. It is important to distinguish between the traditional application of cognitive assessment as a method of obtaining a global IQ score, and contemporary PSW methods that emphasize the exploration of a wide range of cognitive processes for the purpose of hypothesis testing and intervention planning (Decker, Hale, & Flanagan, 2013).

CONCLUSION: BEYOND FORMAL TESTING

In this chapter, we discussed how various models for diagnosing LD could be implemented in adult populations with the WJ IV. We conclude by noting that, like any formal battery, the WJ IV can only assist a clinician part of the way toward an LD diagnosis, especially in adults. What else is needed? First, LD does not begin in adulthood, and so objective historical evidence should be present from childhood. Second, LD does not confine its effects to formal diagnostic tests, and so objective evidence from current real-world settings (i.e., educational, occupational, and everyday life settings) should be present, just as DSM-5 suggests. It is more important that these two sources of data (evidence of childhood onset and current real-world impairment) be added to psychometric batteries than that any particular battery be chosen for formal testing. That said, the WJ IV is an excellent choice for a psychometric battery which, along with other data, can be used for identifying LD in adults under a variety of diagnostic models.

REFERENCES

American Psychiatric Association, (2000). *Diagnostic and statistical manual of mental disorders* (4th ed., text revision). Washington, DC: Author.

American Psychiatric Association, (2013). *Diagnostic and statistical manual of mental disorders* (5th ed.). Arlington, VA: Author.

Brueggemann, A. E., Kamphaus, R. W., & Dombrowski, S. C. (2008). An impairment model of learning disability diagnosis. *Professional Psychology: Research and Practice, 39*(4), 424–430.

Cahan, S., Fono, D., & Nirel, R. (2012). The regression-based discrepancy definition of learning disability: A critical appraisal. *Journal of Learning Disabilities, 45*(2), 170–178.

Caruso, J. C. (2004). A comparison of the reliabilities of four types of difference scores for five cognitive assessment batteries. *European Journal of Psychological Assessment, 20*(3), 166–171.

Consortium for Evidence-Based Early Intervention Practices. (2010). A response to the Learning Disabilities Association of America (LDA) white paper on Specific Learning Disabilities Identification. Retrieved from <http://www.isbe.state.il.us/speced/pdfs/LDA_SLD_white_paper_response.pdf>.

Das, J. P., Naglieri, J. A., & Kirby, J. R. (1994). *Assessment of cognitive processing: The PASS theory of intelligence*. Needham Heights, MA: Allyn and Bacon.

Decker, S. L., Hale, J. B., & Flanagan, D. P. (2013). Professional practice issues in the assessment of cognitive functioning for educational applications. *Psychology in the Schools, 50*(3), 300–313. http://dx.doi.org/10.1002/pits.

Dombrowski, S. C., Kamphaus, R. W., & Reyonlds, C. R. (2004). After the demise of the discrepancy: Proposed learning disabilities diagnostic criteria. *Professional Psychology: Research and Practice, 35*(4), 364–372.

Flanagan, D. P., Alfonso, V. C., & Mascolo, J. T. (2010). A CHC-based operational definition of SLD. In D. P. Flanagan & V. C. Alfonso (Eds.), *Essentials of specific learning disability identification* (pp. 233–299). New York, NY: Wiley.

Flanagan, D. P., Alfonso, V. C., & Ortiz, S. O. (2012). The cross-battery assessment approach: An overview, historical perspective, and current directions. In D. P. Flanagan & P. L. Harrison (Eds.), *Contemporary intellectual assessment: Theories, tests, and issues* (3rd ed., pp. 459–496). New York, NY: Guilford Press.

Flanagan, D. P., & McGrew, K. S. (1997). A cross-battery approach to assessing and interpreting cognitive abilities: Narrowing the gap between practice and cognitive science. In D. P. Flanagan, J. L. Genshaft, & P. L. Harrison (Eds.), *Contemporary intellectual assessment: Theories, tests, and issues* (pp. 314–325). New York, NY: Guilford.

Flanagan, D. P., Ortiz, S. O., & Alfonso, V. C. (2013). *Essentials of cross-battery assessment* (3rd ed.). New York, NY: Wiley.

Fletcher, J. M., Lyon, G. R., Fuchs, L. S., & Barnes, M. A. (2007). *Learning disabilities: From identification to intervention*. New York, NY: Guilford.

Floyd, R., Meisinger, E., Gregg, N., & Keith, T. (2012). An explanation of reading comprehension across development using models from Cattell–Horn–Carroll theory: Support for integrative models of reading. *Psychology in the Schools*, *49*(8), 725–743. http://dx.doi.org/10.1002/pits.21633.

Francis, D. J., Fletcher, J. M., Stuebing, K. K., Lyon, G. R., Shaywitz, B. A., & Shaywitz, S. E. (2005). Psychometric approaches to the identification of LD: IQ and achievement scores are not sufficient. *Journal of Learning Disabilities*, *38*(2), 98–108.

Hale, J. B., & Fiorello, C. A. (2004). *School neuropsychology: A practitioner's handbook*. New York, NY: Guilford.

Hale, J. B., Wycoff, K. L., & Fiorello, C. A. (2010). RTI and cognitive hypothesis testing for identification and intervention of specific learning disabilities: The best of both worlds. In D. P. Flanagan & V. C. Alfonso (Eds.), *Essentials of specific learning disability identification* (pp. 173–202). New York, NY: Wiley.

Harrison, A. G., & Holmes, A. (2012). Easier said than done: Operationalizing the diagnosis of learning disability for use at the postsecondary level in Canada. *Canadian Journal of School Psychology*, *27*, 12–34. http://dx.doi.org/10.1177/0829573512437021.

Haslam, N., Holland, E., & Kuppens, P. (2012). Categories versus dimensions in personality and psychopathology: A quantitative review of taxometric research. *Psychological Medicine*, *42*(5), 903–920.

Kearns, D. K., & Fuchs, D. (2013). Does cognitively focused instruction improve the academic performance of low-achieving students? *Exceptional Children*, *79*(3), 263–290.

Lewandowski, L. J., & Lovett, B. J. (2014a). Learning disabilities. In E. J. Mash & R. A. Barkley (Eds.), *Child psychopathology* (pp. 625–669) (3rd ed.). New York, NY: Guilford.

Lewandowski, L. J., & Lovett, B. J. (2014b). The new Diagnostic and Statistical Manual of Mental Disorders, DSM-5: Implications for accommodations requests. *Bar Examiner*, *83*(1), 42–54.

Lovett, B. J. (2011). On the diagnosis of learning disabilities in gifted students. *Gifted Child Quarterly*, *55*(5), 149–151.

Lovett, B. J. (2013). The science and politics of gifted students with learning disabilities: A social inequality perspective. *Roeper Review*, *35*(2), 136–143.

Lovett, B. J., Gordon, M., & Lewandowski, L. J. Legal conceptions of impairment: Implications for the assessment of psychiatric disabilities. In S. Goldstein & J. A. Naglieri (Eds.), *Assessing impairment: From theory to practice* (2nd ed.). New York, NY: Springer, in press.

Lovett, B. J., & Lewandowski, L. J. (2006). Gifted students with learning disabilities: Who are they? *Journal of Learning Disabilities*, *39*(6), 515–527.

Maki, K. E., Floyd, R. G., & Roberson, T. (2015). State learning disability eligibility criteria: A comprehensive review. *School Psychology Quarterly* Advance online publication. http://dx.doi.org/10.1037/spq000010.

Mapou, R. L. (2008). Comprehensive evaluation of adults with learning disabilities. In L. E. Wolf, H. E. Schreiber, & J. Wasserstein (Eds.), *Adult learning disorders: Contemporary issues* (pp. 247–274). New York, NY: Psychology Press.

Mather, N., & Gregg, N. (2006). Specific learning disabilities: Clarifying, not eliminating, a construct.. *Professional Psychology: Research and Practice*, *37*(1), 99–106.

Mather, N., & Wendling, B. J. (2014). *Examiner's manual: Woodcock–Johnson IV tests of cognitive ability*. Rolling Meadows, IL: Riverside.

McGrew, K. S., LaForte, E. M., & Schrank, F. A. (2014). *Technical manual: Woodcock Johnson IV*. Rolling Meadows, IL: Riverside.

McGrew, K. S., & Wendling, B. J. (2010). Cattell–Horn–Carroll cognitive-achievement relations: What we have learned from the past 20 years of research. *Psychology in the Schools*, *47*(7), 651–675.

Meyer, M. S. (2000). The ability–achievement discrepancy: Does it contribute to an understanding of learning disabilities? *Educational Psychology Review*, *12*(3), 315–337.

Miciak, J., Fletcher, J. M., Stuebing, K. K., Vaughn, S., & Tolar, T. D. (2014). Patterns of cognitive strengths and weaknesses: Identification rates, agreement, and validity for learning disabilities identification. *School Psychology Quarterly*, *29*(1), 21–37. http://dx.doi.org/10.1037/spq0000037.

Naglieri, J. A. (1999). *Essentials of CAS assessment*. New York, NY: Wiley.

Naglieri, J. A. (2010). The discrepancy/consistency approach to SLD identification using the PASS theory. In D. P. Flanagan & V. C. Alfonso (Eds.), *Essentials of specific learning disability identification* (pp. 145–172). New York, NY: Wiley.

Naglieri, J. A., & Das, J. P. (1997). *Cognitive Assessment System. Administration and scoring manual*. Rolling Meadows, IL: Riverside Publishing.

Proctor, B. (2012). Relationships between Cattell–Horn–Carroll (CHC) cognitive abilities and math achievement within a sample of college students with learning disabilities. *Journal of Learning Disabilities*, *45*(3), 278–287. http://dx.doi.org/10.1177/0022219410392049.

Proctor, B., & Prevatt, F. (2003). Agreement among four models used for diagnosing learning disabilities. *Journal of Learning Disabilities*, *36*(5), 459–466.

Reschly, D. J., & Hosp, J. L. (2004). State SLD identification policies and practices. *Learning Disabilities Quarterly*, *27*(4), 197–213.

Schrank, F. A., Mather, N., & McGrew, K. S. (2014a). *Woodcock–Johnson IV tests of achievement*. Rolling Meadows, IL: Riverside.

Schrank, F. A., McGrew, K. S., & Mather, N. (2014b). *Woodcock–Johnson IV*. Rolling Meadows, IL: Riverside.

Schrank, F. A., McGrew, K. S., & Mather, N. (2014c). *Woodcock–Johnson IV tests of cognitive abilities*. Rolling Meadows, IL: Riverside.

Schrank, F. A., McGrew, K. S., & Mather, N. (2015). *The WJ IV Gf–Gc composite and its use in the identification of specific learning disabilities (Woodcock–Johnson IV Assessment Service Bulletin No. 3)*. Rolling Meadows, IL: Riverside.

Siegel, L. S. (1999). Issues in the definition and diagnosis of learning disabilities: A perspective on Guckenberger v. Boston University. *Journal of Learning Disabilities*, *32*(4), 304–319.

Sotelo-Dynega, M., Flanagan, D. P., & Alfonso, V. C. (2011). Overview of specific learning disabilities. In D. P. Flanagan & V. C. Alfonso (Eds.), *Essentials of specific learning disability identification* (pp. 1–19). Hoboken, NJ: Wiley.

Sparks, R. L., & Lovett, B. J. (2009). Objective criteria for classification of postsecondary students as learning disabled: Effects on prevalence rates and group characteristics. *Journal of Learning Disabilities*, *42*(3), 230–239.

Sparks, R. L., & Lovett, B. J. (2013). Applying objective diagnostic criteria to students in a college support program for learning disabilities. *Learning Disability Quarterly*, *36*(4), 231–241.

Stanovich, K. E. (1999). The sociopsychometrics of learning disabilities. *Journal of Learning Disabilities*, *32*(4), 350–361.

Sternberg, R. J., & Grigorenko, E. (2002). Difference scores in the identification of children with learning disabilities: It's time to use a different method. *Journal of School Psychology, 40*(1), 65–83. doi:10.1016/S0022-4405(01)00094-2.

Stuebing, K. K., Fletcher, J. M., Branum-Martin, L., & Francis, D. J. (2012). Evaluation of the technical adequacy of three methods for identifying specific learning disabilities based on cognitive discrepancies. *School Psychology Review, 41*(1), 3–22.

Taylor, A. E. B. (2014). *Diagnostic assessment of learning disabilities in childhood: Bridging the gap between research and practice.* New York, NY: Springer.

United States Office of Education. (1977). Assistance to states for education for handicapped children: Procedures for evaluating specific learning disabilities. Federal Register, 42, G1082–G1085.

Van den Broeck, W. (2002). The misconception of the regression-based discrepancy operationalization in the defining and research of learning disabilities. *Journal of Learning Disabilities, 35*(3), 194–204.

Chapter 10

Use of the Woodcock–Johnson IV Tests of Cognitive Abilities in the Diagnosis of Intellectual Disability

Randy G. Floyd, Isaac L. Woods, Leah J. Singh and Haley K. Hawkins

Department of Psychology, The University of Memphis, Memphis, TN, USA

This chapter focuses on the definition and diagnosis of intellectual disability (ID) and highlights how the Woodcock–Johnson IV Tests of Cognitive Abilities (WJ IV COG; Schrank, McGrew, & Mather, 2014) can be employed to identify elementary school-age children, adolescents, and adults who experience impairment, loss, or risk of loss due to this condition. The chapter does not focus on the psychometric properties of the WJ IV COG as a whole (see Chapter 1) nor does it address using the WJ IV COG with preschool-age children (see Chapter 8).

This chapter is a new contribution to the literature devoted to the Woodcock–Johnson tests. The original version of this edited text (Schrank & Flanagan, 2003) focusing on the Woodcock–Johnson III (WJ III; Woodcock, McGrew, & Mather, 2001) did not include a chapter devoted to the assessment of ID, the *WJ III Technical Manual* (McGrew & Woodcock, 2001) did not contain a study focusing on individuals with ID, and the lead chapter in the Shrank and Flanagan text that provided a review of the literature to date on the validity evidence supporting the WJ III (Floyd, Shaver, & McGrew, 2003) described only one study specifically addressing assessment of ID. Since the publication of the WJ III and the Schrank and Flanagan (2003) text, new guidelines for the identification and diagnosis of ID were offered, some noteworthy research focusing on the WJ III and this population was published, and the *WJ IV Technical Manual* (McGrew, LaForte, & Schrank, 2014) placed increased emphasis on the assessment of ID. Based on this progress, the current chapter begins with an overview of the eligibility and diagnostic criteria for ID, continues to discuss test and score properties that are important when assessing for ID, follows with an evaluation of the WJ IV COG in terms of it addressing these properties, and ends with a case study.

WJ IV Clinical Use and Interpretation. DOI: http://dx.doi.org/10.1016/B978-0-12-802076-0.00011-6

CHARACTERISTICS OF CHILDREN WITH ID AND IMPLICATIONS FOR ASSESSMENT

Across the past century, people with varying levels of severity of ID were labeled as "idiots," "imbeciles," and "morons" (MacMillan & Reschly, 1997; Wehmeyer, 2013). In recent decades, "mental retardation" was the preferred term employed in federal legislation (Individuals with Disabilities Education Improvement Act, 2004), eligibility criteria offered by state departments of education (Bergeron, Floyd, & Shands, 2008; Polloway, Patton, Smith, Antoine, & Lubin, 2009), and diagnostic criteria offered by the American Association on Mental Retardation (2002) and the American Psychiatric Association (APA, 2000). Following the passage of Rosa's Law (2010), which expunged the term mental retardation from all federal laws and regulations, the term ID (which was adopted in its place) has been increasingly employed. For example, the two most prominent modern definitions and diagnostic criteria for the condition now employ the term ID. Details about ID from the American Association on Intellectual and Developmental Disabilities (AAIDD, 2010) and the American Psychiatric Association (APA, 2013) are described in the next sections.

American Association on Intellectual and Developmental Disabilities

In the 11th edition of *Intellectual Disability: Definition, Classification, and Systems of Support*, AAIDD (2010) characterizes ID as a condition associated with significant limitations in intellectual functioning and deficits in adaptive behavior manifesting before age 18 years. According to the AAIDD, intellectual functioning is best represented by a general mental ability. This general mental ability encompasses reasoning, planning, solving problems, thinking abstractly, comprehending complex ideas, learning quickly, and learning from experience. Significant limitations in intellectual functioning are determined by a global composite score (frequently the IQ) from an intelligence test battery that is approximately two standard deviations below the population mean. Adaptive behavior deficits are defined as performance on a norm-referenced measure of adaptive behavior that is approximately two standard deviations below the mean on an overall score or on scores representing conceptual, social, or practical domains of skills. The age of onset criterion requires that ID must originate before the age of 18 years.

Although these core criteria for ID number only three, the AAIDD (2010) recommends a multidimensional and ecological approach to assessment that includes consideration of the interactions of the individual and environment within the domains of intellectual ability, adaptive behavior, health, participation in society, context, and individual support. In this way, the AAIDD conveys that five assumptions must be made during assessment for ID: (i) limitations of present functioning must be considered within context and culture; (ii) valid assessments that consider cultural and linguistic diversity, communication, sensory, motor, and behavior factors must be completed; (iii) a person with ID displays limitations coexisting with strengths; (iv) limitations are important to develop a profile of needed supports; and (v) with the appropriate personalized support for sustained period of time, the life functioning of the person with ID often improves. Users of the WJ IV should be knowledgeable of the multidimensional and ecological approach recommended by the AAIDD.

American Psychiatric Association

The *Diagnostic and Statistical Manual of Mental Disorders-Fifth Edition* (DSM-5; APA, 2013) classifies ID as a neurodevelopmental disorder, which is a condition with onset in the developmental period (often before a child enters grade school) and resulting in impairment in personal, social, academic, or occupational functioning. Like the AAIDD (2010), the APA describes ID as characterized by deficits in general mental abilities and adaptive functioning such that the individual fails to function at a level comparable to same-age peers in conceptual, social, and practical domains.

According to the DSM-5 (APA, 2013) criteria, individuals diagnosed with ID exhibit deficits in reasoning, problem solving, planning, abstract thinking, judgment, academic learning, and learning from experience on clinical assessment and individually administered intelligence test batteries. Although reference to IQs is far less prominent in the DSM-5 criteria than in prior versions of this text, it appears clear that the deficits in intellectual functioning would be generally well represented by such scores (Kranzler & Floyd, 2013). According to the DSM-5, individuals exhibiting such deficits that are two standard deviations or more below the population mean, including a margin for measurement error, are eligible for consideration for ID.

Similar to the approach outlined by the AAIDD (2010), the DSM-5 (APA, 2013) emphasizes the importance of an individual's level of adaptive functioning. Individuals with ID fail to meet developmental and sociocultural standards for personal independence and social responsibility in the practical, social, and conceptual domains when compared to same-age individuals with similar sociocultural backgrounds. Deficits in adaptive functioning limit one or more activities of daily life such as communication, social participation, and independent living across home, work, and school environments. A deficit in adaptive functioning refers to an impairment that is significantly below that of same-age individuals such that ongoing support is required for the individual to perform adequately across environments. The DSM-5 assigns the diagnosis of ID according to specifiers (i.e., mild, moderate, severe, and profound) based on level of adaptive functioning.

With regard to the age criterion, ID emerges in the developmental period, with the age of onset dependent on the severity of brain dysfunction (APA, 2013). Delays in motor and language abilities may be identified within the first 2 years. However, less severe cases of ID become more apparent later in development and during formal schooling when the child must engage in rapid academic learning. Users of the WJ IV should be aware of these noteworthy changes in some of DSM-5 criteria for ID because they are different from those employed during the previous 20 years (APA, 1994).

Implications of the AAIDD and DSM-5 Criteria and Psychometric Standards

Drawing on the AAIDD (2010) and DSM-5 (APA, 2013) criteria for ID as well as general and specific standards for educational and psychological testing (American Educational Research Association [AERA], American Psychological Association, & National Council on Measurement in Education [NCME], 2014), Kranzler and Floyd (2013) offered a checklist for the assessment of ID. It was designed to ensure that intelligence and adaptive behaviors were assessed as accurately as possible, that a medical evaluation was completed, and that levels of needed supports were considered. In this section of the chapter, we highlight the first part of this checklist that focuses on intelligence assessment and also addresses potentially confounding factors associated with this assessment process. Readers interested in learning more about adaptive behavior scales targeting deficits associated with ID (covered in other sections in the Kranzler and Floyd checklist) should review Floyd et al. (2015) and Reschly (2013).

Kranzler and Floyd's (2013) checklist focuses on four issues important for the assessment of intelligence in ID diagnosis and highlights the importance of careful consideration of the psychometric properties of intelligence test batteries. First, it highlights the importance of the recency of the norming data underlying the interpretation of test scores. Although the size and representativeness of normative data are also important to consider when selecting intelligence test batteries for use during ID assessment, the slight variability in these characteristics across the most popular intelligence test batteries is unlikely to produce substantial, systematic differences in norm-referenced scores and seems far less important to consider than the recency of norming data. The recency of such data is, in fact, vital because of the well-established Flynn effect (Flynn, 1984, 1987; Trahan, Stuebing, Hiscock, & Fletcher, 2014), which describes the rising levels of cognitive abilities in the population across time and consequent fluctuation in intelligence test scores for individuals depending on the recency of the test's norming data.

As a result, tests with older norming data tend to produce higher scores than tests with newer norming data; the difference on average is about 3 IQ points per decade between norming dates. When a few points difference in IQs might mean the differences between a diagnosis of ID and no diagnosis, precision in measuring the construct of general mental ability is a high goal (McGrew, 2015b). Kranzler and Floyd recommended using only recently normed intelligence test batteries, which they defined as instruments supported by norms collected within the past decade. Following Alfonso and Flanagan (2009) and Floyd et al. (2015), the norming data could be labeled more precisely in the following ways: *good* when at least some of the norming data (when a range of data collection was reported) were collected within the past 10 years, *adequate* when data were collected within the past 15 years, and *inadequate* when all data were collected more than 15 years ago.

Second, Kranzler and Floyd (2013) focused on reliability—and in particular, internal consistency reliability and test–retest reliability. Internal consistency reliability refers to the relations between test items and the homogeneity (or heterogeneity) of items forming a scale, and test–retest reliability refers to the stability of scores across relatively brief periods of time (viz., 1 month or less). In reference to standards for the assessment of ID, Kranzler and Floyd recommended that internal consistency reliability coefficients for IQ be 0.95 or higher and associated test–retest reliability coefficients be 0.90 or higher. Following Reynolds and Livingston (2014) and Floyd et al. (2015), internal consistency reliability coefficients and short-term test–retest reliability coefficients could be labeled more precisely (as median values across age group or as individual values) using the following scale: *adequate* if they are 0.90 or higher and *inadequate* if they are less than 0.90. Thus, Kranzler and Floyd's criterion level of 0.95 for internal consistency reliability is higher than that otherwise described.

Third, Kranzler and Floyd (2013) highlighted validity evidence supporting the use and interpretation of IQs during the assessment of ID. According to the most recent *Standards for Educational and Psychological Testing* (AERA, American Psychological Association, & NCME, 2014), a body of validity evidence should be accumulated to support the use and interpretation of test scores to address specific questions with specific populations. This validity evidence can be divided into five components. Evidence based on content focuses on item-level themes, wording, and organization and the manner in which they represent the targeted construct in a meaningful (and unbiased) way. Evidence based on response processes focuses on the real or hypothesized actions a person completes when responding to test items, so that the intended pattern is evident and confounds are not (or minimally) evident. Evidence based on internal relations focuses on the correspondence between test items and resulting scores from the test itself, and validity evidence is inferred based about the patterns of these relations. Evidence based on external relations focuses on the association between the scores from a test and other test scores or variables for which they should be highly related (e.g., convergent validity evidence or criterion-related validity evidence) or not (or minimally) related (e.g., divergent validity evidence or absence of test bias). This type of evidence is exceptionally commonly reported to support intelligence test scores. Finally, evidence based on consequences focuses on the intended or unintended effects of testing; this type of validity evidence is generally sparse for most tests, including intelligence tests. In reference to specific populations, the ideal validity evidence informing the assessment of ID would stem from large samples of persons with the disorder.

Fourth, Kranzler and Floyd (2013) directed attention toward scaling of the tasks most closely associated with item-level measurement, the tests composing the intelligence test battery. In particular, it is important to consider how far the lower-end range of norm-referenced scores can fall below the population mean. Seeing the full range of IQs that can fall below 70 and the approximate cutoff required for identification of a deficit in intellectual functioning (also about 70), the common standard for an adequate test floor in the literature is rather forgiving to scaling inadequacies (Bracken, 1987; Bracken, Keith, & Walker, 1998; Bradley-Johnson & Durmusoglu, 2005; Kranzler & Floyd, 2013). An adequate test floor may be evidenced when a test score of 1 produces a norm-referenced score at least two standard deviations below the mean (e.g., a deviation IQ of 70 or lower, a T score of 30 or lower, or a scaled score of 4 or lower).

In addition to these criteria, Kranzler and Floyd (2013) also encouraged examiners to consider the child or adolescent sufficiently motivated to respond during testing and other interfering factors. In particular, seeing the prevalence of sensory and motor difficulties co-occurring with ID (APA, 2000, 2013), it is important that test examiners screen for, adjust for, or accommodate these difficulties. To assist in achieving this goal, Kranzler and Floyd offered the Screening Tool for Assessment (STA), which includes a parent rating form, a teacher rating form, and a screening test to determine if vision, colorblindness, hearing, articulation, or fine motor difficulties are likely to interfere with testing for ID or other conditions.

ASSESSING STUDENTS WITH ID WITH THE WJ IV

Based on the diagnostic criteria for ID from the AAIDD (2010) and DSM-5 (APA, 2013) and psychometric standards for intelligence test batteries described in the previous section, the WJ IV COG offers its most useful contributions to ID assessment in its yielding a global composite called General Intellectual Ability (GIA) and its more narrowly focused alternative, the *Gf–Gc* Composite. This section of the chapter focuses on the norming, reliability, validity evidence, and range of test and composite scaling supporting the use of these scores in the practice of psychology. This chapter does not focus on part scores (including composite scores measuring more narrow abilities than general ability and test scores) due to (i) only minimal reference to these scores in eligibility determination and diagnosis guidelines (cf. National Research Council, 2002), and (ii) cautions against their interpretation during eligibility determination and diagnosis of ID (Bergeron & Floyd, 2006, 2013; McGrew, 2015a).

As described in McGrew et al. (2014), the WJ IV GIA composite appears as a norm-referenced standard score that is yielded from seven tests. These tests include Oral Vocabulary, Number Series, Verbal Attention, Letter-Pattern Matching, Phonological Processing, Story Recall, and Visualization. They appear to measure, in part, seven different broad abilities from the Cattell–Horn–Carroll theory (CHC; Schneider & McGrew, 2012), so the GIA targets general mental ability through the measurement of an array of different content, skills, and mental operations. In comparison, the *Gf–Gc* Composite appears as a norm-referenced standard score yielded from two of the same four tests as the GIA. In addition, it includes two additional tests to measure Fluid Reasoning (*Gf*) and Crystallized Intelligence (*Gc*), which tend to be most closely associated with—both statistically and conceptually—the construct of general mental ability (Carroll, 1993). All in all, the tests contributing to the *Gf–Gc* Composite include Oral Vocabulary, Number Series, General Information, and Concept Formation. The WJ IV GIA stems from a greater number of tests than the *Gf–Gc* Composite and encompasses a greater number of CHC broad abilities than the *Gf–Gc* Composite to ensure that the resulting scores are multidimensional estimates of intelligence. Furthermore, the GIA stems from differential weighting of test scores designed to bolster its accuracy in measuring general mental ability; the *Gf–Gc* Composite stems from equal weighting of tests.

Norming

The norming sample for the WJ IV consists of 7614 males and females (aged 2–90 years) from 46 states and the District of Columbia (McGrew et al., 2014). The average number of individuals in the each of the 22 age groups (spanning 1 year from ages 2 to 19 to a decade beginning at age 20) is 297. Only 4 age groups (2, 60–69, 70–79, and 80+) contained fewer than 200 participants. A stratified norming sample was collected based on the 2010 U.S. Census to reflect sex, country of birth, race, ethnicity, community type, parent education, type of school, type of college, educational attainment, employment status, and occupational level. There was a difference between the census data and the norming data of 5.2% for sex for ages 18–24 years and a difference of 5.9% for sex for ages 65+ years. There were no other differences greater than 5% across all other variables. The norming data were collected in 25 months from December 2009 to January 2012. Based on standards by Alfonso and Flanagan (2009) and Floyd et al. (2015), the WJ IV norming data can be considered good until 2022 and adequate between 2023 and 2027. There was evidence that individuals with ID were included in the norming sample.

Reliability

Internal consistency reliability. Internal consistency reliability coefficients were calculated based on WJ IV norming sample data for all test and cluster scores (McGrew et al., 2014). The GIA composite and *Gf–Gc* Composite exceeded the minimal standard of 0.90 set by Reynolds and Livingston (2014) and Floyd et al. (2015). In fact, the internal consistency reliability estimates for the GIA never fell below 0.95 from ages 5 to 90+ years, and their median value was 0.97 across these age groups. Thus, the GIA uniformly met Kranzler and Floyd's (2013) high internal consistency reliability criterion for IQs used in ID assessment. Based on this range of internal consistency reliability estimates, the reported standard error of measurement (SE_M) for the GIA will always be less than 3.35 (McGrew, 2015a). The internal consistency reliability estimates for the *Gf–Gc* Composite fell below 0.95 for only two, 1-year age groups (ages 11 and 12 years) across ages 5 to 90+ years, and these two exceptions were values of 0.94. Regardless of these exceptions, the median value for the *Gf–Gc* Composite was 0.96 across ages. Again, the *Gf–Gc* Composite typically met Kranzler and Floyd's (2013) internal consistency reliability criterion for IQs used in ID assessment and its reported SE_M will always be less than 3.67.

Test–retest reliability. McGrew et al. (2014) did not report the results of an analysis of test–retest reliability targeting the WJ IV GIA and *Gf–Gc* Composite. Such an analysis was conducted only for data from timed tests collected across a 1-day interval. Results revealed that the median test–retest reliability coefficient for Letter-Pattern Matching (contributing to the GIA) was 0.90 or higher across ages 7–11 years ($n = 47$; $r = 0.91$), ages 14–17 years ($n = 49$; $r = 0.88$), and ages 26–79 years ($n = 50$; $r = 0.91$). The median test–retest reliability coefficient for one of three parts of the Phonological Processing test (contributing to the GIA) was 0.91 or higher across ages 7–11 years ($n = 47$; $r = 0.92$), ages 14–17 years ($n = 49$; $r = 0.91$), and ages 26–79 years ($n = 50$; $r = 0.93$). Regrettably, no definitive statement about the test–retest reliability of WJ IV GIA or the *Gf–Gc* Composite can be made at present.

Validity Evidence

Content and response processes. Because many individuals with ID also experience sensory or motor impairment and some may be English language learners (AAIDD, 2010; APA, 2013), it is important that the WJ IV COG contains features that prevent confounds in assessment from surfacing and that its support materials include descriptions of defensible testing accommodations. As such, McGrew et al. (2014) described several universal design principles that were employed during the development of the test. They include employing stimulus items printed in with bold colors and lines and instructions that are presented in a clear, concise, and simple way for all learners to reduce confounds. In addition, examiners are given increased flexibility during administration because tests can be administered in any order. This flexibility is often needed when testing children with ID.

Internal structure. As described in Chapter 3, McGrew et al. (2014) reported a wide variety of validity evidence supporting the internal structure of the WJ IV. For example, the correlations between all WJ IV test scores and between all of its cluster scores were presented, and the results of a three-stage process of developing and testing models of the WJ IV test interrelations was highlighted. This process included theoretically driven and data-driven analyses, such as cluster analysis, multidimensional scaling, exploratory factor analysis, and confirmatory factor analysis. These results seemed to support measurement of specific abilities measured by tests contributing to the GIA and the *Gf–Gc* Composite as well as general mental ability, which these scores primarily target. The accuracy in which these composite scores measure general mental ability can be estimated by referencing the test *g* loadings, the correlations between test scores and latent variables representing general mental ability (Maynard, Floyd, Acklie, & Houston, 2011). Higher *g* loadings indicate greater accuracy; values of 0.70 or above are typically considered *high*, values between 0.50 and 0.69 are considered *medium*; and values below 0.50 are considered *low* (Floyd, McGrew, Barry, Rafael, & Rogers, 2009; McGrew & Flanagan, 1998).

For the WJ IV tests contributing to the GIA, *g* loadings based on a type of exploratory factor analysis called principal factor analysis ranged (across tests and age groups from 6 to 90 years) from 0.77 (Phonological Processing, ages 40–90+ years) to 0.53 (Story Recall, ages 9–13 years). Across age groups, median values were as follows: Oral Vocabulary, 0.72; Phonological Processing, 0.71; Verbal Attention, 0.64; Number Series, 0.62; Visualization, 0.61; Story Recall, 0.58; and Letter-Pattern Matching, 0.57. As such, smoothed differential weights based on the *g* loadings (obtained from principal component analysis, which is much like principal factor analysis) were reported at 1-year intervals (until age 20 years, after which intervals typically represented a decade). As a result, seven tests contributed to between 7% and 18% of variance to the GIA. For those tests contributing to the *Gf–Gc* Composite, *g* loadings ranged from 0.75 (Oral Vocabulary, ages 40–90+ years) to 0.44 (General Information, ages 6–8 years). Across age groups, median values were as follows: Oral Vocabulary, 0.72; Number Series, 0.62; Concept Formation, 0.66; and General Information, 0.59. Neither the GIA nor the *Gf–Gc* Composite includes primarily tests that are strong measures of general mental ability, but it is highly likely that the sum of these tests measures general mental ability very accurately (Farmer, Floyd, Reynolds, & Kranzler, 2014; Reynolds, Floyd, & Niileksela, 2013).

External relations. McGrew et al. (2014) reported an array of validity evidence based the relations between the WJ IV scores and other variables. For example, they reported cross-sectional growth trajectories for WJ IV scores (including the GIA and *Gf–Gc* Composite) across development. They featured concurrent correlations between the WJ IV GIA and *Gf–Gc* Composite and other measures of general mental ability, such as the Wechsler Intelligence Scale for Children, Fourth Edition (WISC-IV; Wechsler, 2003) Full Scale IQ (FSIQ); the Wechsler Adult Intelligence Scale, Fourth Edition (WAIS-IV; Wechsler, 2008) FSIQ; and the Kaufman Assessment Battery for Children, Second Edition (KABC-II; Kaufman & Kaufman, 2004) Fluid-Crystallized Index (FCI) and Mental Processing Index (MPI). These correlations ranged from 0.57 (WJ IV *Gf–Gc* Composite and the KABC-II MPI) to 0.84 (WJ IV GIA and the WAIS-IV FSIQ) and are well within the range of typical correlations between measures of general mental ability (Floyd, Clark, & Shadish, 2008; Jensen, 1998). In every case, the correlations between the other measures of general mental ability (e.g., from the WISC-IV, WAIS-IV, and KABC-II) and the WJ IV GIA were higher than those between the same measure and the *Gf–Gc* Composite.

McGrew et al. (2014) engaged in several methods to evaluate and eliminate effects of the characteristics associated with race/ethnicity and gender on test scores. In particular, they reported conducting reviews of item content by experts and reviews of items for potential sensitive and biased items. Although it is unclear exactly what scrutiny was given to item content from the WJ IV COG, McGrew et al. (2014) reported consulting with experts (e.g., teachers, university faculty, and psychologists) to generate and evaluate new item content to ensure that it possessed sufficient breadth and did not inadvertently target other skills or abilities. Furthermore, bias and sensitivity reviews of item content led some item content and item formats to be flagged for potential bias and offensiveness. At a statistical level, differential item functioning analysis, which examines the possibility of differential difficulty of items across groups, was conducted. In particular, the Rasch iterative-logit method was employed to compare item-level scores for groups while controlling for ability level (based on scores from other items). Participants were contrasted based on gender (female and male), race (White and non-White), and ethnicity (Hispanic and non-Hispanic). All items producing a significant difference between groups were flagged and evaluated, and the items demonstrating the most apparent bias were eliminated from the final item set. These analyses of external relations support both the construct validity of the GIA and the *Gf–Gc* Composite in measuring general mental ability as well as evidence of absence of or greatly minimized test bias associated with gender, race, and ethnicity.

Adequacy of Test and Composite Floors

Following evaluation guidelines described previously, the floors of tests contributing to the GIA and the *Gf–Gc* Composite were evaluated by entering a raw score of 1 into the WJ IV COG scoring system (Schrank & Dailey, 2014) and evaluating the resultant standard scores (SS; $M = 100$, $SD = 15$) based on age norms. At age 5 years, 0 months, four of the seven WJ IV tests contributing to the GIA demonstrated inadequate floors (Oral Vocabulary SS = 79, Number Series SS = 80, Verbal Attention SS = 83, and Phonological Processing SS = 80). At this age level, findings for the *Gf–Gc* Composite were the same for Oral Vocabulary and Number Series, and Concept Formation also demonstrated an inadequate floor (SS = 75). Thus, three of the four tests contributing to the *Gf–Gc* Composite failed to yield sufficiently low scores at age 5 years, 0 months. Despite this pattern evident in test floors, the raw scores of 1 on all constituent tests still produced a GIA SS of 63 and a *Gf–Gc* Composite SS of 61, which are well below the criterion of 70. Despite the high frequency of insufficient test floors at age 5 years, 0 months, all but one of these test floors was considered adequate at age 6 years, 0 months (Verbal Attention SS = 72). At age 6 years, 0 months, the raw scores of 1 on constituent tests produced a GIA SS of 51 and a

Gf–Gc Composite SS of 46. At age 6 years, 2 months, all tests yielded standard scores of 70 or lower, and at this age level, test raw scores of 1 produced a GIA SS of 46 and a *Gf–Gc* Composite SS of 43, which are more than three standard deviations below the mean. In sum, although the WJ IV GIA and the *Gf–Gc* Composite can produce sufficiently low norm-referenced scores to identify ID beginning age 5-0 years, some of their constituent tests do not do so until early in the sixth year. As a result, it cannot be recommended that the WJ IV be used to assess for ID in low-functioning children younger than age 6 years, 0 months.

Special Study of Children With ID

Despite calls for extensive study of the reliability and validity of intelligence test scores used with children, adolescents, and adults with developmental delays, McGrew et al. (2014) provided only one study targeting the ID population. The sample included 50 participants ages 6–13 years. The sample was roughly evenly split for sex, with 56% being girls. About 92% of children were Caucasian, 6% were Black, and 2% were Asian/Pacific Islander. About 30–46% of their mothers reported completion of high school or additional education, and 24–44% of their fathers reported completion of high school or additional education.

Selected WJ IV tests were administered, but no evidence of the reliability for WJ IV tests or resultant composite scores with this sample was reported. Results primarily reveal validity evidence based on external relations (as discussed previously) for some WJ IV tests and the *Gf–Gc* Composite. First, because the Letter-Pattern Matching and Story Recall tests were not administered to the ID sample as part of the study, GIA scores were not reported or evaluated. Thus, there is no validity evidence in the form of discriminative validity reported for the GIA with samples of children with ID. However, mean scores for four of the five other tests contributing to the GIA were well below two standard deviations below the mean (SS = 70): Oral Vocabulary: $M = 48.4$; Number Series: $M = 54.2$; Verbal Attention: $M = 59.0$; and Phonological Processing: $M = 54.3$. Only the Visualization test produced a mean value above 70 ($M = 75.9$).

Second, scores from the *Gf–Gc* Composite were reported for this sample and evaluated. The mean for this composite was 45.0 ($SD = 19.2$). In addition to the scores from the Oral Vocabulary and Number Series tests reported previously, mean scores for General Information ($M = 60.5$) and Concept Formation ($M = 60.8$) were well below two standard deviations below the mean. This study focusing on the validity of the WJ IV test and composite scores offers a welcomed contribution to the WJ IV literature (cf. McGrew & Woodcock, 2001), but the incomplete nature of the data collection, the rudimentary analysis (yielding only descriptive statistics), and the brief presentation of the results in McGrew et al. (2014) limit its ability to inform users about the strengths and weaknesses of using the WJ IV with the ID population.

CONCLUSION

At the time of writing this chapter, the WJ IV COG has been released only approximately 8 months, and current evidence supporting the use and interpretation of measures of general mental ability from the WJ IV during the assessment of ID is somewhat modest. Following Kranzler and Floyd's (2013) checklist that was based on AAIDD (2010) and DSM-5 (APA, 2013) criteria for ID as well as general and specific standards for educational and psychological testing, the WJ IV COG GIA and *Gf–Gc* Composite certainly meet or exceed the internal consistency reliability standard (based on general population estimates), and their norm-referenced scores are based on some of the most recently gathered norming data of all individually administered intelligence test batteries. In addition, a sizeable body of evidence based on content, internal relations, and external relations (including bias identification studies) supports the construct validity of these two composites in measuring general mental ability. However, there is no test–retest reliability evidence supporting the GIA and *Gf–Gc* Composite, and the scale floors for all their constituent tests are not adequate until age 6 years, 2 months. Although one study was available for review to support the construct validity of the *Gf–Gc* Composite during ID assessment, this study focused only on children, and its results are not comprehensive and substantive. Thus, more evidence is needed to support claims of reliable measurement and construct validity of the WJ IV COG GIA and *Gf–Gc* Composite for children, adolescents, and adults. Future research studies should target the evaluation of such reliability and validity evidence, but in the meantime, practitioners engaging in the assessment of ID should review the reliability and validity supporting alternative measures of general mental ability with the populations they target in their work and employ the WJ IV GIA and *Gf–Gc* Composite cautiously until further evidence has been generated.

CASE STUDY

Reason for Referral

Ronald Thompson was referred to the clinic by his sister, Laura Thompson, because of Ronald's history of academic difficulties in school in a variety of subject areas and an overall lack of focus. The purpose of this assessment was to reassess Ronald for a learning disorder or intellectual disability.

Background Information

Demographic information and family history. Ronald Thompson is a 56-year-old man who is not currently employed and lives alone. Background information was obtained about Ronald's family, medical, developmental, educational, and psychological history through an interview with Ronald's older sister, Laura Thompson, who has power of attorney.

Ronald was previously married, but in 2008, his wife passed away. Prior to her death, Ronald's wife helped Ronald function and complete tasks. Ronald's older sister, Laura, lives in Mississippi and his other sister, Sophia, lives in Arkansas. Laura and Sophia support Ronald financially. Ronald maintains contact with his sisters about once per week via the telephone and visits them several times per year.

Developmental and medical history. Laura reported that her mother's pregnancy with Ronald was difficult due to an Rh blood incompatibility. This incompatibility occurs when the Rh antibodies cross the placenta and attack the fetus's red blood cells. It can lead to hemolytic anemia in the fetus, which is a condition in which red blood cells are destroyed faster than the body can replace them. Ronald was also born with "blue baby syndrome," which is also called methemoglobinemia. Blue baby syndrome occurs when newborn babies have cyanotic heart defects. Laura was unsure of the medical interventions that were used to treat these conditions. No other history of chronic illness, hospitalizations, or abuse was reported.

According to Laura, Ronald has had learning difficulties since birth. Most of Ronald's developmental milestones were met on time, but Ronald's speaking was delayed. Ronald had an electroencephalography (EEG) scan when he was about 4 years old. She stated that the scan showed "low brain activity." Subsequently, he was enrolled in speech therapy and attended twice per week. However, he did not speak well until he was 6 years old and stutters to this day. Laura stated that Ronald wears reading glasses and his last vision screening occurred in the summer of 2014. She did not recall Ronald's last hearing screening.

Educational and psychological history. Laura reported that Ronald was placed in a special education program at 123 Elementary School. Laura recalled that he was evaluated and diagnosed with mild mental retardation, but she could not remember when this evaluation occurred. Ronald remained in the special education program until he graduated from Star Academy in 1974.

Ronald is not currently employed and has not had a job since 2012. He previously held a job working on a box packing line for 20 years, but Laura noted that Ronald was injured on the job and was "let go" due to a lack of focus and ability. Laura reported that Ronald then worked at a mail distribution facility. He worked there for approximately 7 years until he was fired due to an "emotional breakdown." It was after this breakdown that Ronald began receiving psychiatric treatment from Dr. Matthew Wagner at Medical Psychiatric Association.

Ronald is currently seeing Dr. Wagner for anxiety and depression. According to Laura, prior to treatment, Ronald attempted suicide four times. Ronald is currently taking 50 mg of Zoloft and 25 mg of Doxepin daily. He sees Dr. Wagner every 3 months to monitor his medications.

Overall, Laura reported that Ronald has significant difficulty comprehending information, specifically reading and writing. Additionally, Laura stated that Ronald has "never mastered mathematics at any level." Notably, she reported that Ronald has no concept of money. Laura added that if Ronald is in a highly stressful situation, his performance will significantly deteriorate. Laura noted that Ronald must be in a structured environment and needs constant supervision. He can perform well, but he needs very clear instructions, and they must be reinforced. Laura stated that their family has always organized living situations, paid bills, directed medical activities, and helped find jobs for Ronald. He has never lived independently, and Laura stated, "He could never survive on his own."

Assessment Techniques

Semi-structured interview with Laura Thompson
Review of documents regarding Ronald's development provided by Laura Thompson
Screening Tool for Assessment (STA)
   Direct Screening Test Record
   Parent/Caregiver Screening Form
Woodcock–Johnson IV Tests of Cognitive Abilities (WJ IV COG)
Woodcock–Johnson IV Tests of Achievement (WJ IV ACH)
Adaptive Behavior Assessment System, Third Edition (ABAS-3)
   Adult Form completed by Laura Thompson.

Behavioral Observations during Testing

Ronald arrived early for the assessment session and appeared disheveled (e.g., needing a haircut and a shave, having unkempt fingernails, and wearing wrinkled clothing). During the assessment session, Ronald was cooperative and maintained attention to task, but he occasionally gave up when he knew the tasks were beyond his ability. Notably, one test (i.e., Math Facts Fluency) on the WJ IV ACH was not administered due to Ronald's low math ability. His conversational proficiency was also below expectation for his age.

Ronald's intelligibility when speaking was below expectation, and he had difficulty pronouncing some sounds. For example, he pronounced "wreath" as "reef." Additionally, some instances of stuttering were observed in this assessment. Laura also completed two rating scales regarding Ronald's behaviors. Laura appeared to be answering questions honestly, and the general appearance of valid protocols indicates that their results are most likely valid. In general, the results of this assessment appear to be a valid estimate of Ronald's current intellectual functioning, academic achievement, and socio-emotional functioning.

Major Findings

Major Finding #1. Ronald's Woodcock–Johnson IV Tests of Cognitive Abilities (WJ IV COG) GIA score was 53 (90% confidence interval of 51–57).

This score falls in the Extremely Low range and indicates that 99.9% of adults his age would score higher. More specifically, Ronald's score on the *Gf–Gc* Composite was 48 (90% confidence interval of 46–52). This score falls in the Extremely Low range and indicates that 99.9% of adults his age would score higher.

Major Finding #2. Ronald demonstrated a general pattern of low achievement skills relative to peers his age. Ronald's WJ IV Tests of Achievement (ACH) Broad Written Language composite score fell in the Very Low range (SS = 62) when compared to others his age. Specifically, Ronald could create simple sentences based on prompts, but he struggled to spell common words (e.g., "ar" for "are" and "wne" for "when"). Additionally, when writing sentences, Ronald used no punctuation (e.g., no use of periods to conclude sentences), and he inappropriately capitalized letters amidst words (e.g., this is Not wORKing). Results from contributing tests indicate that Ronald's ability to convey ideas in writing, to spell dictated words, and to rapidly produce written sentences is well below other adults his age.

Ronald's WJ IV ACH Broad Reading composite score fell in the Very Low range (SS = 69). Specifically, Ronald could read words on about a third grade reading level, but he struggled to read other words that adults his age can read. When asked to read simple sentences and determine answers to questions at a rapid pace, Ronald completed 41 questions with 4 errors; however, he should be able to complete more than 70 questions based on expectations for adults. Lastly, although Ronald could read some words in a passage, he struggled to draw inferences and understand the passages he read. Results from contributing tests indicate that Ronald's ability to recognize words, read material quickly, and comprehend what he reads is significantly lower than other adults his age.

A WJ IV ACH Broad Mathematics composite score could not be obtained due to Ronald's extremely low score on the Calculation test. Specifically, on the Calculation test, Ronald's score (SS = 19) was in the Extremely Low range. In fact, he was able to complete only two simple addition problems correctly, which places his math calculation skills at about a kindergarten level. Considering his difficulty completing the addition problems, the Math Facts Fluency test was not administered as he would have been unable to complete the required addition, subtraction, and multiplication problems within the time limit. Lastly, Ronald's score on the Applied Problems test (SS = 49) was in the Extremely Low range. This test revealed that Ronald could complete some one-step mathematical word problems, but he struggled to complete any problems that required more than one-step calculations. Additionally, as noted by his sister, he could not calculate problems that were associated with money. Results from contributing tests indicate that Ronald's ability to solve mathematical computations and to solve math problems is well below other adults his age.

Overall, Ronald demonstrated evidence of Very Low academic achievement when compared to others his age. This evidence indicates that Ronald's overall scores in reading and written language, and his test scores in math were in the

Very Low to Extremely Low range. These results are generally commensurate with his scores obtained on the WJ IV COG and are not indicative of a learning disorder in reading, math, or written expression.

Major Finding #3. The Adaptive Behavior Assessment System, Third Edition (ABAS-3) was used to evaluate Ronald's adaptive skills that are important to everyday living. Ronald's sister completed the ABAS-3 Adult Form to assess Ronald's adaptive functioning within the home environment. The ABAS-3 Adult Form yields an overall score, the General Adaptive Composite (GAC). Ronald's GAC fell within the Extremely Low range, with a standard score of 52, when compared to others his age. This score is at the 0.1 percentile compared to peers of Ronald's age; 99.9% of others would score higher. This estimate of general skill level is well below his same-age peers and indicates limited independent functioning.

The ABAS-3 Adult Form also yields three domain scores: Conceptual, Social, and Practical. The Conceptual domain is made up of communication skills (e.g., listening and conversation skills), functional academic skills (basic reading, writing, and math skills), and self-direction (skills needed for independence, following directions, and making choices). Ronald's standard score on the Conceptual domain fell within the Extremely Low range (SS=51). The Social domain is made up of social skills (e.g., having friends and recognizing emotions) and leisure skills (planning recreational activities and playing with others). Ronald's standard score on the Social domain fell within the Extremely Low range (SS=54). The Practical domain is made up of self-care (eating, grooming, and hygiene), home/school living (property maintenance, food preparation, and completing chores), community use (shopping and getting around the community), and health and safety skills (response to illness/injury, using medicines, and showing caution). Ronald's standard score on the Practical domain fell within the Very Low range (SS=65).

All of Ronald's ABAS-3 Adult Form composite scores fell at or below the 1st percentile. These results indicate that Ronald has significant difficulty completing many self-care tasks independently. He needs assistance from others to acquire basic needs for a healthy lifestyle. Without ongoing support, Ronald's adaptive deficits limit his functioning in activities of daily life across home, work, and community environments.

Major Finding #4. Ronald was referred for a psychoeducational evaluation because of concerns regarding his ability to comprehend information and his continued academic difficulties in all areas. Ronald displays significantly subaverage scores in the area of general intellectual functioning as evidenced by his scores on the WJ IV COG. Overall, his intellectual ability is in the Extremely Low range. Additionally, Ronald displayed deficits in adaptive behavior in all areas including conceptual, social, and practical skills, according to his sister's completion of the ABAS-3 Adult Form. His ABAS-3 GAC was in the Extremely Low range, as well. Ronald's subaverage scores in intellectual functioning and adaptive behavior adversely affect his ability to acquire academic skills at the same rate as his nondisabled peers. Ronald's achievement scores also indicate delays in all areas. Specifically, Ronald's broad reading and writing scores were in the Very Low range, and his math test scores were in the Extremely Low range.

Due to limitations regarding general knowledge, reasoning ability, and ability to problem-solve, Ronald may have significant difficulty finding future employment without adequate supports. Therefore, based on Ronald's deficits in intellectual functioning (e.g., reasoning, problem solving, planning, abstract thinking, judgment, and academic learning), as well as deficits in adaptive functioning that result in failure to meet developmental and sociocultural standards for personal independence and social responsibility, Ronald meets the criteria for a diagnosis of ID, moderate (DSM-5 319.00). This diagnosis is the modern-day equivalent of the mental retardation diagnosis that Ronald reportedly received as a child.

REFERENCES

Alfonso, V. C., & Flanagan, D. P. (2009). Assessment of preschool children: A framework for evaluating the adequacy of the technical characteristics of norm-referenced instruments. In B. Mowder, F. Rubinson, & A. Yasik (Eds.), *Evidence based practice in infant and early childhood psychology* (pp. 129–166). New York, NY: Wiley.

American Association on Intellectual and Developmental Disabilities, (2010). *Intellectual disability: Definition, classification, and systems of supports* (11th ed.). Washington, DC: Author.

American Association on Mental Retardation, (2002). *Mental retardation: Definition, classification, and systems of supports* (10th ed.). Washington, DC: Author.

American Educational Research Association, American Psychological Association, & National Council on Measurement in Education, (2014). *Standards for educational and psychological testing*. Washington, DC: American Educational Research Association.

American Psychiatric Association, (1994). *Diagnostic and Statistical Manual of Mental Disorders* (4th ed.). Washington, DC: American Psychiatric Publishing.

American Psychiatric Association, (2000). *Diagnostic and Statistical Manual of Mental Disorders* (4th ed., text revision). Washington, DC: American Psychiatric Publishing.

American Psychiatric Association, (2013). *Diagnostic and Statistical Manual of Mental Disorders* (5th ed.). Washington, DC: American Psychiatric Publishing.

Bergeron, R., & Floyd, R. G. (2006). Broad cognitive abilities of children with mental retardation: An analysis of group and individual profiles. *American Journal of Mental Retardation, 111*(6), 417–432.

Bergeron, R., & Floyd, R. G. (2013). Individual part score profiles of children with intellectual disability: A descriptive analysis across three intelligence tests. *School Psychology Review, 42*(1), 22–38.

Bergeron, R., Floyd, R. G., & Shands, E. I. (2008). State eligibility guidelines for mental retardation: An update and consideration of part scores and unreliability of IQs. *Education and Training in Developmental Disabilities, 43*(1), 123–131.

Bracken, B. A. (1987). Limitations of preschool scales and standards for minimal levels of technical adequacy. *Journal of Psychoeducational Assessment, 5*(4), 313–326.

Bracken, B. A., Keith, L. K., & Walker, K. C. (1998). Assessment of preschool behavior and social-emotional functioning: A review of thirteen third-party scales. *Journal of Psychoeducational Assessment, 16*(2), 153–169.

Bradley-Johnson, S., & Durmusoglu, G. (2005). Evaluation of floors and item gradients for reading and math tests for young children. *Journal of Psychoeducational Assessment, 23*(3), 262–278.

Carroll, J. B. (1993). *Human cognitive abilities: A survey of factor-analytic studies.* New York, NY: Cambridge University Press.

Farmer, R. L., Floyd, R. G., Reynolds, M. R., & Kranzler, J. (2014). IQs are very strong but imperfect indicators of psychometric g: Results from conjoint confirmatory factor analysis. *Psychology in the Schools, 51*(8), 801–813.

Floyd, R. G., Clark, M. H., & Shadish, W. R. (2008). The exchangeability of intelligent quotients: Implications for professional psychology. *Professional Psychology: Research and Practice, 39*(4), 414–423.

Floyd, R. G., McGrew, K. S., Barry, A., Rafael, F. A., & Rogers, J. (2009). General and specific effects on Cattell–Horn–Carroll broad ability composites: Analysis of the Woodcock–Johnson III Normative Update CHC factor clusters across development. *School Psychology Review, 38*(2), 249–265.

Floyd, R. G., Shands, E. I., Alfonso, V. C., Phillips, J., Autry, B. K., Mosteller, J. A., et al. (2015). A systematic review and psychometric evaluation of adaptive behavior scales and recommendations for practice. *Journal of Applied School Psychology, 31*(1), 83–113.

Floyd, R. G., Shaver, R. B., & McGrew, K. S. (2003). Interpretation of the Woodcock–Johnson III tests of cognitive abilities: Acting on evidence. In F. A. Schrank & D. P. Flanagan (Eds.), *WJ III clinical use and interpretation* (pp. 1–46). New York, NY: Academic Press. 403–408.

Flynn, J. R. (1984). The mean IQ of Americans: Massive gains 1932 to 1978. *Psychological Bulletin, 95*(1), 29–51.

Flynn, J. R. (1987). Massive IQ gains in 14 nations: What IQ tests really measure. *Psychological Bulletin, 101*(2), 171–191.

Individuals with Disabilities Education Improvement Act, Pub. L. 108–446 (2004).

Jensen, A. R. (1998). *The g factor: The science of mental ability.* Westport, CT: Praeger.

Kaufman, A. S., & Kaufman, N. L. (2004). *Kaufman assessment battery for children* (2nd ed.). Circle Pines, MN: American Guidance Service.

Kranzler, J. H., & Floyd, R. G. (2013). *Assessing intelligence in children and adolescents: A practical guide.* New York, NY: Guilford Press.

MacMillan, D. L., & Reschly, D. J. (1997). Issues in definition and classification. In W. E. MacLean (Ed.), Jr. *Ellis' handbook of mental deficiency, psychological theory, and research* (3rd ed., pp. 47–74). Mahwah, NJ: Erlbaum.

Maynard, J. L., Floyd, R. G., Acklie, T. J., & Houston, L., III (2011). General factor loadings and specific effects of the Differential Ability Scales, Second Edition composites. *School Psychology Quarterly, 26*(2), 108–118.

McGrew, K. S. (2015a). Intellectual functioning. In E. Polloway (Ed.), *The death penalty and intellectual disability* (pp. 85–112). Washington, DC: American Association on Intellectual and Developmental Disabilities.

McGrew, K. S. (2015b). Norm obsolescence: The Flynn effect. In E. Polloway (Ed.), *The death penalty and intellectual disability* (pp. 155–172). Washington, DC: American Association on Intellectual and Developmental Disabilities.

McGrew, K. S., & Flanagan, D. P. (1998). *The intelligence test desk reference (ITDR): Gf–Gc cross-battery assessment.* Boston: Allyn & Bacon.

McGrew, K. S., LaForte, E. M., & Schrank, F. A. (2014). *Woodcock–Johnson IV technical manual.* Rolling Meadows, IL: Riverside.

McGrew, K. S., & Woodcock, R. W. (2001). *Woodcock–Johnson III technical manual.* Itasca, IL: Riverside.

National Research Council, (2002). *Mental retardation: Determining eligibility for Social Security benefits.* Washington, DC: National Academy Press.

Polloway, E. A., Patton, J. R., Smith, J. D., Antoine, K., & Lubin, J. (2009). State guidelines for mental retardation and intellectual disabilities: A revisitation of previous analyses in light of changes in the field. *Education and Training in Developmental Disabilities, 44*, 14–24.

Reschly, D. J. (2013). Assessing mild intellectual disability. In D. H. Saklofske, C. R. Reynolds, & V. Schwean (Eds.), *Oxford handbook of child and adolescent assessment* (pp. 683–697). New York, NY: Oxford University Press.

Reynolds, C. R., & Livingston, R. B. (2014). A psychometric primer for school psychologists. In P. L. Harrison & A. Thomas (Eds.), *Best practices in school psychology* (6th ed., pp. 281–300). Bethesda, MD: National Association of School Psychologists.

Reynolds, M. R., Floyd, R. G., & Niileksela, C. R. (2013). How well is psychometric g indexed by global composites? Evidence from three popular intelligence tests. *Psychological Assessment, 25*(4), 1314–1321.

Rosa's Law, Pub. L. No. 111–256 (2010).

Schneider, W. J., & McGrew, K. S. (2012). The Cattell–Horn–Carroll model of intelligence. In D. P. Flanagan & P. L. Harrison (Eds.), *Contemporary intellectual assessment: Theories, tests, and issues* (3rd ed., pp. 99–144). New York, NY: Guilford Press.

Schrank, F. A., & Dailey, D. (2014). *Woodcock–Johnson online scoring and reporting [Online format].* Rolling Meadows, IL: Riverside.

Schrank, F. A., & Flanagan, D. P. (Eds.). (2003). *WJ III clinical use and interpretation.* New York, NY: Academic Press.

Schrank, F. A., McGrew, K. S., & Mather, N. (2014). *Woodcock–Johnson IV tests of cognitive abilities.* Rolling Meadows, IL: Riverside.

Trahan, L., Stuebing, K. K., Hiscock, M. K., & Fletcher, J. M. (2014). The Flynn effect: A meta-analysis. *Psychological Bulletin, 140*(5), 1332–1360.

Wechsler, D. (2003). *The Wechsler Intelligence Scale for Children* (4th ed.). San Antonio, TX: Psychological Corporation.

Wechsler, D. (2008). *Wechsler adult intelligence scale* (4th ed.). San Antonio, TX: Pearson Assessments.

Wehmeyer, M. L. (Ed.). (2013). *The story of intellectual disability: An evolution of meaning, understanding, and public perception.* Baltimore, MD: Brookes.

Woodcock, R. W., McGrew, K. S., & Mather, N. (2001). *Woodcock–Johnson III.* Itasca, IL: Riverside.

Chapter 11

Use of the Woodcock–Johnson IV Tests of Cognitive Abilities and Achievement in the Assessment for Giftedness

Steven I. Pfeiffer and Jordy B. Yarnell

Department of Educational Psychology and Learning Systems, College of Education, Florida State University, Tallahassee, FL, USA

INTRODUCTION

This chapter focuses on the use of the Woodcock–Johnson IV Tests of Cognitive Abilities (WJ IV COG; Schrank, McGrew, & Mather, 2014b) and Woodcock–Johnson IV Tests of Achievement (WJ IV ACH; Schrank, Mather, & McGrew, 2014a) in the assessment of students who may be gifted. To provide a context for this discussion, we first tackle the thorny issue of, "who are the gifted?" We then present the readers with the *tripartite model of giftedness*. Next, we discuss the various purposes of assessment of the gifted, basic principles, and fundamental beliefs underlying these assessments. Finally, we examine the unique strengths of the WJ IV COG and ACH for the assessment of the gifted.

As far back as Confucius in China and Plato in Greece, philosophers wrote about "heavenly" or gifted children. Their writings theorized on what high ability constituted and also provided practical recommendations for how society should go about identifying and nurturing these special young citizens (Mönks, Heller, & Passow, 2000). Early philosophers embraced views that giftedness constituted a set of special attributes which we today would view as aspects of cognitive ability (Pfeiffer, 2013a, 2013b).

In the United States, the early roots of the education of individuals who are gifted can be traced to the research conducted by Lewis Terman, a professor at Stanford University. Most readers are familiar with Terman's longitudinal study in California, which followed a large group of students who tested with IQ's at or above 140. Terman collected extensive data on these students over the course of 50 years. He stated that the "twofold purpose of the project was, first of all,

WJ IV Clinical Use and Interpretation. DOI: http://dx.doi.org/10.1016/B978-0-12-802076-0.00012-8

to find what traits characterize children of high IQ, and secondly, to follow them for as many years as possible to see what kind of adults they might become" (Terman, 1925, p. 223; Terman & Oden, 1951, p. 21). Terman concluded that children of high IQ (140 or higher) are healthier, better-adjusted, and higher achievers than unselected children (Robinson & Clinkenbeard, 2008). This early work set the stage for establishing within the education and psychology communities what Dai (2010) calls "a gifted child focus."

There are other early scientific studies and writings on individuals who are gifted, such as Galton's *Hereditary Genius* (1869) and Cattell's *A Statistical Study of American Men of Science* (1906) (Whipple, 1924). However, nothing quite captured the imagination of the public as did Terman's *Genetic Studies of Genius* (Mönks et al., 2000). More than any other individual, Terman's work helped conceptualize giftedness as most practitioners and the lay public understand it, as an individual with a high IQ. Almost a hundred years later, Terman's influence on how we view giftedness remains powerful. The "gifted child focus" emphasizes general intelligence, and assumes that those who are gifted reflect a clearly demarcated and fixed category of exceptional individuals who differ in a number of quantitative and, some argue, qualitative ways from their nongifted peers. The "gifted child focus" dominated twentieth century thinking. A more recent focus is emerging and beginning to challenge the predominant "gifted child focus." It has been labeled a "talent development perspective" (Dai, 2010; Pfeiffer, 2013b; Subotnik, 2009; Subotnik, Olszewski-Kubilius, & Worrell, 2011).

WHO ARE GIFTED INDIVIDUALS?

We now turn to the question of, "who are gifted individuals?" The reader may think that there really is little need to discuss this obviously simple question. Practitioners who works in the schools, know exactly who they are. Students who are gifted are those pupils who meet the eligibility criteria that the school district and state stipulate qualify for the classification of gifted. Graduate students in psychology also know who the gifted are. They are those bright students who have obtained test scores on a standardized cognitive ability measure such as the Stanford Binet, Wechsler Scales, or WJ who exceed a certain threshold, according to what was read in their assessment of intelligence textbook. These are the views of most practitioners and graduate students, according to a recent national survey (McClain & Pfeiffer, 2012) and informal conversations at school psychology conferences and workshops, in the United States and internationally.

The views in this chapter depart somewhat from traditional views and some individuals might argue outdated definition of who are the gifted, and embraces a more nuanced perspective of what we mean by giftedness (Pfeiffer, 2015). "High IQ equals gifted" dominated twentieth-century thinking in the gifted field. Recent research in developmental psychology, the cognitive neurosciences, and the talent development field better informs our understanding of high ability students—who we know as the gifted (Pfeiffer, 2002, 2003, 2013a). Most individuals would agree that the young child who is reading at age 3 years, excelling at competitive chess by age 6 years, or performing violin in an orchestra at age 10 years is a gifted individual. These examples are indicative of children who are developmentally advanced, one hallmark of giftedness (Pfeiffer, 2002, 2012). Most gifted authorities now agree that students who are academically gifted are those in the upper 2–10% compared to their same-age peers in general intellectual ability, distinguished performance in one or more academic domains, and evidence of creative work (Pfeiffer, 2003, 2012, 2013a, 2013b).

There is a genetic influence in the expression of giftedness, at least at the high end of the IQ continuum (Plomin & Spinath, 2004). For example, the fields of music and mathematics have many examples of child prodigies. Evidence also comes from the emergence of eminence among young children from impoverished environments (Nisbett, 2009). However, most developmental psychologists and behavioral geneticists also agree that the unfolding of gifts requires a nurturing and supportive environment, available resources, certain personality characteristics, and even good fortune (Foley Nicpon & Pfeiffer, 2011b; Pfeiffer, 2012, 2013c).

Below is one definition of the child who is gifted. This definition is based on Pfeiffer's *tripartite model of giftedness*, which will be explained shortly.

The gifted child demonstrates a greater likelihood, when compared to other students of the same age, experience and opportunity, to achieve extraordinary accomplishments in one or more culturally valued domains.

(Pfeiffer, 2013b, 2015)

Based on this definition, a child's gifts can be in any culturally valued domain, including academics, athletics, the performing arts, and even civic engagement and community volunteerism. The list of gifts is almost inexhaustible, limited only by what society values and deems important. As the child ages, in most cultures and societies, there is increased opportunity for exposure to a growing number of different domains in which the adolescent can come to excel and gain expertise and even eminence. For example, the young girl who demonstrates precocious mathematical abilities at age 6 years will likely find a wide variety of academic and career domains to excel and become distinguished in as a young adult.

The aforementioned definition reflects the view that the child who is gifted demonstrates a greater likelihood of achieving extraordinary accomplishments in one or more culturally valued domains than others of the same age and opportunity (Pfeiffer, 2013b, 2015). The definition for the *academically gifted student* is conceptually similar to the above definition, but is intentionally more narrowly focused on academics and schooling:

The academically gifted student demonstrates outstanding performance or evidence of potential for outstanding academic performance, when compared with other students of the same age, experience and opportunity…and a thirst to excel in one or more academic domains…the academically gifted student is likely to benefit from special educational programs or resources, especially if they align with their unique profile of abilities and interests.

(Pfeiffer, 2013b, 2015)

The Unmet Academic Needs of Students Who Are Gifted

Frequently, the educational needs of students who are academically gifted are not being met adequately in the classroom or school, and quite often they require specialized programs, services, or activities not ordinarily provided in the regular classroom. This is the primary rationale and justification for assessment of giftedness in the schools—to determine if a student has uncanny intellectual abilities and/or outstanding performance or evidence of potential for outstanding academic performance, frequently indicative of a need for special educational programs or resources not presently available in the regular classroom (Pfeiffer, 2015). Essentially, this is one of the justifications for using the new WJ IV COG and ACH in the assessment of giftedness.

GIFTED AS A SOCIAL CONSTRUCTION

There exists in education of the gifted the belief that giftedness is something real. It is a popular belief among professionals and the lay public. Many practitioners involved in the assessment of IQ in the schools continue to believe that giftedness is real, something concrete, analogous to height, weight, hair color; similar to biomedical conditions such as diabetes, spinal meningitis, or arteriosclerosis. This belief is the hallmark of a "gifted child focus." Many in the gifted field still believe, as Annemarie Roeper (1982) first championed, that the gifted "think, feel and experience" the world differently…giftedness is a greater awareness, a greater sensitivity, and a greater ability to understand and transform perceptions into intellectual and emotional experiences" (p. 21). The position advocated in this chapter is that giftedness is best understood as a socially constructed concept, not anything real in nature like weight, hair color, or diabetes. "Giftedness is not a fact of nature, but, instead, a social construction" (Borland, 2009, p. 237). The concepts of normal, subnormal, and supernormal (gifted) are human inventions, not discoveries of nature. Although we often talk about giftedness as something real, something that children either are or, are not, it is essentially a social construction. It is an invented way of categorizing children using an IQ test or other method (Borland, 2005).

Those who are involved in assessing giftedness using the WJ IV need to appreciate that they are measuring a psychological construct that is a human invention. We need to remember that when we talk about giftedness, we are considering a created concept that can be operationally defined and measured, but not something real in nature. Juvenile diabetes is something real, with clear signs and bio-physiological indicators that differentiate children with and without diabetes. There is a fairly clear distinguishing line (or "joint," as it is called in medicine) that differentiates the child with or without juvenile diabetes. The same is not quite true for giftedness. Those of us who test children in the schools should never forget this important distinction.

The myth that giftedness is something real in nature, and not a social construction has significant implications for the assessment of giftedness and how we interpret test scores on the WJ IV COG and other cognitive ability tests (Kaufman, 2013; Foley Nicpon & Pfeiffer, 2011a, b; Treffinger, 2009). It has huge implications for the rules and regulations we establish when providing programs and services for those students who our cognitive assessments deem as gifted.

TRIPARTITE MODEL OF GIFTEDNESS

The discussion above on giftedness as a social construction and not something that is real leads to the question, "well then, who exactly are the gifted and how should we conceptualize giftedness?" These are important questions which are discussed next. There are many different ways to conceptualize giftedness. There are educational conceptualizations, political conceptualizations, philosophic conceptualizations, and of course, psychometrically driven models. No one conceptualization or model is correct. They are all different ways to view individuals who are in some way special or unique.

The first author of this chapter proposed a model of giftedness called the *tripartite model of giftedness* (Pfeiffer, 2013b, 2015). The model provides three different ways to view students with uncommon, advanced, or exceptionally high ability. The model offers three different ways to assess these three different types of high ability students. The tripartite model incorporates three distinct, but complementary lenses in which one can view giftedness. The three views are three alternative ways to consider assessing and categorizing students of uncommon or high ability.

- Giftedness Through the Lens of High Intelligence
- Giftedness Through the Lens of Outstanding Accomplishments
- Giftedness Through the Lens of Potential to Excel.

The first perspective, the *High Intelligence* viewpoint, is familiar to most readers. Through this first lens, a test such as the new WJ IV COG, Stanford Binet Intelligence Scales-Fifth Edition (SB5; Roid, 2003), or Wechsler Intelligence Scale for Children—Fifth Edition (WISC-V; Wechsler, 2014), or its proxy can be used to assess students who are functioning at a certain level considerably above average intellectually. The criterion for high intelligence giftedness is based on compelling evidence that the student is advanced intellectually when compared to his or her peers on a scientifically sound test of cognitive abilities. This first gifted perspective can follow a general (g) or a multidimensional view of intelligence. The WJ COG (Schrank et al., 2014b) embraces a multidimensional view of intelligence (the Cattell–Horn–Carroll (CHC) abilities model), which other leading IQ test authors and publishers also endorse (Pfeiffer, 2015).

The rationale for programs for gifted individuals based on viewing giftedness through the lens of a high IQ is that students with superior intelligence need and/or are entitled to advanced, intellectually challenging and/or more fast-paced academic material not typically found in the regular classroom. Education of gifted individuals, based on a High Intelligence perspective, consists of a highly accelerated and/or academically advanced and challenging curriculum (Pfeiffer, 2013b, 2015).

The second perspective, the *Outstanding Accomplishments* viewpoint, does not disparage the importance of high intelligence. Many advocates of this second perspective consider an IQ, derived from a test such as the WJ IV COG, useful but not necessarily a central measure when identifying students who may be gifted. This second perspective emphasizes performance in the classroom and on academic tasks as the central or defining characteristic of academic giftedness. According to this second perspective, evidence of academic excellence is the essential characteristic necessary to qualify a student as gifted and to warrant admittance into a gifted program, not high IQ (Pfeiffer, 2013b, 2015).

Psychologists and educators who embrace this second perspective rely on direct academic performance measures to assess students who may be gifted, not tests of intellectual ability that measure cognitive skills but do not necessarily demonstrate direct evidence of "authentic" academic excellence. The new WJ IV ACH (Schrank et al., 2014a) is one measure that could be used to help assess whether a bright student qualifies for the designation within the tripartite model of outstanding accomplishments. The importance of creativity is often emphasized when viewing giftedness through this second lens. Also, the importance of assessing motivation, drive, persistence, and academic passion—clearly nonintellectual factors—is emphasized by many advocates of this alternative way of conceptualizing giftedness (Pfeiffer, 2012, 2013c, 2015). These nonintellectual factors moderate academic accomplishments and talent development of all students, not exclusively students of exceptionally high intellectual ability (Kaufman, 2013; Pfeiffer, 2015).

The rationale for programs for gifted individuals based on an *Outstanding Accomplishments* perspective is that students who excel academically have earned placement in special academic programs because of their outstanding effort and superior classroom accomplishments. Education programs for gifted individuals, based on an *Outstanding Accomplishments* perspective, typically consist of highly enriched and academically challenging curricula (Pfeiffer, 2013b).

The third lens through which the tripartite model conceptualizes giftedness is called, *Potential to Excel*. Some students—for many reasons—have not been provided enough opportunity or the proper intellectual stimulation to develop latent and underdeveloped intellectual and/or academic gifts (Pfeiffer, 2013a,

2013b). Not all students start out on equal footing. Some students from poverty, families in which intellectual and educational activities are neither encouraged nor nurtured in the home, or in which English is not the primary language spoken in the home, students growing up in rural or overcrowded communities where intellectual stimulation and educational opportunities are limited, are all at a distinct disadvantage to develop their gifts (Ford & Whiting, 2008; Nisbett, 2009; Pfeiffer, 2012, 2013b).

Those who advocate for this third perspective view the potential to excel as a defining characteristic of what is termed the "*almost or potentially gifted student*" (Pfeiffer, 2013b, 2015). From this third perspective, the student with high potential to excel is seen as very likely to increase his or her cognitive abilities and academic performance substantially when provided with resources in a special program for gifted students. The assumption is that with time, an encouraging and highly stimulating environment, mentoring, and the proper psycho-educational interventions, these students will actualize their yet unrealized high potential and distinguish themselves from among their peers as gifted. Education for gifted students, based on a *Potential to Excel* perspective, consists of a highly motivating and enriched curriculum that may include compensatory interventions.

It is useful to think of students who are gifted as falling within one or more of the three categories based on the tripartite model. The three categories serve to eliminate much of the acrimony often found when school districts attempt to adopt only one, typically narrowly defined conceptualization of giftedness, most often the high IQ model in which a student needs to score above a predetermined cut-score. The three categories lend themselves to distinct gifted identification/assessment schemes (Pfeiffer, 2002, 2013b, 2015). We will shortly examine the utility of the new WJ IV COG and ACH within the tripartite model.

The first category of giftedness, *students with exceptionally high intelligence*, typically have IQ's in the top 2–5% when compared to other students of the same age.[1] In the early years, these students obtain IQ's of 135–150 or higher, and in middle school when tested "out-of-level" by the regional talent search programs,[2] obtain Scholastic Assessment Test (SAT) or American College Test (ACT) scores in the top 1–2% of the population. It is important to emphasize that there is nothing scientific or exact about a 1% or 2% or 5% threshold or cut-score demarcating those who are gifted from those who are not gifted. If we accept that giftedness is a social construction, not something actually real in nature, then we also can appreciate that where we draw the line separating gifted from not gifted is arbitrary (Pfeiffer, 2012, 2013a, 2013b).

---

1. In many countries the designated cut-score is higher, for example in Singapore and Hong Kong giftedness is defined by intellectual functioning in the top 1%.

2. The talent search model, founded at Johns Hopkins University, is an above-level testing program. Regional talent searches have been conducted at Johns Hopkins, Duke University, and Northwestern University for over 30 years.

The second category of giftedness in the tripartite model, *students with academically outstanding accomplishments*, are academically precocious, do exceptionally well in classroom activities and assignments, enjoy learning and academic challenges, and demonstrate persistence and high motivation when facing academic challenges. When tested, they are found to have above average IQs, most typically 120–130 or higher, enjoy school and schooling, and are highly enthusiastic about learning. They are characteristically among the most capable and top-performing students in the class. Teachers love to have these students in their classroom. These students would be expected to score in the very top range of standardized tests of achievement, such as the new WJ IV ACH. IQ tests such as the WJ IV COG are *not* necessary—although often helpful, in identifying this group of learners who are gifted. Performance in the classroom and on academic tasks and standardized measures are the hallmark of how to identify these academically capable learners.

The third category of giftedness, within the tripartite model, is *students with high potential to excel*. They are often recognized by their teachers and others as bright or quick learners, hardworking, and highly curious about the world around them. They may not test exceptionally well on standardized aptitude or achievement tests. Their IQ's may fall short of established thresholds or cut-scores for gifted consideration, sometimes as low as 110–115. Their achievement test scores and classroom performance also may fall short of the exceptional performance demonstrated by students with *academically outstanding accomplishments*. Yet there is something about these students which conveys latent, partially hidden, and underdeveloped high ability. They are the uncut and unpolished "diamonds-in-the-rough" (Pfeiffer, 2013a, 2013b).

Ratings by teachers on standardized instruments such as the Gifted Rating Scales (GRS; Pfeiffer & Jarosewich, 2003) often pick up characteristics that suggest a youngster with considerable untapped potential. Ipsative analysis using tests such as the WJ IV COG conducted by experienced clinicians can often identify these *students with high potential* (Kaufman, 2009; Pfeiffer, 2015; Silverman, 2013). Experienced teachers also are often quite perceptive and adept in identifying behaviors and attitudes observed in the classroom which indicate that a youngster may have unusually high potential, as yet unrealized or untapped (Pfeiffer, 2015).

The unique challenge with the third category of giftedness, *high potential to excel*, is that it is always a speculative classification. The classification is based on a variety of data sources and contextual information integrated to *infer* that if life circumstances had been different, the student would likely appear as a gifted individual (Pfeiffer, 2013b). This third category of giftedness carries with it a *prediction*. The prediction is that *if* the student is provided comprehensive, intensive, evidence-based psycho-educational interventions—often requiring a home component (think "high-dosage Response to Intervention"), then he or she will ultimately appear indistinguishable, or at least very similar to, any student who is already identified as falling within one of the other two categories of giftedness, *high intelligence* or *academically outstanding accomplishments.* This remains a speculative and untested hypothesis. It is, however, the principle underlying many programs for the gifted designed specifically for students of color and cultural diversity whose test scores do not meet minimum school district criteria for gifted consideration (Ford & Whiting, 2008; Worrell & Erwin, 2011).

In summary, these three categories of students who are gifted constitute different groups of individuals, with different levels and profiles of abilities, and different skill sets and even personality characteristics, although they are not necessarily mutually exclusive. There is, of course, considerable overlap. For example, there are many students with exceptionally high IQs who are academically gifted learners with a burning passion to learn.

There are many extraordinary students with *outstanding academic accomplishments* with IQ's below 120. And there are many students with IQ's at 130 and above who have not distinguished themselves academically in the classroom or on an individually administered test of achievement, for many different reasons.

PURPOSES OF ASSESSMENT FOR GIFTEDNESS

The primary rationale for the identification of giftedness is to recognize and, thus, be able to serve students of exceptional ability or potential who frequently need special educational programs or resources not presently available in the regular classroom. This is the number one purpose for assessment of giftedness in the schools (Pfeiffer, 2012, 2015). However, there are at least eight other purposes for testing a bright student (Pfeiffer, 2013b). When considering the value of the new WJ IV or any other psychological test with students thought to be gifted, it is important to remember that tests can be used for multiple assessment purposes. Below is a list of several other important purposes for assessment of giftedness:

- To provide information to support admission to a special school or gifted program
- To provide data to help better understand the unique strengths and relative weaknesses (asynchronies) of an exceptionally bright child
- To ascertain the degree of giftedness
- To help provide information on growth in areas such as creativity or critical thinking, with implications for curriculum modification, student "fit" within a gifted program, program evaluation, and research
- To assist in the diagnosis of twice exceptionality (e.g., the student who is gifted with a coexisting disability such as Attention Deficit Hyperactivity Disorder, depression, anxiety, or an eating disorder)
- To help identify factors that contribute to or moderate a bright student's underachievement and/or low motivation
- To provide information to parents on homeschooling
- To provide data to help determine appropriate grade placement and/or decisions about grade or course acceleration.

Next, we briefly introduce a set of assessment principles and beliefs that should guide assessment for giftedness. These principles and beliefs are discussed in greater detail in a recent publication by Wiley, *Essentials of Gifted Assessment* (Pfeiffer, 2015).

GUIDING PRINCIPLES AND FUNDAMENTAL BELIEFS ABOUT ASSESSMENT FOR GIFTEDNESS

The topic of guiding principles and fundamental beliefs about assessment for giftedness is, unfortunately, often neglected. It is given short shrift in graduate IQ and psycho-educational assessment courses (Robertson, Pfeiffer, & Taylor, 2011).

Fundamental Beliefs of Assessment for Giftedness

There are at least four fundamental beliefs of assessment for giftedness (Pfeiffer, 2015). The first belief is that giftedness is a useful construct even if giftedness is not something that is real. Earlier in this chapter it was proposed that giftedness is a social construction and that the concepts of intellectually normal, subnormal, and supernormal (or gifted) are human inventions, not discoveries of nature. Giftedness is an invented way of categorizing children (Borland, 2005; Pfeiffer, 2013b). However, even though giftedness is not something that is concrete or real, giftedness is a highly useful concept. The concept of giftedness can serve a constructive purpose—in directing much-needed resources to high ability students in the schools. Also, defining giftedness is valuable in that it encourages research on the talent development of high ability individuals (Pfeiffer, 1980, 2013a, 2013b).

All too often, many very bright students' academic needs are *not* substantially met in the regular classroom. Identification of giftedness is valuable because it directs resources, advanced programs and curricula, to exceptionally bright, "special needs" students. This is one reason why giftedness is a useful concept. Giftedness creates a category of learners in the schools who often require specialized educational interventions to do well, much less thrive and excel.

The second belief is a conviction that we can differentiate high ability and high performing students (i.e., the gifted) from other, less-bright and less accomplished students. Practitioners can differentiate students who are gifted from those who are not by adopting a *high intelligence perspective*. We simply need to establish some IQ or range of IQ's, for example, on multiple measures of cognitive ability falling in the top 2% or 5% when compared to other students of the same age and opportunity. There is no one correct or "true" cut-score or even range that distinguishes gifted from not gifted. The authors of the new WJ IV agree with this view (Branagan, Pfeiffer, Valler, & Burko, 2015). However, this does not mean that a school district cannot justify establishing a set of criteria and decision rules for a gifted categorization based on high intelligence (Pfeiffer, 2013b).

The second type of gifted, the *academically outstanding students*, are scholastically precocious, do exceptionally well in the classroom, enjoy learning, and often demonstrate high persistence and motivation when faced with academic challenges. They are characteristically among the most capable and top-performing students in the class. Practitioners can reliably differentiate students who are gifted from those who are not by adopting this second perspective, as well; the WJ IV ACH can assist in this identification. Those students who consistently are the top two or three performers in their respective classes meet this definition. Schools can decide to be conservative or liberal in the number of high performing students they would like to see with this label and, therefore, select to receive special gifted programs or resources. A school district might decide to be liberal and use a larger "net" in the earlier grades, while employing a more conservative set of criteria for older students in the upper grades (Pfeiffer, 2015).

Finally, we can differentiate students who are gifted from those who are not by viewing those students with the greatest *potential for outstanding accomplishments*. This perspective is the most diagnostically challenging, since we are making predictions about future behavior rather than assessing present ability or performance. The goal here is to identify those students of unusually high potential and promise, the "diamonds-in-the-rough" (Pfeiffer, 2013a, 2013b, 2015). One study reported measuring change over time in a student's profile of abilities using the GRS as a means of identifying the "diamonds-in-the-rough" (Pfeiffer, Kumtepe, & Rosado, 2006).

A third belief is that there are different types/domains and different levels of giftedness. The number of different gifts is limited only by what culture and society value. A student's gifts can be in academics, the performing arts, leadership and student government, athletics, and even community volunteerism. Howard Gardner argues for "multiple intelligences" (Gardner, 1983). The GRS was developed specifically with the goal of assessing up to five different types of gifts: intellectual, academic, artistic, creativity, and leadership (Pfeiffer & Jarosewich, 2003).

There are also different levels or degrees of giftedness. This is equally true whether we are assessing giftedness from a high intelligence, academically exceptional, or potential for outstanding accomplishments perspective (Pfeiffer, 2013b). Students with IQ's above 145, for example, are quite different in a number of educationally relevant and assessable ways from students with IQ's in the 120–130 range.

Francoys Gagné (2005) posits five levels of giftedness: the mildly gifted (top 10%; IQ of approximately 120), moderately gifted (top 1%; IQ approximately 135), highly gifted (145 IQ), exceptionally gifted (155 IQ), and the extremely gifted (165 and above). Terman (1916, p. 79) provided a slightly different four-level classification system when he first published the original Stanford-Binet: 110–120 (superior intelligence), 120–140 (very superior intelligence), and above 140 (near genius or genius).

The fourth and final fundamental belief is that there exist technically adequate tests and procedures to assess for giftedness. There is still considerable work to be done by researchers and test authors to develop new and better psychological tests for the assessments for giftedness. But we are at a point where the field already has many scientifically sound tests that can be used in gifted identification and assessment. Later in this chapter we examine the technical adequacy of the WJ IV.

Key Principles in the Assessment for Giftedness

There are at least six key principles that should guide assessment for giftedness. These principles serve as the foundation for *best practices in gifted identification and assessment* (Pfeiffer, 2013b, 2015).

How We Define Gifted Is Important

How we define giftedness is important. For over 100 years, students who are gifted have been identified by scores obtained on IQ tests (Nisbett, 2009; Pfeiffer, 2002, 2012, 2013b). The majority of states still rely primarily, in some instances almost exclusively, on an IQ (McClain & Pfeiffer, 2012).

Contemporary thinking challenges this view. Past identification models were based on the idea that "being gifted" is something real and permanent; that a student is either gifted (if his/her IQ falls above a certain score), or not gifted. Most authorities today discount this dated view. There is no scientific basis for dichotomizing students into two distinct, mutually exclusive groups, gifted and nongifted (Bronfenbrenner & Ceci, 1994; Ceci & Williams, 1997; Neisser et al., 1996). However, there is an educational and pedagogical justification. Our society should be committed to challenging and inspiring educationally our brightest and most promising students. To this end, it is important to consider how we define giftedness. Because how we define giftedness guides how we go about identifying students who we label as gifted.

Julian Stanley's Talent Search Model (1976) is an example of a different approach to defining giftedness and, therefore, an alternative type of assessment—the above-level "Talent Search" testing program using the SAT or ACT with seventh and eighth graders.

Assessment Should Consider the Types of Available Programs for the Gifted

Assessment for giftedness, when conducted for the purpose of identification, has as its primary goal access to special programs or resources otherwise not available to other students. It should consider the match or congruence between the tests and criteria that we select, and what is expected in terms of the pedagogical approaches, curricular challenges, and learning outcomes available at the local level (Pfeiffer, 2013b). Assessment for gifted identification purposes should never occur in a vacuum independent of context. For example, if the three available options for high school students identified as gifted in a given school district are grade skipping, AP/IB classes, and the opportunity to register for courses offered at a local community college, then it would seem apparent that assessment for giftedness in this school district should include assessment of social maturity.

Ideally, gifted programs should reflect the unique learning needs of high ability students, and should be based on state and national standards and best practices in education for the gifted (Landrum, Callahan, & Shaklee, 2001). There are many different curriculum models and programs for the gifted (Dixon, 2009; Karnes & Bean, 2009; Pfeiffer, 2008; Rakow, 2011). Assessment for giftedness should always consider the type of programs, services and/or resources offered by the school district, and available in the community and online (Pfeiffer, 2015).

Psychometrics Count

When selecting tests for assessing for giftedness, evidence of the reliability, validity, norms, and ceiling effects of each instrument is a critically important consideration (Callahan, Renzulli, Delcourt, & Hertberg-Davis, 2013). We would not want medical doctors to order diagnostic tests of suspect reliability, validity, diagnostic accuracy, or norms, and the same is true for psychological tests—including tests used in assessment for giftedness.

Fortunately, most of the popular and widely-used traditional measures of cognitive ability enjoy strong psychometric qualities, including the WISC-V SB5, and the Differential Ability Scales-2nd Edition (DAS-II; Elliot, 2007). The new WJ IV also enjoys strong reliability, validity, and a representative normative sample. The guiding principle in selecting a test for the assessment of giftedness should be how useful is interpretation of the test score is terms of the specific purposes for and consequences of the testing. Test manuals routinely report evidence based on test content, internal structure, relations to other tests and constructs, and test–criterion relationships. What is infrequently available, however, is evidence based on the consequences of the testing specific to identification of the gifted. No test is valid for all purposes or in all situations (American Educational Research Association [AERA], American Psychological Association [APA], & National Council on Measurement in Education [NCME], 2014).

People, Not Test Scores, Should Make Diagnostic Decisions

The fourth principle is that assessment for giftedness should be guided by sound clinical judgment made by professionals, not based on rigid adherence to test scores. Linda Silverman writes, "…in the diagnosis of giftedness, high stakes decisions frequently are made on the basis of test scores alone (sometimes even group-administered tests)…accurate assessment of giftedness is dependent upon the skill and experience of the examiner in interpreting protocols…" (Silverman, 2013, p. 160). Perhaps surprisingly, David Wechsler was a firm believer of IQ tests as *clinical instruments* (Kaufman, 2013). Nancy Mather and Kevin McGrew, coauthors of the new WJ IV, agree with this view (Branagan et al., 2015).

Multiple Measures

The fifth principle is that there is a diagnostic advantage to consider using multiple measures when assessing any psychological construct, including giftedness (Pfeiffer, 2001b, 2012). When the stakes increase, as they do when making determination of giftedness, it becomes even more imperative to use more than one measure to support the identification process. Assessment of interests, motivation, and self-regulation, passion for learning, frustration tolerance, and comfort with competition should become part of the assessment protocol in middle school and high school (Pfeiffer, 2001b, 2008, 2015).

Recurring Assessment

The sixth principle is that assessment for giftedness in the schools should be a recurring, not one-time, process. Similar to the principle of recurring assessment embraced in the performing arts and in most elite youth sports, students identified as gifted in the schools should be reevaluated at least every two years (Pfeiffer, 2013b). This is consistent with a talent development model (Subotnik, 2009). It is also consistent with a "successive hurdles approach" to assessment, as recommended by Meehl and Rosen (1955) to mitigate against errors of prediction when base rates are low, as they are, by definition, among the gifted.

Students identified as gifted should be reevaluated for evidence that they continue to demonstrate outstanding performance when facing increasingly challenging academic hurdles. Students identified as gifted should also be reevaluated at least every 2 years to determine the extent to which they are benefiting from the special gifted services or programs that they are receiving—essentially an assessment of RTI and program compatibility (Pfeiffer, 2015).

Finally, for those students who are gifted and who are not evidencing expected progress or exceptional performance in the classroom or program for the gifted, the reevaluation should focus on determining the root reasons why—and developing an intervention plan to ameliorate the underlying root causes of the problem, which are likely multidetermined (Pfeiffer, 2013a, 2013b).

Regularly scheduled recurring assessments for giftedness in the schools should also be available to students who may not have been identified as gifted at an earlier time, but who demonstrate recent and compelling evidence that they now should be considered for the program for the gifted. Recurring assessment represents a more valid prediction of future, out-of-school, real-world success (Ackerman, 2013; Kaufman, 2013; Pfeiffer, 2012, 2013b).

THE WJ IV AND ASSESSMENT FOR GIFTEDNESS

Research Using the WJ III with Gifted Students

Over the last hundred years, support surrounding the fundamentals which guide the Woodcock–Johnson's approach to cognitive assessment has grown (Gridley, Norman, Rizza, & Decker, 2003). The WJ closely follows the CHC model of intelligence. As proposed in CHC theory, the WJ assesses an individual's apti-tude across three different levels or strata. At the most fundamental level in CHC theory there exists over 80 "narrow abilities" which fall under 16 "broad abilities" (see Schneider & McGew, 2012 for an update on CHC theory).

The WJ IV COG tests examine performance across seven of these broad abilities, whose names have changed slightly from the WJ III: Comprehension–Knowledge (*Gc*), Fluid Reasoning (*Gf*), Short-Term Working Memory (*Gwm*), Cognitive Processing Speed (*Gs*), Auditory Processing (*Ga*), Long-Term Retrieval (*Glr*), and Visual Processing (*Gv*). Seven of the 10 tests in the standard battery of the WJ IV COG can be administered to obtain a General Intellectual Ability (GIA) score. The GIA is representative of the top-stratum in CHC theory, *g*, or general ability. The GIA is the WJ IV's IQ equivalent.

Research indicates that the WJ III (Woodcock, McGrew, & Mather, 2001) was able to identify relative strengths and weaknesses via intra-ability analyses (Kane, Oakland, & Brand, 2006; Rizza, McIntosh, & McCunn, 2001). Knowing about an individual's differences in specific "narrow abilities" and even "broad abilities" is valuable when developing or modifying a curriculum for students who are gifted (VanTassel-Baska & Brown, 2009). Intra-ability analyses can inform targeted interventions and help identify intellectually or academically outstanding students living with a learning disorder, also known as "twice exceptional," or "2*e*," youth (Foley Nicpon, 2015; Kaufman, 2009; Pfeiffer, 2013c, 2015).

The vast majority of research related to the WJ III's use with individuals who are gifted focused on its significance in the assessment of relative strengths and weaknesses, and identifying underachieving gifted (Kane et al., 2006; Lupart & Pyryt 1996; Mather & Udall, 1985; Rizza et al., 2001). The WJ IV COG and ACH batteries provide in-depth information by exploring specific skills which are not measured by other widely respected assessments (Gridley et al., 2003; Lupart & Pyryt, 1996). For example, the new WJ IV COG measures Auditory Processing (*Ga*), Long-Term Retrieval (*Glr*), and Auditory Memory Span, cog-nitive skills not found in the Stanford Binet. The WJ IV COG has 18 tests (10 of which are included in the standard battery) and the WJ IV ACH has 20 tests (11 of which comprise the standard battery) which an examiner can use to explore a student's strengths and weaknesses. This extensive sampling of cognitive skills can assist the clinician in building a case for giftedness viewed through the lens of "potential to excel" (Pfeiffer, 2013b, 2015).

If the purpose of the assessment is to help identify cognitive strengths and areas of specific weakness within a student who is gifted with learning difficul-ties, the in-depth profile provided by the new WJ IV offers valuable information. In addition to the GIA and broad achievement scores, the WJ IV offers informa-tion at the cluster level (related to broad CHC factors) and test level. Variability can be within or between clusters, and when exploring performance, it is impor-tant to look at both levels. For example, a student who is gifted might perform exceptionally well on Broad Mathematics, but less proficiently on the Broad

Reading cluster. Alternatively, a student's average "Reading" composite score may be inaccurate, due to large variation between the two tests that comprise the cluster. The WJ III offered a view of the discrepancies amongst youth who were learning disabled and gifted (Beck, Spurlock, & Lindsey, 1988), and the new WJ IV likely will prove equally useful. The diagnosis of specific learning disabilities (SLDs) calls for information regarding an individual's academic achievement as well as his/her intellectual ability (American Psychiatric Association, 2013). The new WJ IV batteries can be helpful in these areas, and research has supported its use in the identification of SLD among those who are gifted (Rogers, 2011).

Dombrowski, Kamphaus, and Reynolds (2004) emphasize that the first sign of a SLD is a low score on a norm referenced measure of achievement. In their review of the literature on students who are gifted and those who have SLD, Lovett and Sparks (2013) found that the most common achievement test used in studies to identify giftedness with an SLD was the WJ. The new WJ IV ACH offers three forms parallel in content; each form includes 11 tests in the Standard Battery—ample sampling of academic areas to assist in the diagnosis of the twice exceptional student who is gifted/SLD.

Even when the practitioner is not working with a student who is twice exceptional, information provided by the WJ remains valuable in understanding underachievement among high ability students (Lupart and Pyryt, 1996). According to Nancy Mather and Kevin McGrew, coauthors of the WJ, "the breadth of the test battery and ability to compare Gf (reasoning) and Gc (knowledge) composites with achievement levels" makes it uniquely helpful in identifying "differential patterns of academic and intellectual aptitude" and possible areas of underachievement (Branagan et al., 2015). In other words, customized interventions can be well-informed by the interpretation of performance on the WJ ACH and WJ COG batteries.

Individuals with high levels of intelligence oftentimes show larger differences among narrow and broad abilities than individuals with average or lower levels of cognitive ability (Kane et al., 2006). These greater "peaks and valleys" in a learner who is gifted suggest a wider diversity of potential talents and interests. Higher levels of intelligence afford youngsters more opportunities for differentiated interests (Sampson & Chason, 2008).

In studies where the WJ III was used to assess students purported to be gifted, reports describe the experience for the examinee and examiner as pleasant. Practitioners reported that the students were easy to test using the WJ. These students appreciated the individualized attention they received during WJ assessment and were cooperative. Examiners were able to tell that the students were hungry for learning, and most often found the children to have particular strengths in one or two areas, versus across all abilities (Hanson, 1984).

The literature emphasizes the value of well-researched intellectual assessments, including the WJ, in addressing the multiple purposes for assessment (McIntosh, Dixon, & Pierson, 2012; Pfeiffer, 2001b; Strauss, Sherman, &

Spreen, 2006). The WJ's comprehensive batteries offer considerable information for administrators to corroborate or support a decision to admit the student to an academically accelerated program. Clinicians and educators are able to use the comprehensive clusters and composites offered by the WJ to gain an understanding regarding the degree of giftedness a student is exhibiting, informing academic decisions such as acceleration or grade skipping. Performance on the WJ IV ACH cross-domain clusters, such as broad achievement, offer a general picture of an individual's performance in reading, writing, and mathematics. The academic knowledge cluster informs educators of performance in science, social studies, and humanities. The GIA provided on the WJ IV COG offers insight on an individual's ability to meet the demands of rigorous curricula.

Technical Characteristics of the WJ IV

Earlier we mentioned that several different individual ability tests can be used to identify giftedness through the lens of high intellectual ability. For instance, the WISC-V, SB5, DAS-II, and WJ IV all enjoy strong psychometric properties and have been standardized using representative normative samples.

The WJ IV differentiates among seven different levels of ability, three of the categories (Above Average, Superior, and Very Superior) describe scores beyond the average range. Implications for students who fall within the upper range of Very Superior scores differ from those who fall within the Above Average or Superior ranges. The cutoff scores for these categories provide clear definitions of ability levels, a key principle in the assessment for giftedness.

A recent interview with Nancy Mather and Kevin McGrew provides insight into how the coauthors of the WJ IV view their new test uniquely suited for the assessment for giftedness (Branagan et al., 2015). Mather and McGrew emphasize the value of explicitly incorporating CHC theory as the foundation for development of the WJ IV. Mather emphasizes the value of the new Gf (reasoning)–Gc (knowledge) composite in the identification of giftedness. This composite incorporates the tests which have the highest "g" loadings, and eliminates the impact of processing deficits on estimates of intellectual ability. These authors also remark on the new WJ's breadth of coverage regarding human cognitive abilities. Mather in particular mentions as a unique strength the wide age range (2–90+) on which the test was normed.

McGrew indicates that in addition to CHC theory, the WJ IV is rooted in cognitive neuroscience research. He notes that the WJ IV is particularly useful in identifying students who may be gifted because, "the new WJ IV GIA composite measures a higher level degree of cognitive complexity [than] in the past. Also, it now includes scholastic aptitude clusters that could be used to identify differential patterns of aptitude in certain children (e.g., high math aptitude compared to reading and writing aptitude)" (Branagan et al., 2015).

Some students who are profoundly gifted may not reach a "ceiling" based on the assessment content difficulty. As a result, the test may not allow them to demonstrate their full potential (Pfeiffer, 2001b, 2015). Carvajal, Weaver, and McKnab (1989) mention a particularly important caveat when using the WJ III to compare discrepancies in performance. If individuals are not able to reach a ceiling on a particular test, then it makes it difficult to come to appropriate conclusions regarding their full potential and/or subtle differences between abilities. The reported high ceiling of the WJ IV has standard scores as high as 160; this is a reasonably high ceiling for most exceptionally bright students. In comparison, the WISCIV offers an "Extended Range" of scores for use with exceptionally talented youth ranging to a maximum composite full scale IQ of 192, and the SB5 provides standard scores for FSIQ ranging to 160 (Pfeiffer, 2015; Roid, 2003; Zhu, Clayton, Weiss, & Gabel, 2008).

Technically adequate assessment for giftedness must exist in order to assess talent appropriately. In an article exploring identification and definitional issues in the gifted field, the first author found that experts were hesitant about the reliability and construct validity of most tests used in gifted identification (Pfeiffer, 2001b). Fortunately, the WJ IV assessment battery enjoys strong psychometric support. The normative sample ranged from 2 to 90+ years. A unique strength of the WJ IV is that the cognitive, achievement, and new oral language batteries are all normed using the same standardization sample. Co-normed batteries may offer a psychometric advantage to practitioners exploring discrepancies between areas of cognitive ability and academic achievement.

In terms of reliability and validity, the WJ IV COG clusters all have a median reliability across all age groups of 0.90 or higher, except visual processing (0.86). The WJ IV ACH clusters exhibit a median reliability across all age groups ranging from 0.92 to 0.99. Support regarding the content, construct, concurrent, and predictive validity are provided in the technical manual as well, and summarized in Chapter 1. The WJ IV normative sample includes several clinical validity groups, including a group of students identified as gifted (N=53). The clinical validity group of gifted individuals consisted of students between 5 and 9 years of age (M=8.1, SD=1.1; 54.7% male), who were currently participating in high ability or gifted and talented school curricula, or currently receiving services for the gifted (McGrew, LaForte, & Schrank, 2014, pp. 230, 232). Although the size of the sample is small, the authors are commended for including a "clinical sample" of students considered to be gifted.

The limited use of timed tests and lack of time bonuses on the WJ IV assessments is consistent with current theories regarding the factors that have the highest loadings on g. In the instances where timed tests are used, their purpose is more focused on rate versus level of production (Gridley et al., 2003). The use of a strategically weighted composite of test scores is aligned with the most contemporary views of general intelligence, making the GIA a uniquely informed representation of g (Carroll, 1993). This differs from the more traditional arithmetic mean employed when calculating FSIQ by most other intelligence assessments.

A Practitioner's Perspective: The New WJ IV and Assessment for Giftedness

It is impossible for any test to assess a student's abilities across every culturally valued domain. In our examination of the WJ IV's utility for assessment for giftedness, we focus on the intellectual and academic domains identified within the tripartite model of giftedness. The WJ IV maps well onto multidimensional conceptualizations of giftedness, including the tripartite model. The tripartite model's first type of giftedness explores an individual's ability from the *high intelligence* perspective. The WJ IV COG provides a GIA score representative of *g*. The GIA has a strong correlation with the FSIQ provided by other measures and is understood as the gold-standard by which we judge intellectual ability (Pfeiffer, 2013a; Zhu et al., 2008).

The second type of giftedness that the tripartite model asserts is the *academically outstanding student*. These youngsters demonstrate their prowess through exceptional scholastic ability, extraordinary classroom performance, and a thirst for knowledge. Often, these traits are accompanied by diligent persistence and motivation in the face of challenging academic tasks. The WJ IV ACH provides data in these areas, and can assist in quantifying the level of academic exceptionality.

There are instances when a seemingly bright student does not meet criteria for either of the first two types of giftedness. The skilled clinician has the opportunity to apply the third lens through which the tripartite model conceptualizes giftedness, the *Potential to Excel—the almost/potentially gifted student*. While decisions regarding the first two types can have clear diagnostic criteria, the difficulty with this third category is that it is a speculative classification. This decision is influenced by two important factors: "might environmental factors have limited the development or expression of this youngster's talents?" and "will evidence-based psycho-educational interventions promote this youngster's relative standing comparable to a student who is identified as gifted in either of the first two categories?" Analysis using the WJ assessment batteries can help to answer these questions. The WJ IV COG includes a wide variety of cognitive tasks grouped within clusters (Intellectual Ability, Scholastic Aptitude, CHC Factors, Narrow Ability Clusters, and Clinical Clusters) that provide alternatives for the practitioner, offering multiple ways to operationalize "potential to excel." There is no one correct or best diagnostic cluster that foretells for all students high likelihood of giftedness. In our clinical experience, this varies by student.

The WJ III encouraged qualitative analysis of test performance through a "test session observation checklist" incorporated on the cover of the cognitive and achievement test records. The WJ IV continues this procedure and additionally integrates brief qualitative assessments for 10 (Letter-Word Identification, Applied Problems, Spelling, Passage Comprehension, Calculation, Writing Samples, Word Attack, Sentence Reading Fluency, Math Facts Fluency, and Sentence Writing Fluency) of the 20 academic achievement tests. The qualitative assessments are simple and quick, checkbox-style remarks of observations during the subtest administration. This encourages the examiner to share information regarding the examinee's ease of completion, care taken in giving responses, speed, and accuracy.

Several of the revisions in the Cognitive, Achievement, and Oral Language batteries have implications for assessing whether a student is appropriate for academic programming for gifted individuals. Regarding overall content, the majority of the subtests which appear from the WJ III have remained consistent. There have been very few changes regarding the broad clusters of intelligence and ability which are called upon. Of the 42 subtests found in the standard and extended assessment batteries of the WJ III, 33 subtests reappear, albeit occasionally with different names. Two tests from the WJ III Diagnostic Supplement (Woodcock, McGrew, Mather, & Schrank, 2003) have moved into the WJ IV COG and WJ IV ACH batteries.

The WJ IV ACH battery has three new tests (Oral Reading, Reading Recall, and Word Reading Fluency). The new oral language battery contains nine English tests, four of which were seen on the WJ III ACH battery and three of which were seen on the cognitive battery. Two subtests, Segmentation and Sentence Repetition, are new. The WJ IV COG battery has four new subtests: Verbal Attention, Letter-Pattern Matching, Phonological Processing, and Nonword Repetition. Discussion of the achievement battery and specific subtests on the cognitive battery are covered in other chapters. The important points in terms of assessment of the gifted are that the tests are well-conceived and anchored in current cognitive science theory, attractive and engaging, and have solid psychometric qualities.

Tests presenting with a high cultural loading or cultural bias may mask the expressed ability of a student who may be gifted. One of the test authors, Nancy Mather, notes that test development intentionally sought to screen and eliminate any items which displayed cultural bias. She also points out that the new scale includes three Spanish tests on the oral language battery (moved from the diagnostic supplement) (Branagan et al., 2015). Two subtests in the WJ IV ACH battery demonstrate increased ethnic, gender, and age diversity through the individuals depicted in the images used (Passage Comprehension, Applied Problems).

Each of the Science, Social Studies, and Humanities tests of the WJ IV ACH battery (formerly the Academic Knowledge subtests) has incorporated considerably more diverse topics within each subject area. This should increase their appeal to high ability students. The Science test now spans content covering anatomy, biology, chemistry, geology, medicine, and physics. The Social Studies test contains more items regarding history, economics, geography, government, and psychology. As before, the Humanities test covers literature, art, and music, yet with more depth. While students of average ability may not be impacted by these changes, this allows high ability students with particular interests or advanced knowledge in certain domains to more comprehensively demonstrate their knowledge of those topics which would have been overlooked on previous versions.

Low ceilings can hinder an individual's ability to demonstrate his/her full potential. On timed subtests of the WJ IV, several additional items have been added, raising the ceiling. On others, the progression of difficulty has changed. Items often are of higher complexity and increased difficulty levels from what was seen on the WJ III. This has been done through increased use of advanced language, more open-ended questions, and having complex tasks appear sooner. On the WJ IV ACH, these tests include: Letter-Word Identification, Sentence Reading Fluency, Passage Comprehension, Picture Vocabulary, Oral Comprehension, Editing, Reading Vocabulary, Number Series, Science, and Humanities. On the WJ IV COG, Oral Vocabulary, Number-Pattern Matching, Object-Number Sequencing, Pair Cancellation, and Phonological Processing-Substitution, all have more items. Additionally, on the Reading Vocabulary test, more "correct" options are shared for responses, allowing for youngsters who have particularly expansive vocabularies more options with which to score points.

CONCLUSION

Assessment for giftedness is much more than administering an IQ test and determining whether or not the obtained score exceeds a pre-set criterion demarcating giftedness. In this chapter, we advocate that giftedness is a social construction, not something that is real. We also introduce the tripartite model (Pfeiffer, 2013b, 2015), which provides three different perspectives, or ways, to view giftedness—students with uncommon, advanced, or exceptional ability, aptitude, and/or achievement in culturally valued domains. Each of the three different perspectives within the tripartite model offers slightly different approaches to assessment for giftedness as well as educational programming for those who are identified as gifted.

A second point that we advocated in this chapter is that there are multiple purposes for assessment for giftedness. Identifying students who are gifted is the most frequent and most familiar purpose when testing students of high ability or potential. However, there are other reasons for undertaking this type of assessment, including: providing information to support admission to a special school or program, obtaining data to understand better the unique strengths and relative weaknesses (asynchronies) of an exceptionally bright student, ascertaining the degree of giftedness, providing information to assist in the diagnosis of twice exceptionality, obtaining test data to inform parents on homeschooling, and providing information to help determine appropriate grade placement and/or decisions about grade or course acceleration. When thinking about the new WJ IV and students who may be gifted, all of these different purposes must be considered. It is not enough to consider only how well the new WJ identifies students with high IQ scores.

Our review of the new WJ indicates the following: First, research and clinical experience support the use of the WJ III with high ability students. The WJ III COG (Woodcock et al., 2001) enjoyed wide popularity as an individually administered test of cognitive abilities in identification of the gifted (Pfeiffer, 2013b, 2015). Second, it is too early to know with any certainty whether the new WJ IV will continue to enjoy wide use among practitioners in assessment for giftedness. Our prediction is that it will, but only time will ultimately indicate if this proves to be the case. Third, it is impossible to predict with any certainty what the research will indicate over the next 5–10 years in terms of how well the new WJ works when used for assessment for giftedness. It is our hope that a number of researchers undertake well-designed research studies to explore the validity and utility of the new WJ IV with different cohorts of high ability students. There are so many fascinating and yet unanswered questions about the usefulness of individual (and group) tests of cognitive ability with those individuals who are gifted. We hope that this chapter serves in even a small way to encourage future investigators to pose important research questions using the WJ IV with samples of individuals who may be gifted.

REFERENCES

Ackerman, P. L. (2013). Nonsense, common sense, and science of expert performance: Talent and individual differences. http://dx.doi.org/10.1016/j.intell.2013.04.009.

American Educational Research Association (AERA), American Psychological Association (APA), & National Council on Measurement in Education (NCME), (2014). *Standards for educational and psychological testing*. Washington, DC: American Educational Research Association.

American Psychiatric Association (APA), (2013). *Diagnostic and statistical manual of mental disorders: DSM-5*. Washington, DC: American Psychiatric Association.

Beck, F. W., Spurlock, D. W., & Lindsey, J. L. (1988). The WISC—R and the Woodcock–Johnson Tests of Achievement: Correlations for exceptional children. *Perceptual and Motor Skills*, *67*, 587–590. http://dx.doi.org/10.2466/pms.1988.67.2.577.

Borland, J. H. (2005). Gifted education without gifted children: The case for no conception of giftedness. In R. J. Sternberg & J. E. Davidson (Eds.), *Conceptions of giftedness* (2nd ed., pp. 1–19). New York, NY: Cambridge University Press.

Borland, J. H. (2009). Myth 2: The gifted constitute 3% to 5% of the population. Moreover, giftedness equals high IQ, which is a stable measure of aptitude: Spinal tap psychometrics in gifted education. *Gifted Child Quarterly*, *53*, 236–238.

Branagan, A., Pfeiffer, S., Valler, E., & Burko, J. (2015). Voices of the test authors: A survey of the authors of the leading tests used in gifted assessment.

Bronfenbrenner, U., & Ceci, S. J. (1994). Nature-nurture reconceptualized in developmental perspective: a bioecological model. *Psychological Review*, *101*, 568–586. http://dx.doi.org/10.1037/0033-295X.101.4.568.

Callahan, C. M., Renzulli, J. S., Delcourt, M. A. B., & Hertberg-Davis, H. L. (2013). Considerations for identification of gifted and talented students. In C. M. Callahan & H. L. Hertberg-Davis (Eds.), *Fundamentals of gifted education* (pp. 83–91). NY: Routledge.

Carroll, J. B. (1993). *Human cognitive abilities*. New York, NY: Cambridge University Books.

Carvajal, H., Weaver, K. A., & McKnab, P. (1989). Relationships between scores of gifted children on the Stanford–Binet IV and Woodcock Johnson Tests of Achievement. *Diagnostique, 14,* 241–246.

Cattell, J. (1906). *A statistical study of American men of science.* Whitefish, MT: Kessinger Publishing.

Ceci, S. J., & Williams, W. M. (1997). Are Americans becoming more or less alike? Trends in race, class, and ability differences in intelligence. *American Psychologist, 52,* 1226–1235.

Dai, D. Y. (2010). *The nature and nurture of giftedness.* New York, NY: Teachers College Press.

Dixon, F. A. (2009). *Programs and services for gifted secondary students: A guide to recommended practices.* Waco, TX: Prufrock Press.

Dombrowski, S. C., Kamphaus, R. W., & Reynolds, C. R. (2004). After the Demise of the discrepancy: Proposed learning disabilities diagnostic criteria. *Professional Psychology: Research and Practice, 35,* 364–372. http://dx.doi.org/10.1037/0735-7028.35.4.364.

Elliot, C. D. (2007). *Differential ability scales, 2nd edition: Administration and scoring manual.* San Antonio, TX: Pearson Assessment.

Foley Nicpon, M. (2015). The social and emotional development of twice-exceptional children. In M. Neihart, S. I. Pfeiffer, & T. Cross (Eds.), *The social and emotional development of gifted children. What do we know?.* Waco, TX: Prufrock Press.

Foley Nicpon, M., & Pfeiffer, S. I. (2011a). High ability students: New ways to conceptualize giftedness and provide psychological services in the schools. *Journal of Applied School Psychology, 27,* 293–305.

Foley Nicpon, M., & Pfeiffer, S. I. (Eds.) (2011b). Psycho-educational services and the gifted. Special issue of Journal of Applied School Psychology, 27.

Ford, D. Y., & Whiting, G. W. (2008). Recurring and retaining underrepresented gifted students. In S. I. Pfeiffer (Ed.), *Handbook of giftedness* (pp. 293–308). New York, NY: Springer.

Gagné, F. (2005). From gifts to talents: The DMGT as a developmental model. In R. J. Sternberg & J. E. Davidson (Eds.), *Conceptions of giftedness* (2nd ed., pp. 98–120). Cambridge, UK: Cambridge University Press.

Galton, F. (1869). *Hereditary genius: An inquiry into its laws and consequences.* London: Macmillan.

Gardner, H. (1983). *Frames of mind.* New York, NY: Basic Books.

Gridley, B. E., Norman, K. A., Rizza, M. G., & Decker, S. L. (2003). Assessment of gifted children with the Woodcock–Johnson III. In F. A. Schrank & D. P. Flanagan (Eds.), *WJ III clinical use and interpretation: Scientist-practitioner perspectives* (pp. 285–317). http://dx.doi.org/10.1016/B978-012628982-4/50010-6.

Hanson, I. (1984). A comparison between parent identification of young bright children and subsequent testing. *Roeper Review: A Journal on Gifted Education, 7,* 44–55. http://dx.doi.org/10.1080/02783198409552844.

Kane, H. D., Oakland, T. D., & Brand, C. R. (2006). Differentiation at higher levels of cognitive ability: Evidence from the United States. *The Journal of Genetic Psychology: Research and Theory on Human Development, 167,* 327–341. http://dx.doi.org/10.3200/GNTP.167.3.327-341.

Karnes, F. A., & Bean, S. M. (Eds.). (2009). *Methods and materials for teaching the gifted* (3rd ed.). Waco, TX: Prufrock Press, Inc.

Kaufman, A. S. (2009). *IQ testing 101.* New York: Springer.

Kaufman, A. S. (2013). Intelligent testing with Wechsler's Fourth Editions: Perspectives on the Weiss et al. studies and the eight commentaries. *Journal of Psychoeducational Assessment, 31,* 224–234.

Landrum, M. S., Callahan, C. M., & Shaklee, B. D. (Eds.), (2001). *Aiming for excellence: Gifted program standards.* Waco, TX: Prufrock Press.

Lovett, B. J., & Sparks, R. L. (2013). The identification and performance of gifted students with learning disability diagnoses: A quantitative synthesis. *Journal of Learning Disabilities, 46,* 304–316. http://dx.doi.org/10.1177/0022219411421810.

Lupart, J. L., & Pyryt, M. C. (1996). "Hidden gifted" students: Underachiever prevalence and profile. *Journal for the Education of the Gifted, 20,* 36–53.

Mather, N., & Udall, A. J. (1985). The identification of gifted underachievers using the Woodcock–Johnson Psycho-Educational Battery. *Roeper Review: A Journal on Gifted Education, 8,* 54–56. http://dx.doi.org/10.1080/02783198509552931.

McClain, M. C., & Pfeiffer, S. I. (2012). Identification of gifted students in the U.S. today: A look at state definitions, policies, and practices. *Journal of Applied School Psychology, 28,* 59–88.

McGrew, K. S., LaForte, E. M., & Schrank, F. A. (2014). *Technical manual. Woodcock–Johnson IV.* Rolling Meadows, IL: Riverside.

McIntosh, D. E., Dixon, F. A., & Pierson, E. E. (2012). Use of intelligence tests in the identification of giftedness. In D. P. Flanagan & P. L. Harrison (Eds.), *Co ntemporary intellectual assessment: Theories, tests, and issues* (3rd ed., pp. 623–642). New York, N Y: Guilford Press.

Meehl, P. E., & Rosen, A. (1955). Antecedent probability and the efficiency of psychometric signs, patterns, or cutting scores. *Psychological Bulletin, 52,* 194–216.

Mönks, F. J., Heller, K. A., & Passow, H. (2000). The study of giftedness: Reflections on where we are and where we are going. In K. A. Heller, F. J. Mönks, R. J. Sternberg, & R. F. Subotnik (Eds.), *International Handbook of giftedness and talent* (2nd ed., pp. 839–863). Oxford, UK: Elssevier Science.

Neisser, U., Boodoo, G., Bouchard, T. J., Boykin, A. W., Brody, N., Ceci, S. J., et al. (1996). Intelligence: Knowns and unknowns. *American Psychologist, 51,* 77–101.

Nisbett, R. E. (2009). *Intelligence and how to get it.* New York, NY: Norton.

Pfeiffer, S. I. (1980). The influence of diagnostic labeling on special education placement decisions. *Psychology in the Schools, 17,* 346–350.

Pfeiffer, S. I. (2001a). Emotional intelligence: Popular but elusive construct. *Roeper Review, 23,* 138–142.

Pfeiffer, S. I. (2001b). Professional psychology and the gifted: Emerging practice opportunities. *Professional Psychology: Research and Practice, 32,* 175–180.

Pfeiffer, S. I. (2002). Identifying gifted and talented students: Recurring issues and promising solutions. *Journal of Applied School Psychology, 19,* 31–50.

Pfeiffer, S. I. (2003). Challenges and opportunities for students who are gifted: What the experts say. *Gifted Child Quarterly, 47,* 161–169.

Pfeiffer, S. I. (2008). *Handbook of giftedness in children.* New York, NY: Springer.

Pfeiffer, S. I. (2012). Current perspectives on the identification and assessment of gifted students. *Journal of Psychoeducational Assessment, 30,* 3–9.

Pfeiffer, S. I. (2013a). Lessons learned from working with high ability students. *Gifted Education International, 29,* 86–97.

Pfeiffer, S. I. (2013b). *Serving the gifted: Evidence-based clinical and psychoeducational practice.* New York, NY: Routledge.

Pfeiffer, S. I. (2013c). Treating the clinical problems of gifted children. In L. Grossman & S. Walfish (Eds.), *Translating research into practice: A desk reference for practicing mental health professionals* (pp. 57–63). New York, NY: Springer Publishers.

Pfeiffer, S. I. (2015). *Essentials of gifted assessment.* Hoboken, NJ: Wiley.

Pfeiffer, S. I., & Jarosewich, T. (2003). *The gifted rating scales.* San Antonio, TX: Pearson Assessment.

Pfeiffer, S. I., Kumtepe, A., & Rosado, J. (2006). Gifted identification: Measuring change in a student's profile of abilities using the Gifted Rating Scales. *The School Psychologist*, *60*, 106–111.

Plomin, R., & Spinath, F. M. (2004). Intelligence: Genetics, genes, and genomics. *Journal of Personality and Social Psychology*, *86*, 112–129.

Rakow, S. (2011). *Educating gifted students in middle school*. Waco, TX: Prufrock Press.

Rizza, M. G., McIntosh, D. E., & McCunn, A. (2001). Profile analysis of the Woodcock–Johnson III Tests of Cognitive Abilities with gifted students. *Psychology in the Schools*, *38*, 447–455. http://dx.doi.org/10.1002/pits.1033.

Robertson, S. G., Pfeiffer, S. I., & Taylor, N. (2011). Serving the gifted: A national survey of school psychologists. *Psychology in the Schools*, *48*, 786–799.

Robinson, A., & Clinkenbeard, P. R. (2008). History of giftedness: Perspectives from the past presage modern scholarship. In S. I. Pfeiffer (Ed.), *Handbook of giftedness in children* (pp. 13–31). New York, NY: Springer.

Roeper, A. (1982). How the gifted cope with their emotions. *Roeper Review*, *5*, 21–24.

Rogers, K. B. (2011). Thinking smart about twice exceptional learners: Steps for finding them and strategies for catering to the appropriately. In C. Wormald & W. Vialle (Eds.), *Dual exceptionality* (pp. 57–70). Wollongong, Australia: AAEGT.

Roid, G. H. (2003). *Stanford-Binet intelligence scales* (5th ed.). Itasca, IL: Riverside.

Sampson, J. P., & Chason, A. K. (2008). Helping gifted and talented adolescents and young adults make informed and careful career choices. In S. I. Pfeiffer (Ed.), *Handbook of giftedness in children* (pp. 327–346). New York, NY: Springer.

Schrank, F. A., Mather, N., & McGrew, K. S. (2014a). *Woodcock–Johnson IV tests of achievement*. Rolling Meadows, IL: Riverside.

Schrank, F. A., McGrew, K. S., & Mather, N. (2014b). *Woodcock–Johnson IV tests of cognitive abilities*. Rolling Meadows, IL: Riverside.

Schneider, W. J., & McGrew, K. S. (2012). The Cattell–Horn–Carroll model of intelligence. In D. P. Flanagan & P. L. Harrison (Eds.), *Contemporary intellectual assessment: Theories, tests, and issues* (3rd ed., pp. 99–144). New York, NY: Guilford Press.

Silverman, L. K. (2013). *Giftedness 101*. New York, NY: Springer.

Stanley, J. C. (1976). The case for extreme educational acceleration of intellectually brilliant youths. *Gifted Child Quarterly*, *20*, 66–75.

Strauss, E., Sherman, E. S., & Spreen, O. (2006). *A compendium of neuropsychological tests: Administration, norms, and commentary* (3rd ed.). New York, NY: Oxford University Press.

Subotnik, R. F. (2009). Developmental transitions in giftedness and talent: Adolescence into adulthood. In F. D. Horowitz, R. F. Subotnik, & D. J. Matthews (Eds.), *The development of giftedness and talent across the lifespan* (pp. 155–170). Washington, DC: American Psychological Association.

Subotnik, R. F., Olszewski-Kubilius, & Worrell, F. C. (2011). Rethinking giftedness and gifted education: A proposed direction forward based on psychological science. *Psychological Science in the Public Interest*, *12*, 3–54.

Terman, L. M. (1916). *The measurement of intelligence*. Boston, MA: Houghton-Mifflin.

Terman, L. M. (1925). *Genetic studies of genius. Mental and physical characteristics of a thousand gifted children* (Vol. I). Stanford, CA: Stanford University Press.

Terman, L. M., & Oden, M. H. (1951). The Stanford studies of the gifted. In P. Witty (Ed.), *The gifted child*. Boston, MA: D. C. Heath.

Special Issue: Demythologizing gifted education. Treffinger, D. J. (Ed.), (2009). *Gifted Child Quarterly* (53, pp. 229–288).

VanTassel-Baska, J., & Brown, E. F. (2009). An analysis of gifted education curriculum models. In F. A. Karnes & S. M. Bean (Eds.), *Methods and materials for teaching the gifted* (pp. 75–106) (3rd ed.). Waco, TX: Prufrock Press.

Wechsler, D. (2014). *Wechsler intelligence scale for children* (5th ed.). Bloomington, MN: Pearson.

Whipple, G. M. (Ed.). (1924). *The education of gifted children (23rd Yearbook, Part I). National Society for the Study of Education.* Bloomington, IL: Public School Publishing Company.

Woodcock, R. W., McGrew, K. S., & Mather, N. (2001). *Woodcock–Johnson III.* Itasca, IL: Riverside.

Woodcock, R. W., McGrew, K. S., Mather, N., & Schrank, F. A. (2003). *The diagnostic supplement to the Woodcock–Johnson III tests of cognitive abilities.* Itasca, IL: Riverside Publishing.

Worrell, F. C., & Erwin, J. O. (2011). Best practices in identifying students in gifted and talented education programs. *Journal of Applied School Psychology, 27,* 319–340.

Zhu, J., Clayton, T., Weiss, L., & Gabel, A. (2008). Wechsler intelligence scale for children-fourth edition technical report #7: WISC-IV extended.

Chapter 12

Assessment of Culturally and Linguistically Diverse Individuals with the Woodcock–Johnson IV

Samuel O. Ortiz, Juan A. Ortiz and Rosemary I. Devine
Department of Psychology, St. John's University, Jamaica, NY, USA

INTRODUCTION

Much like its predecessors, the Woodcock–Johnson IV (WJ IV; Schrank, McGrew, & Mather, 2014a) represents perhaps the most technically sophisticated psychometric batteries available to practitioners and offers a wide range of measurement of cognitive, academic, and linguistic abilities. Fair and equitable assessment of individuals from culturally and linguistically diverse populations with the WJ IV, however, continues to require knowledge and comprehension of the many ways varying levels of English language proficiency and acculturative knowledge acquisition can negatively impact test scores and attenuate overall performance.

For various reasons, the manner in which these issues must be understood and accounted for in testing individuals from diverse backgrounds, particularly English language learners (ELLs) also continues to be poorly understood in research and general practice (American Educational Research Association, American Psychological Association, & National Council on Measurement and Evaluation [AERA, APA, & NCME], 2014; Lohman, Korb, & Lakin, 2008; Ortiz, Ochoa, & Dynda, 2012). Assessment efforts with diverse populations are inhibited by several factors including the relative lack of accepted guidelines, conflicting and incoherent research findings, misconceptions regarding test bias, and minimal opportunity for supervised training experiences (Ortiz, 2014; Rhodes, Ochoa, & Ortiz, 2005). Similar to any other ability test, the use of the WJ IV with culturally and linguistically diverse populations requires a thorough understanding of the characteristics of the norming sample and the nature of the tests that comprise the battery relative to an individual examinee's level of

WJ IV Clinical Use and Interpretation. DOI: http://dx.doi.org/10.1016/B978-0-12-802076-0.00013-X
317

developmental English language proficiency and opportunity for the acquisition of acculturative knowledge. These variables are highly related and together have a differential, but systematic and predictable effect on subtest performance for individuals from diverse backgrounds (Cormier, McGrew, & Ysseldyke, 2014). This type of empirical evidence serves as the foundation for the Culture-Language Interpretive Matrix (C-LIM; Flanagan, Ortiz, & Alfonso, 2013; Ortiz & Melo, 2015), which offers practitioners a systematic approach to evaluating the impact of these two important variables on the validity of obtained test scores. Combined with current recommendations for best practices, the C-LIM offers a practical, defensible, and evidence-based approach to evaluating cognitive abilities in culturally and linguistically diverse populations that may be employed by any evaluator using the WJ IV.

The purpose of this chapter is to describe the manner in which cultural and linguistic differences may affect use of the WJ IV with individuals from diverse backgrounds. This is accomplished first by discussing why various traditional approaches to evaluation using standardized tests (including the WJ IV) do not automatically result in valid test scores (Ortiz, 2014). A framework for best practices is then presented that is designed to be responsive to practitioner needs relative to efficient use of time and resources, practicality, legal defensibility, and applicability to all practitioners (Mpofu & Ortiz, 2009; Ortiz & Melo, 2015). Within this framework, use of the C-LIM and its application specifically to the WJ IV Tests of Cognitive Abilities (WJ IV COG; Schrank, McGrew, & Mather, 2014b) will be explained as a systematic method for evaluating the impact of cultural and linguistic variables on the validity of test scores (Flanagan et al., 2013). It should be noted that the most important issue in the use of the WJ IV COG (or any other cognitive battery for that matter) with individuals from diverse backgrounds is the concept of validity. Results that are not valid cannot be interpreted or assigned meaning. Only results that are deemed valid can be defensibly interpreted and ascribed clinical significance. Thus, one of the main reasons and purposes of an evaluation, to determine the presence of a disability, rests entirely on being able to evaluate, establish, and conclude that the results, on which such a diagnosis or conclusion are made, are valid. When confidence can be placed in the validity of test results and when combined with other sources of data and information, an appropriate context is created that is likely to lead to nondiscriminatory conclusions and decisions (Ortiz, 2014).

The Defensibility and Validity of Traditional Assessment Approaches

The cultural, racial, and ethnic diversity of the US population continues to broaden and transform the characteristics of individuals on whom testing is conducted. It is becoming increasingly more likely that any evaluator practicing anywhere will encounter a situation where the examinee's background involves significant developmental differences in experiences and language that may render him/her inadequately represented by a test's norming sample and question the validity of the use of the test or the obtained results. For example, with respect to differences in cultural experiences, Hispanic students enrolled in public schools from pre-K through 12th grade are reaching historical highs and now encompass almost 25% of the population (US Census Bureau, 2014). Moreover, as a group, Hispanics make up one-quarter of 18- to 24-year-old students enrolled in 2-year colleges (US Census Bureau). Being Hispanic also means there is a possibility of the presence of a language other than English (i.e., Spanish) spoken in the home. Statistics indicate that in 2010, there were 37 million Spanish speakers in the United States representing 13% of the overall population (US Census Bureau). For evaluators, the concerns are apparent—to what extent might these differences in culture and language have an effect on test results that render them invalid as indicators of true ability?

This quandary is usually addressed when a test is normed on a sample of appropriate size and stratified along these types of differences, as is typically accomplished by consideration of factors such as population frequency, sex, age, geographic location, socioeconomic status, and race. But race is not the same as culture and does not reliably capture the effect related to the incidental acquisition of acculturative or mainstream knowledge. Moreover, the absence of English language proficiency within the list of stratification variables represents a glaring omission and casts significant doubt on the adequacy of the sample and its appropriateness for diverse individuals, particularly ELLs. Any individual from any race could well be fully assimilated into the mainstream and possess age-expected acculturative knowledge. And in the absence of any consideration of language proficiency differences in the norming sample, practitioners may well feel cornered and unsure how to proceed.

When working with monolingual English speakers with monocultural experiences rooted in the US mainstream, issues related to differences in acculturative learning experiences and developmental language proficiency are effectively controlled via psychometric and sampling procedures that obviate the need for practitioners to be cognizant of them. The same is not true when working with individuals from diverse backgrounds wherein these same differences become absolutely central to understanding the nature of obtained test results and require direct and deliberate consideration (Ortiz, 2014). The difficulty in suddenly having to become aware of these issues that do not typically enter into the consciousness of test users means that evaluators often resort to a host of procedures that lack any validity, but which may "feel" right. For example, one thought may be to turn to the use of a translator/interpreter to administer a test or employ a nonverbal test (Lohman et al., 2008). Or if the evaluator is already bilingual, the usual notion is to use a native language test (Alvarado, 1999), assuming one is available, but similar problems exist with the norming samples (Ortiz, 2014). Yet others feel compelled to alter or modify the testing and test procedures in efforts to help the examinee perform better, but which disregards the fact that doing so undermines the psychometric properties of the test rendering all results invalid (Ortiz, 2014). Still other evaluators seem to believe that the matter is only one of finding the "right" test and administering it. Ochoa, Riccio, Jimenez, Garcia de Alba, and Sines (2004) note that such evaluators are not merely selecting the "wrong" tests, but that in reality there is no "right" one (Ortiz et al., 2012). What all of these actions have accomplished, either by accident or intent, is to permit evaluators to overlook the actual impact that cultural and linguistic differences have on test performance and whether that impact is significant enough to undermine the presumption of score validity. The following section describes briefly the extent to which use of any of the various methods described previously have an evidentiary basis to support them in being able to establish the validity of the test scores and obtained results.

Modified or Altered Methods of Evaluation

One of the more common approaches to the testing of individuals from diverse backgrounds is to modify or alter the test administration or scoring so as to provide a better opportunity for the examinee to exhibit his/her true abilities. This procedure is often referred to as "testing the limits" and may include such changes to the testing protocol as skipping seemingly inappropriate items, explaining or mediating the task prior to administration of actual items, repeating test instructions sometimes in the examinee's native language, accepting responses provided by the examinee irrespective of the language in which it is given, and either extending or eliminating time limits altogether. It seems clear that such modifications are intended to assist the examinee in being able to perform at a level that would be a good and true estimate of his/her actual ability. Some tests provide guidance on such modifications in their various manuals and some expressly permit various alterations. Of course, any alteration of the testing process constitutes a violation of the standardization procedures and, psychometrically speaking, effectively invalidates the test scores and completely precludes any interpretation or the assignment of meaning to them. Most likely it is for this reason that the authors of the WJ IV do not permit acceptance of responses provided in any language other than English.

Another common modification or alteration to testing procedures involves the use of a translator/interpreter for administration. Not only does having someone translate the instructions of a test help in overcoming the language barrier that may exist, it also provides apparent compliance with testing mandates (Individuals with Disabilities Education Act [IDEA], 2004) that may require native language evaluation for individuals who are limited English proficient. Unfortunately, this too also represents a violation of standardization protocol and would similarly undermine test score validity. There is evidence that the presence of a third party in the testing situation (even just an observer) undermines the validity of testing (CPTA, 2007). Moreover, this would be true even in cases where the interpreter might be very highly trained and experienced. The problem is simply that tests are not usually normed in this manner and once again violation of the standardized test protocol introduces error into the testing process. Such error cannot be quantified and thus the extent to which this or any other modification or alteration aided or hindered the performance of the examinee cannot be ascertained. Ultimately, this means that results obtained from testing whenever any modification or alteration is employed, simply cannot be defended as valid.

This is not to say, however, that evaluators should always avoid alterations or modifications to the testing process. Indeed, such procedures are very useful when the goal of evaluation is to derive qualitative information that may assist in understanding performance better or aid in making educational decisions regarding instruction and intervention. The ability to observe individual behavior from a common context, evaluate learning propensity on various tasks, and analyze the nature and process of errors, are all extremely valuable pursuits. Thus, a recommended procedure for evaluators would be to administer all tests in a standardized manner first, something that might later permit interpretation if the results can be assessed as being valid, and then utilize any modifications or alterations that are viewed as possibly being helpful in understanding the performance of the individual further or which may also help to inform the questions and concerns that formed the referral. In short, there is no empirical evidence that the modification or alteration of the testing protocol can reliably produce results that may be considered valid. As such, these procedures must be viewed as secondary and only ancillary procedures in testing where the focus is not on test scores but on qualitative evaluation of performance.

Nonverbal Methods of Evaluation

At first glance, the use of nonverbal methods of evaluation seem to be the perfect panacea to address concerns regarding language differences in examinees. This is, unfortunately, not the case and it is more appropriate to view this approach as being "language-reduced" assessment rather than nonverbal as it is impossible to remove language completely (or its function—communication) from the testing process (Mpofu & Ortiz, 2009).

If it were possible to test individuals without any type or form of language or communication, we might well be able to test most anything rather easily including inanimate objects, let alone animate ones. The reality is that it is impossible to administer any standardized test of ability (including the WJ IV) to an examinee without there being some type of communication between the evaluator and the examinee. Otherwise, how would an examinee know what's a right answer, what's a wrong answer, when to start, when to stop, and when to work quickly? The purpose of spoken language is to facilitate this type of communication and when it is excluded from testing, it is merely replaced with a gestural language that facilitates the very same thing—communication. Thus, administration of a language-reduced test entirely via gestures or pantomime is only free of spoken language, not all language, and the communication function remains completely the same. Teaching an examinee the meaning of various gestures used in the administration of a test is akin to teaching the examinee a new language—one that that the examinee will now have in common with the evaluator to permit administration of the test. Of course, in what manner the meaning of the gestures is communicated to the examinee without the use of spoken or some other language is another issue and it should not be presumed that nonverbal gestures are universal. For example, touching one's nose with a forefinger in the United States is the gesture for "correct" when playing charades, but it has the meaning of "me" when used in Japan.

Other problems remain in the use of language-reduced tests including the fact that the reduction of language used for administration does not reduce concomitantly the cultural knowledge required by or used in the various tasks on the test. Moreover, by definition, language-reduced tests intentionally omit measurement of language-related abilities. As evaluators continue to assess individual strengths and weaknesses, use of language-reduced tests may need to be heavily supplemented to ensure measurement of the full range of cognitive abilities, particularly those with a strong association to core academic skills such as reading and writing (i.e., *Ga*—auditory processing and *Gc*—crystallized intelligence). This may be why language-reduced tests tend to have poor predictive validity as related to academic achievement (Lohman et al., 2008). Beyond these problems, language-reduced tests continue to remain subject to the same concerns regarding norming sample stratification and representation as plague verbal tests.

In summary, language-reduced tests are likely to be every bit as helpful in evaluation of diverse individuals as verbally laden tests when the focus of measurement is primarily on nonverbal type abilities (e.g., *Gv*—visual processing or *Gf*—nonverbal fluid reasoning). In this sense, such tests may even provide good estimates of true ability in those specific areas, but not necessarily in all cases. Even if valid, it would not be prudent to assume that an examinee's other abilities should be comparable and thus estimates of global functioning derived from language-reduced tests should not be used in place of broader indices of intelligence or ability (e.g., General Intellectual Ability [GIA] or Full Scale Intelligence Quotient [FSIQ]). Thus, language-reduced tests appear to have some validity (Suzuki & Aronson, 2005), but it is limited to nonverbal abilities and thus they are not a whole or completely satisfactory solution with respect to fairly measuring the abilities of diverse individuals and may not provide any advantage over using a more comprehensive test that includes measures of the same nonverbal abilities (e.g., WJ IV).

Dominant Language Evaluation: Native Language Assessment

The approach to evaluation of diverse individuals generally refers to assessment that is conducted in whole or part in the individual's native language. There is immense intuitive appeal to native language evaluation for a variety of reasons including the attempt to address test bias issues, provide compliance with legal mandates, and apparent removal of all language barriers to testing. On its face, native language evaluation seems the most appropriate and ideal approach for the evaluation of ELLs, if not for one important fact—ELLs are, by definition, bilingual and therefore are not monolingual speakers and cannot be fairly compared to them (Grosjean, 1989). When students enroll in the US public school system, they are expected ultimately to learn and achieve in English and what they may have learned in their native language is considered, unfortunately, as largely irrelevant. Thus, tests that may be considered as valid for the purpose of evaluating ELLs in the United States must account for the circumstantial bilingualism of such students rather than treat them as monolingual speakers of either the native language or English. At present, there are no standardized tests that not only account for the presence of two languages in US ELLs, but also consider the variability in proficiency in each one as a function of the type and nature of formal instruction received in each language, if any.

The concept of testing language dominance exemplifies the erroneous idea that it is permissible to ignore whatever development might exist in the nondominant language and to dismiss the factors that led to its current level of development in favor of testing in the dominant language. This fallacy in this assumption is based on the mistaken notion that the dominant language is at a level of proficiency that is comparable to other age and grade-based peers and that, as such, will automatically generate test scores that are valid measures of ability (Brown, 2008). The concept of dominance ensures no such conclusions and in reality only provides an estimate as to which language is better developed for the individual, not whether the individual is developing age or grade appropriate abilities. An individual may well be better developed in his/her native language (when entering the school system), but that does not mean his/her proficiency should be considered age appropriate, particularly in cases where the individual may have encountered impediments to normal development (e.g., lack of appropriate language interaction and stimulation, exposure to violence or trauma, neglect due to being orphaned, or residing in refugee camps). For the same individual, 3 years after entering the school system at the kindergarten level, might find him/her to be dominant in English. Yet, once again, it would be a serious mistake to consider him/her as having proficiency and development in English comparable to other 8-year-old, native English-speaking peers for the purposes of testing. Few question the wisdom of attempting to compare the mental abilities of a 3-year-old to those of an 8-year-old, but fewer still recognize the same problem when comparing an 8-year-old ELL with only 3 years of English language development to native English-speaking peers who have had fully 8 years' worth of development. Such are the limitations with using dominance to guide the language of testing without considering the actual developmental proficiency of the individual.

Other problems remain when native language evaluation is considered, whether or not it is chosen on the basis of language dominance. First, evaluation in the native language implies a need for the evaluator to be bilingual so as to be able to administer and score the test. This means that native language evaluation is not an option for the vast majority of evaluators who do not possess the level of proficiency or training required to do so. Second, whether a test is designed to evaluate only in the native language, or with some combination of the native language and English (i.e., presumably "bilingual"), the norming samples, as described, do not provide adequate representation, if any, on the critical variables that are related to differential development. That is, whereas developmental changes and expectations are adjusted by having age-based norms, the same is not true for differences in developmental language proficiency and acculturative learning experiences. Until these variables are somehow included in the stratification and creation of norming samples, neither native language or English language tests can provide a fair and nondiscriminatory basis for measuring and comparing performance of ELLs. And third, problems with current norming samples might be obviated by results from empirical investigations on the performance of ELLs when tested in the native language. Unfortunately, native language assessment with US bilinguals represents a largely untapped and unexplored area of research. There is precious little empirical evidence by which an evaluator might consider patterns of performance for ELLs when they are tested via native language instruments. Without such evidence, the evaluator is left without any guidance regarding what might be appropriate procedures, fair expectations of performance, or other basic standards of practice. In summary, whereas native language assessment has apparent face validity, the reality appears to be that there is no reason to believe that test results generated from this approach are automatically valid or even better than what is obtained from other approaches. Moreover, without an established empirical foundation, there is no way to evaluate the validity of test scores that may be generated via this method.

Dominant Language Evaluation: English Language Assessment

It may seem strange to consider testing an ELL in English since the very purpose of the other methods and approaches already discussed is in direct response to the obvious problems related to administering one of the many widely available and popular standardized tests of ability in English. This approach is far more common than one may think when considering that the current directory of bilingual psychologists compiled by the National Association of School Psychologists (NASP) contains only about 900 names (of which approximately two-thirds are Spanish speakers) in comparison to total membership listed at 24,945 (NASP, 2015). A simple calculation indicates that only about 3–4% of school psychologists identify as such, albeit inclusion on the list does not automatically imply actual competency in native language evaluation. Only two states currently provide bilingual certification at the state level (Illinois and New York) and only one professional organization offers something comparable (California Association of School Psychologists) which means that bilingual competency is based primarily on assessment of one's own skills without any specific point of reference (Sotelo-Dynega, Geddes, Luhrs, & Teague, 2009).

Nevertheless, given the paucity of evaluators who have the requisite ability to administer a test in a language other than English, particularly in a language that is not Spanish, it is not surprising to see that the vast majority of evaluations conducted on US ELLs is likely to be performed by an evaluator who has little choice but to evaluate in English. In addition, employing the concept of testing in the dominant language will mean that when the individual is considered to be more proficient in English than in his/her native language, a common result after a few years of instruction in English only (Thomas & Collier, 2002) and the basis for the withdrawal of English as a Second Language (ESL) services, testing will be performed in English often with little consideration of native language development. The concept of dominance has even found its way implicitly into legal guidelines as current regulations in the IDEA (2004) require some sort of native language evaluation only if the student is still considered "limited English proficient." Once no longer so designated, any ELL may then be legally tested in English only without any necessary requirement for consideration of the native language. Much as was discussed in native language evaluation, such issues continue to highlight an ignorance of the fact that once an ELL, always an ELL, and that no individual suddenly ceases to be bilingual simply because he/she has become English dominant. Or put another way, evaluating bilingual individuals as if they were actually monolingual effectively ignores the nature of their development in language as a whole.

The problems outlined with native language evaluation are equally applicable to testing in English. As before, being dominant in English does not imply age-appropriate development in English or that formal instruction in English has been sufficient to promote age-appropriate development particularly in relation to expectations for higher grade level achievement (i.e., development of Cognitive Academic Language Proficiency[CALP]). In addition, the potential barrier to effective communication and comprehension presented by a language difference and the very same concerns with the use of tests with norming samples drawn primarily on monolingual English speakers are issues that speak against the validity of this method with ELLs. One difference, however, is that evaluation conducted in English does not require that the evaluator speak any other language, albeit there is an implicit requirement regarding competency, including direct training and knowledge in nondiscriminatory assessment techniques and the manner in which cultural and linguistic factors affect test performance. The fact that such competency has not been codified into specific legal regulations and that there are very few restrictions on what constitutes best practice in evaluation of bilingual evaluation, means that assessments will continue to be conducted predominantly in English despite all the inherent problems.

There is another, more significant difference, however, that alters the landscape of evaluation and although it tended to undermine native language evaluation, it does not do so for English language evaluation. And that is that ELLs have an extensive history, spanning a full century, of being tested in English (Naglieri, 2015). Despite the apparent ignorance of the problems already outlined here, or potentially the outright dismissal of them altogether, testing non-native English speakers is a very old idea and has been extremely well explored such that there exists a great deal of empirical evidence on how ELLs perform on tests when they are evaluated in English (Ortiz & Flanagan, 2013; Rhodes et al., 2005). In the current era of evidence-based practice, application of the principles demonstrated within this comprehensive body of literature provides a mechanism by which appropriate activities may be guided and upon which best practices recommendations for evaluation may be established. Moreover, as will be discussed in the following sections, taken collectively, such research provides a reasonable and systematic method for being able to assess the validity of test scores generated via the administration of ability tests in English to bilinguals and English learners alike that can thus permit defensible interpretation and assignment of meaning to the obtained results.

A Recommended Best Practices Approach

Use of the WJ IV in the evaluation of ELLs represents a very narrow issue in that there is a host of other considerations that play a role in nondiscriminatory assessment including assessing the suitability of the test itself for a particular evaluation, determining expectations of performance relative to the developmental factors in the examinee's background, and establishing a comprehensive context within which test scores may be fairly and properly interpreted. Such issues, while of central importance to effective practice, are beyond the scope of this chapter and the reader is referred to other sources for a more detailed discussion (Ortiz, 2014; Rhodes et al., 2005). Nevertheless, when the evaluator considers the use of standardized testing, it becomes necessary to integrate the various approaches and issues discussed in the previous sections of this chapter to help delineate an approach that will result in a method that is practical, systematic, defensible, and evidence-based. To that end, the following section describes a recommended best practices approach to evaluation when standardized tests are to be employed and when the examinee is not a native English speaker. Note that the approach is intended to be equally applicable to any individual for whom English is not the native language, irrespective of current proficiency or dominance in either one.

When standardized tests are considered as part of an evaluation for an examinee who is an ELL, the fundamental obstacle to nondiscriminatory assessment and interpretation rests on the issue of test score validity, specifically the construct validity of the abilities that were targets for measurement. If an examiner is unable to ascertain whether the "thing" that was supposed to be measured by a particular test was in fact the same "thing" that was actually measured, scores must be rendered as invalid because they may not reflect the individual's true ability in the domain in which they were tested. Indeed, the common refrain in testing of ELLs boils this issue down to the simple question of "difference versus disorder." That is, do the test scores reflect performance that is primarily attributable to cultural and linguistic factors which are not the variables that were intended to be measured (and thus scores are invalid) or to an actual intrinsic lack of ability on the dimension that was the target of the measurement (wherein scores are believed to be valid). Until and unless the question of test score validity can be addressed directly, there is no way that quantitative results from standardized testing can be used or interpreted in a manner that is defensible. To do so, even when imploring hollow warnings to the effect that "all scores should be interpreted with extreme caution," is a violation of the psychometric foundations of standardized testing that does not permit interpretation and would render any such conclusions as specious and mere guesses.

Beyond the issue of validity, other considerations bear upon the manner in which testing might be incorporated into a full individual evaluation. Some of these have already been noted; for example, the presence or absence of a research base against which performance may be compared fairly and the need for competency in another language, but to these may be added additional ones, including the reason and purpose of the evaluation, a need to maximize time, effort, and other resources, and compliance with various legal prescriptions. This all seems rather complicated at first; however, their integration into a single framework may be accomplished by application of some basic principles of measurement as well as general logic.

Consider first that the most common reason for and purpose of psychological testing is to identify deficits in cognitive or other abilities. For example, evaluations conducted in schools are invariably driven by IDEA (2004) standards that require the identification of a disability as one criterion that may create eligibility for special education services. Whatever the case, deficits or disabilities are typically supported by the presence of low scores, not those that are generally average or higher. Moreover, on standardized tests of ability, validity is actually more of a concern for low scores than it is for average or higher scores. This is because the psychometric structure of such tests largely eliminates the possibility that performance measured to be in the average range or higher occurred spuriously or by chance. Since the tests are not multiple choice, it is extremely improbable that an examinee could guess his/her way to an average score. As such, test performances in the average range are likely to be reliable and valid, at least to the extent that it does not suggest intrinsic deficits or potential disability. Conversely, test performances that are below average may well be due to factors other than lack of ability. An examinee who is fatigued, unmotivated, hungry, does not understand English well or at all, older or younger than reported, has sensory-motor or perceptual difficulties, and the like, may obtain a score that suggests or indicates a possible deficit but which is actually attributable to one or more of these mitigating factors. These premises permit a simple conclusion—that testing an examinee in just one language (either in English or the native language) means that it is possible to determine with significant confidence that the results indicate no support for the presence of a deficit (i.e., when all test scores are average or higher and thus likely to be valid enough to reject notions of disability). In addition, it cannot yet be determined definitively if the results indicate the presence of a deficit even when some or all test scores are below the average range because low scores require additional information and considerations to confirm their validity.

It should be noted that all test scores that fall below average, whether they were obtained via testing in the native language or in English only, must be validated. As previously discussed, low scores are subject to the influence of a variety of attenuating factors and thus they cannot be presumed to be automatically valid. This is why adherence to the standardized testing protocol is so important—by keeping all extraneous and potentially confounding variables out of the testing situation, we can be more confident that low scores are not the result of poor rapport, improper administration and scoring, health concerns, and so forth. Note, however, that maintaining standardization does not control for the influence of cultural and linguistic differences as defined previously. Thus, when low scores are obtained from the use of standardized tests on ELLs, they must be assessed and evaluated in some manner. It is at this point that testing in English versus the native language begins to provide an advantage in practice.

On the basis of problems with norming samples and other concerns, test scores derived from the administration of tests in the native language cannot be accepted as valid and there is no empirical basis on which test performance might be evaluated or compared fairly. On the other hand, despite similar problems, test scores derived from the administration of tests administered in English can be examined for construct validity and may be compared fairly to the performance of other ELLs because of the existence of an extensive body of research on point. For this reason, the advantage of using standardized tests and administering them in English appears to be a better choice for beginning an evaluation of an ELL. Consider that testing in this manner means that virtually any evaluator can participate in and initiate the assessment because it does not require fluency in another language. Moreover, should all the scores from testing in English happen to fall within the average range or higher, the evaluator may already have sufficient information to conclude that the examinee does not have a cognitive-based deficit and therefore does not have a disability. Only the latter of these can be accomplished when testing is conducted initially in the native language and thus it becomes an obstacle to 96–97% of all evaluators.

Beginning the testing process via the use of English language instruments does not, however, completely permit identification of a disability since low scores obtained from such testing necessarily require some sort of independent evaluation. In other words, how can an evaluator be sure that the low scores were not simply the result of the presence of cultural and linguistic differences as is common in the case of ELLs? Application of the research on the test performance of ELLs (as is accomplished via application of the C-LIM) provides only an initial indication regarding whether the low scores were more likely to be attributable to cultural and linguistic factors rather than something else. This type of analysis also provides legal compliance in that it addresses the exclusionary clause related to identification of Specific Learning Disability (SLD). But the C-LIM is not intended to and cannot verify if the low scores are actually attributable to intrinsic deficits. The C-LIM merely excludes cultural and linguistic factors, but it does not exclude the potential influence of other variables that may have attenuated performance. Again, this highlights the importance of maintaining full standardization in test administration, but it also speaks to the need to provide additional information that can provide some type of independent confirmation regarding whether the low scores do in fact indicate the presence of a deficit.

The need to provide additional evidence of validity to bolster the low scores obtained from testing in English means that it becomes necessary to reexamine the areas noted as potential weaknesses using the native language for cross-linguistic confirmation. There has long been a general consensus among various disciplines that, barring traumatic brain injury or insult, cognitive deficits that exist in one language must also exist in the other (Bialystok, 1991; Paradis, 2014). As such, if there is an intrinsic problem in a particular area of cognitive processing when measured using one language, it will remain evident even when that process is measured using a different language. That is, cognitive deficits are largely language independent. Therefore, if there are areas in which an examinee obtained low scores when tested in English, it is reasonable to reevaluate those same areas using the native language so as to ensure that language differences or limited comprehension did not significantly affect performance. In this manner, it becomes necessary to test an individual in English and the native language in cases where there are areas of suspected deficit which creates the need to provide cross-linguistic confirmation of actual lack of ability. Unlike before, where testing in one language permitted conclusions regarding the *absence* of a disability, testing in two languages is a necessary component of testing for the purpose of being able to defend conclusions regarding the *presence* of a disability. And when an evaluator is reasonably certain that all other feasible variables that may have attenuated test performance were either controlled or not present, native language testing services to confirm that the deficits measured when tested in English are not language-specific and do in fact exist in both languages.

Given all of the preceding considerations, it seems logical that the most practical and defensible approach in using standardized tests with ELLs would be to *begin* testing by using an English administration first and without any sort of modification or alteration. If all test scores indicate that the examinee has no weaknesses, that all abilities fall within the average or higher range (strengths), it is extremely unlikely that the individual has a cognitive-based disability. This conclusion may even render further testing and evaluation as unnecessary when it speaks directly to the nature of the suspected disability that prompted the referral. However, if some or all scores from testing using English administration indicate areas of potential weakness (intrinsic deficits), then it is necessary to *continue* the process of evaluation and to retest the areas found to be suggestive of weaknesses using the native language so as to cross-validate the scores as indicating true and real deficits.

It is important to note further that follow-up evaluation of weak areas using the native language need not be concerned directly or only with quantitative data or scores. The purpose is to provide evidence of difficulty that serves to confirm the low scores from testing conducted in English—scores that have already been determined via the C-LIM to be valid and not due to cultural and linguistic differences. Thus, cross-linguistic confirmation can be accomplished via observation of test performance on the same tasks, analysis of errors, and even via a process or other type of qualitative approach that can all generate information that supports the validity of the original scores obtained from English language administration. Quantitative data, in the form of test scores, may also be helpful but should not be the only or primary focus of the follow up. Remember that native language scores cannot be independently validated. Thus, they gain significance only in relation to what they demonstrate relative to the scores obtained from testing in English. Additional, and perhaps even more valuable, information relevant to supporting the validity of low test scores obtained in English comes from attempts to provide more qualitative data culled from native language evaluation. In short, native language scores are helpful, but not the primary objective. And for this reason, use of the same or similar tests is acceptable as practice effects may well be diagnostic for the purposes of disability evaluations as would be alterations or modifications (including the use of an interpreter) to the testing process.

Best Practices in Evaluation of ELLs with the WJ IV COG

The WJ IV COG provides evaluators with an exceptional tool for evaluation that can examine an extremely wide range of cognitive abilities. When coupled with the co-normed oral language and academic batteries, the range of abilities that can be measured is truly impressive and surpasses all comparable instruments. It is, of course, administered only in English and no longer permits acceptance of responses in a different language Given the preceding framework for best practices in evaluating ELLs, and the rationale for beginning an evaluation using an English language tool, the WJ IV COG remains an ideal first choice battery even when the focus of the evaluation will be on an examinee who is not a native English speaker.

The framework for best practices highlighted the need to adhere strictly to administration and scoring protocol and this remains true even when using the WJ IV COG. Evaluators should have developed sufficient competency in scoring and administration prior to its use in actual practice. Other than this, any evaluation of an ELL may begin in exactly the same way as it would with a native English speaker and does not need to be repeated here. The main difference between evaluation of a native English speaker and an ELL with the WJ

IV COG relates to the need to establish validity of the test scores in light of the presence of cultural and linguistic differences. This procedure is unnecessary when working with native English speakers due to the absence of such differences as well as the norming sample stratification and standardized protocol that control for variation due to other sources. For ELLs, the influence of cultural and linguistic difference on test performance is neither considered nor controlled via stratification or standardization and thus requires a special procedure. This is the purpose of the C-LIM.

Use of the C-LIM with the WJ IV COG

The C-LIM (Flanagan et al., 2013; Ortiz & Melo, 2015) provides evaluators with a practical, systematic method for applying research on ELL test performance to evaluate the extent to which cultural and linguistic variables may have affected the validity of test scores obtained from administration with English language tests. Its development and research foundations are far too broad in scope to permit detailed discussion within this chapter and the reader is referred to the original sources for such information. Its use and application with the WJ IV COG is presented with the assumption that the reader of this chapter is already familiar with the basic principles and guidelines for its use as well as its purpose and rationale.

Recently, the C-LIM was integrated with other Cross-Battery Assessment (XBA) tools (i.e., Data Management, Interpretation, and Analyses [DMIA] and Pattern of Strengths and Weaknesses Analyzer [PSW-A]) into a single software program known as Cross-Battery Assessment Software System (X-BASS; Ortiz, Flanagan, & Alfonso, 2015). Information regarding the abilities measured by the WJ IV COG and Woodcock–Johnson IV Tests of Oral Language (WJ IV OL; Schrank, Mather, & McGrew, 2014a), as well as the cultural and linguistic classifications of tests from these batteries, are available in X-BASS and utilized for the purposes of analysis within the C-LIM module. The classifications are presented in Figure 12.1 and Figure 12.2, respectively, and are based largely on previous classifications (Flanagan, Ortiz, & Alfonso, 2007) associated with previous WJ instruments. Because the WJ IV COG and OL are new batteries, current research is only now underway to assist in establishing the most appropriate classifications relative to ELL test performance. Tests that were carried over to the WJ IV COG from its predecessor will likely retain the same classifications, although recent research has suggested some changes, primarily to tests that tend to fall between the extremes (Cormier et al., 2014). Current research is the basis on which final classifications in the C-LIM are ultimately made as it relies primarily on mean subtest values, particularly when the samples used represent verifiable ELL status, lack of any identified disability, and inclusion of a wide range of English proficiency levels.

Unfortunately, these necessary conditions for establishing and comparing fairly the average and expected performance of an individual ELL to the

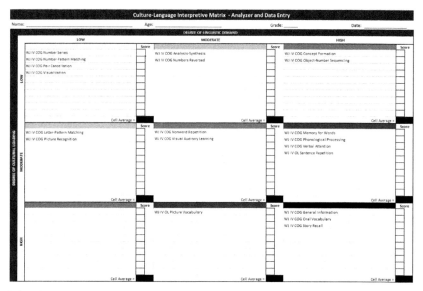

FIGURE 12.1   Culture-Language Classifications of the WJ IV Tests of Cognitive Abilities.

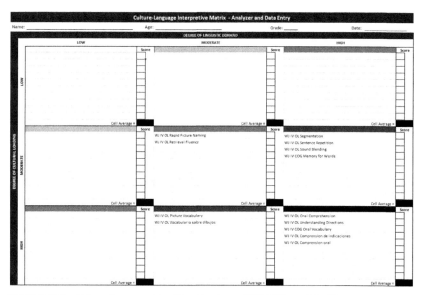

FIGURE 12.2   Culture-Language Test Classifications of WJ IV Tests of Oral Language.

aggregate performance of other similar ELLs are frequently violated and thus result in studies of no value in advancing an understanding of ELL performance or in guiding practice (cf., Styck & Watkins, 2013, 2014). Note also that the C-LIM does not provide any classifications for academic tests and therefore there is no corresponding classification for the Woodcock–Johnson IV Tests of Achievement (WJ IV ACH; Schrank, Mather, & McGrew, 2014b). Part of the reason for not including such tests is that academic skills tasks tend to be measures of manifest ability as opposed to latent abilities typically measured by cognitive ability tests. In addition, measures of academic skills in English are in effect reliable and valid measures of what an ELL can do in English. Such measures do not, of course, indicate what the individual can do in his/her native language, and more importantly they provide no such information regarding the reasons why the scores may be low. And last, to provide an equivalent guide for academic subtests as is provided for cognitive subtests would require an entirely different research base given the direct interaction between formal education and academic skill acquisition that is of less concern in the measurement of cognitive abilities.

Users of the WJ IV COG (and OL) only need enter the test scores into the appropriate cells within the C-LIM and then examine the overall pattern. The C-LIM is intentionally arranged in a manner that examines the influence of cultural and linguistic factors on test performance and compares the individual's results with those established by research. In general, when the individual's scores tend to decline overall, it suggests that test performance was primarily moderated by the presence of cultural and linguistic factors. And when the magnitude of the obtained scores falls within the range that is expected as a function of the degree to which the examinee's cultural and linguistic development differs from that of the norming sample of the test (i.e., primarily native English speakers), it also suggests that the examinee's abilities are commensurate with the abilities of other ELLs with comparable backgrounds who are not disabled and of average ability or higher. The C-LIM provides a variety of graphs that permit visual inspection of the pattern of results and which greatly facilitate interpretation and decision making regarding the validity of the obtained test scores, some of which are presented later in a sample case study.

If the analysis of WJ IV COG and OL test scores indicates that cultural and linguistic influences were the primary reasons why test performance declined, the results should be deemed invalid. That is, they are more likely to be reflections of "difference" than suggestive of "disorder." At this point, there is little reason to continue with any further testing, let alone native language evaluation, because the data indicate the absence of any deficit on which notions of disability could be defended and performance is comparable to the average performance of other ELLs with similar cultural and linguistic backgrounds and development. Thus, when the purpose of evaluation is to identify the presence of a disability, there is little need to conduct further testing as the current test scores have adequately addressed the question. Additional considerations and decisions specific to working with an ELL will arise only when results from English language administrations are deemed to be valid; that is, the overall pattern of scores does not decline as a function of cultural and linguistic factors or when the magnitude of the scores do not reach the levels that would be expected and as established by research with other ELLs of similar cultural and linguistic backgrounds and development. In such cases, it cannot be said that cultural and linguistic factors are primarily responsible for the test score pattern and thus the scores may be deemed to be valid and reasonable estimates of true ability and functioning, with the notable exception of Crystallized Intelligence (*Gc*) which is discussed later. When testing in English results in scores that are deemed to be valid and where there is at least one or more area of identified weakness, the need for follow-up evaluation in the native language presents some new and unique challenges with the WJ IV COG and OL.

Follow Up, Native Language Evaluation with the WJ IV COG and OL

Unlike the previous versions of the WJ, the WJ IV currently has no corresponding Spanish language battery, such as the Batería III Woodcock–Munoz (Batería III; Woodcock, Munoz-Sandoval, McGrew, & Mather, 2004). This means that the easiest option for follow-up evaluation in the native language (using the same tests as used for the English language administration) is not feasible because there is no corresponding native language test and the structure of the WJ IV is not the same as that of the Batería III. This tends to complicate matters somewhat in that the elegant parallel correspondence of the Woodcock–Johnson III (WJ III; Woodcock, McGrew, & Mather, 2001) and Batería III no longer exists. This leaves two options—use a translator/interpreter to administer the same WJ IV COG and OL tests in the native language or adapt the Batería III in the best possible manner to provide relatively equivalent measures of the same broad CHC domains as found on the WJ IV COG and OL.

The former solution is likely to be employed by evaluators who are not bilingual and who may not have access to a bilingual evaluator; albeit, a bilingual evaluator could very well translate the administration instructions on his/her own without the need for an interpreter/translator. There are, of course, significant psychometric problems inherent in on-the-fly translations of tests in English, even when the translator/interpreter is very well trained. But as noted previously, the point of follow-up testing is not to generate valid scores, so much as it is to generate valid data and information that confirms areas of weakness found in English. Therefore, it is neither important nor troublesome to administer the WJ IV COG and OL in this manner when doing so for the expressed and single purpose of cross-linguistic confirmation. It is the generation of qualitative information that is of concern and there are no limitations or restrictions against how such data may be obtained as long as the information is relevant to assessing whether suspected areas of weakness found in English continue to be observed as areas of weakness when evaluated in the native language—irrespective of the method of assessment. Test scores may also provide useful quantitative data, but they should not be viewed as the main or only goal in follow-up evaluation.

The other option, one that can only be employed by evaluators with proficiency in Spanish is to use the Batería III and align measurement with the WJ

IV COG and OL as closely as possible. For example, although they are based on slightly different norming samples, the Fluid Reasoning (*Gf*) domain of the WJ IV COG (which is comprised of the tests, Concept Formation and Number Series) can be reasonably reevaluated using the *Gf* tests from the Batería III (Formación de Conceptos and Analisís-Síntesis). The limitation here, of course, apart from the norming sample, is that the clusters only overlap by one test, not both. For the same reasons that use of a translator/interpreter need not be overly concerned with psychometric equivalency, so too does use of an alternative *Gf* composite from the Batería III provide a clinically sufficient proxy for measurement of the same domain on the WJ IV COG.

Additional Test Score Validity Considerations

Once follow-up testing in the native language is conducted, it becomes necessary to reassess the validity of the obtained results. After all, that was the specific purpose for the follow up; to provide cross-linguistic confirmation of the validity of the original results obtained in English. The possible combinations regarding the nature of results from follow-up evaluation as compared to the original test results creates numerous permutations that necessitate additional procedures that assist in ensuring construct validity across all domains.

It was discussed previously that validity is more of a concern with scores that fall below average than for scores that are average or higher. The same can be said for test results obtained from testing in English or the native language. It has also been argued in the preceding section that in cases where an area of weakness found in English is confirmed as an area of weakness from native language testing, the examiner may confidently conclude that it is likely to be a true deficit for the individual. But what would be the proper conclusion if the native language score not only turns out to be higher than the English language score, but also falls within the average range or higher? On the basis of the psychometric principles and logic used to create the recommended best practices approach coupled with the cross-linguistic requirement of cognitive ability and processing deficits, the native language score would have to be considered valid and the English language score declared invalid. Because the C-LIM only investigates validity relative to cultural and linguistic factors, low scores that suggest areas of weakness may be low due to other extraneous variables. Thus, when native language testing results in a score that measures the same or substantially equivalent domain as that measured in English, it stands to reason that the English language score was invalid—for reasons other than culture and language—but invalid nonetheless. Interpretation of the examinee's ability in a domain where this occurs must then be based on the native language score not the original English language one given that by virtue of falling within the average range, it is not a result that likely occurred by chance and is therefore, valid, and clearly not indicative of a deficit.

Conversely, when the native language score falls below the average range (i.e., suggests an area of deficit), then it merely confirms the validity of the low score (also suggestive of an area of deficit) obtained from testing in English. It would then be appropriate to use the original English language score as that is the one for which validity has been established and not the other way around. These are important considerations for interpretation of data collected in English and the native language and provide guidance for proper interpretation, particularly when scores are involved. It is entirely possible that qualitative analysis and evaluation could cast doubt on the validity of scores obtained in English and there is no necessary requirement that native language test scores be used for this purpose. While they may well prove helpful, the goal of follow-up testing is confirmational in nature and any efforts in accomplishing this task should not be based only or solely on the use of test scores.

The *Gc* Caveat

The preceding method may be used for virtually any ability domain that may be measured in English and the native language. There is one notable exception, however, and that involves the measurement of *Gc*. Unlike all other cognitive abilities, *Gc* is, by definition, cultural knowledge and language ability. The measurement of *Gc* is in every way an attempt to measure an individual's acquisition of culture-specific knowledge as well as his/her development in language. Thus, the measurement of *Gc* cannot be separated from the influence of culture and language because it is itself, culture and language. In some sense, this makes *Gc* much like academic abilities and this notion has little opposition given the degree to which development of *Gc*, particularly as a store of acquired knowledge, is correlated with formal education (Schrank, McGrew, & Mather, 2015). The problem here is compounded by the fact that it is entirely expected that any ELL, even those who are highly proficient in English, are unlikely to obtain scores that are comparable to their same age or grade peers who have vastly more experience with and development in English.

What all of this means is that while the C-LIM may well indicate whether *Gc* abilities (which are nearly always classified as being high in language and culture) for an ELL are within the expected range, should the results be deemed valid, the original *Gc* score would be used as the basis for drawing inferences and making conclusions regarding performance in this area. Given that ELLs tend to score much lower on *Gc* tests than on any other tests, sometimes as much as one to two standard deviations depending on the degree of linguistic difference as compared to the norming sample (Sotelo-Dynega, Ortiz, Flanagan, & Chaplin, 2013), there is a high probability that many ELLs for whom test scores are deemed valid would be considered as having deficits in *Gc* that might suggest difficulties in speech and language.

To prevent the potentially discriminatory interpretation of *Gc* with ELLs when English language scores have been generated, it is recommended that clinical judgment regarding the examinee's functioning be based not on the norming sample of the test (e.g., WJ IV) but instead on the expected range of performance for ELLs as delineated in the C-LIM. This range is illustrated in the various graphs across which a shaded range is presented that corresponds to the mean values for *Gc* subtests drawn from the literature according to degree of difference, primarily the degree of English language proficiency. When the aggregate of *Gc* subtest scores within the high culture/high language cell (the bar farthest to the right in the graphs) falls within the shaded range selected as most appropriate for the individual's level of difference, the proper and equitable interpretation of functioning in the area of *Gc* should be that it is at least within the average range and possibly higher. Engaging in this procedure ensures that the meaning that is ascribed to the obtained score (even when that score is below Standard Score = 90, but not lower than the shaded range on the C-LIM) is fair and represents a nondiscriminatory interpretation of the value.

This method of interpreting *Gc* should only be applied with *Gc* and not to any other areas of suspected weakness found in test scores derived from evaluation in English. This is not to say that other scores will be completely free from the influence of cultural and linguistic factors even when they are deemed valid. The effect of cultural and linguistic variables is always likely to be at the very least a contributory influence on test scores. In this regard, they are insufficient to invalidate the scores and therefore interpretation may proceed in the usual fashion as might be accomplished when working with native English speakers. The same cannot be said for *Gc* which is unique in requiring this type of consideration. Moreover, in cases where the purpose of an evaluation involves identification of SLD within the context of a pattern of strengths and weaknesses (PSW) model, there are additional procedures that may be necessary to ensure that use of the actual score does not also result in discriminatory conclusions on the basis of its lower magnitude (i.e., below the average range). These additional principles will be discussed briefly within the context of the case study that follows.

Legacy Issues in Evaluation of ELLs with the WJ IV COG and OL

The WJ IV COG and OL carry over some remnants of a particular feature that was first developed as part of the Woodcock–Johnson Psycho-Educational Battery-Revised (Woodcock & Johnson, 1989) and the Batería Woodcock–Munoz-Revisada (Batería-R; Woodcock & Muñoz-Sandoval, 1996) known then as the Bilingual-Broad Cognitive Ability (Bilingual BCA; Alvarado, 1999). The concept involved creation of a global ability score (now known as GIA) that was comprised of a combination of tests that were administered in English as well as in Spanish. In some ways, the idea was quite advanced in that it viewed abilities in an integrated linguistic fashion by considering performance in both languages. However, the rationale as to why some abilities should be measured in English whereas others should be measured in the native language was never addressed and probably relied on the mistaken assumption already discussed regarding the presumption of validity of test scores in either language. It cannot be presumed that all ELLs have comparable proficiency in English and neither can it be presumed that all ELLs have comparable proficiency in their native language. No matter what, test scores must be assessed with respect to validity on the basis of the degree to which a given individual differs on the crucial dimensions of acculturative knowledge acquisition and limited proficiency (in whatever language in which they happen to be tested) or else the results are not dependable, preclude determination as valid, and prevent the assignment of defensible meaning or nondiscriminatory interpretation. Therefore, the abilities measured in English may well be deemed valid given the existing research base that forms the foundational principles of the C-LIM, but there is no recourse for ascertaining the validity of tests scores generated via native language testing. And any combination of such scores into a broader composite or amalgam becomes equally problematic.

Although the WJ IV has no partner test in Spanish, there are two clusters on the WJ IV OL that have parallel Spanish versions, Oral Language (standard and extended) and Listening Comprehension, named Lenguaje Oral (standard and amplio) and Comprensión Auditiva, respectively. The standard Oral Language and Lenguaje Oral clusters are made up of the same two tests (Picture Vocabulary/ Vocabulario Sobre Dibjuos and Oral Comprehension/Comprensión Oral). The extended version of the Oral Language and Lenguaje Oral clusters add the same third test to the mix (Understanding Directions/Comprensión de Indicacíones). Similarly, the Listening Comprehension and Compresión Auditiva clusters are made up of the same two tests (Oral Comprehension/Comprensión Oral and Understanding Directions/Comprensión de Indicacíones).

Although the two clusters have different names, it is important to recognize that they share one (standard Oral Language cluster) or two (extended Oral Language cluster) of the same tests depending. This implies that there must be an extremely high intercorrelation between the two and what differences there are, may well be negligible from a theoretical point of view as all are extremely good measures of *Gc*. The only exception is Understanding Directions/Comprensión de Indicacíones, which has a primary loading on working memory with a secondary loading on *Gc* according to Flanagan and colleagues (2013). Exactly how these Spanish language clusters are to be used or in what manner they have a relationship to their English language counterparts is unclear and unspecified in the manual. However, they are very much in line with the best practices framework recommended previously in that they will permit retesting and follow up in the native language in cases where Oral Language and Listening Comprehension were evaluated in English. Because these clusters are measures of *Gc*, the caveats specified in the prior section would come into play and need to be managed accordingly.

One other carry over in the WJ IV related to language issues is continued use of a CALP score that accompanies and is associated with the obtained standard score for a particular subtest. In theory, this score—a sort of criterion-referenced category of functioning—is intended to operationalize the concept originally developed by Cummins (1984). In this regard, it falls somewhat short for reasons having to do with Cummins' own lack of theoretical development of CALP that would permit clear operationalization as well as the fact that it is an entirely different type of language proficiency that emerges only after sufficient formal education (Cummins). This may be confusing to some who will wonder how then it is possible to obtain a CALP score on an examinee in the second grade who by definition, would not be expected to have CALP even begin to emerge until about the fifth grade and beyond. Because the WJ IV is silent on this issue, for all intents and purposes, it seems most reasonable to consider the CALP score as an indication of general language proficiency that is not tied specifically to actual age or grade related developmental proficiency. Within the context of evaluating ELLs, its greatest value may reside in providing a rough empirical estimate of the degree of difference that is most appropriate for an examinee. For example, a CALP level of 1 and 2 would be best considered as "markedly different" in comparison to the norming sample of tests that will be given in English. CALP levels of 3–5 would be roughly equivalent to the "moderately different" category and CALP levels of 6 would suggest that the examinee should be considered only "slightly different."

Apart from the issues presented in this section, use of the WJ IV COG and OL in evaluation of ELLs is relatively straightforward and not unlike that which is typically accomplished when working with native English speakers. The areas of most concern, for example, validity, follow-up evaluation, native language testing, and interpretation of *Gc*, have been discussed in some detail to provide a guide for practice that remains on track with respect to fairness and equity in the evaluation. To provide further illustration of the process, the following section describes a sample case study using the WJ IV COG and OL that may also serve somewhat as a general template that can be followed and replicated, as appropriate, in efforts to conduct evaluations on ELLs in the most nondiscriminatory manner possible.

Case Study: Marosita

Marosita, a 9-year-old 4th grader of Mexican heritage, was evaluated for a possible learning disability by the school psychologist after her teacher observed that she was having significant difficulty compared to her classmates in reading and writing and, to a lesser extent, math. Marosita was born in a rural area of Mexico and came to the United States at the age of 2 years with her family and settled in a small agricultural area in northern Utah. Her mother and father have very limited education and work daily to support the family. Although Marosita's native language and that of her family is Spanish, there was no one available to conduct the evaluation in her native language. However, the school psychologist had been trained and educated in nondiscriminatory assessment methods and procedures, and decided to conduct the assessment as best she could in English. Because Marosita had been raised in the United

States from the age of 2 years, and because she had been instructed in English since Kindergarten, she had developed considerable conversational proficiency and according to recent language testing by the ESL department, she was now dominant in English. Although many people commented that Marosita seemed to speak English well and without an accent, the school psychologist recognized that an accent is a poor indicator of actual proficiency and that indeed Marosita's English language proficiency was unlikely to be commensurate with that of her same age or grade native English-speaking peers. But to what degree Marosita's reported academic problems were due to developmental differences in her English language proficiency or her acquisition of acculturative knowledge, as opposed to being the manifestation of an SLD, could not be answered readily on the basis of the available information.

Initially, the school psychologist sought to evaluate only those abilities that might be related to the areas of suspected disability, namely *Gc*, *Ga*, Short-Term Memory (*Gsm* [the WJ IV COG uses a slightly different label for this ability— *Gwm*]), and Processing Speed (*Gs*), as these abilities have been demonstrated to be significantly related to the development and acquisition of reading and writing skills. However, the school psychologist recognized that the district's use of a PSW model for identification of SLD necessitated additional data that could be used to corroborate possession of overall average general ability and without a full individual evaluation, it might be difficult to substantiate specific deficits in functioning or specify their relationship to academic learning problems. The examiner believed that it was important to gather an extensive array of data, particularly on the seven major domains of cognitive functioning (*Gc*, *Gf*, *Glr* [Long-Term Storage and Retrieval], *Gwm*/*Gsm*, *Gv*, *Ga*, and *Gs*), to be able to examine Marosita's general intellectual functioning and evaluated performance in specific broad cognitive ability areas. Given the preceding constraints and considerations, the school psychologist decided to administer the WJ IV COG which would not require, at least initially, supplemental tests to measure the full range of abilities desired. In addition, the WJ IV COG is conormed with the WJ IV ACH which is typically used within the district to evaluate academic skills.

Marosita's teacher had reported that she did not observe any real difficulties in her ability to decode words efficiently or read aloud. Instead, Marosita's difficulties were noted in the area of comprehension where she seemed unable to recall the meaning of passages after just having read them. This did not seem to affect Marosita's overall ability to retain information in the long run, but it appeared to slow her learning significantly such that she is not able to keep up with the demands of the curriculum. Accordingly, the school psychologist chose to evaluate basic reading and reading comprehension skills as well as written expression and basic calculation skills. Marosita's teacher had not reported significant problems in either area; however, there was some concern that her progress was not at the rate that might be reasonably expected.

Results from administration of selected tests from the WJ IV COG and ACH are presented in Table 12.1 in the format that is generated by the computer

TABLE 12.1 Marosita Case Study Example Compuscore Report for WJ IV Data

Score Report

Name: Marosita
Date of Birth: 08/13/2005
Age: 9-8 (COG)
    9-8 (ACH)
Sex: Female
Date of Testing: 04/22/2015 (COG)
    04/29/2015 (ACH)

School: Washington Elementary
Teacher:
Grade: 4

ID:
Examiners: I.M. Schulsike

TESTS ADMINISTERED

Woodcock-Johnson IV Tests of Cognitive Abilities (Norms based on age 9-8)
Woodcock-Johnson IV Tests of Achievement Form A and Extended (Norms based on age 9-8)

TABLE OF SCORES

Woodcock-Johnson IV Tests of Cognitive Abilities (Norms based on age 9-8)

CLUSTER/Tests	W	AE	RPI	SS (68% Band)
GENERAL INTELLECTUAL ABILITY	492	7-11	61/90	84 (80-88)
BRIEF INTELLECTUAL ABILITY	494	6-9	64/90	85 (80-90)
Gf-Gc COMPOSITE	500	7-11	87/90	89 (83-95)
COMP-KNOWLEDGE (*Gc*)	490	7-1	67/90	83 (79-87)
FLUID REASONING (*Gf*)	508	9-3	82/90	97 (93-101)
S-TERM WORK MEM (*Gwm*)	487	6-1	52/90	77 (72-81)
COG PROCESS SPEED (*Gs*)	501	8-11	77/90	90 (84-95)
AUDITORY PROCESS (*Ga*)	493	9-0	70/90	85 (80-89)
L-TERM RETRIEVAL (*Glr*)	492	8-9	58/90	83 (78-87)
VISUAL PROCESSING (*Gv*)	499	9-1	84/90	88 (82-93)
COGNITIVE EFFICIENCY	499	9-3	87/90	90 (84-95)
Oral Vocabulary	495	7-5	67/90	85 (79-90)
Number Series	507	9-0	81/90	91 (86-95)
Verbal Attention	488	7-3	59/90	76 (69-82)
Letter-Pattern Matching	509	9-8	90/90	94 (86-91)
Phonological Processing	507	9-6	89/90	94 (88-100)
Story Recall	496	6-0	66/90	87 (80-94)
Visualization	495	7-9	70/90	84 (79-89)
General Information	491	6-11	49/90	83 (78-88)
Concept Formation	511	10-7	92/90	102 (98-106)
Numbers Reversed	493	7-5	66/90	80 (75-85)
Pair Cancellation	498	7-10	87/90	89 (83-95)
Nonword Repetition	490	6-3	51/90	77 (72-81)
Visual-Auditory Learning	492	6-5	58/90	79 (74-83)
Picture Recognition	500	7-11	87/90	90 (82-97)

1 of 2

(Continued)

TABLE 12.1 Marosita Case Study Example Compuscore Report for WJ IV Data (Continued)

Score Report

Marosita
April 29, 2015

Woodcock-Johnson IV Tests of Achievement Form A and Extended (Norms based on age 9-8)

CLUSTER/Tests	W	AE	RPI	SS (68% Band)
READING	494	6-9	50/90	84 (80-88)
BASIC READING SKILLS	509	9-7	89/90	98 (94-102)
READING COMPREHENSION	489	5-9	42/90	75 (71-79)
MATHEMATICS	496	7-2	70/90	87 (83-90)
WRITTEN LANGUAGE	495	6-8	67/90	82 (79-85)
ACADEMIC SKILLS	502	7-5	77/90	89 (86-92)
BRIEF ACHIEVEMENT	508	7-9	80/90	93 (90-95)
Letter-Word Identification	504	9-8	90/90	99 (94-103)
Applied Problems	505	9-4	87/90	94 (89-98)
Spelling	499	9-0	80/90	87 (83-90)
Passage Comprehension	482	6-3	52/90	72 (66-77)
Calculation	488	6-9	62/90	82 (77-86)
Writing Samples	486	6-8	58/90	79 (75-83)
Word Attack	504	9-7	88/90	97 (90-103)
Reading Recall	489	6-9	59/90	80 (72-88)

Woodcock-Johnson IV Tests of Achievement Form A and Extended Test Session Observations

Level of conversational proficiency: Advanced

Level of cooperation: Cooperative (typical for age/grade)

Level of activity: Typical for age/grade

Attention and concentration: Attentive to the tasks (typical for age/grade)

Self-confidence: Appeared at ease and comfortable (typical for age/grade)

Care in responding: Prompt but careful in responding (typical for age/grade)

Response to difficult tasks: Generally persisted with difficult tasks (typical for age/grade)

Woodcock-Johnson IV Tests of Achievement Form A and Extended Qualitative Observations

Letter-Word Identification: Identified words rapidly and accurately with little effort (automatic word identification skills)

Applied Problems: Solved initial problems with no observed difficulty but demonstrated slightly more difficulty solving the latter items (typical)

Spelling: Spelled initial items easily and accurately; more difficulty with longer and unfamiliar words (typical

Passage Comprehension: Significant difficulties noted in responses, poor memory and trouble using syntactic and semantic cues)

Calculation: Solved easy problems quickly but appeared to lose process on items requiring longer operations

Reading Recall: Significant difficulty in recalling information, numerous omissions

Word Attack: Correct pronunciation overall, no apparent problems

Writing Samples: Able to form sentences better when referring to cued stimuli, very rote responses, often incorrect

2 of 2

scoring software. Because the WJ IV can only be scored via computer, users are presented with an array of figures and statistics that may be quite daunting at first. Being able to ascertain the effect of culture and language also seems a difficult proposition, but is readily facilitated via use of the C-LIM

Analyzer. Accordingly, the school psychologist utilized the C-LIM Analyzer in the X-BASS and entered the obtained test scores after selecting the WJ IV from the top menu bar to populate the matrix with the tests and their correct classifications. The C-LIM Analyzer automatically calculates cell aggregates and graphs the results for analysis that permitted the school psychologist to examine the validity of the test scores from a perspective that accounts for the impact of cultural and linguistic differences on performance. The main matrix, tiered graph, and primary culture-language graph generated by the C-LIM Analyzer with Marosita's subtest data are shown in Figures 12.3, 12.4, and 12.5, respectively.

Prior to examining the pattern of scores, the school psychologist obtained information from the pre-referral team and the ESL department which had recently completed federally mandated testing to assess progress in English language acquisition in the district's ELL population. Based on a review of the information available, the school psychologist concluded that there were no extremely unusual events or circumstances in Marosita's developmental history and that her experiences were rather typical of other ELLs who were born in the United States (or arrived at an early age), whose parents were of very modest means and low SES, who began schooling in the United States at the age of 5 years, and who received only ESL services without any native language instruction. Accordingly, the school psychologist determined that the most appropriate basis for evaluating Marosita's test performance was the category of "moderately different" and she thus indicated her selection by checking the correct radio button on the C-LIM Analyzer.

Upon evaluation of the pattern of scores from the perspective regarding research that demonstrates an attenuation of performance as tests require increased developmental acculturative knowledge acquisition and English language proficiency, the school psychologist concluded that there did not appear an overall or general pattern of decline across all scores and that there were some cell aggregates where the tests that comprise them did not reach the expected range for ELLs of average ability and similar "moderately different" backgrounds. This indicated that there did not appear to be a primary effect of these cultural and linguistic variables on Marosita's test performance and consequently, the results were deemed valid. The school psychologist noted, however, that the effect being investigated does not simply disappear. Rather, it remains present and may well exert some degree of contributory influence on Marosita's test performance, but not systematic or pervasive enough to render the scores invalid.

Having deemed the results valid, the school psychologist proceeded to evaluate the data using XBA principles to evaluate and enhance the theoretical and psychometric validity of the obtained results. The DMIA module within X-BASS provided the functionality necessary to carry out these procedures, albeit the technical sophistication and strong theoretical foundation of the WJ IV minimized potential concerns in this regard. Indeed, when the data were fully entered into the WJ IV COG and WJ IV ACH test tabs in X-BASS, the only composite that seemed questionable and which might necessitate follow-up testing was in the Auditory Processing (*Ga*) domain. However, careful

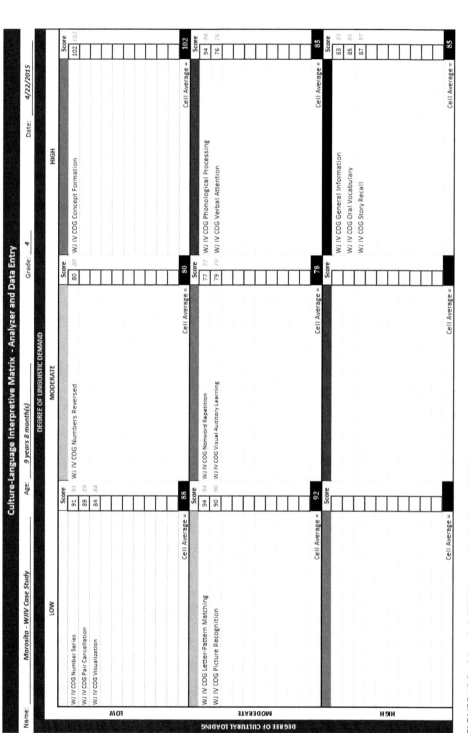

FIGURE 12.3   Marosita's WJ IV case study data in the C-LIM Analyzer.

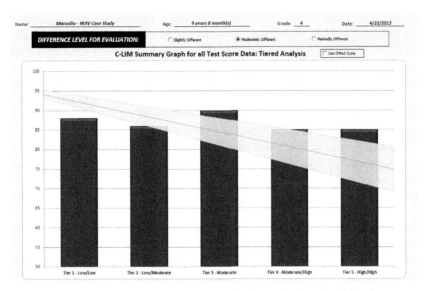

FIGURE 12.4   Marosita's WJ IV case study data in the C-LIM Analyzer Tiered Graph.

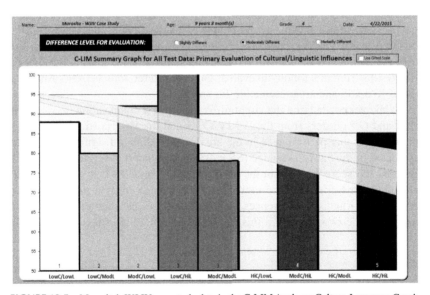

FIGURE 12.5   Marosita's WJ IV case study data in the C-LIM Analyzer Culture-Language Graph.

inspection of the composition of the tests that comprise the *Ga* factor in the WJ IV COG revealed that of the two tests that comprise it (Phonological Processing and Nonword Repetition), the latter was classified as having a primary loading on *Gsm* and only a secondary loading on *Ga*. Further examination of the data also indicated that *Gsm* was in fact an area of possible weakness for Marosita given her score on this factor (SS = 77). However, because her performance on the Phonological Processing test (SS = 94) was consistent with her performance on the Basic Reading Skills cluster of the achievement battery (and which are also good measures of *Ga*), it was clear that Marosita's auditory processing ability was in reality a strength, not a weakness, and that it was attenuated by the presence of the *Gsm* loading of one of the tests. As such, the school psychologist concluded that *Ga* should be considered a strength for the purposes of interpretation and further evaluation of SLD.

In addition to a possible weakness in the area of *Gsm*, the school psychologist noted potential deficits in *Glr* (SS = 83) and *Gc* (SS = 83). The school psychologist then decided to conduct follow-up evaluation of these areas in the native language to provide cross-linguistic confirmation that they are indeed domains that constitute valid weaknesses. In recognition of the *Gc* caveat, the school psychologist first began, by examining *Gc* within the context of the C-LIM Analyzer graphs (Figures 12.4 and 12.5). She then noted that although the magnitude of the *Gc* cluster was low (SS = 83), performance in the high culture/ high language (Tier 5) cell was not only within the shaded and expected range, it was actually slightly above it. This suggested that Marosita's *Gc* abilities were in fact comparable to other ELLs with similar developmental backgrounds and that, like *Ga*, it too should be considered as a "strength" and interpreted as such for the purposes of identifying SLD as well as developing interventions. The school psychologist thus conducted follow-up evaluation in the native language only for *Gsm* and *Glr*, as it was unnecessary to do so for *Gc*, using the Batería III. Results from this follow-up evaluation were entered into the XBA Analyzer tab of X-BASS and are presented in Figure 12.6.

While acknowledging the slight difference in test composition between the *Gsm* and *Glr* clusters from the WJ IV COG and the Batería III, it was nevertheless clear that performance in the area of *Glr* increased significantly when evaluated in the native language (SS = 93) as compared to English (SS = 83). Because the score was within the average range, the school psychologist concluded that the original score must have been attenuated by factors other than cultural and linguistic differences. In fact, the school psychologist was able to recall that the two tests from this cluster had been administered immediately

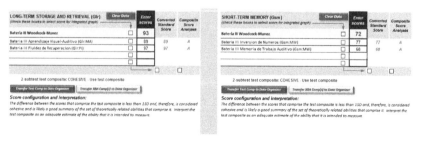

FIGURE 12.6 Marosita's Batería III data from follow-up evaluation entered into the XBA Analyzer.

preceding lunch and a recess break and that this may have caused Marosita to rush through items and lose concentration in an effort to ensure she wouldn't miss being able to eat and play with her friends. Whatever the case may be, the native language *Glr* cluster clearly represented a valid indication of her true ability and rendered the original score from English testing as invalid. Thus, the school psychologist replaced the original cluster with the native language cluster to ensure fair and equitable interpretation and use in further analysis as representing an area of "strength," rather than weakness, as was implied by the original score. In contrast, Marosita's performance in the area of *Gsm* on the Batería III was actually lower (SS = 72) than what was originally obtained when evaluated in English (SS = 77). The school psychologist concluded that this result served to confirm the validity of the original score and, in the absence of any other extraneous variable, that the original cluster was likely to be a valid indicator of difficulties in this domain.

To complete the assessment, the school psychologist next conducted a PSW-based evaluation of SLD using the model and analyses operationalized in the X-BASS and which is based on the Dual-Discrepancy/Consistency model of SLD identification (Flanagan et al., 2013). A summary of the data as organized for the purpose of this analysis is presented in Figure 12.7. Based on the

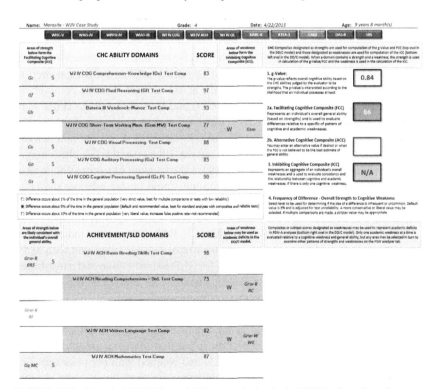

FIGURE 12.7   Marosita's WJ IV/Batería III case study data in the PSW Analyzer Data Summary.

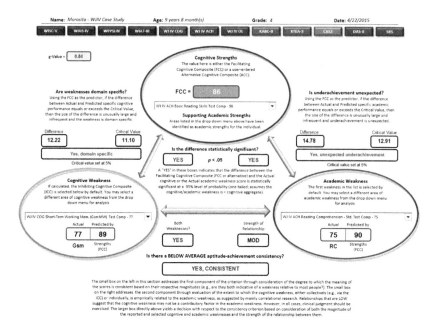

FIGURE 12.8   Marosita's WJ IV case study data in the PSW Analyzer for SLD Identification.

evaluation and decisions regarding the strengths and weaknesses found in Marosita's WJ IV data, the only area of cognitive weakness that appeared to be valid was in the *Gsm* domain and on the academic side, reading comprehension was also significantly weak (SS = 75) and written language skills were also slightly below average (SS = 82) and an area of weakness. In this case, the school psychologist used the original *Gc* score (SS = 83) but had marked it as a "strength" on the basis of the *Gc* caveat. Likewise, the *Glr* cluster from the Batería III (SS = 93) was used to replace the original *Glr* score obtained in English (SS = 83) as the native language score could be defended as valid and it did not confirm *Glr* as an areas of weakness. It too was marked as a strength for the PSW analysis.

When evaluated via the PSW Analyzer in X-BASS, the results indicated that the pattern of strengths and weaknesses for Marosita were consistent with SLD. An illustration of the operational criteria for SLD identification and a test-based summary of the analysis is provided in Figures 12.8 and 12.9. Based on the information provided by the PSW Analyzer, the school psychologist concluded that Marosita's overall pattern of strengths and weaknesses were consistent with SLD and that all necessary criteria for establishing a learning disability had been adequately met. She, therefore, concluded that Marosita met the district's standards for identification as having SLD and coupled with her observed educational need in the area of reading comprehension was likely to be eligible for special education and related services. At the Individualized Educational

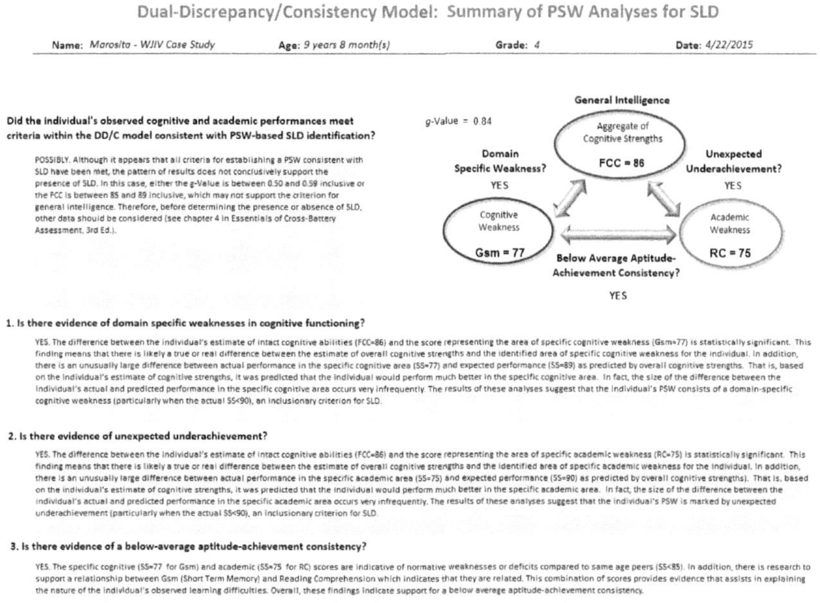

Dual-Discrepancy/Consistency Model: Summary of PSW Analyses for SLD

Name: *Marosita - WJIV Case Study* **Age:** *9 years 8 month(s)* **Grade:** *4* **Date:** *4/22/2015*

Did the individual's observed cognitive and academic performances meet criteria within the DD/C model consistent with PSW-based SLD identification?

POSSIBLY. Although it appears that all criteria for establishing a PSW consistent with SLD have been met, the pattern of results does not conclusively support the presence of SLD. In this case, either the g-Value is between 0.50 and 0.59 inclusive or the FCC is between 85 and 89 inclusive, which may not support the criterion for general intelligence. Therefore, before determining the presence or absence of SLD, other data should be considered (see chapter 4 in Essentials of Cross-Battery Assessment, 3rd Ed.).

g-Value = 0.84

General Intelligence
Aggregate of Cognitive Strengths
FCC = 86
Domain Specific Weakness?
YES
Unexpected Underachievement?
YES
Cognitive Weakness
Gsm = 77
Academic Weakness
RC = 75
Below Average Aptitude-Achievement Consistency?
YES

1. Is there evidence of domain specific weaknesses in cognitive functioning?

YES. The difference between the individual's estimate of intact cognitive abilities (FCC=86) and the score representing the area of specific cognitive weakness (Gsm=77) is statistically significant. This finding means that there is likely a true or real difference between the estimate of overall cognitive strengths and the identified area of specific cognitive weakness for the individual. In addition, there is an unusually large difference between actual performance in the specific cognitive area (SS=77) and expected performance (SS=89) as predicted by overall cognitive strengths. That is, based on the individual's estimate of cognitive strengths, it was predicted that the individual would perform much better in the specific cognitive area. In fact, the size of the difference between the individual's actual and predicted performance in the specific cognitive area occurs very infrequently. The results of these analyses suggest that the individual's PSW consists of a domain-specific cognitive weakness (particularly when the actual SS<90), an inclusionary criterion for SLD.

2. Is there evidence of unexpected underachievement?

YES. The difference between the individual's estimate of intact cognitive abilities (FCC=86) and the score representing the area of specific academic weakness (RC=75) is statistically significant. This finding means that there is likely a true or real difference between the estimate of overall cognitive strengths and the identified area of specific academic weakness for the individual. In addition, there is an unusually large difference between actual performance in the specific academic area (SS=75) and expected performance (SS=90) as predicted by overall cognitive strengths). That is, based on the individual's estimate of cognitive strengths, it was predicted that the individual would perform much better in the specific academic area. In fact, the size of the difference between the individual's actual and predicted performance in the specific academic area occurs very infrequently. The results of these analyses suggest that the individual's PSW is marked by unexpected underachievement (particularly when the actual SS<90), an inclusionary criterion for SLD.

3. Is there evidence of a below-average aptitude-achievement consistency?

YES. The specific cognitive (SS=77 for Gsm) and academic (SS=75 for RC) scores are indicative of normative weaknesses or deficits compared to same age peers (SS<85). In addition, there is research to support a relationship between Gsm (Short Term Memory) and Reading Comprehension which indicates that they are related. This combination of scores provides evidence that assists in explaining the nature of the individual's observed learning difficulties. Overall, these findings indicate support for a below average aptitude-achievement consistency.

FIGURE 12.9 Marosita's WJ IV case study data summary of PSW Analyses for SLD.

Planning (IEP) meeting, the school psychologist advocated for culturally and linguistically appropriate goals and objectives as well as interventions within the general education setting for Marosita to help her manage and ameliorate her deficit in *Gsm* and her difficulties in the development of reading comprehension and to some extent, written language. By ensuring that Marosita receives culturally and linguistically relevant support in the special and general education environments, she will be afforded the opportunity needed to maximize her success in the classroom (Brown & Ortiz, 2014).

SUMMARY

It is important to note that had the school psychologist not followed the recommended best practices approach or fully considered all the steps necessary to ensure fair and equitable assessment described in this chapter and in the case study, she may well have come to the wrong conclusion that Marosita was merely a "slow learner" or that she was of generally low average ability (i.e., mild intellectual disability). For example, had *Gc* been indicated as a weakness rather than strength, and had follow-up native language testing not been conducted in the area of *Glr*, the overall pattern of results would have looked vastly different. Figure 12.10 provides an illustration of the PSW Analyzer Data

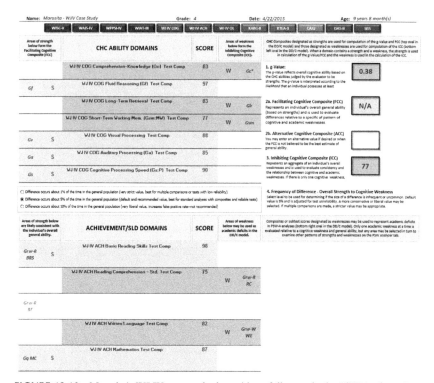

FIGURE 12.10 Marosita's WJ IV case study data without follow up in the PSW Analyzer Data Summary.

Summary as it would appear had both *Gc* been designated as a weakness and the original *Glr* score also designated as a weakness and employed in PSW analysis. In such a case, X-BASS did not even calculate a score to represent Marosita's general intellectual functioning because either the *g*-Value (0.38; an indicator of which and how many abilities are noted as strengths relative to grade level) fell below the range necessary to suggest overall average intelligence (≥0.51) or the composite scores of the strengths that comprise the Facilitating Cognitive Composite (FCC; an indicator of the collective magnitude of cognitive strengths) was below the level that also suggests overall average intelligence (SS ≥ 85). Such a finding not only would preclude identification of SLD, but it may also push consideration of the cause of her academic difficulties quite wrongly in the direction of mild intellectual disability given Marosita's GIA (SS = 84). Only the steps employed prevented such a misclassification.

It is also possible that utilization of the nondiscriminatory steps and procedures outlined in this chapter, particularly use of the C-LIM Analyzer, may have resulted in an overall pattern of test scores from administration of the WJ IV that were invalid. For example, had the overall pattern of test scores shown a general decline, and had the magnitude of all the cell aggregates been within or above the shaded/expected range for other ELLs of similar backgrounds as Marosita, the school psychologist would have had to conclude that the primary reason for the obtained test scores was due to a lack of acculturative knowledge acquisition and limited English language proficiency. At that point, no further evaluation would have been necessary as such a pattern also implies that Marosita's scores were comparable to the performance of other nondisabled, ELLs of average ability with similar developmental backgrounds and experiences. When test scores are be deemed to be invalid, there is an inherent protection against identification of a cognitive-based deficit and thus effectively preclude notions of disability and special education eligibility.

In conclusion, the methods for nondiscriminatory evaluation of culturally and linguistically diverse individuals outlined in this chapter are not necessarily specific to use of the WJ IV. They do illustrate, however, that the WJ IV can be an appropriate and effective tool for evaluation of ELLs, particularly when supplemented with Spanish language tests from the Batería III. When the examinee's heritage language is something other than Spanish, the methods can still be utilized with follow-up evaluation conducted via the aid of a translator/interpreter. When combined with the recommended best practices approach, the WJ IV may well be an ideal tool for any evaluator whose intent is to evaluate diverse individuals in the fairest, most equitable, and nondiscriminatory manner possible.

REFERENCES

Alvarado, C.G. (1999). *A Broad Cognitive Ability—Bilingual Scale for the WJ-R Tests of Cognitive Ability and the Batería Woodcock–Muñoz Pruebas de Habilidad Cognitiva—*Revisada. Research Report Number 2, Riverside Publishing Company.

American Educational Research Association, American Psychological Association, & National Council on Measurement in Education, (2014). *Standards for educational and psychological testing.* Washington, DC: American Educational Research Association.

Bialystok, E. (1991). *Language processing in bilingual children.* New York, NY: Cambridge University Press.

Brown, J.E. (2008). *The use and interpretation of the Batería III with U.S. bilinguals.* Unpublished dissertation, Portland State University, Portland, OR.

Brown, J. E., & Ortiz, S. O. (2014). Interventions for English Language Learners with earning difficulties. In J. T. Mascolo, V. C. Alfonso, & D. P. Flanagan (Eds.), *Essentials of planning, selecting and tailoring intervention* (pp. 267–313). Hoboken, NJ: John Wiley & Sons, Inc.

Cormier, D. C., McGrew, K. S., & Ysseldyke, J. E. (2014). The influences of linguistic demand and cultural loading on cognitive test scores. *Journal of Psychoeducational Assessment, 32*(7), 610–623.

Committee on Psychological Tests and Assessment. (2007). Statement on Third Party Observers in Psychological Testing and Assessment: A framework for decision making. Online document retrieved Nov. 2, 2015. Available from: <http://www.apa.org/science/programs/testing/third-party-observers.pdf>.

Cummins, J. C. (1984). *Bilingual and special education: issues in assessment and pedagogy.* Austin, TX: PRO-ED.

Flanagan, D. P., Ortiz, S. O., & Alfonso, V. C. (2007). *Essentials of cross-battery assessment* (2nd ed.). Hoboken, NJ: John Wiley & Sons, Inc.

Flanagan, D. P., Ortiz, S. O., & Alfonso, V. C. (2013). *Essentials of cross-battery assessment* (3rd ed.). Hoboken, NJ: John Wiley & Sons, Inc.

Grosjean, F. (1989). Neurolinguists beware! The bilingual is not two monolinguals in one person. *Brain and Language, 36*(1), 3–15.

Individuals With Disabilities Education Act, 20 U.S.C. § 1400 (2004).

Lohman, D. F., Korb, K., & Lakin, J. (2008). Identifying academically gifted English language learners using nonverbal tests: A comparison of the Raven, NNAT, and CogAT. *Gifted Child Quarterly, 52*(4), 275–296.

Mpofu, E., & Ortiz, S. O. (2009). Equitable assessment practices in diverse contexts. In E. L. Grigorenko (Ed.), *Multicultural psychoeducational assessment* (pp. 41–76). New York, NY: Springer Publishing Co.

Naglieri, J. A. (2015). Hundred years of intelligence testing: Moving from traditional IQ to second-generation Intelligence Tests. In S. Goldstein, D. Princiotta, & J. A. Naglieri (Eds.), *Handbook of intelligence: Evolutionary theory, historical perspective, and current concepts* (pp. 295–316). New York, NY: Springer.

National Association of School Psychologists (2015). *Online Directory of Bilingual School Psychologists.* Available at: <www.nasponline.org/about_nasp/bilingualdirectory.aspx>. Last retrieved July 24, 2015.

Ochoa, S. H., Riccio, C. A., Jimenez, S., Garcia de Alba, R., & Sines, M. (2004). Psychological assessment of limited English proficient and/or bilingual students: An investigation of school psychologists' current practices. *Journal of Psychoeducational Assessment, 22*(3), 93–105.

Ortiz, S. O. (2014). Best practices in nondiscriminatory assessment. In A. Thomas & J. Grimes (Eds.), *Best practices in school psychology VI.* Washington, DC: National Association of School Psychologists.

Ortiz, S.O., & Flanagan, D.P. (Sect. Eds.) (2013). Section 9: Assessment Theory—Introduction. In B. J. Irby, G. Brown & R. Lara-Alecio (Eds.), *Handbook of educational theories* (pp. 735–738). Charlotte, NC: Information Age Publishing.

Ortiz, S. O., Flanagan, D. P., & Alfonso, V. C. (2015). *Cross-Battery Assessment Software System (X-BASS v1.1) PC and Mac Versions.* Hoboken, NJ: Wiley & Sons, Inc.

Ortiz, S. O., & Melo, K. (2015). Evaluation of intelligence and learning disability with Hispanics. In K. Geisinger (Ed.), *Psychological testing of Hispanics* (pp. 109–134). Washington, DC: APA Books.

Ortiz, S. O., Ochoa, S. H., & Dynda, A. M. (2012). Testing with culturally and linguistically diverse populations: Moving beyond the verbal-performance dichotomy into evidence-based practice. In D. P. Flanagan & P. L. Harrison (Eds.), *Contemporary intellectual assessment, third edition* (pp. 526–552). New York, NY: Guilford Press.

Paradis, M. (2014). *The assessment of bilingual aphasia.* New York, NY: Psychology Press.

Rhodes, R., Ochoa, H. S., & Ortiz, S. O. (2005). *Assessing culturally and linguistically diverse students: A practical guide.* New York, NY: Guilford Press.

Schrank, F. A., Mather, N., & McGrew, K. S. (2014a). *Woodcock–Johnson IV Tests of Oral Language.* Rolling Meadows, IL: Riverside.

Schrank, F. A., Mather, N., & McGrew, K. S. (2014b). *Woodcock–Johnson IV Tests of Achievement.* Rolling Meadows, IL: Riverside.

Schrank, F. A., McGrew, K. S., & Mather, N. (2014a). *Woodcock–Johnson IV.* Rolling Meadows, IL: Riverside.

Schrank, F. A., McGrew, K. S., & Mather, N. (2014b). *Woodcock–Johnson IV Tests of Cognitive Abilities*. Rolling Meadows, IL: Riverside.

Schrank, F. A., McGrew, K. S., & Mather, N. (2015). The WJ IV *Gf–Gc* composite and its use in the identification of specific learning disabilities: *Assessment Service Bulletin Number 3*. Rolling Meadows, IL: Riverside Publishing Co.

Sotelo-Dynega, M., Geddes, L., Luhrs, A., Teague, J. (2009). *What is a Bilingual School Psychologist? A national survey of the credentialing bodes of school psychologists*. Poster presented at the National Association of School Psychologists Annual Conference, Boston, MA.

Sotelo-Dynega, M., Ortiz, S. O., Flanagan, D. P., & Chaplin, W. (2013). English language proficiency and test performance: Evaluation of bilinguals with the Woodcock–Johnson III Tests of Cognitive Abilities. *Psychology in the Schools*, *50*(8), 781–797.

Styck, K. M., & Watkins, M. W. (2013). Diagnostic utility of the Culture-Language Interpretive Matrix for the Wechsler Intelligence Scales for Children—Fourth Edition among referred students. *School Psychology Review*, *42*(4), 367–382.

Styck, K. M., & Watkins, M. W. (2014). Discriminant validity of the WISC-IV Culture-Language Interpretive Matrix. *Contemporary School Psychology*, *18*(3), 168–188.

Suzuki, L. A., & Aronson, J. (2005). The cultural malleability of intelligence and its impact on the racial/ethnic hierarchy. *Psychology, Public Policy, and Law*, *11*(2), 320–327.

Thomas, W. P., & Collier, V. P. (2002). *A national study of school effectiveness for language minority students' long-term academic achievement*. Santa Cruz, CA, and Washington, DC: Center for Research on Education, Diversity & Excellence.

US Census Bureau (2014). Current population survey. Available at <http://www.census.gov/cps/>. Last retrieved July 24, 2015.

Woodcock, R. W., & Johnson, M. B. (1989). *Woodcock–Johnson Psycho-Educational Battery–Revised*. Itasca, IL: Riverside Publishing.

Woodcock, R. W., McGrew, K. S., & Mather, N. (2001). *The Woodcock–Johnson III*. Itasca, IL: Riverside Publishing.

Woodcock, R. W., & Muñoz-Sandoval, A. F. (1996). *Batería Woodcock–Muñoz—Revisada*. Itasca, IL: Riverside Publishing.

Chapter 13

Neurocognitive Applications of the Woodcock–Johnson IV

Daniel C. Miller, Ryan J. McGill and Wendi L. Bauman Johnson
Department of Psychology and Philosophy, Texas Woman's University, Denton, TX, USA

NEUROCOGNITIVE APPLICATIONS OF THE WJ IV

Richard W. Woodcock originally developed the Woodcock–Johnson Psychoeducational Battery—Revised (WJ R; Woodcock & Johnson, 1989) with neuropsychological assessment in mind. Woodcock (1997) noted that "Although the WJ R does not cover all aspects required for a comprehensive neuropsychological evaluation, it does provide more coverage for the assessment and description of deficits and preserved neurocognitive functions than any other single source" (p. 1). The Dean-Woodcock Neuropsychological Model (DWNM) was proposed in 1999, which provided an integration of sensory-motor functioning with the empirically validated cognitive abilities and academic achievement measures from the WJ (Dean & Woodcock, 1999). In 2003, the Dean-Woodcock Neuropsychological Battery was published (DWNB; Dean & Woodcock, 2003) and was based on the DWNM. It provided clinicians and researchers a co-normed assessment tool for neuropsychological assessment.

The most recent version of the Woodcock–Johnson, the Woodcock–Johnson—Fourth Edition (WJ IV; Schrank, McGrew, & Mather, 2014c), is a broad-based battery of cognitive, oral language, and achievement tests based on the Cattell–Horn–Carroll (CHC) theory of cognitive abilities (Schneider & McGrew, 2012). The WJ IV consists of three co-normed test batteries: the Woodcock–Johnson IV Tests of Cognitive Abilities (WJ IV COG; Schrank, McGrew, & Mather, 2014d), the Woodcock–Johnson IV Tests of Oral Language (WJ IV OL; Schrank, Mather, & McGrew, 2014b), and the Woodcock–Johnson IV Tests of Achievement (WJ IV ACH; Schrank, Mather, & McGrew, 2014a).

Schneider and McGrew (2012) noted areas of growth regarding CHC theory and its application to cognitive assessment and labeled this growth as "beyond CHC theory" (p. 109). The WJ IV has incorporated additional neuropsychological

WJ IV Clinical Use and Interpretation. DOI: http://dx.doi.org/10.1016/B978-0-12-802076-0.00014-1

constructs into the overall battery such as enhanced auditory processing, working memory, and fluency measures. Schneider and McGrew stated:

> *The most active CHC "spillover" has been in the area of neuropsychological assessment… It is our opinion that CHC-based neuropsychological assessment holds great potential. Much clinical lore within the field of neuropsychological assessment is tied to specific tests from specific batteries. CHC theory has the potential to help neuropsychologists generalize their interpretations beyond specific test batteries and give them greater theoretical unity.* (p. 109)

The purpose of this chapter is to review the application of the WJ IV batteries from a neuropsychological perspective. The first section of the chapter presents a reclassification of the WJ IV tests into a neuropsychological conceptual framework. The second section of the chapter provides a review of what basic neurocognitive constructs are addressed and assessed by the WJ IV tests of cognitive, oral language, and achievement. The final section of the chapter provides an example of how the learning and memory tests may be interpreted from a neuropsychological perspective.

WJ IV TESTS CLASSIFIED ACCORDING TO A NEUROPSYCHOLOGICAL MODEL

Flanagan, Alfonso, Ortiz, and Dynda (2010) were the first to present a classification of the subtests from the major tests of cognitive abilities and pediatric neuropsychological measures using either a Lurian theoretical model, the school neuropsychological conceptual model (Miller, 2007), or the CHC nomenclature. Flanagan and colleagues referred to this as an integrated framework. In 2013, Miller updated his school neuropsychological conceptual model by providing additional integration between neuropsychological constructs and CHC theory. Miller's revised model, now referred to as the Integrated School Neuropsychological/Cattell–Horn–Carroll (Integrated SNP/CHC) Model (Miller, 2013) is based on current psychometric theory and research (Flanagan, Alfonso, & Ortiz, 2012; Horn & Blankson, 2012; Keith & Reynolds, 2012; Schneider & McGrew, 2012; Schrank & Wendling, 2012) and ongoing discussions with the CHC theorists and cross-battery researchers.

The Integrated SNP/CHC Model encompasses four major classifications: (i) basic sensorimotor functions; (ii) facilitators and inhibitors for cognitive processes and acquired knowledge skills; (iii) basic cognitive processes; and (iv) acquired knowledge. In addition to these four major classifications, the test results must be interpreted within the context of the child's social–emotional, environmental, and cultural backgrounds. Within each of these major classifications, the neuropsychological constructs are classified further into broad areas, and classified even further into second-order classifications and then third-order classifications, as appropriate. As an example, tests within the broad classification of sensorimotor functions can be classified further into the second-order classifications of: lateral preference, sensory functions, fine-motor functions, visual-motor integration skills, visual scanning, gross motor functions, and qualitative behaviors. Some of these second-order classifications can be sub-divided further into third-order classification such as the sensory functions domain, which can be subdivided into auditory and visual acuity, tactile sensation and perception, kinesthetic sensation and perception, and olfactory sensation and perception. For the sake of simplifying the Integrated SNP/CHC Model for this chapter, only the broad and second-order classifications of the model are presented in Table 13.1 along with the classifications of the WJ IV tests.

TABLE 13.1 Coverage of the Basic Neurocognitive Constructs by the WJ IV Tests of Cognitive Abilities, Oral Language, and Achievement

Integrated SNP/ CHC Broad Classifications	Integrated SNP/ CHC Second-Order Classifications	WJ IV Test	WJ IV Battery
Basic Sensorimotor Functions	Lateral preference Sensory functions Fine-motor functions Visual-motor integration skills Visual scanning/tracking (indirect measures)	Pair Cancellation Number-Pattern Matching (New)	Cognitive Cognitive
	Gross motor functions Quantitative behaviors		
Cognitive Processes: Visuospatial	Visuospatial perception Visuospatial reasoning	Visualization (New)	Cognitive
Cognitive Processes: Auditory/ Phonological	Sound discrimination and auditory/phonological processing	Sound Awareness Nonword Repetition (New) Phonological Processing (New) Segmentation (New) Sound Blending	Oral Language Cognitive Cognitive Oral Language Oral Language
Cognitive Processes: Learning and Memory	Rate of learning		
	Immediate verbal memory	Memory for Words Sentence Repetition Story Recall	Cognitive Oral Language Cognitive
	Visual immediate memory Delayed verbal memory Delayed visual memory	Picture Recognition	Cognitive
	Verbal–visual associative learning and recall	Visual–Auditory Learning	Cognitive

(Continued)

TABLE 13.1 Coverage of the Basic Neurocognitive Constructs by the WJ IV Tests of Cognitive Abilities, Oral Language, and Achievement (Continued)

Integrated SNP/ CHC Broad Classifications	Integrated SNP/ CHC Second-Order Classifications	WJ IV Test	WJ IV Battery
Cognitive Processes: Executive Functions	Cognitive flexibility		
	Concept recognition and generation		
	Problem solving, fluid reasoning, and planning	Concept Generation	Cognitive
		Analysis/Synthesis	Cognitive
		Number Matrices (New)	Achievement
		Number Series	Cognitive
	Response inhibition		
Facilitators/Inhibitors: Allocating and Maintaining Attention	Selective/focused and sustained attention	Pair Cancellation	Cognitive
	Attentional capacity	Sentence Repetition	Oral language
		Memory for Words	Cognitive
		Story Recall	Cognitive
Facilitators/Inhibitors: Working Memory	Working memory	Object-Number Sequencing	Cognitive
		Numbers Reversed	Cognitive
		Verbal Attention (New)	Cognitive
Facilitators/ Inhibitors: Speed, Fluency, and Efficiency of Processing	Performance fluency	Letter-Pattern Matching (New)	Cognitive
		Number-Pattern Matching	Cognitive
		Rapid Picture Naming	Cognitive
	Retrieval fluency	Retrieval Fluency	Cognitive
	Acquired knowledge fluency	Oral Reading (New)	Achievement
		Word Reading Fluency (New)	Achievement
		Sentence Reading Fluency	Achievement
		Sentence Writing Fluency (new)	Achievement
		Math Facts Fluency	Achievement

(Continued)

TABLE 13.1 Coverage of the Basic Neurocognitive Constructs by the WJ IV Tests of Cognitive Abilities, Oral Language, and Achievement (Continued)

Integrated SNP/ CHC Broad Classifications	Integrated SNP/ CHC Second-Order Classifications	WJ IV Test	WJ IV Battery
Acquired Knowledge: Acculturation Knowledge	Semantic memory (general information)	Oral Vocabulary General Information	Cognitive Cognitive
Acquired Knowledge: Language Abilities	Oral expression	Picture Vocabulary	Cognitive
	Receptive language (listening comprehension)	Oral Comprehension Understanding Directions	Oral Language Oral Language
Acquired Knowledge: Reading Achievement	Basic reading skills: Phonological decoding	Letter-Word Identification Word Attack	Achievement Achievement
	Reading comprehension skills	Passage Comprehension Reading Recall (New) Reading Vocabulary	Achievement Achievement Achievement
Acquired Knowledge: Written Language Achievement	Written expression	Editing	Achievement
	Expository composition Orthographic spelling	Writing Samples Spelling Spelling of Sounds	Achievement Achievement Achievement
Acquired Knowledge: Mathematics	Mathematical calculations	Calculations	Achievement
	Mathematical reasoning	Applied Problems	Achievement

Note: Integrated SNP= Integrated School Neuropsychological, CHC= Cattell–Horn–Carroll.

In this chapter, the tests from the WJ IV Tests of Cognitive Abilities, Oral Language, and Achievement are classified according to the Integrated SNP/CHC Model (Table 13.1). See Miller (2013) for how other common neuropsychological tests are classified into the Integrated SNP/CHC Model. The purposes of the Integrated SNP/CHC Model are to: (i) facilitate clinical interpretation by providing an organizational framework for the assessment data; (ii) strengthen the linkage between assessment and evidence-based interventions; and (iii) provide a common frame of reference for evaluating the effects of neurodevelopmental disorders on neurocognitive processes (Miller, 2013). The complete SNP Model includes the integration of social–emotional functioning with the major neuropsychological assessment components (see Miller, 2013, and Miller & Maricle, 2012, 2014, for comprehensive reviews).

COVERAGE OF BASIC NEUROCOGNITIVE CONSTRUCTS BY THE WJ IV TESTS OF COGNITIVE ABILITIES, ORAL LANGUAGE, AND ACHIEVEMENT

Table 13.2 also provides a list of the WJ IV tests classified according to the Integrated SNP/CHC Model, but adds additional information to aid in clinical interpretation. Each test includes a brief description of the task(s), the CHC narrow ability(ies) measured by the task, the input, processing, and output demands of the task, as well as, the primary neuroanatomical regions of the brain associated with the task. The input, processing, and output requirements of each WJ IV measure were derived by conducting demand analyses (Fiorello, Hale, & Wycoff, 2012; Hale & Fiorello, 2004). Tests can be grouped in the same conceptual classification, but can yield very different results due to the subtle changes in the input, processing, or output demands of the task. In a later section of this chapter, the differences in the demand characteristics of learning and memory tests will be discussed.

Basic Sensorimotor Functions. The WJ IV does not provide direct measures of basic sensorimotor functions. The sensory-motor portion of the DWNB was developed to be a companion to the Woodcock–Johnson III Normative Update Tests of Cognitive Abilities (Woodcock, McGrew, & Mather, 2001, 2007a) and the Tests of Achievement (Woodcock, McGrew, & Mather, 2001, 2007b). The DWNB provides a comprehensive assessment of sensory-motor functioning; however, the test has not been re-normed with the WJ IV. If sensorimotor deficits are suspected within a neuropsychological evaluation, it is recommended that additional tests be administered such as the sensorimotor subtests from the NEPSY-II (Korkman, Kirk, & Kemp, 2007).

The WJ IV COG has two tests, Pair Cancellation and Number-Pattern Matching, which indirectly measure, or require, good visual scanning skills to complete the tasks. Poor visual scanning skills can negatively impact the ability to read words on a line, or write text on a straight line, or efficiently search for embedded visual information with an array of data (Miller, 2013). When using the WJ IV, sensory-motor functions must be inferred from qualitative observational data and known historical medical information. The WJ IV does not require fine-motor manipulative tasks, unlike other tests of cognitive abilities, such as Wechsler Intelligence Scale for Children—Fifth Edition (WISC-V; Wechsler, 2014), which require tasks such as Block Design.

TABLE 13.2 Input, Processing, and Output Demands Required for WJ IV Cognitive, Achievement, and Oral Language Tests Classified According to Miller's Integrated School Neuropsychological—CHC Conceptual Model

Test	Task Description	Narrow CHC Ability	Input Demands	Processing Demands	Output Demands	Primary Neuroanatomical Regions
Cognitive Processes: Visuospatial (Gv)						
COG-7: Visualization	Identify two or more pieces that go together to form a complete target shape and ability to select the two sets of blocks that are rotated versions of the target pattern	• Visualization (VZ)	Visual (objects on a page)	Visuospatial reasoning (recognizing spatial configurations with and without mental rotations)	Verbal (stating numbers of correct answers) or motor response (pointing to correct answers)	Bilateral frontal parietal network (mental rotations); right occipital–temporal region—ventral stream (recognition of objects)
Cognitive Processes: Auditory/Phonological (Ga)						
COG-5: Phonological Processing	Three part task involving phonemic word recall, word retrieval, and phonemic substitution	• Phonetic Coding (PC) • Speed of Lexical Access (LA)	Verbal (words)	Phonological processing	Verbal (creation of words based on phonetic rules, word retrieval, and phonetic substitution)	Bilateral posterior-superior temporal

(Continued)

TABLE 13.2 Input, Processing, and Output Demands Required for WJ IV Cognitive, Achievement, and Oral Language Tests Classified According to Miller's Integrated School Neuropsychological—CHC Conceptual Model (Continued)

Test	Task Description	Narrow CHC Ability	Input Demands	Processing Demands	Output Demands	Primary Neuroanatomical Regions
COG-12: Nonword Repetition	Listen to a nonsense word then repeat it exactly	• Phonetic Coding (PC) • Memory for Sound Patterns (UM) (Auditory) Memory Span (MS)	Verbal (nonsense words)	Phonological processing in verbal immediate memory	Verbal (nonsense word)	Ventral aspect of the inferior parietal cortex
OL-3: Segmentation	Listens to words and identifies word parts	• Phonetic Coding (PC)	Verbal (segmented words)	Phonological processing	Verbal (parts of words or whole words)	Bilateral posterior–superior temporal
OL-7: Sound Blending	Identifying a whole word base on the sum of the individual phonemes	• Phonetic Coding (PC)	Verbal (phonemes)	Phonological processing	Verbal (word)	Bilateral posterior–superior temporal
OL-9: Sound Awareness	Deleting word parts and phonemes from orally presented words	• Phonetic Coding (PC)	Verbal (words and phonemes)	Phonological processing	Verbal (words and phonemes)	Bilateral posterior–superior temporal

Cognitive Processes: Learning and Memory (*Glr*)

COG-6: Story Recall	Details recalled from verbally presented stories	• Meaningful Memory (MM) • Listening Ability (LS)	Verbal (passages)	Immediate verbal memory and recall	Verbal (passage)	Anterior temporal lobes, dorsomedial prefrontal cortex, and areas along the middle and superior temporal gyri and inferior frontal cortex
COG-13: Visual–Auditory Learning	Learning visual–verbal associations and then recalling them	• Associative Memory (MA)	Paired visual (rebuses) and auditory (words)	Verbal–visual associative learning and recall	Verbal (words to form sentences)	Left fusiform gyrus and left inferior parietal lobe
COG-14: Picture Recognition	Identifying previously seen pictures embedded in a set of similar pictures	• Visual Memory (MV)	Visual (pictures)	Immediate visual memory and recall	Verbal (numbers of pictures) or motoric (pointing to pictures)	Left ventrolateral prefrontal cortex
COG-18: Memory for Words	Repeat a list of unrelated words in sequence	• Memory Span (MS)	Verbal (words)	Immediate verbal memory and recall	Verbal (sequence of words)	Right dorsolateral frontal cortex and the bilateral posterior parietal cortex
OL-5: Sentence Repetition	Recall of sentences of increasing length and complexity	• Memory Span (MS) • Listening Ability (LS)	Verbal (sentences)	Immediate verbal memory and recall	Verbal (sentences)	Right dorsolateral frontal cortex and the bilateral posterior parietal cortex

(Continued)

TABLE 13.2 Input, Processing, and Output Demands Required for WJ IV Cognitive, Achievement, and Oral Language Tests Classified According to Miller's Integrated School Neuropsychological—CHC Conceptual Model (Continued)

Test	Task Description	Narrow CHC Ability	Input Demands	Processing Demands	Output Demands	Primary Neuroanatomical Regions
Cognitive Processes: Executive Functions (*Gf*)						
COG-2: Number Series	Determining a number missing in a sequence	• Quantitative Reasoning (RQ) • Induction (I)	Visual (numeric)	Recall and manipulation of internal number line and applying numerical reasoning to solve problem	Verbal (a number)	Horizontal intraparietal sulcus within the parietal cortex (number sense) and left frontal parietal and left basal ganglia (reasoning)
COG-9: Concept Formation	Determining and applying categorization rules	• Induction (I)	Visual (drawings)	Executive functions of categorization based on rules using inductive reasoning	Verbal (definition of a conceptual rule)	Prefrontal–striatal–thalamus loop
COG-15: Analysis–Synthesis	Analyzing if then visual relationships to deduce missing elements	• General Sequential Reasoning (RG)	Visual (drawings)	Executive functions of deductive reasoning	Verbal (words)	Left frontal parietal and left basal ganglia

Test	Description	Constructs	Visual	Fluid reasoning	Verbal	Brain region
ACH-13: Number Matrices	Ability to analyze the relationship among numbers and identify the missing number	• Quantitative Reasoning (RQ)	Visual (numeric)	Fluid reasoning: quantitative reasoning	Verbal (a number)	Horizontal intraparietal sulcus within the parietal cortex (number sense) and left frontal parietal and left basal ganglia (reasoning)
Facilitators/Inhibitors: Allocating and Maintaining Attention						
COG-17: Pair Cancellation	Matching target stimuli from a large visual array under time constraints	• Attentional Control (AC) • Perceptual Speed (P) • Spatial Scanning (SS)	Visual (picture icons)	Selective/focused and sustained attention; proactive interference	Motoric (circle responses)	Right prefrontal and anterior cingulate
Facilitators/Inhibitors: Working Memory						
COG-3: Verbal Attention	Answering questions about the order of intermingled list of animals and digits	• Working Memory Capacity (WM) • Attentional Control (AC)	Verbal (words and numbers)	Verbal working memory and attentional capacity	Verbal (animal name or digit)	Left supramarginal gyrus in the inferior parietal lobes and the lateral frontal (premotor) region
COG-10: Numbers Reversed	Holding a span of numbers in immediate memory then performing a mental operation on them	• Working Memory Capacity (WM) • Attentional Control (AC)	Verbal (numbers)	Short-term verbal working memory and attentional capacity	Verbal (number sequence)	Left supramarginal gyrus in the inferior parietal lobes and the lateral frontal (premotor) region

(Continued)

TABLE 13.2 Input, Processing, and Output Demands Required for WJ IV Cognitive, Achievement, and Oral Language Tests Classified According to Miller's Integrated School Neuropsychological—CHC Conceptual Model (Continued)

Test	Task Description	Narrow CHC Ability	Input Demands	Processing Demands	Output Demands	Primary Neuroanatomical Regions
COG-16: Object-Number Sequencing	Holding a set of intermingled words and numbers in memory then recall them regrouped into ordered sequences	• Working Memory Capacity (WM)	Verbal (words and numbers)	Verbal working memory and recall	Verbal (number or word sequence)	Left supramarginal gyrus in the inferior parietal lobes and the lateral frontal (premotor) region
Facilitators/Inhibitors: Speed, Fluency, and Efficiency of Processing—Cognitive Processing Speed (Gs)						
COG-4: Letter-Pattern Matching	Locate and circle two identical letter patterns in a row	• Perceptual Speed (P)	Visual (letters on a page)	Perceptual speed, a function of processing speed	Motoric (circle items on a page)	White matter organization in parietal and temporal lobes and connections to lateral prefrontal cortex
COG-11: Number-Pattern Matching	Locate and circle two identical numbers in a row of numbers	• Perceptual Speed (P)	Visual (numbers on a page)	Perceptual speed, a function of processing speed	Motoric (circle items on a page)	White matter organization in parietal and temporal lobes and connections to lateral prefrontal cortex

OL-4: Rapid Picture Naming	Naming quickly pictures of common objects across rows	• Naming Facility (NA) • Speed of Lexical Access (LA)	Visual (Pictures)	Speed of lexical access	Verbal (words)	Left temporal lobe (lexical access)
OL-8: Retrieval Fluency	Naming words as quickly as possible, which start with a particular letter or fit in the same category	• Ideational Fluency (FI) • Speed of Lexical Access (LA)	Auditory (directions only)	Speed of word and semantic lexical assess	Verbal (words)	Left temporal lobe (lexical access)
ACH-8: Oral Reading	Reading sentence for accuracy and fluency of expression of increasing lengths and difficulty	• Reading Decoding (RD) • Verbal (printed) Language Comprehension (V)	Visual (sentences)	Reading fluency: rapid phonological decoding	Verbal (sentences)	Left occipital and fusiform gyrus (fluency)
ACH-9: Sentence Reading Fluency	Rapidly reading short, simple sentences and circles yes or no if they make sense over a 3-min interval	• Reading Speed (RS) • Reading Comprehension (RC)	Visual (sentences)	Reading fluency: rapid phonological decoding	Verbal (sentences)	Left occipital and fusiform gyrus (fluency); right inferior longitudinal fasciculus and the superior longitudinal fasciculus (reading comprehension)

(Continued)

TABLE 13.2 Input, Processing, and Output Demands Required for WJ IV Cognitive, Achievement, and Oral Language Tests Classified According to Miller's Integrated School Neuropsychological—CHC Conceptual Model (Continued)

Test	Task Description	Narrow CHC Ability	Input Demands	Processing Demands	Output Demands	Primary Neuroanatomical Regions
ACH-11: Sentence Writing Fluency	Producing, in writing, simple sentences that are legible	• Writing Speed (WS) • Writing Ability (WA)	Auditory (directions and prompts)	Writing fluency	Motoric (written sentences)	Left basal ganglia
ACH-10: Math Facts Fluency	Solving simple math problems quickly	• Mathematic Achievement (A3) • Number Facility (N)	Visual (math problems)	Mathematics fluency	Motoric (solving math problems)	Horizontal segment of the intraparietal sulcus
ACH-15: Word Reading Fluency	Rapidly reading words and marking the two semantically related words in each row	• Reading Comprehension (RC) • Reading Speed (RS)	Visual (words)	Reading fluency	Motoric (slash marks)	Left occipital and fusiform gyrus (fluency)
Acquired Knowledge: Acculturation Knowledge						
COG-1: Oral Vocabulary	Knowledge of synonyms and antonyms	• Lexical Knowledge (VL) • Language Development (LD)	Auditory questions	Semantic memory activation and retrieval and verbal analogical reasoning	Verbal (saying a word)	Middle temporal gyrus and inferior temporal gyrus

COG-8: General Information	Knowledge of what and where questions	• General Verbal Information (K0)	Auditory questions	Semantic memory activation and retrieval from declarative (semantic) memories	Verbal (one word or up to a sentence answer)	Inferior frontal gyrus and the anterior cingulate
ACH-18: Science	Knowledge of information related to science	• General Verbal Information (K0) • General Science Information (K1)	Auditory questions with visual stimuli	Semantic memory of domain-specific knowledge	Verbal	Inferior frontal gyrus and the anterior cingulate
ACH-19: Social Studies	Knowledge of information related to social studies	• General Verbal Information (K0) • Knowledge of Culture (K2) • Geography Achievement (A5)	Auditory questions with visual stimuli	Semantic memory of domain-specific knowledge	Verbal	Inferior frontal gyrus and the anterior cingulate
ACH-20: Humanities	Knowledge of information related to humanities and the arts	• General Verbal Information (K0) • Knowledge of Culture (K2)	Auditory questions with visual stimuli	Semantic memory of domain-specific knowledge	Verbal	Inferior frontal gyrus and the anterior cingulate

(Continued)

TABLE 13.2 Input, Processing, and Output Demands Required for WJ IV Cognitive, Achievement, and Oral Language Tests Classified According to Miller's Integrated School Neuropsychological—CHC Conceptual Model (Continued)

Test	Task Description	Narrow CHC Ability	Input Demands	Processing Demands	Output Demands	Primary Neuroanatomical Regions
Acquired Knowledge: Language Abilities						
OL-1: Picture Vocabulary	Recognize and name pictured objects	• Lexical Knowledge (VL) • Language Development (LD)	Visual (picture)	Oral expression: vocabulary knowledge	Verbal (word)	Left prefrontal cortex, with contributions from the temporal, anterior cingulate, and cerebellum
OL-2: Oral Comprehension	Listening to a short passage and providing the missing word	• Listening Skills (LS)	Verbal listening skills	Receptive language and semantic memory activation and retrieval	Verbal (missing word)	Left hemisphere temporoparietal region "Wernicke area" and left prefrontal cortex (retrieval)
OL-6: Understanding Directions	Listening to instructions and then pointing to objects in pictures	• Working Memory Capacity (WM) • Listening Skills (LS)	Verbal listening skills	Verbal working memory and receptive language skills	Nonverbal "pointing" response	Left hemisphere temporoparietal region "Wernicke area" and left supramarginal gyrus in the inferior parietal lobes

Acquired Knowledge: Reading Achievement

ACH-1: Letter-Word Identification	Reading words in isolation	• Reading Decoding (RD)	Verbal (words)	Basic reading skills: phonological decoding	Verbal (words)	Left inferior frontal and inferior parietal
ACH-7: Word Attack	Reading phonetically regular nonsense words orally	• Reading Decoding (RD) • Phonetic Coding (PC)	Verbal (nonsense words)	Basic reading skills: phonological decoding	Verbal (nonsense words)	Supramarginal gyrus
ACH-4: Passage Comprehension	Reading a passage silently and provides the missing word	• Reading Comprehension (RC)	Visual (reading passages)	Reading comprehension skills	Verbal (word)	Right inferior longitudinal fasciculus (ILF) and superior longitudinal fasciculus (SLF) tracts
ACH-12: Reading Recall	Ability to read a story silently and retell as much of the story as possible	• Reading Comprehension (RC) • Meaningful Memory (MM)	Visual (reading passages)	Reading comprehension skills	Verbal (story recall)	Right inferior longitudinal fasciculus (ILF) and superior longitudinal fasciculus (SLF) tracts
ACH-17: Reading Vocabulary	Orally producing synonyms, antonyms, or verbal analogies	• Reading Comprehension (RC) • Lexical Knowledge (VL)	Verbal (directions and prompts) with visual (word cues)	Reading comprehension skills	Verbal (word)	Right inferior longitudinal fasciculus (ILF) and superior longitudinal fasciculus (SLF) tracts

(Continued)

TABLE 13.2 Input, Processing, and Output Demands Required for WJ IV Cognitive, Achievement, and Oral Language Tests Classified According to Miller's Integrated School Neuropsychological—CHC Conceptual Model (Continued)

Test	Task Description	Narrow CHC Ability	Input Demands	Processing Demands	Output Demands	Primary Neuroanatomical Regions
Acquired Knowledge: Written Language Achievement						
ACH-14: Editing	Ability to use proper punctuation and capitalization and identify writing mistakes	• English Usage (EU)	Visual (sentences)	Written expression skills	Oral (editing details)	Left prefrontal (retrieval)
ACH-6: Writing Samples	Producing meaningful written sentences	• Writing Ability (WA)	Verbal (directions) and visual (text)	Expository composition skills	Motoric (writing)	Cerebellum and frontal areas of language-dominant hemisphere
ACH-3: Spelling	Ability to spell words from dictation	• Spelling Ability (SG)	Verbal (words)	Orthographic spelling skills	Motoric (writing)	Left fusiform gyrus, left supramarginal gyrus, and inferior frontal cortex
ACH-16: Spelling of Sounds	Ability to spell nonsense words that conform to conventional phonetics	• Spelling Ability (SA) • Phonetic Coding (PC)	Verbal (letters and words)	Orthographic spelling skills	Motoric (writing)	Left fusiform gyrus, left supramarginal gyrus, and inferior frontal cortex

Acquired Knowledge: Mathematics Achievement

			Visual (numbers)	Mathematical calculation skills	Motoric (writing)	
ACH-5: Calculations	Performing a variety of math calculations	• Mathematical Achievement (A3)	Visual (numbers)	Mathematical calculation skills	Motoric (writing)	*Addition and multiplication facts*: Left perisylvian area along the temporal lobe *Subtraction*: Bilateral occipital–temporal regions *Number recognition*: Fusiform gyrus Estimation skills, fractions, and division: Bilateral inferior parietal regions
ACH-2: Applied Problems	Analyzing and solving practical math problems	• Mathematical Achievement (A3) • Quantitative Reasoning (RQ)	Verbal (questions) and Visual (numbers and text)	Mathematical reasoning skills	Verbal (answers)	Horizontal intraparietal sulcus within the parietal cortex (number sense) and left frontal parietal and left basal ganglia (reasoning)

Cognitive processes. In the Integrated SNP/CHC Model, Miller (2013) identified four principal cognitive processes: visuospatial, auditory/phonological, learning and memory, and executive functions. These basic cognitive processes are influenced by basic sensory functions, are modulated by the facilitators and inhibitors, and influence acquired knowledge.

Visuospatial. The WJ IV authors include the Visualization and Picture Recognition tests as measures of *Gv* or Visual Processing. The Visualization test consists of two subtests: Block Rotation and Spatial Relations, which require recognizing spatial configurations with and without mental rotations. The right occipital–temporal region, called the ventral stream, is the area of the brain responsible for recognition of objects (Ungerleider & Mishkin, 1982). The bilateral frontal parietal network in the brain is activated during the performance of mental rotation tasks similar to the ones used on the WJ IV (Millivojevic, Hamm, & Corballis, 2009). It is also important to note that more complex visual rotational tasks (e.g., dual axis rotations) place additional demands on executive processes thus simultaneously activating cortical areas within the dorsolateral prefrontal cortex (Just, Carpenter, Maguire, Diwadkar, & McMains, 2001).

In the Integrated SNP/CHC Model, Miller (2013) classifies the Picture Recognition test as an example of a visual immediate memory task, rather than a *Gv* test. The Picture Recognition test does require visuospatial *Gv* skills at a rudimentary level, but the key processing demands of the task involve visual immediate memory. From a neurocognitive perspective, the *Gv* abilities are not fully assessed by the WJ IV and should be supplemented with other cross-battery measures as needed (see Miller, 2013 for a comprehensive list).

Auditory/Phonological. The test authors have significantly enhanced the measurement of auditory processing (*Ga*) in the revision from the WJ III NU to the WJ IV. *Ga* abilities have become more widely recognized as playing a major scaffolding role in language development and in general cognitive abilities (Conway, Pisoni, & Kronenberger, 2009). From a neuropsychological perspective, *Ga* can be divided into separate omnibus processing streams, a spatial stream that originates in the caudal part of the superior temporal gyrus and projects to the parietal cortex, and a pattern or object stream originating in the more anterior portions of the lateral belt (Rauschecker & Tian, 2000).

Ga is measured by the new WJ IV COG Nonword Repetition and Phonological Processing tests, and by the WJ IV OL Sound Awareness, Segmentation, and Sound Blending tests. The narrow ability of phonetic coding (PC) is the principal cognitive skill required for all of these tests, which requires activation of the bilateral posterior–superior temporal regions of the brain (Hickok & Poeppel, 2000). Schneider and McGrew (2012) added an additional narrow ability to *Ga* called memory for sound patterns (UM), which is a cognitive processing requirement for the WJ IV COG Nonword Repetition test. UM seems to be related to processing within the ventral aspect of the inferior parietal cortex (Ravizza, Delgado, Chein, Becker, & Fiez, 2004).

Learning and Memory. A thorough assessment of learning and memory processes is very complex. Some tests focus on only one aspect of learning and memory such as immediate memory or working memory. Miller (2013) classified the broad area of learning and memory into six second-order classifications: rate of learning, verbal immediate memory, visual immediate memory, delayed verbal memory, delayed visual memory, and verbal–visual associative learning and recall. The WJ IV provides assessment of learning and memory in the areas of verbal and visual immediate memory, and verbal–visual associative memory, but does not provide any tests designed to measure rate of learning or delayed recall or recognition. If a clinician is concerned about an examinee's learning and memory, additional cross-battery assessment of these constructs would be warranted and can be obtained by administering one of the stand-alone learning and memory tests such as the Wide Range Assessment of Memory and Learning—Second Edition (WRAML-2; Sheslow & Adams, 2003), the Test of Memory and Learning—Second Edition (TOMAL-2; Reynolds & Voress, 2007), or the Wechsler Memory Scale—Fourth Edition (WMS-IV; Wechsler, 2009).

The WJ IV COG Story Recall test measures the narrow ability of Meaningful Memory (MM). This MM task requires the comprehension of narratives, which involves multiple brain regions such as those areas along the middle and superior temporal gyri and inferior cortex for general language processing (Ferstl & von Cramon, 2001). In addition, specific regions such as the anterior temporal lobes (Ferstl, Neumann, Bogler, & von Cramon, 2007) and the dorsomedial prefrontal cortex (Hasson, Nusbaum, & Small, 2007) are also involved due to the cognitive demands necessary for comprehension of text.

The narrow ability of Visual Memory (Gv-MV) is measured by the WJ IV COG Picture Recognition test. The left ventrolateral prefrontal cortex seems to be involved in the processing of immediate memory for pictures (Sanefuji et al., 2011). Finally, the narrow ability of Memory Span (MS) is measured by the WJ IV COG Memory for Words and the WJ IV OL Sentence Repetition tests. The left ventrolateral frontal cortex is preferentially active during the encoding of words of sentences, but these regions do not retrieve the information. It is the right dorsolateral frontal cortex and the bilateral posterior parietal cortex that are active in memory retrieval (Tulving, Kapur, Craik, Moscovitch, & Houle, 1994).

Executive Functions. The WJ IV COG has four measures of executive functions, which are viewed as synonymous with the CHC broad ability of fluid reasoning (Gf). Number Matrices and Number Series were taken from the WJ III Diagnostic Supplement (Woodcock, McGrew, Mather, & Schrank, 2003, 2007) and added to the WJ IV COG. The WJ IV COG Concept Formation test is a measure of inductive reasoning and involves the prefrontal–striatal–thalamus loop (Liang et al., 2010). The WJ IV COG Analysis–Synthesis test measures the narrow ability of General Sequential Reasoning (RG), which involves the left frontal parietal and basal ganglia regions of the brain (Prado, Chadha, & Booth, 2011). Interestingly, a series of recent empirical studies (Au et al., 2014; Chuderski, 2013; Colom et al., 2015) suggests that performance on executive functioning tasks such as *Gf* is governed by number of intermediary cognitive processes such as *Gwm* and *Gs*. Thus, clinicians should be mindful of the potential influence of these and other related facilitating cognitive factors when appraising an individual's performance on higher order measures of executive functioning on the WJ IV.

WJ IV COG Number Series and WJ IV ACH Number Matrices tests measure the narrow ability of Quantitative (or numerical) Reasoning (RQ). Wilson and Dehaene (2007) have suggested that tasks that involve RQ involve manipulation of the internal number line, which activates the horizontal intraparietal sulcus within the parietal cortex (number sense). The reasoning aspects of these two tasks also involve the left frontal parietal and left basal ganglia regions of the brain.

Facilitators/Inhibitors. The Integrated SNP/CHC Model (Miller, 2013) includes a broad classification called facilitators/inhibitors, which comprises three broad categories: (i) allocating and maintaining attention; (ii) working memory; and (iii) speed, fluency, and efficiency of processing. These three processes act to either facilitate or inhibit higher order cognitive processes such as executive functions and learning and memory.

Allocating and Maintaining Attention. Attentional skills are a prerequisite skill for the majority of the WJ IV tasks; however, the WJ IV COG Pair Cancellation test is the only test that specifically measures selective/focused and sustained attention. The right prefrontal and the anterior cingulate of the brain are related to allocating and maintaining attentional control (Posner & Raichle, 1994). Clinicians must exercise caution when interpreting higher order cognitive skills, such as learning and memory or executive functions, when an underlying attentional processing deficit is present. This is because selective/focused attention mediates all cognitive processing tasks (Cowan, 1988). If poor performance on these tasks is observed, additional assessment may be needed so that clinicians can determine the underlying neurocognitive mechanism responsible for the observed performance. If attentional processing deficits are suspected as part of the referral question(s), the clinician should add additional cross-battery tests from the NEPSY-II (Korkman et al., 2007), such as the Auditory Attention and Response Set test or select tests from the Test of Everyday Attention for Children (TEA-Ch; Manly, Robertson, Anderson, & Nimmo-Smith, 1999).

Working Memory. A welcome change to CHC nomenclature from the WJ III to the WJ IV was the relabeling of the broad CHC ability, short-term memory (*Gsm*) to working memory (*Gwm*) (Schneider & McGrew, 2012). The revised working memory label is more consistent with the neuropsychology literature. In contrast to other contemporary cognitive batteries (e.g., WISC-V), the WJ IV provides users with an array of *Gwm* assessment measures beyond traditional digit span (forward and backward) tasks. An additional test, Verbal Attention, was added to the WJ IV COG to strengthen the assessment of working memory. In addition to the Verbal Attention test, the WJ IV COG has the Object-Number Sequencing test (formerly called Auditory Working Memory) and the Numbers Reversed test. Each of these three tests measure verbal working memory, which involves a left hemispheric network consisting of the lateral frontal (premotor region) and the inferior parietal lobes (supramarginal gyrus) (Ravizza et al., 2004). For a thorough assessment of working memory, it is recommended that the clinician also assess visual working memory using tests from other cognitive batteries (e.g., Symbolic Working Memory test from the WRAML-2; Sheslow & Adams, 2003).

Speed, Fluency, and Efficiency of Processing. The neurocognitive constructs of processing speed, fluency, and efficiency have been poorly defined up until the recent past (Miller, 2013). Based on a synthesis of many exploratory and confirmatory factor analytic studies, McGrew (2005), McGrew and Evans (2004), and Schneider and McGrew (2012) concluded that processing speed (*Gs*) might be best considered as a set of hierarchically organized speed taxonomy. Miller (2013) expanded on the idea of a multifaceted model of processing speed and proposed a broad classification of facilitators/inhibitors for speed, fluency, and efficiency of processing. Miller took this broad classification and subclassified it into four second-order classifications: (i) performance fluency; (ii) retrieval fluency; (iii) acquired knowledge fluency; and (iv) fluency in relation to accuracy.

Performance fluency "is defined as the ability to quickly perform simple, repetitive tasks," which do not require assessing prior learning (Miller, 2013, p. 399). The WJ IV COG has three tests that can be classified as performance fluency measures: Letter-Pattern Matching, Number-Pattern Matching, and Rapid Picture Naming. Letter-Pattern Matching is a new test to the WJ IV and measures the narrow CHC ability of perceptual speed (P). Number-Pattern Matching (formerly called Visual Matching on the WJ III NU) is also a measure of the narrow ability of P. Efficient perceptual speed seems to be related to the white matter organization in the parietal and temporal lobes and to connections between these areas and the lateral prefrontal lobes (Ferrer et al., 2013; Turken et al., 2008). Rapid Picture Naming measures the narrow abilities of Naming Facility (NA) and Speed of Lexical Access (LA), which are processes related to the left temporal lobe region of the brain for lexical access (Shaywitz, Shaywitz & Pugh, 1995).

Retrieval fluency "is defined as how quickly information can be retrieved from long-term memory" (Miller, 2013, p. 399). The WJ IV OL Retrieval Fluency test is designed to measure the narrow abilities of Ideational Fluency (FI) and Speed of Lexical Access (LA), which is again related to left temporal lobe functions (Shaywitz et al., 1995). Acquired Knowledge Fluency "relates to the automaticity of academic achievement including: reading fluency, writing fluency, and mathematics fluency" (Miller, 2013, p. 399). The WJ IV ACH test battery has five measures of acquired knowledge fluency: Oral Reading, Word

Reading Fluency, Sentence Reading Fluency, Sentence Writing Fluency, and Math Facts Fluency.

The WJ IV ACH Oral Reading test measures the narrow abilities of Reading Decoding (RD) and Verbal (printed) Language (V). This test also has a strong fluency component. Reading fluency is further assessed on the WJ IV ACH using the Sentence Reading Fluency and the Word Reading Fluency Test. These reading fluency measures tap a variety of cognitive processes including reading decoding, reading comprehension, and reading speed. The reading fluency aspect is related to the left occipital/fusiform gyrus regions of the brain (Benjamin & Gabb, 2012), and the reading comprehension component of these tasks relates to the right inferior longitudinal fasciculus and the superior longitudinal fasciculus (Horowitz-Kraus, Grainger, DiFrancesco, Vannest, & Holland, 2014).

Writing fluency is measured by the WJ IV ACH Sentence Writing Fluency test, which is related to left basal ganglia functions within the brain (Swett, Contreras-Vidal, Birn, & Braun, 2010). The WJ IV ACH Math Fluency test measures the narrow abilities of Number Facility (N) and Mathematic Achievement (A3). The horizontal segment of the intraparietal sulcus is activated whenever a mathematical operation needs to access a quantitative representation of numbers, such as what is required in math fluency tasks (Dehaene, Piazza, Pinel, & Cohen, 2005).

Acquired Knowledge. Acquired knowledge is the broad term used in the Integrated SNP/CHC Model (Miller, 2013), which encompasses the acculturation knowledge, language abilities, and reading, writing, and mathematics achievement. This next section of the chapter reviews the WJ IV tests associated with each of these five types of acquired knowledge.

Acculturation Knowledge. Horn and Blankson (2012) first used the term acculturation knowledge to describe *Gc*, and is synonymous with CHC label comprehension-knowledge. Within the acculturation knowledge broad classification, Miller (2013) defined a second-order classification called semantic memory, which includes verbal comprehension and general information knowledge. The WJ IV COG Oral Vocabulary test measures the narrow abilities of Lexical Knowledge (VL) and Language Development (LD). This test requires the examinee to retrieve synonyms and antonyms for words, which involves lexical access within the middle temporal gyrus and the inferior temporal gyrus (Binder et al., 2000). The WJ IV COG General Information test requires semantic memory activation and retrieval, while the WJ IV ACH tests of Science, Social Studies, and Humanities require retrieval of specific content knowledge. Retrieval of factual knowledge requires the inferior frontal gyrus and the anterior cingulate (Borst & Anderson, 2013).

Language Abilities. Miller (2013) identified two second-order classifications of Language Abilities: (i) oral expression, and (ii) receptive language or listening comprehension. The WJ IV OL Picture Vocabulary test measures the CHC narrow abilities of Lexical Knowledge (VL) and Language Development (LD).

The ability to recognize and name pictured objects requires retrieval of vocabulary knowledge, which is related to left prefrontal cortex functions with contributions from the temporal, anterior cingulate, and cerebellum (Binder et al., 1997). The WJ IV OL Oral Comprehension test measures the CHC narrow ability of Listening Skills (LS), which is related to the left temporoparietal region (Wernicke's Area) for receptive language processing and the left prefrontal cortex for retrieval (Berl et al., 2010). The WJ IV OL Understanding Directions test measures two CHC narrow abilities: Listening Skills (LS) and Working Memory Capacity (WM). Based on the neurocognitive demands of this test, it could be classified as either a component of Acquired Knowledge: Language Abilities or as a Facilitator/Inhibitor: Working Memory task. The listening skills part of the task requires the left temporoparietal region (Wernicke's Area) and the working memory part of the task requires the left supramarginal gyrus in the inferior parietal lobes and the lateral frontal (premotor) region of the brain (Ravizza et al., 2004).

Reading Achievement. Tests from each of the WJ IV batteries (COG, OL, and ACH) contribute to a broad assessment of reading achievement and the cognitive skills predictive of reading achievement. Reading disorders in children are widely believed to reflect an underlying weakness in phonological awareness (PA), which is the ability to recognize and manipulate the sound structure of words (Wagner & Torgesen, 1987). The WJ IV ACH tests of Letter-Word Identification and Word Attack were designed to measure aspects of PA. Verbal–visual associative learning is an important prerequisite skill for reading fluency (Newman & Joanisse, 2011), which in turn influences reading comprehension. The WJ IV COG Visual–Auditory Learning test was designed to measure verbal–visual associative learning.

Some children with reading disorders also have deficits in rapid automatized naming (RAN), either in isolation or in combination with PA deficits (Katzir, Kim, Wolf, Morris, & Lovett, 2008). RAN is the speed that one can name out loud a series of visually presented familiar stimuli such as colors, letter, numbers, or words. The WJ IV OL Rapid Picture Naming test was designed to be a RAN measure. RAN measures reflect the automaticity of processes, which are important for reading (Norton & Wolf, 2012). Wolf and Bowers (1999) proposed the double-deficit hypothesis where RAN and PA may either independently, or combined, be the cause of reading disorders in children. Subsequently, a host of empirical evidence has since confirmed the role of these foundational neurocognitive constructs with respect to development of reading difficulties across the lifespan (Cronin, 2013). Norton et al. (2014) used functional magnetic resonance imaging (fMRI) to explore the functional neuroanatomical basis of the double-deficit hypothesis model of developmental dyslexia. PA tasks activated the left inferior frontal and inferior parietal regions of the brain, whereas the RAN tasks activated the right cerebellar VI region of the brain.

The WJ IV ACH Passage Comprehension, Reading Recall, and Reading Vocabulary are tests designed to measure reading comprehension.

Reading comprehension is typically thought to rely on the automatic recognition of language, which in turn is generally thought to reflect left hemispheric processing (Horowitz-Kraus et al., 2014). Horowitz-Kraus and colleagues found that the known language tracts in the brain, the right inferior longitudinal fasciculus and the superior longitudinal fasciculus tracts were positively correlated with scores from the WJ III Passage Comprehension test (Woodcock et al., 2001, 2007a). They also reported that imaging data collected during reading comprehension tasks showed greater activation in the right hemisphere, than previously expected.

Written Language Achievement. The WJ IV ACH includes four tests of written language: Editing, Writing Samples, Spelling, and Spelling of Sounds. Editing skills are related to the recall and application of the rules for proper punctuation and capitalization and the application of those rules. Precise location of this function within the brain is not known at this time, but the retrieval of the rules and the application of the rules is likely related to left prefrontal activity. Writing is a complex process that includes phonological and orthographical functioning, the lexical level of functioning, syntax, and pragmatics. The frontal lobes must be able to retrieve specific linguistic information upon demand, hold that information in working memory, and assemble that information using a logical motoric output (Feifer, 2013). The frontal areas of the language-dominant hemisphere and the cerebellum are the broad-based regions of the brain activated during writing tasks. In fMRI studies, spelling tasks activated the left fusiform gyrus, left supramarginal gyrus, and the inferior frontal cortex (Norton, Kovelman, & Petitto, 2007).

Mathematics Achievement. The WJ IV ACH includes two tests, Calculations and Applied Problems, designed to measure several narrow abilities related to mathematics achievement. These tests measure the CHC narrow ability of Mathematical Achievement (A3), while the Applied Problems test also measures Quantitative Reasoning (RQ). The brain structures associated with mathematical computations and mathematical reasoning involve the frontal, left, and right hemispheres (Maricle, Psimas-Fraser, Muenke, & Miller, 2010). Neuroimaging studies (Cohen, Dehaene, Chochon, Lehericy, & Naccache, 2000) found that left frontal, inferior parietal, perisylvian region, and basal ganglia regions were all related to mathematical functions. Feifer and De Fina (2005) suggested that the region of the brain being activated varies depending upon the type of mathematical calculation being performed.

INTERPRETING THE WJ IV FROM A NEUROPSYCHOLOGICAL PERSPECTIVE

Due to the page constraints of a book chapter, it is not possible to include a sample of a complete neuropsychological report, which integrates the WJ IV tests as the core battery. However, it is possible to provide an example of how one section of learning and memory within a comprehensive neuropsychological evaluation could be examined from a neuropsychological perspective. Table 13.3 presents the WJ IV tests that are classified according to the Integrated SNP/CHC Model (Miller, 2013) as measures of learning and memory. Table 13.3 also presents the demand characteristics of each of these tests.

In Table 13.3, note that three of the WJ IV tests measure immediate verbal memory and recall: WJ IV COG Memory for Words, WJ IV OL Sentence Repetition, and WJ IV COG Story Recall. Each of these tests has a verbal input requirement, but varies in its complexity. There is a marked increase in the quantity of verbal input as the tasks increase from presenting words in isolation, to words in sentences, and finally to entire paragraphs. As a result of the changes to the verbal input of these three tasks, the processing and output demands change, as well. Some examinees benefit from the additional semantic loading or contextual cues (e.g., memory for stories > memory for sentences > memory for words). Examinees with these results typically benefit from learning new material that can be related to broad thematic topics or points of reference.

Other examinees struggle with the additional verbal content or semantic loading (e.g., memory for words > memory for sentences > memory for stories). Examinees with these results learn best by memorizing small chunks of information in isolation and become quickly overwhelmed by too much verbal information. It may be the case that examinees with this type of learning profile are capable of learning more complex material, but most likely their poor attention processing is hindering their learning capabilities. Performance on these three measures is also sensitive to changes in the processing requirements related to attentional capacity. Examinees who have significant attentional processing difficulties often achieve average scores on the Memory for Words test, but their performance suffers on the other two immediate verbal memory tests as the verbal complexity increases (Miller, 2013).

It is important for the clinician to evaluate other potential differences within the learning and memory domain, such as, the potential difference between the three tests that measure immediate verbal memory and performance on the WJ IV COG Picture Recognition test, which measures immediate visual memory and recall. Deficits in auditory processing often cause, or are related to, deficits in verbal memory. Likewise, deficits in visual–spatial processing often cause, or are related to, deficits in visual memory. It is important for the clinician to evaluate both the verbal and visual modalities of immediate memory. Instructional implications will vary depending upon any performance differences between verbal and visual immediate memory tasks.

Finally, within the learning and memory domain, it is important for clinicians to evaluate the learning and memory capabilities when verbal and visual information must be associated with each other. Paired associative learning is a prerequisite skill for the acquisition of good reading skills (Miller, 2013). Some examinees will perform in the average range for learning and memory of verbal or visual information in isolation, but stumble on verbal–visual associative

TABLE 13.3 Example of a Demand Analysis for the WJ IV Learning and Memory Tests

Test	Task Description	Input Demands	Processing Demands		Output Demands
COG-18: Memory for Words	Repeat a list of unrelated words in sequence	Verbal (words)	Immediate verbal memory and recall		Verbal (sequence of words)
OL-5: Sentence Repetition	Recall of sentences of increasing length and complexity	Verbal (sentences)	Immediate verbal memory and recall	Increased contextual cues and semantic loading	Verbal (sentences)
COG-6: Story Recall	Details recalled from verbally presented stories	Verbal (passages)	Immediate verbal memory and recall		Verbal (passage)
COG-13: Visual–Auditory Learning	Learning visual–verbal associations and then recalling them	Paired visual (rebuses) and auditory (words)	Verbal–visual associative learning and recall		Verbal (words to form sentences)
COG-14: Picture Recognition	Identifying previously seen pictures embedded in a set of similar pictures	Visual (pictures)	Immediate visual memory and recall		Verbal (numbers of pictures) or motoric (pointing to pictures)

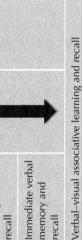

learning tasks. From a neuropsychological perspective, it is important for clinicians to understand the neurocognitive demands of the tasks as reported by the test authors, as well as, any variations in strategies that an individual examinee may employ during the completion of tasks. Although a comprehensive review of demands analysis is beyond the scope of the present chapter, a number of useful resources (Carroll, 1976; Floyd & Kranzler, 2012; Hale & Fiorello, 2004) are available for clinician's to consult. The ultimate goal of a comprehensive assessment is to determine the examinee's strengths and weaknesses and tailor subsequent evidence-based interventions.

Despite the illusion of orthogonality provided by psychometric interpretive frameworks (e.g., CHC), some have characterized attempts to disentangle the different features of cognition is akin to "slicing smoke" (Horn, 1991). Accordingly, we encourage clinicians to be mindful of the fact that all cognitive tasks require an examinee to utilize multiple neurocognitive abilities simultaneously. An integrated neuropsychological assessment and interpretive model, as we have articulated in the present chapter, potentially provides WJ IV users with an evidence-based framework for making more clinically useful inferences about the multitude of quantitative and qualitative factors that mediate the performance that is observed on individual psychoeducational tasks.

SUMMARY

Compared to all of the other major co-normed tests of cognitive abilities and academic achievement, the WJ IV provides the most coverage across the classifications defined by the Integrated SNP/CHC Model. While the WJ IV batteries cover a comprehensive representation of the broad and narrow neurocognitive processes and skills as outlined in the Integrated SNP/CHC Model (Miller, 2013), administering only those tests does not constitute a comprehensive neuropsychological assessment. Some processing domains are not covered by the WJ IV such as sensorimotor functions and other domains of processing, which are not covered in great detail, such as tests of attention or learning and memory. The WJ IV tests typically serve as baseline testing for a more comprehensive neuropsychological assessment. Hypotheses about an examinee's strengths and weaknesses are generated based on the WJ IV tests results and then the clinician chooses additional cross-battery assessments to validate or refute those hypotheses.

The WJ IV authors missed an important opportunity to add to the clinical utility of their tests during the revision by not including more qualitative behaviors. Some qualitative behaviors are included in the WJ IV ACH tests, but the authors and publisher do not include standardization sample base rates for those qualitative behaviors. It is valuable to have the capability of making statements such as, "only 16% of children of the same age as the examinee engaged in this qualitative behavior." A trained clinician can certainly note qualitative behaviors during task administrations, but the base rate data would have been invaluable, as well.

Finally, a word of caution must be made about test interpretation in general. Test developers try to create tests that maximize the measurement variance of a particular skill or cognitive process. However, in any measurement there will be error variance that must be accounted for as well, and construct irrelevant cognitive processes or skills that may also account for some of the reliable variance (Schneider, 2013). Just because an examinee is presented with a verbal task that requires working memory and a verbal output does not mean that the examinee will utilize those same cognitive processes to complete the task. An important step in any assessment is to administer tests in a standardized manner, but then to ask the examinee why certain tasks are more difficult for them than others, and why some tasks are easier than others. This allows the administrator to explore with the examinee what kinds of unique strategies were employed to complete the tasks. This qualitative information provides critical details as to the processes underlying the standardized score and is a foundational feature of modern neuropsychological assessment (cf., Kaplan, 1990). When coupled together, the qualitative data with the outcome scores provides the clinician the ability to develop a more meaningful profile of the examinee's neurocognitive strengths and weaknesses.

REFERENCES

Au, J., Sheehan, E., Tsai, N., Duncan, G. J., Buschkuehl, M., & Jaeggi, S. M. (2014). Improving fluid intelligence with training on working memory: A meta-analysis. *Psychonomic Bulletin and Review* Advance online publication. http://dx.doi.org/10.3758/s13423-014-0699-x.

Benjamin, C. F. A., & Gaab, N. (2012). What's the story? The tale of reading fluency told at speed. *Human Brain Mapping, 33*(11), 2572–2585.

Berl, M. M., Duke, E. S., Mayo, J., Rosenberger, L. R., Moore, E. N., Vanmeter, J., et al. (2010). Functional anatomy of listening and reading comprehension during development. *Brain and Language, 114*(2), 115–125.

Binder, J. R., Frost, J. A., Hammeke, T. A., Bellgowan, P. S. E., Springer, J. A., Kaufman, J. N., et al. (2000). Human temporal lobe activation by speech and non-speech sounds. *Cerebral Cortex, 10,* 512–528.

Binder, J. R., Frost, J. A., Hammeke, T. A., Cox, R. W., Rao, S. M., & Prieto, T. (1997). Human brain language areas identified by functional magnetic resonance imaging. *Journal of neuroscience, 17*(1), 353–362.

Borst, J. P., & Anderson, J. R. (2013). Using model-based functional MRI to locate working memory updates and declarative memory retrievals in the fronto-parietal network. *Proceedings of the National Academy of Sciences of the United States of America, 110*(5), 1628–1633.

Carroll, J. B. (1976). Psychometric tests as cognitive tasks: A new structure of intellect. In L. B. Resnick (Ed.), *The nature of intelligence* (pp. 27–56). Hillsdale, NJ: Erlbaum.

Chuderski, A. (2013). When are fluid intelligence and working memory isomorphic and when are they not? *Intelligence, 41,* 244–262.

Cohen, L., Dehaene, S., Chochon, F., Lehericy, S., & Naccache, L. (2000). Language and calculation with the parietal lobe: A combined cognitive, anatomical, and fMRI study. *Neuropsychologia, 38,* 1426–1440.

Colom, R., Privado, J., Garcia, L. F., Estrada, E., Cuevas, L., & Shih, P. (2015). Fluid intelligence and working memory capacity: Is time for working on intelligence problems relevant for explaining their relationship? *Personality and Individual Differences, 79,* 75–80.

Conway, C. M., Pisoni, D. B., & Kronenberger, W. G. (2009). The auditory scaffolding hypothesis. *Current Directions in Psychological Science, 18*(1), 275–279.

Cowan, N. (1988). Evolving conceptions of memory storage, selective attention, and their mutual constraints within the human information-processing system. *Psychological Bulletin, 104,* 163–191.

Cronin, V. S. (2013). RAN and double-deficit theory. *Journal of Learning Disabilities, 46,* 182–190.

Dean, R. S., & Woodcock, R. W. (1999). *The WJ-R and Bateria-R in neuropsychological assessment* (Research Report No. 3). Itasca, IL: Riverside.

Dean, R. S., & Woodcock, R. W. (2003). *Dean-Woodcock neuropsychological battery.* Itasca, IL: Riverside Publishing.

Dehaene, S., Piazza, M., Pinel, P., & Cohen, L. (2005). Three parietal circuits for number processing. In J. I. D. Campbell (Ed.), *Handbook of mathematical calculation* (pp. 433–453). New York, NY: Psychology Press.

Feifer, S. G. (2013). The neuropsychology of written language disorders: A framework for effective interventions. Middleton. MD: School Neuropsych Press, LLC.

Feifer, S. G., & DeFina, P. A. (2005). *The neuropsychology of mathematics disorders: Diagnosis and intervention.* Middletown, MD: School Neuropsych Press.

Ferrer, E., Whitaker, K. J., Steele, J. S., Green, C. T., Wendelken, C., & Bunge, S. A. (2013). White matter maturation supports the development of reasoning ability through its influence on processing speed. *Developmental Science, 16*(6), 941–951.

Ferstl, E. C., & von Cramon, D. Y. (2001). The role of coherence and cohesion in text comprehension: An event-related fMRI study. *Cognitive Brain Research, 11,* 325–340.

Ferstl, E. C., Neumann, J., Bogler, C., & von Cramon, D. (2007). The extended language network: A meta-analysis of neuroimaging studies on text comprehension. *Human Brain Mapping, 29*(5), 581–593.

Fiorello, C. A., Hale, J. B., & Wycoff, K. L. (2012). Cognitive hypothesis testing. In D. P. Flanagan & P. L. Harrison (Eds.), *Contemporary intellectual assessment: Theories, tests, and issues* (pp. 484–496) (3rd ed.). New York, NY: Guilford Press.

Flanagan, D. P., Alfonso, V. C., & Ortiz, S. O. (2012). The cross-battery assessment approach. In D. P. Flanagan & P. L. Harrison (Eds.), *Contemporary intellectual assessment: Theories, tests, and issues* (pp. 459–483) (3rd ed.). NY: The Guilford Press.

Flangan, D. P., Alfonso, V. C., Ortiz, S. O., & Dynda, A. M. (2010). Integrating cognitive assessment in school neuropsychological evaluations. In D. C. Miller (Ed.), *Best practices in school neuropsychology: Guidelines for effective practice, assessment, and evidence-based intervention* (pp. 101–140). Hoboken, NJ: Wiley & Sons, Inc.

Floyd, R. G., & Kranzler, J. H. (2012). Processing approaches to interpretation of information from cognitive ability tests. In D. P. Flanagan & P. L. Harrison (Eds.), *Contemporary intellectual assessment: Theories, tests, and issues* (3rd ed., pp. 497–525). New York, NY: Guilford Press.

Hale, J. B., & Fiorello, C. A. (2004). *School neuropsychology: A practitioner's handbook.* New York, NY: Guilford Press.

Hasson, U., Nusbaum, H. C., & Small, S. L. (2007). Brain networks subserving the extraction of sentence information and its encoding to memory. *Cerebral Cortex, 17*(12), 2899–2913.

Hickok, G., & Poeppel, D. (2000). Towards a functional neuroanatomy of speech perception. *Trends in Cognitive Sciences, 4*(4), 131–138.

Horn, J. L. (1991). Measurement of intellectual capabilities: A review of theory. In K. McGrew, J. K. Werder, & R. W. Woodcock (Eds.), *WJ-R technical manual* (pp. 197–232). Itasca, IL: Riverside Publishing.

Horn, J. L., & Blankson, A. N. (2012). Foundations for better understanding of cognitive abilities. In D. P. Flanagan & P. L. Harrison (Eds.), *Contemporary intellectual assessment: Theories, tests, and issues* (3rd ed., pp. 73–98). New York, NY: The Guilford Press.

Horowitz-Kraus, T., Grainger, M., DiFrancesco, M., Vannest, J., & Holland, S. K. (2014). Right is not wrong: Dti and fMRI evidence for the reliance of reading comprehension on language-comprehension neworks in the right hemisphere. *Brain Imaging and Behavior* Retrieved from: http://ezproxy.twu.edu:2079/10.1007/s11682-014-9341-9.

Just, M. A., Carpenter, P. A., Maguire, M., Diwadkar, V., & McMains, S. (2001). Mental rotation of objects retrieved from memory: An fMRI study of spatial processing. *Journal of Experimental Psychology: General, 130*, 493–504.

Kaplan, E. (1990). The process approach to neuropsychological assessment of psychiatric patients. *Journal of Neuropsychiatry and Clinical Neurosciences, 2*, 72–87.

Katzir, T., Kim, Y. S., Wolf, M., Morris, R., & Lovett, M. W. (2008). The varieties of pathways to dysfluent reading: Comparing subtypes of children with developmental dyslexia at letter, word, and connected text levels of reading. *Journal of Learning Disabilities, 41*(1), 47–66.

Keith, T. Z., & Reynolds, M. R. (2012). Using confirmatory factor analysis to aid in understanding the constructs measured by intelligence tests. In D. P. Flanagan & P. L. Harrison (Eds.), *Contemporary intellectual assessment: Theories, tests, and issues* (pp. 758–799). NY: The Guilford Press.

Korkman, M., Kirk, U., & Kemp, S. (2007). *NEPSY-II: A developmental neuropsychological assessment*. San Antonio, TX: The Psychological Corporation.

Liang, P., Mei, Y., Jia, X., Yang, Y., Lu, S., Zhong, N., et al. (2010). Brain activation and deactivation in human inductive reasoning: An fMRI study. In Y. Y. Yao (Ed.), *Brain Infomatics 2010, Lecture Notes in Computer Sciences, 6334* (pp. 387–398). Berlin: Springer-Verlag.

Manly, T., Robinson, I. H., Anderson, V., & Nimmo-Smith, I. (1999). *Test of everyday attention for children (TEA-Ch)*. San Antonio, TX: Harcourt.

Maricle, D. E., Psimas-Fraser, L., Muenke, R. C., & Miller, D. C. (2010). Assessment and intervention with children with math disorders. In D. C. Miller (Ed.), *Best practices in school neuropsychology: Guidelines for effective practice, assessment, and evidence-based intervention* (pp. 521–550). Hoboken, NJ: Wiley & Sons, Inc..

McGrew, K. S. (2005). The Cattell–Horn–Carroll theory of cognitive abilities: Past, present, and future. In D. P. Flanagan & P. L. Harrison (Eds.), Contemporary intellectual assessment: Theories, tests, and issues (3rd ed., pp. 136–181). New York, NY: Guilford Press.

McGrew, K. S., & Evans, J. J. (2004). Internal and External Factorial Extensions to the Cattell–Horn–Carroll (CHC) Theory of Cognitive Abilities: A Review of Factor Analytic Research Since Carroll's Seminal 1993 Treatise. Institute for Applied Psychometrics.

Miller, (2007). Essentials of school neuropsychological assessment. Hoboken, NJ: Wiley.

Miller, D. C. (2013). Essentials of school neuropsychological assessment (2nd ed.). Hoboken, NJ: Wiley.

Miller, D. C., & Maricle, D. E. (2012). The emergence of neuropsychological constructs into tests of intelligence. In D. P. Flanagan & P. L. Harrison (Eds.), *Contemporary intellectual assessment: Theories, tests, and issues* (3rd ed., pp. 800–819). New York, NY: Guilford Press.

Miller, D. C., & Maricle, D. E. (2014 for comprehensive reviews).

Millivojec, B., Hamm, J. P., & Corballis, M. C. (2009). Functional neuroanatomy of mental rotation. *Journal of Cognitive Neuroscience, 21*(5), 945–959. http://dx.doi.org/10.1162/jocn.2009.21085.

Newman, R. L., & Joanisse, M. F. (2011). Modulation of brain regions involved in word recognition by homophonous stimuli: an fMRI study. *Brain Research*, *1367*, 250–264.

Norton, E. S., Black, J. M., Stanley, L. M., Tanaka, H., Gabrieli, J. D. E., Sawyer, C., et al. (2014). Functional neuroanatomical evidence for the double-deficit hypothesis of developmental dyslexia. *Neuropsychologia*, *61*, 235–246.

Norton, E. S., Kovelman, I., & Petitto, L. A. (2007). Are there separate neural systems for spelling? New insights into the roles of rules and memory in spelling from functional magnetic resonance imaging. *Mind, Brain, and Education*, *1*(1), 48–59.

Norton, E. S., & Wolf, M. (2012). Rapid automatized naming (RAN) and reading fluency: Implications for understanding and treatment of reading disabilities. *Annual Review of Psychology*, *63*(1), 427–452.

Posner, M. L., & Raichle, M. E. (1994). *Images of mind*. New York, NY: W. H. Freeman.

Prado, J., Chadha, A., & Booth, J. R. (2011). The brain network for deductive reasoning: A quantitative meta-analysis of 28 neuroimaging studies. *Journal of Cognitive Neuroscience*, *23*(11), 3483–3497.

Rauschecker, J. P., & Tian, B. (2000). Mechanisms and streams for processing of "what" and "where" in auditory cortex. *Proceedings of the National Academy of Sciences*, *22*, 11800–11806.

Ravizza, S. M., Delgado, M. R., Chein, J. M., Becker, J. T., & Fiez, J. A. (2004). Functional dissociations with the inferior parietal cortex in verbal working memory. *Neuroimage*, *22*, 562–573.

Reynolds, C. R., & Voress, J. K. (2007). *Test of memory and learning* (2nd ed.). Austin, TX: Pro-Ed.

Sanefuji, M., Takada, Y., Kimura, N., Torisu, H., Kira, R., Ishizaki, Y., et al. (2011). Strategy in short-term memory for pictures in childhood: A near-infrared spectroscopy study. *Neuroimage*, *54*(3), 2394–2400.

Schneider, W. J. (2013). Principles of assessment of aptitude and achievement. In D. H. Saklofske, C. R. Reynolds, & V. L. Schwean (Eds.), *The Oxford handbook of child psychological assessment*. New York, NY: Oxford University Press.http://dx.doi.org/10.1177/0734282913478046.

Schneider, W. J., & McGrew, K. S. (2012). The Cattell–Horn–Carroll model of intelligence. In D. P. Flanagan & P. L. Harrison (Eds.), *Contemporary intellectual assessment: Theories, tests, and issues* (pp. 99–144) (3rd ed.). NY: The Guilford Press.

Schrank, F. A., Mather, N., & McGrew, K. S. (2014a). Woodcock–Johnson IV tests of achievement. Rolling Meadows, IL: Riverside.

Schrank, F. A., Mather, N., & McGrew, K. S. (2014b). Woodcock–Johnson IV tests of oral language. Rolling Meadows, IL: Riverside.

Schrank, F. A., McGrew, K. S., & Mather, N. (2014c). Woodcock–Johnson IV. Rolling Meadows, IL: Riverside.

Schrank, F. A., McGrew, K. S., & Mather, N. (2014d). Woodcock–Johnson IV tests of cognitive abilities. Rolling Meadows, IL: Riverside.

Schrank, F. A., & Wendling, B. J. (2012). The Woodcock–Johnson III Normative Update. In D. P. Flanagan & P. L. Harrison (Eds.), *Contemporary intellectual assessment: Theories, tests, and issues* (3rd ed., pp. 297–335). New York, NY: The Guilford Press.

Shaywitz, B. A., Shaywitz, S. E., Pugh, K. R., et al. (1995). Localization of semantic processing using functional magnetic resonance imaging. *Human Brain Mapping*, *2*, 149–158.

Sheslow, D., & Adams, W. (2003). *Wide range assessment of memory and learning—second edition*. Wilmington, DE: Wide Range, Inc.

Swett, B. A., Contreras-Vidal, J. L., Birn, R., & Braun, A. (2010). Neural substrates of graphomotor sequence learning" A combined fMRI and kinematic study. *Journal of neurophysiology*, *103*(6), 3366–3377.

Tulving, E., Kapur, S., Craik, F. I. M., Moscovitch, M., & Houke, S. (1994). Hemispheric encoding/retrieval asymmetry in episodic memory: Positron emission tomography finding. *Proceedings of the National Academy of Sciences of the United States of America, 91*, 2016–2020.

Turken, A. U., Whitfield-Gabrieli, S., Bammer, R., Baldo, J. V., Dronkers, N. F., & Gabrieli, J. D. E. (2008). Cognitive processing speed and the structure of white matter pathways: Convergent evidence from normal variation and lesion studies. *NeuroImage, 42*(2), 1032–1044.

Ungerleider, L. G., & Miskin, M. (1982). Two cortical visual systems. In D. J. Engle, M. A. Goodale, & R. J. Manfield (Eds.), *Analysis of visual behavior* (pp. 529–586). Cambridge, MA: MIT Press.

Wagner, R. K., & Torgesen, J. K. (1987). The nature of phonological awareness and is causal role in the acquisition of reading skills. *Psychological Bulletin, 101*, 192–212.

Wechsler, D. (2009). *Wechsler memory scale* (4th ed.). Bloomington, MN: PsychCorp.

Wechsler, D. (2014). Wechsler intelligence scale for children (5th ed.). Bloomington, MN: PsychCorp.

Wilson, A. J., & Dehaene, S. (2007). Number sense and developmental dyscalculia. In D. Coch, G. Dawson, & K. Fischer (Eds.), *Human behavior, learning, and the developing brain: Atypical development* (pp. 212–238). New York, NY: Guilford.

Wolf, M., & Bowers, P. G. (1999). The double-deficit hypothesis for the developmental dyslexias. *Journal of Educational Psychology, 91*(3), 415–438.

Woodcock, R. W. (1997). *The WJ-R in neuropsychological assessment.* Tolovana Park, OR: Measurement/Learning/Consultants, LLC.

Woodcock, R. W., & Johnson, M. B. (1989). *Woodcock–Johnson psychoeducational battery—Revised.* Chicago: Riverside.

Woodcock, R. W., McGrew, K. S., & Mather, N. (2001, 2007a). *Woodcock–Johnson III Tests of Cognitive Abilities.* Itasca, IL: Riverside Publishing.

Woodcock, R. W., McGrew, K. S., & Mather, N. (2001, 2007b). *Woodcock–Johnson III tests of achievement.* Itasca, IL: Riverside Publishing.

Woodcock, R. W., McGrew, K. S., Mather, N., & Schrank, F. A. (2003, 2007). *The diagnostic supplement to the Woodcock–Johnson III tests of cognitive abilities.* Itasca, IL: Riverside Publishing.

Chapter 14

Use of the Woodcock–Johnson IV in a Response to Intervention Service Delivery Model

Karen E. Apgar and Justin L. Potts
Eugene (Oregon) School District 4J, Eugene, OR, USA

In this chapter, we provide direction regarding the use of the Woodcock–Johnson® IV (WJ IV; Schrank, McGrew, & Mather, 2014c) assessments in a Response to Intervention (RtI) instructional delivery system. We discuss the core components of RtI, demonstrate how components of the WJ IV can be used to identify specific areas in need of targeted academic intervention, and illustrate the use of the WJ IV in a full and comprehensive evaluation of students who fail to respond adequately to well-designed instructional intervention.

RTI AS AN EDUCATIONAL INITIATIVE

Among the multitude of initiatives that have rolled across the educational landscape, few have been as far reaching, as instructionally relevant, and perhaps as misunderstood as Response to Intervention or RtI. At its heart, RtI is a simple proposition with a founding in decades of instructional problem-solving research and public health intervention models. However, this surface-level simplicity and common sense activity masks a complex interaction between the functions of the public school systems, special education services, and professional development. Compounding this complexity is the fact that RtI does not have a standard protocol for design and implementation. Since its inclusion in the Individuals with Disabilities Education Act (IDEA, 2004), RtI has spawned nearly as many "flavors" as there are states, and nearly as many variations in the legal code around them. Adding to the challenge of implementation is that the systems-level change required of RtI carries significant cost to educational systems that are already stressed (Fuchs, Fuchs, & Compton, 2012). While RtI can be considered to be a continual work in progress, there are effective ways to use well-researched, standardized assessment tools with which practitioners

WJ IV Clinical Use and Interpretation. DOI: http://dx.doi.org/10.1016/B978-0-12-802076-0.00015-3

have many years of experience in conjunction with nearly any district's model for a tiered intervention system.

RTI BASICS

In order to use the WJ IV effectively in an RtI system, which we will refer to here as an academic multitiered system of supports (MTSS), we first need to understand the components of such a system. At its most basic, an academic MTSS can be described as an instructional system of increasingly targeted interventions, designed to address academic skill deficits and provide instructional support without delay. Most systems employ multiple tiers of service, with each tier providing increasingly intense and targeted academic skill instruction (Fuchs, Compton, Fuchs, Bryant, & Davis, 2008). Each student's academic needs are addressed using two, three, or more tiers of instruction within the educational system, with Special Education services determined either within a tier or separate from the tiers. Student progress is monitored regularly in order to determine whether or not the student's specific skills are improving. Based on that progress-monitoring data, student interventions are changed, increased or decreased in intensity, or discontinued. In addition, data can be aggregated by classroom, grade, school building, or at the district level in order to provide a snapshot of progress for whole groups of students.

Note the importance of the word *system* in multitiered systems of supports: MTSS is not something that is done to a student, or for a student, and it is not a set of hoops to jump through in order to direct a child into special education programs. Rather, true MTSS is a school-wide (preferably, district-wide) set of activities, interactions, and interventions that are used for all students, according to their academic skills. It is part of the school or district's General Education model. As Lichtenstein (2008) stated, in order for instructional interventions to be effective, they need to be "embedded within a well-designed and institutionalized multitiered service delivery system."

In addition to providing timely academic support to students with skill deficits, MTSS is also essential for helping educational teams make data-based instructional decisions. It is incumbent upon educators to look beyond teacher observations and high-stakes test scores to determine educational changes—for an individual child, a classroom, a grade level or an entire school. Without the baseline, progress and outcome data that is the bread and butter of an MTSS system, it is difficult for academic teams to make decisions about how best to instruct individual students, how to adjust curricula, how to select academic supports, or whether or not to consider special education for a student.

IDEA 2004

Although measuring student skills and altering instruction accordingly is not a new concept, the term RtI became an instant buzzword upon the publication of the federal guidelines related to the 2004 reauthorization of IDEA 2004. Although RtI might refer to any type of behavioral, social or academic intervention process, the 2004 IDEA reauthorization focused the field of school psychology on RtI as a method for special education identification under the Specific Learning Disability (SLD) eligibility category. The regulations provided two distinct references to intervention response in the SLD regulations.

First, the regulators specified that, as an alternative to the traditional ability–achievement discrepancy approach, states must allow an SLD to be determined when a student does not make sufficient progress to meet academic standards "when using a process based on the child's response to scientific, research-based intervention" (Federal Register, 34 CFR §300.309(2)(a)(i)). In some states, this method for determining SLD is the only option provided in state regulations; in other states, this "response to scientific, research-based intervention" is an option, along with the ability–achievement discrepancy method, and/or "a pattern of strengths and weaknesses…that is determined by the group to be relevant to the identification of a specific learning disability" (34 CFR §300.309(2)(a)(ii); Hauerwas, Brown, & Scott, 2013). As a result, many states have embarked upon creating and establishing MTSS in order to make decisions regarding SLD identification.

Second, and important to those states that allow a method other than MTSS for SLD identification, the federal regulators required that all teams responsible for determining eligibility must demonstrate that a student's skill deficits are not primarily due to lack of appropriate instruction in reading or math. To accomplish this, teams are required to verify that appropriate instruction was provided by qualified personnel in the regular education setting (34 CFR §300.309(b)(1)). Teams are also required to provide "data-based documentation of repeated assessments of achievement at reasonable intervals, reflecting formal assessment of student progress during instruction" (34 CFR §300.309(b)(2)).

The collection of data-based, repeated assessments of student academic progress that reflects formal instruction can be satisfied by the progress-monitoring data provided by MTSS. Therefore, it behooves school districts to adopt an academic MTSS in order to meet the minimal requirements of federal and state regulations pertaining to SLD identification and to use MTSS as a sound and beneficial instruction practice.

KEY ELEMENTS OF AN ACADEMIC MTSS

In spite of the regulatory references to RtI processes for the "appropriate instruction" exclusionary factor and, in some cases, as the sole method of SLD identification, the regulators decline any further specification.

There are many RtI models and the regulations are written to accommodate the many different models that are currently in use…. The Department does not mandate or endorse any particular model.

(34 CFR §300.307 p46653)

Regardless of the model a district chooses, there are several essential components to creating and implementing a successful MTSS that yields actionable data at the district, school, classroom, and individual levels. According to Johnson, Mellard, Fuchs, and McKnight (2006), a strong MTSS uses:

- High-quality, research-based classroom instruction
- Universal (school-wide) screening
- Ongoing progress monitoring
- Evidence-based interventions
- Fidelity measures.

In addition, we suggest that an effective MTSS also requires:

- Precise school-wide scheduling for intervention time
- Well-trained interventionists and progress monitors
- Research-based decision rules

High-quality classroom instruction. First and foremost, MTSS systems are predicated on the school or district using scientific, research-based curricula in the classroom. In addition, teachers must be well trained and highly skilled—not only in the curriculum itself, but also in the ability to differentiate instructional techniques to meet the needs of the various students in the classroom while implementing the chosen curriculum. The provision of the classroom curriculum is often referred to as *Tier 1* of an MTSS system (National Center on Response to Intervention [NCRTI], 2010).

Universal screening. An effective MTSS must provide for school-wide screening of academic skills in order to identify struggling learners. A universal screener is a relatively quick measure of a skill and is administered to every student. For instance, all kindergarteners may be universally screened regarding their knowledge of letter sounds, or older students may be universally screened regarding their skill at solving basic math facts. Some districts use published screening tools, while others design their own. A review of aggregate screening results can help determine what skills need to be given extra attention across a grade level. A review of results comparing each student to his/her grade level peers can help determine which students are the best candidates for extra support. It is essential, therefore, that each school building have a mechanism to review, analyze, and discuss the screener results, and then make decisions based on that data. In many MTSS systems, each building has an RtI Team or a Data Team composed of teachers, administrators, and specialists for this purpose (Wright, 2010).

Progress monitoring. In addition to the initial, universal screener that helps teams determine which students need additional intervention, an MTSS needs a reasonable way to measure progress regularly throughout the delivery of interventions. For instance, if a student is receiving an intervention in word-level reading, a measure of that skill should be administered at regular intervals. Progress monitoring tools need to be fairly quick to administer and, more importantly, need to be sensitive enough to measure small changes in skill development. Measures of progress must be equivalent; that is, each version of the measure must have the same level of difficulty. Otherwise, it is impossible to demonstrate whether a student's skills have improved, decreased, or remained static. Using appropriate progress monitoring tools allows the data to be graphed in a linear fashion, with the slope of this progress line indicating the rate at which a student is making progress. These graphs provide useful visual tools for MTSS data teams, as well as effective graphics for conveying student progress to parents or other stakeholders. Many commercially available progress monitoring tools provide these graphs, which can be easily printed or viewed electronically (National Center on Intensive Intervention [NCII], 2015).

Evidence-based interventions. The crux of an MTSS system is the selection of instructional interventions to address academic skill deficits. A student struggling to make progress in a specific skill, despite general education instruction, is a student who needs specific instruction to target the skill. This may require a school or a district to design research-based intervention materials, such as using rhyming games, sound-deletion practice, and letter sound discrimination activities to help students increase their phonemic awareness (Moats & Tolman, 2009). Conversely, a school or district may choose to address a student's phonemic awareness with a published curriculum that research demonstrates will increase phonemic awareness for the age group in question (Institute of Education Sciences, 2009). Other interventions would be required to address other skills, such as reading fluency, reading comprehension, math calculation, or writing.

The creation or acquisition of intervention tools may be determined, in part, by which type of MTSS the district chooses to practice. To summarize Shapiro (2009), in a Standard Protocol MTSS model, an intervention is provided to all students who demonstrate a general need, based on universal screening data. In such a system, there might be one reading fluency intervention (usually a published curriculum) provided to a group of students who are not yet reading fluently. This generally occurs in a moderately sized intervention group (6–10 students) without an in-depth analysis of their skill errors. Conversely, in a Problem-Solving Protocol, an intervention is chosen or designed on a student-by-student basis, based on that student's individualized skill deficits. This may be delivered in small groups of fewer than five students. Also, some districts choose to combine these types of intervention, at different tiers, to address student needs better (Shapiro, 2009).

Fidelity checks. An effective MTSS must employ measures of fidelity across the system. This includes creating methods for ensuring that interventions are delivered effectively and consistently, for the correct amount of time and the correct number of sessions, and that this occurs for every student, every time (Kovaleski, Marco-Fies, & Bonashefski, 2013). Similarly, the administration of progress monitoring measures must be routinely audited to ensure consistency of practice across time, across settings, and across students. Absence of fidelity renders data points inaccurate, as discrepancies in delivery or measurement may impact the demonstration of student skill. In essence, progress cannot be accurately measured without evidence of procedural fidelity (NCRTI, 2010).

Precise school-wide schedule. A promising MTSS can be easily derailed by an inadequate instructional schedule. Since interventions supplement rather than supplant grade-level curriculum, intervention times must be created outside the regular instructional time for each subject (Liu, Alonzo, & Tindal, 2011). A schedule must be designed in which each grade receives their intervention at a time different than their regular class reading instruction time. This often results in multiple complications for the staff members in charge of creating a building to schedule; however, MTSS only works if each student receives interventions *in addition* to regular grade-level instruction (NCRTI, 2010).

Well-trained interventionists and progress monitors. Even with a well-designed intervention schedule, an MTSS can be disrupted when the professionals providing the interventions are not thoroughly trained in the instructional aspects of the intervention and in the appropriate measurement of student progress. Most commercially available intervention curricula require the teacher to engage in formal or self-study training to familiarize themselves with the instructional procedures, activities, and lessons required by the program. Similarly, the selection of appropriate progress tools and the consistent and accurate administration of the measures may require training and practice time (Scanlon, 2013). In many systems, staff members other than the interventionist administer the progress monitoring measures. In these cases, it is imperative that the progress monitor is adequately trained and has practice administering the progress measures.

Decision rules. In an MTSS, the ability to make instructional and educational decisions relies on everyone in the system adhering to a set of decision rules. These rules help teams determine what steps to take after analyzing a set of data. For instance, after analyzing the rate of progress for an individual student, how does the team determine whether or not to continue with the intervention or make a change? Decision rules must be established regarding:

- which students receive interventions, based on universal screening results
- how long to implement an intervention before reviewing a student's progress data
- what level of progress indicates an intervention be continued, discontinued or changed
- at what point a comprehensive evaluation for special education be considered.

ACADEMIC MTSS IN ACTION

While each district may implement an MTSS slightly differently, a basic system might look like this (adapted from Curtis, Sullivan, Alonzo, & Tindal, 2011):

Tier 1—comprehensive core instruction. The school district must adopt research-based curricula for use in the regular classroom, adequately train staff to teach the curricula, and provide ongoing professional development to ensure appropriate application of the curricula. This research-based curricular instruction should address the learning needs of the majority of students at each grade level. All students access this level of general education curriculum and, early in the school year, universal screeners are administered to every student. Examples of possible universal screening tools include easyCBM, DIBELS, and AimsWeb (NCII, 2015). Equivalent screening measures can also be administered mid-year, to "catch" additional students who may have fallen behind since the beginning of the school year.

The Data Team then reviews the results at each grade level and, based on already established decision rules, selects students to receive additional intervention beyond the general education program. For example, first-graders whose universal screening performance fell below the 20th percentile on a screening measure of Word Reading Fluency may be selected for additional intervention. This level of intervention is often referred to as *Tier 2*.

Tier 2—small group interventions. Intervention groups are established based on universal screening results and standard interventions are provided for a predetermined length of time. The standard intervention is often derived from the supplemental support materials provided by the publisher of the research-based curriculum. Measurements of progress occur for each student at regular intervals, using established progress monitoring measures. For example, for a school using the *Treasures* (McGraw-Hill, 2006) reading curriculum, the first-graders in the above example can receive additional instruction in groups of six to eight, using the curriculum's supplemental instruction program, *Triumphs* (McGraw-Hill, 2006). These students' Word Reading Fluency improvement can be measured, once every 2 weeks, using easyCBM progress monitoring tools (Lai, Alonzo, & Tindal, 2013; University of Oregon, 2006).

After the prescribed amount of intervention time, the Data Team reviews each student's progress to determine if the intervention has impacted academic skill growth. Based on the decision rules, each student's intervention is discontinued, continued, or changed. For example, the first-grade students' Word Reading Fluency improvement rates can be determined using the data from the easyCBM progress monitoring probes. While at least three data points are required to establish a graphical trend line for each student's performance, a minimum of 6 data points, or 12 weeks of intervention data, is often recommended (Curtis et al., 2011). For students whose data indicate strong progress and at or near grade-level performance, interventions are usually discontinued, with the expectation that regular classroom instruction will be sufficient for continued growth. For students whose data indicate steady progress, but whose skills are still not yet near grade level, Tier 2 intervention is continued. The expectation is that the intervention will continue to result in steady progress and that the student will soon reach grade level. For students whose data indicate little or no progress, interventions are usually adjusted, or additional interventions added, to provide more targeted and intensive instruction. This is often referred to as Tier 3 intervention.

Tier 3—targeted interventions. This level of support generally follows a Problem-Solving Protocol (Shapiro, 2009), and requires that additional assessment data be gathered in order to target the student's skill deficit sufficiently. For example, rather than providing an overall literacy or reading intervention, a Tier 3 intervention focuses specifically on one or two specific elements of reading with which each student struggles, such as vowel sounds, consonant digraphs, or multisyllable words. This requires some level of diagnostic assessment.

Use of the Woodcock–Johnson IV Tests of Achievement (WJ IV ACH; Schrank, Mather, & McGrew, 2014a) *at Tier 3.* For students who fail to make adequate progress, despite Tier 1 instruction and Tier 2 intervention, individual assessment of specific academic skills helps Data Teams design highly targeted interventions. For students who continue to struggle with reading, the team may choose to administer the Basic Reading Skills Cluster (Test 1: Letter-Word Identification+Test 7: Word Attack) from the WJ IV ACH to determine if the student stumbles over individual letter sounds, sound blends, vowel sounds, or other specific decoding challenges. The team may choose to administer the Reading Fluency (Test 8: Oral Reading+Test 9: Sentence Reading Fluency) and the Reading Rate (Test 9: Sentence Reading Fluency+Test 15: Word Reading Fluency) clusters to determine if a student's fluency challenges are related more to decoding errors or to reading speed. A student who has not responded well to Tiers 1 and 2 in math may need the Math Calculations cluster (Test 5: Computation+Test 10: Math Facts Fluency) to determine if the student needs additional help with math facts or specific procedural rules.

Results from the above assessment data can be used to design interventions to target the specific skills the student needs in order to make progress. For example, consider the first-grade students who have not been improving their Word Reading Fluency despite Tier 2 intervention. Each student's WJ IV ACH Basic Reading Skills and Reading Fluency cluster results can be analyzed to determine what specific reading-related skill deficit is impeding their progress. Those students who have been found to have difficulty with actual letter sounds and sound blends might be provided targeted instruction, in a group of two or three students, using a *Reading Mastery* (SRA/McGraw-Hill, 2001) intervention to focus on those skills. This might be offered daily in short sessions, or three times per week in longer sessions (Curtis et al., 2011). Those students who have been found to struggle not with the pronunciation of words, but rather with fluidity and prosody of reading, might be provided targeted instruction using a *Read Naturally* (Read Naturally, Inc., 2015) intervention. Of course, in both groups, student progress must be continually monitored at regular intervals, as in Tier 2.

It should be noted that while the WJ IV ACH have different forms (Forms A, B, and C), they will not suffice as a true progress-monitoring tool. The limited number of equivalent WJ IV ACH measures available does not provide enough options to monitor a student's progress for several weeks in a row, and the WJ IV ACH is not designed to be sensitive to small changes over short periods of time.

However, a district or school might choose to use the three forms of the WJ IV ACH as occasional benchmark measures, or as pre- and postintervention summative assessments. In this case, it would be important for the team to use only growth indicators on the WJ IV ACH (the Relative Proficiency Index, RPI), rather than standard scores, because standard scores are tied to student age or grade level, not to absolute skill growth (*WJ IV Technical Manual*; McGrew, LaForte, & Schrank, 2014). The district or school would need to establish criteria for sufficient growth, based on changes in RPI scores.

Returning to the Tier 3 students, after a prescribed amount of intervention determined by the team and based on recommendations and research from the intervention's publisher, the Data Team reviews and analyzes the rate and amount of growth for each student. Based on the results and the established decision rules, the team may decide to discontinue the intervention due to successful progress. The student may then return to a Tier 2 intervention or, in the case of substantial progress, may no longer need any interventions. Alternately, the team may determine that the Tier 3 intervention appears to be effective, but that the student needs continued intervention at this level in order to approach grade level. Finally, the team may determine that the student has made little or no growth, despite intensive targeted intervention and a referral for a special education evaluation may be in order. For example, a first grader who continues to fall below the 10th percentile rank on the easyCBM Word Reading Fluency progress measure and/or who is not making a rate of progress that would allow him or her to approach grade level performance within the next year may be demonstrating an educational disability, which requires a comprehensive individual evaluation. Before drawing this conclusion, however, the Data Team must be vigilant in their exploration of other possible factors that may be impacting the student's rate or level of progress, such as the following:

- Was the student's progress being monitoring at his/her instructional level, rather than grade level? Monitoring at the instructional level, even if below the student's actual grade, will allow the student to demonstrate small increments of progress. Grade level measures may still be above this student's skill level, in which case progress will not be seen, even when small increments are actually occurring.
- Was the student frequently absent and, therefore, missed multiple intervention sessions? It is not appropriate to draw a conclusion about a student's skills when that student has not received the full number of intervention sessions.
- Was the intervention provided consistently and accurately for all students in the group and was the progress monitoring measure administered accurately and on schedule? If not, data may not be accurate. Fidelity measures should be employed to address this.
- Was the intervention targeting the appropriate skill deficits for this student? The team must examine the student's diagnostic assessments and ensure that

the intervention provided was reasonably designed to address the student's specific skill deficit(s).

- Do all three tiers of instruction align to support this student's instructional needs? While a student is receiving Tier 3 interventions, Tiers 1 and 2 must continue. This provides the student continued access to the core curriculum, as well as supplemental supports.
- Are there other factors that may be limiting the student's growth? The team should consider the student's culture, language, behavior, and emotional and mental health before moving forward.

If these possibilities have been ruled out, the team may suspect an educational disability and must proceed with a comprehensive evaluation to determine whether or not the student requires special education services in order to make educational progress.

COMPREHENSIVE INDIVIDUAL EVALUATION

There are currently many school districts and states that rely on the results of MTSS as the primary factor in determining a student's eligibility for special education services under the category SLD, without pursuing any additional individual assessment (Zirkel & Thomas, 2010). This has been a source of much disagreement and discourse in the field of school psychology. In addition to the requirement that students be provided with a full and individual evaluation (34 CFR 300.304-300.311) before determining a disability, the failure to pursue cognitive evaluation is contrary to the federal definition of SLD: "a disorder in one or more of the basic psychological processes involved in understanding or in using language, spoken or written, that may manifest itself in an imperfect ability to listen, think, speak, read, write, spell, or to do mathematical calculations…" (34 CFR §300.8(10) (i)). Similarly, recent years of educational and neurological research concurs that SLDs involve neurological deficits in cognitive processes that interfere with the acquisition of specific academic skills (NASP, 2007). Knowing this, professionals must attempt to evaluate the functioning of a student's psychological/cognitive processes in order to determine if failure to respond to interventions is due to an SLD.

Other professional organizations support this position. The National Joint Committee on Learning Disabilities (NJCLD) states that data from RtI/MTSS could be an important component of an evaluation for special education, but such data are not sufficient to identify a learning disability (NJCLD, 2005). Similarly, the Learning Disabilities Association of America (LDA) specifically notes that RtI data and methods should not be the only, or the most important, method for identifying learning disabilities. By eliminating tests of cognition, language, and perception, educators are ignoring years of empirical research on the nature and origins of learning disabilities (LDA, 2006). Furthermore, forgoing evaluation of psychological processing deficits and using the MTSS data to conclude that a child has a learning disability, fails to help the team determine why the interventions were not effective. It also makes it difficult to distinguish SLD from mild Intellectual Disability (ID), and it does not focus on the student's strengths in addition to his or her weaknesses (Wodrich, Spencer, & Daley, 2006). Finally, the United States Department of Education's Office of Special Education Programs (OSEP) states that, "the use of RtI strategies cannot be used to delay or deny the provision of a full and individual evaluation" if a disability is suspected (Musgrove, 2011). Therefore, OSEP makes a clear distinction between RtI/MTSS procedures and comprehensive evaluation for possible special education eligibility. This directive from OSEP indicates that failure to respond to well-designed interventions is not sufficient to make a determination of SLD and, thus, additional evaluation is required. Therefore, while we strongly support the use of MTSS to provide early and targeted interventions to promote student learning and success, we also insist that a full, individual and comprehensive evaluation be conducted beyond analysis of MTSS data.

USE OF THE WJ IV ASSESSMENT TOOLS IN THREE MTSS-BASED USE CASE SCENARIOS

As previously mentioned, a myriad of instructional intervention and progress monitoring methods may be employed in any given district model, with each tier of intervention representing a wide range of possible services and criteria for measuring response (Fuchs et al., 2012). While commonalities existed between models, in Jenkins and colleagues' (2013) survey across 62 districts in 17 states, wide variation was identified in RtI/MTSS practice, intervention intensity, and implementation of services for general and special education students. Whether the end intent of multitiered intervention systems is solely for the identification of an SLD or to inform and enhance instructional changes, the use of standardized assessment tools is still valuable to school teams and to parents in understanding individual students. The role of the standardized test may vary based on the needs of the team, the methodologies employed, and local policies and procedures. Given the inherent variability in these procedures, narrowing the range of options down to a few particular use case scenarios may be the most helpful for the typical school psychologist practitioner.

MTSS and measurement of chronic under achievement with the WJ IV. In this case scenario, the district defines services and decision points based on the identification of a student's chronic underachievement. While most MTSS benchmarking and progress-monitoring tools use a normative sample to calculate percentile ranks, they are not standardized assessments and do not utilize a common metric. The choices of criteria measures and cut points can greatly impact decisions in disability classification systems (VanDerHeyden, 2011). For some measures, the distribution of performance may be bimodal and/or skewed, so formulating decision points on individual measures becomes problematic. The benefit of including a standardized measure such as the WJ IV ACH is to produce a variety of common metrics that can be used to determine a threshold for absolute underachievement.

For example, student A has, in the parlance of intervention terminology, "flatlined" on his curriculum-based benchmarking measures (CBM). This means that the team interpreting progress data has determined that progress is not being made. If administered at the typical three-times-per-year interval, the error of measurement on such a tool may encompass the entire growth range of a typical student during the course of an instructional year (Christ & Silberglitt, 2007). This may cause teams to provide intervention when it is not necessarily needed or perceive that the student is demonstrating growth when he actually may not be. With the ability to administer up to three alternate forms of the WJ IV ACH (note: only the first 11 tests are alternate forms between the A, B, and C measures), a limited investment of assessment time would allow a team to develop a measure of achievement compared to a national norm base. In addition to age and grade-based norms, the ability to utilize the RPI and descriptive developmental zones of the WJ IV ACH, practitioners could develop a more nuanced set of decision rules for intervention change or special education referral and/or identification thresholds. A school team could additionally use the Roster Reports available for the WJ IV ACH to assist with student intervention grouping. Following a specified time frame for intervention, the intervention group could be readministered the appropriate WJ IV ACH alternate form and the student in question could be compared to the rest of the intervention group to determine relative performance.

MTSS and cross-battery assessment with the WJ IV ACH. Much has been debated and described on the use of cross-battery assessment because of the complexity involved in comparisons and calculations (Glutting, Watkins, & Youngstrom, 2003; Ortiz & Flanagan, 2002a, 2002b), but the use of technology tools such as the Cross-Battery Assessment Software System (X-BASS; Flangan, Ortiz, & Alfonso, 2015) has greatly reduced the technical threshold for a typical practitioner's entry into evaluating statistical data across a variety of measures. In this scenario, a team has targeted a culturally and linguistically diverse (CLD) third grader (student B) for additional evaluation following her Tier 2 and Tier 3 intervention efforts. The use of benchmarking and progress monitoring tools with CLD students still requires careful consideration and unique application (Esparza Brown & Sandford, 2011).

Cross-battery assessment (Flanagan, Ortiz, & Alfonso, 2013) utilizes the Cattell–Horn–Carroll theory of cognitive abilities that relies on substantial factor analysis conducted across different standardized test batteries. In this case, the student was administered the Clinical Evaluation of Language Fundamentals-4 (CELF-4; Semel, Wiig, & Secord, 2003), which includes a phonological awareness subtest. Using the WJ IV Tests of Oral Language (WJ IV OL; Schrank, Mather, & McGrew, 2014b) battery as a supplement, the results from the single CELF-4 subtest could be combined with the two-subtest cluster for Phonetic Coding (Test 3: Segmentation and Test 7: Sound Blending) to provide measures that confirm a suspected weakness in this area. Given the CLD status of the student, a cross-battery model assessment need not be confined to a specific tool.

The WJ IV OL also includes Spanish clusters to calculate a Comparative Language Index (CLI) to assist in determining language dominance issues. If multiple core test batteries are given, the subsequent results can be entered, compared, and analyzed using a system such as the X-BASS to look for emergent patterns that suggest an underlying problem. The results can then be reviewed for patterns consistent or inconsistent with the cultural and linguistic demands for each test administered. The three testing batteries of the WJ IV contain 50 tests that can be constructed into 45 different clusters or composites across academic, cognitive, and language domains. All final assessment measures were interpreted using the Culture-Language Interpretive Matrix (C-LIM) (Ortiz, 2005), which examines the degree to which linguistic demands and cultural loading may explain patterns of performance across multiple standardized assessments.

MTSS and a hybrid hypothesis testing model with the WJ IV ACH. Given that integrity and fidelity checks in RtI systems continue to be an area of ongoing concern (Hardcastle & Justice, 2010), the role of standardized assessment tools with strong reliability and validity to supplement the data from intervention responsiveness cannot be understated. Various models of hypothesis testing that utilize cognitive measures have been proposed including Discrepancy/Consistency (Naglieri, 1999, 2014) and Cognitive Hypothesis Testing (Fiorello, Hale, & Snyder, 2006). These methodologies tend to begin with a hypothesis about the underlying weaknesses or strengths that would be predicted given the achievement data gathered through benchmarking and progress measures of an MTSS.

An example of this scenario is student C who has demonstrated a difficulty in math computation, with evidence of poor number sense and difficulty with mental measurement. Presuming that Tier 1 core instruction has been adequately delivered, Tier 2 or supplemental instruction would take place that follows the general sequence of core instruction, but would be scaffolded for scope and complexity in a group-level intervention. In this model, Tier 2 instruction would be delivered by the student's regular teacher, but during the regular instructional time for math. Tier 2 would also include regular checks of progress using a tool designed to be sensitive to intervention efforts, such as Numbers and Operations probes from easyCBM. By Tier 3, the student would be receiving the regular and supplemental instruction, but in addition to the core time allotted to math, would receive targeted small group separate instruction. Tier 3 interventions typically utilize materials that have diagnostic measures to identify missing skills and structured methods of instructional delivery. While the student may not make progress, or may make progress only with such intensive and ongoing efforts, the information gained thus far does not confirm "why" the student is not progressing. It also involves such complexity in scheduling and instruction that to assume an underlying weakness in a cognitive process that describes a learning disability would be inadequate without formulating a hypothesis and actually testing it.

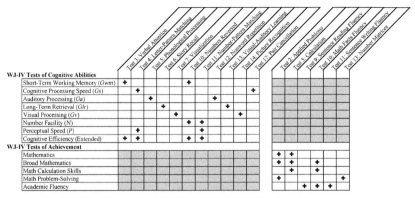

Source: Adapted from WJ IV Tests of Achievement and Tests of Cognitive Abilities Examiner's Manuals, Riverside Publishing Company, 2014.

FIGURE 14.1 Example grid for selective testing using the WJ IV Achievement and Cognitive batteries.

A hybrid model shares a number of features with the under-achievement and the cross-battery scenarios. It adds *a priori* selection of standardized assessments that would capture the most probable underlying cognitive processes involved in basic computation problems as well as other areas where potential strengths can be identified. Using the principle of convergent validity, the model seeks to triangulate with multiple sources of data on the student's strengths and weaknesses (see Eugene School District 4J Model described in Flanagan et al., 2013). When weaknesses are identified consistent with the learning problem area, and strengths are found in unrelated or minimally related areas, the school team has strong evidence to support a learning disability identification.

For student C, the team understands that the processes of working memory and processing speed have been implicated in math-related learning problems (Geary, Hoard, Byrd-Craven, Nugent, & Numtee, 2007). Additionally, attention has been found to be a mediating process for basic computational skill development (DeHaene, Molko, Cohen, & Wilson, 2004). Utilizing the achievement and cognitive batteries of the WJ IV, the following tests were selected to minimize assessment time and maximize the number of clusters available for analysis (Figure 14.1).

While the number of tests administered in the table appears daunting, there are actually only 17 tests total across batteries. These 17 tests will effectively yield 8 cognitive clusters and 5 achievement clusters. While additional achievement measures could be added to establish more comprehensive achievement levels in reading and writing, the Academic Fluency cluster provides basic skill development information.

Student C would be expected to demonstrate weaknesses in the processing speed and working memory clusters, but potential strengths or at least average performance in auditory processing and visual processing clusters.

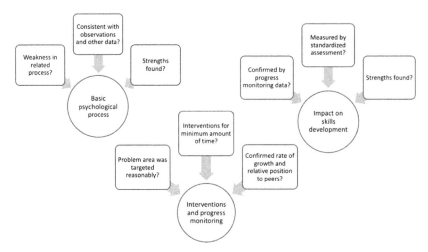

FIGURE 14.2   Illustration of factors in identifying SLD using convergent validity principles.

The achievement clusters would serve to confirm absolute achievement weaknesses in basic calculation skills and could be combined with the criterion-referenced progress-monitoring measures to evaluate slope of growth (Figure 14.2).

Regardless of the model or use case scenario used, the WJ IV provides a dynamic range of options that can be used to supplement the data obtained from MTSS implementations. It also provides a stable normative base and set of metrics that are not dependent on a specific type of MTSS.

CONCLUSION

The lively debate around the best way to identify learning disabilities, in the context of systemic intervention systems, has continued to provide momentum for the discovery of new and better methodologies. Ongoing research efforts continue to implicate a strong research-based connection between learning disabilities and their neurological underpinnings (Fletcher-Janzen & Reynolds, 2008). Even in strong MTSS implementations with rigorous responsiveness to intervention components, it would ignore decades of research to exclude psychometrically validated instruments such as the WJ IV as an integral part of any Special Education eligibility process, and even as part of an ongoing problem-solving model (Flanagan, Fiorello, & Ortiz, 2010). These instruments have received significant updates over the last decade to reduce bias, improve correlations with other instructional outcomes and enhance educational planning efforts. If the field is to progress toward a more unified and consistent model for practitioners, then the collection of data from the best of our instruments is crucial. Our ability to answer the what, the why, and the how of learning problems can only be enhanced by collection of ecological and student-centered data evaluation.

REFERENCES

Christ, T. J., & Silberglitt, B. (2007). Estimates of the standard error of measurement for curriculum-based measures of oral reading fluency. *School Psychology Review*, *36*(1), 130–146.

Curtis, Y., Sullivan, L., Alonzo, J., & Tindal, G. (2011). The context and process of implementation of the University of Oregon—Eugene School District 4J RTI model. In E. S. Shapiro, N. Z. Zigmond, T. Wallace, and D. Marston (Eds.), *Models for implementing response to intervention: Tools, outcomes and implications*. New York, NY: The Guildford Press.

DeHaene, S., Molko, N., Cohen, L., & Wilson, A. J. (2004). Arithmetic and the brain. *Current Opinion in Neurobiology*, *14*, 218–224.

Department of Education, (2006). 34 CFR Parts 300 and 301 Assistance to states for the education of children with disabilities and preschool grants for children with disabilities; Final rule. *Federal Register*, *71*(156), 46540–46845.

Esparza Brown, J., & Sanford, A. (March 2011). *RTI for English language learners: Appropriately using screening and progress monitoring tools to improve instructional outcomes*. Washington, DC: U.S. Department of Education, Office of Special Education Programs, National Center on Response to Intervention.

Fiorello, C. A., Hale, J. B., & Snyder, L. E. (2006). Cognitive hypothesis testing and response to intervention for children with reading problems. *Psychology in the Schools*, *43*(8), 835–853.

Flanagan, D. P., Fiorello, C. A., & Ortiz, S. O. (2010). Enhancing practice through application of Cattell–Horn–Carroll theory and research: A "Third Method" approach to specific learning disability identification. *Psychology in the Schools*, *47*(7), 739–760.

Flanagan, D. P., Ortiz, S. O., & Alfonso, V. C. (2013). *Essentials of cross-battery assessment* (3rd ed.). New Jersey: John Wiley & Sons, Inc.

Flanagan, D. P., Ortiz, S. O., & Alfonso, V. C. (2015). *Cross-battery assessment software system* (X-BASS) [Computer Software]. New Jersey: John Wiley & Sons, Inc.

Fletcher-Janzen, E., & Reynolds, C. R. (2008). Neuropsychological perspectives on learning disabilities in the era of RTI: Recommendations for diagnosis and intervention. New Jersey: John Wiley & Sons, Inc.

Fuchs, D., Fuchs, L. S., Compton, D. C., Bryant, J., & Davis, G. N. (2008). Making "secondary intervention" work in a three-tier responsiveness-to-intervention model: Findings from the first-grade longitudinal reading study at the National Research Center on Learning Disabilities. *Reading and Writing: An Interdisciplinary Journal*, *21*(4), 413–436.

Fuchs, D., Fuchs, L. S., & Compton, D. L. (2012). Smart RTI: A next-generation approach to multilevel prevention. *Exceptional Children*, *78*(3), 263–279.

Geary, D. C., Hoard, M. K., Byrd-Craven, J., Nugent, L., & Numtee, C. (2007). Cognitive mechanisms underlying achievement deficits in children with mathematical learning disability. *Child Development*, *78*(4), 1343–1359.

Glutting, J. J., Watkins, M. W., & Youngstrom, E. A. (2003). Multifactored and cross-battery ability assessments: Are they worth the effort?. In C. R. Reynolds & R. W. Kamphaus (Eds.), *Handbook of psychological and educational assessment of children: Intelligence and achievement*. New York: Guilford.

Hardcastle, B., & Justice, K. (2010). *Fidelity and RtI: Strategies to ensure intervention integrity in your schools*. Horsham, PA: LRP Publications.

Hauerhas, L. B., Brown, A., & Scott, A. N. (2013). Specific learning disability and response to intervention: State-level guidance. *Exceptional Children*, *80*(1), 101–120.

Individuals With Disabilities Education Act, 20 U.S.C. § 1400 (2004).

Institute of Education Sciences, (2009). Assisting students struggling with reading: Response to intervention (RtI) and multitier intervention in the primary grades. Washington, DC: U.S. Department of Education.

Jenkins, J. R., Schiller, E., Blackorby, J., Thayer, S. K., & Tilly, W. D. (2013). Responsiveness to intervention in reading: Architecture and practices. *Learning Disability Quarterly, 36*(1), 36–46.

Johnson, E., Mellard, D. F., Fuchs, D., & McKnight, M. A. (2006). *Responsiveness to intervention (RTI): How to do it.* Lawrence, KS: National Research Center on Learning Disabilities.

Kovaleski, J.F., Marco-Fies, C.M., & Boneshefski, M.J. (2013). *Treatment integrity: Ensuring the I in RTI.* Retrieved March 1, 2015, from <http://www.rtinetwork.org/getstarted/evaluate/treatment-integrity-ensuring-the-i-in-rti>.

Lai, C. F., Alonzo, J., & Tindal, G. (2013). *easyCBM reading criterion related validity evidence: Grades k-1.* Eugene, OR: Behavioral Research and Teaching, University of Oregon. (Technical Report 1309).

Learning Disabilities Association of America (LDA). (2006). *Position paper on response to intervention.* Retrieved March 22, 2015, from <http://ldaamerica.org/advocacy/lda-position-papers/response-to-intervention-rti/>.

Lichtenstein, R. (2008). Best practices in identification of learning disabilities. In A. Thomas & J. Grimes (Eds.), *Best practices in school psychology V.* Bethesda, MD: National Association of School Psychologists.

Liu, K., Alonzo, J., & Tindal, G. (2011). Implementation and outcomes. In E. S. Shapiro, N. Z. Zigmond, T. Wallace, and D. Marston (Eds.), *Models for implementing response to intervention: Tools, outcomes and implications.* New York, NY: The Guildford Press.

McGraw-Hill, (2006). *Treasures reading program.* New York, NY: MacMillan/McGraw-Hill.

McGrew, K. S., LaForte, E. M., & Schrank, F. A. (2014). *Technical manual: Woodcock–Johnson IV.* Rolling Meadows, IL: Riverside.

Moats, L., & Tolman, C. (2009). Language essentials for teachers of reading and spelling (LETRS): The speech sounds of English: Phonetics, phonology, and phoneme awareness (Module 2). Boston, MA: Sopris West.

Musgrove, M. (2011). Memorandum to state directors of special education: A response-to-intervention process (RTI) cannot be used to delay–deny an evaluation for eligibility under the Individuals with Disabilities Education Act (IDEA). Washington, DC: U.S. Department of Education Office of Special Education Programs.

Naglieri, J. A. (1999). *Essentials of CAS assessment.* New York, NY: Wiley.

Naglieri, J. A. (2014). *Cognitive assessment system* (2nd ed.). Texas: PRO-ED, Inc.

National Association of School Psychologists (NASP), (2007). Identification of students with specific learning disabilities (Position Statement). Bethesda, MD: NASP.

National Center on Intensive Intervention, (February 2015). *Academic progress monitoring tools chart.* Washington, DC: American Institutes for Research.

National Center on Response to Intervention (NCRTI), (March 2010). *Essential components of RTI—A closer look at response to intervention.* Washington, DC: U.S. Department of Education, Office of Special Education Programs.

National Joint Committee on Learning Disabilities (NJCLD). (2005). *Responsiveness to Intervention and Learning Disabilities.* Retrieved March 22, 2015, from <http://www.ldonline.org/article/11498>.

Ortiz, S. O. (2005). The Culture-Language Test Classifications (C-LTC) and Culture-Language Interpretive Matrix (C-LIM). St. Johns University: Samuel O Ortiz, Ph.D.

Ortiz, S. O., & Flanagan, D. P. (2002a). Cross battery assessment revisited: Some cautions concerning "some cautions" (part 1). *Communiqué*, *30*(7), 32–34.

Ortiz, S. O., & Flanagan, D. P. (2002b). Cross battery assessment revisited: Some cautions concerning "some cautions" (part II). *Communiqué*, *30*(8), 36–38.

Read Naturally, Inc., (2015). *Read naturally, live*. St. Paul, MN: Author.

Scanlon, D. M. (2013). Assessing RTI Strategies: The trouble with packaged and scripted interventions. *Reading Today*, 20–21. Aug–Sep 2013.

Schrank, F. A., Mather, N., & McGrew, K. S. (2014a). *Woodcock–Johnson IV tests of achievement*. Rolling Meadows, IL: Riverside.

Schrank, F. A., Mather, N., & McGrew, K. S. (2014b). *Woodcock–Johnson IV tests of oral language*. Rolling Meadows, IL: Riverside.

Schrank, F. A., McGrew, K. S., & Mather, N. (2014c). *Woodcock–Johnson IV*. Rolling Meadows, IL: Riverside.

Semel, E., Wiig, E. H., & Secord, W. A. (2003). *Clinical evaluation of language fundamentals— fourth edition*. Sn Antonio, TX: The Psychological Corporation.

Shapiro, E. S. (2009). *The two models of RTI: Standard protocol and problem solving*. Bethlehem, PA: Center for Promoting Research to Practice, Lehigh University.

SRA/McGraw Hill, (2001). *Reading Mastery*. Columbus, OH: The McGraw-Hill Companies.

University of Oregon, (2006). *easyCBM*. Rolling Meadows, IL: Hougton Miffllin Harcourt–Riverside.

VanDerHeyden, A. M. (2011). Technical adequacy of response to intervention decisions. *Exceptional Children*, *77*(3), 335–350.

Wodrich, D. L., Spencer, M. L. S., & Daley, K. B. (2006). Combining RTI and psychoeducational assessment: What we must assume to do otherwise. *Psychology in the Schools*, *43*(7), 797–806.

Wright, J. (2010). *Frequently Asked Questions About...RTI Problem-Solving Teams*. Retrieved March 10, 2015, from <www.interventioncentral.org/sites/default/files/rti_team_faqs.pdf>.

Zirkel, P. A., & Thomas, L. B. (2010). State laws and guidelines for implementing RTI. *Teaching Exceptional Children*, *43*(1), 62–73.

Index